The Didache

Compendia Rerum Iudaicarum ad Novum Testamentum

SECTION III

JEWISH TRADITIONS IN EARLY CHRISTIAN LITERATURE

Volume I
PAUL AND THE JEWISH LAW; HALAKHA IN THE LETTERS
OF THE APOSTLE TO THE GENTILES
Peter J. Tomson

Volume 2
JEWISH HISTORIOGRAPHY AND ICONOGRAPHY
IN EARLY AND MEDIEVAL CHRISTIANITY
Heinz Schreckenberg – Kurt Schubert
Translations from the German: Paul A. Cathey

Volume 3
PHILO IN EARLY CHRISTIAN LITERATURE; A SURVEY
David T. Runia

Volume 4
THE JEWISH APOCALYPTIC HERITAGE IN EARLY CHRISTIANITY
Edited by James C. VanderKam and William Adler

Volume 5
THE DIDACHE; ITS JEWISH SOURCES AND ITS PLACE
IN EARLY JUDAISM AND CHRISTIANITY
Huub van de Sandt – David Flusser

Published under the auspices of the
Foundation Compendia Rerum Iudaicarum ad Novum Testamentum
Amsterdam

The Didache

Its Jewish Sources and its Place in Early Judaism and Christianity

Huub van de Sandt and David Flusser

2002
Royal Van Gorcum, Assen
Fortress Press, Minneapolis

Printed in the Netherlands by Royal Van Gorcum, Assen, The Netherlands

Contents

I THE TWO WAYS TRACTATE: DID 1-6

Editors' Foreword

It is with sadness and joy that we present this volume to our readers. Sadness prevails now that, over a year after the decease of one of the authors of this book and just before publication, we had to register the loss of one of the pillars of the Foundation that supports our project.

After reaching the age of retirement, Bob Levisson retained positions of global influence in the world of printing and remained an active member of the Dutch Jewish community, making also a marked contribution to the teaching and study- ing of Jewish tradition in the many 'houses of study' that are scattered across the Netherlands and are populated mainly with Christians. If the chairmanship of the Compendia Foundation was a natural extension of these activities, Bob Levisson has made the function unforgettable by the resources of wit and energy with which he filled it for 18 years. Mingling irony and wisdom in his persevering interest in the progress of the several components of the project, he came to be appreciated by the editors not as a mere organiser of financial support but as a true source of inspiration and energy.

In David Flusser, we have lost one of the most creative and prolific scholars in the field of ancient culture and religion, in particular in its Jewish and Christian manifestations. He was also among the creative forces behind the *Compendia* as from its conception in the 1960's. In a large part, it was his intimate knowledge of the classical Greek, Latin, Hebrew and Aramaic sources and the thrust of his erudite imagination that inspired the designing and production of the various sections and volumes.

The studying and describing anew of the Christian beginnings within its Jewish context presented a double challenge. Firstly, the catastrophic dimensions of the Shoa and the apparent involvement in it of European Christians revealed the dimensions of Christian anti-Judaism and the need to strive for a correction. This included the domain of historical and theological scholarship. More than ever it became a top priority for Christian scholars to integrate the large body of rabbinic literature, an area they hitherto largely ignored and left to Jewish scholars, into their discussion. Secondly, the discovery of the Dead Sea scrolls necessitated the effort to study them closely and to integrate them into the overall image of ancient Judaism. As it happened, these two challenges appeared on the agenda almost simultaneously. It was necessary at the same time to re-read rabbinic halakha and midrash in comparison with the Qumran laws and exposition, and to re-interpret the gospels and epistles with reference to the renewed picture of Judaism – the matrix of Christianity – emerging from that comparitive re-reading.

This two-fold process of integration required, and still requires, the limitless curiosity and perceptiveness of gifted scholars like the late David Flusser. The first anniversary of his death having passed, it is not only sad to remember our loss, but also a joy to establish a memorial to his life by presenting another fruit of his intellectual labours. Due largely to the sustained efforts of Huub van de Sandt, Flusser's original idea to write a monograph on the Didache and its Jewish background has now been realised. Insofar as the richness and the benefits of Flusser's learned explorations have as yet remained little known in the world of New Testament and Patristic studies, the present work is an excellent opportunity to remedy this.

The present study on the Didache may be seen as an epitome of the *Compendia* undertaking. It results from the close collaboration of a Jewish and a Christian scholar; it involves the integrated implementation of scholarly expertise in Greek, Latin, Hebrew and Aramaic sources; and it utilises the information from rabbinic literature no less than that of the Qumran scrolls or the writings of the church fathers. Also, the Christian work under discussion integrates what a consensus of scholars considers to be an independent Jewish document, the so-called 'Two Ways'; the elucidation of its place in ancient Jewish culture is no doubt one of the important contributions of the present work.

As it is, this study moves on the boundaries between ancient Judaism and Christianity, an area mined with prejudice and apprehension. Unflinchingly, its authors trace the development from the written 'Jewish source', through the stages of a composite Judaeo-Christian text, and on to the document of an anti-Jewish gentile church which they discern in the Didache. The prize of objective scholarship, the strived-for 'purity of science', is not in the pretended absence of special interests of the scholar. It is in the ability to manage such interests – for they are absent in no one – and to make them subservient to the aim of gathering knowledge in the quest for truth. This, David Flusser once said on the occasion of the appearance of one of his books, is a sacred mission directly linked to the duty of fostering peace in the world. If we are not mistaken, such purity is one of the qualities of the present book, and in it, some major aims of our undertaking are being fulfilled.

The editors feel extremely indebted to Dr. Huub van de Sandt for his incessant and meticulous efforts in bringing the project to its completion. Presently involved in teaching and research at Tilburg University, the Netherlands, Dr. Van de Sandt began his scholarly career under the aegis of Flusser's esteemed colleague and early collaborator in the project, W.C. van Unnik, and he complemented it by a two year study period with Flusser in Jerusalem. Dr. Van de Sandt has not just carried out the difficult task of bringing the ideas of his elder colleague and teacher to their full and clear expression; he has at the same time done a great deal in integrating scholarly developments that went beyond the perception of the master. In effect, Dr. Van de Sandt has written most of the following pages, often dealing with topics that were only discussed orally between the two authors. Furthermore, the scholarly documentation is his work.

The editors are happy to conclude that the *Compendia* project, which began nearly forty years ago, has made another significant stride forward. Even if the road is longer than originally projected and involves complications unforeseen, the main course is still correct and, we feel, ever commendable. In fact, the recent proliferation of similar projects demonstrates the relevance of our undertaking and the growing recognition of the aims we have been pursuing all along. We hope that those who in the past hesitated about the project will allow themselves to be convinced of its positive aspects, and that those who have been sympathetic will not miss the adjustments made in course and method. We have learned that it is wise to refrain from making announcements about future publications. Nevertheless the reader can be assured that such publications are being prepared and will in due time be available.

In addition to the acknowledgements made in the author's preface, we wish to express our special gratitude to the Greek Patriarchate in Jerusalem for providing the photographs of the Jerusalem Manuscript of the Didache, and for the permission to publish them. We also want to state our debt to Mrs. Doris Lambers-Petry for her important intervention in this matter.

Finally, we wish to thank the Foundation Board for the patience and the confidence they have granted us, and the team of Van Gorcum's for staying faithful even when things went slower than what sensible publishers know is advisable.

The Editors

Preface

The Didache, a first-century Christian manual probably composed in Syria-Palestine, is a goldmine of information on the nascent Christian church and early Judaism. Because it offers rules for ecclesiastical praxis one might characterize the Didache as a handbook of church morals, ritual and discipline. To a certain extent, these rules obviously reflect local reality. The manual offers a glimpse of the earliest details with regard to the actual practice of the catechumenate, baptism, and the Eucharist in a specific Christian community (Did 1-10) and provides us with data about the functioning of leadership in that primitive community (Did 11-15).

The booklet does not, however, merely preserve archaic traditions of a particular Christian locality in patristic times. Anybody who consults the text will observe that it is profoundly Jewish. The traditions embodied in the earliest layers of the Didache text partly originate from a Jewish milieu and partly emerge from Jewish Christian circles, that is, from Jews who believed in Jesus and were seen as part of the Jewish community. Of course, those who made Jesus the core of their understanding of Judaism were aware of their being distinct in some sense. In the manual's developing proces, however, the lines of demarcation were still fluid and the borders so fuzzy that we are not allowed to speak of 'Judaism' and 'Christianity' as single entities yet unless it regards the last layer of composition. Therefore, a study of the Didache will not only benefit Christian research but, conversely, may also contribute to our knowledge of first-century Judaism.

These observations are meaningful for the approach adopted in the present study. Two methodological features characterize our research. First of all, instead of looking at the Didache only as an independent unit (belonging to Patristic Studies) we will see it as part of a larger environment of Jewish and Christian religious and cultural history. As the world of biblical studies expanded and segmented itself into specialized fields, the work has on the whole been carried out in separate, watertight compartments. We will attempt to maintain a broad perspective and relate the findings of the distinct areas (for example the New Testament, Second Temple Judaism, Liturgy, Patristic Studies) to one another.

Second, this study utilizes historical methodology – being historical, the questions are answered on historical grounds. There is a broad scholarly consensus that the document is a compilation of several older sources which already had a separate existence and a corresponding meaning before their incorporation into the Didache. A more exact understanding of the text thus requires a critical historical study, which must examine in each case the extent, age, origin, and meaning of the unit of tradition. We must make proper historical distinctions and thus sufficiently differentiate between the Didache as the result of an author's (here: the Didachist's) redactorial activity, the actual materials used by the Didachist, and the traditions behind these materials. Form Criticism and Redaction Criticism will prove important for the analysis of the various sections. Form Criticism sets itself the task of studying the formation of the various sections of the Didache prior to the writing of the manual. We will be looking for constant elements, phenomena which recur repeatedly in all sorts of documents. By a comparative analysis of 'forms' we will attempt to disentangle the traditional materials embodied in the Didache and to find the real-life situation (*Sitz im Leben*) of each particular literary form. Redaction Criticism attempts to determine how the composer used and reshaped these traditions within the document.

This monograph consists of two major parts. After a general *Introduction* in the Didache as a whole, the "ethical" section of Did 1:1-6:1, the Two Ways, is dealt with in *Part I*. The main concern of this first Part lies with the Jewishness of these chapters. The Two Ways, occurring here in a Christian post-apostolic writing, represents a document which is almost en bloc Jewish. For the most part, it was taken over from a Jewish original which is lost. In search of the earliest form of this moral instruction, we will compare the Two Ways in the Didache with other early Christian versions (Chap. 2). In the subsequent chapter (Chap. 3), it will be shown that a Two Ways document remained in existence as a separate model for baptismal instruction up to and including mediaeval times. Once we have observed the independent circulation of the Two Ways tradition in a form similar to the one underlying the Didache and other early Christian versions, an attempt is made to reconstruct the lost Greek prototype of the Two Ways (Chap. 4). What remains to be discussed in a next chapter, however, is the Jewish life situation of the Two Ways. Although a consensus has been reached about its Jewish character in the last few decades, scholarly opinion is still divided about the genre and provenance of the Two Ways. The hypothetical reconstruction, also designated as the *Greek Two Ways* (*GTW*), will be the basis for determining the milieu in which the Two Ways was composed and transmitted originally (Chap. 5).

Part II deals with materials coming from Jewish Christian circles. We will see how the knowledge of Jewish traditional materials in the Didache benefits an understanding of first-century Christianity. This, of course, holds true for Chaps. 1-6 in the Didache in the first place. Once we have reconstructed the Jewish form, conclusions can be drawn concerning the editorial activity of the Christian composer of the manual. But the Jewish Two Ways may also contribute to finding a way out of redactional critical problems appearing in other Christian texts. A number of scholars have noticed significant agreements between a part of the Two Ways documents and the antithetical section in Matt 5:17-48 as they both share structure and argument (see below, Chap. 6, n. 3). Unanimity has not been reached as yet as to what precisely is tradition and what are interpolations and later expansions in Matthew. If we take the Jewishness of the Two Ways document seriously, however, we are in a position to determine what is redactional and what is source material in this gospel section and thus restore the text in its fuller Jewish meaning (Chap. 6).

Once Jewish Christians who were responsible for the composition of the earlier layers of the Didache had adopted the Two Ways, the instruction primarily came to serve as an instruction to gentile converts. This becomes apparent in the addition of the remarkable passage in Did 6:2-3. These verses represent a considerable shift in focus as compared with the Jewish prohibitions that were offered in Did. 1:1-6:1. There is strong evidence that the passage reflects a separate tradition of the Apostolic Decree mentioned in Acts 15:20.29; 21:25. In this context, the Noachide laws and their (pre-) rabbinic equivalents become particularly relevant (Chap. 7). Jewish traditions are also significant in the Didache's handling of Baptism, the Lord's Prayer and the Eucharist. Special attention will be paid to the account of the Eucharist in Did 9-10 because it hardly harmonizes with the evidence of the New Testament traditions. It will become clear that the specific nature of the eucharistic prayers is ultimately shaped after Jewish models (Chap. 8). In Did 11-15, the focus will primarily be upon the character and functioning of the teachers, apostles and prophets within the Didache community. We will see how the Jewish impact on the function of these figures is still clearly recognizable (Chap. 9).

Since I had the joy of being taught by David Flusser in the years I was studying at the Hebrew University in Jerusalem (1973-1975), I sincerely express my deep appreciation here for his abundant creative genius, his huge memory, and his rich intuition. Besides the gift of insight into the philology and thought of late antiquity, he also possessed an unusual sensitivity to the individual characters of his friends and students. His keen perception and wisdom mingled with a tremendous sense of humour and a bit of irony. When he died on 15 September last year, the world lost a brilliant scholar.

From June 1994 onward, I was honoured to work closely with David Flusser as a co-author of this monograph. We were engaged in an extended dialogue both through annual conversations in Jerusalem and a steady correspondence over the years. The results of our cooperation are presented in this book. David Flusser wrote the first draft of the Section about 'The Manuscript of Jerusalem' in Chapter 1 (pp. 16-24) and the outlines of Chapters 4, 5 and 8. These elementary sketches were revised, rewritten and extensively expanded. I also wrote Chapters 1, 2, 3, 6, 7 and 9, although I am obliged to Flusser for a number of helpful suggestions and improvements.

Acknowledgements

I am indebted to the Theological Faculty of Tilburg University, the Netherlands, for supporting me in writing this book. My work on the Didache was carried out while I had the usual teaching responsibilities. I would like to express my gratitude to my colleagues in Biblical Studies at the Tilburg Theological Faculty for their patience. Yvonne van den Akker, Door Brouns, Pierre van Hecke, Jan Holman (retired), Albert Kamp, Ron Pirson, Didier Vandersnickt, Wim Weren, and Ellen van Wolde took a constant interest in my studies. In the present context, it is fitting to record two other debts of gratitude. First, I must express my appreciation to the desk librarians of our faculty for having gently and efficiently acquired sources, monographs, and journal articles for me. They deserve admiration. In the second place, I wish to record my sincere thanks to Pieter van der Horst for reading and commenting on the manuscript. Likewise, the friendly advice and constructive criticism by Peter Tomson were very much appreciated. He showed painstaking care in reading the manuscript and his sharp questions forced me to reconsider many points.

I express my grateful acknowledgment to the managing directors of the editors of *Supplements to Novum Testamentum* and *Sources Chrétiennes* for the kind permission to incorporate in this volume materials that were previously published:

- A. Cody, 'The *Didache:* An English Translation', in C.N. Jefford, (ed.), *The Didache in Context. Essays on Its Text, History and Transmission.* (NovTSup 77) Leiden-New York-Köln 1995, 3-14
- the edition of the Doctrina Apostolorum (including the critical apparatus) in W. Rordorf et A. Tuilier, *La Doctrine des douze Apôtres (Didachè).* (SC 248 bis) Paris [2]1998, 207-210

I also thankfully acknowledge the permission to reproduce the manuscript passage of *Biblioteca Apostolica, Pal. Lat. 485*, fol. 91ro-92ro from the Department of manuscripts of the Vatican Library, Rome.

Huub van de Sandt
March 2001

Chapter One

Introduction:
History and Text of the Didache

Although the Didache is a composite document, containing elements from different backgrounds and stages of development, in this introductory chapter it will be
treated as an unity. Our views on topics like the Didache's reputation, its textual
witnesses, division, goal, use of Scriptural materials, time, and place will all be
briefly introduced as these judgments are often assumed, discussed, and defended
in the chapters which follow. We will draw attention to the wide popularity of the
Didache in the early church (pp. 1-6), examine the Codex H which contains the
only known complete form of the manual and give a translation of this manuscript
(pp. 6-28), consider the manual's sources and the intention behind the arrangement
of these pre-didachic materials (pp. 28-35), study the sayings and traditions in the
Didache which are closely related to the New Testament (pp. 35-48), and make
a reasonable guess at the date and provenance of the compilation as a whole (pp.
48-52).

The Prominence and Decline of the Didache
in Early Christianity

No copy of the Didache was known to exist until Philotheos Bryennios brought
the manuscript (now preserved in Jerusalem) to light in 1883. Until then the
Didache was considered a lost work which was referred to only by some accidental
witnesses. Eusebius of Caesarea (c. 265-339) in his Ecclesiastical History, for
example, mentions "the alleged teachings of the apostles" (τῶν ἀποστόλων
αἱ λεγόμεναι Διδαχαί) among the 'spurious' (νόθα) books of the New Testament,
together with the Acts of Paul, the Shepherd of Hermas, the Apocalypse of Peter,
the Epistle of Barnabas, and the Revelation of John. Eusebius notes that, although
these writings are not included in the canon, they do enjoy respect as they "are
familiar to most churchmen." A similar statement is found in the Festal Letters of
Athanasius. In his Festal Letter 39 (367 CE), Athanasius of Alexandria lists the
"so-called Teaching of the Apostles" (Διδαχὴ καλουμένη τῶν ἀποστόλων) with
the Wisdom of Solomon, Ben Sira, Esther, Tobit, and the Shepherd among the
writings sanctioned for religious instruction to catechumens.[1]

---

[1] For the instances in Eusebius and Athanasius, see below, Chap. 3, pp. 86-87.

Quotations in early Church literature may cast some further light on the influence of the Didache. Pseudo-Cyprian with a reference to the "Doctrinae apostolorum" (Teachings of the Apostles) renders a quotation that combines Did 14:2 and 15:3 in Chap. 4 of his De Aleatoribus ("About Dice-players"):

> And in the teachings of the apostles: if a brother offends in the church and disobeys the law, let him not be considered until he does penance, nor received, lest he defile and obstruct your prayer.[2]

The quoted text probably is considered to have the status of (sacred) Scripture as it is listed among citations from Paul. Nonetheless, it is clear that around 300 CE, when Pseudo-Cyprian's De Aleatoribus was composed,[3] a Latin version of the Didache existed which probably bore the title 'Doctrinae Apostolorum'. Similarly, Augustine also witnessed to the existence of a Latin translation of the Didache in the fourth or fifth century. In his commentary on the Psalms, he quotes the saying about the "sweating alms" found in Did 1:6 several times. Once he even introduces the sentence by explicitly referring to "Scripture."[4] So, both Pseudo-Cyprian (De Aleatoribus) and Augustine probably knew the Didache in Latin and the designation and use of the Didache in these writings implies its canonical or near-canonical status.

The importance of the Didache during the first Christian centuries is shown by its use in later church orders as well. Like the Didache, these works present authoritative 'apostolic' rules on matters of moral conduct, liturgical practice, and ecclesiastical organization. It is possible but not at all certain that the compiler of the Didascalia Apostolorum was familiar with our Didache and occasionally utilized it as a source.[5] This work was probably composed in Northern Syria during the first half of the third century.[6] Another famous church order which indubitably

---

[2] "Et in doctrinis apostolorum: si quis frater delinquit in ecclesia et non paret legi, hic nec colligatur donec poenitentiam agat, et non recipiatur, ne inquinetur et inpediatur oratio vestra;" cf. Hartel, *S. Thasci Caecili Cypriani* 3, 92-104, esp. 96. See also Von Harnack, *Die Lehre der zwölf Apostel*, Prolegomena, 20-21; Audet, *La Didachè*, 79-81 and Niederwimmer, *Die Didache*, 21-22.

[3] Altaner-Stuiber, *Patrologie*, 177.

[4] See his commentary on Ps 146:17: "Utrumque dictum est, fratres mei, et: Omni petenti te da, modo lectum est; et alio loco Scriptura dicit: Sudet eleemosyna in manu tua, quousque invenias iustum cui eam tradas" ("And again it is said, my brothers, also: Give to everyone who asks you, as we just read; and alsewhere Scripture says: Let your alms sweat in your hand until you find a just person to whom to give it"); cf. Dekkers-Fraipont, *Sancti Aurelii Augustini Enarrationes*, 2135. For other quotations from Augustine's Enarrationes, see idem, 1462 (on Ps 102:12) and 1509 (on Ps 103:10). For post-Augustinian and mediaeval Christian literature, see Audet, *La Didachè*, 277-79; Niederwimmer, *Die Didache*, 25.

[5] For the use of the compiler of the Didascalia, see a.o. Connolly, 'The Use of the Didache'; Muilenburg, *The Literary Relations*, 36-38; Vokes, *The Riddle of the Didache*, 67-71.

[6] Because most of the original Greek text has been lost, our main knowledge of the document is dependent on two early translations, one into Latin (preserved partially) and one into Syriac (preserved completely). For the latest edition of the Syriac version, with English translation, see Vööbus, *The Didascalia Apostolorum*. For the Latin version, cf. Tidner, *Didascalia Apostolorum* and for remnants of the Greek original, see Bartlet, 'Fragments of the Didascalia'.

drew on the Didache is the Apostolic Constitutions. It is commonly agreed that this composite Greek document, probably dating from the end of the fourth century, was written in Syria. It contains the Didascalia (forming book 1-6 of the writing), the Didache (book 7), and the Apostolic Tradition attributed to Hippolytus[7] (book 8). As far as the Didache is concerned, this church order is grafted on the traditional material of the Didache circulating within one or more communities and forming part of their heritage and tradition. At the same time, the text of the Didache was subjected to revision and rewriting to reflect changing historical and cultural circumstances.[8]

The Oxyrhynchus papyrus fragments, the Coptic remnant, and the parts retained from the Ethiopic version, likewise attest to the Didache's circulation. These will be dealt with in the next section of this chapter. This evidence indicates that the Didache was widely known and highly esteemed in the first Christian centuries. Unfortunately, however, after the fifth century the Didache was no longer part of church tradition and fell into obscurity. What the manual had to say was not the sort of material which later generations wanted to preserve; the moral teaching (Chaps. 1-6), the liturgical part (Chaps. 7-10), and the church order proper (Chaps. 11-15) were no longer relevant to their needs. Furthermore, there were clear signs which suggested that the liturgy described in Did 9-10 could not represent an actual eucharist as it was very different from the accounts in the New Testament. The instructions for the eucharist reverse the order of bread and wine universally used by the later church and, moreover, omit of the words of institution commonly pronounced during a eucharistic ritual in the later church. The absence of priests in the manual, the lack of any indication that ecclesiastical authority rests in a monarchial bishop, and its "primitive" concern with itinerant apostles, prophets, and teachers undoubtedly added to the decrease of popular interest in the Didache. The meagre ethical, ritual, and ecclesiastical provisions were too archaic to be reconciled with contemporary practice and the text ceased to appear in the later canonical collections. The manual is still referred to as an apocryphal work in early canonical catalogues such as the List of Sixty Canonical Books (c. 600 CE) and the Stichometry of Nicephorus (c. 850 CE),[9] but by the Middle Ages it had become a lost work.

Another reason for its decline is that apostolic fiction ceased to be used as a source of authority within the church. The Didache bears two designations, a short title ("Doctrine of the Twelve Apostles") and a longer subtitle ("Doctrine of the Lord to the nations through the twelve apostles"). The title and subtitle of the Didache as retained in the Jerusalem manuscript indicate that the "Twelve Apos-

---

[7] For this work, see Altaner-Stuiber, *Patrologie*, 82-84; 557-58; Quasten, *Patrology* 2, 180-94. It is not completely sure, however, whether this composition was indeed originally written by Hippolytus in c. 215 CE; see Drobner, *Lehrbuch der Patrologie*, 102 and, more recently, Metzger, 'Nouvelles perspectives pour la prétendue *Tradition apostolique*'.

[8] This will be discussed in the next section below.

[9] For these works, see Audet, *La Didachè*, 87-90 and Rordorf-Tuilier, *La Doctrine des douze Apôtres*, 107-110.

tles" are to be taken as the source for the Didache. The content of the document itself, however, does not substantiate this identification. On the contrary, even when apostles are directly considered in Did 11:3-6, the Twelve are not mentioned. In Chapter 3, we will see that neither the short nor the long title belonged to the original text of the Didache.[10] The reason for connecting the twelve apostles with the Didache is evident. In purporting to come from the apostles themselves, the document emphasizes the authority of its prescriptions. In fact, as the above titles show, most of the church orders[11] adopted the convention of claiming apostolic authority in order to enhance the binding nature of their ordinances and to add weight to their directives.[12]

From the fourth and fifth centuries onward, however, these pseudo-apostolic injunctions ceased to be relevant for two reasons. First, it was almost impossible to further develop a regulation that is said to derive from the apostles without losing its credibility. Their 'apostolic' descent needed to be more firmly corroborated by more forceful assertions if they were to continue to have any authority. Any alteration or adaption of specific precepts in a church order as a result of emerging problems might very well increase the danger of this manual being exposed as a forgery. In that case, the authenticity of these writings would be questioned and eventually their legitimizing status challenged. Second, since the third century the recognized source and power for establishing liturgical and ecclesiastical matters were increasingly focussed in separate offices, councils, and synods. These became the bodies having administrative and legislative power. From then onward, the collections of canon law and liturgical texts which were produced derived their authority from individual living bishops and genuine synodical assemblies. The last mention of the "Teaching of the Apostles" (Διδαχὴ ἀποστόλων) from personal knowledge[13] was made by Patriarch Nicephoros of

---

[10] Instead, it is likely that the shorter title became the title of the *Christianized* Two Ways treatise at a relatively early period. When this treatise became part of the Didache – or at some later point – this title too came to be attached to the Didache; cf. Niederwimmer, *Die Didache*, 82. Below, in Chap. 3, pp. 84-87, we will see that the Two Ways in some of its Latin versions continued to exist without ascribing it to the authority of the apostles. See also Rordorf-Tuilier, *La Doctrine des douze Apôtres*, 14-15

[11] The Didache in many respects resembles these later church orders. It might, however, be somewhat misleading to designate the first century manual that way. It is especially G. Schöllgen who has argued against the idea that the Didache is a comprehensive church manual. The document probably embodies only a selective collection of rules seeking to settle particularly controversial questions in the sphere of community discipline. It does not represent an accurate picture of all aspects of life of the community behind the document. See Schöllgen, 'Die Didache als Kirchenordnung', 20; cf. also id., 'Die literarische Gattung'.

[12] Cf. Steimer, *Vertex Traditionis*, 342-50 and, with respect to the Didache, 25-27; Walls, 'A Note on the Apostolic Claim', 86-91; Schöllgen, ('Pseudapostolizität und Schriftgebrauch') emphasizes that the pseudo-apostolic framework of the earliest church orders (Didache, the Traditio Apostolica and Syrian Didascalia) could serve to legitimize their authority because these manuals were considered to be a continuation of evangelical tradition (cf. esp. the summary on pp. 119-121)

[13] For (later) Byzantine authors who do mention the Didache but probably were not acquainted with the document itself, see Niederwimmer, *Die Didache*, 32-33.

Constantinople (d. 829 CE). In the list of apocryphal New Testament writings, he refers to this document and reports its stich number as 200.[14] According to Rordorf and Tuilier, the length of the Didache in Nicephoros' information is approximately that of the number of stichoi in the Jerusalem Manuscript (204 stichoi) and probably refers to an ancient uncial text.[15] Nevertheless, after this mention, the Didache disappeared from history till its recovery at the end of the nineteenth century when Bryennios published the Jerusalem manuscript.

We have to be careful, however, not to oversimplify matters. It is not as easy a task as it may seem to map out the use of the Didache in the early Christian centuries: early writers and compilers do neither provide sufficient control for determining what work they precisely have in mind, nor do they attach an accurate label to the materials quoted. They often refer to a writing known as the "Teaching" (Didache, Doctrina) or "Teachings" (Didachai, Doctrinae) "of the Apostles." Since the exact excerpts are not mentioned, there is no way of telling with any confidence what exactly these ancient authors are referring to.

This observation is of importance because, as will be demonstrated in Chaps. 2-5 below, early Christian literature attests to the separate circulation of a Two Ways ethic that is closely related to Did 1:1-6:1 (but without the materials in 1:3b-2:1). An independent form of the Didache's first six chapters is found in a Latin version, the Doctrina Apostolorum, and in the final chapters of the Letter of Barnabas. It thus is possible that Eusebius, in referring to "the alleged teachings of the apostles," may have had in mind the Didache (as suggested above), but it is likewise conceivable that he meant an independent Two Ways treatise. The early Christians must, in any case, have been familiar with an autonomous Two Ways edition since the manual served for centuries as a pre-baptismal instruction. It is found in a more or less reworked form in early church orders such as the Apostolic Church Order (c. 300) and the related Epitome of the Canons of the Holy Apostles, in the Ps.-Athanasian Syntagma Doctrinae (c. 350-70), the Fides CCCXVIII Patrum or Fides Nicaena (c. 375), the Apostolic Constitutions (as part of the Didache), and the fifth-century Arabic Life of Shenoute.[16]

Like the Didache, the Two Ways also had a long and complicated history. The latter document, however, did not vanish until the eleventh century as it kept circulating in the West down to the Carolingian period. It draws on a lost Jewish source and basically consists of the double love command and the Golden Rule which are then worked out through the second table of the Ten Commandments. Of course, the exact form of the Two Ways teaching may have varied from place to place, but it was somehow utilized in the Rule of Benedict and the Rule of the

---

[14] Διδαχὴ ἀποστόλων στιχ. σ´; cf. Preuschen, *Analecta*, 2,64.

[15] *La Doctrine des douze Apôtres*, 109-110 (105-07).

[16] For these writings, see below, Chap. 2. Furthermore, we will see in Chap. 3, that the designation "so-called teaching (Διδαχή) of the apostles" or "the teaching of the catechesis of the apostles," at variance with the widespread conviction, often refers to the separate existence of the Two Ways. In the same chapter, we will ascertain that there are several quotations of Didache-like material which in fact are derived from the Two Ways.

Master, in the Fifteenth Sermon of Ps.-Boniface and, finally, in the Second Catechesis of the Ratio de Cathecizandis Rudibus.[17] Especially the two Latin manuscripts with the title "(De) Doctrina Apostolorum" are important in this respect.
One of these, dating from the ninth or tenth centuries, is only a fragment while the
other, stemming from the eleventh century, appears to form a complete whole.[18]
Because it is not appropriate to pursue this matter here and now, we will postpone
further discussion until chapters 2 and 3, where an historical survey will be
provided of the influence the teaching wielded from the time of its origin onward.

The Text of the Didache

This section first presents a translation of the complete text of the Didache. Next,
it discusses those textual authorities which are indispensable for the establishment
of the text of the Didache. We have already seen that the Bryennios manuscript
is the only complete Greek text of the Didache which has been left to us. Other
direct textual witnesses can be found in fragments such as the Oxyrhynchus
papyrus covering merely a few verses of the Didache and the extracts from translations of the Didache in Coptic and Ethiopic. The writings collected under the
heading 'Indirect Textual sources' include two different types of materials: first,
an extensive reworking of the Didache as a whole in the Apostolic Constitutions
and, second, a number of versions representing the separate Two Ways treatise
before it was incorporated into the Didache.

A TRANSLATION OF THE CORRECTED JERUSALEM MANUSCRIPT

The entire English text below (including its heading) is based on the translation
by A. Cody, 'The *Didache:* An English Translation.'[19] The underlying Greek text
has been established by Willy Rordorf and André Tuilier on the basis of the most
complete direct textual source, which is the Jerusalem Ms. H from the 11th
century.[20] As a result of extensive critical comparisons with one or more direct and
indirect witnesses, Rordorf and Tuilier have made several restorations. And
although realizing that much must remain undecided, we have attempted to make
some further corrections which will be accounted for in the notes. The words in
square brackets [ ] are not found in the source but are added to clarify and interpret
the Greek text. The words in pointed brackets < > are not contained in Ms. H
either, but indicate corrections by Rordorf and Tuilier to the text of H.

---

[17] For these writings, see below, Chap 3, pp. 89-111.
[18] See below, Chap. 4, p. 113.
[19] In Jefford, *The Didache in Context* (in the NovTSup Series), 3-14; esp. 5-8. We gratefully acknowledge the kind permission of Brill (Leiden) to use this translation.
[20] About the value of this MS, see pp. 16-24 below.

The Jerusalem Manuscript (H), fol. 76ʳᵒ. Lines 1-4 from bottom: First and second Title; Did. *1:1-2.*

Fol. 78ro: Did. *5:1-7:4.*
5:1, Beginning of the Way of Death.
6:2f. (line 14f.), Jewish-Christian section on food.

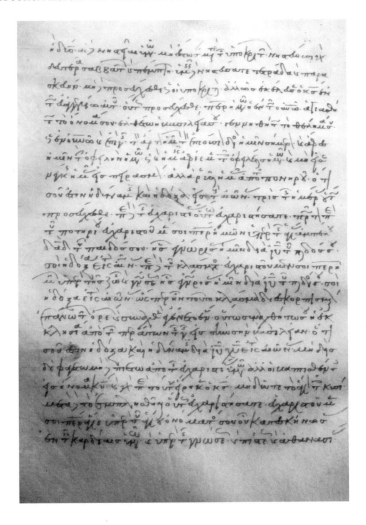

Fol. 78ᵛᵒ: Did. *8:1-10:2.*
8:1 (line 1) on Fasting; 8:2 on the Lord's Prayer (lines 4-10); 9:1ff., on the Eucharist (line 10ff.).

DOCTRINE OF THE TWELVE APOSTLES

Doctrine of the Lord [Brought] to the Nations
by the Twelve Apostles

1:1   There are two ways, one of life, the other of death, and between the two ways there is a great difference.

   2   Now the way of life is this: you shall love first the God who created you, then your neighbour as yourself, and do not yourself do to another what you would not want done to you.

   3   Here is the teaching [that flows] from these words. Bless [pl. throughout verse 3] those who curse you and pray for your enemies, fast for those who persecute you. What kind of favour is it when you love those who love you? Do not even the nations do that? Just love those who hate you and you will not have any enemy.

   4   Avoid the fleshly and bodily passions. If someone strikes you on your right cheek, turn your other one to him too, and you will be perfect. If someone presses you into one mile of service, go along with him for two. If someone takes your cloak, give him your tunic as well. If someone takes away from you what is yours, do not demand it back since you cannot do so anyway.

   5   Give to everyone what he asks of you, and do not ask for it back, for the Father wants people to share with everyone the gifts that have been freely granted to them. Blessed is the person who gives according to the commandment, for he is guiltless. Alas for the person who takes. If someone takes something because he is in need, he is guiltless, but if he is not in need, he shall have to defend his reason for taking it and the use for which he intends it; if he is imprisoned, he shall be interrogated about what he has done, and he shall not go free until he has paid back the last penny.

   6   But then about this sort of thing it has also been said, "Let your charitable gift sweat in your hands until you know to whom you are giving it."

2:1   The second commandment of the doctrine:

   2   You shall not murder. You shall not commit adultery, You shall not corrupt children, You shall not fornicate. You shall not steal. You shall not practise magic. You shall not use the confections of a sorcerer. You shall not murder a child, whether by [procuring its] abortion or by killing it once it is born. You shall not covet what belongs to your neighbour.

   3   You shall not swear falsely. You shall not bear false witness. You shall not speak evil of anyone. You shall not harbour resentment.

   4   You shall not equivocate, either in what you think or in what you say, for equivocation is a mortal snare.

   5   Your word shall not be false or empty but shall be fulfilled in what you really do.

   6   You shall not be given to greed, or swindling, or hypocrisy, or malice, or pride. You shall not plot evil against your neighbour.

   7   You shall not hate anyone. Some people, though, you shall call to task, and for them you shall pray. Others you shall love more than yourself.

3:1   My child, flee from all evil and from everything like it.

   2   Do not be an angry person, for anger leads to murder; nor should you be a zealot or a quarrelsome or hot-tempered person, for from all of these [traits of character] flow murderous acts.

3 My child, do not be a person given to passion, because passion leads to fornication; nor should you be given to obscene speech or to bold gazes, for from all of these [actions] flow acts of adultery.

4 My child, do not practise soothsaying, because this leads to idolatry; nor should you be an enchanter, or an astrologer, or a person who performs purificatory rituals; you should not even want to see <or hear> such things, for from all of these [activities] idolatry is spawned.

5 My child, do not be a liar, because lying leads to theft; nor should you be given to avarice or to vainglory, for from all these [traits of character] theft is spawned.

6 My child, do not be a grumbler, because this leads to slander; nor should you be stubbornly willful or disposed to think evil of people, for from all these [attitudes] slanderous behaviour is spawned.

7 On the contrary, be mild tempered, since those who are mild tempered will inherit the land.

8 Be patient and merciful, without guile, tranquil and good, holding constantly in awe the words you have heard.

9 You shall not exalt yourself or let yourself be arrogant. You shall not attach yourself to those who are highly placed but shall associate with those who are just and humble.

10 Accept the experiences that come your way as good ones, knowing that nothing happens without God.

4:1 My child, you shall be mindful day and night of the one who speaks to you the word of God. You shall honour him as the Lord, for at the source of discourse on lordship the Lord is there.

2 You shall seek out the holy persons every day to find support in their words.

3 You shall not cause division; instead, you shall reconcile those who quarrel. You shall judge justly. You shall not show partiality in calling people to task for their faults.

4 You shall not show indecision [in determining] whether [something] shall be or shall not be.

5 Do not be the sort of person who holds out his hands to receive but draws them back when it comes to giving.

6 If you have [something] through the work of your hands, you shall give [something as] redemption of your sins.

7 You shall not hesitate to give, and when you give you shall not grumble, for you will know who the paymaster is who gives good wages.

8 You shall not turn away anyone who is in need; on the contrary, you shall hold everything in common with your brother, and you shall not say that anything is your own, for if you [pl.] are partners in what is immortal, [should you not be so] all the more in things that perish?

9 You shall not be remiss in guiding your son or your daughter, but shall teach them reverence for God from [the days of] their youth.

10 You shall not show your harsh side when you give a command to your slave or your maid, those who hope in the same God, lest they stop revering the God who is over both [you and them]. For he comes not to call [people] according to their personal status but [to call] those on whom he has prepared the spirit [to descend] [or, (he comes) rather upon those whom the spirit has prepared].

11 As for you [pl.] who are slaves, with respect and reverence you shall be subject to your masters as replicas of God.

12 You shall hate all hypocrisy and all that is not pleasing to the Lord.

13 You shall not abandon the commandments of the Lord but shall keep what you have received, without adding or subtracting anything.

14 In the assembly you shall confess your faults, and you shall not approach with a bad conscience to make your prayer. This is the way of live.

5:1 And the way of death is this. Above of all, it is evil and full of accursedness; [Characteristic of it are] acts of murder, adultery, passion, fornication, theft, idolatry, magic, sorcery, robbery, false witness, hypocrisy, duplicity, guile, pride, malice, willful stubbornness, avarice, obscene speech, jealousy, insolence, arrogance, boastfulness, <irreverence>.

2 [Characteristic of it are also] people who persecute the good, who hate truth, who love falsehood, who do not know money earned in a just way, who do not adhere to what is good or to just judgment, who stay up late at night for purposes that are not good but evil, who are far from being mild tempered and patient, who love what is futile, who are out for money, who do not show mercy to a poor person, who are not distressed by [the plight of] the oppressed, who do not know him who made them, [who are] child murderers, who abort what God has formed, who reject the needy person, who oppress the person who is distressed, [who are] defenders of the rich [and] unjust judges of the poor--[people who are] sinners in everything that they do. Children, from all this may you [pl.] be preserved.

6:1 See to it that no one leads you astray from this way of the doctrine, since [the person who would do so] teaches apart from God.

2 If you can bear the entire yoke of the Lord, you will be perfect, but if you cannot, do what you can.

3 As for food, bear what you can, but be very much on your guard against food offered to idols, for it is [related to] worship of dead gods.

7:1 As for baptism, baptize this way. Having said all this beforehand [i.e., all that is written above], baptize in the name of the Father and of the Son and of the Holy Spirit, in running water.

2 If you [sing. through verses 2-4] do not have running water, however, baptize in another kind of water; if you cannot [do so] in cold [water], then [do so] in warm [water].

3 But if you have neither, pour water on the head thrice in the name of Father and Son and Holy Spirit.

4 Before the baptism, let the person baptizing and the person being baptized – and others who are able – fast; tell the one being baptized to fast one or two [days] before.

8:1 Let your fasts not [coincide] with [those of] the hypocrites. They fast on Monday and Thursday; you, though, should fast on Wednesday and Friday.

2 And do not pray as the hypocrites [do]; pray instead this way, as the Lord directed in his gospel:

"Our Father in heaven,
May your name be acclaimed as holy,

> May your kingdom come,
> May your will come to pass on earth as it does in heaven.
> Give us today our bread for the morrow,
> And cancel for us our debt [owed for sin],
> As we cancel [debts] for those who are indebted to us,
> And do not bring us into temptation,
> But preserve us from evil [or, from the evil one].
> For power and glory are yours forever."

3 Pray this way thrice daily.

9:1 As for the eucharist* [thanksgiving], give thanks this way.

2 First, with regard to the cup:
> We thank you, our Father,
> For the holy vine of David your servant
> which you made known to us
> through Jesus your servant.
> To you be glory forever.

3 And with regard to the fragment:
> We thank you, our Father,
> For the life and knowledge
> which you made known to us
> through Jesus your servant.
> To you be glory forever.

4 As this fragment lay scattered upon the mountains
> and became a single [fragment] when it had been gathered,
> May your church be gathered into your kingdom
> from the ends of the earth.
> For glory and power are yours,
> through Jesus Christ, forever.

5 Let no one eat or drink of your eucharist save those who have been baptized in the name of the Lord, since the Lord has said, "Do not give to dogs what is holy."

10:1 When you have had your fill, give thanks this way:

2 We thank you, holy Father,
> For your holy name,
> which you made dwell in our hearts,
> And for the knowledge and faith and immortality,
> which you made known to us
> through Jesus your servant.
> To you be glory forever.

3 You, almighty Lord, created all things for the sake of your name,
> and you gave food and drink to human beings for enjoyment,
> so that they would thank you;
> But you graced us with spiritual food and drink and eternal life

---

* We have replaced the noun 'thanksgiving' in the translation of A. Cody here and in 9:5 by 'eucharist' since the ritual meal described in Chaps. 9-10 is a celebration of the Eucharist (see below, chapter 8, pp. 298-304).

through ‹Jesus› your servant.

4   For all things[*] we thank you, Lord, because you are powerful.
To you be glory forever.

5   Be mindful, Lord, of your church,
to preserve it from all evil [or, from every evil being]
and to perfect it in your love.
And, once it is sanctified, gather it from the four winds,
into the kingdom which you have prepared for it.
For power and glory are yours forever.

6   May favour [or, grace] come, and may this world pass by.
Hosanna to the God of David!
If anyone is holy, let him come.
If anyone is not, let him repent.
Our Lord, come! Amen.

7   Allow the propets, though, to give thanks as much as they like.

11:1   Accordingly, receive anyone who comes and teaches you all that has been said above.

2   If the teacher himself turns to teaching another doctrine [which will lead] to destruction, do not listen to him, but [if it will lead] to an increase of justice and knowledge of the Lord, receive him as the Lord.

3   In the matter of apostles and prophets, act this way, according to the ordinance of the gospel.

4   Let every apostle who comes to you be received as the Lord.

5   He shall stay <only> one day, or, if need be, another day too. If he stays three days, he is a false prophet.

6   When the apostle leaves, let him receive nothing but [enough] bread [to see him through] until he finds lodging. If he asks for money, he is a false prophet.

7   Do not test any prophet who speaks in spirit, and do not judge him, for every [other] sin will be forgiven, but this sin will not be forgiven.

8   Not everyone who speaks in spirit is a prophet but only the one whose behaviour is the Lord's. So the false prophet and the prophet will be recognized by their behaviour.

9   Any prophet who gives orders for a table [i.e., a meal] in spirit shall not eat of it; if he does, he is a false prophet.

10   If any prophet teaching the truth does not do what he teaches, he is a false prophet.

11   No prophet, examined and found true, who acts for the earthly mystery of the church but does not teach [others] to do everything that he himself does, shall be judged by you, for his judgment is with God. The ancient prophets acted in the same way.

12   You shall not listen to anyone who says in spirit, "Give me money, or something," but if he is asking that something be given for others who are in need, let no one judge him.

---

[*] Read "for all things (περὶ πάντων)" with the Coptic translation. For arguments, see below, Chap. 8, p. 298, n. 87; p. 314 and n. 130. This variant is to be preferred to the version πρὸ πάντων in the Jerusalem Ms. The latter reading is found in Rordorf-Tuilier (*La Doctrine des douze Apôtres*, 180) and was translated by Cody as "above all."

12:1 Let everyone who comes in the name of the Lord be received, and then, when you have taken stock of him, you will know [what he is like], for you will have right and left perception [i.e., perception of what is good and bad about him].

2 If the person who comes is just passing through on the way to some other place, help him as much as you can, but he shall not stay with you more than two or three days – if that is necessary.

3 If he wants to settle in with you, though, and he is a craftsman, let him work and [thus] eat.

4 If he has no craft, you shall use your insight to provide a good way for him to avoid living with you as a Christian with nothing to do.

5 If he is unwilling to do what that way calls for, he is using Christ to make a living. Be on your guard against people like this.

13:1 Every true prophet who wants to settle in with you deserves his food.

2 In the same way, a true teacher, too, deserves his food, just as a worker does.

3 So when you [sing.] take any firstfruits of what is produced by the wine press and the threshing floor, by cows and by sheep, you [sing.] shall give the firstfruits to the prophets, for they are your [pl.] high priests.

4 If, however, you [pl. through verse 4] have no prophet, give [them] to the poor.

5 If you [sing. through verses 5-7] make bread, take the firstfruits and give them according to the commandment.

6 Likewise, when you open a jar of wine or oil, take the firstfruits and give them to the prophets.

7 Take the firstfruits of money and clothing and whatever [else] you own as you think best and give them according to the commandment.

14:1 Assembling on every Sunday of the Lord, break bread and give thanks, confessing your faults besides so that your sacrifice may be clean.

2 Let no one engaged in a dispute with his comrade join you until they have been reconciled, lest your sacrifice be profaned.

3 This is [the sacrifice] of which the Lord has said: "'to offer me a clean sacrifice in every place and time, because I am a great king,' says the Lord, 'and my name is held in wonder among the nations.'"

15:1 Select, then, for yourselves bishops and deacons worthy of the Lord, mild-tempered men who are not greedy, who are honest and have proved themselves, for they too perform the functions of prophets and teachers for you.

2 So do not disregard them, for they are the persons who hold a place of honour among you, together with the prophets and the teachers.

3 Correct one another not in anger but in peace, as you have it [written] in the gospel; and let no one speak to anyone who wrongs another – let him not hear [a word] from you – until he has repented.

4 Perform your prayers and your almsgiving and all that you undertake as you have it [written] in the gospel of our Lord.

16:1 Keep vigil over your life. Let your lamps not go out and let your waists not be ungirded but be ready, for you do not know the hour at which our Lord is coming.

2 You shall assemble frequently, seeking what pertains to your souls, for the whole time of your belief will be of no profit to you unless you are perfected at the final hour.

3 For in the final days false prophets and corruptors will be multiplied, and the sheep
   will turn into wolves, and love will turn into hate.
4 As lawlessness increases, they will hate and persecute and betray one another, and
   at that time the one who leads the world astray will appear as a son of God and will
   work signs and wonders, and the earth will be given into his hands, and he will do
   godless things which have never been done since the beginning of time.
5 Then human creation will pass into the testing fire and many will fall away and
   perish, but those who persevere in their belief will be saved by the curse itself [or,
   by the very one who is (under?) a curse?].
6 And then the signs of truth will appear, first, the sign of extension [of the cross?]
   in heaven, next, the signal of the trumpet call, and third, resurrection of the dead –
7 not of all, however, but, as it has been said, "The Lord will come and all the holy
   ones with him."
8 Then the world will see the Lord coming upon the clouds of heaven...

THE DIRECT TEXTUAL SOURCES

An (almost) complete text of the Didache has survived in only one manuscript,
an eleventh century minuscule, the Manuscript of Jerusalem (Hierosolymitanus
54), which was published in 1883. Because the quality of the text in
Hierosolymitanus 54 is a controversial point, most of our discussion below will
focus on its antiquity and reliabilty. In the remainder of this subsection, attention
will be given to other direct witnesses to the text of the Didache: two parchment
fragments from the fourth century discovered in Oxyrhynchus, a Coptic papyrus
sheet from the fifth century found in Cairo and some parts of the Didache which
were inserted into the Ethiopic Church Order.

The Manuscript of Jerusalem (H)

In 1873, the metropolitan of Serres (Serrae) in Macedonia, Philotheos Bryennios,
discovered a Greek parchment manuscript in the monastery of the Holy Sepulcre
in Constantinople. The document contained several early Christian writings,
including the text of the famous Didache. He edited the treatise in 1883. In 1887,
the manuscript was transferred to the Greek patriarchate in Jerusalem where it is
still preserved today.[21] Although the Didache text is mostly studied in isolation

---

[21] Under the signature Κῶδ. πατρ. 54. A microfilm of the whole manuscript is available in the Library
of Congress in Washington; see Prigent-Kraft, *Épître de Barnabé*, 50, n. 2. Photos of the folios 51b-76a
(containing the Clementine epistles) were published in Lightfoot, *The Apostolic Fathers* I/1, 425-74.
A photocopy of the Didache part (76a-80b) appeared in the appendix to Harris, *The Teaching of the
Apostles*. A photograph of three pages of the Jerusalem Manuscript (folios 51b, 76a and 120a) are
printed in Harris, *Three Pages of the Bryennios Manuscript*. See above pp. 7-9.

from other works of the Jerusalem Manuscript, it will presently be shown that consultation of the manuscript as a whole may be useful as well.[22]

The Quality of the Manuscript. In the colophon (fol. 120[ro]) the name of the scribe and the date are preserved. "Leon[23] the scribe and sinner" (Λέων νοτάριος καὶ ἀλείτης) was the one who produced this codex which he completed on Tuesday, 11 June 1056. The manuscript contains the following items:

a) Ps.-Chrysostom's Synopsis Veteris et Novi Testamenti: fol.1[ro]-38[vo];
b) Epistle of Barnabas: fol. 39[ro]-51[vo];
c) First Epistle of Clement: fol. 51[vo]-70[ro];
d) Second Epistle of Clement: fol. 70[ro]-76[ro];
e) A list of the "names of (biblical) books used by the Hebrews" (ὀνόματα τῶν βιβλίων παρ' ἑβραίοις). Both the titles (transliterated from Hebrew[24] into Greek) and the Greek equivalents are written in red ink: fol. 76[ro];
f) Didache: fol. 76[ro]- 80[vo];
g) The letter by Maria of Cassoboloi to Ignatius of Antioch: fol. 81[ro]-82[ro];
h) Twelve letters by Ignatius of Antioch in the secondary, longer version:[25] fols. 82[ro]-120[ro].
    The colophon is followed by a treatise on the genealogy of Jesus: fol. 120[ro]-120[vo].

Hierosolymitanus 54 is the only manuscript containing a full version of the Didache (except for the final lines). At the same time, however, considerable doubt can be expressed with respect to its textual value since it is a mediaeval document. A series of alterations, such as interpolations and harmonizations, are to be expected from the time of a text's first emergence to its final reproduction in the eleventh century. So the value of the Jerusalem codex, not surprisingly, was challenged in the course of time. It was considered to reflect a late recension and was assumed to contribute very little to the reconstruction of the original text. Because they believed the recension of H to be corrupt, Erik Peterson and J.-P. Audet consequently introduced a considerable number of changes in the H-text.[26] Klaus Wengst is also sceptical about the reliability of the Jerusalem manuscript and was so committed to this conviction that he excluded the evangelical section (Did 1:3b-2:1), added the prayer for the myrrh in 10:8, and completed the ending

---

[22] In the conviction that further examination of the Jerusalem Codex H can help to dispel certain misconceptions about the Didache text, David Flusser has recently used several occasions to inspect the entirety of the manuscript itself in the Greek patriarchate in the Old City of Jerusalem. The following observations result from these visits.

[23] In the original, the name Leon is clearly legible (pace Niederwimmer, *Die Didache*, 33, n. 3).

[24] Below we will return to the Greek transcription of the supposed Aramaic titles in this list.

[25] The Greek text of the letter by Maria of Cassoboloi to Ignatius and the longer version of the latter's epistles are reprinted in Ruiz Bueno, *Padres Apostólicos*, 503-569.

[26] Peterson, 'Über einige Probleme', 181 (summarizing) and Audet, *La Didachè*, 52-78.

of the eschatological portion in 16:8 on the basis of the conclusion in the Apostolic Constitutions.[27]

Here, nevertheless, the choice was made to adopt the Jerusalem Manuscript as a basis for study, not in the last place because sufficient alternative manuscript material is lacking. Indeed, a cautious testing of particular instances by a continuous collation against the Jerusalem Ms. ought to be carried out. The oldest manuscripts which are of value for the text of the Didache, however, are merely a half-dozen fragments existing in Greek, Coptic, Ethiopic and Latin. Their diminutive size disqualifies them from being useful evidence in assessing the degree to which our 11th century copy replicates the original. Moreover, it is dangerous to assign too much weight to the readings of the Apostolic Constitutions since this work presents an expanded and, unfortunately, paraphrased text of the Didache.[28] Because these fragments providing a collation against the Jerusalem Ms. are so few in number, it would be impossible to really establish a secure critical text of the Didache.

In addition to this negative argument, there are also positive considerations for accepting the Jerusalem document. Firstly, the value of the Jerusalem Ms. is endorsed by the fact that it offers a unique collection. It is the sole manuscript containing the Didache and both the Epistle of Barnabas and the First Epistle of Clement. It is also is the only document which has preserved the complete text of the Second Epistle of Clement. In the Codex Alexandrinus the latter Epistle ends with 12:5. This too must be taken into account when evaluating the fundamental reliability of our manuscript in the literary transmission of the Didache. Despite the late date of its origin, the Jerusalem codex in some respects measures up to the Alexandrinus and the Sinaiticus. The second reason is linked to the optimistic judgment of Willy Rordorf and André Tuilier about the value of the Jerusalem Manuscript. They take the text of H to be one that is based on a source from the fourth and fifth century[29] and thus to offer a very ancient recension of the Didache. In the next pages, evidence will be provided which supports and enhances their position.[30] A closer examination of the Jerusalem Manuscript considered to its full extent will help solve problems about the twofold title of the Didache, its abrupt ending in 16:8, and the quality of the manuscript.

The Antiquity of the List of "Names of Books Used by the Hebrews". Before looking at the composition of the manuscript in a more specific fashion, it is useful to just briefly review the question of the curious list of the Old Testament books

---

[27] Wengst, (*Didache [Apostellehre]*), 6; and for the three passages mentioned here, cf. 18-20; 57-59 and 20. For the latter change, see also Aldridge, 'The Lost Ending'. For a summary and support of Wengst's alterations, see Dehandschutter, 'The Text of the *Didache*'.

[28] Niederwimmer, *Die Didache*, 46-47; Schöllgen-(Geerlings), *Didache. Zwölf-Apostellehre*, 92-93.

[29] Rordorf-Tuilier, *La Doctrine des douze Apôtres*, 102-110 (104-07) and a similar position was represented previously by Audet, *La Didachè*, 32.

[30] Moreover, since they have provided a cautious and critical edition of the Didache as presented in H, we adopt this text (see above, pp. 10-16).

in the Jerusalem Manuscript (fol. 76ʳᵒ).[31] It has already been noted that the same inventory of transliterated Hebrew titles with Greek equivalents, though wholly recast, also appears in Epiphanius' small treatise On Weights and Measures.[32] In addition, two other Greek lists of the Jewish Old Testament books survived, one by Melito, the bishop of Sardis (ca. 170 CE) and the other by Origen (ca. 185-254 CE). Both catalogues are incorporated in Eusebius' Ecclesiastical History. While Melito's list is in Greek only (Eccl. Hist. IV, 26, 14),[33] Origen's list provides a transliteration of the Hebrew names and the Greek equivalents (Eccl. Hist. VI, 25, 2).[34]

It is clear that these series of titles of biblical books, enumerated in Origen's list and preserved in the Jerusalem Manuscript, were composed in order to answer the question of which books belonged to the Jewish Bible (παρ' ἑβραίοις). Jews were asked about their canon because Christians had to decide which Jewish books should be considered canonical in the Old Testament. Since various lists may have been in circulation, there probably was a need to establish a reliable norm for the names, order and number of sacred writings.

The lists in our manuscript and that of Epiphanius are somewhat problematic. Of course, it is only natural that they both present mistakes. Transcription from a foreign language almost inevitably results in new graphical errors. Moreover, errors may also arise from faulty reception. The scribe taking dictation in a foreign language is prone to misinterpret what he has heard. But how are we to explain the various Aramaic elements, present in the transliterations of most of the titles of the sacred books? The Semitic names in Origen's list are clearly Hebrew[35] but

---

[31] See the discussion in Audet, 'A Hebrew-Aramaic List' and Torrey-Eissfeldt, 'hebräisch-aramäisches Verzeichnis'. The list in our manuscript (cf. Audet, 'A Hebrew-Aramaic List', 136) runs as follows (the numbers were added by Audet to facilitate reference):

ὀνόματα τῶν βιβλίων παρ' ἑβραίοις

1. βρισίθ · γένεσις. 2. ἐλσιμόθ · ἔξοδος. 3. ὀδοικρά · λευϊτικόν. 4. διιησοῦ · ἰησοῦ υἱοῦ ναυή. 5. ἐλεδεββαρί · δευτερονόμιον. 6. οὐιδαβίρ · ἀριθμοί. 7. δαρούθ · τῆς ῥούθ. 8. διώβ · τοῦ ἰώβ. 9. δάσοφτιμ · τῶν κριτῶν. 10. σφερτελίμ · ψαλτήριον. 11. διεμμουήλ · βασιλειῶν α'. 12. διαδδουδεμουήλ · βασιλειῶν β'. 13. δαμαλαχήμ · βασιλειῶν γ'. 14. ἀμαλαχήμ · βασιλειῶν δ'. 15. δεβριιαμίν · παραλειπομένων α'. 16. δεριιαμίν · παραλειπομένων β'. 17. δαμαλεώθ · παροιμιῶν. 18. δακοέλεθ · ἐκκλησιαστής. 19. σιρὰ σιρίμ · ἆσμα ἀσμάτων. 20. διερέμ · ἰερεμίας. 21. δααθαρσιαρ · δωδεκαπρόφητον. 22. δησαίου · ἠσαίου. 23. διεεζεκιήλ · ἰεζεκιήλ. 24. δαδανιήλ · δανιήλ. 25. δέσδρα · ἔσδρα α'. 26. δαδέσδρα · ἔσδρα β'. 27. δεσθής · ἐσθήρ.

[32] De mensuris et ponderibus, Chap. 23.9. For the text of Epiphanius' inventory, see Audet, 'A Hebrew-Aramaic List', 138.

[33] Melito writes about his visit to Palestine. He presents here the earliest surviving Christian list of the Old Testament books. For Eusebius' Eccl. Hist. IV, 26, 14, see Schwartz, Eusebius II: Die Kirchengeschichte: II/1, 388. The list is also reproduced in: Hall, Melito of Sardis, 66.

[34] For Eusebius' Eccl. Hist. VI, 25, 2, see Schwartz, Eusebius II: Die Kirchengeschichte: II/2, 572.574.576. The lists in the Jerusalem Manuscript, in Epiphanius, and in Origen conclude by mentioning Esther, a title missing in Melito's rendering. For the latter phenomenon, see Ellis, 'The Old Testament Canon', 659 and n. 34.

[35] The importance of knowing whether these semitic designations are transliterations from the Hebrew or Aramaic may be illustrated by the following example. In our list, the book of Proverbs is named δαμαλεώθ; in Epiphanius, it is called δμεαλώθ. The vocabulary is similar to Origen's title μελώθ. Since Origen's list is evidently independent from ours, the only possible suggestion is that all three terms

the ones in our (and Epiphanius') list are usually taken to be Aramaic titles transliterated into Greek.[36]

It is obvious that some of the titles in our list kept a purely Hebrew form in transcription (the five books of the Pentateuch, Psalms, the Song of Songs and the two books of Chronicles). The remainder of the items (18 out of 27 titles), however, seem to be Aramaic in form since the letter *d* has been attached as a prefix to the specific titles. This syllable, being the transcription of the Aramaic genitive particle, has the possessive meaning which in English is expressed by the preposition "of". So in all 18 cases the titles can be understood as something like "the book of Ruth" (δαρούθ · τῆς ῥούθ) / "the book of Job" (διώβ · τοῦ ἰώβ.) / "the book of Judges" (δάσοφτιμ · τῶν κριτῶν) / "the book of ... (etc)." It has been suggested, not improbably, that the lists, transmitted by the Jerusalem Manuscript and Epiphanius, are dependent on a common source which may be attributed to the first half of the second century CE.[37]

The question remains, however, how to account for this Aramaic form of the Hebrew titles. This presents us with a riddle which can be pointed out but for which no solution can be provided here. For it does not make any sense whatever to translate the Hebrew names of the Jewish scriptures into Aramaic when one is speaking about the *Hebrew* Bible (ὀνόματα τῶν βιβλίων παρ' ἑβραίοις). The one and single name in our list which surely was transmitted in Aramaic, is that given to the Twelve (minor) Prophets: δαθαριασαρά[38] (δωδεκαπρόφητον), i.e., דתרי עשׂרא. This remains their current name to this day.[39] No plausible explanation for this ancient anomaly has yet been found.

A final consideration in this paragraph concerns the relevance of this list in the attempt to solve the problem of the two titles borne by the Didache. It has already been mentioned above that the list of titles for the books of the Hebrew Bible in the manuscript was written in red ink. The red colour probably shows them precisely to be titles and it is this fact which has particular importance for the

---

reflect the Hebrew מלות, a *status constructus* of מלים. Admittedly, this form does not appear at the beginning of the Book of Proverbs nor elsewhere in the Hebrew Bible.

On the other hand, if we assume an Aramaic background behind δαμαλεώθ / δμεαλώθ, these two terms suggest we are dealing with a corruption. For this reason, the copyist of the Syriac translation of Epiphanius' De mensuris et ponderibus has suggested it be read *dm'th'lōth* (דמחלוה; cf. Audet, 'A Hebrew-Aramaic List', 137) instead of δαμαλεώθ / δμεαλώθ. He probably took these titles to reflect a noun form derived from the Aramaic *mᵉthal*, and thus a *thêta*, corresponding to the Aramaic *taw* (מתל = parable, riddle, etc.), would have been lost in the course of transmission.

[36] Audet, 'A Hebrew-Aramaic List', 140-41. 144–54; Torrey-Eissfeldt, 'hebräisch-aramäisches Verzeichnis', 251-52; Niederwimmer, *Die Didache*, 34.

[37] Cf. Audet, 'A Hebrew-Aramaic List', 141-45 and Torrey-Eissfeldt, 'hebräisch-aramäisches Verzeichnis', 251-52 and n. 10.

[38] So in the Epiphanius' list. In our manuscript, the name is somehow corrupt (see above, note 31, nr. 21).

[39] In bBB 14b-15a, the order of the biblical books and their dates of composition are discussed. The printed edition of the Babylonian Talmud has the title of the Twelve (minor Prophets) adjusted to the Hebrew one (שנים עשׂר), but in the manuscripts their name is written in Aramaic.

By the way, the list of Origen does not the mention the Twelve Prophets.

question which of the twofold headings of the Didache is the original one. The book, in fact, has two titles. The first is the shorter (Διδαχὴ τῶν δώδεκα ἀποστόλων), while the second is a longer name (Διδαχὴ κυρίου διὰ τῶν δώδεκα ἀποστόλων τοῖς ἔθνεσιν). It has long been a topic of great debate which of the two titles is the authentic one. Against this background, it is of particular interest to see that, in our manuscript, the Didache begins with the short title on the next line immediately after the end of the list of the books of the Hebrew Bible. The short title follows the previous work with no intervening space in a separate line and, like the list, it is written in red ink. Additionally, a cross is used as a mark in the margin. The longer name, however, constitutes the beginning of the text itself and continues in the same line with ὁδοὶ δύο ("two ways"). Moreover, it is rendered in black ink. The conclusion to be drawn from this evidence is that in the eyes of the scribe the first, shorter name was the real title, while he considered the longer name as belonging to the tractate. This graphical aspect shows the shorter title to be the usual designation of the Didache, a fact which is corroborated by the superscription of the Latin translation of the Jewish source behind the Two Ways tractate, that is, The Teaching of the Apostles (Doctrina apostolorum).[40]

The Antiquity of the Central Part of the Jerusalem Codex. An examination of the actual composition of the manuscript as a whole may shed further light on the antiquity of the document. Moreover, it may enable us to deal more adequately with the question why the final chapter of the Didache breaks off in the middle of fol. 80[vo] while leaving blank one-third of the page.

First some chronological data with regard to the individual works contained in our manuscript are needed. John Chrysostom lived between 347-407 CE and because the Synopsis Veteris et Novi Testamenti was written later, it has been wrongly attributed to him.[41] The Epistle of Barnabas was probably composed at the beginning of the second century CE. The First Epistle of Clement was conceived ca. 96 CE while the Second Epistle of Clement stems from the first half of the second century CE. As to the Didache itself, it was surely edited before this date. The secondary, longer version of the correspondence of Ignatius of Antioch was not composed before the late fourth century CE.[42]

At this point, it is already clear enough that the 'subapostolic' writings (produced before 150 CE) in our manuscript, i.e., Barnabas, 1-2 Clement, and the Didache, comprise one sequel. Moreover, it has been suggested above that also the bilingual list of the Jewish Old Testament writings, located between 2 Clement and the Didache, may have originated in the first part of the the second century CE. On the other hand, the works copied at the beginning of our codex (the Synopsis

---

[40] The witnesses testifying to this title are mentioned in the survey in Audet, *La Didachè*, 92-93 and Niederwimmer, *Die Didache*, 81, n. 5. For a discussion on the independent Two Ways tractate, see below, Chap 2, pp. 56-59; Chap. 3, pp. 82-89; Chap. 4, pp. 117-30.

[41] Altaner-Stuiber, *Patrologie*, 328; Quasten, *Patrology* 3, 472 and Bardenhewer, *Geschichte* 3, 352.

[42] The long recension of the Ignatian letters appeared in the latter part of the fourth century. For this recension, cf. Schoedel, *Ignatius of Antioch*, 1-2.4 and Fischer, *Die Apostolischen Väter*, 111-13.

Veteris et Novi Testamenti[43] on fol. 1ro-38vo) and at the end (the long recension of the Epistles of Ignatius of Antioch on fol. 82ro-120ro) are both inauthentic and late.

The situation indicates that the scribe Leon used a very old codex, although this source, of course, must stem from a later date than the subapostolic age. In his copy, he prefaced this precious collection of authentic ancient writings with Pseudo-Chrysostom's work containing the presentation of biblical books and supplemented it by adding a collection of an extra subapostolic author, the Pseudo-Ignatian epistles, at the end. He may have had doubts about the antiquity and genuineness of these two works but, nevertheless, utilized them because they both treated subjects which were also dealt with in his ancient source.

The external form of the Jerusalem manuscript confirms the above internal analysis. It has already been mentioned that the remaining lines of the page where the text of the Didache ends are left unused.[44] Because fol. 80[vo] contains 16 written lines and the standard number per page is 23, we may assume that 7 lines are missing here. The usual explanation for this omission is that the conclusion of the Didache is lost. It is mostly assumed that Leon left the rest of the page blank so as to show that the document he was copying was defective. Sometimes it is even suggested that the number of empty lines indicates the quantity of text left out.[45] Indeed, the Didache's ending, breaking off when recounting Christ's return, stops abruptly and cannot be complete. It is unlikely, however, that the scribe Leon allocated the remainder of the page to the missing material. He probably did not know how much space was needed to copy these materials. We might push things even further. In our opinion, the remaining one-third page of fol. 80[vo] is not left blank in order to draw attention to the defectiveness of his copy. The reason for the omission is related to the scribe's habit of reproducing his sources. After he had finished copying a codex, he left the rest of the page empty and began to copy the following source at the top of the next page.

The first example of this practice in our document is on fol. 29[ro]. Having completed his copy of the first manuscript of Pseudo-Chrysostom, Leon started reproducing the second manuscript of the work on the following page (fol. 29[vo]). Because it begins with Isaiah – which is the first book of the prophetical portion in the Christian canon – the second codex is likely to have contained the treatment of the prophetical books of the Old Testament. Once he had finished copying this manuscript (fol. 38[vo]), Leon began (on fol. 39[ro]) to reproduce the ancient codex of the Apostolic Fathers while leaving no blanks in the text from this place onward! Each new work begins on the next line following the previous work without intervening space. His precious manuscript contained at least five ancient Christian

---

[43]   This introduction to Scripture with a detailed account of the content of each book is incomplete. A lot of materials, especially on the books of the New Testament, are still missing.

[44]   See Niederwimmer, *Die Didache*, 34-35; Rordorf-Tuilier, *La Doctrine des douze Apôtres*, 107 and 199, n. 3; Wengst, *Didache (Apostellehre)*, 20.

[45]   So Audet, *La Didachè*, 75-78: "Mais alors il devient d'un grand intérêt de se demander si, comme il était normal, le blanc de sept lignes dans le ms. de Bryennios n'a pas été calculé approximativement d'après le contenu possible du folio perdu. L'hypothèse a pour elle toutes les vraisemblances." (75).

writings: the Epistle of Barnabas (fol. 39ro-51vo), the first Epistle of Clement (fol. 51vo-70ro), the second Epistle of Clement (fol. 70ro-76ro) and a list of the Jewish books of the Old Testament - in red ink (fol.76ro). This list is directly followed by the Didache (fols. 76ro-80vo).

At this point, we again have arrived at fol. 80vo with the omission of 7 lines. Given the fact that the scribe was not in the habit of leaving spaces before starting a copy of a new codex, one may reasonably surmise that it was on this spot that the copy he was reproducing broke off. Here the valuable manuscript of the Apostolic Fathers, which the scribe copied in our manuscript on fols. 39ro-80vo, ceased. On top of fol. 81ro, the scribe commences copying the longer, secondary text of Ignatius of Antioch, and this is concluded by the colophon with the name of the scribe (fol. 120ro-120vo). Leon apparently was the one and single scribe of the entire manuscript. Comparing the addition after the colophon with the preceding pages, one can detect no difference in the script. In order to leave no space in the manuscript unused, he also filled the remaining portion of this final folio (after his name and date) with a genealogical exposition about Jesus.

W. Rordorf and A. Tuilier have suggested that the text of our eleventh-century minuscule, discovered by the metropolitan Bryennios, rests on a source from the fourth or fifth century CE.[46] It now appears that we should narrow down the ancient textual basis of the manuscript to its central part only. The source of this text, extending from Barnabas to the end of the Didache (fol. 39ro-80vo), should probably be assigned to an earlier period than was previously thought. It may have originated in the patristic period and contained a major part of the so-called Apostolic Fathers.[47] We have already established that the end of the Didache, the last part of the precious manuscript, was lost at the time Leon was copying it. And, of course, it is a well-known fact that the ends of codices and scrolls are frequently

---

[46] Rordorf-Tuilier, *La Doctrine des douze Apôtres*, 105-107.

[47] Our manuscript was completed on June 11th, 1056, two years after the official beginning of the schism between the Roman and Byzantine Church (July 16th, 1054). In the year when the manuscript was copied, the last representative of the so-called Macedonian dynasty died: Theodora, the daughter of the Byzantine emperor Constantine VIII. Because the new period of Byzantine art in the tenth century has strongly been influenced, stimulated and promoted by the Macedonian dynasty, it is often called the 'Macedonian renaissance'. It was an age characterized by a renewal of study, especially of classical antiquity and ancient hellenistic art. Today's scholarship and knowledge of the 'Macedonian renaissance' are primarily based on the research of illuminated manuscripts which in turn are assumed to be copies or compilations of valuable illuminated Greek manuscripts of classical authors. This clearly shows how important the practice of copying ancient manuscripts was for the revival of classical learning and education in the period of the Macedonian dynasty. Unfortunately, present scholarship mostly is interested in the 'pagan' aspect of such revivals. Although such a renaissance evidently is also characterized by a return to the Bible and early Christian sources, scholars do not pay sufficient attention these days to the renewal of Christianity in such renaissances.

A standard work about the revival of classical learning and about the practice of copying ancient pre-Christian Greek literature in that period is Lemerle, *Le premier humanisme byzantin*. We are not familiar with any study about the reproduction of patristic Greek works in those days. The prehistory of the Jerusalem manuscript of the Didache, however, evidences to the tendency of copying ancient Christian manuscripts in the 'Macedonian renaissance'.

mutilated or missing. It is quite possible, then, that the lost end of Leon's outstanding source contained more than just the end of the Didache. Originally, still another subapostolic treatise, like for example the Shepherd of Hermas, may have succeeded the text of the Didache. However that may be, it is well conceivable that the person who in the 11th century discovered the 'patristic' codex (and this may have been Leon himself), immensely enjoyed his discovery.[48]

The Two Oxyrhynchus Fragments (P)

There are also other, though incomplete and fractional, witnesses to the text of the Didache. In 1922, two fragments, discovered in Oxyrhynchus, were published (POxy 1782).[49] The parchment leaves, which are abraded, probably belonged to some small fourth-century codex.[50] They preserve the text of Did 1:3c-4a and 2:7b-3:2a and amount to just 64 words. The text offered in P is important since these fragments, being about 650 years older than the Jerusalem manuscript, are the most ancient witnesses of the direct textual tradition. As compared with H, the textual variants in P do show clear variations and some significant expansion in Did 1:4. All this might indicate that the latter manuscript is based on an archetype divergent from H.[51] For our reconstruction of the Greek Two Ways (below, Chap. 4), these fragments will not play a significant role.[52]

The Coptic Fragment

Two years after the publication of the Oxyrhynchus Fragments, a papyrus was edited by G.W. Horner.[53] The text, written in Coptic, corresponds to Did 10:3b-

---

[48]   Audet (*La Didachè*, 1, n. 2), compares the excitement caused in 1883 by the publication of the Didache with the general excitement after the discovery of the Dead Sea Scrolls. It is not likely, however, that the discovery of the codex of the Apostolic Fathers awoke a similar interest in the 11th century because in that period the sense for history was not as developed as it is in modern times.

[49]   Grenfell-Hunt, *The Oxyrhynchus Papyri*, no. 1782.

[50]   For further reading, see Audet, *La Didachè*, 26-27, n. 2.

[51]   Cf. Niederwimmer, *Die Didache*, 38 and 39. See also Audet, *La Didachè*, 28.

[52]   The first leaf of P (containing Did 1:3c-4a) comprises part of the passage which belongs to the Christian interpolation in the Two Ways (below, pp. 40-48). The second leaf of P has the remarkable textual variant ἀπὸ παντὸς πράγματος πονηροῦ against the reading ἀπὸ παντὸς πονηροῦ in Did 3:1 in the Jerusalem Ms. The longer expression in P, however, rather seems to be a secondary clarification. See, also for minor variants, Audet, *La Didachè*, 28 and Niederwimmer, *Die Didache*, 39.

[53]   Horner, 'A New Papyrus Fragment', 226-29 (text) and 230-31 (English translation). Since the Horner edition, the fragment has been issued another three times. In 1925, C. Schmidt published his edition ('Das koptische Didache-Fragment') with a German translation (84-89) and a supplementary discussion (90-99); then, in 1952, L.-Th. Lefort edited, translated, and commented upon the text in his *Les Pères apostoliques* 1, 32-34 (text) and 2, 25-28 (French translation). The most recent edition was published by F.S. Jones and P.A. Mirecki, 'Considerations on the Coptic Papyrus', 52-67 (text with English translation) and 58-87 (commentary and discussion).

12:2a. It turned up for the first time in Cairo and is preserved now in the British Museum in London (PLond Or. 9271). The question why the text ends where it does must be left open. An attempt has been made to prove that the ending point of the Coptic version in 12:2a reflects the actual conclusion of a papyrus roll which contained the Didache.[54] This conclusion, however, was challenged convincingly. The text was not used as the end of a roll but was cut from a roll of papyrus in order to serve as a double-leaf intended for a codex.[55]

The Coptic Fragment, which probably dates from the fifth century, offers many textual variants as compared to H which will not be investigated here.[56] When dealing with the Eucharistic prayers, however, we will discuss two interesting divergences (see below, Chap. 8, n. 87). The Coptic text offers an 'ointment' or μύρον blessing in 10:8, which is not paralleled in H. This prayer, occurring in the Apostolic Constitutions VII, 27,1-2 as well, is often considered to be an authentic text of the Didache.[57] There are, however, good reasons to question its genuineness.[58] The other textual divergence will appear to be closer to the original text than the reading in H, as it reflects a formulation in the Birkat Ha-Mazon, the Jewish prayer which lies behind this eucharistic prayer. The variant "for all things" (περὶ πάντων) of the Coptic translation at Did 10:4 is to be preferred to the reading "above all" (πρὸ πάντων) in the Jerusalem manuscript.[59] Generally speaking, however, the text-critical value of the Coptic Fragment should not be exaggerated. It is useful to a limited degree only for the establishment of the text of the Didache.[60]

The Version in the Ethiopian Church Order

In addition to the Oxyrhynchus Fragments and the Coptic papyrus, also the Ethiopic Church Order or Ethiopic Canones Ecclesiastici preserves portions of the Didache. The existence of parts of the Didache in the Ethiopic version exclusively

---

[54] Cf. Patterson-Jefford, 'A Note on *Didache* 12,2a'; Patterson, '*Didache* 11-13: the Legacy'. See also below, Chap. 9, pp. 332-333.

[55] Cf. Jones-Mirecki, 'Considerations on the Coptic Papyrus', 74-83.

[56] But see Bihlmeyer, *Die Apostolischen Väter*, XVIII-XIX; Audet, *La Didachè*, 33-34; Niederwimmer, 'Textprobleme der Didache', passim.

[57] See Bihlmeyer, *Die Apostolischen Väter*, 20; Gero, 'The so-called Ointment Prayer'; Wengst, *Didache (Apostellehre)*, 57-59.

[58] For the Coptic text, cf. Jones-Mirecki, 'Considerations on the Coptic Papyrus', 52-57; esp. 52-53, column 1, lines 15-20. The "ointment prayer" was considered secondary by Vööbus, *Liturgical Traditions*, 51-60; Rordorf-Tuilier, *La Doctrine des douze Apôtres*, 47-48; Niederwimmer, *Die Didache*, 205-09; Schöllgen-(Geerlings), *Didache. Zwölf-Apostellehre*, 54-55, among others. Further, see below, Chap. 8, n. 87.

[59] For the Coptic version, see Jones-Mirecki, 'Considerations on the Coptic Papyrus', 52-57; esp. 52-53, column 1, lines 4-6. Further, see below, Chap. 8, n. 87.

[60] Niederwimmer, *Die Didache*, 42-43 and Jones-Mirecki, 'Considerations on the Coptic Papyrus', 84-86.

and the absence of these portions from the Coptic and Arabic versions of this church order, suggests that these segments are borrowed from an Ethiopic translation of the text of the Didache as a whole. The complete version, however, has been lost to us and all that is preserved is Did 11:3-13:7 and 8:1-2a (in this order) in can. 52.[61] These sections might have been incorporated into the Ethiopic version of the Canones Ecclesiastici in the middle of the fourth century.[62] The bearing of this witness on the reconstruction of the original text is meagre. For it remains debatable whether the text was rendered directly from a Greek or a Coptic source. Moreover, the version often gives preference to paraphrase over translation. Below, in Chapter 7 (p. 243), the Ethiopic Church Order will be helpful as a witness to the traditional understanding of the prescriptions of Did 6:2-3.[63]

THE INDIRECT TEXTUAL SOURCES

The following two types of texts, though related to the Didache, deviate from the manual in that they cannot be characterized as presenting (a piece of) the Greek text or a translation of the extant form of the Didache. The first one (the Apostolic Constitutions) embodies an extensively adapted and rewritten form of the Didache as a whole, while the second type is represented by a number of Two Way versions which are more original in form than the one represented by Did 1-6. Whereas the work of Apostolic Constitutions is relevant to the history of the Didache as a whole, the early representatives of the Two Ways shed light on the development of only a part of the Didache prior to its incorporation into the manual. As far as the establishment of the genuine text of the Didache is concerned, however, these materials may be considered indirect sources at best.

---

[61]   Cf. Horner, *The Statutes of the Apostles*, 193,7-194,23 and 194,24-29, respectively.

[62]   See Audet, *La Didachè*, 34-45; esp. 43.

[63]   Perhaps the Georgian version of the Didache should be discussed here as well. It concerns a collation from a manuscript that contained the whole Didache (and some other texts) in Georgian translation. In Constantinople, this version was copied from a nineteenth century codex in 1923 by Simon Pheikrishvili. In 1932, a collation against the Greek version of H from this copy (not the copy itself) was published by Gregor Peradse ('Die "Lehre der zwölf Apostel,"' 115-16; the text is also provided by Vokes, *The Riddle of the Didache*, 25-26 and Audet, *La Didachè*, 47-50). The codex from which Pheikrishvili had copied, however, has since completely disappeared. Rordorf and Tuilier reject the idea that the Georgian version would have any independent value in restoring the original Didache text. In their opinion, the vanished Constantinople codex is but a translation made in the nineteenth century on the basis of the Codex H (*La Doctrine des douze Apôtres*, 115-16, n. 2). As late as 1887, the latter codex was transferred from Constantinople to Jerusalem. Although their view that the text of the Pheikrishvili codex is directly dependent on the Jerusalem Ms. might not be correct (Niederwimmer, *Die Didache*, 44-45; Schöllgen-[Geerlings], *Didache. Zwölf-Apostellehre*, 89-92; Wengst, *Didache [Apostellehre]*, 12), we are nevertheless faced here with a modern translation. Moreover, since the Georgian reading can no longer be verified, the text-critical value of the Georgian translation should be minimized.

The Apostolic Constitutions

The Greek Apostolic Constitutions appears to have originated between 375 and 380 CE. The compilation covers the whole of the Didache in the major part of the seventh book (7/1,2-32,4)[64] albeit in a revised version. Similarly, these Constitutions comprise an adapted form of the Didascalia in the Books 1-6 and a modified shape of the Apostolic Tradition ascribed to Hippolytus in Book 8. The work was compiled by an Syrian author who utilized these older sources and reworked them into the church discipline and liturgical practice of his time.

The basic text of the Didache has been amended thoroughly. On account of the frequent paraphrases, citations from both testaments in the bible and interpretations, the text reads more like a commentary. The compiler repeatedly adjusted the text to bring it into harmony with the contemporary church in his own situation. A few examples will suffice. The regulation with regard to Baptism in Did 7 was expanded. It is introduced by the anointing with ἔλαιον and concluded by the anointing with μύρον. Nothing is said, however, about the alternative modes of being baptized in Did 7:1c-3, directives which have their parallels in Jewish halakhic instructions (see below, Chap. 8, pp. 281-83). Moreover, the eucharistic prayers in Did 9 are revised to fit a sacramental Eucharist with the sequence bread-cup, an order which in the meantime had become the official line in the church (see below, Chap. 8, pp. 304-09). And finally, the archaic rules governing apostles and prophets in Did 11-12 (see below, Chap. 9, pp. 353-60) are severely cut down because in the time of the compiler these itinerant preachers had long since been figures of the past. Because the Apostolic Constitutions or its immediate predecessors introduced these and numerous other alterations in the source to make the document conform to contemporary conditions, the work is valuable for the history rather than for the reconstruction of the text of the Didache.

The Various Forms of the Two Ways in Did 1-6

Indirect evidence of the text of the Two Ways is found in a number of different recensions. They do not have a direct bearing on the establishment of the Didache text in these chapters, since the recension behind the source of all these versions is different from the H recension in omitting the specifically Christian passages in 1:3b-2:1 and 6:2-3. In the next chapter, we will discuss extensively these early Christian Two Ways versions since they are important witnesses to the history of the Two Ways before this doctrine was incorporated in the Didache. In the same chapter, we will also attempt to describe the more precise genealogical relation-

---

[64] For the following discussion, see Audet, *La Didachè*, 5-51; Wengst, *Didache (Apostellehre)*, 7; Kraft, *The Apostolic Fathers*, 58-59; Rordorf-Tuilier, *La Doctrine des douze Apôtres*, 120-22; Schöllgen-(Geerlings), *Didache. Zwölf-Apostellehre*, 92-93; Niederwimmer, *Die Didache*, 45-47.

ships between the Two Ways version in the Didache, Barnabas, Doctrina Apostolorum, the Canons of the Apostles and the Epitome

Composition and Purpose of the Didache

One may divide the text of the Didache into several main topical sections, each of which has enough internal coherence to stand alone. In fact, the Didache is a compilation of several older sources, and this is especially true of the first six chapters. But why are these sections presented as a unified document? Does the fact that the work is constructed out of separate blocks of tradition presuppose a minimal intervention of the (single) redactor? In order to determine the extent of editorial activity in the text, an examination of the Didache from a form-critical point of view is needed. In identifying the different layers of composition, one might perceive the particular occasions and core problems prompting the editor to produce this compilation. Especially on pp. 31-35, we will attempt to discover the hand of the final editor – called the Didachist – modifying an older tradition. As he felt forced to make the transmitted traditions conform to the needs of the community in his time, his particular interest emerges where he is responding to the actual historical problems in his community.

COMPOSITION

Throughout our analysis of the Didache, it will become quite evident that this booklet cannot be considered a homogeneous text. The Didache is a compilation of several older sources which are structured into four clearly separated thematic sections: the Two Ways document (Chaps. 1-6 with later additions in 1:3b-2:1 and in 6:2-3), a liturgical treatise (Chaps. 7-10), a treatise on church organization (Chaps. 11-15 with a later expansion in 11-13) and an eschatologial section (Chap. 16). Each individual part belongs to a different literary genre, has evolved over a period of time, and makes up a coherent unity. Since all this will be corroborated further below in the remaining eight chapters of this study, some introductory observations may suffice at this point.

The opening line of the Didache, "There are two ways, one of life, the other of death" (1:1), introduces the subject treated in its first part. The Way of Life (Did 1-4) contains moral instruction which is expounded at greater length than the Way of Death, which contains a mere list of warnings (Did 5). The Way of Life begins with a conventional summary of Law consisting of the double love command (the "love of God" and the "love of neighbour") and the Golden Rule in its negative form ("do not yourself do to another what you would not want done to you"). The topic clause in 1:3a ("Here is the teaching [that flows] from these words") shows the following part to be interpretation. This interpretation continues all the way through three chapters before reaching its conclusion in 4:14b. It includes first a series of positive admonitions found in the verses 3b-2:1 which reflect some of the radical requirements of the Sermon on the Mount and are particularly close to the Synoptic tradition.[65] Then follows a list of precepts intended to cover the essentials of the second table of the Ten Commandments (2:2-7) and, finally, two chapters dealing with morals, humility and constructive social behaviour (3-4). The Way of Death in fact represents a catalogue consisting of twenty-three vices in the first part and a list of nineteen evildoers in the second (5:1-2). After these inventories, the Two Ways doctrine comes to a close in 6:1 with a warning to sustain and observe the aforesaid prescriptions.[66]

Did 6:2-3, reflecting an atmosphere of concession, is probably a supplement to the original Two Ways teaching. The passage is directed to gentile Christians who already have accepted the faith in Jesus Christ, urging them to observe the Mosaic Law as far as they can. It probably represents a (larger) source listing the various relevant food laws which the Jerusalem Council had adopted from pre-rabbinic equivalents of Jewish Noachide Laws for sympathizing gentiles (see Acts 15:20.29; 21:25).[67] Section 6:2-3 may have been added to the Two Ways instruction in a Jewish-Chistian milieu where the Tora was still faithfully observed by Christians of Jewish origin. It is not likely, therefore, that this addition came from the pen of the Didachist who was responsible for the extant edition of the Didache. This is because, as will be seen below, the layer of the Didache reflecting the date and milieu of his days shows a community which appears to have alienated itself from its Jewish background and to have taken on the character of a gentile Christian group.[68]

Did 7 is linked to the first section by the guideline in 7:1b which says that the Two Ways doctrine should provide the material for pre-baptismal teaching. It is likely that in the days of the Didachist the Two Ways as presented in Chapters 1-6 served as a basic catechetical instruction preceding baptism.[69] Baptism is to be performed after a brief fast by the candidate and the celebrant. The practice of immersion in cold, running water is preferred but also still water (pools an cisterns) may be used. Even mere affusion is allowed in case water is scarce. The mention of a pre-baptismal fast in 7:4 appears to have prompted the observation about fasting as an independent phenomenon in 8:1, that is, the stationary fast. In the next verse, the Christians are required to recite the Lord's Prayer three times a day (8:2-

---

[65] See below, pp. 40-48.

[66] For further details on the establishment of an earlier form of the Two Ways and its versions in early Christian literature, see below, Chap. 2 (passim); for its influence in Christian literature up to and including the early Middle Ages, see Chap. 3; for the (hypothetical) reconstruction of the Two Ways, see Chap. 4; for its genre, its provenance and the circles within which it was preserved and transmitted, see Chap. 5; and, finally, for its effect on finding a way out in the redactional critical problems of distinguishing between tradition and redaction in Matt 5:17-48, see Chap. 6.

[67] See below, Chap. 7, passim.

[68] Below, Chap. 8, pp. 291-96 and 325-29; Chap. 9, pp. 350-51 and n. 67.

[69] See below, Chap. 8, pp. 280-81 and Chap. 3, pp. 87-89. The remainder of the latter chapter also shows that materials with close affinities to the basic principles of the Two Ways are found in a setting of pre-baptismal teaching in monastic Rules, the sermon of Ps.-Boniface, and in the second instruction of the Ratio de Cathecizandis Rudibus (ca. 800).

3). The version of this prayer written out in full here, varies from Matt 6:9-13 in some details only but, even so, probably is not dependent on Matthew.[70] Chapters 9 and 10 present the prayers, rubrics and regulations for the Eucharist. Binding formulae are given for the prayer over the cup (9:2), over the broken bread (9:3-4) and after the meal proper (10:2-6). There is no general agreement on the nature of the rite dealt with here. It is considered to be a Eucharist, an Agape, a combined Agape and Eucharist, or some other kind of meal. Below, in Chapter 8, we will argue for a eucharistic celebration consisting of the following elements. The liturgy is introduced in 9:2-4 by blessings over the cup and the bread based on Jewish prayers of blessing, a full meal comes next (10:1) and this again is followed by a prayer modelled on the Jewish prayer after meals (10:2-5). Surprisingly, there is no reference to the death and resurrection of Jesus or to the Last Supper and the ritual order is cup – bread.[71]

What follows next is the section comprising Chaps. 11-15 with guidelines for good order and church discipline. Turning to the instructions concerning the reception of itinerant outsiders, the apostles are the first class of visitors considered here. They are persons sent out on a mission from elsewhere and because they were in transit, they were not allowed to stay longer than two days or to ask for money (11:4-6). The second class of strangers dealt with here are the prophets. It was rather difficult, however, to equip the community with criteria enabling them to differentiate between true and false prophets. Since prophets were regarded as speaking in the Spirit, they had a privileged status which distinguished them from other teachers. The Didache, however, sanctions the prophetic gifts without endangering the community. While preserving the high valuation of speaking in the Spirit, the manual recommends an examination of a prophet's lifestyle as a chief criterion for credibility (11:7-12). Discussing ordinary people, who come to the community and claim to be Christians, the Didache in the next chapter demands a further testing and setting of conditions as well. If a travelling Christian layman wants to settle in the community, the general rule is that such a person must earn his own living with a trade (12:1-5). This instruction does not apply, however, in the case of a teacher and a genuine prophet. When true prophets desire to settle down in the community, they are to be given material support as a reward for their labours (13:1-2). The 'firstfruit' section elaborating on this fundamental principle in 13:3-7 probably reflects an adapted Jewish halakhic tradition.[72]

Having dealt with the reception of outsiders, the text of the third major section of the Didache about church organization has not ended yet. It now comes to discuss some themes of internal community life which are loosely related to the preceding questions. In Did 14, the confession of sins and reconciliation is the central theme. The Eucharist is understood here as a sacrifice and anyone who neglected to confess his or her transgressions prior to the Eucharist on the "Sunday

---

[70] See below, Chap 8, pp. 294-95.
[71] See below, Chap 8, pp. 296, 304-09 etc.
[72] See below, Chap. 9, pp. 360-64.

of the Lord" could not be considered as offering the "pure sacrifice" which the Lord required.[73] The succeeding passage gives some information about bishops and deacons (15:1-2). It reveals that they were elected from local community members and, in addition to the more general qualification of being "worthy of the Lord," it mentions the most important prerequisites for these offices. They are to be honest, unassuming and not greedy. After the digression in 15:1-2, the text proceeds to the theme which to a certain extent was dealt with in 14:1-3: the *correctio fraterna*, implying a friendly confrontation of someone with an error he or she has committed. If the errant brother or sister, despite this correction, persists in sin, the members of the community are prohibited to further relate to him or her until the moment of repentance (15:3).

The concluding section in Chap. 16, which is incomplete in the manuscript left to us (H), contains an eschatological premonition to ensure obedience to the provisions preceding in Did 1-15. As will be shown below (pp. 35-40), it contains eschatological warnings and a brief conventional apocalypse.

PURPOSE

The Didache must not be treated, however, as a fragmented collage of materials only, for since as a whole it is a community rule, intended to regulate the behaviour of the community, the manual deserves to be considered as a coherent systematic unity as well. One might ask why the constituent parts of the manual (Chapters 1-5, 7-10, 11-15 and 16) are placed in the order given. What are the Didache's setup, stategy and concerns? What was the purpose of the composition of the Didache?

It has already been mentioned above that the Two Ways doctrine put forward in Did 1:1-6:1 (without 1:3b-2:1) has for a long time circulated independently. The Didachist conceivably took this teaching as the basic framework. The transition to baptism by means of the phrase "Having said all this beforehand" in Did 7:1b shows the Two Ways teaching to be a prerequisite for baptism. It is thus likely that the Two Ways teaching already served in some form as a pre-baptismal instruction within the community whose traditions are reflected in the Didache. There is a good possibility that at this stage the passage of Did 6:2-3 was already part of the Two Ways and thus describes a minimum of commandments for believing gentiles. So, in Did 1:1-6:1 (less 1:3b-2:1), the Didachist may simply have set down as a regulation here what was common practice within his community.

On the other hand, considering the world of the Didachist, the character of the clause in 7:1b must not be played down as merely describing established practice. It apparently was intended as a prescriptive code principally for gentiles rather than for Jews who, as a result of their education, grasped what God required of them. When it came to gentiles, however, who had grown up in households in which pagan gods and pagan standards of morality abounded, the line of former beliefs

---

[73] See below, Chap. 8, p. 304.

and conduct had to be changed. For this reason, the doctrine of the Two Ways after its short title may have been prefaced in the Didache with a supplementary long title as well: "Doctrine of the Lord [brought] to the Nations by the Twelve Apostles." It thus follows that both the ethical catechesis incorporated in the Didache (the Two Ways *plus* Did 6:2-3) and the Didache itself envisage converts to Christianity from paganism. And since the basic norms of conduct displayed in the early form of Did 1-6 might equally be suited for training a gentile to become a Jew,[74] it probably was the composer of the Didache who added the evangelical section in Did 1:3b-2:1.

But for what reason did the editor endeavour to compile a rule book containing additional directories for liturgical prayer and community order as well? It is hard to know his intention. Nevertheless, one may assume that the function of the Two Ways instruction, i.e., the ethical catechesis for any candidate preceding his or her baptism, accounts for the shift from the Two Ways tradition to the ritual of baptism in Chap. 7. It further may be useful to notice a correspondence between Chaps. 8-15 of the Didache and Chaps. 2-3 of the First Letter to Timothy. In his construction of Did 8-15, the Didachist may have drawn upon a model used by 1 Tim 2:1-3:13 as well,[75] for, with the exclusion of Did 11-13, the materials of Did 8-15 represent the same sequel of topics as 1 Tim 2:1-3:13, that is, instructions regarding praying (Did 8:2-10:7 and 1 Tim 2:1-7), ethical conditions of a congregational worship (Did 14 and 1 Tim 2:8-15), and directives with regard to bishops and deacons (Did 15 and 1 Tim 3:1-13). The agreement suggests that the sequence of topics in Did 8-15 (without Chaps. 11-13) and 1 Tim. 2:1-3:13 was arranged according to a common traditional pattern.[76]

This model might have been ancient but the instructions themselves apparently are changed and amplified to meet the different situations. Some glimpse of the pressing problems which inspired the Didachist to formulate the text which we have before us is given first of all in Did 8-10. The community whose traditions at least partially appear in the Didache is likely to have been composed initially of Judeo-Christians. The ritual of baptism, the Lord's Prayer, and the eucharistic celebration, are deeply affected by the pattern of Jewish daily worship.[77] At the time the Didache was finally edited, however, things had apparently changed. The text shows clear indications of a community having distanced itself from Judaism. In Did 8, directions are given for set times of fasting and of prayer. The members of the Didache group are required to fast on Wednesdays and Fridays, disassociating them this way from the pious Jews who fasted on Mondays and Thursdays: "Let your fasts not [coincide] with [those of] the hypocrites" (8:1). The Jews are disparagingly characterized as 'hypocrites' here and once again in the next verse.

---

[74] Milavec, 'The Pastoral Genius of the Didache', 121-123.
[75] For the following, see Dibelius, *Geschichte der urchristlichen Literatur*, 151-52; Id. *Die Pastoralbriefe*, 5 and Vielhauer, *Geschichte der urchristlichen Literatur*, 727-28. See also Stempel, 'Der Lehrer', 214.
[76] See below, Chap. 9, pp. 339-40.
[77] See below, Chap. 8.

The Christians, so it says in 8:2, should "not pray as the hypocrites [do]" but are required to recite the Lord's Prayer. The Lord's Prayer is offered in an obligatory text without mentioning or quoting additional prayers. This circumstance, and the requirement to say the Lord's Prayer three times a day may indicate that this prayer takes the place of the Jewish *tefilla*, which was was recited three times a day as well.[78] One may assume that individual members of the Didache community still prayed the *tefilla*, and when the number of gentiles in the community increased, this practice doubtlessly caused a strong tension between non-Jewish Christians and Judaizing Christians in that congregation. The prayer formulary in Did 8 may have served as a means to prevent people within the Christian community from imitating Jewish practices.

Some evidence of gentile Christian influence may also be recognized in the description of the Eucharist in Did 9-10. Of course, the meal blessings of Did 9 are akin to Jewish table blessings, and the content and themes of the prayers of Did 10 show a close affinity to the Birkat Ha-Mazon, the prayer that concludes the Jewish ritual meal. But these prayers represent some vestiges of gentile Christian usage as well. The petitions in Did 9:4 and 10:5 regarding the gathering of the church are bound up with the biblical expectation of salvation that the dispersed of Israel will be collected in the day of salvation (Deut 30:3-5a; Isa 11:12b-c; Ezek 37:21). Later this desire was kept alive in the tenth benediction of the *tefilla*. The transfer of this concept to the Christian church in Did 9:4 and 10:5, however, involving a gathering of the church without further reference to the Jewish people, is a conspicuous characteristic of gentile Christian refashioning. Admittedly, the prayers do not yet presage the ecclesiology of the second-century Christian tradition claiming Israel as a whole to be dispossessed and gentiles taking its place.[79] And even the gospel of Matthew is couched in more extreme phraseology when it states in no uncertain terms the rejection of the people of Israel. In the parable of the labourers in the vineyard, Jesus announces that the kingdom of God will be taken from Israel and given to a (new) people (Matt 21:43). And those entering the kingdom, so Jesus asserts, will come from the remote corners of the world: "I tell you, many" (non-Jews) "will come from east and west and sit at table with Abraham, Isaac, and Jacob in the kingdom of heaven, while the sons of the kingdom" (Israel) "will be thrown into the outer darkness; there men will weep and gnash their teeth" (Matt 8:11-12).[80] The Didache does not show any indication of viewing Israel as condemned. At the same time, however, it is also clear that a petition for the gathering of the dispersed people of Israel is beyond the liturgic range of the community of the Didache. The formulation reflects a gentile, rather than a particular Jewish position and perspective. One may therefore assume that the supplications in Did 9:4 and 10:5 were formulated in a predominantly gentile

---

[78] The Mishnah required all freemen to recite the Jewish *tefilla* and "if not, an abstract of the Eighteen" (mBer 4:3) three times a day (4:1.7); see also below, Chap. 8, p. 294 and n. 77.

[79] See also below, Chap. 8, pp. 325-28.

[80] See below, Chap. 6, n. 35.

Christian community. These liturgical components may date from the last two decades of the first century CE and appear to reflect the fact that, as the Didache group won more and more gentiles, it gradually alienated itself from its Jewish background.

Besides the attempt to define the new Christian group as distinct from Judaism, there might also have been another reason prompting the author to create the Didache. Above, it was suggested that the Didachist basically framed the entirety of Chapters 8-15 (without 11-13) according to a traditional design, which is reflected in 1 Timothy as well. If this view is correct, it follows that Did 11-13 was added later to the pristine pre-Didache form. And, indeed, as will be supported in the discussion below in Chapter 9 of this study, Did 11-13 (dealing with wandering apostles and prophets) presupposes a new development in the history of the community. One thus has to distinguish between two different layers in the text of the Didache reflecting corresponding stages in the history of the Didache community. The first is concerned with directives regarding confession of sins, reconciliation and the offices of bishops and deacons (Did 14-15). The second layer, reflecting a later phase, reveals the older rules to be updated in order to meet the problems involved in the offices of itinerant apostles and prophets. Visiting prophets (and even traveling apostles) are still active in the church by the time of the redaction of the Didache and this phenomenon fits the general mobility of contemporary religious teachers of popular Hellenistic religion. At the time of the Didachist, the number of itinerant religious propagandists appears to have increased to such an extent, however, that it opened the door for abuses to set in. Because Christians were generally expected to offer a generous and cordial welcome to guests and strangers, this hospitable attitude could easily be misused. It was these circumstances which caused the Didachist to modify and expand the section about the church organization with a set of practical norms which would enable the reader to check potential charlatans, crooks and annoying foreigners.

In their given order, the subsequent sections of the present Didache display a deliberate progression. The first section specifies how new gentile members are to be instructed prior to baptism (Did 1-6/7). Then a section follows giving rules for those having been baptized and providing the required text of the Lord's prayer and the Eucharist (Did 7-10). It is not unrealistic to assume that in the last stage of the development of the Didache, the community included a variety of groups. There probably was an increasing quantity of gentiles grown up in non-Jewish households, a number of members who were Jewish in their own self-conception and halakhic practice, and various shades of other believers-in-Jesus in the middle. The Didachist attempts to overcome the tension between these groups and movements by replacing Jewish traditions and prayers which might have been operative earlier in his community with a modified and transformed worship reflecting the liturgical traditions that were maintained by the majority in his own time. In this light, we also have to consider the Didachist's concern in displaying the entire set of eucharistic prayers in Did 9-10. One may suppose that he took great pains to present the well-defined formulae in order to enforce the complete text of the eucharistic prayers in Did 9-10 as a substitute for the Jewish

Birkat Ha-Mazon.[81] The presentation of the required Christianized pre-baptismal catechesis, the Lord's Prayer, and the complete set of eucharistic prayers are intended to prevent a seemingly irreversible division within the community.

Resuming our comment on the developing coherence within the Didache, a few words about the next two sections may suffice. In addition to the admission of gentiles into the Didache community, also the hospitable treatment of transient outsiders caused significant problems. The additional regulations in the third section (Did 11-15) specify how certain classes of visitors must be tested so as to protect the community from troublesome visitors. Did 16, finally, may be regarded as a reaffirmation of the grave importance of the instructions given in the preceding chapters. To sum up: since the Didache was composed in a time of transition, its major concern was to safeguard the unity and identity of his community against threats from the inside and outside world. The bold novelty of the manual consists in offering the required content of pivotal prayers and in integrating an appropriate set of rules to prevent the community's hospitality from being exploited.

The Eschatological Conclusion of the Didache (Did 16)

The eschatological section, concluding the Didache in Chap. 16, consists of two distinct parts. First there is a parenetic passage, which includes two concrete admonitions, i.e., a call for vigilance (16:1a) and an admonition to meet "frequently" (16:2a).[82] Both incentives are substantiated eschatologically. The admonitions are followed by a succinct apocalyptic scenario (16:3-8) which portrays the events at the end of time, starting with the multiplication of false prophets and corrupters. Because its style is quite different from the tone of the preceding text, this little apocalypse might well have been a separate tradition once. In that case, the terminology in 16:2b ἐὰν μὴ ἐν τῷ ἐσχάτῳ καιρῷ τελειωθῆτε ("unless you are perfected at the final hour") must have urged the composer to connect this material with the apocalyptic portion beginning with the wording ἐν γὰρ (!) ταῖς ἐσχάταις ἡμέραις ("For in the final days" in 16:3a). If somebody renounces his Christian faith in the last hour, so it says in Did 16:2, the fact that he was a believer for years will not suffice to outweigh his eventual apostasy. The "final hour" is

---

[81] It is difficult to escape the impression that also Did 14:1 must be expounded as directed against judaizing Christians. The gathering of the community for the breaking of the bread and thanksgivings should, according to this verse, take place on the "Lord's day of the Lord." The doublet may be considered to affirm the Sunday as the day of the eucharistic celebration against those who preferred the Sabbath as the day for the celebration; cf. Rordorf-Tuilier, *La Doctrine des douze Apôtres*, 64-65. See also below, Chap. 9, n. 67 and Chap. 8, n. 99.

[82] Or "in large numbers;" cf. Knopf, *Die Lehre der zwölf Apostel*, 38; Wengst, *Didache (Apostellehre)*, 89, n. 127. For our translation, see (in addition to Cody, 'The *Didache*', 13) Von Harnack, *Die Lehre der zwölf Apostel*, 61; Rordorf-Tuilier, *La Doctrine des douze Apôtres*, 195; Audet, *La Didachè*, 468; Giet, *L'Énigme de la Didachè*, 245; Niederwimmer, *Die Didache*, 256.

the central concept for the concluding apocalypse. The idea in v. 2b that ethical perfection is to be assessed only in the time of the eschaton leads to this elaboration.[83]

The description of the apocalyptic disturbances and calamities in 16:3-8 is neatly ordered in subsequent periods by the use of the temporal adverb τότε (then). Besides the increase in the number of false prophets, also the image of sheep turning into wolves and of love transforming into hate are manifestations of an unbalanced and deranged social era within the Christian communities of the Last Days (vv. 3-4a). The second phase is characterized by the appearance of the "world-deceiver", the arrival of the Antichrist[84] impersonating the "son of God" and doing "godless things" (v. 4). Next, in the third phase (v. 5), the final crisis takes place before the triumphal advent of the Lord. In the burning process of the decisive test, it will become clear whether one's loyalty to the Lord is paramount or whether one – under the pressures of the last days – will go astray from Christian faith, apostatize and perish. Those who remain firm in their faith will be saved by the "curse itself," which might refer to Jesus as an "accursed person,"[85] as the one who was cursed during the dominion of the world-deceiver.[86]

After the conclusive trial (vv. 3-5), it is the "signs of truth," contrasting with the lies of the deceiver, which will appear: the "sign of extension in heaven," the sound of the trumpet and the resurrection of the dead (vv. 6-7). The "sign of the extension" according to many commentators must refer to the cross.[87] With the help of a quotation of Zech 14:5, the resurrection of the dead is specified in the next verse as a reawakening to life of the "holy ones," probably of those who have suffered and endured the above hardships. The limitations of the resurrection to only the saints suggests that the Didache does not know (yet) a general resurrection.[88] The last phase of the eschatological events (v. 8), at least as far as recorded in H, is concerned with the arrival of the Lord. The title "Lord" (Κύριος) replaces the wording υἱὸς ἀνθρώπου ("Son of man") in the foundational passage (Dan 7:13 LXX). At this point, one would expect a portrayal of the final judgment but, as we have seen above (pp. 22-24) the conclusion of the apocalypse is unfortunately lost in the Jerusalem Manuscript. To be sure, an ending with an explicit reference to the final judgment is supported by textual sources such as the Georgian version of the Didache and the Apostolic Constitutions. It is hard to decide,

---

[83] Bammel, 'Pattern and Prototype, 369-70.

[84] The term "world-deceiver" (κοσμοπλανής) is a hapax legomenon. But see 2 John 7: ὁ πλάνος καὶ ὁ ἀντίχριστος. The "Antichrist" figure, however, frequently occurs in apocalyptic literature; cf., e.g., Dan 7:25; 11:36-39; 2 Thess 2:8; 1 John 2:18; Rev 13.

[85] Pardee, 'The Curse That Saves', 175.

[86] See, for example, Von Harnack, *Die Lehre der zwölf Apostel*, 62-63; Wengst, *Didache (Apostellehre)*, 99, n. 137; Rordorf-Tuilier, *La Doctrine des douze Apôtres*, 197-98, n. 6.

[87] See e.g. Köster, *Synoptische Überlieferung*, 190; Stommel, 'Σημεῖον ἐκπετάσεως', 25-26; Butler, 'The Literary Relations', 276-80; Rordorf-Tuilier, *La Doctrine des douze Apôtres*, 198–99, n.1; Niederwimmer, *Die Didache*, 265; Schöllgen-(Geerlings), *Didache. Zwölf-Apostellehre*, 79; Draper, 'The Development', 14-15.

[88] See also Seeliger, 'Erwägungen zu Hintergrund', 189-90.

however, to what extent these versions – even in combination – may be helpful to reconstruct in detail the ending of the Didache.[89]

It has often been argued that the text of Did 16 was the original conclusion of the Two Ways tractate.[90] Because the form of the Two Ways available in Barnabas and the Apostolic Church Order (ACO) is provided with an eschatological conclusion, it has been contended that both the warning and the apocalyptic part of Did 16 was displaced from its original position at the end of the Two Ways to be retained in the conclusion of the Didache document as a whole. Two objections, however, are to be raised against the position that Did 16 in its present form represents the original conclusion of the Two Ways tractate.

First, it is of importance to note some genealogical data. In the next chapter, we will see that early Jewish and Christian literature attests to a separate circulation of a Jewish Greek Two Ways source which is best represented by the source

---

[89] Above we have seen that one has to be cautious in accepting the reading of the Apostolic Constitutions. Similarly, it is doubtful whether the Georgian translation might be considered a separate corroborating witness to the originality of the a restored ending (see above, n. 63).

In an interesting article, Aldridge ('The Lost Ending') draws attention to a third source, one that might have been used by Boniface of Mainz (ca. 680-754), "the apostle of Germany," in his sermon 'Renunciation'. This sermon has frequently been edited (cf. also Aldridge, 'The Lost Ending', 8, n. 20) and below, in Chap. 3, this discourse will be discussed extensively under the heading 'The Fifteenth Sermon of Ps.-Boniface'. An earlier recension of this sermon, found in the Vatican library with the signature *Bibl. Apostolica, Pal. lat. 485*, fol. 91[ro]-92[ro] will be rendered there as well. Aldridge, who was probably unfamiliar with this version which we will call "Audite" in view of its incipit, has not utilized it.

According to Aldridge, the text of the sermon may be useful in reconstructing the end of the little apocalypse in Did 16:3-8 since he takes the Bonifacian address to be dependent on the whole of the Didache. The sermon, so he claims, first renders the Way of Death, next abbreviates "the Didache's middle chapters into a list of Christian duties" (9) and thereafter appears to reflect some version of the missing ending of Chap. 16. The latter part strongly agrees with the conclusion of the Apostolic Constitutions and partially conforms with the Georgian version. And, indeed, at first sight, the parousial passage about the arrival of the Lord, the punishment of the wicked and blessful happiness of the righteous in the Bonifacian sermon might represent a somewhat reworked version of the Didache's genuine ending. This view might even be corroborated by the sermon's earlier version which will be presented in Chap. 3. In this anterior form of the discourse, the parousial section actually represents the real ending of the sermon's text (cf. Chap. 3, p. 103)

On the other hand, it is questionable whether the sermon really summarizes the entire Didache. In the same Chap. 3, we will establish that its structure and content show close parallels to the Two Ways doctrine which is reflected in Did 7-16. The echoes of Did 7-16, however, – and this was already pointed out by Schlecht (*Doctrina XII Apostolorum* [1901] 77) – are very scanty and scarce indeed. It thus is doubtful whether the sermon covers the Didache as a whole. Instead, the Bonifacian sermon might ultimately be traced back to a later form of the Two Ways tractate which was also utilized by Barnabas and the Apostolic Church Order. Another possibility is that the eschatological part was added to the sermon in some later period to enhance its teaching on the moral conduct expected of catechumens. In neither case, however, can the discourse be used to reconstruct the authentic ending of the Didache.

[90] See, e.g., Drews, 'Untersuchungen zur Didache', 68-73; Creed, 'The Didache', 379; Baltzer, *Das Bundesformular*, 132-33; Kamlah, *Die Form der katalogischen Paränese*, 214; Kraft, *Barnabas and the Didache*, 12-16; Bammel, 'Pattern and Prototype', 368-72. Opposed to this view, among others (see below), is Van Eijk, *La résurrection des morts*, 20-21.

underlying the Latin Doctrina Apostolorum and Did 1:1-6:1 (but without the material in 1:3b-2:1). Also the other extant Two Ways forms in early Christian literature ultimately depend on this moral Jewish instruction, which is lost to us. If this view is correct, the ending of the original Jewish Two Ways document cannot have contained more than an eschatological tinge at most, since the conclusion of the Two Ways as represented in Doctrina 6:4-5 just faintly echoes some allusion to the End while the Didache's rendering of the Two Ways' conclusion lacks any eschatological preoccupation.[91]

In comparison with the Doctr. / Did tradition, however, the last part of the Two Ways in the Letter of Barnabas (= Barn. 21) and the Apostolic Church Order (= ACO 14) show an apocalyptic part charged with present eschatological drama. We will say more on these witnesses to the history of the Two Ways in the next chapter, but for now it is in order to note that Barn. 18-21 and the Apostolic Church Order 4-14 contain a Two Ways text which, as compared with its rendering in the Doctrina an Didache, was reworked in other respects as well. Although Barn. 18-21 and ACO 4-14 are obviously closely related to the Two Ways in the Doctrina / Didache source, they exhibit a slightly different stage in the development of the Two Ways tradition. Both versions must have been derived from a later Two Ways form which linked the basic instruction to the emphasis on the nearness of the End, involving both judgment and reward.

So, at some later date, the Greek Two Ways (also) circulated in connection with an apocalyptic appendix as reflected in Barnabas and ACO. Does Did 16 then reproduce the ending of this later version of the Greek Two Ways?[92] At this point

---

[91] "Didache 1-6 shows no real interest in eschatology. ... In the Didache eschatology either is subsumed under liturgy (8:2; 9:4; 10:5-6) or forms an appendix (ch. 16);" cf. Kraft, *Barnabas and the Didache*, 7. Cf. Rordorf-Tuilier, *La Doctrine des douze Apôtres*, 82 (2nd reason); Seeliger, 'Erwägungen zu Hintergrund', 188. Further, see below, Chap. 2. We will suggest below (Chap. 7, p. 241) that the Didachist copied a form of the Two Ways which already included Did 6:2-3.

[92] There are some elements in Did 16 which seem to be related to an older Two Ways doctrine. The admonition to watchfulness in 16:1a "over your life" (Γρηγορεῖτε ὑπὲρ τῆς ζωῆς ὑμῶν) might have introduced an appropriate concluding warning to keep the Way of Life. Furthermore, there is a clear relationship between Did 16:2b and Barn. 4:9
The wording is almost verbally identical:
Didache
οὐ γὰρ ὠφελήσει ὑμᾶς ὁ πᾶς χρόνος τῆς πίστεως ὑμῶν,
ἐὰν μὴ ἐν τῷ ἐσχάτῳ καιρῷ τελειωθῆτε.
Barnabas
οὐδὲν γὰρ ὠφελήσει ἡμᾶς ὁ πᾶς χρόνος τῆς ζωῆς καὶ τῆς πίστεως ἡμῶν,
ἐὰν μὴ νῦν ἐν τῷ ἀνόμῳ καιρῷ καὶ τοῖς μέλλουσιν σκανδάλοις, ὡς πρέπει υἱοῖς θεοῦ, ἀνιστῶμεν.
According to a number of scholars (see Ehrhard, *Die altchristliche Litteratur*, 51; Creed, 'The Didache', 379; Kraft, *Barnabas and the Didache*, 15), this agreement points to a derivation from the original conclusion to the Two Ways source. In our view, it is possible that both Barn. 4:9 and Did 16:2b stem from the conclusion to the secondary TW source which underlied Barn. and ACO. The lack of additional similarities, however, rather indicates these verbal links to be accidental agreements. The parallels are not so extensive as to cause us to think of a genuine literary dependence on such a common source.

we come to a second objection to the view that Did 16 was once part of the Two Ways tractate: the eschatological appendix in Did 16 barely shares any verbal affinities with the eschatological ending of the Two Ways in Barnabas and ACO. The conclusion seems therefore justified that the final redactor of the Didache (the Didachist) probably was not familiar with an eschatological epilogue of a Two Ways tractate either in its original or in its secondary recension.

Where, then, do the materials in Did 16 come from? Several scholars have observed that the apocalyptic 'appendix' in Did 16 has words, phrases and motifs in common with the Synoptic gospels. It is closely related to the Synoptic Apocalypse in Matt 24-25 and Mark 13.[93] The majority of parallels, however, are with the so-called 'little apocalypse' of Matt 24 and the obvious question, then, is how to interpret these similarities. Are the agreements between Did 16 and Matt 24 indicative of the fact that the Didachist quoted Matthew and/or some other Synoptic gospel[94] *or* is the eschatological Chapter 16 completely independent of the Synoptics, resting on a source or sources common to both Matthew 24 and the Didache?[95] Since an extremely large portion of the Synoptic material is not included in Did 16, and moreover, since there is evidence that the text of Did 16 probably represents an independent pre-gospel tradition, the latter option seems the better alternative. To be more specific, Did 16 reveals no dependence upon either Mark or Matthew as we know it but rather represents a tradition upon which Matthew drew.[96] It is likely, therefore, that both Matthew and the Did 16 are grafted upon a common early collection of apocalyptic materials.

We may continue our investigation by asking in what circles these apocalyptic materials emerged. The question at first sight seems superfluous, since the pattern and content of Did 16:3-8, like any other primitive Christian apocalypse, is Jewish in origin. The section, nevertheless, also has certain features which show indications of having been constructed by a Christian editor rather than just highlighting traits of a Jewish pre-history: the characterization of the world-deceiver as "son of God" (v. 4; appearing only here in the Didache); the curse in v. 5 as probably referring to Jesus who was cursed by the enemies; the "sign of the extension" (v. 6) presumably aiming at the cross and the replacement of the "Son of man" by the "Lord" (v. 8). These specific "Christian" elements do not show any sign of being intrusive in Did 16. On the contrary, they embody the backbone of the exposition

---

[93] Cf. Köster, *Synoptische Überlieferung*, 173-90. See also 1 Thess 4:13-5:11; 2 Thess 2:1-12; 1 Cor 15:23-28; Jude; 2 Pet 2-3; Rev 3-22.

[94] Massaux, *Influence de l'Évangile*, 631-38; see also Prigent, 'Une thèse nouvelle sur la Didachè', 303; Butler, 'The Literary Relations', 280-81; Giet, *L'Énigme de la Didachè*, 244-45 and n. 16; Tuckett, 'Synoptic Tradition in the Didache', 95-104.

[95] For the different possibilities, suggested by scholars, see Rordorf-Tuilier, *La Doctrine des douze Apôtres*, 89-90; Niederwimmer, *Die Didache*, 250-56.

[96] See Audet, *La Didachè*, 180-82; Glover, 'The *Didache*'s Quotations', 21-25; Köster, *Synoptische Überlieferung*, 184.189-190; esp. 184; Rordorf-Tuilier, *La Doctrine des douze Apôtres*, 90; Kloppenborg, 'Didache 16,6-8'; Draper, 'The Development', 14-15; Rordorf, 'Does the Didache contain Jesus Tradition', 412-21.

and thus reveal this tradition as having originated in Christian circles. This observation, by the way, also serves to corroborate the above arguments against considering Did 16 in its present form as the original conclusion of the Two Ways tractate.[97] It would be inconceivable for a Jewish treatise to have contained from its beginning an ending of Christian origin.

We have seen that, in the parenetic passage of vv. 1-2, eschatology functions as a warning to the reader for the retribution at the end of time. It is this tenor which appears to govern the chapter as a whole. The theme of the "last days " or "final hour" in Chap. 16 does not deal with a real situation of anxiety and peril. For the time of "the last days" is in the future rather than in the present. The section was not meant to admonish and comfort a community suffering from tension and repression, nor were the eschatological events, pictured in vv. 3-8, meant to supplant the ethical teaching. Of course, the parenesis of Did 16:1-2 was united with a terse apocalypic scenario to provide a simple piece of teaching about the last things.[98] Nevertheless, its eschatology has become but a subordinate aspect of ethics.[99] Similar compositions are noticeable in the Jewish and Christian traditions, where collections of parenesis often end with an eschatological warning to reinforce teaching on the morality expected in this present age.[100] Did 16 was deliberately crafted to advance the instructions given in the preceding chapters of the Didache. It was a method to keep the reader watchful and to inculcate rules for righteous living.

The Evangelical Section (Did 1:3b-2:1)

Section 1:3b-2:1, unlike the greatest part of the first five chapters of the Didache, undoubtedly derives from more recent sources. It clearly interrupts the connection between Did 1:3a and 2:2 and it stands out from the immediate context in Chaps. 1-6 with respect to its high number of close parallels to the gospels of Matthew and Luke. Moreover, the omission of this section in an important part of textual tradition (Barnabas 18-20, the Doctrina Apostolorum and other early Two Ways renderings) clearly indicates that Did 1:3b-2:1 is a later addition to the basic tradition of the Jewish Two Ways.[101] There is a good possibility that the section was inserted into Did 1-6 at the time when the earlier Two Ways form was incorporated in the Didache as a whole.[102] By inserting the evangelical section right

---

[97] See Vielhauer, *Geschichte der urchristlichen Literatur*, 731.

[98] Cf. also Vielhauer, 'Das Schlusskapitel der Didache', 536-37.

[99] Wengst, 59-61; Schoellgen, 75; Lohmann, *Drohung und Verheissung*, 49-50; cf. Niederwimmer, *Die Didache*, 258-59.

[100] Bammel, 'Pattern and Prototype', 364-66 and 368, n. 27.

[101] Further arguments will be provided below, in Chap 2, pp. 57-58, 70.

[102] Cf., e.g., Nautin, 'La composition de la "Didachê"', 200-201; Köster, *Synoptische Überlieferung*, 238-39; Rordorf-Tuilier, *La Doctrine des douze Apôtres*, 100; Rordorf, 'Le problème de la transmission', 153; Niederwimmer, *Die Didache*, 94. The other options are less likely. It is doubtful that the

after 1:3a, the explanation of the double love command and the Golden Rule (1:2) was Christianized while the traditional Jewish interpetration in Did 2:2-7 accordingly became the 'second commandment'.[103] It is especially the radical exposition about the love of one's neighbour as love of one's enemies which recalls Synoptic tradition in Matt 5:44.46-47 and Luke 6:27-28.32-33. Besides this paragraph (Did 1:3b-d), the evangelical insertion includes two additional units which respectively articulate the prohibition of violent resistance (Did 1:4; cf. Matt 5:39-41; Luke 6:29) and the parenesis about right giving which is concluded by a scriptural quotation (Did 1:5-6; cf. Matt 5:42. 25c-26; *Herm. Man.* II, 4-6; Luke 6:30; 12:58c-59).

Where do the items in the evangelical section come from? The above materials establish a close relationship with the Sermon on the Mount in Matthew (5:3-7:27) and the Sermon on the Plain in Luke (6:20-49). Must we assume that the final composer of the Didache knew one or two of the finished Synoptic gospels? This question will be addressed in the following pages. Many scholars support the view that the evangelical section draws on the gospels of Matthew and Luke as we have them,[104] especially those who give a rather late date to the final edition of the Didache.[105] And indeed, a Didache which was composed in the second half of the 2nd century or later would present a strong case for the use of finished gospels since, by that time, one of the canonical gospels might have attained an authoritative position in the Didache community. In recent scholarship, however, a new consensus is emerging for a date about the turn of the first century CE. If, however, the Didache was redacted that early, dependence of the document on (one of) the Synoptic gospels becomes uncertain. Admittedly, the evangelical section itself offers a passage in Did 1:5b-c which is similar to *Herm. Man.* II, 4-6, and the assignation of the latter writing to the middle of the 2nd century CE would suggest a late date for the redaction of the Didache too. But even in this case, the facts are far from clear. There is no need to suppose that the section is literarily dependent

---

section was part of the Two Ways prior to its embodiment into the whole of the Didache since there is no independent Two Ways tradition available containing any traces of an evangelical section. It is also improbable that the interpolation represents a later insertion since no version of the Didache has been preserved without it. The section is found in the Jerusalem Ms., the Oxyrhynchus papyrus, the Apostolic Constitutions and – at least if it were clear that this document used Did 1:3d and 1:5c – also in the Didascalia Apostolorum. Nevertheless, the latter position, holding that the section was interpolated in the original materials during the history of transmission of the Didache, has some serious defenders, including Von Harnack, *Die Apostellehre*, 31-32; Streeter, 'The Much-Belaboured Didache', 369-70; Creed, 'The Didache', 374-79; Audet, *La Didachè*, 261-80; Vielhauer, *Geschichte der urchristlichen Literatur*, 733 and Wengst, *Didache (Apostellehre)*, 18-20. Wengst is so convinced that the section is a subsequent interpolation in the original Didache that he transfers it in whole to a footnote in his edition of the text (66.68).

[103]   See below, Chap. 5, pp. 161-62.

[104]   Massaux, *Influence de l'Évangile*, 608-13; Layton, 'The Sources'; Köster, *Synoptische Überlieferung*, 217-239; esp. 238; Neirynck, 'Paul', 298-99; Tuckett, 'Synoptic Tradition', 110-28.

[105]   E.g. J.A. Robinson, *Barnabas, Hermas and the Didache*, 47-50; Connolly, 'Canon Streeter', 367-70; Vokes, *The Riddle of the Didache*, 51-61.

on Hermas, since it is more likely that both Hermas and the Didache draw on a common tradition.[106]

As recent studies have argued in detail,[107] it might be appropriate to suggest that the Synoptic gospels were not used as a source for the evangelical section in the Didache. The interpolation in Did 1:3b-2:1 shows a certain affiliation with Matthew and Luke, but the parallel material does not display the precise vocabulary nor word order of the gospels. The wording of the evangelical section in some respects is even in clearer correspondence with the collection of material in Justin (*1 Apology* 15-16) than with either Matthew or Luke.[108] The relevance of this phenomenon becomes all the more evident when one realizes that the text of the evangelical section is delivered to us in an eleventh century manuscript. One may thus expect that, in the intervening ten centuries, the temptation to harmonize discordant parallels must have intensified since copyists became increasingly familiar with the written gospels and their authority in church practice. In general,[109] then, the divergences in the Didache from the canonical texts are significant and must be taken serious as witnesses to an independent tradition.

Did1:3b Bless those who curse you and pray for your enemies, fast for those who persecute you.
3c What kind of favour is it when you love those who love you? Do not even the nations (ἔθνη) do that?
3d Just love those who hate you and you will not have any enemy.
4a Avoid the fleshly and bodily passions.
4b If someone strikes (δῷ ῥάπισμα) you on your right cheek, turn your other one to him too, and you will be perfect.
4c If someone presses you into one mile of service, go along with him for two.
4d If someone takes (ἄρῃ) your cloak (τὸ ἱμάτιόν σου), give him your tunic (τὸν χιτῶνα) as well.
4e If someone takes away from you what is yours, do not demand it back (ἐὰν λάβῃ τις ἀπὸ σοῦ τὸ σόν, μὴ ἀπαίτει) since you cannot do so anyway.
(5a Give to everyone what he asks of you, and do not ask for it back [παντὶ τῷ αἰτοῦντί σε δίδου, καὶ μὴ ἀπαίτει]...)

The material in 1:3b-4 is about the attitude of Christians to those who are ill-disposed towards them. The various elements are closely related to the teachings assigned to Jesus in the Synoptic tradition, particularly in Matt 5:43-48 + 38-42 and Luke 6:27-28.32-36 + 29-30, but the precise nature of the relationship is hard

[106] Jefford, *The Sayings of Jesus*, 50-51; Kraft, *Barnabas and the Didache*, 140-41; Schöllgen-(Geerlings), *Didache. Zwölf-Apostellehre*, 32; Niederwimmer, *Die Didache*, 108-09.
[107] Rordorf, 'Le problème de la transmission'; Draper, 'The Jesus Tradition in the Didache'; Glover, 'The *Didache*'s Quotations', 12-17; Köhler, *Die Rezeption des Matthäusevangeliums*, 46-47.
[108] See the extra-canonical materials in Stroker, *Extracanonical Sayings*, 200-04.227-29 and the tables in Koester, *Synoptische Überlieferung*, 220.227.231; Draper, 'The Jesus Tradition in the Didache', 79-81.
[109] "... unless," of course, "it can be demonstrated that a later redactor would have had a motive in altering the form of the text;" Draper, 'The Jesus Tradition in the Didache', 75.

to establish. First, in comparison to the Synoptic versions, the Didache text is remarkably shorter. Second, several features of vocabulary, content, and ordering make the witness of the Didache unique. Did 1:3b agrees with Luke 6:28, but the injunction to "bless those who curse you" is missing in Matthew. The admonition "pray for your enemies" agrees with Justin, *1 Apol.* 15:9 (Εὔχεσθε ὑπὲρ τῶν ἐχθρῶν ὑμῶν)[110] against Matthew and Luke. The third admonition of this verse, which mentions fasting for persecutors, has no parallel in Synoptic tradition.

In order to evaluate these and the following findings correctly, one must differentiate between the knowledge of a work in its final form and the knowledge of the traditions underlying it. Between the original words of Jesus and the final gospels lie a number of oral and written stages, one of which accounts, in large part, for the similarities and differences in the version of the Didache. The evangelical section, though showing a manifest likeness to certain parts of the Sermon on the Mount, is sufficiently different so as to demonstrate that the composer depended on traditions similar to those used by Matthew and Luke (and Justin), rather than on Matthew, Luke, or Justin themselves. These sources, though their exact form may have varied from place to place, are likely to have circulated in the first century CE in both oral and written forms. Luke and Matthew possessed these sources and they were, at least partially, available to Justin.

Turning now to v. 3c-d, it is important to note that the three directives in 3b are given a sound basis in v. 3c. It would be nothing special to love one's friends because the nations or pagans (ἔθνη) do that too. Christians are exhorted to exceed the standard of love utilized by "the nations." In examining this clause with respect to its parallels – found in Matt 5:46-47; Luke 6:32-33 and Justin, *1 Apol.* 15:9 – it may be particularly instructive to focus on the label ἔθνη in Did 1:3c. Because the Didachist who inserted the evangelical section was not well-disposed towards Jews[111] and probably was a pagan himself, the anti-gentile bias of this statement is surprising. In this light, the divergence between the variant readings like ἔθνη (Did), ἐθνικοί (Matt 5:47), on the one hand, and ἁμαρτωλοί (Luke 6:33), πόρνοι (Justin), on the other, becomes relevant. Because Luke and Justin wrote their works for communities where the gentiles were numerous, they refrain from presenting them as a bad example here in order to maintain good relations. Matthew may have hesitated about altering the tradition since he offers ἐθνικοί in 5:47,[112] but has opted for the more contemptible class of the tax collectors (τελῶναι) in the

---

[110] Goodspeed, *Die ältesten Apologeten*, 35. See also Glover, 'Patristic Quotations and Gospel Sources', 239-40.
Niederwimmer, (*Die Didache*, 95; 101, n. 39; 102, n. 44) with reference to Grenfell-Hunt (*The Oxyrhynchus Papyri*, fol. 2ʳᵒ, col. 1) mentions that the variant κ]αὶ π[ρ]οσεύχεσθε ὑπὲρ [τῶν ἐχθ]ρῶν ὑμῶν is found in P.Oxy.1224; see also Stroker, *Extracanonical Sayings*, 201-02.
[111] See below, Chap. 8, pp. 293, 295-96.
[112] See, however, the number of Mss. supporting τελῶναι at this instance as well. B.M. Metzger views this situation as follows: "In later witnesses, followed by the Textus Receptus, the reading τελῶναι appears to have been substituted for ἐθνικοί in order to bring the statement into closer parallelism with the preceding sentence" (*A Textual Commentary*, 14).

preceding verse 46. In any case, both the thoughtless manner of speaking by the Didachist and the apparent inadequacy of the other texts to agree on a clear-cut surrogate "suggests that the Didache's reading could be the original one."[113] Addressing the logion in v. 3d, we establish that the beginning of the statement reflects Matt 5:44 and Luke 6:27 (= Q), but that the remainder of the clause "and you will not have any enemy" is completely absent in the Synoptics.

After a short statement in v. 4a stressing the need to be free from "fleshly passions,"[114] the text continues with four logia (4b-e) which make up a unit in terms of structure and content. Each clause begins with ἐάν and they all deal with the subject of non-retaliation. Unit 4b-d presents a text which is close to Matt 5:39b-41. This especially obtains for Did 1:4b and Matt 5:39b, although the somewhat awkward wording of striking (δῷ ῥάπισμα) someone on his right cheek in 1:4b is slightly different from its stylistically better Matthean counterpart (ῥαπίζει). The Didache's simple way of putting it, however, may corroborate the impression that this version has retained the more primitive text.[115] Did 1:4c is also essentially similar to Matt 5:41, while it does not have any analogue phrase in the paralleling text of Luke 6:29. The number of corresponding clauses between the Didache and Matthew turns out to be limited, however, when one examines the next phrases. The version of Did 1:4d is unmistakenly closer to Luke 6:29b. First, it displays a succession of the items τὸ ἱμάτιόν σου ("your cloak") and τὸν χιτῶνα ("the tunic") which clearly is the reverse of that in Matthew and, second, the Matthean construction of participle and infinitive θέλοντί ... κριθῆναι ("wanting to sue...") is lacking in Did 1:4d and Luke 6:29b. On the other hand, it is only fair to say as well that the Didache version does not correspond to Luke completely since it offers the aorist subjunctive ἄρῃ ("to take") instead of the Lukan participle αἴροντος.

While in 4c and 4d the one oppressed or robbed gives the aggressor even more than asked for, clauses 4e and 5a fit one another in that the victim abstains from making any demand for restitution. The logion in Did 1:4e ("If someone takes away from you what is yours, do not demand it back"/ ἐὰν λάβῃ τις ἀπὸ σοῦ τὸ σόν, μὴ ἀπαίτει) also recalls Luke because it is in partial agreement with Luke 6:30b ("[Give to every one who begs from you; and] of him who takes away your goods do not demand them back"/ [παντὶ αἰτοῦντί σε δίδου, καὶ] ἀπὸ τοῦ

---

[113] Glover, 'The *Didache*'s Quotations', 14. Other studies too (Rordorf-Tuilier, *La Doctrine des douze Apôtres*, 85; Rordorf, 'Does the Didache contain Jesus Tradition', 402-03; Draper, 'The Jesus Tradition in the Didache', 82 and Jefford, *The Sayings of Jesus*, 46-47) point to the antiquity of the tradition in the Didache here. We should also note in passing that the first element in v. 3c ("What kind of favour is it" /ποία γὰρ χάρις) is sometimes considered to betray Lukan redaction; cf. Tuckett, 'Synoptic Tradition', 120-22. For a different understanding of the passage, see Rordorf, 'id.', 403-04; Draper, ibid.

[114] The combination of "fleshly" with "bodily passions/desires" (τῶν σαρκικῶν καὶ σωματικῶν ἐπιθυμιῶν) as found in the Ms. H might not be the original wording since καὶ σωματικῶν is not found in the text of the Oxyrhynchus fragments (P) nor in the 'Constitutions'; cf., e.g., Niederwimmer, *Die Didache*, 104-05.

[115] Glover, 'The *Didache*'s Quotations', 14-15; Rordorf-Tuilier, *La Doctrine des douze Apôtres*, 85.

αἴροντος τὰ σὰ μὴ ἀπαίτει). Whereas Matthew lacks the equivalent for Did 1:4e, Luke has preserved the same sense in 6:30b in a shorter form. However, the conclusion of this logion in the Didache ("since you cannot do so anyway"/ οὐδὲ γὰρ δύνασαι) whose exact meaning is problematic, has no parallel in the Synoptic tradition. Did 1:5a agrees with Luke 6:30 in rendering the wording μὴ ἀπαίτει against Matthew (μὴ ἀποστραφῇς) and they both have retained the παντί which is absent in Matthew.[116]

Admittedly, the successive clauses in Did 1:4e and 5a create some difficulties[117] for someone wanting to uphold and defend the claim that the evangelical section represents a line of tradition which is independent of the Synoptic gospels. For, if we take the text at its face value, it may derive from an original commandment in Luke 6:30 that has been disbanded, broken up and re-arranged to become two separated directives in Did 1:4e and 5a.[118] On the other hand, there is no need to suppose that Did 1:4e shows literary dependence on Luke 6:30 since this logion might also represent an assimilation to the preceding logion in 1:4d for mnemo-technical reasons.[119] Moreover, if the logia of Did 1:4e-5a did draw on Luke's text, why, then, is the order of the clauses in Luke 6:30 a and b reversed in the Didache? And, finally, why has the stronger verb αἴρω ("to take away") in Luke 6:30b been replaced by the weaker λαμβάνω ("to take") in Did 1:4e? The latter question becomes all the more acute since this stronger verb probably would have made avoidable the hopeless complaint in the final clause "since you cannot do so anyway" of Did 1:4e.[120] No sound case that the passage in 1:4e and 1:5a reflects Luke's redactional work can therefore be made.

Did1:5a   Give (δίδου) to everyone what he asks of you, and do not ask for it back
    5b   for the Father wants people to share (δίδοσθαι) with everyone the gifts that
        have been freely granted to them.
    5c   Blessed is the person who gives (ὁ διδούς) according to the commandment,
        for he is guiltless. Alas for the person who takes. If someone takes something
        because he is in need, he is guiltless, but if he is not in need, he shall have
        to defend his reason for taking it and the use for which he intends it;
    5d   if he is imprisoned, he shall be interrogated about what he has done, and he
        shall not go free until he has paid back the last penny.
    6a   But then about this sort of thing it has also been said (εἴρηται),

---

[116] Justin has both παντί and ἀποστρέφομαι: ... Παντὶ τῷ αἰτοῦντι δίδοτε καὶ τὸν βουλόμενον δανείσασθαι μὴ ἀποστραφῆτε. ... (1 Apol. 15:10; cf. Goodspeed, Die ältesten Apologeten, 36.

[117] "The net result of the discussion of this section" (= 1:4d-5a) "is that the Didache here appears to presuppose Luke's redactional work and hence Luke's finished gospel;" cf. Tuckett, 'Synoptic Tradition in the Didache', 127.

[118] See Manson, The Sayings of Jesus, 50; Köster, Synoptische Überlieferung, 228-29; cf. also Giet, L'Énigme de la Didachè, 59-60.

[119] Cf. Wrege, Die Überlieferungsgeschichte der Bergpredigt, 78, n. 2.

[120] See Rordorf, 'Does the Didache contain Jesus Tradition', 407. Elsewhere Rordorf states that the two commandments of Did 1:4e-5a, apart from being combined in Luke 6:30, circulated independently as well; cf. 'Le problème de la transmission', 146, n. 1.

6b   "Let your charitable gift sweat in your hands until you know to whom you
      are giving it."
2:1   The second commandment of the doctrine: ...

The logion in Did 1:5a introduces the final unit dealing with the question of alms
giving (1:5a-6b). First, the basic ethical tenet – also found in a similar wording
in the Synoptic tradition (Matt 5:42; Luke 6:30 = Q?) and in Justin, *1 Apol.* 15:10
– is formulated: "Give to everyone what he asks of you, and do not ask for it back."
The subsequent commentary on this traditional rule tones down this advice and
reduces the force of its meaning. This saying of the Lord is discussed and tempered
with respect to the attitude of Christians in two ways. First, in Did 1:5c-d, it is the
recipient who is held responsible for his behaviour and, second, the quotation in
1:6 hints at some kind of responsibility on the part of the giver as well.

The first approach in mitigating the transmitted saying of Jesus is formulated
in Did 1:5c. Verses 5b-c represent a blending of traditional passages which are
attached to Did 1:5a by means of the catchword "to give" (δίδωμι). The statement
in 1:5b resembles the last phrase of the Greek Two Ways (GTW) 4:8, which, as
we will see below in Chapter 4, constitutes the earlier form of the Two Ways in
the Didache. This phrase, a common Jewish statement, is still present in its original
position in the text of the Doctrina Apostolorum which closely parallels the Greek
Two Ways: "For the Lord wants to give to all of his gifts." Because the interpolator
of Did 1:3b-2:1, however, assigned this verse part to Did 1:5b, it is no longer found
in the Did 4:8 (further, see Chapter 4, pp. 136-37). Moreover, in Did 1:5b, he has
accredited the motivation for claiming indiscriminate generosity to Jesus (in
referring to the "Father"). An additional demand of charity occurs in almost
identical form in the first lines of *Herm. Man.* II, 4-6:

> Give to all (Πᾶσιν δίδου), for God wishes that all be in receipt of his own gifts. Those
> then who receive shall be accountable to God for why they received and for what
> purpose; for those who received while in distress will not be condemned, but those who
> receive in hypocrisy shall pay a penalty. He therefore who gives is innocent: ....

It is difficult to escape the impression that the correspondence of the wording in
Did 1:5b-c with the above quotation was meant to soften the requirement of the
Jesus saying. With the help of the tradition in *Herm. Man.* II, 4-6, which probably
was known to both the composer of Hermas and the interpolator of the Didache,
an attempt is made to discourage those persons who take alms without needing
them. Because a detailed treatment of the text would extend beyond the scope of
this chapter, attention will be paid to some basic points only. The passage in 1:5b-c
parallels the directive in Hermas which, after the imperative "give to all," in a
similar way stresses the moral liability of the beneficiary and concludes with the
observation that those who receive will account to God for why they received and
for what. Those who receive hypocritically will have to pay a penalty.[121] The

---

[121]   *Herm. Man.* II, 4b-6a; for the Greek text, cf. (Körtner-) Leutzsch, *Papiasfragmente. Hirt des
Hermas*, 192.

common source is provided with a conclusion in Did 1:5d which again recalls Synoptic tradition (Matt 5:25c-26; Luke 12:58c-59) – though in a radically different context – as it mentions somebody being imprisoned and affirms in a parallel close to Matt 5:26 that "he shall not go free until he has paid back the last penny." We should note in passing that the composer of the Didache in his reflection on the command of almsgiving is not likely to have derived his materials from the extant versions of the Synoptic gospels. The variety of constituents point to the Didachist's drawing on some collection of Jesus sayings.

The second line of argumentation in limiting the introductory directive on giving is a warning against indiscriminate charity in 1:6 by quoting a saying that might have come from Sir 12:1. The saying appears to advocate a deliberate selectivity on the part of the alms giver, and it is reasonable to suppose that a quotation from Scripture was needed here in order to allow for human realism as a substitute for the visionary teaching of Jesus.[122] The citation formula εἴρηται suggests that the verse being quoted was borrowed from Scripture, although it has not been possible to establish its source with definitive literary evidence. We cannot enter into details here. Suffice it to say that the saying probably originates from a version of Sir 12:1 which is independent of the LXX.[123]

Did 2:1, finally, is a transitional verse leading the reader back again to the materials of the earlier Two Ways form. Its introduction relegates the original explanation (which is the list of precepts 2:2-7, at least, and Chaps. 2-4, at most) of the initial summary of the Law in 1:2 to being the second commandment. It is likely that the person who was responsible for the adoption of the evangelical portion formulated this verse in an attempt to integrate the section into the Two Ways.

---

[122] Cf. Schöllgen-(Geerlings), Didache. Zwölf-Apostellehre, 33-35.

[123] Cf. e.g. Audet, La Didachè, 275-80; Skehan, 'Didache 1,6 and Sirach 12,1'; Layton, 'The Sources', 367-69. But see also the criticism of Niederwimmer, Die Didache, 113-14 and Bridge, 'To Give or Not to Give?', 558-60. According to Bridge, the traditional interpretation of Did 1:6 creates a contradiction between the directive in 1:5a-b urging indiscriminate generosity and the saying in 1:6 encouraging restraint and caution. He levels criticism against the Didache-Sirach relationship and deliberately proposes an interpretation that is not affected by Sir 12:1 nor by its immediate context. At variance with usual scholarly opinion, he not only takes the quotation in 1:6 to be in agreement with 1:5, but suggests that it even goes beyond it in scope: "Let your almsgiving bring sweat to your hands until you know (γνῷς) to whom you give." The charitable activity should bring perspiration to the hands in the tireless effort of giving alms. But how can the second clause of the quotation be explained? In Bridge's view, the phrase parallels the wording "you shall know (γνώσῃ) who is the good repayer of wage" in Did 4:7. A comparison of the two phrases to get at the meaning of the second part of Did 1:6 makes it clear that the reference in this clause is to God: "... until you know that it is to God to whom you are giving" (564). This explanation is ingenious but hazardous since God is considered to bestow and not to receive payments in Did 4:7. Moreover, the precise origin of the saying remains equally uncertain in this exegesis. And finally, the quotation in 1:6 is understandable in the present context as referring to Sir 12:1. For the commandment in 1:5a-b, taken from the Jesus tradition, may have been intentionally transformed and tempered in view of the social reality predominant in the churches at the time of the Didachist. One must understand this exegetical tour de force as a biblical justification of standard practice in the Didache community. See also below.

To sum up this long discussion: Did 1:3.4.5a and 5d reflect logia from the Jesus tradition, but their variation in order and wording (and to some extent this also pertains to Justin) in comparison to the canonical gospels indicates that the Didache has preserved a Jesus tradition independently of the gospels of Matthew and Luke. The unit in Did 1:3b-4, discussing the attitude of a Christian toward those who display aggressive behaviour against him, probably goes back to a block of sayings close to Synoptic tradition but circulating separately.[124] The second unit (1:5-6) may have been produced by the Didachist himself. He may have used the same sources as our gospels did (1:5a.d), a common Jewish statement about charitable activity (1:5b) which subsequently was tempered by materials available to (at least) Hermas and the Didachist (1:5c) and by some unknown Greek version of Sir 12:1 (1:6b). The Didachist, by this exegetical procedure, shows his intention to restrict the appeal to unconditional almsgiving in his time and milieu. The Didache community apparently experienced the saying of the Lord as too difficult a burden to be observed in their time and region. Unscrupulous charlatans could easily take advantage of the precept of indiscriminate generosity. And, indeed, a central concern of the Didachist in the altered circumstances of his time was to protect the community against frauds and swindlers.

Date and Provenance

In making a statement about the date and place of origin of the Didache, no answer can pretend to be better than a reasonable guess. The many differing opinions show how meagre and puzzling are the clues given by the Didache. Some think that the composition of the text in its present form must have been undertaken between 50 and 70 CE;[125] others suggest an editorial date at the first half of the second century[126] while still others, mostly English researchers, argue for the second half of the second century.[127] An ever-growing consensus emerging in recent scholarship is that the text was composed by the turn of the first century CE.[128] The

---

[124] Cf. Rordorf, 'Le problème de la transmission', 146; Id., 'Does the Didache contain Jesus Tradition', 410.

[125] Cf. Audet, *La Didachè*, 187-210; esp.199. See also J.A.T. Robinson (*Redating the New Testament*, 96-100 and 322-27) who dates the Didache between 40 and 60 CE.

[126] E.g. Quasten, *Patrology* 1, 37; Altaner-Stuiber, *Patrologie*, 81; Barnard, *Studies in the Apostolic Fathers*, 99; Niederwimmer, *Die Didache*, 79.

[127] E.g. J.A. Robinson, *Barnabas, Hermas and the Didache*, 69-83; esp. 82 (in his view it might even be a third-century document); Kraft, *Barnabas and the Didache*, 76-77; S.E. Johnson, 'A Subsidiary Motive', 108; Vokes, *The Riddle of the Didache*, 86; Connolly, 'The Didache and Montanism'; Massaux, *Influence de l'Évangile*, 6. 604-05. 654-55.

[128] E.g. Adam, 'Erwägungen zur Herkunft', 70; Vielhauer, *Geschichte der urchristlichen Literatur*, 735-37; Wengst, *Didache (Apostellehre)*, 62-63; Rordorf-Tuilier, *La Doctrine des douze Apôtres*, 91-99; esp. 96 and 232; Köhler, *Die Rezeption des Matthäusevangeliums*, 29-30; Steimer, *Vertex Traditionis*, 20. See also Schaff, *The Oldest Church Manual*, 119-25; esp. 122; Ehrhard, *Die altchristliche Litteratur*, 65 etc.

provenance of the Didache is usually assigned alternatively to Egypt, to the Syria-Palestine region, or more specifically to Antioch. An increasing number of modern authors attribute the text to Syria-Palestine.

Obviously, the literary dependence of the Didache on other early Christian writings could be a significant point in establishing its date. The version of the Two Ways in Did 1-6 has often been considered to be literarily dependent on the Epistle of Barnabas, while an individual verse like Did 1:5 (in the evangelical section) has frequently been taken to draw, at least partially, upon the Shepherd of Hermas.[129] If the Didache has used Barnabas and Hermas, it surely must be dated later than those sources, and, in that case, the text could not have been composed prior to 140. Today it is widely accepted, however, that the manual did not utilize the Two Ways material from Barnabas nor resort to Hermas. Most scholars agree that the version of the Two Ways in the Didache goes back to an originally Jewish basic model, while it is felt that it is also conceivable that the textual agreement between Did 1:5 and Hermas reflects a common tradition.[130]

Evidence for the dating of the Didache to the middle of the 2nd century or later has also long been inferred from an alleged influence of New Testament texts, especially of the canonical gospels. And, indeed, if we take the text at its face value, the Didache would seem to be rather extensively familiar with the Synoptic gospels, especially Matthew's gospel (cf. Did 1:4b-d; 8:2; 9:5b; 15:3.4; 16:3-8). However, the view that the Didache – even in its latest redactional layer – alludes to or quotes from the canonical version of the New Testament is highly controversial. Above, on pp. 35-48 of this chapter, we have opted for independence on the part of the Didache in the eschatological conclusion (Did 16) and the evangelical section (Did 1:3b-2:1).[131]

It is more difficult, however, to determine the nature of the formulation in those instances which explicitly refer to "the gospel" in Did 8:2; 11:3; 15:3.4. A number

---

[129] For the alleged dependence of the Did 1-6 on Barnabas, see below, Chap. 2, pp. 60-61; for the supposed dependence of Did 1:5b-c on *Herm. Man.* II, 4-6, see, e.g. Hennecke, 'Die Grundschrift der Didache', 71; Muilenburg, *The Literary Relations*, 33. 46. 167; Vokes, *The Riddle of the Didache*, 51-61; Connolly, 'Canon Streeter on the Didache', 377-79; Layton, 'The Sources', 361-67.

[130] For the common tradition of Did 1:5 and Hermas, cf. Ropes, *Die Sprüche Jesu*, 64-71; Kraft, *Barnabas and the Didache*, 140-41; Glover, 'The *Didache*'s Quotations', 15-16; Köster, *Synoptische Überlieferung*, 230-31; Audet, *La Didachè*, 163-66 and 271-72; Niederwimmer, *Die Didache*, 108-11; Schöllgen-(Geerlings), *Didache. Zwölf-Apostellehre*, 32. See also below, Chap. 4, pp. 136-37.

[131] It was established that these segments, Did 1:3b-2:1 and Did 16, probably represent independent pre-gospel traditions drawing upon materials which preceded the final forms of the Synoptic gospels. It is also unlikely that, in its other parts, the Didache is indebted to any of the New testament writings as we know them (e.g., Did 8:1and Matt 6:16; Did 8:2 and Matt 6:5 [for these, see below, Chap. 8, pp. 291-96]; Did 8:2 and Matt 6:9-13 [= The Lord's Prayer; see below, ibid.]; Did 9:5 and Matt 7:6; Did 11:7 and Matt 12:31; Did 15:3 and Matt 18:15-17); cf. Glover, 'The *Didache*'s Quotations', 17-29 (and Id., 'Patristic Quotations and Gospel Sources', esp. 240.247-48); Audet, *La Didachè*, 166-83; Rordorf-Tuilier, *La Doctrine des douze Apôtres*, 84-89; Rordorf, 'Does the Didache contain Jesus Tradition', 421-23; Draper, 'The Jesus Tradition in the Didache', 76-79.85-86; Jefford, *The Sayings of Jesus*, 91.130-45; Court, 'The Didache and St. Matthew's Gospel', 109-113.

of scholars have assumed here the use of at least the gospel of Matthew.[132] Do these expressions really betray literary dependence on one of the known gospels? Below, in Chapters 8 and 9, they will be discussed within their proper contexts. We will see that the expression in 8:2 ("as the Lord directed in his gospel") introduces the Lord's Prayer, which in form and wording strongly agrees with the version transmitted in Matthew. On the other hand, if we are dealing here with a prayer that was recited thrice daily in the Didache community (Did 8:3), it is hard to believe that the manual quotes directly from the written gospel text of Matthew.[133]

A similar situation obtains with respect to Did 15:3.4.[134] These injunctions regulate some aspects of internal community life and their substance is buttressed twice by the formula "as you have it in the gospel (of our Lord)." Although the duplicate expression clearly suggests a document in which these requirements were written down, we will see that the context of these references only faintly reflects some materials in a gospel (cf., for example, Matt 18:15-17). Instead, they turn out to presuppose ideas and wordings which occur in circles close to the Qumran sectarians. The evidence, then, does not support the hypothesis that one of the canonical gospels had acquired an authoritative position in the Didache community by the time of the manual's final redaction.[135] It is clear, as a result, that the gospels cannot serve as a foundation for the basic theories discussing the date of its composition.

Egypt and Syria are the most frequently proposed as the likely candidates for the provenance of the Didache. The text provided by Clement of Alexandria (ca. 150-215 CE) would suggest an early use of the Didache material in Egypt. Clement's quotations and allusions are not undisputed, however, since they may have derived from an independent Two Ways treatise.[136] Certainly, the Papyrus Oxyrhynchus and the Coptic version provide ample evidence that our form of the Didache was in circulation in fourth-century Egypt,[137] but these textual sources

---

[132] E.g. Massaux, *Influence de l'Évangile*, 604-646; Köhler, *Die Rezeption des Matthäusevangeliums*, 29-30; Wengst, *Didache (Apostellehre)*, 24-32 and 61-63 etc.

[133] It is more likely that a Christian writer would have cited the form of the prayer in use in his community; cf. also below, Chap. 8, pp. 294-95.

[134] Cf. below, Chap. 9, p. 352.

[135] Admittedly, it is difficult to ascertain what exactly the term 'gospel' alludes to, but its usage as a technical term is not likely in these instances for "it is inherently improbable that any word should so speedily acquire a new and exclusive meaning" (Glover, 'The *Didache*'s Quotations', 28). In fact, nothing in the context of these references indicates the presence of materials which were derived from any known gospel in writing. In these cases, this designation is probably best understood as a reference to oral or written collections of sayings (cf. Rordorf-Tuilier, *La Doctrine des douze Apôtres*, 86-89).

[136] Cf. below, Chap 3, pp. 82-87; esp. pp. 82-83; see also above, pp. 5-6.

[137] We do not consider the contacts between Origen and the Didache to rest on literary dependence; cf. Niederwimmer, *Die Didache*, 20.

do not help us to further determine the area whence the Didache originated two or three centuries before.[138]

Elements in the Didache which speak in favour of a descendance from Syria or Palestine are the geographical allusions in the prayer of 9:4 (presupposing hillsides or mountains) and the regulation about baptism in 7:2-3 (implying a region lacking water). Indeed, these details suggest an origin in Syria-Palestine. The section in Did 7-10 may very well have preserved materials that stem from a community as it existed prior to the composition of the Didache. At the same time, however, it should be emphasized that the Didache is a composite document. The date and region of the sewing together of the Didache as a whole must thus be distinguished from the time and area of the four independent sections so utilized. What we are looking for here and now is the date and the provenance that apply to the final and overall editing of the Didache text.

When viewed without proper investigation, the directives in the Didache make the impression of being timeless and impersonal. However, the analysis on pp. 28-35, above, made it clear that the manual was not edited in a historical vacuum. The redactor of the Didache intended to communicate a specific message to a particular audience which experienced pressing social problems. We have concluded that the two major concerns of the Didache at the level of redaction can be found in the attempt to define a new (religious) position distancing itself from Judaism and to equip the community in the face of the influence of potential troublesome visitors. The first objective does not carry much weight in assessing the date and geographical origin of the Didache since the endeavour to differentiate Christian practice from Jewish rituals has not necessarily taken place in every region at the same speed.

The other editorial concern is reflected in the section of Did 11-13 where rules are set forth to help the community deal with troublesome visitors. Although we acknowledge the tentative nature of the following observations, the data surveyed above, on pp. 28-35, and below, in Chapter 9 (pp. 340-50), may permit some conclusions in the light of contemporary evidence. First, the familiarity of the Did 11-13 with the real-life situation of the community is likely to exempt its provenance in Egypt. Even though Hellenistic wandering teachers, for example, Cynic philosophers and teachers, are found in other parts of the Greco-Roman world as well, it appears that this type of itinerant Christian preacher flourished primarily in Syria. Similar traditions of radical itinerancy are found in Lucian of Samosata's *De morte Peregrini*, in the gospel of Thomas, and in the Ps-Clementine letters *Ad Virgines*.

Second, as a result of the increasingly questionable behaviour of itinerants who did not belong to the community of the Didache, guidelines were formulated in

---

[138] "Für Ägypten konnte angeführt werden, dass viele gerade der frühesten antiken Textzeugen aus dieser Region stammen; doch klafft zwischen Abfassung und ältestem Textzeugen, dem *Papyrus Oxyrhynchus 1782* (P), ein Zeitraum von mehr als 200 Jahren;" Schöllgen-(Geerlings), *Didache. Zwölf-Apostellehre*, 84.

the editorial section of Did 11-13 on behalf of the local congregation *vis-à-vis* these wanderers. Some of the instructions are similar to the ones in the gospel of Matthew. Closer examination of that gospel suggests that the Matthean community was also a settled congregation which, like the community of the Didache, was visited by itinerant prophets, some of which were illegitimate (Matt 7:15-23; 10:5-15.40-42; 24:11.24). In Did 11-13, there are still wandering apostles and prophets, although a number of the latter ones are in the process of becoming resident (13:1-2). Moreover, we have seen that, also with respect to other important elements, the Didache reveals a strong affinity with sayings of the Matthean gospel. It is not far-fetched to suppose, therefore, that the text of the Didache was compiled in fairly close contact with the community in which Matthew's gospel arose. Since arguments have been advanced for the Syrian provenance of Matthew,[139] it is only natural to suggest a similar geographical and chronological setting for the Didache.

Third, the type of ministry showing the continued existence of traveling apostles and prophets alongside a resident ministry of teachers, deacons, and bishops does not reflect the high degree of organizational structure of larger Christian communities in urban areas. The rudimentary character of these institutions points to a rural or semi-rural origin, rather than to an urban one. In this respect, the following is also of interest. The Didache is very explicit about the nourishment of an apostle when leaving the community and continuing his journey: he is to be provided with food for one day only (11:4-6). This rule, rather than applying to an area in which long distances between big cities had to be bridged, must have been operative first of all in a semirural region.[140] In sum, it appears that the setting for the Didache is likely to be found in one of the congregations within a network of villages and small towns. The community for which the manual was composed probably was a rural Christian congregation in some Greek speaking part of (Western) Syria or, possibly, in the borderland between Syria and Palestine at the close of the first century.

---

[139] According to Luz (*Das Evangelium nach Matthäus*, 1, 73) scholars agree on Syria as the area whence Matthew's gospel originated: "Konsens ist: Matthäus stammt aus dem syrischen Raum." The composition of the gospel of Matthew is often ascribed to Antioch; cf. Meier, *Law and History in Matthew's Gospel*, 8-9; Kingsbury, *Matthew*, 96-107. However, other places for the composition of the gospel have been suggested as well. For a survey of the various proposals, cf. Stanton, 'The Origin and Purpose of Matthew's Gospel', 1941-42; Davies-Allison, *The Gospel according to Saint Matthew* 1, 138-47; Saldarini, 'The Gospel of Matthew', 26, n. 8. See also Sim (*The Gospel of Matthew*, 40-62), who considers the pros and cons of the various suggested locations and finally identifies Antioch on the Orontes as the gospel's place of composition.

[140] In addition, one may also refer to the directions for the distribution of the firstfruits in Did 13:3-7, reflecting an agricultural economy. However, since this section represents a tradition which existed at one time as a separate unit (see below, Chap. 9, pp. 360-64) and does not stem from the redactor's hand, it will play no part in this discussion.

I The Two Ways Tractate:

Didache 1-6

Chapter Two

The Jewish Source of Didache 1-6:
the Two Ways

The section of moral instruction in Chaps. 1-6 of the Didache differs from the remainder of the work (7:1-16:8), which is concerned with church order and practice. The following pages will briefly discuss the contents of Did 1-6 (pp. 55-56). Next, it will be demonstrated that the materials in Did 1-6 suggest at least two layers of composition, representing two different stages of the literary history of the Two Ways. It will further become apparent that the earlier layer (without Did 1:3a-2:1 and 6:2-3) is closely connected with a Jewish pattern of the Two Ways (pp. 56-59). In a subsequent section, we will see that this earlier layer, perceived in the first part of the present Didache, appears as an independent composition in Two Ways sections of other extant Christian writings. These sections may accordingly be qualified as representing the ancient Two Ways tradition (pp. 59-70).[1] Finally, in search of the tradition's earliest form, the interrelationship will be discussed between the Didache, the Doctrina Apostolorum, the Letter of Barnabas, and the Apostolic Church Order as far as their Two Ways passages are concerned (pp. 70-80).

The Contents of the Two Ways Section in Did 1-6

After an introduction (1:1), the first division of Did 1-6 teaches the Way of Life (Chaps.1-4), which is described at greater length than the Way of Death (Chap. 5). It begins with the double love commandment (the "love of God" and the "love of neighbour"), which is followed by the Golden Rule in its negative form. Then a series of positive admonitions is found in verses 3b-2:1, which, reflecting some radical requirements of the Sermon on the Mount, display Christian concerns rather strictly. The segment calls upon the reader/hearer to love his enemy, to abandon retaliation and to give to the needy. The acceptance of unnecessary charity and the unconditional dispensation of alms, however, probably as a result of contemporary abuses, are condemned.

---

[1] We are only concerned here with the literary agreements. This is not to deny the relevance of oral tradition to our subject but, given the fact that only literary documents are brought into focus, an oral tradition is not considered here; cf. also Niederwimmer, *Die Didache*, 56-57, n. 49.

Moreover, there may have been additional developments of the tradition of the Two Ways or extra intermediary stages of its transmission. We are dealing here, however, with the reconstruction of the transmission as far as this can be deduced from the available sources.

After a second introduction, a list of prohibitions is presented in 2:2-7. Although this parenetic catalogue is expanded with specific additional elements, it is in fact a development of the more general themes of the second table of the Decalogue. Thus the commandment not to commit adultery is extended to include a prohibition on pederasty and fornication. Also other items expressing a firm stand against the danger of contemporary threats can be explained as modifications of the Decalogue. These prohibitions include magic, sorcery, murdering children, and abortion. The next passage, Did 3:1-6, stands out as a distinctive literary unit. The verses in 3:2-6 present five negative admonitions on major transgressions (as in 2:2-3), which are viewed each in its turn as the utmost consequences of transgressing light precepts. They begin with the address "My child" (τέκνον μου) and are constructed in a strophic and repetitive pattern. This pattern is not extended to the next verses. Instead, the passage in Did 3:7-10 gives a series of positive admonitions which, with respect to their content, are basically characterized by the motif of humble meekness.

Did 4 is the concluding chapter of the Way of Life and can be divided into three parts. The first part (4:1-8) focusses on the precepts governing social relationships within the religious community. They include the reverence toward the teacher of the word of God, a warning of separation and division, insistence on an unbiased judgment in internal community conflicts and generosity between the brethren. The second part (4:9-11) contains "household exhortations" which remind the parents, masters and slaves of their specific duties. In the third part (4:12-14), a general admonition is found which, among other things, warns the reader to keep the Lord's commandments by neither adding nor subtracting anything from them.

The Way of Death in Did 5 is introduced by a short designation, expressing its peculiar evil character. It is described next by lengthy lists of features typifying the nature of a wicked existence. After a catalogue of twenty-three vices (5:1), which is mainly a concise repetition of the materials presented in 2:1-7, a list of nineteen evildoers (5:2) is offered. The Way of Death ends with a wish or prayer that the reader may be preserved from "all this." Then, after the warning in 6:1 to be on one's guard against false teachers who may lead the readers/hearers away from the teaching of the Two Ways, the subsequent verses (6:2-3) present a reduction of the previous standards for those who are unable to "bear the entire yoke of the Lord."

The Didache Form of the Two Ways Tradition and the Tradition's Ancestry

Two things may be noted about the form of the Two Ways in Did 1-6. Firstly, one would expect that the exhortation in 6:1 concludes the Two Ways section of the Didache in its entirety: "See to it that no one leads you astray from this way of the doctrine, since [the person who would do so] teaches apart from God." Both formulation and content suggest that this statement is the final verse; this impression is strengthened by the predominant concessive tenor in the next verses (6:2-3), which appear to strike out on a new course. For at the end of the comprehensive ethical treatise, Did 6:2 rather suddenly grants that also a partial compliance with all previous admonitions suffices. Furthermore, with respect to food, everyone is allowed to determine what is to be eaten and only a minimum requirement is laid down (6:3). A number of scholars have drawn attention to the affinity of Did 6:2-3 with the Apostolic Decree in Acts 15;[2] in another chapter of this book,[3] it will be argued that the directives in these verses may reflect the position of the mother church in Jerusalem with regard to the gentile Christians. For the present, however, it suffices to notice that the statements in Did 6:2-3 appear to be a later addition to a basic tradition of the Two Ways.

A second remarkable feature occurs in Did 1:3b-2:1. In the above survey, it was already suggested that the specific themes in this passage remind us of sayings in the synoptic tradition (especially the Sermon on the Mount). This observation is the more striking because a similar accumulation of traditional gospel motifs is absent from the remainder of the Two Ways manual of Did 1-6. The situation in fact is such that apart from the evangelical section in 1:3b-2:1 (and, of course the concessive items in 6:2-3), there is hardly any[4] reference to the specific Christian doctrine in the Two Ways manual of the Didache. Nowhere does one come across obvious soteriological and Christological motifs such as the passion, death and resurrection of Christ. On the other hand, it has been observed that the text in Did 1:1-3a. 2:2-6:1 is closely related to traditional Jewish materials in *T. Asher*, Ps.-Clem. Hom. VII, 3,3ff; 7,1ff and the Sentences of Pseudo-Phocylides.[5] For these reasons, it has been argued as early as the end of the previous century that this or

---

[2] See e.g. Taylor, *The Teaching of the Twelve Apostles*, 46-48; Vokes, *The Riddle of the Didache*, 95-96; Stuiber, '"Das ganze Joch"', 326-327; Rordorf-Tuilier, *La Doctrine des douze Apôtres*, 32; Wengst, *Didache (Apostellehre)*, 96, n. 53; Jefford, *The Sayings of Jesus*, 96-98; Mitchell, 'Baptism in the Didache', 237-242.

[3] See below, Chap. 7.

[4] The wording Ἐν ἐκκλησίᾳ in Did 4:14 – omitted in the Doctrina, the Letter of Barnabas and the Epitome – is probably a rare exception. It must be a later insertion. It is unlikely, however, that the double love commandment in Did 1:2 (cf. Doctr. 1:2; ACO 4:2-3 and Epitome 1) is a later Christianization of Jewish materials (see below, p. 73).

[5] Cf. Rordorf-Tuilier, *La Doctrine des douze Apôtres*, 24; Niederwimmer, *Die Didache*, 57-58 and 84-87.

It is difficult to evaluate the relationship of the Two Ways to Pseudo-Phocylides and to the Oath of Asaph the Physician. With regard to Ps.-Phocylides, one may argue that both instructions, like many others, belong to the gnomic literary genre; cf. Berger, 'Hellenistische Gattungen', 1058-59 and Küchler, *Frühjüdische Weisheitstraditionen*, 236-302. Furthermore, both the Two Ways and Ps.-Phocylides are confined to fairly general, comprehensive and universal moral exhortations reflecting particularly Jewish concerns but also commonplaces of Greek teaching. It is obvious, though, that both writings are interested in ethics, not in theology.

Shlomo Pines ('The Oath of Asaph the Physician') was the first to discover a connection between some verses of the Hebrew 'Oath of Asaph the Physician' and certain passages in the Two Ways part of the Didache. It might be that some physician(s) have appropriated the (gnomic) version of the Two Ways instruction for the "exigencies of the medical profession" (255).

a similar form of the Two Ways is a derivative from a Jewish origin.[6] The facts do indeed appear to support the view that a Jewish tradition, in which Did 1:3a was linked with 2:2, stands behind the present form of the Two Ways in the Didache.

The theme of the Two Ways, however, is not limited exclusively to Judaism or to the text of the Didache. The next section will point out that this teaching has various parallel texts in the literature of the early church. Moreover, the Two Ways device was widespread in the early Mediterranean world. The usages of the metaphor are quite common in classical antiquity. The best-known example is the famous myth "the Choice of Heracles," created by the sophist Prodicus of Ceos and told by Xenophon, our main source of the Prodicus tradition.[7] In this story, Heracles is called upon to choose between two ways, each of which is represented by a woman, symbolizing virtue (ἀρετή) and vice (κακία). In the light of this evidence and other data[8] attesting the wide popularity of the Two Ways metaphor, it would seem reasonable to think that the instruction in Did 1-6 is just another witness to the flourishing of this type of teaching in Greek antiquity.

On the other hand, considering the numerous links of the Two Ways form in the Didache with materials in sources of early Judaism, one may assume that an ancient Jewish recension stands behind the Christian counterpart. It is therefore only natural to look for similar Jewish foms of instruction that would qualify as its direct ancestry. The data in the Hebrew Bible and LXX[9] might be relevant in this regard, since the topos of the Two Ways frequently occurs in such passages as Deut 11:26-28; 30:15-19; Jer 21:8; Pss 1:1.6; 119 (118):29-30; 139 (138):24; Prov 2:13; 4:18-19; 11:20; 12:28 (LXX), and so forth. Yet, these places do not provide immediate ties with the form of the Two Ways as represented in Did 1:1-3a; 2:2-6:1. They do not show the same basic structure, and it is unlikely that any of them actually represents the direct source of the text we are concerned with. Admittedly, some of them, especially Deut. 30:15-19[10] and Ps 1,[11] may have played a role in the development of the tradition, but even these do not evidence a Two

---

[6] It is especially the work of C. Taylor (*The Teaching of the Twelve Apostles*) which has been most influential in this respect. For the history of research of the Didache, cf. Ehrhard, *Die altchristliche Litteratur*, 37-68; Vokes, 'The Didache – Still Debated', 57-62; Jefford, *The Sayings of Jesus*, 1-17; Draper, 'The Didache in Modern Research: an Overview'.

[7] Cf. *Memorabilia*, II, 1, 21-34. For the dissemination of the Two Ways theme, see Bergman, 'Zum Zwei-Wege-Motiv'. See also Alpers, *Hercules in Bivio*; Becker, *Das Bild des Weges*; Panofsky, *Hercules am Scheidewege*, 42-52; Gladigow, 'Der Makarismus des Weisen', 423-24; Harms, *Homo viator in bivio*; etc.

[8] Further references in Niederwimmer, *Die Didache*, 83-84; Berger, 'Hellenistische Gattungen', 1090-91.

[9] The metaphor of the Two Ways appears with extraordinary frequency in the LXX; cf. Knopf, *Die Lehre der zwölf Apostel*, 4.

[10] Cf. TgPs-Yon on Deut 30:15 and TgNeof on Deut 30:19; see below, Chapter 5, pp. 143-44.

[11] K. Berger claims that the Geniza Wisdom Manuscript (in 3:17.18; 4:1.2; cf. 1:1) contains a peculiar type of Two Ways instruction connected with Ps 1; cf. *Die Weisheitsschrift*, 182-204. He argues that the work was composed at the end of the first century, but this date is highly controversial. H.P. Rüger takes the writing to be "ein Produkt des mittelalterlichen jüdischen Neuplatonismus;" cf. *Die Weisheitsschrift*, 1-19; esp. 17. See also Ebersohn, *Das Nächstenliebegebot*,133.

Ways tradition in that they contain separate lists of virtues and vices, such as is found in the present Two Ways form of the Didache. They do not fill the gap between the initial rudimentary stages of the Two Ways metaphor in the Hebrew Bible / LXX and the specific type preserved in the Didache.

The discovery of the Qumran scrolls stimulated research in another direction. In this respect, the contribution of Jean-Paul Audet, published in 1952,[12] is of overriding importance. He demonstrated for the first time that a pattern of the Two Ways tradition – with the parenetic form of a double catalogue – was incorporated in the Manual of Discipline (1QS 3:13-4:26).[13] In order to really appreciate the relevance of this post-biblical Jewish Two Ways tradition, two things have to be taken into account: firstly, the sharply deterministic and dualistic tone in the Qumran model and, secondly, the plurality of the Christian Two Ways forms.

According to 1QS 3:13-4:26 God has predetermined the moral history of men. Under the influence of two antagonistic heavenly spirits the world is divided into two opposing forces of good and evil, light and darkness. On earth, the conflict is seen between two classes or groups of people, the sons of light and the sons of darkness, who are involved in this type of cosmic struggle. In this framework, the double catalogue of virtues and vices represent the traits by which each spirit leads man aright or astray. Eventually, however, the spirit of light and its "side" will be victorious.[14] It is important to note that this antagonistic line of development is not recognizable in the Two Ways instruction of the Didache. On the other hand, the Two Ways tradition is retained in various additional early Christian writings, some of which might show this tradition in a stage of its development which is nearer to the form of the Two Ways in the Manual of Discipline. Thus, in order to trace the connecting link between the Qumran document and the Christian Two Ways versions, it is necessary to survey (in addition to the Two Ways in the Didache) also these extant documents and manuscripts and to trace their interrelationship as far as they concern the Two Ways materials. As a matter of fact, it will become clear that these versions are witnesses to a separate circulation of a Two Ways tradition and in some cases represent a closer connection with 1QS 3:13-4:26 than does the Didache.

Other Forms of the Two Ways Tradition in Early Christian Literature

Materials similar to the Two Ways manual in Did 1-6 are found in other Christian writings from the first through the fifth centuries. The extensive use of the Two

---

[12] 'Affinités littéraires et doctrinales du <Manuel de Discipline>'.

[13] Cf. Barnard, *Studies in the Apostolic Fathers*, 97: "However, the Manual of Discipline version is of great value in demonstrating, for the first time, that a *written* Two Ways manual or expository sermon, containing lists of virtues and vices, was known in Judaism in the pre-Christian era."

[14] See, for example, Licht, 'An Analysis'.

Ways in early Christian literature shows the pervasive influence of this tradition once it had entered Christianity. In the following pages, the relevant versions of the Two Ways will be discussed as they appear in extant documents.[15] Because we have dealt with the Two Ways of the Didache above, that version is left aside here. The present section will consider the Letter of Barnabas, the Doctrina, the Apostolic Church Order, the Epitome of the Canons of the Holy Apostles, the Arabic Life of Shenoute, the Ps.-Athanasian Syntagma Doctrinae and the Fides CCCXVIII Patrum. The wide ramifications of the Two Ways instruction in these writings, which include church orders, letters, and monastic writings, attest to the popularity of this tradition and prove that it was widely known in the first Christian centuries.

THE LETTER OF BARNABAS

Although the theme of the Two Ways pervades the entire Letter of Barnabas,[16] which was composed in c.130 CE, it is especially the concluding Chaps. 18-20 that contain an extensive account of the Two Ways. Admittedly, Barnabas 18-20 and Did 1-6 reveal a significant difference with respect to their major outlines and the sequence of items. Moreover, the materials of the evangelical section in Did 1:3b-2:1, the strophic passage in Did 3:1-6, and the passage paralleling Did 6:1-3 are missing here. Yet, there are minute agreements in wording between Barn. 18-20 and the first five chapters of the Didache. These agreements are so close that one cannot refrain from describing their connection in terms of a literary relationship.

In order to account for this undisputed literary affinity between the two forms of the tradition, scholars often have assumed that either (a) Barnabas might have created the materials which subsequently were used by the Didache, or (b) that Barnabas used the Didache.[17] An argument involved in both alternatives is the primitive, respectively chaotic order in Chaps. 18-19 of Barnabas' Two Ways section corresponding to Did 1-4. The rather loose topical organization of Barnabas by comparison with the systematic manner in which the items are presented in the Didache has often been noted. The question, then, is whether Barnabas has preserved the primitive order reflecting a not yet strictly fixed tradition of the original

---

[15] Only those writings in which the respective Two Ways sections show a close literary affinity are dealt with. The Two Way instructions which clearly display the influence of the Didache as a whole will not be considered here. This implies that the Didascalia Apostolorum which was possibly related to the Didache (as two instances in this writing might reflect Did 1:3d and 1:5c) and the Apostolic Constitutions VII, 1,2-32,4 which incorporated the entire Didache (with additions, paraphrases and alterations) will not be discussed. For both the Didascalia Apostolorum and the Apostolic Constitutions, see above, Chap. 1, p. 2 and 27, respectively.

[16] Kraft, *Barnabas and the Didache*, 5-6 and Prigent-Kraft, *Épître de Barnabé*, 15.

[17] Early advocates of Barnabas' originality include Ph. Bryennios and A. von Harnack, and this position received a new impulse by J.A. Robinson (*Barnabas, Hermas and the Didache*, 69-70). They were followed by Muilenburg (*The Literary Relations*, 140-158), Connolly ('The *Didache*') and others. The priority of the Didache was defended by scholars like Th. Zahn, P. Sabatier and, especially, F.X. Funk.

Two Ways, which subsequently was reworked into the form as shown in the present Didache, or whether the Didache represents the earliest Greek form, which order has been disturbed by Barnabas.

Neither of these alternative solutions, however, has turned out to be satisfactory. Apart from the fact that each hypothesis presents obstacles as such,[18] they both have to contend with the difficulty that they do not explain why the additional materials in Barnabas 1-17 would have been omitted in the Didache or, *vice versa*, why Barnabas does not show any traces of Didache 7-16.[19] The literary relationship between Barnabas and the Didache is restricted to the mere section of the Two Ways. It is mainly this limited agreement which underlies the standard view in modern research that the Two Ways materials in the two documents are dependent upon a common source which was used by the Didachist and the author of Barnabas.[20] The present forms in the Didache and Barnabas presuppose a separate written tractate of the Two Ways in Greek.

THE DOCTRINA APOSTOLORUM

The Latin version of the Two Ways will be dealt with extensively below in Chapter 4. It has survived in two mediaeval manuscripts, the *Monacensis lat. 6264* and the *Mellicensis 597*, which go back to a common archetype. It is interesting to see that this archetype, known as the Doctrina Apostolorum, offers essentially the same account and follows the same sequence as Did 1-6. For a long time, even after the discovery of the complete text of the Two Ways in the *Monacensis*, the Doctrina was believed to be a translation of the first chapters of the Didache.[21] Today,

---

[18] The argument used preeminently in support of the originality of Barnabas is the pervasiveness of the Two Ways in Chaps. 1-17 of this letter as well. The overall influence of this theme in the entire letter underscores the literary unity of this work (Prigent-Kraft, *Épître de Barnabé*, 15). In the opinion of Robinson, Connolly, and Muilenburg, the Two Ways materials were consequently an original contribution of Barnabas. However, this literary unity has no relevance whatsoever with regard to the sources of the letter. What can be argued at most is that the letter presupposes the Two Ways instruction, which may have been employed by one and the same author (cf. Audet, *La Didachè*, 124-25; Prigent-Kraft, *Épître de Barnabé*, 15). Furthermore, the awkward transition from the second person plural to the second person singular in Chaps. 19-20 and again to the plural in Chap. 21 would be difficult to explain if the author of Barnabas were not drawing on a source here (Audet, *La Didachè*, 125-26).
Against the priority of the Didache, the objection may be raised that the evangelical section (Did 1:3b-2:1) is unlikely to have been present in Barnabas' source. Why would a Christian author like Barnabas have left out such a distinctive Christian passage? (Wengst, *Didache [Apostellehre]*, 19).
[19] The item in Barn. 4:9 which is similar to Did 16:2 may have belonged to a common source on which both Barnabas and the Apostolic Church Order (ACO) drew. See, however, above, Chap. 1, n. 92.
[20] Niederwimmer, *Die Didache*, 49; Wengst, *Didache (Apostellehre)*, 21; Audet, *La Didachè*, 131.
[21] So also Schlecht, *Doctrina XII Apostolorum* (1901) 9-10 and Wohleb, *Die lateinische Übersetzung*, passim; Streeter, 'The Much-Belaboured Didache', 274.

however, it is widely accepted that the Doctrina offers a Two Ways version whose source is not the Didache. This position, first of all, is taken on the basis of its shape, i.e., that of a document which is confined to the Two Ways manual only. Moreover, the Doctrina shows significant differences from its supposed original which can hardly be explained by virtue of translation: the wording of Did 1:5b seems to be reflected in Doctr. 4:8c ("omnibus enim dominus dare uult de donis suis"); the evangelical section (Did 1:3b-2:1) is lacking in the Doctrina; and the opening words of the Didache ("There are two ways, one of life, the other of death, and between the two ways there is a great difference") are formulated in the Doctrina as follows: "There are two ways in the world, one of life, the other of death, one of light, the other of darkness; upon them two angels are appointed, one of righteousness, the other of iniquity, and between the two ways there is a great difference (1:2)."[22] Instead of being a translation, the Doctrina is more likely to be derived from an independent Greek original of the Two Ways.[23] This prior document, which has been lost, initially circulated separately from the rest of the Didache.

If the Doctrina, despite its closeness to the Two Ways in the Didache, represents a separate instruction, one may ask next which of the two writings represents the tradition's earlier form. For several reasons, preference is given here to the Doctrina version. It was stated above that the evangelical section is atypical of the remainder of the chapters in Did 1-6. As it appears now, this part is missing here as well as in the Two Ways section of Barnabas (and, as will become clear, also in other early witnesses to the Two Ways). Both the incongruity of the evangelical section with its context in the Didache and its absence from other main known examples of the Two Ways strongly suggest that it is an interpolation.[24] This is to say that initially the Two Ways circulated in a form without these Christian materials.

Additional evidence supporting the assumption that the Doctrina offers a more faithful form of the original Two Ways tradition than does the Didache is its affinity to the Judaism of its origin. At many points of difference with Did 1-6,

---

[22] "Viae duae sunt in saeculo, uitae et mortis, lucis et tenebrarum; in his constituti sunt angeli duo, unus aequitatis, alter iniquitatis; distantia autem magna est duarum uiarum" (1:1). For these and other differences between the Two Ways form in the Didache and the Doctrina, see Audet, 'Affinités littéraires et doctrinales', 225; Niederwimmer, *Die Didache*, 50, n. 16; Wengst, *Didache (Apostellehre)*, 13 (n. 40) and 21-22.

[23] The date of origin of the Doctrina cannot be determined with certitude but the recension undoubtedly stems from very early times and may be older than the beginning of the third century; cf. Schlecht, *Doctrina XII Apostolorum* (1901), 68 and Wohleb, *Die lateinische Übersetzung*, 86; Altaner, 'Zum Problem',167.

[24] It is difficult to tell whether this insertion took place in the final stage of the editing of the Didache (and as such is a redactional passage), or whether it occurred in the Two Ways tradition before the Didache was edited, or whether it was added once the Didache was edited (and as such is no more than a subsequent gloss; the latter view is expressed by Wengst, *Didache [Apostellehre]*, 18-19 who leaves it out of his edition). Above, in Chap, 1, p. 32, we suggest that it was the composer of the Didache who incorporated this portion in Did 1:3a-2:1.

the Doctrina has traits reflecting a Jewish pre-Christian tradition[25] and as such is still easily recoverable as a Jewish document. Some items in the Doctrina strongly remind us of the dualistic concept which is predominant in the Qumran Manual of Discipline. The dualistic introduction of the two ways in 1:2 as being "one of light, the other of darkness," on which "two angels are appointed, one of righteousness, the other of iniquity," bears the stamp of the sharply antithetical construction of the Two Ways pattern in 1QS 3-4. In the Didache, these elements of dualistic cosmology and angelology are missing. The absence of these elements from the Didache might have occurred by accident in the course of transmission or might have been the result of a deliberate attempt to ethicize the tradition. Another particular point of parallel is the presence of the wording "in saeculo" that has dropped out of other sources but is retained in Doctr. 1:1 and reminds of the expression בתבל in 1QS 4:2. These parallels prove that the recension of the Two Ways as represented in the Doctrina is closer to its Jewish origin than its counterpart in the Didache, which shows clearly recognizable traces of Christianization. The related literary framework and the general line of development in the Doctrina thus make clear that the original Greek text of the Latin version is a Jewish document which is particularly dependent upon 1QS.

THE APOSTOLIC CHURCH ORDER AND THE EPITOME OF THE CANONS
OF THE HOLY APOSTLES

Two related recensions corresponding with the Way of Life[26] in Doctr./Did 1-4 are found in the Apostolic Church Order (ACO), also known as the Ecclesiastical

---

[25] Cf. •   "*sanctam* terram" in 3:7;
   •   "*dominus*" for θεός in 4:1.9.10a.10b, which echoes the LXX κύριος;
   •   "omnibus enim *dominus* dare vult de donis suis" in 4:8b. This phrase was probably omitted in Did 4:8 because it was inserted in a similar wording in Did 1:5: πᾶσι γὰρ θέλει δίδοσθαι ὁ πατὴρ ἐκ τῶν ἰδίων χαρισμάτων (cf. above, Chap. 1, p. 46, and below, Chap. 4, pp. 136-37).
For these and other Jewish features, lacking in the Did 1-6, see Audet, *La Didachè*, 132-35; cf. also Butler, 'The "Two Ways"', 35.

[26] Although the opening words of the Apostolic Church Order (4:1) and the Epitome of the Canons of the Holy Apostles (1) explicitly refer both to the Way of Life and to the Way of Death, they only describe the former. Barnard (*Studies in the Apostolic Fathers*, 104) declares that the omission "was probably due to a desire to avoid a repetition of what was already present, as negative prohibitions, in the *Via Vitae*." Rordorf-Tuilier suppose that the disappearance resulted from the rise of gnosticism, a heresy that evoked fierce reactions on the part of the early church: "Cette disparition progressive commence effectivement, semble-t-il, avec le triomphe définitif de la réaction anti-gnostique à partir du IIIᵉ siècle ..." (*La Doctrine des douze Apôtres*, 119, n. 1). Wengst suggests that the one-sided rendering is connected with the express apostolic assignment, "den Weg zum Leben und nicht den zum Tode (zu) verkünden" (*Didache (Apostellehre)*, 10). Niederwimmer, finally, states: "der Text bricht ab, wenn die Liste erschöpft ist" (*Die Didache*, 52, n. 27).

Canons of the (Holy) Apostles (Chaps. 4-13),[27] and the Epitome of the Canons of the Holy Apostles (E).[28] The text of ACO, dating from the beginning of the fourth century and originating from Syria or Egypt,[29] forms the first part of a longer manual. After an introduction (Chaps. 1-3), this manual offers materials paralleling Did 1:1-3a plus 2:2-4:8 (Chaps. 4-13), regulations governing the organization of the Christian community and church offices (Chaps. 15-28) and a conclusion (Chaps. 29-30).[30] It has been debated whether E represents the original text of the Two Ways section in ACO[31] or whether the latter version, being first in priority, was excerpted by E.[32] The present tendency, however, is to assume that ACO and E are connected in their dependence on a common ancestor.[33] The existence of an (ultimate) common ancestor is indicated not only by the fact that the Two Ways section in ACO and E is limited to the Way of Life. Both writings also share the characteristic that this teaching is sectioned off and put into the mouth of eleven individual apostles,[34] who one after the other enunciate a passage from the Two Ways.

It is thus probable that ACO and E have taken their materials from an earlier manuscript which merely presented the instructions of the Way of Life in the form of small speech sections, pronounced by single apostles. The common source may thus be designated as an "Elfapostelmoral" [35] and it is obvious that its stylistic design must be the result of a revision of preexisting Two Ways materials.[36] By splitting up the Two Ways materials into apostolic sayings, it gives the impression of an official document that commemorates the words spoken during an apostolic

[27] [Αἱ διαταγαὶ αἱ διὰ Κλήμεντος καὶ] κανόνες ἐκκλησιαστικοὶ τῶν ἁγίων ἀποστόλων.
Editions: Bickell, *Geschichte des Kirchenrechts*, 107-132; Von Harnack, *Die Lehre der zwölf Apostel*, Proleg., 225-237; Funk, *Doctrina duodecim Apostolorum*, 50-73; Schermann, *Die allgemeine Kirchenordnung*, 12-34.
Especially in French scholarship, this document is referred to with various titles; see Steimer, 'Die apostolische Kirchenordnung (CEA)', in id., *Vertex Traditionis*, 60-71; esp. 60-61.
[28] Ἐπιτομὴ ὅρων τῶν ἁγίων ἀποστόλων καθολικῆς παραδόσεως. Edition: Schermann, *Eine Elfapostelmoral*, 16-18.
[29] See, for example, Quasten, *Patrology* 2, 119; Bardenhewer, *Geschichte* 2, 259-261; Faivre, 'Le texte Grec', 32.
[30] For its contents, cf. Funk, 'Die Apostolische Kirchenordnung', 237; Bardenhewer, *Geschichte* 2, 257-58; Quasten, *Patrology* 2, 119; Maclean, *The Ancient Church Orders*, 26-28; Faivre, *Naissance d'une hiérarchie*, 143-153; id., 'La documentation canonico-liturgique', 278-79; id., 'Le texte Grec'; Vööbus, 'Die Entdeckung der alteste Urkunde'.
[31] Cf. Schermann, 'Eine neue Handschrift', 407-08 and id., *Eine Elfapostelmoral*, passim.
[32] Von Harnack, *Die Lehre der zwölf Apostel*, Proleg., 220-22, n. 43.
[33] Rordorf-Tuilier, *La Doctrine des douze Apôtres*, 119; Wengst, *Didache (Apostellehre)*, 8-10; Niederwimmer, *Die Didache*, 52, esp. n. 27.
[34] In addition to the moral part of ACO, this characteristic also applies to the items of the disciplinary part and the conclusion of this writing in Chaps. 15-30. For a list of the apostles and their sayings in the whole of ACO, cf. Giet, *L'Énigme de la Didachè*, 127.
[35] Schermann, *Eine Elfapostelmoral*; cf. also Wengst, *Didache (Apostellehre)*, 10; Steimer, 'Die apostolische Kirchenordnung (CEA)', 69.
[36] Cf. also Niederwimmer, *Die Didache*, 51: "eine sicher nachträgliche Stilisierung des Stoffes."

assembly.[37] This brings up the question whether we can determine the source that has been revised in the (postulated) "Elfapostelmoral". Since ACO and E largely agree in both text and sequence with the Didache recension of the Two Ways, the "Elfapostelmoral" might be dependent on the Didache.[38] What is of significance, however, is that the Two Ways section in both derivatives (ACO and E) lack the evangelical section. It is thus reasonable to suppose that they represent an earlier stage of the Two Ways than does the present form in the Didache and attest to an independent circulation of a particular form of the Two Ways which was similar to that of the Doctrina.[39]

One problem, which has not been discussed so far, is the extent of the treatment of the Way of Life, the *Via Vitae,* as presented by the apostles in ACO and E by comparison with its occurrence in the Two Ways version of the Didache and the Doctrina. In ACO, the Way of Life is less fully described than in E. The passage runs from 4:1 to 13:4 and parallels Doctr./Did 1:1-4:8 (without the evangelical section). Then, in 14:1 Bartholomew, the eleventh apostle, delivers a statement, which apart from the clause in 14:3b (φυλάξεις ἃ παρέλαβες μήτε προσθεὶς μήτε ὑφαιρῶν = Did 4:13),[40] contains items analoguous to Barn. 21:2c-4.6a; 19:11b. In E 1-11, the Way of Life section first equates Doctr./Did 1:1-4:8 but continues in v. 11 with additional materials, analoguous to Doctr./Did 4:9-14. Bartholomew, being the eleventh and last apostle in the series here as well, pronounces sayings, reflecting the concluding paragraph of the Way of Life in Doctr./Did 4. Thus, whereas the closing statements of theWay of Life in ACO reflect the last chapter of the Letter of Barnabas, the final words in E represent the last part

---

[37] Cf. Schöllgen-(Geerlings), *Didache. Zwölf-Apostellehre,* 19; Steimer, 'Die apostolische Kirchenordnung (CEA)', 69.

[38] See also the wording in ACO 12:3: ἠξίωσέν σοι δοθῆναι πνευματικὴν τροφὴν καὶ ποτὸν καὶ ζωὴν αἰώνιον, which seems to echo the expression ἡμῖν δὲ ἐχαρίσω πνευματικὴν τροφὴν καὶ ποτὸν καὶ ζωὴν αἰώνιον διὰ τοῦ παιδός σου in Did 10:3c. According to Niederwimmer, who refers to Von Harnack (*Die Lehre der zwölf Apostel,* Proleg., 210-11, n. 34), "Can." (= ACO) "würde zeigen, dass sein Verf. auch den zweiten Teil der Did. kennt und das würde die Annahme literarischer Abhängigkeit im *ersten* Teil unterstützen" (*Die Didache,* 51, n. 24). Since we are dealing with the usage of a liturgical formulation here, however, Niederwimmer supposes that ACO is not necessarily drawing upon the Didache.

[39] Here and there, reminiscences of the Letter of Barnabas are found which will be discussed below, pp. 74-76.
There is no conclusive evidence to assume that the very *same* Greek original which is now only known in the Latin Doctrina Apostolorum underlies "the Elfapostelmoral." It is makes more sense, instead, to suppose that it was a *similar* form since the opening lines of ACO and E are more in keeping with the Didache version of the Two Ways than with that of the Doctrina (and Barnabas). Moreover, ACO and E have additional elements, which are present in the Didache but not found in the Doctrina. We are referring to the clauses in ACO 6:4 (περὶ ὧν δὲ προσεύξῃ) plus E 3 (περὶ ὧν δε καὶ προσεύξῃ), which are paralleled in Did 2:7, and the admonitions in ACO 8:1 plus E 5, which (in a somewhat modified wording) are analoguous to Did 3:3.

[40] Cf. also ACO 30: φυλάξαι τὰς ἐντολὰς μηδὲν ἀφαιρούντας ἢ προστιθέντα; cf. Did 4:13: φυλάξεις δὲ ἃ παρέλαβες, μήτε προστιθεὶς μήτε ἀφαιρῶν; see also Doctr. 4:13: "Custodi ergo, fili, quae audisti neque appones illis contraria neque diminues."
See below, n. 80.

of the Way of Life as seen in the extant versions of the Doctrina and Didache. Nevertheless, the items in E 11 expressing this conclusion are framed in a particular order. They are cast in a sequence of positions that varies from the parallel positions in Doctr./Did as follows: 4:9. 14a. 13a. 14b. 12. 13b. 14c.[41] So far no satisfactory solution has been brought forward for the disagreement between these two versions, both of which draw upon the "Elfapostelmoral". It is unlikely, however, as has often been suggested,[42] that the words of Bartholomew in ACO 14:1-3 are taken directly from Barnabas. In the final section of this chapter, this matter will be discussed.

THE ARABIC LIFE OF SHENOUTE

Shenoute (Sinuthius) was an abbot of the famous White Monastery of Atripe in Upper Egypt.[43] When he died around 466 at the age of 118, his life was written by his successor, the abba Besa. In the form of a memorial speech, Besa idolizes the personality of his great teacher and idealizes his achievements. The account, which was thus a hagiography rather than an ordinary biography, was written in Sahidic Coptic and served as a source for translations into Syriac, Arabic and the Bohairic dialect. The text in the Bohairic dialect dates from the Middle Ages and was first published by Émile Amélineau[44] in the late nineteenth century and again by Iohannes Leipoldt in 1906.[45] For our present study, the Arabic text of the Life of Shenoute is of significance because only this translation includes a version of the Two Ways. After the publication of the Arabic text as a whole by É. Amélineau[46] in 1888, it was L.E. Iselin who identified the very beginning of this hagiography as a form of the Two Ways instruction.[47]

The Two Ways form in the Arabic Life of Shenoute, like the Apostolic Church Order, leaves out the materials which are presented in Doctr./Did 4:9-14. This does not mean, however, that the Arabic version was indebted in this respect to ACO. For ACO (and the Epitome for that matter) omits the Way of Death passage as

---

[41] Cf. Wengst, *Didache (Apostellehre)*, 7.

[42] Von Harnack, *Die Lehre der zwölf Apostel*, Proleg, 211; Wengst, *Didache (Apostellehre)*, 10, n. 23: "KO" (= ACO) "zeigt sicher Kenntnis des Barnabasbriefes, nicht aber E." Contra: Niederwimmer, *Die Didache*, 59-61 and see below, pp. 74-77.

[43] For the following, see Quasten, *Patrology* 3, 185-187; Altaner-Stuiber, *Patrologie*, 268-269; Bell, *Besa: The Life of Shenoute*, 1-35 (Introduction); Davis, 'The *Didache* and early Monasticism', 353-358.

[44] *Mémoires* 4.1, 1-91: 'Vie de Schnoudi'.

[45] We had only access to the following publication: Leipoldt, *Sinuthii Vita Bohairice* (1951). A Latin translation (completed by L.T. Lefort) is found in Wiesmann, *Sinuthii Vita Bohairice* (1951).

[46] *Mémoires*, 4.1: *Monuments*, 289-478 and for the Two Ways, see esp. 291-296.

[47] *Eine bisher unbekannte Version des ersten Teiles der "Apostellehre"* (1895) with a German translation from A. Heusler. An English translation of the Life's Two Ways section ("from the rendition of the French translation by Émile C. Amélineau") is found in Davis, 'The *Didache* and early Monasticism', 365-367.

well, which in an abbreviated shape is present in the Arabic version. Another outstanding feature in this design of the Two Ways is that the "τέκνον" sayings are not limited to the passage that corresponds with Doctr./Did 3:1-6. In the Life of Shenoute, the hearers/readers are addressed as "my son" from the phrase which runs parallel to Doct./Did 2:6 and this stylistic device (with exceptions in the parallel passages to 3:9-10; 4:7) is maintained as far as the saying analoguous to 4:8. However, the distinctive repetitive pattern which characterizes all five literary units in Doctr./Did 3:1-6 is lacking here. Finally, the present form of the writing, referring to "Jesus Christ" (cf. the parallel item in Doctr./Did 2:5 and, possibly, in 4:14c) and "Jesus" (cf. id., 4:7), shows some obvious instances of Christian editing.

Amélineau supposed that the Arabic text of the Life of Shenoute is a faithful translation from the Sahidic Coptic original. Modern scholarship, however, no longer accepts this view and believes that the Arabic Life represents an adaptation and elaboration of the Sahidic Coptic archetype.[48] The revision may date from the late seventh century. Besa (or "Visa" in the Arabic version), on the other hand, composed his original in the second half of the fifth century. It is clear that these data concerning the process of tradition and transmission do not inspire confidence with regard to a well-founded judgment on the earlier shape of the present text. This much is clear, however, that the monks in the White Monastery in Atripe had a Coptic version of the Two Ways at their disposal.[49] This version was not a secondary elaboration of this instruction, like, for example, the Apostolic Church Order. For despite the additions, omissions, and alterations, the Arabic text has many items in common with the Doctr./Did 1:1-5:1[50] and these agreements largely occur in the same sequence. The Coptic Two Ways treatise as seen in the Arabic translation betrays a feature of its primitiviness in omitting the evangelical section of Did 1:3b-2:1. It may thus be considered a witness to a Two Ways form that circulated independently of the Didache and was closely related to the one in the Doctrina.

---

[48] See Bell, *Besa: The Life of Shenoute*, 4. For the view of Amélineau, cf. *Mémoires* 4.1: *Monuments*, LII-LVIII.
[49] Cf. also Davis, 'The *Didache* and early monasticism', 358.
[50] Goodspeed traced seventy-seven corresponding items; cf. 'The Didache', 237.

THE PS.-ATHANASIAN SYNTAGMA DOCTRINAE AND THE FIDES CCCXVIII PATRUM

The Ps.-Athanasian Syntagma Doctrinae[51] and the Fides CCCXVIII Patrum[52] are textually akin, although scholarly opinion is divided on the question how they are related to one another.[53] In 1685, the first document was attributed to Athanasius (c. 295-373) by its first editor André Arnold, who, for this attribution, relied upon the title of this work in his manuscript.[54] The document has ever since been connected with the name of this bishop of Alexandria and outstanding theologian in the fourth century. Bernard de Montfaucon, however, who shortly afterward edited all works by Athanasius, showed this ascription to be incorrect.[55] The second writing, the Fides Patrum, exists in a Greek and a Coptic version.[56] The Greek

---

[51] The title in full: Τοῦ ἐν ἁγίοις πατρὸς ἡμῶν ᾿Αθανασίου ἀρχιεπισκόπου ᾿Αλεξανδρείας σύνταγμα διδασκαλίας πρὸς μονάζοντας καὶ πάντας χριστιανοὺς κληρικούς τε καὶ λαϊκούς. Editions: Migne, PG, 28, 835-45 and see also below, nn. 54 and 55; Batiffol, 'Le Syntagma Doctrinae', 121-128.

[52] The title varies in the different editions, as they are based on disparate mss.:

- Πίστις τῶν ἁγίων τριακοσίων δέκα καὶ ὀκτὼ ἁγίων θεοφόρων Πατέρων τῶν ἐν Νικαίᾳ· καὶ διδασκαλία πάνυ θαυμαστὴ καὶ σωτήριος περὶ τῆς ἁγίας Τριάδος; cf. PG, 28, 1637A. The text in PG, 28, 1637A-1644C is a reproduction of the first edition by Mingarelli, Graeci codices manuscripti apud Nanios (1784).

- ῎Εκθεσις πίστεως ἁγίων τιη´ πατέρων τῶν ἐν Νικαίᾳ καὶ διδασκαλία πάνυ θαυμαστὴ καὶ ὠφέλιμος ‹ ὠφήλιμος › τοῦ μεγάλου Βασιλείου; cf. Batiffol, 'Canones Nicaeni Pseudepigraphi', 134. In addition to the different rendering of the title, this version also differs from the one in Migne, PG, in many other respects.

- ῎Εκθεσις πίστεως τῶν ἁγίων τιη´ πατέρων τῶν ἐν Νικαίᾳ καὶ διδασκαλία πάνυ θαυμαστή; cf. Batiffol, Didascalia CCCXVIII patrum pseudepigrapha, 7.

[53] Goodspeed ('The Didache', 233), Barnard (The Apostolic Fathers, 105) and Connolly ('The Use of the Didache', 156) believe that the Fides Patrum is based on the Syntagma Doctrinae, whereas Von Harnack (Geschichte der altchristlichen Litteratur, 87) and Batiffol ('Le Syntagma Doctrinae', 135) suggest that both writings are dependent on a common source. Cf. Niederwimmer, Die Didache, who adds: "Die ganze Frage (einschliesslich der Einordnung der versio coptica der Fides patr.) bedürfte einer neuen Untersuchung" (54).

[54] The text of Arnold's edition (Athanasii archiep. Alex. Syntagma) is based on a manuscript preserved in Leiden with the signature Voss. Gr. F. 46 (Fols. 161ᵛ-164ᵛ; cf. De Meyier, Bibliotheca Universitatis Leidensis. Codices Manuscripti, 52-53) and is also found in PG 28, 836A-845B. The most recent edition of the Syntagma Doctrinae according to the 'Vossianus graec.' is from Batiffol, 'Le Syntagma Doctrinae'.

[55] Athanasii archiep. Alexandrini Opera omnia (1698) 3, 358-64. He discovered that the language of Athanasius differed substantially from the wording in the Syntagma Doctrinae: "Nobis itaque omnino spurium videtur hoc opusculum, tum ob styli genus, quod ab Athanasii ἐνεργεία mirum quam remotum sit, tum ob multas voculas quae sequioris aevi notam praeferunt, ...(360);" This argument is reproduced in PG, 28, 835-36.

[56] For the Greek editions, see above, n. 52. For the Coptic version, see Revillout, Le concile de Nicée 1 (fasc. 1), 33ff (text) and 2, 475-489 (French translation). Like the Syntagma Doctrinae, the Fides Patrum has (mistakenly) been assigned to the church leader Athanasius by Revillout. In his opinion, the collection which incorporates this document represents proceedings of the synod of Alexandria in 362 CE, which were formulated by Athanasius (Le concile de Nicée 2, 489-92). According to Batiffol ('Le Syntagma Doctrinae', 136), however, this Coptic collection does not remind us of anything we know about this synod from other sources.

version has been published in various forms but a critical edition based on all extant manuscripts is as yet to be desired.

Just as the Arabic version of the Life of Shenoute is addressed first of all to the monks of the White Monastery, so the Syntagma Doctrinae ("Summary of Doctrine") and the Fides Patrum, though intended for all Christians in principle, present rules for monastic life. There is, however, a marked difference between the Life of Shenoute and the latter two writings. Although each of these compositions contains teachings which obviously depend on a Two Ways tradition, the Life of Shenoute does not show any effort to adapt the original wording (as reflected in the Doctr./Did form) to the audience addressed. There is no allusion at all to monastic life. Moreover, it was established above that this Arabic text displays a high degree of verbatim and sequential agreement with the Doctrina (and the Didache). On the other hand, the reminiscenses of the Two Ways in the Syntagma Doctrinae and the Fides Patrum clearly serve as a part of a complete directory for monks. The scattered Two Ways phraseology in these writings, usually in a parallel arrangement,[57] follows the order of items represented by the Doct./Did form, but is interspersed throughout by elaborate instructions offering guidance for religious conduct.[58]

It must be noted that the materials in the two documents parallel the Two Ways only, without showing any clear knowledge of Did 7-16.[59] The omission of Did 1:3a-2:1 is again of significance. Above, we have noted the haphazard occurrences of the Doctr./Did materials. There is no doubt, however, that the extended passage in Syntagma Doctrinae I,4-5 and in Fides Patrum III[60] reflects the version of the Two Ways as represented in Doctr. 1:2b-2:2. In the Syntagma Doctrinae, it says: "Love the Lord, your God, from all your heart and all your soul and your neighbour as yourself. You shall not murder, you shall not commit adultery, you shall not fornicate, you shall not corrupt children, you shall not practise sorcery ...etc."[61] A similar text is found in the Fides Patrum.[62] The evident omission of the evangeli-

---

[57] Apart from the place in Fides Patrum III (ed. Batiffol, 'Canones Nicaeni Pseudepigraphi') = 1639C (ed. Migne, *PG* 28) = 10,17-18 (ed. Batiffol, *Didascalia CCCXVIII patrum pseudepigrapha*), which corresponds with Doctr./Did 6:1 but is lacking in the Syntagma Doctrinae. For the Greek editions of the Fides Patrum, see above, n. 52.

[58] The agreements between the Syntagma Doctrinae and the Fides Patrum, on the one hand, and the Didache (but the Doctrina as well) on the other, can be studied conveniently in the survey as offered by Niederwimmer, *Die Didache*, 55; cf. also the items listed in Goodspeed, 'The Didache', 233. Moreover, it is worth noticing that the statements in the Fides Patrum, paralleling the Doctr./Did, are confined to the moral part of this writing (i.e. the second half) only.

[59] See the discussion in Goodspeed, 'The Didache', 233 and Niederwimmer, *Die Didache*, 55.

[60] III (in Batiffol, 'Canones Nicaeni Pseudepigraphi') = 1639C (in Migne, *PG* 28) = 10,5-11,4 (in Batiffol, *Didascalia CCCXVIII patrum pseudepigrapha*); see above, n. 52.

[61] (᾽Αγωνίζονται μετὰ τοῦ) Κύριον τὸν θεόν σου ἀγαπήσεις ἐξ ὅλης καρδίας σου, καὶ ἐξ ὅλης τῆς ψυχῆς σου, καὶ τὸν πλησίον σου ὡς σεαυτόν· Οὐ φονεύσεις, οὐ μοιχεύσεις, οὐ πορνεύσεις, οὐ παιδοφθορήσεις, οὐ φαρμακεύσεις... κτλ.

[62] • καὶ τὸν κύριον ἡμῶν ᾽Ιησοῦν Χριστὸν ἀγαπήσεις αὐτὸν ἐξ ὅλης τῆς καρδίας σου, καὶ ἐξ ὅλης τῆς ψυχῆς σου· καὶ τὸν πλησίον σου ὡς σεαυτόν· οὐ φονεύσωμεν· οὐ μοιχεύσωμεν· οὐ παιδοφθορήσωμεν· οὐ φαρμακεύσωμεν· οὐ κλέψωμεν· οὐ ψευδομαρτυρήσωμεν... κτλ. (ed. *PG*, 28, 1639C);

cal section indicates that these writings were related to an independent Greek form of the Two Ways, a form known to us in the Latin translation of the Doctrina Apostolorum.

Toward the Earliest Form of the Two Ways Tradition in Early Christian Literature

The evidence given so far supports the view that the Jewish instruction of the Two Ways was taken over by early Christians. It was a Greek form of this tradition from which the last part of the Letter of Barnabas, the Doctrina, and the first chapters of the Didache are derived. Each particular shape of the Two Ways in these writings represents an independent witness to this ancient tradition. The Two Ways tradition in the later recensions as represented by the Apostolic Church Order, the Epitome of the Canons of the Holy Apostles, the Life of Shenoute, the Ps.-Athanasian Syntagma Doctrinae, and the Fides CCCXVIII Patrum, demonstrate numerous links with the contents and structure of the Doctrina and the Didache. With respect to the Didache, however, they show neither familiarity with Did 7-16 nor acquaintance with the evangelical section in Did 1:3b-2:1. The obvious explanation for this phenomenon is that these writings are somehow affiliated with a form of the Two Ways tradition lacking these parts. This basic tradition circulated in Christian communities apart from its eventual incorporation and modification in the Didache. An early representative of the form, reflected in the later witnesses, is the original Greek version of the Two Ways behind the Doctrina which is lost to us. This recension embodies an earlier form of the Jewish Two Ways that was somehow akin to the Manual of Discipline (1QS 3:13-4:26).

The Letter of Barnabas reproduces early Two Ways materials too. Although the order of presentation of the Two Ways diverges from the arrangement of the items in the Doctrina and the Didache, Barnabas has many verbal links with both documents and, in addition, one point of unique agreement in common with the Doctrina only. This parallel is of special importance. We have shown above that the dualistic introduction of the Two Ways in the Doctrina, framed in the form of a dualistic cosmology and angelology, reminds us of a Jewish ancestor that is closely related with the Qumran Manual of Discipline (1QS 3-4). It is noteworthy,

---

- ... καὶ ταῦτα φυλάττειν, μετὰ τὸ ἀγαπῆσαι κύριον τὸν θεὸν ἡμῶν ἐξ ὅλης (τῆς) ψυχῆς καὶ ἐξ ὅλης τῆς καρδίας, καὶ τὸν πλησίον ὡς ἑαυτούς· οὐ φονεύσομεν – Batiffol mentions, however, that the ms. itself has the reading φονεύσωμεν and the same ending – ωμεν, so he states, is found in the rendering of the next verbs too – οὐ πορνεύσομεν, οὐ παιδοφθορήσομεν· οὐ φαρμακεύσομεν· οὐ κλέψομεν· οὐ ψευδομαρτυρήσομεν·... κτλ. (ed. Batiffol, 'Canones Nicaeni Pseudepigraphi', 136);

- ... καὶ ταῦτα φυλάττειν μετὰ τὸ ἀγαπῆσαι κύριον τὸν θεὸν ἐξ ὅλης τῆς καρδίας καὶ ψυχῆς, καὶ τὸν πλησίον ὡς ἑαυτούς. οὐ φονεύσωμεν, οὐ μοιχεύσωμεν, οὐ πορνεύσωμεν, οὐ φαρμακεύσωμεν, οὐ παιδοφθορήσωμεν, οὐ κλέψωμεν, οὐ ψευδομαρτυρήσωμεν·... κτλ. (ed. Batiffol, *Didascalia CCCXVIII patrum pseudepigrapha*, 10,12-16).

then, that a similar dichotomy of the Way of Light and the Way of Darkness, controlled by two opposite groups of angels, is found in the first lines of the instruction in the Letter of Barnabas. The distinct shape of this introduction thus marks the primitiveness of the tradition presented here.[63]

There are thus good grounds for arguing that Barnabas made use of an early form of the Two Ways. In this light, it is remarkable, to say the least, that neither the Doctrina nor the Didache nor the later Christian recensions present its particular Two Ways items in the order of the Letter of Barnabas. How is this phenomenon to be understood? To answer this question, it is important first of all to make clear that a view on the interrelationship between the early Two Ways forms will be supported here that (in divergent forms) has been expressed by several scholars.[64] We mean the proposition that the Two Ways form in Barnabas (and in later Christian writings as well) is dependent upon (a version of) an original Greek tradition behind the Doctrina and the Didache. The Doctrina has preserved the earliest form in the textual transmission of the Christian Two Ways, because the Latin translation of this treatise betrays nearness to the traditional Jewish instruction of the Two Ways and is related to the Manual of Discipline. If this is correct, the Jewish Two Ways tradition was mediated to the early church through the Greek form behind the Doctrina and Didache. This hypothetical version, which is to be reconstructed in chapter 4, is labelled from here onwards the *"Greek Two Ways" (GTW)*.

Although it is certainly correct to suppose that the Doctrina presents a more reliable preservation of this source (for example in its opening words, its omission of the evangelical section, and its closing lines) than does the text of the Didache, there are good grounds for arguing that the text of the Latin Doctrina does not verbatim reproduce the wording of its Greek source. The translation appears to be inaccurate in many respects. This is indicated by the presence of quite a few items in Two Ways sections of Barnabas and the Didache which are not found in the Doctrina. The Doctrina, Barn. 18-20, and Did 1-6 are independent witnesses to a prior Two Ways document, and verbal similarities between the Didache and Barnabas (against the Doctrina), shows the Latin translation to be frequently incorrect.[65] The poor quality of the specific wording in the Latin translation may

---

[63] In Barnabas, the Two Ways instruction appears at the end of the letter and the author states that he is rendering extant catechetical materials. In 18:1, he writes as follows: "Now let us pass on to another lesson and teaching (διδαχήν)," thereby indicating that his source was called "didache" or "teaching".

[64] Cf. Goodspeed, 'The Didache', 234-35; Barnard, *Studies in the Apostolic Fathers*, 98-99; Altaner, 'Zum Problem', 161; Audet, *La Didachè*, 122-163; esp. 161; cf. also Warfield, 'Text, Sources and Contents of "The Two Ways"'; Taylor, *The Teaching of the Twelve Apostles*; Savi, 'La dottrina degli apostoli'.

[65] Some examples:
- "division": Did 4:3a and Barn. 19:12; *Doctr.:* plur.
- "You shall not show partiality in calling people to task for their faults:" Did 4:3c; cf. Barn. 19:4e; *Doctr.:* diff.
- "you will know": Did 4:7b and Barn. 19:11b; *Doctr.:* participle "knowing"
- "for if you are partners:" Did 4:8d and Barn. 19:8c; *Doctr.:* "for if *we* are partners"

be due to a defective transmission or a translator's inaccuracy. In any case, because also the Two Ways in the Didache represents a primitive, though Christianized, offshoot from the ancient common literary stock, we may invoke the help of this version in reconstructing the GTW, paralleling the materials of Did 1:1-3a and 2:2-6:1 in the Doctrina.[66]

The hypothesis regarding the Doctrina's priority is more complicated as far as Barnabas is concerned. Before going into the subject, however, it is of significance to take notice of the haphazard presentation of the Two Ways materials in Barnabas (especially in Chaps. 18-19) in comparison to the systematic arrangement in the Doctr./Did form (esp. Chaps. 1-4). It is difficult to decide whether the present form of the instruction in Barnabas reflects its source or whether the author of Barnabas muddled the original order of items. We are dealing here, in fact, with the same difficulties as referred to above, when the priority of the Two Ways in either Barnabas or the Didache was discussed. In this case, the problem is difficult to solve. Yet, if Barnabas' Two Ways section were a faithful representation of the earliest form of this manual in a Christian writing,[67] it would be hard to imagine how the Two Ways instruction, contained in the Doctr./Did form, could emerge from this chaotic original. It cannot reasonably be supposed that the Doctrina and Didache form, which does not show any vestige of an artificial composition, was created by unravelling the muddle of materials in the source of Barnabas so as to obtain a perfectly coherent literary pattern.[68] It is inconceivable, therefore, that the Two Ways in Barnabas reveals an earlier form of this tradition which in a later stage may have been replaced by a different line of transmission represented by the Doctr./Did form. It makes much more sense that Barnabas rewrote and extensively reworked his source with respect to its sequence.

We return to the question concerning the relationship between Barnabas and the Doctrina. The hypothesis that the Greek form of the Two Ways, which was

---

- "your son:" Did 4:9 and Barn. 19:5; *Doctr.:* plur.
- "You shall not abandon the commandments of the Lord...:" Did 4:13a; cf. Barn. 19:2h; *Doctr.:* om.
- "you shall confess your faults:" Did 4:14a; cf. Barn. 19:12c; *Doctr.:* om.
- "duplicity:" Did 5:1o; cf. Barn. 20:1h; *Doctr.:* om.
- "guile:" Did 5:1p; cf. Barn. 20:1n; *Doctr.:* om.
- "defenders of the rich:" Did 5:2p; cf. Barn. 20:2u; *Doctr.:* om.
- "unjust judges of the poor:" Did 5:2q; cf. Barn. 20:2v; *Doctr.:* diff.
- "sinners in everything that they do:" Did 5:2r; cf. Barn. 20:2w; *Doctr.:* om.

[66] For the Two Ways source of the Didache reflecting the Greek treatise behind the Doctrina, see Wengst, *Didache (Apostellehre)*, 13 and 22.

[67] So Wengst, *Didache (Apostellehre)*, 21 and n. 77; 22, n. 81; id., *Tradition und Theologie*, 58-59; Jefford, *The Sayings of Jesus*, 35, n. 39; Kloppenborg, 'The Transformation of Moral Exhortation', 92.

[68] See Audet, *La Didachè*, 11-12. 128. 320; Barnard, 'The Problem of the Epistle of Barnabas', 218-221 and Niederwimmer, *Die Didache.*, 61-63, n. 74: "Die alternative Annahme, erst der Redaktor von C" (i.e. the Doctr./Did source) "hätte den Text in jene Ordnung gebracht, die wir in Did. etc. finden, ist weniger gut: die Abschnitte des Weges-Traktats, wie sie in Did. aufeinanderfolgen, gehören jeweils verschiedenen genera dicendi an; dergleichen stellt man schwerlich nachträglich her. ... ."

the Doctr./Did source, also underlies the Two Ways section of Barnabas is certainly not accepted by a consensus of modern scholarly opinion. On the contrary, it is quite commonly felt that Barnabas used an earlier form of the Two Ways tradition than the one attested by the Doctr./Did form. In this view, the Two Ways instruction in Barnabas derives from an earlier form of the Two Ways instruction which, in a later stage of transmission and in a modified form, became the source of the Doctrina (and Didache). The main argument adduced in support of this position concerns the striking differences between the Two Ways tradition in Barnabas and that in the Doctrina / Didache. The omission of the double love commandment (cf. Doctr./Did 1:2a) and the τέκνον-passage (cf. Doctr./Did 3:1-6) in Barnabas is held to be so significant that Barnabas' Two Ways section is believed to derive from an earlier stage of the manual.[69] The presence of these elements in the Doctr./Did form (lacking in the present text of Barnabas) would seem to be the result of a later development which took place independently of the form of the Two Ways known to Barnabas.

This argument, however, does not necessarily prove the priority of Barnabas. It is clear that a double love commandment left no imprint in Barnabas. Because this logion is found in Mark 12:30-31; Matt 22:37-39, and Luke 10:27, it is often suggested that its wording ("πρῶτος ... δεύτερος" or "primo ... secundo") represents a later Christianization in Doctr./Did with regard to the version in Barnabas.[70] However, the terminology in which the combination of the two precepts of love is phrased in the Doctr./Did form differs from the Synoptic tradition to such an extent that it need not be indebted to this tradition. It is far more preferable to consider the double commandment in the Doctr./Did as attesting to a tradition which is independent of the Synoptic gospels.[71] Moreover, the juxtaposition of these two precepts is not unknown in first-century Judaism.[72] With repect to the τέκνον-passage in Doctr./Did 3:1-6,[73] which has no parallels in Barnabas, it is assumed that this segment was lacking in the Two Ways source of Barnabas.[74] This

---

[69] Kraft, *Barnabas and the Didache* 9; Niederwimmer, *Die Didache*, 57-58 (n. 53) and 63. Wengst *(Didache [Apostellehre])*, Jefford *(The Sayings of Jesus)* and Kloppenborg ('The Transformation') support the priority of Barnabas on account of its loose topical organisation.

[70] Butler, 'The "Two Ways"', 29-30; Giet, *L'Énigme de la Didachè*, 66, 70; Niederwimmer, *Die Didache*, 57-58, n. 53; 63; 91; etc.

[71] Cf. Niederwimmer, *Die Didache*, 89-91.

[72] Cf., for example, Kraft, *Barnabas and the Didache* 137; Berger, *Die Gesetzesauslegung Jesu*, 142-165; Nissen, *Gott und der Nächste*, 230-44; Rordorf-Tuilier, *La Doctrine des douze Apôtres*, 29, n. 1; Niederwimmer, *Die Didache*, 91, n. 11; Kloppenborg, 'The Transformation', 98, n. 41; etc. For a similar numerical schema, see Flavius Josephus, who in connection with the Essene doctrine states: πρῶτον μὲν εὐσεβήσειν τὸ θεῖον, ἔπειτα τὰ πρὸς ἀνθυρώπους δίκαια φυλάξειν *(Bellum* 2,139). Cf. also *T. Dan* 5:3; *T. Issa.* 5:2; 7:6; *T. Zeb.* 5:1 and *T. Jos.* 11:1. See further below, Chap. 5, pp. 156-57 and esp. n. 57.

[73] Did 3:3-4a is lacking in the the Doctr. and the omission of these clauses may be due to the transmission of the tradition.

[74] According to Niederwimmer, *Die Didache*, 124 and implied by Kloppenborg, 'The Transformation', 90, n. 11.

may be the case, but it may be argued with equal reason that Barnabas, who probably rewrote his source, did not preserve these materials.[75]

On the other hand, there is evidence supporting the priority of the Doctr./Did source. The view that Barnabas borrowed his Two Ways materials from the Doctr./Did source is indirectly corroborated by the form of the Two Ways tradition in the Apostolic Church Order. Although the wording and sequence of the instruction in ACO, in the main, agrees with the Doctr./Did form, this document in some particular instances has verbal links with Barnabas' Two Ways section which are missing in the Doctrina and the Didache.[76] At first sight, these unique agreements seem to imply that the Two Ways form in Barnabas and ACO derive from a common source that is not represented by the Doctr./Did form. This, then, would indicate that the moral instruction in the Doctr./Did source does not underlie the Two Ways of Barnabas. In the following pages, we will firstly present the agreements of ACO (and in one instance of E as well) with Barnabas one by one. Secondly, we will try to show that these verbal links do not undermine the priority of the Doctr./Did source with respect to Barnabas' Two Ways instruction. On the contrary, it will become clear that these materials, shared by Barnabas and ACO, reflect a later revision of the Two Ways tradition which was used by Barnabas and – in a later stage – by ACO (or, eventually, by the "Elfapostelmoral").

The first example, the wording in ACO 14:1-3, closely corresponds to Barn. 21:2-4c.6a.8b but is lacking in Doctr./Did:

Barn. 21:2-4c.6a. 8b	ACO 14:1-3
(2) ἐρωτῶ τοὺς ὑπερέχοντας, εἴ τινά μου γνώμης ἀγαθῆς λαμβάνετε συμβουλίαν· ἔχετε μεθ᾽ ἑαυτῶν, εἰς οὓς ἐργάσησθε τὸ καλόν· μὴ ἐλλείπητε. (3) ἐγγὺς ἡ ἡμέρα, ἐν ᾗ συναπολεῖται πάντα τῷ πονηρῷ· ἐγγὺς ὁ κύριος καὶ ὁ μισθὸς αὐτοῦ.	(1) ... ἐρωτῶμεν ὑμᾶς, ἀδελφοί, ὡς ἔτι καιρός ἐστι καὶ οὐκ ἔχετε εἰς οὓς ἐργάζεσθε μεθ᾽ ἑαυτῶν, μὴ ἐκλίπητε ἐν μηδενί, ἐξουσίαν ἐὰν ἔχητε. (2) ἐγγὺς γὰρ ἡ ἡμέρα κυρίου, ἐν ᾗ συναπολεῖται πάντα σὺν τῷ πονηρῷ· ἥξει γὰρ ὁ κύριος καὶ ὁ μισθὸς αὐτοῦ.

---

[75] "...much of it – murder, lust, enchantment, magic, lying, avarice, grumbling – are covered elsewhere in Barnabas, chh. 18-21, mostly in *positive* command, adjusted to a loftier plane of Christian living: ...Moreover Barnabas presents not so much vices to be shunned as virtues to be cultivated, a far superior method, of course. The average Christian then as now does not so much need to be told not to murder, rob, lust or lie, as to be kind, generous, pure and true. ... He was not writing to <the heathen> but to a public so familiar with the Hebrew scriptures that they would enjoy the allegories of Barn 1-17, and naturally so advanced in the Christian life that some rudimentary morals might be taken for granted;" Goodspeed, 'The Didache', 235-36.

For the Jewish *Sitz im Leben* of the materials in Doctr./Did 3:1-6, see Van de Sandt, 'Didache 3,1-6: A Transformation'.

[76] According to Barnard (*The Apostolic Fathers*, 103) and Prigent-Kraft (*Épître de Barnabé*, 17), ACO may have inserted here reminiscences of Barnabas. This possibility, however, as will be made clear below, must be excluded. See also Niederwimmer, *Die Didache*, 59-61 and Kloppenborg, 'The Transformation', 90-91, n.14.

(4) ἔτι καὶ ἔτι ἐρωτῶ ὑμᾶς· ἑαυτῶν   (3) ἑαυτῶν γίνεσθε νομοθέται,
γίνεσθε νομοθέται ἀγαθοί, ἑαυτῶν   ἑαυτῶν γίνεσθε σύμβουλοι ἀγαθοι,
μένετε σύμβουλοι πιστοί· ... (6) γίνεσθε   θεοδίδακτοι· (φυλάξεις ἃ παρέλαβες
δὲ θεοδίδακτοι ἐκζητοῦντες ... (8)... μὴ   μήτε προσθεὶς μήτε ὑφαιρῶν).[78]
ἐλλείπητε μηδενὶ αὐτῶν κτλ....[77]

One might suppose that ACO is indebted here to the Letter of Barnabas[79] but it
is more likely that the texts in Barnabas and ACO draw on a common literary
source which was reworked by Barnabas.[80] The dependency of Barnabas and ACO
upon a common ancestor is corroborated by the random appearance of verbal
agreements, lacking again in Doctr./Did, in the following examples. It is difficult
to imagine these analogies as intentional references to precisely Barnabas.

Barn.1:1	ACO proem
Χαίρετε, υἱοὶ καὶ θυγατέρες, ἐν ὀνόματι	Χαίρετε υἱοὶ καὶ θυγατέρες ἐν
κυρίου τοῦ ἀγαπήσαντος ἡμᾶς ἐν εἰρήνῃ.	ὀνόματι κυρίου 'Ιησοῦ Χριστοῦ.

The resemblance between the opening sentence in ACO and that of Barnabas
stands out, the more so since the form of address "sons and daughters" apparently
occurs in a very few instances in early Christian literature.[81]

---

[77] For the text of Barnabas, cf. 'Barnabasbrief' in Wengst, *Didache (Apostellehre)*, 138-195. The
English text reads: "(2) I urge those who are in a high position, if you accept any of my well-intentioned
advice: have among you those to whom you may do that which is good. Do not fail. (3) The day is near
in which all things will perish together with the Wicked one. The Lord is near, and his reward. (4) Again
and again I urge you: be your own good lawgivers, remain your own faithful advisers, ... (6) Be taught
by God, ... (8) ... do not fail in any respect...etc."

[78] For the text of the Apostolic Church Order, cf. Schermann, *Die allgemeine Kirchenordnung*, 12-34.
The English text reads: "(1) ... We urge you, brethren, while there is yet time and you have not among
you those for whom you may work, do not fail in any respect if you have the power. (2) For the day
of the Lord is near in which all things will perish with the Wicked one. For the Lord is coming and his
reward. (3) Be your own lawgivers, be your own good advisers, taught by God. (keep what you received,
neither adding nor subtracting anything)." For the latter phrase, see below, n. 80.

[79] Cf. for example, Prigent-Kraft, *Épître de Barnabé*, 214-15, n. 2: "Le parallélisme avec *Did./Doctr.*
est terminé et, si les *Canons Ecclésiastiques* ... connaissent quelque chose d'approchant, sans doute faut-
il l'expliquer par un contact littéraire avec notre épître: ...Il faut donc sans doute renoncer à chercher
dans le *Duae Viae* primitif la matière de ce chapitre dont la paternité doit être attribuée à Barnabé lui-
même."

[80] The phrase φυλάξεις ἃ παρέλαβες μήτε προσθεὶς μήτε ὑφαιρῶν ("keep what you received,
neither adding nor subtracting anything") in the closing statement of ACO 14:3 is also found in the final
lines of the Two Ways section in E 11 (φυλάξη δὲ ἃ παρέλαβες μήτε προσθεὶς μήτε ὑφαιρῶν) and
in the conclusion of the whole of the Apostolic Church Order in Chap. 30 as well: φυλάξαι τὰς
ἐντολὰς μηδὲν ἀφαιροῦντας ἢ προστιθέντας... The original position of this clause in the Two Ways
is likely to have been in a parallel position of its present place in Doctr./Did 4:13 (or Barn. 19:11). The
composer of the "Elfapostelmoral" probably transferred the phrase to the conclusion of the Two Ways
(echoed in ACO 14:3 and E 11), while the composer of ACO finished his work by repeating it (with
some divergencies). For the diffusion of this clause in early Jewish, Christian and pagan literature, cf.
Van Unnik, 'De la Règle Μήτε προσθεῖναι μήτε ἀφελεῖν'.

[81] See Wengst, *Didache (Apostellehre)*, 196, n. 2.

Barn. 19:2a	ACO 4:2	Did 1:2a	Doctr. 1:2a
You shall love him who made you, fear him who formed you, δοξάσεις τόν σε λυτρωσάμενον ἐκ θανάτου (glorify him who redeemed you from death).	First, you shall love the God who made you with all your heart καὶ δοξάσεις τὸν λυτρωσάμενόν σε ἐκ θανάτου	First, you shall love the God who made you: (second, ...)	First, you shall love the eternal God who made you: (second, ...)

Whereas the double love commandment appears in the Doctrina and the Didache, the elements of the 'love of God' and of the 'love of the neighbour' are found separately in Barn. 19:2a and 5c. To be sure, in ACO 4:2 the two commandments do occur in juxtaposition but the insertion of the wording δοξάσεις τὸν (σε) λυτρωσάμενόν (σε) ἐκ θανάτου shows a knowledge of the document which also Barnabas used.

Barn. 19:9b-10a	ACO 12:1 = E 9	Did 4:1a = Doctr. 4:1a
ἀγαπήσεις ὡς κόρην ὀφθαλμοῦ σου πάντα τὸν λαλοῦντα σοι τὸν λόγον κυρίου. μνησθήσῃ ἡμέραν κρίσεως νυκτὸς καὶ ἡμέρας κτλ[82] ...	τέκνον (τέκνον om.: E), τὸν λαλοῦντά σοι τὸν λόγον τοῦ θεοῦ καὶ παραίτιόν σοι γινόμενον τῆς ζωῆς καὶ δόντα σοι τὴν ἐν κυρίῳ σφραγῖδα ἀγαπήσεις (αὐτὸν add.: E) ὡς κόρην ὀφθαλμοῦ σου, μνησθήσῃ δὲ (δὲ om.: E) αὐτοῦ νύκτα καὶ ἡμέραν (νυκτὸς καὶ ἡμέρας: E), τιμήσεις (δὲ add.: E) αὐτὸν ὡς τὸν (τὸν: om. E) κύριον.[83]	τέκνον μου (om.: Doctr.), τοῦ λαλοῦντός σοι τὸν λόγον τοῦ θεοῦ (domini dei: Doctr.) μνησθήσῃ νυκτὸς καὶ ἡμέρας (die ac nocte: Doctr.), τιμήσεις δὲ αὐτὸν ὡς κύριον.[84]

ACO and E have a more elaborate version than either Barnabas, the Doctrina or the Didache. The admonition to love the one who speaks the word of God "as the apple of his eye," a clause that must have been part of the "Elfapostelmoral" (cf. ἀγαπήσεις ὡς κόρην ὀφθαλμοῦ σου in ACO and ἀγαπήσεις αὐτὸν ὡς κόρην ὀφθαλμοῦ σου in E), agrees verbally with Barn. 19:9b. On the other hand, the phrase to be mindful of the proclaimer of God's word (cf. Doctr. / Did 4:1) is

---

[82] "Love as the apple of your eye all who speak the Lord's word to you. Remember the day of judgment night and day."

[83] "Child, love as the apple of your eye the one who speaks to you God's word and is partly the cause of life for you and gives to you the seal in the Lord, remember him night and day, honour him as the Lord."

[84] For the text, cf. Rordorf-Tuilier, *La Doctrine des douze Apôtres*, 140-98 and id., 207-210, respectively.

modified in Barnabas, where the day of judgment is introduced. Because this reference interrupts the line of thought in this particular place in Barnabas, it is likely that Doctr., Did, ACO and E represent the source here on which Barnabas drew.[85]

What is the point of presenting this list of these occasional striking verbatim agreements between Barnabas and ACO? In the first place, they make clear that despite the usual affinity in text and sequence between Doctr./Did and the "Elfapostelmoral", Barnabas and ACO at some points (and at one point also E) show an apparent literary relationship. There is also a second significant feature that may be observed in these materials. The Two Ways version in ACO starts with the epistolary formula Χαίρετε which is a key-term in Greek letters:[86]

Χαίρετε υἱοὶ καὶ θυγατέρες ἐν ὀνόματι κυρίου Ἰησοῦ Χριστοῦ.

Almost the same formula is found in the first line of the Letter of Barnabas:

Χαίρετε, υἱοὶ καὶ θυγατέρες, ἐν ὀνόματι κυρίου τοῦ ἀγαπήσαντος ἡμᾶς ἐν εἰρήνῃ (1:1)

It deserves attention that the form of address υἱοὶ καὶ θυγατέρες is atypical of the remainder of the Letter of Barnabas. In the other instances, the audience to which the letter is directed is addressed as τέκνα or ἀδελφοί. On the other hand, it is remarkable that a church order like ACO is presented in the form of a letter. Instructions in church manuals are usually presented as timeless guidelines to successive generations in the community. There is a good possibility, then, that the author of Barnabas found this form of address in his Two Ways source and that this source was used by the composer of ACO as well. The author of Barnabas changed its original position but retained it in the introduction to his work as a whole. After all, the pervasiveness of the Two Ways materials in the first part of Barnabas (Chaps. 1-17) shows that this tradition played a formative role in the composition of this letter.[87]

The observation about the opening of the Two Ways in the source gains weight when one also takes notice of its closing section as represented in Barnabas and ACO. After a transitional verse in 21:1 Barnabas concludes his letter as follows:

> I urge (ἐρωτῶ) those who are in a high position, if you accept any of my well-intentioned advice: have among you those to whom you may do that which is good. Do not fail. The

---

[85] Cf. Prigent-Kraft, *Épître de Barnabé*, 207-208, nn. 5 and 6.

[86] See Conzelmann, 'χαίρω, χαρά, συγχαίρω κ.τ.λ.', 351 and 384; cf. also Berger, 'Apostelbrief und apostolische Rede', 191-207.
The following observations with regard to the conspicuous traits of the Two Ways form in Barnabas and ACO are inspired by an interesting article of Hennecke, 'Die Grundschrift der Didache und ihre Recensionen', 58-72; esp. 62-66.

[87] Cf. Kraft, *Barnabas and the Didache*, 5-6 and Prigent-Kraft, *Épître de Barnabé*,15. It is not likely, therefore, that the opening sentence in ACO is derived from the first line in Barnabas as stated by Goodspeed, 'The Didache', 232-33 and Barnard, *The Apostolic Fathers*, 103. See Niederwimmer, *Die Didache*, 61-63.

day is near in which all things will perish together with the Wicked one. The Lord is near, and his reward. Again and again I urge you (ἔτι καὶ ἔτι ἐρωτῶ ὑμᾶς·...)... .

The Two Ways version in ACO ends by presenting Bartholomew as the one who addresses the ἀδελφοί:

> We urge you, brethren (ἐρωτῶμεν ὑμᾶς, ἀδελφοί), while there is yet time and you have not among you those for whom you may work, do not fail in any respect if you have the power. For the day of the Lord is near in which all things will perish with the Wicked one. For the Lord is coming and his reward. Be your own lawgivers, be your own good advisers taught by God. (keep what you received, neither adding nor subtracting anything).

In the above (pp. 74-75) printed parallel columns of this passage, one can ascertain the numerous verbal links between ACO 14:1-3 and Barn. 21:2-4c.6a.8b. Again, it is likely that both ACO and Barnabas used the same document as a source which was reworked, enlarged, and expanded (cf. the double ἐρωτῶ and ἔτι καὶ ἔτι ἐρωτῶ // μὴ ἐλλείπητε and μὴ ἐλλείπητε μηδενί // συναπολεῖται and cf. also 21:1) by Barnabas with additional materials.[88]

The epistolary formula in the beginning and the final request at the end (in the first person plural in ACO: ἐρωτῶμεν ὑμᾶς, ἀδελφοί and in the first person singular in Barnabas: ἐρωτω and ἔτι καὶ ἔτι ἐρωτῶ ὑμᾶς) makes two things clear. First, in the source of both documents, the simple Two Ways manual has taken the form of a letter.[89] It is of importance here to emphasize that in the early church the Two Ways teaching preceded the performance of baptism. The candi-

---

[88] "The chapter" (i.e. Barn. 21:1-9) "reads as though it had been expanded in various stages, possibly by uniting an older conclusion to chapters 1 – 17 (21:2-5?) with the Two Ways conclusion.... In fact, CO's" (= ACO's) "version of 21:2 ff. resolves much of this awkwardness: does it reflect an older form?"; cf. Kraft, *Barnabas and the Didache*, 162, n.

See also Niederwimmer: "Mann wird sich schwerlich davon überzeugen können, dass Can" (= ACO) "14 direkt aus Barn. stammt. Der text in Can. wirkt unmittelbarer; eher gehen die Epiloge in Can. 14 und Barn. 21 auf eine gemeinsame Quelle zurück. Vermutlich liegt dem Text von Can. der Schluss einer der Rezensionen des Wege-Traktats zugrunde; einen ähnlichen las auch Barn. (...); doch hat Barn. verändert und erweitert" (*Die Didache*, 59).

This propensity for rewriting transmitted materials may also have been at work in Barnabas' treatment of the Two Ways proper and thus supports the assumption that he arbitrarily disrupted the original sequence of its items.

[89] Prostmeier (*Der Barnabasbrief*) rejects this view: "Weil also eine direkte Rezeption des Barn seitens des CEA" (= ACO) "-Kompilators nicht auszuschliessen ist, vermögen die wörtliche Übereinstimmung zwischen CEA proœm. und Barn 1,1 sowie die Berührungen zwischen CEA 14 und Barn 21,2-4.6a nicht die Beweislast dafür zu tragen, dass bereits die Zwei-Wege-Vorlage, auf die der Barn zurückgreifen konnte, mit dieser signifikanten Leseranrede und einem aufs engste mit Barn 21,2-4.6a verwandten eschatologischen Abschluss eingefasst war" (110; see also 51-55). Prostmeier supposes that the agreements between ACO and Barnabas against Doctr./Did are due to the use of Barnabas as an additional source by the composer of ACO. This solution, however, is not convincing. For ACO generally agrees, both in wording and sequence, with the Doctr./Did form, while showing verbal links with Barnabas against Doctr./Did in rare cases only. It would be difficult to explain why ACO used Barnabas of all documents, and even more awkward to clarify why precisely these instances in Barnabas of all instances.

date who applied for baptism was instructed in the ethical cathechesis as contained in the Two Ways tradition. In addition to other evidence,[90] this is explicitly stated in Did 7:1, a verse that follows right after the rendering of the Two Ways section: "As for baptism, baptize this way. Having said all these things beforehand (ταῦτα πάντα προειπόντες), baptize ...."

Now, it has been established above that the casual similarities between Barnabas and ACO are based on a common source and that the introductory part and the concluding section of this source, occurring in the common materials in Barnabas and ACO, reflect a particular type of literary composition. The tradition of the Two Ways is no longer transmitted and kept alive in the instruction to catechumens, but has developed into an epistolary genre with a personal message. This modified form of the tradition was appropriated by the "apostles" and "Barnabas", respectively.[91] It is likely, therefore, that the common source of Barnabas and ACO (and possibly of the "Elfapostelmoral"[92]) represents a later stage in the development of the Two Ways tradition than does the pre-baptismal teaching in the Doctrina.

The second conclusion concerns the eschatological sections in Barnabas and ACO. On account of the above evidence, it will be clear that we do not take the passages in both Barn. 21 and ACO 14 to be original to the Two Ways, but, instead, consider them as later additions which derive from the common source used by Barnabas and ACO. The Two Ways section in Barnabas and ACO is set within a framework which anticipates the time when the evil one and his works will be destroyed, that is, the final moment of God's eschatological judgment. The evidence thus appears to indicate that such an eschatological section came to be incorporated as an appendix in the epistolary Two Ways composition. This basic form, in which the Two Ways took the shape of a letter, circulated separately and was used as a source by Barn. 21 and ACO 14.

It is important to keep in mind that ACO (and E for that matter) usually agrees both in text and structure with the Doctr./Did form of the Two Ways. At the same time, also Barnabas shows many similarities in text – though not in the arrangement of the materials – with the Didache. For this reason, one may assume that the original form of the source, used by Barnabas and ACO, must have been in substance the Doctr./Did source. The order of items in the source of Barnabas followed the sequence of Doctr./Did form but was extensively reworked by Barnabas himself. It is impossible, however, to determine when this Doctr./Did form of the Two Ways tradition assumed the form of the letter which became known to Barnabas and ACO. The introduction of the Two Ways section in

---

[90] See below, Chapter 3, pp. 88-89.

[91] J.A. Draper even argues that the Letter of Barnabas displays a polemical thrust against Jewish Christianity. He suggests that its author recasts these Two Ways materials as advanced (post-baptismal) gnosis for the elite. See his 'Barnabas and the Riddle'.

[92] It is difficult to decide whether the same conclusion applies to the common source of ACO and E. The briefly worded version as extant in E has one (though relatively large) passage in common with ACO and Barnabas (E 9). E, however, lacks an introduction, and its conclusion parallels Doctr./Did 4:9-14 (in a modified sequence of items), which is missing in ACO (see above, pp. 65-66).

Barnabas certainly suggests an early stage. Accordingly, Barnabas may have preserved elements of the Two Ways form which are more primitive than the corresponding elements in the Latin Doctrina.[93] ACO, instead, though representing the same line of descent as does Barnabas, reflects quite a different phase in the transmission of the Two Ways tradition. One may presume that the materials found in the common epistolary source of Barnabas and ACO went through a significant amount of development and intermediary stages of transmission before it was finally incorporated in the present form of ACO.

It thus appears that the Two Ways source of Barnabas was not the connecting link between the Jewish and Christian tradition of the Two Ways. The earliest form is found in the Doctr./ Did source and the Doctrina gives us the best idea of its contents.

---

[93] As is shown above (pp. 71-72, n. 65) where various items and wordings are mentioned, present in Barnabas and in the Didache but missing in the Doctrina.

Chapter Three

The Influence of the Two Ways
in Christian Literature

Chapter 2 has shown that materials similar to those in Didache 1-6 are found in a number of other early Christan writings. The close affinities between these different versions of the Two Ways (including Did 1-6) are generally explained in modern research by their – direct or indirect – dependence upon a Jewish Two Ways document which is no longer known to us. This original manual, which in some form lived on in a number of Greek versions, was probably written in Greek. The most accurate form of the lost Two Ways document, however, is retained in its Latin version, in the Doctrina Apostolorum, which survived in two mediaeval manuscripts, the *Monacensis lat. 6264*, fol. 102vo-103vo and the *Mellicensis 597*, fol. 115vo.[1]

The present chapter is divided into two parts. The first part traces the influence of the Two Ways in the early church beyond the scope of the above-mentioned compilations. Because in addition to its incorporation in the Didache and in most of the other writings mentioned above, the Two Ways tradition is interpolated into other materials as well, it is hardly conceivable that the Two Ways document never existed apart from its presence in these compositions. In order to corroborate this assumption, it is of importance to know whether the indirect Christian tradition attests to the diffusion of the original Greek document and/or of its Latin translation. Are there quotations and testimonies of church fathers and of other Christian writings available evidencing an independent Two Ways tradition? A related question regards the life situation *(Sitz im Leben)* of this teaching within early Christianity. Of course, one might refer to its increased impact as a moral code, once a version of Two Ways was presented as sayings of individual apostles (the "Elfapostelmoral") and was incorporated in a public regulation of the church

---

[1] Further, see below, Chap. 4, pp. 113-14. For the date of the *Monacensis*, see also Rordorf-Tuilier, *La Doctrine des douze Apôtres*, 203. The text of this Doctrina version is edited by Schlecht, *Doctrina XII Apostolorum* (1901) 101-104.

For the date of the *Mellicensis* and last edition of its Doctrina version, cf. also Niederwimmer, 'Doctrina Apostolorum (Cod. Mellic. 597)'.

A recension of the *Doctrina*, as represented in these mss., is found in Lietzmann, *Die Didache* and, more recently, Rordorf-Tuilier, *La Doctrine des douze Apôtres*, 207-210.

(Apostolic Church Order).[2] Our concern, however, here is with the function of the
Two Ways manual in its first Christian setting. The second part of this chapter
investigates the influence of the Two Ways manual on the Latin church literature
dating from later (Merovingian and Carolingian) periods.

The Early Christian Period

Our search for traces of the Two Ways begins in the post-apostolic period. In
Stromateis I, 20, 100, 4 Clement of Alexandria quotes the following phrase: υἱέ,
μὴ γίνου ψεύστης· ὁδηγεῖ γὰρ τὸ ψεῦσμα πρὸς τὴν κλοπήν ("Child, do not
be a liar, for lying leads to theft"). Although Clement does not specify his source,
the text is very similar to Did 3:5 (Τέκνον μου, μὴ γίνου ψεύστης, ἐπειδὴ
ὁδηγεῖ τὸ ψεῦσμα εἰς τὴν κλοπήν). However, considering the similar version
of Doctr. 3:5 ("Noli fieri mendax, quia mendacium ducit ad furtum"), it is not clear
whether the quotation can be traced back to our Didache, or whether Clement may
have been tributary to a separate Greek Two Ways manual instead.[3] Other places
in Clement's writings are relevant in this respect as well. In his rendering of the
commandments of the Decalogue, he sometimes appears to allude to the text in
Did 2:2: οὐ φονεύσεις, οὐ μοιχεύσεις, οὐ παιδοφθορήσεις, οὐ πορνεύσεις,
οὐ κλέψεις... ("You shall not murder, you shall not commit adultery, you shall
not corrupt children, you shall not fornicate, you shall not steal..."). On account
of the repeated inclusion of the clause οὐ παιδοφθορήσεις in *Stromateis* III, 4,
36, 5; *Protrepticus* X, 108, 5; *Paedagogus* II, 10, 89 and III, 12, 89,[4] which is
missing in the biblical Decalogues, Clement may have had a passage in view like
the one in Did 2:2. The same expression, however, is found in the Latin Doctr. 2:2
("non puerum violabis") in a similar list of precepts. What the discussion about
these references comes down to is that Clement may have had the Didache or the
Greek Two Ways document in mind here. Because he does in fact not give evidence of any acquaintance with Did 7-16,[5] it is more likely that his source was not

---

[2] See above, Chap. 2, pp. 63-66. For an explanation of the church ordinances claiming apostolic
authority, see above, Chap. 1, pp. 3-5 and cf. Schöllgen-(Geerlings), *Didache. Zwölf-Apostellehre*,
13-21.

[3] From the preceding phrase ὑπο τῆς γραφῆς most commentators conclude that Clement considered
the text from which he quotes as Scripture. For a discussion, see Niederwimmer, *Die Didache*, 19.

[4] Preceding this rendering of the (second table of) the Decalogue (ἡ δεκάλογος in 12,89) in the last
passage, we find the positive form of the Golden Rule and the double love commandment (12,88). This
structure (although the Golden Rule and double love commandment appear in reverse order here)
corresponds with the teaching of the Two Ways. Nevertheless, since the Golden Rule is formulated in
a way which is similar to Matt 7:12 and the additional two elements are interspersed with Matthean
quotations, it is difficult to decide whether this larger part of Clement's instruction is really based upon
the Two Ways.

[5] It is true, the expression τὸν οἶνον, τὸ αἷμα τῆς ἀμπέλου τῆς δαβίδ, ἐκχέας ("pour out the wine,
the blood of the vine of David") in Clement's *Quis dives salvetur?* (29,4) echoes Did 9:2. In accordance
with Niederwimmer (*Die Didache*, 20), however, we consider this terminology to be liturgical. It is

the composite Didache document but some form of the Two Ways manual. This source probably still circulated in Clement's days apart from its presence in the Didache and the Letter of Barnabas.

Indications of an independent existence of the Two Ways teaching in the West, like the one which is offered in the Doctrina Apostolorum, are found in several quotations. The earliest extant witness to a Latin version of the Two Ways manual might be represented by the Gesta apud Zenophilum (c. 320),[6] where it says: "tamen secundum dei uoluntatem, qui dixit: quosdam diligo super animam meam, ..."[7] The statement closely corresponds with Doctr. 2:7: "(Neminem hominum oderis,) quosdam amabis super animam tuam."[8] If a quotation is involved here,[9] it has been modified in the Gesta. The major love of one's neighbour is formulated in the first person and attributed to God himself, while being worded in the second person in the Doctrina and imparted as an instruction to men.

The next reference comes from Optatus, bishop of Milevis in Numidia in the fourth century. In his work Libri VII contra Parmenianum Donatistam I,21, he writes: "Denique inter cetera praecepta etiam haec tria iussio diuina prohibuit: non occides, non ibis post deos alienos, et in capitibus mandatorum: non facies scisma"[10] ("finally, among other commandments, these three the divine regulation forbade as well: you shall not kill, you shall not run after other gods, and in the chapters of commandments: you shall not cause division"). The prohibition to cause division, presented here as a divine injunction which is handed down in a writing with the title 'capita mandatorum' ('chapters of commandments'), is repeated as a divine saying in III,7: "non sacrificabis idolis idem deus locutus est et: non facies scisma et ..."[11] ("you shall not sacrifice to idols, as God has said, and: you shall not cause division, and ..."). Both quotations are reminiscent of Doctr. 4:3: "Non facies dissensiones, ..."[12] It is true, the term "dissensiones" is not repeated in Contra Parmenianum. Berthold Altaner[13] suggests that the substitution of "scisma" for the wording "dissensiones" results from the purpose of Optatus' writing. Because he is fighting a schism, created by the Donatists, Optatus seems to have deliberately opted for the word "scisma", which is a basic Scriptural motif.

---

therefore conceivable that both Clement and the Didache knew this text from their respective church traditions. For other possible but improbable repetitions in Clement, see Hitchcock, 'Did Clement of Alexandria know'; Giet, *L'Énigme de la Didachè*, 36, n. 96; Rordorf-Tuilier, *La Doctrine des douze Apôtres*, 125, n. 1.

6 Cf. also for the following, Altaner, 'Zum Problem'.

7 See Ziwsa, 'Gesta apud Zenophilum', 192.

8 Did 2:7 could refer to the same source: (...) οὓς δὲ ἀγαπήσεις ὑπερ τὴν ψυχήν σου. See also Barn. 19:5: ἀγαπήσεις τὸν πλησίον σου ὑπὲρ τὴν ψυχήν σου.

9 Niederwimmer (*Didache*, 23) characterizes the passage as "problematisch". However, it is obvious that the writer of this letter did not have Jer. 31:3 and 1 John 4:9 in mind, to which Ziwsa in his edition of the 'Gesta apud Zenophilum' refers.

10 Cf. Ziwsa, *Optatus von Mileve*, 23.

11 Cf. Ziwsa, *Optatus von Mileve*, 88-89.

12 Cf. Did 4:3: Οὐ ποιήσεις σχίσμα,... (= Barn. 19:12).

13 'Zum Problem', 163.

On the other hand, it may be worthwhile to stress that the Latin Doctrina is a translation of the Greek Two Ways tractate which has been retained for us by mere chance. Additional Latin versions may have circulated.

The last passage offered here occurs in the Epistula Ps.-Titi, which presumably originated in Spain in the fifth century.[14] In the lines 262-63 it says: "... praeconante prudencia gesta futura hoc est quod mandat semper dicens: Fuge, filiole, omnem malum et ab omne simile illi, ..."[15] ("while wisdom announces the future, this is what it always requires by saying: Flee, my child, from every evil person and from everyone like him"). This statement corresponds closely with that in Doctr. 3:1 ("Fili, fuge ab homine malo et homine simulatore") and when it comes to determining the Epistula's source, it lends support to an independent use of the Duae Viae document. According to Altaner, who has the firm conviction that the author of Epistula Ps.-Titi everywhere employs Latin writings exclusively,[16] this quotation did not proceed from the Didache but from a Latin Two Ways manual.

The above discussion indicates that several versions of the Latin Duae Viae may have circulated as a piece of instruction in the fourth and fifth centuries. Another essential point, emerging from the materials dealt with so far, is the absence of a fixed title for this Duae Viae document. Optatus of Milevis refers to the 'capita mandatorum', which would be a suitable heading for our manual, and the Epistula Ps.-Titi attributes its quotation to the 'Prudencia'.[17] In this respect, also the testimony of Rufinus of Aquileia (c. 345-410) is important. In Chap. 36 of his Commentary on the Apostles' Creed, called the Expositio Symboli, he offers a list of canonical works and a series of ecclesiastical reading books.[18] As to the latter type, he states that the writings for the Old Testament consist of the additional books of the LXX (later accepted as deuterocanonical). He then assigns the following reading books to the New Testament: "...libellus qui dicitur Pastoris siue Hermae, et is qui appellatur Duae uiae, uel Iudicium secundum Petrum, ..."[19] ("the little book which is called 'of the Pastor' or 'of Hermas', and the one called 'Two Ways', or 'Judgment according to Peter'"). It is clear that the title 'Duae viae' refers to the incipit of the Two Ways and Rufinus must have had a version of this document in mind.[20] The variety of titles attributed to the Two Ways manual thus suggests

[14]   Cf. Altaner-Stuiber, *Patrologie*, 140-41.

[15]   De Bruyne, 'Epistula Titi, Discipuli Pauli', 54.

[16]   "Dass der lateinisch schreibende Verfasser der Epistula Titi nur lateinische Schriften benützt und zitiert, kann als sicher gelten; ...;" cf. Altaner, 'Zum Problem', 164, n. 10.

[17]   It must be admitted, however, that also in Epistula Ps.-Titi, line 209 and 420, the 'Prudencia' introduces a quotation from an unknown source (Sir 20:4?) and Sir 30:19, respectively; cf. De Santos Otero, 'Der Pseudo-Titus-Brief', 59, n. 47. This fact on the one hand indicates that its author did not set aside the term "prudencia" for a particular reference to the Two Ways but seems to imply that he was not familiar with a specific title of the document on the other.

[18]   See Stenzel, 'Der Bibelkanon des Rufin', 57.

[19]   Simonetti, *Rufin. Opera*, 171.

[20]   This is also the opinion of Stenzel, 'Der Bibelkanon des Rufin', 58. That the expression "Duae viae" does not point to a Latin version of the whole of the Didache may be derived from the fact that Rufinus seems to reserve for the latter work the explicit reference of 'Doctrina quae dicitur apostolorum' ("The

that, at least in some of its Latin versions, this writing was not ascribed to the authority of the apostles: it did not exist as a Doctrina *apostolorum* but was transmitted anonymously.

There is reason to suppose that the absence of apostolic authority in these Latin witnesses[21] probably reflects the earliest stage in the transmission of the Two Ways document in the church. The manual was incorporated – albeit it thoroughly modified – in the Letter of Barnabas. The author of this letter introduces his lengthy rendering of the Two Ways in 18:1 as follows: "Now let us pass on to another lesson and teaching (διδαχήν)." These words indicate that Barnabas' source was called "didache" or "teaching". Moreover, the content of the instruction in Barn. 18-20 is devoid of any allusion to the apostles. They are mentioned neither in Did 1-6 nor in the Doctrina. Therefore, it is likely that the reference to the "apostles" in the Doctrina's heading was added afterwards[22] in order to provide the manual with a canonical status. It was probably moulded in imitation of the phrase in Acts 2:42 (προσκαρτεροῦντες τῇ διδαχῇ τῶν ἀποστόλων / "devoting themselves to the apostles' teaching").[23] In its original form, however, the document appears to have circulated in Christian communities with various titles, one of wich was "Didache". We have no exact information when apostolic authority was assigned to our Two Ways document. It has been proposed more than once that it reached this position before it became a part of the Didache.[24] The Didache, then, might have adopted the title "Teaching of (the) Apostles" when its materials were prefaced with the Two Ways.

Nevertheless, in spite of its insertion in the Didache, the Two Ways manual maintained an independent existence with the title Διδαχῇ (τῶν) ἀποστόλων or

---

Teaching called 'of the Apostles'") in his translation of the phrase τῶν ἀποστόλων αἱ λεγόμεναι Διδαχαί in Eusebius' Ecclesiastical History III, 25, 4; (cf. Schwartz, *Eusebius II: Die Kirchengeschichte*, 253; see below, n. 29). In that case Rufinus probably changed the plural Διδαχαί of Eusebius' text into the singular 'Doctrina' (see Rordorf-Tuilier, *La Doctrine des douze Apôtres*, 108-109). On the other hand, it is also possible that Eusebius' expression τῶν ἀποστόλων αἱ λεγόμεναι Διδαχαί ("the alleged teachings of the apostles") in fact did not refer to the Didache but to the Two Ways treatise (see below). It is not clear whether Rufinus in mentioning "Duae uiae, uel Iudicium secundum Petrum" points to two separate books or to one only; cf. Rordorf-Tuilier, *La Doctrine des douze Apôtres*, 108, n. 5; Niederwimmer, *Die Didache*, 18 and recently Aldridge, 'Peter and the "Two Ways"', 238-45.

[21] R.E. Aldridge has suggested that the title 'Iudicium secundum Petrum' connects the Two Ways with the apostle Peter. In a long article ('Peter and the "Two Ways"'), he attempts to demonstrate that in the early church there was indeed a tradition associating Peter with the Two Ways.

[22] A reference to an instruction of the apostles was probably also lacking in the Coptic version of the Two Ways, which the monks in the White Monastery in Atripe had at their disposal (see above, Chap. 2, pp. 66-67). In the Arabic text of the Life of Shenoute, which is a translation from a Coptic original, "fehlt sowohl am Anfang wie am Ende der Aufzählung von Satzungen ganz wie im Barnabasbrief der Hinweis darauf, dass Lehren der Apostel vorliegen. Das ist um so bemerkenswerter, als eine solche Einführung ganz im Sinne Schnudi's gewesen wäre, der sonst manche seiner Verfügungen durch besondere Offenbarungen und Visionen, die er angeblich von Propheten und Aposteln erhalten hatte, zu stützen suchte;" cf. Iselin, *Eine bisher unbekannte Version*, 12.

[23] Cf. Rordorf-Tuilier, *La Doctrine des douze Apôtres*, 15 and Steimer, *Vertex Traditionis*, 25.

[24] Cf. Goodspeed, 'The Didache', 231; Köster, *Synoptische Überlieferung*, 218; Nautin, 'La Composition de la 'Didachê', 213; Niederwimmer, *Die Didache*, 82.

"Doctrina Apostolorum."[25] This is not only apparent from its separate occurrence and its designation in the two extant mediaeval manuscripts. The early testimony of the Apostolic Church Order (ACO) and the Epitome (E) demonstrates this as well. In each of these writings, the materials of the Two Ways are divided into separate instructions, pronounced by eleven individual apostles. Because these documents present our Two Ways in the form of apostolic sayings, they are considered to be dependent upon a common source (the "Elfapostelmoral") which was a revision of the Two Ways document.[26] Since it cannot have been the content of the Two Ways document itself, which – as stated above – does not make any reference to an apostle at all, it must have been the title of the document which induced the redactor of the "Elfapostelmoral" to put these instructions into the mouth of the apostles.[27] This source, then, which served as a fundament to the Apostolic Church Order and the Epitome, testifies to the continuous preservation of the Two Ways with the title "Teaching of (the) Apostles."

If the Two Ways document remained in existence as an independent text and was known (at least in some versions) as the "Teaching of (the) Apostles," one wonders whether some testimonies in the early Christian literature, referring to the Διδαχὴ / Διδαχαὶ (τῶν) ἀποστόλων, might not point to a form of the Two Ways document rather than – as is mostly assumed – to the Didache. Because a treatment of all places that ought to be considered in this context would extend beyond the scope of this chapter, attention will here be focussed upon three occurrences only.[28] The first one, found in the Ecclesiastical History III, 25, 4 (c. 315-325) of Eusebius of Caesarea (c. 265-339),[29] mentions "the alleged teachings of the apostles" (τῶν ἀποστόλων αἱ λεγόμεναι Διδαχαί). There is a good possibility that Eusebius has a version of the Two Ways in mind and qualifies the manual as "alleged" because its content does not authenticate its apostolic origin.

Athanasius of Alexandria refers to the "so-called teaching of the apostles" (Διδαχὴ καλουμένη τῶν ἀποστόλων) in the Festal Letter 39 (367).[30] It is not certain, however, whether his added καλουμένη manifests the same distrust concerning its apostolic parentage as does the wording in Eusebius' work. As a matter of fact, he includes the seven Catholic Letters of the New Testament among the canonized writings while characterizing them as ἐπιστολαὶ καθολικαὶ

---

[25] For the reading "De Doctrina Apostolorum," which occurs in the *Monacensis*, see below, Chap. 4, n. 3.

[26] Cf. Wengst, *Didache (Apostellehre)*, 7-11 and Niederwimmer, *Die Didache*, 51-52.63. See also above, Chap. 2, pp. 63-66.

[27] Cf. Audet, *La Didachè*, 95-96. Audet, however, believes that this title was transferred from the Didache to the Two Ways.

[28] For some of these and other references – although mostly related with the Didache –, see Audet, *La Didachè*, 81-88; Rordorf-Tuilier, *La Doctrine des douze Apôtres*, 108. 126; Wengst, *Didache (Apostellehre)*, 5; Niederwimmer, *Die Didache*, 15-18.

[29] Schwartz, *Eusebius II: Die Kirchengeschichte*, 250-52. Rufinus in his translation has the singular "Doctrina" here; cf. above, n. 20.

[30] The surviving portion of the Greek text of Athanasius' letter has been edited by P.-P. Joannou in his *Fonti* 2, 71-76. See also *PG*, 1437-1440 and Preuschen, *Analecta* 2, 45.

καλούμεναι as well.[31] That the reference Διδαχὴ καλουμένη τῶν ἀποστόλων may indicate an independent Two Ways manual instead of the Didache is supported by its context. In addition to other writings (Wis, Sir, Esth, Jdt, Tob and *Herm.*), Athanasius in this Festal Letter lists the Διδαχὴ καλουμένη τῶν ἀποστόλων among those documents that were considered appropriate reading for baptismal candidates. They were appointed for τοῖς ἄρτι προσερχομένοις, for those who want to κατηχεῖσθαι τὸν τῆς εὐσεβείας λόγον, in short for the "catechumens."[32] Whereas Did 7-16 contains directives on rituals (like baptism and eucharist) and church discipline, it is only the Two Ways part in Did 1-6 which offers a model for initial instruction. Moreover, it is obvious that the liturgical and disciplinary part in Did 7-16, as reflecting the conditions and circumstances of a primeval community, were not relevant to later ages. That these chapters lost their practical worth and importance may be inferred from their supersession by later church orders like the Apostolic Church Order and the Apostolic Constitutions.

The last testimony in this series apparently links up with Athanasius' purpose of listing documents, designated for those under instruction for baptism. In his Commentary on Ecclesiastes 78,22, Didymus the Blind or Ps.-Didymus (c. 313-398) refers to "the teaching of the catechesis of the apostles" ([ἐν] τῇ Διδαχῇ τῆς κ[ατη]χ[ή]σεως τῶν ἀποσ[τ]όλων).[33] The supposed educational value of the instruction here is likely to point to the practical worth of the Two Ways for later ages as well.

In the above discussion, Athanasius (and to a certain extent Didymus) is a core witness in establishing the *Sitz im Leben* of the Two Ways instruction. In fourth-century Egypt, it was used as a pre-baptismal teaching, as a basic instruction about Christian life to those who were preparing for church membership. It is possible to trace the baptismal use of this manual even further back. In the church of the first centuries, the teaching of the Two Ways probably formed part of a catechesis that was related to the ritual of baptism as well. Evidence for this instruction to be given prior to the performance of baptism is found in Did 7:1-4. In addition to the description of the proper wording and correct practice regarding the ritual of

---

[31] Cf. Audet, *La Didachè*, 85.

[32] Cf. ... ἔστι καὶ ἕτερα βιβλία τούτων ἔξωθεν, οὐ κανονιζόμενα μέν, τετυπωμένα δὲ παρὰ τῶν πατέρων ἀναγινώσκεσθαι τοῖς ἄρτι προσερχομένοις καὶ βουλομένοις κατηχεῖσθαι τὸν τῆς εὐσεβείας λόγον; cf. Festal Letter 39 (Joannou, *Fonti* 2, 75). See also Rordorf-Tuilier, *La Doctrine des douze Apôtres*, 31 and Niederwimmer, *Die Didache*, 16.

[33] Ps.-Didymus mentions the clause εἰρηνεύσεις μαχομένους here, alluding to a version of the Two Ways like the one in Doctr./Did 4:3; cf. Gronewald, *Didymos der Blinde* 2, 70. The same words are quoted in his Commentary on Psalm 34:20 and introduced as follows there: "ἐν τῇ Διδαχῇ τῇ βίβλῳ τῆς κατηχήσεως λέγεται· ...;" cf. Gronewald, *Didymos der Blinde* 3, 398. See also Lührmann, 'Das Bruchstück', 276. According to B.D. Ehrman who maintains that the Didache is quoted "canonically" and is granted a Scriptural stature here, it is only of incidental interest that Didymus refers to the Didache as a catechetical book. "Apparently", so he states, "the term κατήχησις is a functional description having nothing to do, necessarily, with a book's canonical status. These books were simply those out of which young converts in Alexandria could and did receive their basic Christian instruction" ('The New Testament Canon', 21 [n. 16] and 16-17).

baptism, which follows right after the teaching of the Two Ways as recorded in Did 1-6, it is especially the wording "after having said these things" (7:1) which is important. It is explicitly stated here that the catechetical instruction, offered in Chaps. 1-6, is to precede baptism.[34]

The information on the specifics of (at least) part of pre-baptismal instruction reflected in Did 7:1 is consistent with indications in two other sources that date from the beginning of the second century.[35] First, there is the well-known letter of Pliny to Trajan, written about 112 in Bithynia. In this letter Pliny, talking about Christians, who were examined by him, states:

> They also declared that the sum total of their guilt or error amounted to no more than this: they had met regularly before dawn on a fixed day to chant verses alternately among themselves in honour of Christ as if to a god, and also to bind themselves by oath, not for any criminal purpose, but to abstain from theft, robbery and adultery, to commit no breach of trust and not to deny a deposit when called upon to restore it (...sed ne furta ne latrocinia ne adulteria committerent, ne fidem fallerent, ne depositum adpellati abnegarent). (Ep. Ad Traj. X, 96, 7)[36]

The meaning of this passage is much debated[37] but it seems reasonable to suppose that in mentioning the morning service the author alludes to some baptismal ritual. It most probably was a formal oath ceremony involving solemn vows which may have been performed in a river or a stream. "Important indirect evidence for this conclusion," according to D.H. Tripp, "lies in the fact that Pliny is clearly very interested in initiations."[38] If the interpretation is correct that converts are making a baptismal vow here to refrain from the above list of vices, this ceremonial act presupposes a baptismal instruction.

Also Hippolytus in his Refutatio omnium Haeresium – Κατὰ πασῶν αἱρέσεων ἔλεγχος – (IX,13-17) states that in the Judeo-Christian teaching of Elchasai,[39] a

---

[34] Cf. Benoit, *Le Baptême Chrétien*, 6-7 and Mitchell, 'Baptism in the *Didache*', 236-37. Audet, *La Didachè*, 58-62 and 358-367 disputes the authenticity of this wording. See, however, Nautin, 'La Composition', 206-207; De Riedmatten, 'La Didachè', 423; Rordorf-Tuilier, *La Doctrine des douze Apôtres*, 30-32.

[35] For the following, see Kretschmar, 'Die Geschichte des Taufgottesdienstes', 44; Rordorf, 'Un chapitre d'éthique', 165-68.

[36] For the Latin text and the English translation, see Radice, *Pliny*, 289. The whole of the Christian oath in Pliny's Letter to Trajan is very similar to the passage in Aristides, *Apology* 15,4; cf. Geffcken, *Zwei griechische Apologeten*, 24 (lines 3-6) and see his commentary on pp. 87-88. See also below, Chap. 5, n. 152.

[37] See Merkelbach, 'Der Eid der Bithynischen Christen'.

[38] Tripp, 'The letter of Pliny', 52. See also Id., 'Pliny and the Liturgy', 582-84; Lietzmann, 'Die liturgischen Angaben des Plinius'; Van Beeck, 'The Worship of Christians', 124; Peterson, 'Die Behandlung der Tollwut', 224, n. 5.

[39] Or is it Alcibiades to whom reference is made? It is usually held that it is the Elchasaites who are referred to in this passage; cf. Irmscher, 'Das Buch des Elchasai', 622 and, recently, Mimouni (*Le judéo-christianisme ancien*, 295-307; esp. 304-05) who believes IX, 15,5-6 to be one of four quotations from the Book of Elchasai in Hippolytus' Refutatio. According to Luttikhuizen, (*The Revelation of*

Christian sinner, before being rebaptized, should cleanse himself and make a solemn promise. Hippolytus in his quotation reports among other things:

> Behold, I call to witness the heaven and the water, and the holy spirits, and the angels of prayer, and the oil, and the salt, and the earth. I testify by these seven witnesses that I shall sin no more: I shall not commit adultery, nor steal, nor be guilty of injustice, nor be greedy, nor be hateful nor be scornful, nor shall I take pleasure in any wicked [deeds] (...οὐ μοιχεύσω, οὐ κλέψω, οὐκ ἀδικήσω, οὐ πλεονεκτήσω, οὐ μισήσω, οὐκ ἀθετήσω, οὐδὲ ἐν πᾶσι πονηροῖς εὐδοκήσω). (Ref. IX, 15,5-6)[40]

The oath, being sworn in the water, was part of a purification ceremony preceding the rebaptism for the remission of sins. Prior to this baptism, the repentant sinner presumably had to purify himself and solemny swear before seven witnesses never to sin again.[41]

One may assume that the sins rejected in the above passages correspond with the ethical exhortation preceding the baptismal ritual. They also have much in common with the text of the catechetical instruction of the Two Ways. In either case, we are presented with short lists of vices which show close affinities with those in Doctr./ Did 2:2-6; 3:2-6 and 5:1. With repect to the next section, it is also relevant to observe that these catalogues are based on the second table of the Decalogue. To sum up this discussion, the data seem to indicate that the teaching of the Two Ways is to be located in a pre-baptismal instruction[42] during the first Christian centuries.

The Merovingian and Carolingian Period

If a version of the Two Ways called the Doctrina Apostolorum apparently was copied until the eleventh century in the West, it is of significance to know how it was used in the Merovingian and Carolingian periods. Did a Latin version of the Two Ways affect the moral exhortations and liturgical observances in Christian

---

Elchasai, 54) Hippolytus in fact refers to Alcibiades of Apamea, whose teachings and activities in Rome are attacked in IX,13-17.

[40] For the Greek text, see Marcovich, *Hippolytus*, 361, lines 28-33.

[41] Luttikhuizen, *The Revelation of Elchasai*, 67-78. According to Peterson ('Die Behandlung der Tollwut', esp. 228-35) the immersion is a means to bridle one's sexual passions. It corresponds, so he writes, with "die judenchristliche (durch Elchasai bezeugte) Auffassung, dass das Tauchbad gegen die Konkupiszenz vorgeschrieben und neben der Taufe nötig ist ..." (234). And, indeed, there is reason to believe that the abjuration of sins was considered an antidote against sexual desire, metaphorically represented as a bite by a rabid dog (cf. the Introduction in IX,15,4 and 2). According to Luttikhuizen (75-78), however, it is Hippolytus who tries to prove that Alcibiades and his adherents made use of magical formulas. Hippolytus describes the abjuration of sins before the seven witnesses as an invocation of magical names on account of his polemical intention to suggest that the whole procedure taught by Alcibiades (abjuration of sins, purification rite, second baptism) is merely a magical trick.

[42] It is not suggested here, though, that the use of the Two Ways teaching was restricted to the catechetical instruction prior to baptism only. That it was used otherwise as well is shown by its insertion into the Letter of Barnabas, which was written to baptized Christians.

writings in these times? In order to answer this question, some documents which are often referred to in this connection but have never been seriously considered in detail will be examined for possible vestiges of the Two Ways tradition: The Rule of Benedict and the Rule of the Master, the Fifteenth Sermon of Ps.-Boniface and, finally, the Second Catechesis in the Ratio de Cathecizandis Rudibus.

THE RULE OF BENEDICT AND THE RULE OF THE MASTER

The Rule that Benedict of Nursia (c. 480-547) wrote at Monte Cassino towards the end of his life was intended to serve as a guide for monks. In the seventh and eighth centuries, its impact became widespread among the Anglo-Saxon and Frankish peoples in Europe.[43] Outside Southern Italy and Rome, the Rule diffused its influence throughout England after the Synod of Whitby in 664 and was promulgated as obligatory for the monasteries in the whole Carolingian empire at the Frankish Synods of 743 and 744. The main factors firmly establishing monastic life according the *Rule of Benedict* (*RB*) were the missionary work of Anglo-Saxon monks, especially the zeal of Boniface of Mainz (ca. 680-754), and the favourable patronage of the Carolingian sovereigns.

Although the *RB* by itself is not ordered in a strict systematic arrangement, one might structure its contents into the following sections: the Prologue with the nature of the monastic life (Chaps. 1-3), the spiritual art (Chaps. 4-7), communal prayer (Chaps. 8-20), the internal administration of the monastery (Chaps. 21-52), the relationship between the monastery and the world (Chaps. 53-57), the renovation of the monastic community (Chaps. 58-65), a concluding Chapter 66 and, finally, the Appendix (Chaps. 67-73).[44] The arrangement of the directories in the *RB* is closely related to the pattern of organization in the anonymous *Rule of the Master* (*RM*), an elaborate monastic rule which is three times the size of the *RB*. Although the *RB* has for a long time been taken to be the source of the *RM*, it is now almost generally believed that the latter document holds first place. The *RB* is not only posterior to the *RM* but probably dependent on it as well.[45] This is not to say that Benedict himself did not revise and adapt the materials transmitted to him. He modified, abbreviated, and expanded the text while leaving out those elements which did not suit his ideas. Yet, the examination of the two documents has made clear that he was influenced by the *RM* in the topics of his directories, their sequence, their style and their vocabulary. The *RB* is especially related to its source in the Prologue (vv. 5-45.50), in Chap.1 (vv. 1-11), Chap. 2 (1-18a. 18b-25. 30. 35-37), Chap. 4 (1-7. 9-59. 62-74) and Chaps. 5-7.

---

[43] See Faust, 'Benediktiner, Benediktinerinnen'; Jaspert, 'Die Regula Benedicti-Forschung' and Steidle, *Die Benediktusregel*, 7-52.

[44] Cf. Steidle, *Die Benediktusregel*, 31-34.

[45] Cf. Steidle, *Die Benediktusregel*, 21; Jaspert, 'Die Regula Benedicti-Forschung', 141-43; Faust, 'Benediktiner, Benediktinerinnen', 90; De Bruyne, 'La première Règle', 330; Rochais-Manning, *Règle de Saint Benoît*, VI.

The question whether or not the *RB* may be influenced by some form of the Two Ways is especially relevant with regard to Chap. 4 of this document. On the one hand, the materials in this chapter are clearly akin to the Two Ways, but it is difficult to prove that this correlation transcends a mere phenomenogical similarity, on the other.[46] Before going into detail, it is important to note that the directories in *RB* 4 to a large extent correspond verbally with those in *RM* 3, and on the basis of this evidence one may safely assume that Benedict used the Rule or the Master as a source here.[47] In *RB* 4 (74 verses), he summarizes Chaps. 3-6 from *RM* (116 verses) in just one chapter, mainly focussing his attention on *RM* 3. *RB* 4 is entitled "What are the Instruments of Good Works? (Quae sunt instrumenta bonorum operum?)" and in this respect it differs from the probably original heading in *RM* 3, which is phrased in this way: 'What is the Holy Art which the abbot ought to teach his disciples? (Quae est Ars Sancta, quam docere debet abbas discipulos in monasterio?).'"[48]

At the outset of the treatise in *RB* 4, the double love commandment is found, the love of God and that of the neighbour, followed by a long series of directories elaborating on these principles. Both chapters, *RB* 4 and *RM* 3, are meant to serve as a preamble to the subsequent topics of obedience, silence, and humility, which are set forth in *RB* 5-7 and *RM* 7-10, respectively. It is interesting to see, however, that almost all statements in these introductory chapters are formulated in broad and general terms[49] which tend to give to these texts the distinct character of a summary of universal morals rather than an introduction to monastic discipline. The general tenor of the directories suits the life of a secular Christian better than rules governing the conduct and activities of monks. Even more than in *RB* 4, one notices the lack of monastic peculiarities in the corresponding chapters of *RM* 3-6. Benedict apparently modified some maxims for the benefit of his fellow-monks, but evidently left untouched the major part of his source. That the practical worth of the catalogue of Good Works in *RB* 4 appealed to the imagination of many Christians at an early date may be concluded from the fact that it was also transmitted independently of *RB* as a separate segment to be used for the instruction of lay people.[50]

It is likely that the universal moral code of conduct in *RB* 4 and *RM* 3, at least partially, is derived from a preexisting document. Its literary style and genre

---

[46] J. Schlecht was the first to propose that RB 4 was based on the first part of the Didache; cf. *Doctrina XII Apostolorum* (1901) 86-90. This opinion is supported (although without a reference to Schlecht's work) by Boehmer, ('Hat Benedikt von Nursia') and was recently endorsed by Rordorf, 'Un chapitre d'éthique', 173. Schlecht's judgment has been rejected, however, by Butler, 'The Rule of St Benedict'. Niederwimmer recommends "die genaueren Bezüge unseres Traktats" (i.e. the Two Ways manual in its Latin translation) "zur Regula Magistri und zur Regula Benedicti neuerlich zu untersuchen" (*Die Didache*, 64, n. 80).

[47] Cf. De Vogüé, *La Règle de Saint Benoît* 7, 126-134.

[48] Cf. De Vogüé, *La Règle de Saint Benoît* 4, 181-190.

[49] For the following, see De Vogüé, *La Règle de Saint Benoît* 7, 124-128.

[50] Cf. Hallinger, 'Das Kommentarfragment', 226-227.

distinguishes this collection of sayings on natural ethics from its context and seems to fit better in a distant past.[51] If, however, *RM* 3 is not a product of the Master, one wonders what document or documents this catalogue of directories is borrowed from. In this respect, Adalbert de Vogüé has pointed out its correspondence with the Prologue to *RM*.[52] This Prologue, which is largely a commentary on the Lord's Prayer and the Psalms, displays a similar general and neutral tenor as the Holy Art catalogue of *RM* 3. In fact, it expounds at length upon the conversion of the unbeliever and his baptism. It is likely, therefore, that the Prologue to *RM* is dependent upon a document containing baptismal instruction.[53] Because some details in *RM* 3 reveal a close resemblance with the Prologue and because its Holy Art catalogue essentially provides an elementary catechesis, also the teaching in this third chapter may originally have formed part of the document used for the moral instruction of new converts. This is to say that the same type of document as the one underlying the Prologue to the *RM* was also the source of *RM* 3 and (indirectly) of *RB* 4.[54]

According to Joseph Schlecht,[55] Benedict borrowed his Good Works treatise in *RB* 4 as a whole from the Didache to incorporate it, albeit in a modified form, in his Rule. In his opinion, Benedict employed a Greek recension of the Didache because the version in *RB* 4 showed many deviations from the Latin version of the Two Ways that he himself had discovered and published in 1900 and 1901. In order to prove this thesis, he printed in parallel columns the sayings in *RB* 4 and the corresponding passages in the Greek Didache. However, relatively few articles agree with those in the Didache.[56] Since it is difficult to prove that the Good Works treatise is an overall derivative from the Didache, it might be more useful to give prior attention to separate passages from *RM* 3 // *RB* 4.

---

[51] Cf. Wilmart, 'Le Discours de Saint Basile', 233, n. 1.

[52] *La Règle de Saint Benoît* 4, 128-130. In fact, the introduction to *RM* is usually divided into 'Prologus' (vv. 1-57) and 'Thema' (the remaining part).
Here the term 'Prologue' is used only.

[53] For the baptismal features in the Prologue, see also Lambert, 'Autour de la Règle du Maître' and Manning, 'Une catéchèse baptismale'.

[54] Cf. De Vogüé, *La Règle de Saint Benoît* 4, 131-32; see also Manning, who suggests that three passages in the eighth treatise of St. Augustine's Epistola Ioannis ad Parthos underlie *RB* 4 (and *RM* 3), 13-17. Augustine himself mentions that this exposition was delivered during the first week after Easter, the period which was appropriate for the instruction of new converts. Moreover, these sermons are interspersed with baptismal allusions. Having displayed the agreement between the two documents, Manning concludes: "Nous savons que l'enseignement donné aux néophytes comportait l'obligation d'apprendre (...) les vertus à pratiquer et les vices à éviter. C'est sans doute dans cette direction qu'il faut chercher l'origine de nos trois textes. ..." (cf. 'Un texte de S. Augustin', 332-33.

[55] *Doctrina XII Apostolorum* (1901) 86-90.

[56] "... out of St Benedict's seventy instruments" (precepts or rules), "to hardly a dozen can any kind of even seeming parallel be adduced from the *Didache*;" cf. Butler, 'The Rule of St Benedict' (1911), 285.

Cyprian Davis recently has endorsed the view of De Vogüé that the following maxims in *RB* 4,63-69 (= *RM* 3,69-74) are based upon the Didache:[57] "Live by God's commandments every day. Treasure chastity. Harbour neither hatred nor jealousy of anyone, and do nothing out of envy. Do not love quarreling. (Shun arrogance)."[58] They do indeed show a resemblance with Did 2:7 but might equally be identified as references to Doctr. 2:7.[59] What is of importance, however, is that these directories, which come at the end of both the treatise on the Good Works in *RB* 4 and the one on the Holy Art in *RM* 3, in a certain sense resume their beginnings where the love commandment is rendered. Since they cover the initial and final topics of a chapter, they form a thematic inclusion around the enclosed materials. The same phenomenon applies to the Two Ways as reflected in the Didache and the Doctrina. The saying in Doctr./Did 2:7, which comes at the end of a separate section (1:1-2:7), corresponds with the love commandment of 1:2.[60]

In his article, Davis pays due attention to the concluding maxims of *RB* 4 and *RM* 3 but, unfortunately, refers to the list of precepts at the beginning of these units only in passing. It is noteworthy, however, that also the first nine sayings of *RM* 3 (and of *RB* 4 as well) appear to be closely akin to the first part of the Two Ways. The passage in *RM* 3,1-9 is as follows:[61]

1. Quae haec est ars sancta: primo credere, confiteri et timere Deum Patrem et Filium et Spiritum Sanctum, unum Deum in Trinitate et trinum in unitate, trinum in una deitatis substantia et unum in trina magestatis potentia. Ergo hunc ex toto corde et ex tota anima diligere.
2. Deinde in secundis diligere proximum tamquam seipsum.
3. Deinde non occidere,
4. non adulterare,
5. non facere furtum,
6. non concupiscere,
7. non falsum testimonium dicere,
8. honorare patrem et matrem,
9. et quod sibi quis non uult fieri, alio ne faciat.

The trinitarian confession of faith in v. 1 is printed in small type here because it was added at a later stage and it is likely that Benedict retained its previous

---

[57] 'The *Didache* and early Monasticism', 360-361. This agreement has also be noticed by Schlecht, *Doctrina XII Apostolorum* (1901) 89. Whether *RM* 80 is really related to Did 14:1-3, as proposed by Davis (cf. pp. 361-64), is open to question.

[58] "Praecepta Dei factis cotidie adimplere. Castitatem amare. Nullum odire. Zelum non habere. Invidiam non exercere. Contentionem non amare. (Elationem fugere);" cf. *RB* 4,63-69 / *RM* 3,69-74. The last clause (of *RB* 4,69) is placed within brackets here because it is missing in *RM*.

[59] Did 2:7: Οὐ μισήσεις πάντα ἄνθρωπον, ἀλλὰ οὓς μὲν ἐλέγξεις, περὶ ὧν δὲ προσεύξῃ, οὓς δὲ ἀγαπήσεις ὑπὲρ τὴν ψυχήν σου (You will not hate anyone, but some you will reconcile, and others you will pray for, and still others you will love more than your own soul).
In Doctr. 2:7 it says here: "Neminem hominum oderis, quosdam amabis super animam tuam."

[60] Cf. Davis, 'The *Didache* and early Monasticism, 360-61 and De Vogüé, '"Ne haïr personne"', 3-4.

[61] For the text, see De Vogüé, *La Règle du Maître* 1, 364.

version.[62] The chapter proper starts with the two great commandments of love (3,1-2), and are followed by six Decalogue commandments (3,3-8) and the negative form of the Golden Rule (3,9). These three elements are found in Doctr./Did 1:1-2:6 as well. It is noticeable, however, that *RM* 3 (and *RB* 4), unlike the materials in Did 1:1-2:6, do not refer to any sayings of Jesus. This absence suggests that *RM* 3,1-9 (*RB* 4,1-9) is more akin to the form of the Two Ways as preserved in the Latin version of Doctr. 1:1-2:6 than to its counterpart in the Didache. While in Did 1:1-2:6 the double love commandment and Golden Rule are separated from the Decalogue commandments by a lengthy Christian interpolation in 1:3b-2:1, the evangelical section is missing both in the Doctrina and in the ancient catalogue of *RM* 3 and *RB* 4.

Admittedly, the order of the second (Decalogue commandments) and third element (Golden Rule) are reversed in *RM* 3 (and *RB* 4). Moreover, the Decalogue section of Doctr. 2:2-6 is abbreviated here (although expanded with the love of parents in the fourth commandment) and is probably adapted to its occurrence in the New Testament (Matt 19:18-19 and Luke 18:20). Nevertheless, – and this has already been stressed by De Vogüé – it is striking that the combination of the double love commandment, the second half of the Decalogue, and the negative form of the Golden Rule is found nowhere in the New Testament but recurs in Doctr. 1:1-2:7 as well as in *RM* 3,1-9 (*RB* 4,1-9).[63] The collocation of these specific elements in *RM* 3 and *RB* 4 is apparently based upon a Latin recension of the Two Ways.[64] This view is corroborated by the close link of the text in *RM* 3,69-74 and *RB* 4,63-69 with Doctr./Did 2:7, which is discussed by De Vogüé and Davis. It appears that the ancient catalogue of Holy Art or Good Works in the two Rules is surrounded by two passages which reflect the materials in Doctr. 1:1-2:6 and Doctr. 2:7 respectively.

Apart from possible additional parallels between the Two Ways and the two monastic Rules, one may draw the following conclusion. The common source, which underlies the version of *RM* 3 and *RB* 4 and appears to have been linked up originally with the manual that formed the foundation of the Prologue to *RM*, was related to a version of the Two Ways. It is likely that this source was enclosed in Two Ways materials. It contained a rudimentary catechesis and many features of its present form in the two monastic Rules suggest that it represented a pre-

---

[62] See De Vogüé, *La Règle de Saint Benoît* 4, 190-93. Chapter 4 of the *RB* start as follows: "Inprimis dominum deum diligere ex toto corde, tota anima, tota uirtute;" cf. Hanslik, *Benedicti Regula*, 29.

[63] "En fait, l'assemblage des deux commandements, soit avec le Décalogue, soit avec la Règle d'or, ne se trouve pas dans les Évangiles. Cet ensemble caractéristique constitue un trait d'union entre le *Duae Viae* et ses dérivés d'une part, et nos Règles de l'autre;" cf. *La Règle de Saint Benoît* 4, 132-33.

[64] The specific linkage of the double love commandment, the Decalogue and the Golden Rule is attested in other sources as well, in particular in Clement of Alexandria's *Paed.* III, 12, 88-89 (see note 4) and Justin's *Dial.* 93,1-2. In these places, the sequence of the three elements is not carried out as consistently as in Doctr. 1:1-2:7 and *RM* 3, 1-9 // *RB* 4,1-9, respectively (cf. also Aristides, *Apol.* 15,2-5 [Greek]; Theoph. of Antioch, *Ad Autol.* 2,34; Tertullian, *Adv. Marc.* 4,16,17). Furthermore, the occurrence of the three essential similarities in these additional sources may be due to their dependence upon the Two Ways tradition.

baptismal instruction. Apparently the instruction to neophytes was the setting in which this secular catalogue functioned and was transmitted.

THE FIFTEENTH SERMON OF PS.-BONIFACE

The sermon attributed to Boniface which will be discussed here is transmitted in the two manuscripts which also contain the Latin version of the Two Ways, i.e., the *Cod. Lat. Monacensis 6264* (fol. 102[rv]) and the *Mellicensis 597* (fol. 114[ro]-115[ro]). The *Monacensis 6264* (F) was previously called the *Frisingensis 64*. It stems from the eleventh century, belonged to St. Mary's abbey of Freising in Bavaria, and is found nowadays in the Staatsbibliothek at Munich. The manuscript was edited for the first time by Schlecht in 1900[65] and an expanded edition appeared in 1901.[66] The *Mellicensis 597* (M) was designated nr. *914* and before that: *Q 52*. It dates from the early tenth or, possibly, from the ninth century and is kept in the Stiftsbibliothek at Melk, Austria.[67]

The two documents have preserved the fifteenth sermon of St. Boniface, dealing with the "Baptismal Renunciation" ("De abrenuntiatione in Baptismate") of Satan at the moment of baptism,[68] almost immediately before their presentation of the Two Ways. The two manuscripts, however, have more in common. In addition to the sermon and a version of the Two Ways, which belong to the concluding sections of the two documents, they mainly offer a collection of homilies for each Sunday and for the feastdays throughout the church year. The homilies are arranged according the same calender in either manuscript, but the *Mellicensis*, unlike the *Monacensis*, only has part of this schedule and starts with the Sunday after Pentecost.[69] The questions to be discussed in this section regard the character of these documents. How are they related to one another? Does the sermon indeed give evidence of the way Boniface preached? And, last but not least, what is its connection with the Two Ways tradition? Our first concern, however, will be to

---

[65] *Doctrina XII apostolorum, una cum antiqua versione latina prioris partis de Duabus viis.* Freiburg im Breisgau 1900.

[66] J. Schlecht, *Doctrina XII apostolorum. Die Apostellehre in der Liturgie der katholischen Kirche*, Freiburg i. B. 1901, 101-104. For the date of the *Monacensis*, see Rordorf-Tuilier, *La Doctrine des douze Apôtres*, 203.

[67] For the date of the *Mellicensis*, cf. Niederwimmer, 'Doctrina Apostolorum (Cod. Mellic. 597)', 269.

[68] Although the titles differ somewhat from one another. The heading of the *Monacensis* says: "Incipit ad" (sic!) "Amonitio S. Petri sive praedicatio sancti Bonifatii ep. de abrenuntiatione in baptismate" ("The Warning of St. Peter or the Preaching of St. Boniface the Bishop on Baptismal Renunciation;" cf. Schlecht, *Doctrina XII Apostolorum* [1901] 37.124) whereas the sermon in the *Mellicensis* is entitled as follows: "Ammonitio sive predicatio (sic!) sancti Bonifacii episcopi de abrenuntiatione in baptismatae" (sic!) (cf. Niederwimmer, 'Doctrina Apostolorum [Cod. Mellic. 597]', 269).

[69] For a complete survey of the content in the *Monacensis 6264*, cf. Schlecht, *Doctrina XII Apostolorum* (1901) 22-39, and for the *Mellicensis*, cf. Funk, 'Zur alten lateinischen Uebersetzung', 651-653.

briefly rank the compilations of homilies of the two above manuscripts among other extant homily collections (homiliaries) from the Carolingian age.

Usually the homiliaries from the seventh to the tenth centuries are divided into two categories: patristic and Carolingian. The Carolingian homilies, in contrast to the patristic ones which first of all were meant to be read during public worship, were designed for private devotion and study or for the use of oral instruction.[70] To the latter type belong the two manuscript homiliaries, the *Mellicensis* and the *Monacensis*, which offer the sermon[71] attributed to Boniface as well. In the homiletic manuscript tradition, these two collections, as a matter of fact, are witnesses to a specific compilation of sermon materials which were mistakenly attributed to the Anglo-Saxon Bede (672-735) by their first editor J. Gymnicus in 1535.[72] The homiliary of Ps.-Bede, written in the beginning of the ninth century in (probably) Bavaria,[73] was widely diffused and the extent of this spread is attested to by their partial or complete preservation in many manuscripts. Besides the above *Monacensis* and *Mellicensis*, Henri Barré has located other witnesses to this ancient Ps.-Bedan homiliary in Munich (*Staatsbibl. Monacensis lat. 14410* – part of which will be discussed in our next section – and *14472*), in Oxford (*Bodl. Laud. Misc. 427*), Cologne (*Bibl. Capit. 172*), Avranches (*Bibl. Mun. 29*, fol. 1-98) and Trier (*Stadtbibl. 216*).[74] The Ps.-Bedan homiliary contains 124 homilies or "explanationes lectionum seu epistolarum," ranging from the vigil of Christmas up to All Saints' Day. As far as this collection deals with the New Testament, it is unique in that its homilies are based on the Pauline writings only. Whereas homiliaries commonly present collections of sermons about appropriate gospels and epistles for the day (arranged according to the liturgical cycle), the Ps.-Bedan collection merely confines itself to Paul's Epistles.

The sermon attributed to Boniface, preserved in the *Mellicensis* and *Monacensis*, however, does not belong to the substance of the Ps.-Bedan homiliary. It is not classified as connected with a lecture of a specific day in the liturgical calender but is found among materials which are attached at the end of both manuscripts by way of appendix. Since 1733, this sermon has been transmitted as part of a larger collection of sermons, all of which are attributed to Boniface. In that year, E. Martène and U. Durand[75] published a collection of fifteen sermons by St. Boniface, which have been edited as a collective body ever since. The last one (the

---

[70] See Longère, *La Prédication Médiévale*, 35-36.

[71] The terms 'sermon' and 'homily' are used without distinction here, since both categories are applicable to these Carolingian 'explanationes', in which moral exhortation succeeds Scriptural interpretation or even replaces it; cf. McKitterick, *The Frankish Church*, 92 (and n.1).

[72] "Homiliae Venerabilis Bedae, presbyteri Anglosaxonis, theologi celeberrimi, in D. Pauli epistolas et alias veteris et novi testamenti lectiones tam de tempore quam de sanctis, ut per totum annum in templis leguntur, nunc primum excussae;" cf. Barré, *Les Homéliaires Carolingiens*, 7.

[73] Longère, *La Prédication Médiévale*, 44.

[74] *Les Homéliaires Carolingiens*, 8. See also Schlecht, *Doctrina XII Apostolorum* (1901) VI-IX.

[75] *Collectio amplissima*, col. 185-218; cf. 'Sermones Sancti Bonifatii' in *PL* 89, 843-872. See, also for the following, Bouhot, 'Alcuin',184-191.

fifteenth) of these homilies is identical with the sermon on the renunciation of Satan in the above manuscripts. The two editors took it from an edition of B. Pez,[76] who in his turn had copied it from the codex in the cloister-library at Melk. The preceding fourteen sermons in this compilation are probably borrowed from the *Lat. 10741* (nowadays in the Bibliothèque Nationale in Paris), the only manuscript in which these are preserved collectively.[77] These sermons correspond in many respects with the homilies of a celebrated preacher in the church of the fifth century, Caesarius of Arles (c. 470-542).[78] Their authenticity was often challenged[79] and defended[80] in the past, and is rejected today. Except for the fifteenth sermon, they probably date from the middle of the ninth century and are considered to have served as a manual for preaching.[81]

The fifteenth sermon in this collection, which in accordance with its incipit will be called "Audite" in the succeeding discussion, is from an earlier date than the first fourteen.[82] We have already mentioned that it is presented in the *Monacencis* and *Mellicencis*. It is found anonymously and in a shorter version in an additional manuscript as well. This manuscript is presently found in the Vatican library with the signature *Biblioteca Apostolica, Pal. lat. 485*. In fol. 91ro-92ro, it preserves the sermon in an earlier recension. Nevertheless, despite the recension's antiquity, it is quite unlikely that even the "Audite" sermon reflects an authentic address by St. Boniface. Its style deviates from the characteristically Bonifacian letters and the content does not refer at all to the historical context in which he worked.[83]

Yet, the sermon "Audite" is important in the attempt to uncover traces of a persistent use of the Two Ways. In 1887, J. Rendel Harris reproduced the fifteenth sermon from Pez's edition in order to show that it depends upon the Didache "from beginning to end" and his conclusion is clear: "Hence we are entitled to say that

---

[76] *Thesaurus anecdotorum nouissimus* 4, pars 2, col. 3-5; Cf. Bouhot, 'Alcuin', 184, n. 22. The cols. 5-6 offer the first edition of the Two Ways according the Codex *Mellicensis* as well, although at that time this phenomenon could not be judged on its true merits.

[77] Paris, *B.N.*, lat. 10741 (*Olim*: Suppl. lat. 205), fol. 102vo-129; (cf. Bouhot, 'Alcuin', 186-7). These sermons are partially preserved in three mss., written in the twelveth and sixteenth centuries (cf. id., 190).

[78] Longère, *La Prédication Médiévale*, 50.

[79] Cf. for example, Hahn, 'Die angeblichen Predigten des Bonifaz'; Flaskamp, *Die Missionsmethode des hl. Bonifatius*, 38: "Die als 'Predigten des heiligen Bonifatius' geführten 15 lateinischen Reden sind in ihrer Echtheit angefochten, ja man darf sagen: erledigt."

[80] Cruel, *Geschichte der deutschen Predigt*, 23-27; Schlecht, *Doctrina XII Apostolorum* (1901) 76.

[81] Cf. Bouhot, 'Alcuin': "Aucun détail ne permet de rapporter ces prédications" (i.e. the collection of fourteen sermons) "à un moment particulier du ministère de saint Boniface ... auprès des peuples de Germanie, ni même de tenir pour assuré qu'elles ont été adressées à des chrétiens récemment convertis et baptisés. Enfin les témoins de la tradition manuscrite n'invitent pas à faire remonter la composition de ce recueil avant le milieu du IXe siècle, ..." (191); Cf. also Longère, *La Prédication Médiévale*, 50.

[82] See also Aldridge, 'The Lost Ending of the *Didache*', 10, n. 22. We do not accept, however, his contention that this sermon covers the entire Didache. The points of contact are too few in number to justify this view (see below).

[83] "... le texte ne fournit pas d'indices significatifs du style et des préoccupations de l'apôtre de la Germanie;" cf. Bouhot, 'Alcuin', 186.

The most authentic extant witness to the Fifteenth Sermon of Ps. Boniface ("Audite"), probably written in Lorsch before 875 (Vatican ms. Biblioteca Apostolica, Pal. lat. 485, fol. 91ro-92ro).

exquirere strigas. &fictos luposcredere. dominis inoboe-
dientesee philacteria habere. haec&his similia mala
operasunt diaboli. &hisomnibus inbaptismo renuntiastis. &sicut apostolus dicit. Quitalia agunt digni sí
morte. &regnum di nonconsequentur. Sed credimus
p̅misericordiam di. ut hisomnibus malis superius conp̅
hensis corde&opere renuntietis &p̅confessionem &dig-
non paenitentiam emendetis ut ueniam consequi me-
reamini. haec sunt ergo quae inbaptismo promisistis
&custodire debetis. primitus enim promisistis credere
indm̅ patrem omnipotentem. &inihm̅ xp̅m filium
eius &insp̅m̅ sc̅m. qui est unus ds ̅omnipotens intrini-
tate perfecta. haec sunt ergo mandata di quaefacere
&custodire debetis. ut ipsum dm̅ quem confessi estis.
diligatis extoto corde. extota anima. extota uirtute. extota mente. deinde proximos uestros
tamquam uosmet ipsos. quia in his duobus mandatis tota lex pendet &prophetae. estote patientes.
estote misericordes. benigni. casti. inpolluti. filios
acfilias uras docete. ut dm̅ timeant filium ur̅m
similiter. discordes pacate. iuste iudicate. munera
iniusta non accipiatis quia munera obcecant &iam
sapientes. diem dominicum obseruate. adecclesiam
conuenite. ibi orantes &non uerbositantes. elimosinas dare iuxta uires. hospitales inuicem. peregrinos
suscipite. infirmos uisitate. uiduis &pupillis ministrate. decimas adecclesias reddite. &quod tibinon
uis alio nefacias. dm̅ solum ubiq. timete. serui
sub dr̅ia estote dominis. &domini iustitia conseruate

92

seruis. Orationem dominicam & symbolum quod est
credo indñm omnino tenere. & filius uris tradere & filio
lis uris quos inbaptismo fide iussores extitistis. ieiunium
amare. iustitiam diligere. Diabulo semper resistere.
eucharistiam per tempora sumere. haec sunt opera
quaedñ iussit facere & conseruare & his similia. uentu
rum xpm credere & carnis resurrectionem. & iudicium
omnium hominum ibi discernuntur impii a forte iusto
rum & mittuntur in ignem aeternum. iusti autem inui
tam aeternam. ibi est uita cum dõ sine morte ibi aeterna
gloria sine fine. ibi fulgebunt iusti sic sol. ibi omnia
bona quae oculus non uidit. nec auris audiuit nec incor
hominis ascendit quam tum praeparauit dñs diligentibus
se quod ipse praestare dignetur qui uiuit interre pfecta
uiuit & regnat dñs in saecula saeculorum amen

INCIPIUNT CAPITULA

Sicut sca sinodus nicena interdicit. Nullus umquam
presbr indomo sua habitare secum per mittat mulie
rem extraneam. praeter matrem & sororem atque
amittam uel matertertam uel eam ad secretum cubiculi
uel cellario. Nullus presbiter feminam aliquam adire
pmittat. Quod si fecerit post haec scicit se abhonore presbi
teratus deponi. quia haec frequenter secundum canoni
cam instructionem phibuimus & pleniter a presbiteris ob
seruatum non fuit. Ideoq. praecipimus ut qui gradus hono
rissui retinere uult omnibus modis a familiaritate ex
tranearum mulierum se abstinere faciat. ut nulla occa
sio inimico pateat suggerendi peccatum & famam malam
a populo nullus eorum incurrat.

if Boniface was the apostle of Germany, the Teaching" (i.e. the Didache) "must have been his text-book."[84] Fourteen years later, Joseph Schlecht[85] reedited the text of the sermon on the basis of a collation of the *Monacensis* (edited in J.P. Migne, *PL* 89, 870A-872A), the *Mellicensis* (in the form in which this manuscript was published by Pez) and the *Pal. lat. 485* (the variant readings of which he received from a Benedictine monk, B. Albers) with a similar purpose. In his evaluation of the interrelationship between the Didache and the sermon, he, independently of Harris[86], established that the double love commandment, the Golden Rule, and the catalogue of sins – the last one in a more developed shape – in the first two chapters of the Didache are in agreement with elements in the sermon of Boniface. He was, however, less confident than Harris that Chaps. 7-16 of the Didache were at the basis of the sermon, and believed that the dependence upon the Didache was confined to the Two Ways only. The remaining question was which form of this ancient manual was used. He did not consider it likely that Boniface was acquainted with the Greek Didache as presented in the Bryennios manuscript.[87] At the same time he found out that the text of the sermon in the parts corresponding with the Two Ways differed from the Latin version in his own edition of the manual. He therefore concluded that the sermon was based on a different recension of the Two Ways.

In the argumentation of Schlecht, the three elements which were also found in Benedict's Rule (double love commandment, catalogue of sins, and Golden Rule) play a significant role. It is also important to consider that the sermon, as the document underlying *RM* 3 (and *RB* 4) probably was, is related to baptism. In the following discussion, we will try to corroborate Schlecht's judgment about the sermon's dependence upon the Two Ways. In turning to the text of the sermon, it is first of all noteworthy that the version printed here at length has not been published so far. It is a transcript of the text in *Pal. Lat. 485,* the manuscript which probably was written in Lorsch before 875[88] and is described by B. Bischoff.[89] In

---

[84]   *The Teaching of the Apostles*, London-Baltimore 1887, 60. See also the position of Aldridge ('The Lost Ending', 8-9): "This is *De abrenuntiatione in baptismate* ("Baptismal Renunciation"), an eighth century catechetical sermon of St. Boniface, reminding new converts of their baptismal vows in connection with the approaching Advent season, and clearly based upon the *Didache*."
[85]   *Doctrina XII Apostolorum* (1901) 124-126.
[86]   "Ich hatte diese Beobachtung unabhängig von *Harris* gemacht und meine Gegenüberstellung der korrespondierenden Texte bereits angefertigt, als ich seine Nachweise zu Gesicht bekam" (76).
[87]   Schlecht (wrongly) took the Latin form of the Two Ways to be a translation of the Bryennios' Didache; cf. *Doctrina XII Apostolorum* (1901) 9-10.
[88]   According to Bischoff, 'Paläographische Fragen', 113; cf. Bouhot, 'Alcuin', 185; Id., 'Un florilège sur le symbolisme', 172-73.
[89]   "Pal. lat. 485. Kalendarium, Liturgica, Canones, etc.; 113 Bl., ca. 255x185 mm (ca. 190x120 mm), 29 oder 30 Zeilen. Von zahlreichen Händen. Der Grundbestand ist teils in charakteristischer schmälerer Schrift (...) geschrieben, teils in einem offenen Typ, selbst ohne re-Ligatur (26ᵛ ff., 64ʳ ff.). Gelegentlich insulares »enim«-Symbol. Sorgfältige Rustica und Unziale; die kräftige Unziale auf fol. 55ᵛᵒ ff. ähnlich jener der Erlangen-Augsburger Sakramentarfragmente und des Clm 21218 (vgl. z.B. das A). Es steht im Einklang mit dem Schriftcharakter, dass die Kalendareinträge zum 8. X. (Schlacht bei Andernach 875) und 20. I. (Tod Ludwigs des Jüngeren 882) von zweiter Hand geschrieben sind. Das Jahr 875 ist Terminus ad bzw. ante quem. ...;" cf. Bischoff, *Die Abtei Lorsch*, 55.

fol. 91ro-92ro this document appears to have preserved a more original form of the sermon:

fol. 91ro

Audite, fratres, et adtentius cogitetis. quid in baptismo renuntiastis. abrenuntiastis enim diabolo et omnibus operibus eius. haec sunt opera eius quae renuntiastis. superbiam. inuidiam. odium. detractionem. mendacium. periurium. fornicationem. adulterium. homicidium. furtum. falsum testimonium. rapinam. auaritiam. gulam. et ebrietatem. turpiloquia. contentiones. ira. ueneficia. incantationes. et sortilegos	Listen, brothers, and attentively think. What did you renounce at baptism. You renounced the devil and all his works. These are his works which you renounced: pride, jealousy, hatred, slander, lie, perjury, fornication, adultery, murder, theft, false witness, robbery, avarice, greed, drunkenness, obscene speech, quarrels, rage, poisonings, sorceries,

fol. 91vo

exquirere strigas et fictos lupos credere. Dominis inobedientes esse. philacteria habere. haec et his similia mala opera sunt diaboli. et his omnibus in baptismo renuntiastis. et sicut apostolus dicit. Qui talia agunt digni sunt morte. et regnum dei non consequentur. Sed credimus per misericordiam dei ut his omnibus malis superius conprehensis corde et opere renuntietis et per confessionem et dignam paenitentiam emendetis ut ueniam consequi mereamini. haec sunt ergo quae in baptismo promisistis et custodire debetis. primitus enim promisistis credere in deum patrem omnipotentem. et in iesum christum filium eius et in spiritum sanctum. qui est unus deus omnipotens in trinitate perfecta. haec sunt ergo mandata dei quae facere et custodire debetis. ut ipsum deum quem confessi estis diligatis ex toto corde. ex tota anima. ex tota uirtute. ex tota mente. Deinde proximos uestros tamquam uosmet ipsos. quia in his duobus mandatis tota lex pendet et prophetae. Estote patientes. estote misericordes. benigni. casti. impolluti. filios ac filias uestras docete. ut deum timeant filiam *(familiam?)* uestram similiter. discordes pacate. iuste iudicate. munera iniusta non accipiatis quia munera obcecant etiam sapientes. Diem	consulting fortune-tellers, believing in witches and werewolves, being disobedient to his masters, wearing amulets. These and bad works similar to these belong to the devil. And all these you renounced at baptism. And as the Apostle says: "those who do such things" deserve death and "shall not inherit the kingdom of God" *(Gal 5:21)*. But we believe that through the mercy of God you have renounced all these wicked things, listed above, with your heart and action and that by confession and appropriate repentance you improve (yourselves) so that you might deserve to acquire forgiveness. These then are the things which you promised at baptism and which you should keep. First of all, you promised to believe in God the almighty father and in Jesus Christ his son and in the Holy Spirit, who is the one almighty God in perfect trinity. These are the injunctions óf God which you should perform and keep, namely that you love God whom you have professed with all your heart, with all your soul, with all your strength and with all your mind. Then your neighbours as yourselves. Since on these two commandments depend all the law and the prophets. Be

dominicum obseruate. ad ecclesiam
conuenite. ibi orantes et non
uerbositantes. elimosinas date iuxta uires.
hospitales inuicem. peregrinos suscipite.
infirmos uisitate. uiduis et pupillis
ministrate. Decimas ad ecclesias reddite.
et quod tibi non uis alio ne facias. Deum
solum ubique timete. Serui subditi estote
dominis. et domini iustitiam conseruate

fol. 92ro

seruis. Orationem dominicam et
symbolum quod est credo in deum
omnino tenete. et filiis uestris tradite et
filiolis uestris quos in baptismo fide
iussores extitistis. ieiunium amate.
iustitiam diligite. Diabulo semper
resistite. eucharistiam per tempora
sumite. haec sunt opera quae deus iussit
facere et conseruare et his similia.
Uenturum christum credite et carnis
resurrectionem. et iudicium omnium
hominum. ibi discernuntur impii a sorte
iustorum et mittuntur in ignem aeternum.
iusti autem in uitam aeternam. ibi est uita
cum deo sine morte ibi aeterna gloria
sine fine. Ibi fulgebunt iusti sicut sol. ibi
omnia bona quae oculus non uidit. nec
auris audiuit nec in cor hominis ascendit
quantum preparauit deus diligentibus se
quod ipse praestare dignetur qui in
trinitate perfecta uiuit et regnat deus in
saecula saeculorum amen.

patient, be merciful, kind, chaste,
immaculate. Teach your sons and
daughters that they fear God. (Teach)
your slaves (?) similarly. Pacify the
discordants, judge fairly, do not accept
unjust presents because presents also
dazzle the wise. Keep the Lord's day.
Come together to church in order to
pray there, not to chatter. Give
according to your power, be mutually
hospitable, receive strangers, visit the
sick, support widows and orphans, give
tithes to the churches and what you
don't want (done) to you, do not (do) to
another. Fear everywhere God only. As
slaves be obedient to (your) masters and
as masters observe justice (being

done) to (your) slaves. Hold on entirely
to the Lord's Prayer and the confession
of faith which is the creed. And teach
(these) to your children and your little
ones, of whom you became godparents
at baptism. Observe fasting with
gladness, love righteousness, always
resist the devil, and receive the
Eucharist in due time. These are the
works which God ordered (you) to
perform and keep and works similar to
these. Believe in Christ's coming, the
resurrection of the flesh, and the
judgment of all men. In that place, evil
men are distinguished from the lot of
the righteous men and are assigned to
eternal fire. The righteous, however, to
eternal life. In that place, there is life
with God without death. There eternal
glory [is] without end. There the
righteous will shine like the sun. There
[will be] all good things which "no eye
has seen, nor ear heard, nor has arisen
in man's heart what God has prepared
for the ones who love him" *(1 Cor 2:9)*,
which he himself condescends to
provide who lives and reigns in perfect
trinity, God for ever and ever, amen.

In addition to some other minor changes, it is striking that this version is shorter than the one published by Schlecht and Migne. The two latter editions offer a fifteenth sermon which has affixed instructional materials from other great preachers to the original Sermon's ending. The passage in Schlecht's (126) and Migne's (*PL* 89, 870A-872A) edition "Hoc etiam moneo vos fratres carissimi ... / / ... ad eternam beatitudinem feliciter pervenire" to a large extent corresponds with the concluding sentences of a sermon of Caesarius of Arles[90] while the subsequent and final paragraph in Schlecht's edition "Hec" (haec) "est fides, que" (quae) "paucis verbis tenenda ... / / ... corde mundato quod credant intelligant" is (some details excepted) borrowed from St. Augustine's De Fide et Symbolo 25.[91]

Turning to the content of the text in *Pal. Lat. 485*, we ascertain that the sermon is addressed to converted Christians. It reminds the audience of their formal declaration at the baptismal ritual when they were required to renounce the devil ("abrenuntiatio") and swear their adherence to Christ ("promissio" or "confessio"). This repudiation of the devil, his works, and his corteges (often also: his angels)[92] *and* the promise of loyalty to Christ were essential elements in the baptismal liturgy of the Carolingian period.[93] The renunciation was a liturgical act which suggests that sin was not so much an offence against God and intrinsically objectionable but rather a result of Satan's influence. It is the power of the devil which is responsible for the transgressions and violations of man. Satan was the adversary of Christ. Renunciation and adherence, in fact, were basic conditions for the believer to be seized from the rule of the devil and to be incorporated in God's kingdom. Because the devil was thought capable of taking the shape of pagan idols, the Germanic gods were considered as demons. This explains why a Saxon catechism required the catechumens to forsake his old gods, Thuner, Uuoden, and Saxnote, and believe in the Trinity instead.[94] The antagonistic contrast between the kingdom of God and that of the devil in the baptismal formula has a long

---

[90] See the italics in the following text:" ... *Hoc* enim *ammonuimus, fratres, ut quia natalis domini inminet,* tamquam ad nuptiale et caeleste convivium *ab omni luxuria* nitidi et bonis operibus adornati per Christi adiutorium nos praeparemus, elemosynas pauperibus erogemus, *iracundiam vel odium velut venenum* diaboli *de cordibus* nostris *respuamus. Castitatem etiam cum propriis uxoribus* fideliter *conservate, ad conviviola vestra pauperes frequentius revocate,* ad vigilias maturius convenite, in ecclesia stantes aut orate aut psallite; verba otiosa aut saecularia nec ipsi ex ore vestro proferte, et eos qui proferre voluerint castigate: *pacem cum omnibus custodite,* et quos *discordes* agnoscitis, ad concordiam revocate. *Haec si fideliter Christo adiuvante volueritis implere, et in hoc saeculo ad altare domini* cum *secura* conscientia poteritis *accedere, et in futuro ad aeternam beatitudinem feliciter pervenire*: ipso adiuvante, qui vivit et regnat in saecula saeculorum. Amen" (serm. 188,6; cf. Morin, *Sancti Caesarii Arelatensis Sermones,* 769-70).

[91] "Hec est fides, que paucis verbis tenenda in symbolo novellis christianis datur, que pauca verba fidelibus nota sunt. ut credendo subiugati recte vivant. recte vivendo cor mundent. corde mundato quod credant intelligant;" cf. Schlecht, *Doctrina XII Apostolorum* (1901) 126 and see also Zycha, *Sancti Aureli Augustini,* 32, line 12-16. This fact has been revealed by a marginal note in red ink in the *Monacensis* (cf. Schlecht's edition, 126, n. 4).

[92] For the formulae, see Kirsten, *Die Taufabsage,* 38-74.

[93] See Kirsten, *Die Taufabsage,* passim; Kretschmar, 'Die Geschichte des Taufgottesdienstes', 311.

[94] Cf. Kirsten, *Die Taufabsage,* 44; Angenendt, *Kaiserherrschaft und Königstaufe,* 49-57.

history, having already been recorded in the baptismal rite of the early church from Tertullian onwards.[95] In the framework of this study, it even seems possible that the liturgical rite of renunciation and adherence reaches even further back in time and has its roots in the dualism of the original Two Ways, which is presided over by the angels of justice and injustice, respectively.

A closer look at the text of Ps.-Boniface shows our sermon to be dependent on a Two Ways version – or upon a tradition linked up with such a version – in precisely this respect. The sermon presents the "abrenuntiatio" and "confessio" as a means of admonition for the baptized Christians. Joseph Schlecht has put the materials of the Sermon and the Didache in a parallel order but, by doing so, he has taken the phrases from the Didache up and down in such a manner that they suggest a lack of any structural parallelism between the two documents. It is of significance to see that the materials in the sermon are not only frequently analogous with the Latin version of the Two Ways but are arranged according to the definite pattern of this manual as well. The sermon clearly is subdivided into the two topics italicized here:

> Audite, fratres, et adtentius cogitetis. *quid in baptismo renuntiastis.* abrenuntiastis enim diabulo et omnibus operibus eius. haec sunt opera eius quae renuntiastis. ... // ... haec et his similia mala opera sunt diaboli

and

> *haec sunt ergo quae in baptismo promisistis et custodire debetis.* primitus enim promisistis credere in deum patrem omnipotentem. et in iesum christum filium eius et in spiritum sanctum. qui est unus deus omnipotens in trinitate perfecta. haec sunt ergo mandata dei quae facere et custodire debetis. ... // ... haec sunt opera quae deus iussit facere et conseruare et his similia.

It is important to notice, however, that not only the double theme of the sermon *quid in baptismo renuntiastis* ("What did you renounce at baptism") and *haec sunt ergo quae in baptismo promisistis et custodire debetis* ("these then are the things which you promised at baptism and which you should keep"), but also the specific materials, attached to either theme, echo the two opposing principles of the Two Ways. The particular items in the sermon are a development in detail of the characteristics which in the Two Ways serve as an explication of the Way of Life and the Way of Death.

The first part of the sermon mentioning the works of the devil ("superbiam. inuidiam. odium [pride, jealousy, hatred]. ... / / ... dominis inobedientes esse. philacteria habere [being disobedient to his masters, wearing amulets].") reflects the catalogue of sins in Doctr. 5:1, consisting of nothing but substantives, which illustrates the Way of Death in the Doctrina.[96]

---

[95] Cf. Dölger, *Die Sonne der Gerechtigkeit*, passim; Kirsten, *Die Taufabsage*, 9-37.

[96] The list ("superbiam, ..., fornicationem, ..., homicidium, furtum, falsum testimonium, rapinam, ...") partly agrees with Doctr. 5:1 although the occurrence of these substantives is rendered in the plural there.

The second part of the sermon, dealing with the promise to God, at first renders the trinitarian creed. It then, however, links up with the Two Ways again as is shown by the italicized references: "ut ipsum deum quem confessi estis diligatis ex toto corde. ex tota anima. ex tota uirtute. ex tota mente. Deinde proximos uestros tamquam uosmet ipsos *(cf. Doctr. 1:2)*. quia in his duobus mandatis tota lex pendet et prophetae. Estote patientes. estote misericordes. benigni. casti. impolluti. *(cf. Doctr. 3:7-8)* filios ac filias uestras docete. ut deum timeant familiam uestram similiter *(cf. Doctr. 4:9-10)*. discordes pacate. iuste iudicate. munera iniusta non accipiatis quia munera obcecant etiam sapientes *(cf. Doctr. 4:3)*. Diem dominicum obseruate. ad ecclesiam conuenite. ibi orantes et non uerbositantes. elimosinas date iuxta uires *(cf. Doctr. 4:7)*. hospitales inuicem. peregrinos suscipite. infirmos uisitate. uiduis et pupillis ministrate. Decimas ad ecclesias reddite. et quod tibi non uis alio ne facias *(cf. Doctr. 1:2)*. Deum solum ubique timete. Serui subditi estote dominis *(cf. Doctr. 4:11)*. et domini iustitiam conseruate seruis *(cf. Doctr. 4:10)*. Orationem dominicam et symbolum quod est credo in deum omnino tenete. et filiis uestris tradite et filiolis uestris quos in baptismo fide iussores extitistis. ieiunium amate. iustitiam diligite. Diabulo semper resistite. eucharistiam per tempora sumite."

The double love commandment in the sermon's second part is presented as a summary of the law, which in Doctr. 1:2 is stated to be the content of the Way of Life ("primo....secundo"). The subsequent lines in the sermon offer a list of admonitions which, just as in Doctr.2:1-7, immediately succeed the foregoing law summary without any bearing upon the evangelical section that is apparent in Did 1:3b-2:1. The negative form of the Golden Rule is found here too. It does not, however, appear in juxtaposition with the double love commandment (cf. Doctr. 2:2) but forms part of the list of admonitions. At the same time, one sees that these admonitions are not based upon a review of the second table of the Decalogue (cf. Doctr. 2:2-6). The replacement may have served to prevent a series of repetitional statements since the list of Doctr. 2: 2-6 displays a doublet of the catalogue of sins in Doctr. 5:1. Nevertheless, to a large extent these admonitions in the sermon reflect directories which are scattered in the additional commentary of Doctr. 3:1-4:14.[97] Moreover, it is noteworthy that many admonitions in the sermon (second person plural) are worded in the literary style of the second table of the Decalogue.

In the above discussion, it was established that, in its first part, the sermon "Audite" offers a list of vices, some of which parallel the second table of the Decalogue, and, in its second part, collocates the double love commandment, a series of virtues, partially rendered in the style of the Decalogue, and the negative form of the Golden Rule. Although the presence itself of these particular elements reveal important agreements with the Two Ways, it is especially the similar arrangement of the materials in either case which supports the evident relationship between the two documents. The sermon casts the motifs of the renunciation of the devil and the promise to God, including their distinctive features, into a dualist-

---

[97] Cf. Schlecht, *Doctrina XII Apostolorum* (1901) 77-78.125.

ic framework in a manner that is consistent with the Latin version of the Two Ways, representing the Way of Death (Doctr. 1:1 and 5:1) and the Way of Life (Doctr. 1:1-2:6 / 4:14), respectively, the first one being controlled by the angel of iniquity and the second one by the angel of justice.

The recension of the Two Ways used in the sermon "Audite" probably differed from the one we have in the codex *Monacensis* and *Mellicensis*. Yet, the correspondence in style, content, and structure of the sermon with the Latin version of the manual clearly shows that the sermon of Ps.-Boniface is a witness to a similar Two Ways tradition. This conclusion is underscored by the transmission of the sermon in combination with the Latin Doctrina in both the *Monacensis* and *Mellicensis*, a characteristic that might be explained as an early awareness of the interrelationship between the sermon and the Two Ways.

THE SECOND CATECHESIS OF THE RATIO DE CATHECIZANDIS RUDIBUS

Another document displaying possible traces of the Two Ways tradition is the Decalogue instruction in the series of the six catechetical teachings, entitled Ratio de cathecizandis Rudibus. J.M. Heer published the text of the Ratio in 1911 from the *Monacensis lat. 14410* fol 85[vo]-92, which dates from the beginning of the ninth century.[98] The manuscript belonged to the monastery of St. Emmeram in Regensburg and was transferred to the Staatsbibliothek in Munich where it is preserved nowadays. Just like the *Monacensis 6264* and *Mellicensis*, it is a witness to the homiliary of Ps.-Bede in that it mainly contains homilies on the New Testament letters of Paul. These homilies cover the part of the liturgical year from the vigil of Christmas till Ascension Day (fol. 1-77[vo]).[99] The Ratio may have been composed, as Heer suggested, to serve as a guide for missionaries in their initial instruction of pagans (Avars or Saxons) who were willing to accept Christianity.[100] In order to fully comprehend the relevance of this document, it is worthwhile to see how it fits into the historical context.

During the early phase of the Carolingian period (seventh, and especially eighth centuries), Anglo-Saxon missionaries came to the continent to convert the Frankish peoples. Their customary practice was to introduce them to the rudiments of Christian belief and, after their baptism, to continue their instruction.[101] However, the expansion of Christianity under Carolingian rulers, especially under Charle-

---

[98]   Heer, *Ein Karolingischer Missions-Katechismus*.
Concerning the date and provenance of this ms.: "Ganz von einer Hand aus dem ersten Drittel des IX. Jhs. geschrieben, entweder in Oberitalien oder in Bayern;" cf. Bischoff, *Die südostdeutschen Schreibschulen*, 241.
[99]   Barré, *Les Homéliaires Carolingiens*, 8; Heer, *Ein Karolingischer Missions-Katechismus*, 55.
[100]   Cf. Bouhot, 'Explications du rituel baptismal', 296.
[101]   Cf. Kilger, 'Die Taufvorbereitung in der frühmittelalterlichen Benediktinermission'; Kretschmar, 'Die Geschichte des Taufgottesdienstes', 309 and (also for the following) Sullivan, 'Carolingian Missionary Theories'.

magne, often was coupled with the use of forceful methods; by the employment of ruthless constraint, large masses of pagans were left no other choice but accept the new religion. It is obvious that in such circumstances there was no room for an appropriate pre-baptismal instruction. They were not allowed to get acquainted with the essentials of Christian faith in a gradual teaching process.[102]

In these trying times, the Anglo-Saxon scholar Alcuin (c. 735-804) requested Charlemagne to meet this severe inadequacy. In 796, after the victory over the Avars, he demanded from the king a sensible missionary policy so as to prevent the Christianization of the Avars from resulting in disaster. In his letter to the king, Alcuin explicitly refers to a writing of Augustine, called De Catechizandis Rudibus. The adjective "rudis", in fact, refers to a newly converted pagan before his admission to the stage of being a catechumen. Although in the age of Augustine a catechumen received a more extensive pre-baptismal instruction, the church father's treatise is focussed upon this initial catechetical activity only. Alcuin, however, was concerned with the whole period of pre-baptismal teaching. His instruction, which has the immortality of the soul and its dependence on the deeds in life upon earth as its central topic, did not correspond with the substance of Augustine's manual either. His reference to the writing of the authoritative Augustine seems first of all intended to provide a safeguard for his recommendation to Charlemagne.[103]

This rapid survey allows us to determine the position of the cycle of six catechetical instructions of our Ratio de cathecizandis Rudibus in their historical context. The title is reminiscent of Augustine's manual, referred to by Alcuin, and seems to indicate that the topics treated in the work ought to be taught to pagans before their baptism. In Heer's opinion, the monk who wrote this manual about 800 made use of Augustine's work in his first catechetical instruction only. In his selection of these materials, he evidently was influenced by Alcuin's letter.[104] This first instruction deals with the transitoriness of earthly goods and the eternal value of heavenly securities. The only way to save one's soul is to give up the temporal reward to gain eternal life. The second catechesis, which will be discussed below, confronts the pagan with the Decalogue as a means by which he is in a position to reach glory and happiness. Next, the third instruction opposes the idol cult, while the fourth, fifth and sixth addresses focus the attention on the devotion to the true God. What is striking in all six catecheses is that next to nothing is said about the specific Christian doctrine.

---

[102] Cf. Fisher, *Christian Initiation*, 60.

[103] Bouhot, 'Alcuin', 230; Longère, *La Prédication Médiévale*, 52.
    This letter of Alcuin underlies the later exposition of pre-baptismal instruction, the *Ordo de cathecizandis rudibus vel quid sint singula quae geruntur in sacramento baptismatis*, composed in the beginning of the ninth century, of which the authentic version is preserved in Rouen; cf. Bouhot, 'Explications du rituel baptismal', 283-85 and for a detailed description of the different recensions of the *Ordo de cathecizandis rudibus*, see Bouhot, 'Alcuin', 194-200).

[104] Heer, *Ein Karolingischer Missions-Katechismus*, 36.

The second instruction in this cycle runs as follows[105]:

De decem praeceptis legis.
Si ergo perfecte christianus esse desideras, magnas ignorantiae et infidelitatis poteris
euadere tenebras. Nam si diuinae legis praecepta seruare potueris, recte christianus eris.
Quae si responderit obseruare posse, dices ei: Bene quidem promittis, sed opus est, ut
teneas promissionem tuam, quam deus, qui ubique praesens est audit. uide ergo ut
custodias quod auditurus es: Deus omnipotens qui nos ad imaginem et similitudinem
suam fecit, ipse dedit nobis legem, ut sciamus, quemadmodum uiuere et deum colere
debemus. Sic ergo ait per Moysen sanctum famulum suum:
Idola non coles. non homicidium facies. non moechaberis. falsum testimonium non dicis.
non facies furtum. non praecantabis. non auguriabis non ad montes. non ad arbores. non
ad fontes. non ad flumina. non ad angulos sacrificia facies. non in ullo alio loco, nisi ad
sanctam ecclesiam sacrificium tuum defer, ut ibi pro te serui dei ác pro omnibus tuis qui
christiani esse uoluerint, deo soli sacrificium offeras, et pro praesenti ac pro aeterna tua
salute dei clementiam imploras *(sic)*.
Honora patrem tuum. et matrem tuam. Diliges dominum deum tuum ex toto corde tuo.
et ex omni memoria tua. et ex omni mente tua. et amplius quam uel temetipsum. Quia
si deum ex intimo corde dilexeris, tunc etiam temetipsum recte diligis, quia propter istam
transitoriam. sed et propter aeternam uitam et salutem tuam, et deum et temetipsum
debes diligere. Deinde diliges proximum tuum sicut temetipsum. et quod tibi non uis
fieri, alio ne facias. Et bonum quodcumque tibi esse uolueris, nemini inuideas.
Ista sunt decem praecepta legis dei, quae omnes homines haec obseruantes ad tantam
gloriam ad tantamque beatitudinem et ad tantam perducunt beatitudinem, quae nec
carnalibus oculis quis ualet uidere, nec auris carnalis audire, nulla umquam ualet edissere
(sic) lingua, quam magna et qualia sunt, quae praeparauit deus his qui diligunt eum.
Unde cum summo studio cum magnamque *(sic)* diligenti laborare debes, ut haec
praecepta custodias et ut deo propitiante ualeas tanta bona mereri. Quod ipse non solum
tibi, sed et omnibus recte eum colentibus et in eum recte credentibus paratus est dare.
Deus omnipotens qui uiuit et regnat in saecula[106].

---

[105] Heer, *Ein Karolingischer Missions-Katechismus*, 80-82.
[106] *About the ten commandments of the law.*
If you wish to be perfectly Christian, you can escape the big darkness of ignorance and disloyalty. For
if you can keep the commandments of the divine law, you are properly Christian. And if someone
answers that he can keep these, you will say to him: "It is fine, indeed, that you promise but it is
necessary that you keep your promise which God, who is present everywhere, hears." See, then, to it
that you hold what you are going to hear: the almighty God himself who made us "in his image and after
his likeness" *(Gen 1:26)*, gave us the law so that we might know in what way we should live and
worship God. Thus he spoke by means of his holy servant Moses: you shall not worship idols, you shall
not kill, you shall not commit adultery, you shall not bear false witness, you shall not steal, you shall
not work magic, you shall not foretell events, not from mountains, not from trees, not from fountains,
not from rivers. You will not make sacrifices at remote corners, not to any other place you will move
your sacrifice unless to the holy church so that you, servants *(plur.!)* of God, may offer a sacrifice to
the only God there for you and for all those of yours who are willing to be Christians, and beseech the
mercy of God for your present welfare and eternal salvation. Honour your father and mother. You shall
love the Lord your God with all your heart, and with all your recollection and with all your mind. And
(this) more than yourself. Because if you have loved God from the very depth of your heart, then you
also love yourself properly, because, on account of this transitory life but also on account of eternal life
and your salvation, you should love both God and yourself. Next: you shall love your neighbour as

The subdivision of the sermon, as presented above, is ours. Subsequent to the list of precepts reproducing five of the Ten Commandments ("Idola non coles. non homicidium facies. non moechaberis. falsum testimonium non dicis. non facies furtum."), the presentation of the Law of Moses is continued with admonitions, warnings against superstitious practices such as engaging in incantations, auguries and idolatrous sacrifices ("non praecantabis. non auguriabis non ad montes. ... / / ... et pro praesenti ac pro aeterna tua salute dei clementiam imploras").[107] The only place where sacrifices are to be offered and the one God is to be worshipped is the church. The conversion of the pagan people from their gods in the Carolingian time apparently was not an easy task. Pagan beliefs obviously were so firmly entrenched in traditional customs that they were difficult to counter. Criticism of idolatry is found not only here but recurs preeminently in the third catechesis.

After its digression on the acts of offering and devotion in accordance with the new faith, the catechesis turns back to the Decalogue in stating the Commandment of honouring one's parents. Finally, the exhortation is concluded with the double love commandment and the negative form of the Golden Rule. It should be noticed, however, that the commandment to love God is not yoked with loving one's neighbour here but is interrupted by a summons to love God more than oneself. This moral principle is regarded as being the best guarantee to secure man's own happiness in the mortal world and in eternal life. In spite of the peculiar wording of this passage, the author of this catechesis probably found the double love commandment (love of God, love of neighbour) in juxtaposition in his source. He himself might have inserted the portion about self-love since the subject of the worthlessness of earthly life and valuableness of eternal life was prominent in the first catechesis as well.

It is hard to know, however, whether the author of the second catechesis arranged the Decalogue, the double love commandment, and the negative form of the Golden Rule in their extant form or whether this collocation represents a tradition in which these elements were already combined. Because the same elements are attached to the Way of Life in the Doctrina, one is inclined to conclude that their composition is related to a version of the Two Ways. There are, however, some noticeable discrepancies between the second catechesis and the Doctrina. In spite of its abbreviated version of the Decalogue and its expansion

---

yourself, and what you don't want to happen to you, do not do to another. And don't begrudge anybody the good which you want to be yours. These are the ten commandments of the law of God which bring all people who keep these to such a great glory and to such a great bliss and to such great bliss – which nobody is able to see with carnal eyes, nor a carnal ear can hear, nor a tongue is able to utter ever – as the quantity and quality are of those things "which God has prepared for those who love him" *(1 Cor 2:9).* Therefore you must work with sheer hard work and with utmost care that you may observe these commandments and that you, while God is favourably disposed (toward you), may be able to deserve such great goods. And he himself is determined to give this not only to you but to all who worship him correctly and believe in him properly, he, the almighty God who lives and reigns for ever.

[107] For the following, see Heer, *Ein Karolingischer Missions-Katechismus*, 18-22 and Sullivan, 'Carolingian Missionary Theories', 284-85.

with additional elements, the catechesis is entitled "About the Ten Command-ments of the law (De decem praeceptis legis)", a designation that recurs after the last clause concerning the Golden Rule in this arrangement ("Ista sunt decem praecepta legis dei..."). Moreover, while the double love commandment and the Golden Rule are explained in the Doctrina with a review of the commandments of the second table of the Decalogue, they are not considered as a summary here, but are part of the Ten Commandments themselves.

Nevertheless, there are two reasons for believing that the combination of the Decalogue, the double love commandment, and the negative form of the Golden Rule represents a tradition which is related to the Two Ways source. Firstly, the same three elements are also found in *RM* 3, *RB* 4 and the Fifteenth sermon of Ps.-Boniface, i.e. in materials which are closely akin to a Two Ways manual in other respects as well. Secondly, within the short scope of this second catechesis, the three items occur in a setting of pre-baptismal teaching. In addition to the witnesses mentioned in the first part of this chapter, it is again the monastic Rules and the sermon of Ps.-Boniface which show the persistence of the Two Ways tradition in the Mediaeval West in baptismal instruction. This instruction was not only deliv-ered to those who were initiated into the new religion but was continued after baptism as well. One may therefore assume that behind the presence of the Decalo-gue, the double love commandment and the negative form of the Golden Rule in the second catechesis of the Ratio, there stands the same ancient Two Ways manual or a related tradition.

The evidence surveyed here shows that the above-mentioned Merovingian and Carolingian documents in their own order and in their own way reproduce features of a Two Ways tradition. It is not our contention, however, to argue that the above materials are to be considered as a direct derivation of the Two Ways manual. What is of importance is that they prove each time the influence of a tradition which is at least closely related to the Two Ways. Therefore the conclusion is inescapable that the original Two Ways manual, known in Judaism in the pre-Christian era, not only survived in two mediaeval manuscripts, the *Monacensis 6264* and the *Mellicensis 597,* but somehow also served as a model for basic instruction of neophytes and Christian believers in the Merovingian and Carol-ingian periods.

Chapter Four

A Reconstruction of the Two Ways

In the previous chapters, we have seen that Did 1-6 and Barn. 18-20 are independent witnesses to a prior Two Ways document. In fact, it appeared that a number of other early Christian writings also attest to a separate circulation of a form of the Two Ways, closely related to Did 1-6 but without the Christian materials in 1:3b-2:1 and 6:2-3. It was further observed that, among the extant Two Ways witnesses, the earliest form of this ethical catechesis is best represented by the Doctrina Apostolorum. This is also the form of the Two Ways doctrine which can be found reflected in Merovingian and Carolingian documents. The recension of the Doctrina Apostolorum contains no trace of Christian interpolation and is nearest both in literary framework and general line of development to the Qumran teaching in 1QS 3:13-4:26. In certain respects, the document thus exhibits the oldest preserved witness to the Jewish Two Ways tradition.

The objective of the following pages is, primarily, to render the full text of the Doctrina as it was published in a separate appendix to the Didache edition of W. Rordorf and A. Tuilier[1] (pp. 114-16). Next, we will briefly outline the specific features of this document in comparison to the Two Ways version of the Didache (pp. 117-20). Notwithstanding its traditional character, however, the Doctrina Apostolorum is less reliable as far as the precise wording is concerned. Indeed, although it shows clear traits of being a Jewish arrangement of moral teaching, it does not, as noted in Chap. 2, present a verbatim translation of its Greek source. The Doctrina is not simply the archetypical source of Did 1-6 translated into Latin. It is, rather, another version in Latin translation of what must have been the Greek source for Did 1-6. The primary purpose, then, of the second half of this chapter is to present a hypothetical reconstruction of the original Greek text of the composition behind the Doctrina, the Didache and Barnabas, although – as was observed above[2] – the latter does not appear to have been acquainted with the source shared by the Didache and the Doctrina. Apart from the above-mentioned Christian additions in Did 1:3b-2:1, Did 6:2-3, and some other divergences, the reconstructed text, displayed in the second section, will be very similar to the extant version in the Didache. An English translation will follow this hypothetical Greek manual (pp. 128-30), while a final subdivision will discuss some points of the Greek reconstruction, which have not or only partly been dealt with in modern editions of the Didache (pp. 131-39).

---

[1] Rordorf-Tuilier, *La Doctrine des douze Apôtres*, 207-10.
[2] See above, Chap. 2, pp. 74-80.

The Doctrina Apostolorum

The Doctrina Apostolorum has survived in two mediaeval manuscripts, the *Monacensis lat. 6264* (fol. 102vo-103vo) and the *Mellicensis 597* (fol. 115vo).[3] Both documents exhibit interesting similarities in terms of text and sequence and, in fact, are to be classified among the witnesses to an ancient Ps.-Bedan homiliary.[4] Each one contains a collection of homilies to the lections read on particular days of the liturgical year. Another important common feature of the manuscripts is their preservation of a copy of a sermon assigned to St. Boniface, preceding the rendering of the Doctrina Apostolorum. Interestingly, this homily, serving as an admonition for baptized Christians, shows important affinities with the subsequent Doctrina in style, content, and structure. In Chapter 3, we have seen that for someone to whom the pseudonym of St. Boniface was ascribed, the Two Ways somehow functioned as a textbook in his catechetical teaching. For the present, some notes on the modern history of the two manuscripts with respect to the Doctrina Apostolorum may suffice.

The *Monacensis* (in accordance with its former designation abbreviated as F) presents the complete text of the Latin version, paralleling (in general) Did 1:1-3a. 2:2-6:1. The *Mellicensis* (M) offers an incomplete text and goes as far as Doctr. 2:6.[5] The editing of the latter manuscript has gone through a complicated history.[6] Having been published as early as 1723 by B. Pez,[7] it fell back into oblivion. After the Didache had been edited by Bryennios, O. von Gebhardt was one of the first scholars to call attention to the significance of this fragment; however, since he could not trace the original manuscript, he reedited it in 1884 according to the edition of Pez.[8] Whereas the manuscript was considered lost, it was F.X. Funk who recovered it in the abbey of Melk. In 1886, he presented a description of its

---

[3] The *Mellicensis* offers the title "Doctrina Apostolorum," whereas the *Monacensis* has "De Doctrina Apostolorum," and it is difficult to decide which heading is original. It is possible, however, that the titles of the preceding texts in the *Monacensis* has incited the copyist of this manuscript to add the preposition "de" in this place as well; cf. fol. 99ro: "Omelia s. Augustini de alleluja;" 100ro: "De resurrectione fidelium;" ibid.: "Omelia de fide;" 102vo: "Incipit ... sancti Bonifatii ep. de abrenuntiatione in baptismate;" see Wohleb, *Die lateinische Übersetzung*, 5-6 and 6, n. 1.

[4] On these mss. and the homiliary, see above, Chap. 3, pp. 95-97.

[5] Above, it has been specified that the *Monacensis* stems from the eleventh century, is found in the Staatsbibliothek at Munich, and was first published by Joseph Schlecht in 1900. The *Mellicensis*, on the other hand, might stem from the ninth century and is kept in the Stiftsbibliothek at Melk, Austria (see Chap. 3, p. 95).

[6] For our account of the fate the Two Ways fragment in this manuscript, cf. Audet, *La Didachè*, 9-10 and, especially, Niederwimmer, 'Doctrina Apostolorum (Cod. Mellic. 597)', 266-67.

[7] *Thesaurus anecdotorum novissimus* 4 (1723), pars 2, col. 5-8.

[8] 'Ein übersehenes Fragment der Διδαχή in alter lateinischer Übersetzung'. He published this fragment as an appendix to A. von Harnack's edition and comprehensive commentary of the Didache (*Die Lehre der zwölf Apostel*, 275-86).

content,[9] and in 1887 he published it.[10] The versions of the Latin *Two Ways* in the *Monacensis* and the *Mellicensis* show only a few (insignificant) divergencies; therefore both versions must surely go back to a common archetype.

THE TEXT OF THE DOCTRINA APOSTOLORUM

A recension of the Doctrina Apostolorum, as represented in the *Monacensis* and the *Mellicensis*, was given by H. Lietzmann. Below we will render the more recent edition with apparatus by Rordorf-Tuilier.[11] The verse numbers in the text that follows refer to the standard chapter and verse divisions for the Didache.

	De Doctrina Apostolorum	1
(1:1)	Viae duae sunt in saeculo, uitae et mortis, lucis et tenebrarum; in his constituti	2
	sunt angeli duo, unus aequitatis, alter iniquitatis; distantia autem magna est	3
	duarum uiarum.	4
(1:2)	Via ergo uitae haec est : primo diliges deum aeternum qui te fecit, secundo	5
	proximum tuum ut te ipsum; omne autem, quod tibi fieri non uis, alii ne	6
	feceris.	7
(1:3a)	Interpretatio autem horum uerborum haec est:	8

In apparatu: F = Ms. Monacensis lat. 6264
                F ^{1}, F ^{2} = corrections, to be attributed to a secondary, third hand
                M = Ms. Mellicensis 597
                Schlecht = J. Schlecht, *Doctrina XII apostolorum. Die Apostellehre in der Liturgie der katholischen Kirche*, Freiburg i. B. (1901) 101-104.

Ceterae abbreviationes: *a sec. m.* = a secunda manu; *ac* = ante corruptionem; *add.* = additus, addidit, addiderunt; *des.* = desinit; *edd.* = editores; *exp.* = expunxit; *om.* = omisit, omiserunt; *pc* = post correctionem; *ras.* = rasura; *sup.l.* = supra lineam; *transp.* = transposuit; *ut uid.* = ut uidetur.

Titulus : De *ante* Doctrina *om.* M || 5: deum F (*add. sup. l.*) M *om.* M^{ac} || 6: fieri *post* non uis *transp.* M || alii (*secundum* i *factum ex* o *a sec. m.*) F (*secundum* i *factum ex* o) M : alio F^{ac}M^{ac} || ne M : non F ||8: Interpretatio — est (*in ras. a sec. m.*) FM

---

[9]   Cf. Funk, 'Zur alten lateinischen Übersetzung'.
In 1898 Schlecht has studied this fragment in Melk (cf. *Doctrina XII apostolorum* [1901] 43, n. 2) and as a result was able to insert in his edition (pp.16-17) a synopsis of the *Monacensis* and the *Mellicensis*.
[10]   *Doctrina duodecim apostolorum*, LXIII-LXVII and 102-104.
The last edition of this fragment in the *Mellicensis* can be found in Niederwimmer, 'Doctrina Apostolorum (Cod. Mellic. 597)', 270-71.
[11]   *La Doctrine des douze Apôtres*, 207-210. We gratefully acknowledge the kind permission of the editors to use the materials from the Sources Chrétiennes Series.

(2:2)	Non moechaberis, non homicidium facies, non falsum testimonium dices,	1
	non puerum uiolabis, non fornicaberis, non magica facies, non medicamenta	2
	mala facies, non occides filium in abortum nec natum succides, non con-	3
	cupisces quicquam de re proximi tui.	4
(2:3)	Non periurabis, non male loqueris, non eris memor malorum factorum.	5
(2:4)	Nec eris duplex in consilium dandum, neque bilinguis, tendiculum enim	6
	mortis est lingua.	7
(2:5)	Non erit uerbum tuum uacuum nec mendax.	8
(2:6)	Non eris cupidus nec auarus nec rapax nec adulator nec contentiosus nec	9
	malemoris. Non accipies consilium malum aduersus proximum tuum.	10
(2:7)	Neminem hominum oderis, quosdam amabis super animam tuam.	11
(3:1)	Fili, fuge ab homine malo et homine simulatore.	12
(3:2)	Noli fieri iracundus, quia iracundia ducit ad homicidium, nec appetens eris	13
	malitiae nec animosus, de his enim omnibus irae nascuntur.	14
(3:4)	Noli esse mathematicus neque delustrator, quae res ducunt ad uanam super-	15
	stitionem; nec uelis ea uidere nec audire.	16
(3:5)	Noli fieri mendax, quia mendacium ducit ad furtum; neque amator pecuniae,	17
	nec uanus, de his enim omnibus furta nascuntur.	18
(3:6)	Noli fieri murmuriosus, quia ducit ad maledictionem. Noli fieri audax nec	19
	male sapiens, de his enim omnibus maledictiones nascuntur.	20
(3:7)	Esto autem mansuetus, quia mansueti possidebunt sanctam terram.	21
(3:8)	Esto patiens et tui negotii, bonus et tremens omnia uerba quae audis.	22
(3:9)	Non altabis te nec honorabis te apud homines nec dabis animae tuae super-	23
	biam, non iunges te animo cum altioribus, sed cum iustis humilibusque	24
	conuersaberis.	25
(3:10)	Quae tibi contraria contingunt, pro bonis excipies, sciens nihil sine deo fieri.	26
(4:1)	Qui loquitur tibi uerbum domini dei, memineris die ac nocte, reuereberis eum	27
	quasi dominum ; unde enim dominica procedunt, ibi et dominus est.	28
(4:2)	Require autem facies sanctorum, ut te reficias uerbis illorum.	29
(4:3)	Non facies dissensiones, pacifica litigantes, iudica iuste, sciens quod tu	30
	iudicaberis. Non deprimes quemquam in casu suo.	31
(4:4)	Nec dubitabis, uerum erit an non erit.	32
(4:5)	Noli esse ad accipiendum extendens manum et ad reddendum subtrahens.	33
(4:6)	Si habes per manus tuas redemptionem peccatorum.	34

2: uiolabis Schlecht : uiolaberis F uiolaueris M ‖ fornicaberis F : fornicaueris M
magica F : mag M ‖ 3: abortum M : auortum F ‖ 4: quicquam F : quidquam M ‖ 5: periurabis
M : peiurabis F ‖ 6: Nec F : non M ‖ 8: uacuum F uacu]u[m M^{pc} : uacum M^{ac} ‖ 9: ad]u[lator
(u *a sec. m. sup.l.*) F : adolator FM ‖ contentiosus F : conten M ‖ *post* conten *des.* M ‖ 10:
malemoris F^{pc} : male moris F^{ac} ‖ 11: oderis (*ras. inter* d *et* e) F : odieris (*ut uid.*) F^{ac} ‖ 12:
simulatore (ulatore *in ras. a sec. m.*) F : simili illi (*ut uid.*) F^{ac} ‖ 14: irae *edd.* : ire F ‖ 15:
delustrator F : delusor *glossa sup. l.* F ^{2} ‖ 19: murmuriosus F^{ac} : murmurosus (i *exp. a sec.
m.*) F ‖ 23: altabis (i *eras. inter* t *et* a) F : altiabis F^{ac}

(4:7)   Non dubitabis dare nec dans murmuraueris, sciens, quis sit huius mercedis   1
         bonus redditor.   2
(4:8)   Non auertes te ab egente, communicabis autem omnia cum fratribus tuis nec   3
         dices tua esse; si enim <in im> mortalibus socii sumus, quanto magis hinc   4
         initiantes esse debemus? Omnibus enim dominus dare uult de donis suis.   5
(4:9)   Non tolles manum tuam a filiis, sed a iuuentute docebis eos timorem domini.   6
(4:10)   Seruo tuo uel ancillae, qui in eundem sperant dominum, in ira tua non   7
         imperabis, timeat utrumque, dominum et te; non enim uenit, ut personas   8
         inuitaret, sed in quibus spiritum inuenit.   9
(4:11)   Vos autem serui subiecti dominis uestris estote tamquam formae dei cum   10
         pudore et tremore.   11
(4:12)   Oderis omnem affectationem et quod deo non placet, non facies.   12
(4:13)   Custodi ergo, fili, quae audisti neque appones illis contraria neque diminues. 13
(4:14)   Non accedas ad orationem cum conscientia mala. Haec est uia uitae.   14

(5:1)   Mortis autem uia est illi contraria. Primum nequam et maledictis plena: 15
         moechationes, homicidia, falsa testimonia, fornicationes, desideria mala,   16
         magicae, medicamenta iniqua, furta, uanae superstitiones, rapinae, affectatio- 17
         nes, fastidia, malitia, petulantia, cupiditas, impudica loquela, zelus, audacia, 18
         superbia, altitudo, uanitas.   19
(5:2)   Non timentes, persequentes bonos, odio habentes ueritatem, amantes menda-   20
         cium, non scientes mercedem ueritatis, non applicantes se bonis, non haben-   21
         tes iudicium iustum, peruigilantes non in bono, sed in malo, quorum longe   22
         est mansuetudo et superbia proxima, persequentes remuneratores, non   23
         miserantes pauperum, non dolentes pro dolente, non scientes genitorem   24
         suum, peremptores filiorum suorum, abortuantes, auertentes se a bonis   25
         operibus, deprimentes laborantem, aduocationes iustorum deuitantes. Abstine 26
         te, fili, ab istis omnibus.   27

(6:1)   Et uide, ne quis te ab hac doctrina auocet, et si minus, extra disciplinam   28
         doceberis.   29
(6:4)   Haec in consulendo si cottidie feceris, prope eris uiuo deo; quod si non   30
         feceris, longe eris a ueritate.   31
(6:5)   Haec omnia tibi in animo pone et non deciperis de spe tua, sed per haec   32
         sancta certamina peruenies ad coronam.   33
(6:6)   Per dominum Iesum Christum regnantem et dominantem cum deo patre et   34
         spiritu sancto in saecula saeculorum. Amen.   35

1: murmuraueris (u *in ras. a sec. m.*) F : murmuraberis *(ut uid.)* F[ac] || quis *(ut uid.)* F[ac] : quia
(a *in ras. a sec. m.*) F || mer]cedis F [2] *sup. l.* : mercis F || 3: auertes F : auert]a[s F [2] *sup. l.*
|| 4: <in im> mortalibus Schlecht : mortalibus F || 9: *post* spiritum *a sec. m. add.* humilem
F *sup. l.* || 20: deum *ante* Non *a sec. m. add.* F *sup. l.* || 25: abortuantes Schlecht : auortuantes
F || 32: dec]i[peris F [2] *sup. l.* : deceperis F

LITERARY FEATURES OF THE DOCTRINA APOSTOLORUM

In seeking to discover the outline of the Latin Two Ways without imposing one somewhat arbitrarily upon the material, one must look for pivotal phrases, crucial concepts, and thematically related materials. The literary disposition of the Doctrina is clearly recognizable since the variety of subunits is interpretatively framed within connecting formulas:

- *"Via ergo uitae haec est"* (1:2 / line 5): introduction to the definition of the Way of Life.
- *"Interpretatio autem horum uerborum haec est:"* (1:3a / line 8): interpretation of the preceding definition of the Way of Life and this clarification continues through 2:2-4:14a
- *"Haec est uia uitae"* (4:14b / line 14): conclusion of the specifics on the Way of Life.
- *"Mortis autem uia est illi contraria"* (5:1 / line 15): introduction to the catalogue of vices and sinners that makes up the Way of Death
- *"Et uide, ne quis te ab hac doctrina auocet, ..."* (6:1 / line 28): preface to the final conclusion.

These formulas are obvious indicators of the literary pattern and leave us with a basic division of the Doctrina which is rather remarkable. Although the set of ethical admonitions is organized according to the doctrine of the Two Ways, the Way of Life takes up a much bigger part than the Way of Death, which is described far more tersely. After the Way of Life is defined, its clarification continues through three chapters before reaching a conclusion (4:14b), whereas the Way of Death, consisting of little more than a list of sins followed by a list of evildoers, is not mentioned until chapter 5. In fact, rather than presenting the readers with an existential choice between the Way of Life and the Way of Death, the Doctrina seems to presume a high degree of concern about the former option.

The composition of the Way of Life consists of two divisions, the first of which confines itself to the definition of the Way of Life in Doctr. 1:2, and the second one of which, 'explaining' the definition of the Way of Life, takes up the specifics in the remainder of the unit (2:2-4:14). Within this 'explanation',[12] several clues as to further groupings occur, some of which appear to have circulated as independent units once. The first segment 2:2-7 contains a list of precepts which is clearly meant to illustrate, expand, and expound the second half of the Decalogue which was commonly seen as the moral essence of Judaism in the Second Temple period. The Doctrina lists adultery, murder, false witness, covetousness (theft is omitted here), and a similar listing of these Decalogue materials is found in the vices rendered in Doctr. 5:1. The authority of the second half of the Decalogue is evident to the extent that the text applies these traditional commandments to a new situation and appears to address these practices in gentile society. Many offences going beyond the prohibitions of the Decalogue are enumerated here within the Decalogue

---

[12] For the term 'explanation' as a translation of the word "interpretatio" in Doctr. 1:3a, see the Commentary below, p. 132.

commandments, namely pederasty, magic, sorcery, abortion, and exposure of infants. These are commonly found, however, in Jewish literature.[13]

The second part, specifying the Way of Life, concerns Doctr. 3:1-6. This section, which is not found in the Two Ways of Barnabas, stands out as a separate unit. It displays a carefully structured tradition of prohibitions which is wholly unlike the rest of the Two Ways. The unit appears to stem from an early independent source, originally containing a pattern of five single prohibitions, that came to be incorporated into the Two Ways. In the present Doctrina form, the prohibitions are four in number and have become twofold each.[14] The third part of the Way of Life is made up by Doctr. 3:7-10, a separate traditional unit which differs in form and focus from the former one. The admonitions offered here are very similar to the cautions in 1QS 4:2b-4a, although they have become more honed, refined, and polished in our passage.[15] The concept of humility, perceived as the opposite of self-exaltation and arrogance, is central to these verses. The last division of this larger section is Doctr. 4:1-14 which presents a series of admonitions governing social relationships. Closer examination will make clear that it exhibits the characteristic emphases of the rabbinic Derekh Erets literature. In chapter 5, the various literary units of the Way of Life will be discussed at some length in order to provide a basis for a better understanding of the life situation of the Two Ways, its historical development, and the identity of the groups handing on this doctrine.

One conclusion with respect to the Letter of Barnabas may be drawn at this point. In chapter 2, we have seen that both the Doctrina and the Didache, at variance with Barnabas, essentially offer the same account of the Ways of Life and Death. It was established that both Two Ways versions share a source that must have been derived from an earlier form of the Two Ways tradition than the one underlying the Two Ways tradition in the letter of Barnabas. The likelihood of the Doctr./Did priority is supported by the following consideration. The arrangement of the smaller separate units shows signs of argumentative structure and purpose. Apparently, the Two Ways source was not composed from merely scattered single sentences collected at random, but from various clusters of admonitions which might be viewed as redactional units. The organization of such passages as Doctr. 1:2; 2:2-7; 3:1-6; and 3:7-10, which are paralleled in Jewish tradition with respect to their themes and/or external form, stands in marked contrast to the arbitrary disregard for its order and content of the same materials in Barnabas. If this is correct, it is obvious even from this point of view that the sequence of the Two Ways in the Doctrina and the Didache is closer to its Jewish ancestor than the amorphous order in Barn. 18-20.

A comparison with the Didache, however, reveals that the Doctrina much more faithfully preserves the original substance of the Two Ways source than does the

---

[13] Rordorf-Tuilier, *La Doctrine des douze Apôtres*, 149-51 (nn.); Geffcken, *Zwei griechische Apologeten*, 87-88.

[14] See also below, Chap. 5 pp. 165-72.

[15] See also below, pp. 148-49.

Didache. The Doctrina has a number of features, lacking in the Didache, which look less like a reflection of Christian interest than a familiarity with peculiarities from the Jewish pre-history of the Two Ways tradition. The document has retained the vestiges from its earlier stage which become obvious as we see that the Didache has applied traditional Jewish materials to the new Christian setting in which it came to serve.

In Doctr. 1:1, the sharply dualistic wording stands out:

> There are two ways in the world, one of life, the other of death, one of light, the other of darkness; upon them two angels are appointed, one of righteousness, the other of iniquity, and between the two ways there is a great difference.

Although the options proposed remain human free choice in the Doctrina, the reference to hostile spiritual powers is a conspicuous characteristic and closely reflects the characterization of the two spirits in 1QS (cf. Chap. 5). The opening line of the Didache, on the other hand, simply announces that "there are two ways, one of life, the other of death, and between the two ways there is a great difference." The disappearance of the light-darkness dichotomy and the powerful angels in the latter introduction, which come down to a significant reduction of the cosmic dualism in the earlier Two Ways, might reflect a deliberate effort to ethicize and demythologize a type of traditional materials. This way the reader increasingly is confronted with his autonomous choice between the moral standards corresponding to the Way of Life and the Way of Death.

The Doctrina omits the evangelical section (Did 1:3b-2:1) and in perfect sequence passes on to the Decalogue commandments in 2:2-7. Its Way of Life begins with a definition in 1:2 (the double love commandment and the Golden Rule) and what follows is said to be the 'explanation' of this principle. Everything contained in chapters 2-4 is understood to be its exposition, and it is worth noting that in Judaism too such a comprehensive principle of moral conduct (love one's neighbour or the Golden Rule) is spelled out in further distinct commandments (see Chap. 5, pp. 156-62). The Didache, on the other hand, provides us with a new interpretation of the definition by inserting extraneous materials which seriously interferes with the structural pattern (Did 1:3b-2:1). In order to fit the traditional material into its new context, an editorial expansion was needed, qualifying the list of precepts that was based on the second half of the Decalogue as "the second commandment" (2:1a). We have seen that the Doctrina, but other extant Christian writings as well, show knowledge of the Two Ways without this material.

It is likely that the conclusion of the earlier form of the Jewish Two Ways is preserved more accurately in the Doctrina Apostolorum, although without the final doxology in 6:6:

> 1. See to it that no one leads you astray from this instruction, otherwise you will be taught apart from the (right) teaching. (*verses Did 6:2-3 are lacking*) 4. If you will act in this manner every day, you will be near to the living God; (but) if you will not act so, you will be far from the truth. 5. Put all this in your heart and you will not be deceived in your hope but through this holy contest you will reach the wreath.

The concluding remark of the Doctrina,[16] warning against false teachers and encouraging a stringent observance of the preceding precepts, undoubtedly supports the weight of the preceding instruction. The Didache, however, does not show this endeavour as it closes its Two Ways version with the following three verses which are largely omitted in the Doctrina (and in other Christian versions of the Two Ways as well):

> 1. See to it that no one leads you astray from this way of the doctrine, since [the person who would do so] teaches apart from God. 2. If you can bear the entire yoke of the Lord, you will be perfect, but if you cannot, do what you can. 3. As for food, bear what you can, but be very much on your guard against food offered to idols, for it is [related to] worship of dead gods.

The rendering of the Two Ways in the Didache definitely represents a concession. The unit's first part agrees with the Doctrina in cautioning against anyone who "leads you astray from this way of the doctrine," but it ends with the statement that the reader is not required to measure up to the preceding guidelines. This means we should treat 6:2-3 with great caution as being evidence of a concessional attitude. It is hard to believe that after it presents rigorous teaching in a comprehensive ethical blueprint and imposes a high standard for the Way of Life, the manual would, in the end, offer a concession as if suggesting that a partial compliance would suffice. As will be supported further in chapter 7, the passage in Did 6:2-3 must be an addition to the Jewish document, which can be explained as a response by Jewish-Christians to viewpoints expressed and considered by gentile believers.

In the Didache, the clause "Having said all this beforehand" (7:1) marks the preceding Two Ways section as a pre-baptismal catechesis, but it is far from clear that a similar setting belonged to the primary Jewish document. It is not by necessity implied that the text was originally used in early Judaism as a pre-baptismal instruction, or was intended for gentiles who wanted to associate themselves with Judaism. Indeed, we will see that the teaching, without any link to a functional context as provided in the Didache, was constructed, preserved, and handed on within pious Jewish circles which maintained highly refined ethical standards (Chap. 5).

A Reconstruction of the Greek Two Ways

In sum, the Doctrina is probably our best guide to the Jewish Two Ways edition that was most widely known in ancient times. While the document provides us with the most primitive form of the manual, the Didache and Barnabas represent independent adaptations of the original scheme. It must be admitted, however, that

---

[16] It is not likely, however, that the final doxology in 6:6 ("Through the lord Jesus Christ who reigns and rules with god the father and the holy spirit for ever and ever. Amen") belonged to the Doctrina proper.

many elements of the Two Ways represented in the Didache and Barnabas are more primitive than the corresponding ones in the Latin Doctrina. This becomes clear when the extent of verbal similarities is considered in the versions of the Didache and Barnabas and compared with the Doctrina. In spite of their great disparity in order, it is striking that the Didache and Barnabas versions share several minute agreements in wording which are absent from the Doctrina.[17] Thus, although the Doctrina gives us the best access to the tradition's earliest general form, it is by no means a pure witness to the pre-Christian text of the Two Ways. The most plausible explanation of this phenomenon is that the Latin translation was made some centuries after the original Greek source which it translates was written (cf. Chap. 3, pp. 83-84). Many accurate wordings may have been lost from the Greek original as a result of the process of textual transmission, or as a consequence of the translation activity itself.[18] Admittedly, we do not have a copy of the original source extant and our knowledge is at best indirect, being only deducible from the Doctrina, Didache, and Barnabas.

The next reconstruction of the source text is based on the following presuppositions:

1. The evidence of the texts in the Doctrina, Didache, and Barnabas is best explained if the Greek source were a written text, not just a body of oral tradition; otherwise it is difficult to explain such long stretches of verbatim and near-verbatim Didache-Doctrina and Didache-Barnabas agreements. Prior to reaching its fully developed form in the Greek source, however, the teaching probably underwent expansion as it gradually collected smaller blocks of material, some of which might have originally been oral in nature. In chapter 5, we will see that the formation of the GTW has been a longer and much more complex process than just a one stage redaction of simply random materials at the level of the final text.

2. The presentation of the materials in the version of the Greek source concurs with the order of the Latin translation. That is to say that, as was established in chapter 2, our reconstructed text follows the order of items shared by the Doctrina and the Didache (against Barnabas) while, on the other hand, lacking the christianized sections of 1:3b-2:1 and 6:2-3 (against the Didache). It is the (lost) document behind the Latin Doctrina which represents the earliest stage of the Two Ways tradition and not the version of the Didache.

3. While it is thus assumed that the Greek original equals the framework of the Latin Doctrina, we will generally rely on the Greek text of the Didache contained in the Jerusalem manuscript H[19] as a core witness for our textual reconstruction. Our confidence in the text-critical value of the Didache recension as

---

[17] See above, Chap. 2, n. 65.

[18] Doctr. 3:1 may serve as a marked example of this poor translation; cf. below, pp. 113-34. For another instance, see Doctr. 4:13 (below, p. 137).

[19] Although the Jerusalem manuscript H has to be regarded with caution, its fundamental integrity is accepted by Rordorf-Tuilier, *La Doctrine des douze Apôtres*, 102-110; Niederwimmer, *Die Didache*, 35-36; Schöllgen-(Geerlings), *Didache. Zwölf-Apostellehre*, 85-94. See also above, Chap. 1, pp. 21-24.

a means to correct the readings in the Doctrina is based on the assumption that both the Doctrina- and the Didache-forms of the Two Ways are dependent upon one common literary source. Of course, the Jewish document contained in the Didache did not survive without further (specifically Christian) editing; usually, the need for corrections of the text in the Didache will be accounted for in the subsequent commentary (pp. 131-39). At the same time, the extent of the similarities between the three documents can be studied in the apparatus at the bottom of the following pages. The likelihood that the Didache in many cases reflects the precise wording of the hypothetical Greek Two Ways is enhanced by its textual correspondence with Barnabas. Even though the two documents differ in the order of their various elements, the numerous minute verbal correspondences between the Didache and Barnabas[20] certify that the text offered below is close to the original version of the lost Two Ways teaching. Because it is impossible, however, to establish scientifically justifiable criteria to distinguish between the genuine source of the Two Ways, on the one hand, and interpolations, modifications and expansions of later redactors, on the other, our reconstruction of the text behind the Doctr./Did, of course, remains a hypothetical composition.

THE TEXT OF THE RECONSTRUCTED GREEK TWO WAYS

In the following pages, the wording of the hypothesized GTW that differs from the text of the Christian Didache as presented by the Jerusalem manuscript is *italicized*. Omissions are not indicated in the text but mentioned in the apparatus only.

---

[20] To mention just a few examples (but see also the verbal similarities in the versions of the Didache and Barnabas diverging from the Doctrina mentioned in Chap. 2, n. 65):

- οὐ λήψῃ πρόσωπον ἐλέγξαι ἐπὶ παραπτώμασιν (Did 4:3; ed. Rordorf-Tuilier, *La Doctrine des douze Apôtres*) – οὐ λήμψῃ πρόσωπον ἐλέγξαι τινὰ ἐπὶ παραπτώμασιν (Barn. 19:4c; ed. Prigent-Kraft, *Épître de Barnabé*)
- Οὐκ ἀρεῖς τὴν χεῖρά σου ἀπὸ τοῦ υἱοῦ σου ἢ ἀπὸ τῆς θυγατρός σου, ἀλλὰ ἀπὸ νεότητος διδάξεις τὸν φόβον τοῦ θεοῦ (Did 4:9) – Οὐ μὴ ἄρῃς τὴν χεῖρά σου ἀπὸ τοῦ υἱοῦ σου ἢ ἀπὸ τῆς θυγατρός σου, ἀλλὰ ἀπὸ νεότητος διδάξεις φόβον κυρίου (Barn. 19:5e)
- Οὐ κολληθήσεται ἡ ψυχή σου μετὰ ὑψηλῶν, ἀλλὰ μετὰ δικαίων καὶ ταπεινῶν ἀναστραφήσῃ. Τὰ συμβαίνοντά σοι ἐνεργήματα ὡς ἀγαθὰ προσδέξῃ, εἰδὼς ὅτι ἄτερ θεοῦ οὐδὲν γίνεται (Did 3:9b-10) – Οὐδὲ κολληθήσῃ ἐκ ψυχῆς σου μετὰ ὑψηλῶν, ἀλλὰ μετὰ δικαίων καὶ ταπεινῶν ἀναστραφήσῃ . Τὰ συμβαίνοντά σοι ἐνεργήματα ὡς ἀγαθὰ προσδέξῃ, εἰδὼς ὅτι ἄνευ θεοῦ οὐδὲν γίνεται (Barn. 19:6b-c)
- Οὐκ ἐπιτάξεις δούλῳ σου ἢ παιδίσκῃ, τοῖς ἐπὶ τὸν αὐτὸν θεὸν ἐλπίζουσιν, ἐν πικρίᾳ σου, μήποτε οὐ μὴ φοβηθήσονται τὸν ἐπ' ἀμφοτέροις θεόν· οὐ γὰρ ἔρχεται κατὰ πρόσωπον καλέσαι, ἀλλ' ἐφ' οὓς τὸ πνεῦμα ἡτοίμασεν (Did 4:10) – Οὐ μὴ ἐπιτάξῃς δούλῳ σου ἢ παιδίσκῃ ἐν πικρίᾳ, τοῖς ἐπὶ τὸν αὐτὸν θεὸν ἐλπίζουσιν, μή ποτε οὐ φοβηθῶσιν τὸν ἐπ' ἀμφοτέροις θεόν· ὅτι ἦλθεν οὐ κατὰ πρόσωπον καλέσαι, ἀλλ' ἐφ' οὓς τὸ πνεῦμα ἡτοίμασεν (Barn. 19:7c) etc.

(1:1) Ὁδοὶ δύο εἰσίν ἐν κόσμῳ, μία τῆς ζωῆς καὶ μία τοῦ θανάτου, μία τοῦ   1
φωτὸς καὶ μία τοῦ σκότους ἐφ' ἧς μὲν γάρ εἰσιν τεταγμένοι ἄγγελοι   2
δύο, ὁ μὲν τῆς δικαιοσύνης ὁ δὲ τῆς ἀνομίας· διαφορὰ δὲ πολλὴ μεταξὺ   3
τῶν δύο ὁδῶν.   4

(1:2) Ἡ μὲν οὖν ὁδὸς τῆς ζωῆς ἐστιν αὕτη· Πρῶτον ἀγαπήσεις τὸν θεὸν τὸν   5
ποιήσαντά σε, δεύτερον τὸν πλησίον σου ὡς σεαυτόν, καὶ πᾶν ὃ μὴ   6
θέλεις γίνεσθαί σοι καὶ σὺ ἄλλῳ οὐ ποιήσεις.   7

(1:3a) Τούτων δὲ τῶν λόγων ἡ ἑρμηνεία ἐστιν αὕτη·   8

(2:2) Οὐ φονεύσεις, οὐ μοιχεύσεις, οὐ παιδοφθορήσεις, οὐ πορνεύσεις, οὐ   9
κλέψεις, οὐ μαγεύσεις, οὐ φαρμακεύσεις, οὐ φονεύσεις τέκνον ἐν   10
φθορᾷ οὐδὲ γεννηθὲν ἀποκτενεῖς, οὐκ ἐπιθυμήσεις τὰ τοῦ πλησίον σου.   11

(2:3) Οὐκ ἐπιορκήσεις, οὐ ψευδομαρτυρήσεις, οὐ κακολογήσεις, οὐ   12
μνησικακήσεις.   13

(2:4) Οὐκ ἔσῃ διγνώμων οὐδὲ δίγλωσσος· παγὶς γὰρ θανάτου ἡ διγλωσσία.   14

(2:5) Οὐκ ἔσται ὁ λόγος σου κενός, οὐδὲ ψευδής.   15

In apparatu: H = Didache, secundum Hierosolymitanus 54;
                P = Didache, secundum Pap. Oxyrhynchus 1782;
                Ba = Barnabae Epistula, ed. Prigent-Kraft, *Épître de Barnabé*;
                Dc = Doctrina Apostolorum, ed. Rordorf-Tuilier, *La Doctrine des douze Apôtres*, 207-10;
                Comment. = Textual Commentary (below, on pp. 131-39).
N.B. Because of the haphazard and random occurrences of the Doctr. / Did materials in Barnabas, the references to the latter will be specified.
1: ἐν κόσμῳ in saeculo Dc (cf. 1QS 4:2); om. H (cf. infra, Comment.) ‖ 1-2: μία ... σκότους: μία τοῦ φωτὸς καὶ μία τοῦ σκότους: om. H; ἥ τε τοῦ φωτὸς καὶ ἡ τοῦ σκότους Ba 18:1; vitae et mortis, lucis et tenebrarum Dc ‖ 2-3: ἐφ' ἧς ... ἀνομίας: om. H; ἐφ' ἧς μὲν γάρ εἰσιν τεταγμένοι φωταγωγοὶ ἄγγελοι τοῦ θεοῦ, ἐφ' ἧς δὲ ἄγγελοι τοῦ σατανᾶ Ba 18:1; in his constituti sunt angeli duo, unus aequitatis, alter iniquitatis Dc (cf. 1QS 3:18-21) ‖ 3: μεταξὺ H; om. Ba 18:1; Dc ‖ 5: μὲν οὖν H; οὖν Ba 19:1; ergo Dc ‖ τὸν θεὸν H; om. Ba 19:2; deum aeternum Dc ‖ 5-6: τὸν ποιήσαντά σε H; Ba 19:2; qui te fecit Dc ‖ 6-7: δεύτερον ... ποιήσεις: om. Ba ‖ καὶ πᾶν... ποιήσεις: πάντα δὲ ὅσα ἐὰν θελήσῃς μὴ γίνεσθαί σοι, καὶ σὺ ἄλλῳ μὴ ποίει H; omne autem, quod tibi fieri non uis, alii ne feceris Dc ‖ 8: ἡ ἑρμηνεία: διδαχή H; interpretatio Dc; cf. supra p. 117 et infra, Chap. 5, pp. 161-62 ‖ (1:3b-2:1): om. Ba and Dc; interpolatio christiana in H (cf. supra, Chap. 2, pp. 57.70 et infra, Comment.) ‖ 9-11: Οὐ φονεύσεις ... τοῦ πλησίον σου: ordo et peccata secundum H ‖ 9: Οὐ φονεύσεις, οὐ μοιχεύσεις: non moechaberis, non homicidium facies Dc (cf. infra, Comment.) ‖ non falsum testimonium dices post non homicidium facies add. Dc ‖ οὐ κλέψεις om. Dc ‖ 11: πάλιν ante γεννηθὲν add. Ba 19:5 ‖ γεννηθὲν Ba 19:5; natum Dc; γεννηθέντα H ‖ ἀποκτενεῖς H; ἀνελεῖς Ba 19:5 ‖ τοῦ πλησίον σου Ba 19:6; proximi tui Dc ‖ 12-13: Οὐκ ἐπιορκήσεις... οὐ μνησικακήσεις ordo et peccata secundum H ‖ οὐ ψευδομαρτυρήσεις om. Dc ‖ οὐ μνησικακήσεις H; οὐ μὴ μνησικακήσεις Ba 19:4 ‖ 14: ἐστὶν post θανάτου add. Ba 19:7 ‖ διγλωσσία H; Ba 19:7; lingua Dc ‖ 15: om. Ba ‖ ψευδής, οὐ κενός, ἀλλὰ μεμεστωμένος πράξει H; uacuum nec mendax Doc (cf. infra, Comment.)

(2:6)   Οὐκ ἔσῃ πλεονέκτης οὐδὲ ἅρπαξ οὐδὲ ὑποκριτὴς οὐδὲ κακοήθης οὐδὲ   1
        ὑπερήφανος· οὐ λήψῃ βουλὴν πονηρὰν κατὰ τοῦ πλησίον σου.   2
(2:7)   Οὐ μισήσεις πάντα ἄνθρωπον, ἀλλὰ οὓς μὲν ἐλέγξεις, περὶ ὧν δὲ   3
        προσεύξῃ, οὓς δὲ ἀγαπήσεις ὑπὲρ τὴν ψυχήν σου.   4

(3:1)   Τέκνον μου, φεῦγε ἀπὸ παντὸς πονηροῦ καὶ ἀπὸ παντὸς ὁμοίου αὐτοῦ.   5
(3:2)   Μὴ γίνου ὀργίλος, ὁδηγεῖ γὰρ ἡ ὀργὴ πρὸς τὸν φόνον, μηδὲ ζηλωτὴς   6
        μηδὲ ἐριστικὸς μηδὲ θυμικός· ἐκ γὰρ τούτων ἁπάντων φόνοι   7
        γεννῶνται.   8
(3:3)   Τέκνον μου, μὴ γίνου ἐπιθυμητής, ὁδηγεῖ γὰρ ἡ ἐπιθυμία πρὸς τὴν   9
        πορνείαν, μηδὲ αἰσχρολόγος μηδὲ ὑψηλόφθαλμος· ἐκ γὰρ τούτων   10
        ἁπάντων μοιχεῖαι γεννῶνται.   11
(3:4)   Τέκνον μου, μὴ γίνου οἰωνοσκόπος, ἐπειδὴ ὁδηγεῖ εἰς τὴν   12
        εἰδωλολατρίαν, μηδὲ ἐπαοιδὸς μηδὲ μαθηματικὸς μηδὲ περικαθαίρων,   13
        μηδὲ θέλε αὐτὰ βλέπειν *μηδὲ ἀκούειν* ἐκ γὰρ τούτων ἁπάντων   14
        εἰδωλολατρία γεννᾶται.   15
(3:5)   τέκνον μου, μὴ γίνου ψεύστης, ἐπειδὴ ὁδηγεῖ τὸ ψεῦσμα εἰς τὴν   16
        κλοπήν, μηδὲ φιλάργυρος μηδὲ κενόδοξος· ἐκ γὰρ τούτων ἁπάντων   17
        κλοπαὶ γεννῶνται.   18
(3:6)   Τέκνον μου, μὴ γίνου γόγγυσος, ἐπειδὴ ὁδηγεῖ εἰς τὴν βλασφημίαν,   19
        μηδὲ αὐθάδης μηδὲ πονηρόφρων· ἐκ γὰρ τούτων ἁπάντων βλασφημίαι   20
        γεννῶνται.   21

(3:7)   Ἴσθι δὲ πραΰς, ἐπεὶ οἱ πραεῖς κληρονομήσουσι τὴν *ἁγίαν* γῆν.   22
(3:8)   Γίνου μακρόθυμος καὶ ἐλεήμων καὶ ἄκακος καὶ ἡσύχιος καὶ ἀγαθὸς καὶ 23
        τρέμων τοὺς λόγους διὰ παντός, οὓς ἤκουσας.   24

1: οὐκ ... ἅρπαξ H; non eris cupidus nec auarus nec rapax Dc ‖ 1-2: Οὐκ ... ὑπερήφανος
om. Ba ‖ οὐδὲ κακοήθης οὐδὲ ὑπερήφανος H; nec contentiosus nec malemoris Dc ‖ 2:
λήψῃ H; λημψῃ Ba 19:3 ‖ 3-4: ἀλλὰ ... προσεύξῃ H; *om.* Dc ‖ περὶ ὧν δὲ P; περὶ δὲ ὧν
H; οὕς δὲ H; quosdam Dc ‖ 3-4: Οὐ μισήσεις ... οὓς δὲ *om.* Ba ‖ (3:1-6) *om.* Ba ‖ 5: ἀπὸ
παντὸς πονηροῦ H; ἀπὸ παντὸς πράγματος πονηροῦ P; ab homine malo Dc ‖ καὶ ἀπὸ
παντὸς ὁμοίου αὐτοῦ H; καὶ ὁμοίου αὐτοῦ P; et homine simulatore Dc ‖ 6: ὁδηγεῖ γὰρ
ἡ ὀργὴ H; ἐπειδὴ ὁδηγεῖ ἡ ὀργὴ P; quia iracundia ducit Dc ‖ 6-7: μηδὲ ζηλωτὴς μηδὲ
ἐριστικὸς μηδὲ θυμικός H; nec appetens eris malitiae nec animosus Dc ‖ 7: φόνοι H; irae
Dc ‖ 9-11: *om.* Dc ‖ 12: Τέκνον μου H; *om.* Dc ‖ μὴ γίνου οἰωνοσκόπος H; noli esse
mathematicus neque delustrator Dc (3:4a) ‖ ἐπειδὴ H; quae res Dc ‖ 13: μηδὲ ἐπαοιδὸς
H; *om.* Dc ‖ μηδὲ μαθηματικὸς μηδὲ περικαθαίρων H (3:4b); *om.* Dc 3:4b *sed cf.* Dc 3:4a
‖ 14: μηδὲ ἀκούειν *om.* H; *conj.* Bihlmeyer, *Die Apostolischen Väter;* Audet, *La Didachè;*
Rordorf-Tuilier, *La Doctrine des douze Apôtres;* Wengst, *Didache (Apostellehre);*
Niederwimmer; 'Der Didachist und seine Quellen', 25; *cf.* nec audire Dc ‖ 14-15: ἐκ γὰρ
... γεννᾶται H; *om.* Dc ‖ 16: τέκνον μου H; *om.* Dc ‖ 19: τέκνον μου H; *om.* Dc ‖ 20: μηδὲ
H; noli fieri Dc ‖ 22: ἐπεὶ ... γῆν: *om.* Ba ‖ ἁγίαν *om.* H; sanctam Dc (*cf. etiam* Audet, *La
Didachè,* 132-33 *et infra,* Comment.) ‖ 23: Γίνου ... ἄκακος *om.* Ba (*de his verbis, vide
etiam infra,* Comment.) ‖ Γίνου μακρόθυμος H; Esto patiens et tui negotii Dc ‖ καὶ
ἐλεήμων καὶ ἄκακος H; *om.* Dc ‖ καὶ ἡσύχιος H; ἔσῃ ἡσύχιος Ba 19:4; *om.* Dc ‖ καὶ
ἀγαθὸς H; *om.* Ba; bonus Dc ‖ 23-24: καὶ τρέμων H; ἔσῃ τρέμων Ba 19:4; et tremens Dc
‖ 24: τοὺς λόγους διὰ παντός H; τοὺς λόγους Ba 19:4; omnia verba Dc ‖ οὓς ἤκουσας
H; Ba 19:4; quae audis Dc

(3:9) Οὐχ ὑψώσεις σεαυτὸν οὐδὲ δώσεις τῇ ψυχῇ σου θράσος. *Οὐ κολληθήσῃ*   1
       τῇ ψυχῇ σου μετὰ ὑψηλῶν, ἀλλὰ μετὰ δικαίων καὶ ταπεινῶν   2
       ἀναστραφήσῃ.   3
(3:10) Τὰ συμβαίνοντά σοι ἐνεργήματα ὡς ἀγαθὰ προσδέξῃ, εἰδὼς ὅτι ἄτερ   4
       θεοῦ οὐδὲν γίνεται.   5
(4:1) *Τὸν λαλοῦντά* σοι τὸν λόγον τοῦ θεοῦ μνησθήσῃ νυκτὸς καὶ ἡμέρας,   6
       τιμήσεις δὲ αὐτὸν ὡς κύριον· ὅθεν γὰρ ἡ κυριότης λαλεῖται, ἐκεῖ ὁ   7
       θεός ἐστιν.   8
(4:2) Ἐκζητήσεις δὲ καθ' ἡμέραν τὰ πρόσωπα τῶν ἁγίων, ἵνα ἐπαναπαῇς τοῖς   9
       λόγοις αὐτῶν.   10
(4:3) Οὐ *ποιήσεις* σχίσμα, εἰρηνεύσεις δὲ μαχομένους· κρινεῖς δικαίως, οὐ   11
       λήψῃ πρόσωπον ἐλέγξαι ἐπὶ παραπτώμασιν.   12
(4:4) Οὐ διψυχήσεις, πότερον ἔσται ἢ οὔ.   13
(4:5) Μὴ γίνου πρὸς μὲν τὸ λαβεῖν ἐκτείνων *τὴν χεῖρα,* πρὸς δὲ τὸ δοῦναι   14
       συσπῶν.   15
(4:6) Ἐὰν ἔχῃς διὰ τῶν χειρῶν σου, δώσεις λύτρωσιν ἁμαρτιῶν σου.   16
(4:7) Οὐ διστάσεις δοῦναι οὐδὲ διδοὺς γογγύσεις· γνώσῃ γὰρ τίς ἐστιν ὁ   17
       τοῦ μισθοῦ καλὸς ἀνταποδότης.   18

1: nec honorabis te apud homines *post par.* Οὐχ ὑψώσεις σεαυτὸν *add.* Dc = *fort.* Οὐκ
ἀρεῖς ἐπὶ σεαυτὸν δόξαν Ba 19:3? || οὐδὲ H; οὐ Ba 19:3; nec Dc || Οὐ H; Οὐδὲ Ba 19:6;
non Dc || 1-2: κολληθήσῃ τῇ ψυχῇ σου: κολληθήσεται ἡ ψυχή σου H; κολληθήσῃ ἐκ
ψυχῆς σου Ba 19:6; iunges te animo Dc; *vide etiam* Wohleb, *Die lateinische Übersetzung
der Didache,* 95 (*ad loc.*) || 4: ἄτερ H; ἄνευ Ba 19:6; sine Dc || 6: *incip.* Τέκνον μου H;
om. Dc et Ba 19:9 || Τὸν λαλοῦντά: Τοῦ λαλοῦντός H; πάντα τὸν λαλοῦντά Ba 19:9;
qui loquitur Dc || τοῦ θεου H; κυρίου Ba 19:9; domini dei Dc || μνησθήσῃ H; μνησθήσῃ
ἡμέραν κρίσεως Ba 19:10; memineris Dc || νυκτὸς καὶ ἡμέρας H; Ba 19:10; die ac nocte
Dc || 7-8: τιμήσεις ... ἐστιν *om.* Ba || 7: τιμήσεις δὲ H; reuerberis Dc || ἡ κυριότης
λαλεῖται H; dominica procedunt Dc || ἐκεῖ H; ibi et Dc || 7-8: ὁ θεός: κύριός H; dominus
Dc; *(sed vide etiam infra,* Comment.) || 9: Ἐκζητήσεις δὲ H; καὶ ἐκζητήσεις Ba 19:10;
require autem Dc || καθ' ἡμέραν H; καθ' ἑκάστην ἡμέραν Ba 19:10; *om.* Dc ||
ἐπαναπαῇς: H; te reficias Dc || 9-10: ἵνα ... αὐτῶν *om.* Ba || 11: ποιήσεις Ba 19:12; facies
Dc; ποθήσεις H || σχίσμα H; Ba 19:12; dissensiones Dc || δὲ *om.* Dc || συναγαγών *post*
μαχομένους *add.* Ba 19:12 || sciens quod tu iudicaberis *post par.* δικαίως *add.* Dc || 12:
λήψῃ H; λήμψῃ Ba 19:4 || 11-12: οὐ λήψῃ πρόσωπον ἐλέγξαι H; non deprimes
quemquam Dc || 12: τινὰ *post* ἐλέγξαι *add.* Ba 19:4 || παραπτώμασιν H; παραπτώματι
Ba 19:4; casu suo Dc. || 13: Οὐ διψυχήσεις H; Οὐ μὴ διψυχήσῃς Ba 19:5; nec dubitabis
Dc || πότερον ἔσται ἢ οὔ H; Ba 19:5; verum erit an non erit Dc || 14: τὴν χεῖρα: τὰς
χεῖρας H; Ba 19:9; manum Dc; *cf. etiam* Wengst, *Didache (Apostellehre),* ad loc. || 16:
δώσεις H; ἐργάσῃ εἰς Ba 19:10; *om.* Dc || λύτρωσιν H; λύτρον Ba 19:10; redemptionem
Dc || 17: γνώσῃ γὰρ H; γνώσῃ δὲ Ba 19:11; sciens Dc || ἐστιν H; *om.* Ba; sit Dc || ὁ Ba
19:11; ἡ H (ὁ *emend.* Bryennios)

(4:8) Οὐκ ἀποστραφήσῃ τὸν ἐνδεόμενον, συγκοινωνήσεις δὲ πάντα τῷ 1
ἀδελφῷ σου καὶ οὐκ ἐρεῖς ἴδια εἶναι· εἰ γὰρ ἐν τῷ ἀθανάτῳ κοινωνοί 2
ἐστε, πόσῳ μᾶλλον ἐν τοῖς θνητοῖς; *πᾶσι γὰρ θέλει δίδοσθαι ὁ κύριος* 3
ἐκ τῶν ἰδίων χαρισμάτων. 4

(4:9) Οὐκ ἀρεῖς τὴν χεῖρά σου ἀπὸ τοῦ υἱοῦ σου ἢ ἀπὸ τῆς θυγατρός σου, 5
ἀλλὰ ἀπὸ νεότητος διδάξεις *αὐτοὺς* τὸν φόβον τοῦ *κυρίου.* 6

(4:10) Οὐκ ἐπιτάξεις δούλῳ σου ἢ παιδίσκῃ, τοῖς ἐπὶ τὸν αὐτὸν θεὸν 7
ἐλπίζουσιν, ἐν πικρίᾳ σου, μήποτε οὐ μὴ φοβηθήσονται τὸν ἐπ᾽ 8
ἀμφοτέροις θεόν· οὐ γὰρ ἔρχεται κατὰ πρόσωπον καλέσαι, ἀλλ᾽ ἐφ᾽ οὓς 9
τὸ πνεῦμα ἡτοίμασεν. 10

(4:11) Ὑμεῖς δὲ οἱ δοῦλοι ὑποταγήσεσθε τοῖς κυρίοις ὑμῶν ὡς τύπῳ θεοῦ ἐν 11
αἰσχύνῃ καὶ φόβῳ. 12

(4:12) Μισήσεις πᾶσαν ὑπόκρισιν καὶ πᾶν ὃ μὴ ἀρεστὸν τῷ *θεῷ.* 13

(4:13) Οὐ μὴ ἐγκαταλίπῃς ἐντολὰς κυρίου, φυλάξεις δὲ ἃ παρέλαβες, μήτε 14
προστιθεὶς μήτε ἀφαιρῶν. 15

(4:14) Ἐξομολογήσῃ τὰ παραπτώματά σου καὶ οὐ προσελεύσῃ ἐπὶ προσευχήν 16
ἐν συνειδήσει πονηρᾷ. Αὕτη ἐστὶν ἡ ὁδὸς τῆς ζωῆς. 17

1: Οὐκ ... ἐνδεόμενον H; *om.* Ba ‖ συγκοινωνήσεις H; κοινωνήσεις Ba 19:8; communicabis Dc ‖ δὲ H; *om.* Ba; autem Dc ‖ πάντα H; ἐν πᾶσιν Ba; omnia Dc ‖ 1-2: τῷ ἀδελφῷ σου H; τῷ πλησίον σου Ba 19:8; fratribus tuis Dc ‖ 2: ἀθανάτῳ H; ἀφθάρτῳ Ba 19:8; mortalibus Dc ‖ 3: ἐστε H; Ba; sumus Dc ‖ ἐν τοῖς θνητοῖς H; ἐν τοῖς φθαρτοῖς Ba 19:8; hinc initiantes esse debemus Dc ‖ 3-4: πᾶσι γὰρ θέλει δίδοσθαι ὁ κύριος ἐκ τῶν ἰδίων χαρισμάτων *om.* H; Ba; omnibus enim dominus dare uult de donis suis Dc (*vide etiam infra,* Comment.)) ‖ 5: Οὐκ H; οὐ μὴ Ba 19:5; non Dc ‖ ἀρεῖς H; ἄρῃς Ba 19:5; tolles Dc ‖ ἀπὸ τοῦ υἱοῦ σου H; Ba 19:5; a filiis Dc ‖ ἢ ἀπὸ τῆς θυγατρός σου H; Ba 19:5; *om.* Dc ‖ 6: αὐτοὺς *om.* H; Ba; docebis eos Dc ‖ τὸν *om.* Ba ‖ κυρίου: θεοῦ H; κυρίου Ba 19:5 domini Dc; *cf. etiam* Audet, *La Didachè,* 133-34 ‖ 7: Οὐκ ἐπιτάξεις H; Οὐ μὴ ἐπιτάξῃς Ba 19:7; non imperabis Dc ‖ 8: ἐν πικρίᾳ σου H; ἐν πικρίᾳ Ba 19:7; in ira tua Dc ‖ 8: μήποτε οὐ μὴ φοβηθήσονται H; μή ποτε οὐ φοβηθῶσιν Ba 19:7; timeat Dc ‖ 8-9: τὸν ἐπ᾽ ἀμφοτέροις θεόν H; Ba 19:7; utrumque, dominum et te Dc ‖ 9: οὐ γὰρ ἔρχεται H; ὅτι ἦλθεν οὐ Ba 19:7; non enim uenit Dc ‖ κατὰ πρόσωπον H; Ba 19:7; personas Dc ‖ 9-10: ἀλλ᾽ ἐφ᾽ οὓς τὸ πνεῦμα ἡτοίμασεν H; Ba 19:7; sed in quibus spiritum inuenit Dc ‖ 11: Ὑμεῖς δὲ οἱ δοῦλοι H; *om.* Ba ‖ ὑποταγήσεσθε τοῖς κυρίοις ἡμῶν H (ὑμῶν *emend.* Bryennios); ὑποταγήσῃ κυρίοις Ba 19:7; subiecti dominis uestris estote Dc ‖ 13: πᾶσαν ὑπόκρισιν καὶ H; *om.* Ba 19:2; omnem affectationem et Dc ‖ πᾶν ὃ μὴ ἀρεστὸν τῷ κυρίῳ H; πᾶν ὃ οὐκ ἔστιν ἀρεστὸν τῷ θεῷ Ba 19:2; quod deo non placet Dc; *et add.* non facies Dc. ‖ 14: Οὐ μὴ ἐγκαταλίπῃς ἐντολὰς κυρίου H; Ba 19:2; *om.* Dc ‖ φυλάξεις H; Ba 19:11; custodi Dc ‖ δὲ H; ergo Dc; *om.* Ba ‖ fili *post* ergo *add.* Dc ‖ 14-15: μήτε προστιθεὶς μήτε ἀφαιρῶν H; Ba 19:11; neque appones illis contraria neque diminues Dc ‖ 16: Ἐν ἐκκλησίᾳ *ante* Ἐξομολογήσῃ *add.* H; *om.* Ba; Dc (*cf. infra,* Comment.) ‖ Ἐξομολογήσῃ ... καὶ *om.* Dc ‖ τὰ παραπτώματά H; ἐπὶ ἁμαρτίαις Ba 19:12 ‖ καὶ H; *om.* Ba 19:12 ‖ προσελεύσῃ H; προσήξεις Ba 19:12; accedas Dc ‖ σου *post* προσευχήν *add.* H; *om.* Ba; Dc ‖ 17: Αὕτη ... ζωῆς *om.* Ba

(5:1) Ἡ δὲ τοῦ θανάτου ὁδός ἐστιν αὕτη· Πρῶτον πάντων πονηρά ἐστι καὶ 1
κατάρας μεστή· φόνοι, μοιχεῖαι, ἐπιθυμίαι παράνομοι, πορνεῖαι, 2
κλοπαί, εἰδωλολατρίαι, μαγεῖαι, φαρμακίαι, ἁρπαγαί, ψευδομαρτυρίαι, 3
ὑποκρίσεις, διπλοκαρδία, δόλος, ὑπερηφανία, κακία, αὐθάδεια, 4
πλεονεξία, αἰσχρολογία, ζηλοτυπία, θρασύτης, ὕψος, ἀλαζονεία, 5
ἀφοβία θεοῦ· 6
(5:2) διῶκται ἀγαθῶν, μισοῦντες ἀλήθειαν, ἀγαπῶντες ψεῦδος, οὐ 7
γινώσκοντες μισθὸν δικαιοσύνης, οὐ κολλώμενοι ἀγαθῷ οὐδὲ κρίσει 8
δικαίᾳ, ἀγρυπνοῦντες οὐκ εἰς τὸ ἀγαθόν, ἀλλ᾿ εἰς τὸ πονηρόν· ὧν 9
μακρὰν πραΰτης καὶ ὑπομονή, μάταια ἀγαπῶντες, διώκοντες 10
ἀνταπόδομα, οὐκ ἐλεοῦντες πτωχόν, οὐ πονοῦντες ἐπὶ καταπονουμένῳ, 11
οὐ γινώσκοντες τὸν ποιήσαντα αὐτούς, φονεῖς τέκνων, φθορεῖς 12
πλάσματος θεοῦ, ἀποστρεφόμενοι τὸν ἐνδεόμενον, καταπονοῦντες τὸν 13
θλιβόμενον, πλουσίων παράκλητοι, πενήτων ἄνομοι κριταί, 14
πανθαμάρτητοι· ῥυσθείητε, τέκνα, ἀπὸ τούτων ἀπάντων. 15

1: Ἡ δὲ τοῦ θανάτου ὁδός H; Ἡ δὲ τοῦ μέλανος ὁδός Ba 20:1; Mortis autem uia Dc
‖ αὕτη H; om. Ba; illi contraria Dc ‖ Πρῶτον πάντων H; om. Ba; Primum Dc ‖ 1-2:
πονηρά ἐστι καὶ κατάρας μεστή H; σκολιὰ καὶ κατάρας μεστή Ba 20:1; nequam et
maledictis plena Dc ‖ 2-5: φόνοι ... ἀλαζονεία: *peccatorum ordo sec.* H ‖ 2: Ὅλως γάρ
ἐστιν ὁδὸς θανάτου αἰωνίου μετὰ τιμωρίας, ἐν ᾗ ἐστὶν τὰ ἀπολλύντα τὴν ψυχὴν
αὐτῶν *post* μεστή add. Ba 20:1 ‖ φόνοι, μοιχεῖαι H; *ordo verborum invert* Dc (*cf. infra,*
Comment. *ad 2:2*) ‖ ἐπιθυμίαι παράνομοι: ἐπιθυμίαι H; om. Ba; desideria mala Dc (*cf.
infra,* Comment.) ‖ 2-3: πορνεῖαι, κλοπαί H; om. Ba ‖ 3: εἰδωλολατρίαι H;
εἰδωλολατρεία Ba 20:1; om. Dc ‖ μαγεῖαι H; μαγεία Ba 20:1; magicae Dc ‖ φαρμακίαι
H; φαρμακεία Ba 20:1; medicamenta iniqua Dc ‖ ἁρπαγαί H; ἁρπαγή Ba 20:1; rapinae
Dc ‖ ψευδομαρτυρίαι H; om. Ba; falsa testimonia Dc ‖ 4: ὑποκρίσεις H; ὑπόκρισις Ba
20:1; affectationes Dc ‖ διπλοκαρδία H; Ba 20:1; om. Dc ‖ δόλος H; Ba 20:1; om. Dc ‖
5: αἰσχρολογία H; om. Ba; impudica loquela Dc; ζηλοτυπία H; om. Ba; zelus Dc ‖ ὕψος
H; ὕψος δυνάμεως Ba 20:1; altitudo Dc ‖ ἀλαζονεία H; om. Ba; uanitas Dc ‖ 6: ἀφοβία
θεοῦ Ba 20:1; om. H; non timentes Dc (F¹) 5:2; deum non timentes: Dc (F²); (*cf. infra,*
Comment. *et* Rordorf-Tuilier, *La Doctrine des douze Apôtres,* 167, n. 6) ‖ 7: διῶκται
ἀγαθῶν H; διῶκται τῶν ἀγαθῶν Ba 20:2; persequentes bonos Dc ‖ 8: μισθὸν
δικαιοσύνης H; Ba 20:2; mercedem ueritatis Dc ‖ ἀγαθῷ H; Ba; bonis Dc ‖ οὐδὲ κρίσει
H; οὐ κρίσει Ba 20:2; non habentes iudicium Dc ‖ 9: εἰς τὸ ἀγαθόν H; εἰς φόβον θεοῦ
Ba 20:2; in bono Dc ‖ εἰς τὸ πονηρόν H; ἐπὶ τὸ πονηρόν Ba 20:2; in malo Dc ‖ 10: καὶ
πόρρω *post* ὧν μακρὰν add. Ba 20:2 ‖ 10: μάταια ἀγαπῶντες H; *ordo verborum invert*
Ba 20:2; om. Dc ‖ 10-11: διώκοντες ἀνταπόδομα H; Ba 20:2; persequentes remuneratores
Dc ‖ 12-13: φθορεῖς πλάσματος θεοῦ H; Ba 20:2; abortuantes Dc ‖ 13: τὸν ἐνδεόμενον
H; Ba 20:2; a bonis operibus Dc ‖ 14: πλουσίων παράκλητοι H; Ba 20:2; aduocationes
iustorum deuitantes Dc ‖ πενήτων ἄνομοι κριταί H; Ba 20:2; om. Dc ‖ 15:
πανθαμάρτητοι H; πανταμάρτητοι Ba 20:2; om. Dc ‖ ῥυσθείητε ... ἀπάντων om. Ba
‖ 15: ῥυσθείητε τέκνα H; abstine te, fili: Dc

(6:1) Ὅρα, μή τίς σε πλανήσῃ ἀπὸ ταύτης τῆς διδαχῆς, ἐπεὶ παρεκτὸς *τῆς*   1
      διδαχῆς σε διδάσκει.   2

(6:4) *'Εὰν μὲν συμβουλεύων ταῦτα ποιῇς καθ' ἡμέραν, ἐγγὺς θεοῦ ζῶντος*   3
      ἔσει· ἐὰν δὲ μὴ ποιῇς, μακράν ἀπ' ἀληθείας ἔσει.   4

(6:5) *Ταῦτα πάντα εἰς τὸ πνεῦμα σου ἐνβάλλων οὐ πεσεῖ ἀπὸ τῆς ἐλπίδος*   5
      σου (ἀλλὰ διὰ τουτούς ἁγίους ἀγῶνας στέφανον λήψει).   6

1-6: *om.* Ba ‖ 1: Et *ante par.*Ὅρα *add.* Dc ‖ ἀπὸ ταύτης τῆς διδαχῆς: ἀπὸ ταύτης τῆς ὁδοῦ τῆς διδαχῆς H; ab hac doctrina Dc ‖ ἐπεὶ H; et si minus Dc ‖ 1-2: τῆς διδαχῆς: θεοῦ H; extra disciplinam Dc (*cf. infra*, Comment.) ‖ – (6:2-3) Εἰ μὲν γὰρ δύνασαι βαστάσαι ὅλον τὸν ζυγὸν τοῦ κυρίου, τέλειος ἔσῃ· εἰ δ᾽ οὐ δύνασαι, ὃ δύνῃ, τοῦτο ποίει. Περὶ δὲ τῆς βρώσεως, ὃ δύνασαι βάστασον· ἀπὸ δὲ τοῦ εἰδωλοθύτου λίαν πρόσεχε· λατρεία γάρ ἐστι θεῶν νεκρῶν H; *om.* Dc (*cf. supra, pp. 119-20 et infra*, Comment.; *vide etiam* Niederwimmer; 'Der Didachist und seine Quellen', 28, n. 21) – ‖ 3-6: 'Εὰν μὲν ... στέφανον λήψει: haec in consulendo si cottidie feceris, prope eris vivo deo; quod si non feceris, longe eris a veritate. Haec omnia tibi in animo pone et non deciperis de spe tua sed per haec sancta certamina pervenies ad coronam: Dc *sola; Versus 4 et 5 in textibus Graecis non exstant* ‖ 6: ἀλλὰ διὰ τουτούς ἁγίους ἀγῶνας στέφανον λήψει: *additio Christiana?* (*cf. infra*, Comment.) ‖ 6: *post* λήψει doxologia *non genuina* per dominum Iesum Christum regnantem et dominantem cum deo patre et spiritu sancto in saecula saeculorum. Amen *add.* Dc 6:6

THE ENGLISH TRANSLATION OF THE RECONSTRUCTED GREEK TWO WAYS

The following translation is based upon the work of A. Cody, O.S.B., 'The *Didache:* An English Translation.'[21]. The words in parentheses are not found in the Greek reconstruction but have been added to help the English reader understand the probable meaning of specific texts.

(1:1) There are two ways *in the world,* one of life, the other of death, *one of light, the other of darkness; upon them two angels are appointed, one of righteousness, the other of iniquity,* and between the two ways there is a great difference.

(1:2) Now the way of life is this: you shall love first God who created you, then your neighbour as yourself, and *do not do to another what you do not want to be done to you.*

(1:3) The *explanation* of these words is as follows:

(2:2) You shall not murder. You shall not commit adultery. You shall not corrupt children. You shall not fornicate. You shall not steal. You shall not practise magic. You shall not use the confections of a sorcerer. You shall not murder a child, whether by [procuring its] abortion or by killing it once it is born. You shall not covet what belongs to *your* neighbour.

---

[21] Jefford, *The Didache in Context*, 3-14; esp. 5-8.

(2:3)   You shall not swear falsely. You shall not bear false witness. You shall not speak evil of anyone. You shall not harbour resentment.

(2:4)   You shall not equivocate, either in what you think or what you say, for equivocation is a mortal snare.

(2:5)   Your word shall not be *empty or false.*

(2:6)   You shall not be given to greed, or swindling, or hypocrisy, or malice, or pride. You shall not plot evil against your neighbour.

(2:7)   You shall not hate anyone. Reprove some people, pray for others, and others you shall love more than yourself.

(3:1)   My child, flee from all evil and from everything like it.

(3:2)   Do not be an angry person, for anger leads to murder; nor should you be a zealot or quarrelsome or hot-tempered person, for all of these [traits of character] flow murderous acts.

(3:3)   My child, do not be a person given to passion, because passion leads to fornication; nor should you be given to obscene speech or to bold gazes, for from all these [actions] flow acts of adultery.

(3:4)   My child, do not practise soothsaying, because this leads to idolatry; nor should you be an enchanter, or an astrologer, or a person who performs purificatory rituals; you should not even want to see *or hear* such things, for from all these [activities] idolatry is spawned.

(3:5)   My child, do not be a liar, because lying leads to theft; nor should you be given to avarice or to vainglory, for from all of these [treats of character] theft is spawned.

(3:6)   My child, do not be a grumbler, because this leads to slander; nor should you be stubbornly willful or disposed to think evil of people, for from all these [attitudes] slanderous behaviour is spawned.

(3:7)   On the contrary, be meek, since those who are meek will inherit the *holy* land.

(3:8)   Be patient and merciful, without guile, tranquil and good, holding constantly in awe the words you have heard.

(3:9)   You shall not exalt yourself or let yourself be arrogant. *You shall* not *attach yourself mentally* to those who are highly placed but shall associate with those who are just and humble.

(3:10) Accept the experiences that come your way as good ones, knowing that nothing happens without God.

(4:1)   You shall be mindful day and night of the one who speaks to you the word of God. You shall honour him as the Lord, for at the source of discourse on lordship *God* is there.

(4:2)   You shall seek out the holy persons every day to find support in their words.

(4:3)   You shall not *cause* division; instead, you shall reconcile those who quarrel. You shall judge justly. You shall not show partiality in calling people to task for their faults.

(4:4)   You shall not show indecision [in determining] whether [something] shall be or shall not be.

(4:5)   Do not be the sort of person who holds *his hand* to receive, but draws it back when it comes to giving.

(4:6)   If you have [something] through the work of your hands, you shall give [something as] redemption of your sins.

(4:7)   You shall not hesitate to give, and when you give you shall not grumble, for you will know who the paymaster is who gives good wages.

(4:8)   You shall not turn away anyone who is in need; on the contrary, you shall hold everything in common with your brother, and you shall not say that anything is your own, for if you are partners in what is immortal, [should you not be so] all the more in things that perish? *For the Lord wants that one shall give to all from His own gracious gifts.*

(4:9)   You shall not be remiss in guiding your son or your daughter, but shall teach *them* reverence for the *Lord* from [the days of] their youth.

(4:10) You shall not show your harsh side when you give a command to your slave or your maid, those who hope in the same God, lest they stop revering the God who is over both [you and them]. For he comes not to call [people] according to their personal status but [to call] those for whom he has prepared the spirit.

(4:11) As for you who are slaves, with respect and reverence you shall be subject to your masters as replicas of God.

(4:12) You shall hate all hypocrisy and all that is not pleasing to *God*.

(4:13) You shall not abandon the commandments of the Lord but shall keep what you have received without adding or subtracting anything.

(4:14) You shall confess your faults and you shall not approach with a bad conscience to make a prayer. This is the way of life.

(5:1)   And the way of death is this: Above all it is evil and full of accursedness; [characteristics of it are] acts of murder, adultery, *forbidden* passions, fornication, theft, idolatry, magic, sorcery, robbery, false witness, hypocrisy, duplicity, guile, pride, malice, willful stubbornness, avarice, obscene speech, jealousy, insolence, arrogance, boastfulness, *lack of fear of God*.

(5:2)   [Characteristic of it are also] people who persecute the good, who hate truth, who love falsehood, who do not know money earned in a just way, who do not adhere to what is good or to just judgement, who stay up late at night for purposes that are not good but evil, who are far from being mild-tempered and patient, who love what is futile, who are out for money, who do not show mercy to a poor person, who are not distressed by [the plight of] the oppressed, who do not know him who made them, [who are] child murderers, who abort what God has formed, who reject the needy person, who oppress the person who is distressed, [who are] defenders of the rich [and] unjust judges of the poor - [people who are] sinners in everything what they do. Children, from all this may you be preserved.

(6:1)   See to it that no one leads you astray from this instruction, since [the person who would do so] teaches apart from the *[right] instruction.*

(6:4)   *If you will act with this in mind every day, you will be near to the living God, [but] if you will not act so, you will be far from the truth.*

(6:5)   *Put all this in your mind and you will not be deceived in your hope (but through these holy contests you will reach a wreath).*

TEXTUAL COMMENTARY ON THE RECONSTRUCTED GREEK TWO WAYS

The following notes represent a selection from the wealth of issues which might be considered in reconstructing the text of the Greek Two Ways. Our focus is upon the textual variants, parallel terminology, Jewish and Hellenistic motifs, and other materials which have as yet not – or just partly – been found in contemporary studies about the Didache.

The title of the Jewish treatise

The shorter title *Teaching of the Apostles* (Διδαχὴ τῶν ἀποστόλων) is evidently the usual designation of the Two Ways treatise. Above, in Chaps. 1 (pp. 5.21) and 3 (pp. 85-86), it became clear that this was also the superscription of the Greek manuscript of the Two Ways which was translated into Latin, the "Doctrina Apostolorum" (regarding the title "De Doctrina Apostolorum," see above, n. 3). It is highly unlikely, however, that the "Apostles" had already been mentioned in the title of the Jewish treatise. It was only after the Jewish Two Ways document came to be considered as authoritative within Christian circles that it was regarded as coming from the apostles. The title "the Teaching of the Apostles" was apparently borrowed from Acts 2:42: "And they devoted themselves to the apostles' teaching" (τῇ διδαχῇ τῶν ἀποστόλων). Barn. 18:1 begins the paraphrase of the two sources by speaking about "another teaching" v. "teaching" (διδαχή). (See also above, Chap. 3, p. 85).

(1:1) in the world:

"In saeculo" (Doctr. 1:1). The word was omitted by the Didachist, although it corresponds to the Hebrew in the Treatise of the Two Spirits in 1QS 3:13-4:26 (ואלה דרכיהן בתבל); cf. 1QS 4:2; see also below, Chap. 5, pp. 148).

(1:1) one of life, the other of death, one of light, the other of darkness

The double antithetical formulation in two pairs is taken from Doctr. (see also the apparatus). In 1QS 3:17-21 and Barn. 18:1 the realms of Light and Darkness are found but the Life-Death dichotomy is absent from both the entirety of the Dead Sea Scrolls and Barn. 18:1. (See, however, Barn. 20:1).

(1:1) upon them two angels are appointed, one of righteousness, the other of iniquity

The clause is omitted by Did, but see Barn. 18:1b! It is translated here from Doctr. The wording is in keeping with 1QS 3:18-19: וישם לו שתי רוחות להתהלך בם ... הנה רוחות האמת והעול ... ("and designed for him two spirits in which to walk ..., namely the spirits of truth and of deceit / iniquity"). (See below, Chap. 5, pp. 153-54).

(1:2) The two Great Commandments

The "double love commandment" appears in conjunction with the so-called "Golden Rule." Although it is well known that the requirements to love God and to love thy neighbour appear in tandem in Matt 22:34-40, Mark 12:28-34, and Luke 10:25-28, there are also purely Jewish sources attesting to their juxtaposition (see below, Chap. 5, pp. 156-58 and Flusser, 'A New Sensitivity in Judaism', 474-480. For the Golden Rule, see Dihle, *Die Goldene Regel* and recently, Alexander, 'Jesus and the Golden Rule'. Cf. Matt 7:12 and Luke 6:31). The Golden Rule occurs in a positive and negative form. We decided for the negative form not only because it is attested by the Doctrina but also because it is predominant throughout the tradition of the Golden Rule (see Dihle, *Die Goldene Regel*, 107).

(1:2) (God) who created you:

These words were added under the influence of Sir 7:30a (cf. below, Chap. 5, pp. 156-57 and nn. 52 and 53).

(1:3a) The explanation of these words is as follows:

The Doctrina omits the evangelical section, the Christian interpolation of Did 1:3b-2:1, which is also lacking in Barnabas. In order to reconstruct the Greek text of 1:3a, one may adopt the phrase from the Doctrina ("interpretatio autem horum verborum haec est") and consider the next precepts as a detailed exposition of the general principles mentioned in 1:2. It follows that, in this case, only the word "teaching" in the Didache has to be replaced by "explanation" (Lat. "interpretatio") which equals the Greek noun ἑρμηνεία. The pertinent Greek verb ἑρμηνεύω means "interpret, explain, put into words, describe, articulate" (cf. Luke 24:27; see Bauer, *A Greek-English Lexicon*, 310). It is parallel to the Hebrew פרש (cf. CD 2:12-13 and 6:14. See also below, Chap. 5, pp. 161-62 and n. 73). According to bShab 31a, Hillel summarized the essence of the whole Law by rendering the negative form of the Golden Rule ("Whatever is hateful to you, do it not unto your fellow") and adding: "the rest is a mere specification" (ואידך פירושה היא). This reduction of the laws to basic principles very much resembles our passage in 1:2-3. In 1:2, the essential core of the Way of Life is found in the double love commandment combined with the negative form of the Golden Rule. These three precepts which have special prominence and serve as the basic elements of the Way of Life are then followed by the clause: "The explanation of these words is as follows." As the Way of Life is practically identical to the Way of the (Jewish) Law, the similarity is striking (see also below, Chap. 5, pp. 155-60).

(2:2) You shall not murder. You shall not commit adultery

In the Latin Doctrina 2:2 (the beginning of the explication of the Way of Life) and 5:1 (the beginning of the Way of Death), the seventh commandment of the Decalogue precedes the sixth one. The reversed order also appears in the Greek Bible and other witnesses. The Two Ways of the Didache, however, in both instances (2:2 and 5:1) reflects the Masoretic sequence. The Didache is likely to have preserved this order of the two commandments because its source, the Greek Two Ways, also reflected an ordering identical to the Masoretic tradition (see Flusser, '"Do not commit adultery"', 221-222).

(2:2) You shall not murder a child, whether by [procuring its] abortion or by killing it
        once it is born:

For this expansion of the commandments of the second table of the Decalogue with
regard to contemporary accusations against gentile society, see the list of references in Rordorf-Tuilier, *La Doctrine des douze Apôtres*, 149, n. 7. Further, see
Justin Martyr, *1 Apol.* 27:1: ʽΗμεῖς δέ, ἵνα μηδὲν ἀδικῶμεν μηδὲ ἀσεβῶμεν,
ἐκτιθέναι καὶ τὰ γεννώμενα πονηρῶν εἶναι δεδιδάγμεθα· .../ "Lest we do
anything wrong or commit sin ourselves, we have been taught that it is wicked to
expose even newly-born children, ..." (for the Greek text, cf. Marcovich, *Iustini
Martyris Apologiae*, 72, lines 1-2 and the references in the related note there).

(2:5) Your word shall not be empty or false

The reading in the Didache (= H) is: Οὐκ ἔσται ὁ λόγος σου ψευδής, οὐ κενός,
ἀλλὰ μεμεστωμένος πράξει. It was already suggested by Schlecht with reference
to the Doctr. text, that the wording ἀλλὰ μεμεστωμένος πράξει probably is an
addition (cf. his *Doctrina XII apostolorum* [1901] 48). The extension in the
Didache is likely to also have caused the Didachic inversion of κενός and ψευδής
as compared to the order in the Doctr.: "Non erit uerbum tuum uacuum nec
mendax" (see Wengst, *Didache (Apostellehre)*, 69, n. 12; similarly Niederwimmer,
Die Didache, 120-21 and Dehandschutter, 'The Text of the *Didache*', 41).

(3:1-6)

The symmetrical strophic pattern of this unit has led many scholars to conclude
that this passage existed as a separate block before it was incorporated into the
Jewish Two Ways. The fact that it is lacking in the Barnabean Two Ways is not
decisive in delineating this unit's history since its absence may be the result of
Barnabas' ideosyncratic employment of traditions. Moreover, the priority of the
order of the Doctr./Did source has already been noted above. However, there are
indications that in the Greek original or even in an earlier stratum of the tradition,
the unit did not occur as it appears in the present form of the Doctr. and Did. The
distinctive repetitive pattern in each strophe suggests the existence of older and
less complex traditional statements behind the present passage. At some stage in
its history, single-lined phrases may have constituted this unit, and rather than being
bipartite, the original structure of the unit in GTW 3:1-6 may well have consisted
of five simple strophes. The major offenses in this list are five of the seven commandments for the sons of Noah recorded in bYoma 67b and Sifra, Aharei Moth
9,10, on Lev. 18:4. Thus, our unit (GTW 3:1-6) reflects the trespasses against the
common or "natural" ethical law (further, see below, Chap. 5, pp. 165-72). The
preamble "My child, flee from all evil and from everything like it" (3:1) is a
common rabbinic moral rule whose *Sitz im Leben* is in the Derekh Erets literature
(cf. Yir'at Het I,13 according to Van Loopik, *The Ways of the Sages*,194-97 [with
commentary] = Massekhet Derekh Erets I,12 according to Higger, *The treatises
Derek Erez* 1, 63 [Hebr.] and 2, 35 [ET]). The Latin translation of GTW 3:1 in the
Doctrina ("Fili, fuge ab homine malo et homine simili illi [aut: simulatore])" is an

outstanding example of either the inadequate textual transmission or inability of the Latin translator (The text of the Doctrina is also unsatisfactory in that it omits GTW 3:3). Instead, see Did 3:1 and compare also Job 1:1 (LXX); 1 Thess 5:21-22 and 1 Cor 6:18.

> (3:4) do not practise soothsaying, because this leads to idolatry; nor should you be an
> enchanter, or an astrologer, or a person who performs purificatory rituals

See the list in Deut 18:10-11, especially in the Greek translation and 2 Chr 33:6. See also Or. Sib. III 225 in Kurfess, *Sibyllinische Weissagungen*, 82 (οὐ μάντεις, οὐ φαρμακούς, οὐ μὴν ἐπαοιδούς,..) and 293 (note); see also Gauger, *Sibyllinische Weissagungen*, 76, line 225. For the latter passage and its immediate context, see in particular Van der Horst, 'Jewish Self-Definition', 95-110; esp. 106-07. For the same text (οὐ μάντεις, κτλ.), compare Tertullianus, *Apologeticum* 43,1 ("Plane confitebor, quinam, si forte, uere de sterilitate Christianorum conqueri possint. Primi erunt lenones, perductores, aquarioli, tum sicarii, uenenarii, magi, item haruspices, harioli, mathematici") in Dekkers, *Tertulliani Opera* 1, 158; see also Tertullianus, *Adversus Marcionem*, I,18,1 (in *Id.*, 459) and Tertullianus, *De Idololatria*, 9,2-3.8 in Gerlo, *Tertulliani Opera* 2, 1107-09. The Jewish Sages referred to magic and superstitious practices as "the ways of the Amorites;" see Alon, 'Hahalakha ba-Torat 12 ha-Shelihim', 280-81 (ET: 174-75); and 2 Apoc. Bar. 60:1 in Bogaert, *Apocalypse de Baruch* 1, 507 and 2, 113-114; cf. Schürer, *The History of the Jewish People* 3/1, 342-47.

> (3:7-8) On the contrary, be meek, since those who are meek will inherit the holy land.
> Be patient and merciful, without guile, tranquil and good, ...

The first four adjectives "meek, patient and merciful, without guile" - even with regard to the order of the terms - appear in close proximity to 1QS 4:3. The first of the four adjectives in GTW 3:7, however, is expanded by the addition "since those who are meek will inherit the holy land." This expansion is dependent upon Ps 37:11a (MT), "and the meek shall inherit land/earth" (= 36:11a, LXX), a text which has been used in Matt 5:5 too, but presented there in the form of a macarism. The only difference, albeit a significant one for the ultimate meaning of the phrase, appears in the word "holy". We chose to follow here the Latin Doctrina 3:7 ("Esto autem mansuetus, quia mansueti possidebunt sanctam terram") and thus to supply the adjective "holy" which by implication suggests the object of the promise to be the physical land of Israel. The Didache (and Matt 5:5), on the other hand, may well have omitted the specification "holy" under the influence of the parallel text in Ps 37:11. What was decisive for our "patriotic" or national-political interpretation, however, was the specific emphasis found in 4Qp Ps[a] (4Q 171) 3:9-11, where the words in Ps 37:22 ("... those who are blessed [... will in]herit the land, ...") are interpreted in the sense that "the congregation of the poor ones ... will take possession of the high mountain of Isra[el, ...]" and this, of course, refers to the temple of Jerusalem. The political hopes of the sectarian community were to be realized in a near eschatological future. For the translation of 4Qp Ps[a] 3:9-11, see Horgan, *Pesharim: Qumran Interpretations*, 197; see also Pardee, 'A Restudy of the

Commentary', 165. There is only a hint to GTW 3:7-8 in Barn. 19:4b. - For interesting parallels, see *Herm. Man.* II, 1 (...᾽ Ἁπλότητα ἔχε καὶ ἄκακος γίνου, καὶ ἔσῃ ὡς τὰ νήπια τὰ μὴ γινώσκοντα τὴν πονηρίαν τὴν ἀπολλύουσαν τὴν ζωὴν τῶν ἀνθρώπων / "Have simplicity and be innocent and you shall be as the children who do not know the wickedness that destroys the life of men") and *T. Dan* 6:9b (ἔστι γὰρ ἀληθὴς καὶ μακρόθυμος, πρᾶος καὶ ταπεινός, καὶ ἐκδιδάσκων διὰ τῶν ἔργων νόμον θεοῦ / "for he is true and longsuffering, meek and lowly, and teaching the law of God through his works").

> (4:1) You shall be mindful day and night of the one who speaks to you the word of God. You shall honour him as the Lord, ...

See Barn. 19:9b-10a (cf. above, Chap. 2, pp. 76-77) and Yir'at Het II,4: "Sit before the Elders and incline your ear and hear their words ...;" cf. Van Loopik, *The Ways of the Sages*, 220 = Massekhet Derekh Erets I,21 according to Higger, *The treatises Derek Erez* 1, 71 (Hebr.) and 2, 36 (ET).

> (4:1, end) ... for at the source of discourse on lordship God is there.

Here we accepted the reading "God", but even so, it was difficult to make a decision. For the idea, see mAv 3:3: "... But if three have eaten at one table and have spoken over it words of the Law, it is as if they had eaten from the table of God, ...;" similarly mAv 3:6 and see also ARN a 8 (= Schechter, *Aboth de Rabbi Nathan*,18b) and ARN b 18 (= Schechter, 20b) and 34 (= Schechter, 37b); for more relevant rabbinic material, cf. Str-B 1, 794-95. According to the main thrust of these sayings, the Shekhina will be present wherever men convene to occupy themselves with the study of the Tora (see also Flusser, 'I am in the midst'). For the common perspective shared by GTW and Ignatius, *Eph.* 6:1, see Jefford, 'Did Ignatius of Antioch', 344-345.

> (4:4) You shall not show indecision [in determining] whether [something] shall be or shall not be.

The διψυχ-root appears in the New Testament in Jas 1:8; 4:8 (adj. δίψυχος) only. In the light of the parallels, the warning in 4:4 refers to uncertainty regarding the fulfilment of prophecies or doubtfulness in prayer; see Rordorf-Tuilier, *La Doctrine des douze Apôtres*, 159, note 6. Compare also the following parallels:

> But in order that 'the name of God might be glorified' they (these visions) have been, and shall be, revealed to you because of the double-minded who dispute in their heart (διὰ τοὺς διψύχους, τοὺς διαλογιζομένους ἐν ταῖς καρδίαις αὐτῶν) whether these things are so or not (*Herm. Vis.* III 4,3)

and

> Remove from yourself double-mindedness, and be not at all double-minded about asking (Ἆρον ἀπὸ σεαυτοῦ τὴν διψυχίαν καὶ μὲν ὅλως διψυχήσῃς αἰτήσασθαί) anything from God, saying in yourself, How can I ask anything from the Lord and receive it after having sinned so greatly against him? Do not have these thoughts but 'turn to the Lord with all your heart', and ask from him without doubting, and you shall know his great

mercifulness, that he will not desert you, but will fulfil the petition of your soul (*Herm. Man.* IX, 1-2 and see also Bauer, *A Greek-English Lexicon*, 200-201).

(4:8) For the Lord wants that one shall give to all from His own gracious gifts

The Doctrina has this clause in the present position but it does not occur in a parallel position in the Didache, an omission which may have resulted from the editorial activities of the Didachist. He obviously transferred this clause from GTW 4:8 to the evangelical section of Did 1:3b-2:1 (Did 1:5b; see also Wengst, *Didache [Apostellehre]*, 95, n. 38 and Dehandschutter, 'The Text of the *Didache*', 41). Furthermore, the reading "Lord" of the Doctr. is to be preferred to the variant "Father" in Did 1:5b. The demand of charity with regard to the poor – considering that God is the giver of all riches – was a common Jewish statement and is almost verbally paralleled in *Herm. Man.* II, 4: (πᾶσιν δίδου·) πᾶσιν γάρ ὁ θεὸς δίδοσθαι θέλει ἐκ τῶν ἰδίων δωρημάτων / "give to all, for to all God wishes gifts to be made of his own bounties;" see Brox, *Der Hirt des Hermas*,195-196. A similar demand occurs in Ps.-Phocylides 29 too: "Of that which God has given to you (ὧν σοι ἔδωκε θεός), give of it to the needy" and cf. *T. Zeb.* 6:7; 7:2. See also Philo, *Quis heres*, 103-105:

> First it (*the wording 'take for me' in Gen 15:9*) says to us 'you have no good thing of your own, but whatever you think you have, Another has provided' (ἔτερος παρέσχηκεν). Hence we infer that all things are the possession of God who gives, ...The second is 'even if you take, take not for yourself, but count that which is given a loan or trust and render it back to Him who entrusted and leased it to you, ...'. For vast is the number of those who repudiate the sacred trusts and in their unmeasured greed use up what belongs to Another as though it was their own. ...; (cf. Colson, *Philo* 4 [LCL 261], 332-33)

and Midrash Canticum Zuta:

> If you have given an alm, you have not given from your property but from (the property) of God, as it is written (Hag 2:8): 'The silver is mine and the gold is mine' (see also I Chron 29:14): 'Every thing comes from You and we have given you only what comes from Your hand' (cf. Buber, *Midrasch suta*, 18)

and also Yir'at Het II,12:

> And know the difference between today and tomorrow, in connection to what is yours and to what is not yours (what is yours is in reality not yours), as for what is (not) yours, how you can regard it as yours? (cf. Van Loopik, *The Ways of the Sages*, 226-27 = Massekhet Derekh Erets I, 24 according to Higger, *The treatises Derek Erez* 1, 76 [Hebr.] and 2, 37 [ET])

and cf. Yir'at Het II, 26 (Van Loopik, *The Ways of the Sages*, 234 = Massekhet Derekh Erets I,29 according to Higger, *The treatises Derek Erez* 1, 82-83 [Hebr.] and 2, 39 [ET]) and mAv 5:10: "He who says 'What is mine is thine and what is thine is thine' is a saint (hassid);" see also Justin Martyr, *1 Apol.* 14:2-3 (= Marcovich, *Iustini Martyris Apologiae*, 52-53 [lines 10-18]).

For the clause preceding this final phrase in GTW 4:8 ("for if you are partners ... things that perish?"), which provides a rational ground for a mitigated form of sharing goods, see below, Chap. 5, pp. 182-90. See also Niederwimmer, *Die Didache*, 108-110, and Draper, 'The Jesus Tradition' (1996), 84.

(4:10)   ... your slave or your maid, those who hope in the same God, ...

One may assume that in the latter part of the Second Temple period no Jewish or "Hebrew" slaves were held by Jewish masters. The sources give the impression that the majority of slaves, if not all, in Jewish Palestine were of foreign origin. A non-Jewish slave who belonged to a Jew became a part of the Jewish nation. He was circumcised (manservants) or underwent ritual immersion (maidservants). The male servant's obligation to perform the commandments was the same as that of a Jewish woman. If a foreign slave was emancipated, he or she became an Israelite with all the rights and obligations that involved (see Stern, 'Aspects of Jewish Society', 628-29 and Safrai, 'Home and Family', 751-52; cf. also Büchler, 'Hearot al matsav ha-dati').

(4:11)   as replicas of God

See Loewenstamm, 'Beloved is Man', 48-50; esp. nn. 5, 5a. He has called attention to an Assyrian text in which the king is said to resemble the very image of the deity: "The shadow of the god (is) a free man. [And] the shadow of a free man (is) a slave. The king: He is li[ke] the image of a god" (48). See also Heintz, 'Royal Traits and Messianic Figures', 62. The concept was known as late as the Hellenistic period. This is evidenced in the Neo-Pythagorian text of the treatise about the kingship by the Pseudo-Ecphantus, composed probably in the first or the second century CE:

> (On the earth and among us man has the best nature of all; however the king is more divine ... he was made by the best craftsman), who wrought him using himself as a model. Thus the king is the one and only creature to represent the king of heaven, ... (ὅς ἐτεχνίτευσεν αὐτὸν ἀρχετύπῳ χρώμενος ἑαυτῷ. κατασκεύασμα δὴ ὦν ὁ βασιλεὺς ἓν καὶ μόνον ἐντὶ οἷα τύπος τῶ ἀνωτέρω βασιλέως, ...); cf. Stern, *Greek and Latin Authors*, 33-37.

See also Col 3:22-24 and Eph 6:5-9.

(4:13)   ... without adding or subtracting anything

See Deut 4:2; 13:1. Cf. Niederwimmer, *Die Didache*, 145. The Latin translator of the Doctrina did not understand the sentence; he writes: "neque appones illis contraria" (Doctr. 4:13). "... durch diese Ergänzung" (contraria) "ist nicht ein Zusetzen zu den Herrenworten schlechthin verboten, sondern nur die Einfügung *widersprechender* Lehren, ..." (Schlecht, *Doctrina XII apostolorum* [1901], 59).

(4:14)   You shall confess your faults ...

This phrase is lacking in the Doctrina (see Schlecht, *Doctrina XII apostolorum* [1901], 59-61). We have omitted the wording ἐν ἐκκλησία ("in the assembly" or "in the church"). The expression ἐν ἐκκλησίᾳ may indeed have figured in the pre-Christian stage of the Two Ways (see Rordorf-Tuilier, *La Doctrine des douze Apôtres*, 165, note 5 and Niederwimmer, *Die Didache*, 145, note 14) but since it appears only in the manuscript of the Didache (= H), it might just as well be a Christian addition here (see also Barn. 19:12b).

(5:1) acts of murder, adultery

The beginning of the list at this point in the Didache – "acts of murder, adultery" – follows the order of the Hebrew text of the Decalogue, whereas the Latin Doctrina – "moechationes, homicidia" – presents the sequence of Greek Bible. The same phenomenon occurs above, in 2:1.

(5:1) forbidden passions

The sin of "idolatry" is lacking in the Doctrina, apparently because this transgression was considered to be the equivalent of "desideria mala," a wording found here only.

(5:1, end) lack of fear of God

This phraseology is missing in the Jerusalem manuscript of the Didache (= H). The Doctr. offers: "deum non timentes" (where a secondary hand – F^2 – inserted the word "deum" above the line). See Schlecht, *Doctrina XII apostolorum* (1901), 61-62. We opted for ἀφοβία θεοῦ as found in Barn. 20:1. On the other hand, the reconstruction of Wengst, *Didache (Apostellehre)*, 75 (οὐ φοβούμενοι τὸν θεόν; cf. his note 50, too), which is mainly based on the Doctrina, may also be correct. To the whole list of vices in GTW, Chap. 5, see the parallels in 3 Baruch 4:17; 8:5 and 13:4 (cf. Harlow, *The Greek Apocalypse of Baruch (3 Baruch)*, 79-80 + notes).

> (6:1) See to it that no one leads you astray from this instruction, since [the person who would do so] teaches apart from the [right] instruction

The Didache offers the reading "from this way of the instruction" (ἀπὸ ταύτης τῆς ὁδοῦ τῆς διδαχῆς; cf. 2 Pet 2:15.21), but in our context, a phrase like "from the instruction of the Way" (ἀπὸ ταύτης τῆς διδαχῆς τῆς ὁδοῦ [namely τῆς ζωῆς]) would be more conceivable. Here, a reading is accepted that offers the closest parallel with the Doctrina ("ab hac doctrina"). As a consequence, it is likely that the final clause of this verse was originally stated in a similar wording: ἐπεὶ παρεκτὸς τῆς διδαχῆς σε διδάσκει (cf. the Doctr. which renders "extra disciplinam" [the Didache has παρεκτὸς θεοῦ]. See also Schlecht, *Doctrina XII apostolorum* (1901), 63. Compare Deut 13:6b).

(6:2-3)

These verses do not belong to the Greek Two Ways but form an addition to the Jewish document (see above, pp. 119-20 and below, Chap. 7). The original Jewish ending is preserved in the Latin Doctrina.

(6:4a)   If you will act with this in mind every day

Doctr.: "Haec in consulendo si cottidie feceris." The possibility cannot be excluded that Doctr. 6:4a originates from Josh 1:8 (see also Barn. 21:2a: λαμβάνετε συμβουλίαν and cf. Id., 21:4).

(6:5b)   but through these holy contests you will reach a wreath

It is not clear whether this phrase belongs to the Jewish source or whether it was added in the (Christian) translation. The final doxology in the next verse of the Doctrina, on the other hand, is apparently Christian.

Chapter Five

The Two Ways as a Jewish Document

The genre and provenance of the Two Ways have been the subject of debate since the first decades of the twentieth century. Shortly after the publication of the Didache in 1883, Charles Taylor[1] and J.R. Harris[2] argued for the Jewishness of the Two Ways with reference to parallels which were to be found in rabbinic literature. This position received a new impulse from both Paul Drews[3] and Alfred Seeberg.[4] They held that the Two Ways once formed part of a primitive Jewish proselyte catechism which was adopted and appropriated by the early Christians as baptismal instruction. This thesis associating the Two Ways with a Jewish instruction for gentile converts, however, which was defended in various modifications by several scholars,[5] has not gone unchallenged.[6] The Jewish character of the Two Ways was substantiated and confirmed by the monumental contribution of Jean-Paul Audet[7] who provided irrefutable documentation that the Two Ways sections in the Didache and Barnabas are grafted on the model of the Treatise of the Two Spirits in the Manual of Discipline or Community Rule (1QS 3:13-4:26). Audet's work has exerted a lasting influence upon subsequent scholars and is an important building block for students even today.

A brief summary of modern views on the type of literary composition and the original *Sitz im Leben* of the Two Ways shows that present scholarly opinion is still divided over the issue. Klaus Baltzer[8] sought to recognize a specific genre of an ancient Covenant formula behind the Two Spirits Treatise at Qumran and the

---

[1] *The Teaching of the Twelve Apostles.* For summaries of the history of research, see Ehrhard, *Die altchristliche Litteratur* 1, 37-68; Audet, *La Didachè*, 1-21; Prigent-Kraft, *Épître de Barnabé*, 12-20; Rordorf, 'Un chapitre d'éthique judéo-chrétienne', 156-58; Draper, 'The Didache in Modern Research', 8-16.

[2] *The Teaching of the Apostles.*

[3] 'Untersuchungen zur Didache', 54.

[4] *Der Katechismus der Urchristenheit*; Id., *Das Evangelium Christi*; Id., *Die Beiden Wege und das Aposteldekret*; Id., *Die Didache des Judentums.*

[5] Klein, *Der älteste christliche Katechismus,* 137-83 (as will become clear below, this work contains many insights which are still valuable today); Daube, *The New Testament*, 106-107; Adam, 'Erwägungen zur Herkunft', 53-54. The theory was also brought forward some time before the publications of Drews and Seeberg by Von Harnack, *Die Apostellehre*, 14 and 29-31.

[6] Cf. the criticism of Alon, 'Ha-halakha ba-Torat 12 ha-Shelihim', 275-79; (ET: 167-72); Wibbing, *Die Tugend- und Lasterkataloge,* 5-8; Michaelis, 'ὁδός κτλ.', 92 and 99; Niederwimmer, *Die Didache*, 56-57, n. 49; Rordorf-Tuilier, *La Doctrine des douze Apôtres,* 31, n. 5 (correcting Rordorf's former position reflected in 'Un chapitre d'éthique', 159-60; 161-168 [ET: 152 and 153-59]).

[7] See his article 'Affinités littéraires et doctrinales' and his commentary in *La Didachè*, 121-63.

[8] *Das Bundesformular.*

various forms of the Two Ways teaching. According to Ehrhard Kamlah,[9] these materials, and some early Christian virtue and vice lists as well, belong to a common genre that has been modified by Jewish-Christian literature under the influence of a dualistic Iranian mythology. M.J. Suggs, supporting this view, subsequently argued that the Two Ways originally belonged to the type of community rules which maintained "a strong sense of in-group awareness"[10] like the one advanced in the dualistic Two Spirits passage at Qumran. Drawing upon Kamlah's conclusions, he examined the various forms of the Two Ways tradition and believed the common genre established by Kamlah (i.e., the Two Spirits section, the Two Ways pattern, and some virtue and vice catalogues), reflected a progressive development. He contends that these materials exhibit an evolutionary process from the sharply dualistic tone in the Qumran Scrolls (still present in the Two Ways section in Barnabas) through the more ethicized and individualized form in the Testament of Asher to the purely ethical instruction in the Didache.

Suggs' solution to the problem has been criticized by Willy Rordorf and André Tuilier. They believe that it would be an oversimplification to regard the various forms of the Two Ways tradition as a chronological evolution reflecting an increasing elimination of dualistic elements. In their opinion, dualistic Two Ways traditions and non-dualistic ones existed simultaneously in early Judaism and both forms were adopted by early Christianity.[11] Finally, we mention Jonathan A. Draper who has identified important similarities between the Two Ways in the Didache and the Two Spirits Treatise.[12] He does not believe, however, that the Two Ways unilaterally proceeds from a dualistic Essene tradition since the parallels do not reflect the distinctive ideas and expressions which are unique to the Qumran ideology. Rather, he considers the tradition to be more congenial with Two Ways echoes found in rabbinic writings.[13]

---

[9] *Die Form der katalogischen Paränese.*

[10] 'The Christian Two Ways Tradition', 67 and see also 70-71: "Whatever the author of the epistle" (of Barnabas) "intended in taking up the Two Ways teaching into his 'letter', the Two Ways tradition upon which he depends seems still to serve the function identified for 1QS: it is an instrument of group identity, meant to separate 'us' from 'them'."

[11] Rordorf-Tuilier, *La Doctrine des douze Apôtres*, 26-28; esp. 26-27: "Il serait trop simple de croire que l'effacement progressif de la conception dualiste constitue un critère pour le classement chronologique des différentes recensions des *Deux voies* dans le christianisme primitif. Dans le judaïsme en effet, les traditions dualiste et non dualiste existaient déjà simultanément et rien ne permet d'affirmer que l'une est antérieure à l'autre à partir d'une certaine époque." See also Rordorf's earlier contribution, published – like Suggs' article – in 1972: "Etant donné la complexité du problème de la provenance du *duae viae*, il faudra surtout éviter les solutions simplistes, unilatérales; il ne semble pas, en effet, que le *duae viae* (dans *toutes* ces formes) vienne de Qumran, ni qu'il dérive uniquement de l'instruction donnée aux prosélytes juifs, ni encore qu'il soit une expression tardive de la morale de l'alliance ancrée dans le *Bundesformular*." ('Un chapitre d'éthique', 160 [ET: 152-53]).

[12] *A Commentary on the Didache*, 76-79 and 116-20.

[13] Draper, 'The Didache in Modern Research: an Overview', 15. Berger ('Hellenistische Gattungen', 1139) defines the literary type of the Two Ways in Did 1-6 as προτρεπτικὸς λόγος. In his opinion, the schema of the Two Ways, governing the section as a whole, and the listings of virtues and vices embody the essential characteristics of this type of composition.

This brief summary indicates that the questions concerning genre and provenance of the Two Ways certainly have not been answered fully and need further examination. Previous research shows that one of the major problems in establishing the genre, provenance, and concrete life situation of the Two Ways is the mixed type of Judaism displayed by this doctrine. On the one hand, the teaching betrays affinities with the parenetic character of Israel's practical wisdom, but it also embraces doctrines found in the teaching of Qumran. In this chapter, an attempt will be made to show that the confluence of a sapiential and dualistic stream in the Two Ways reflects the outlook of the pious Jewish circles from which the tradition emanated.

We will take the following steps.[14] Because the earliest form of the Two Ways tradition echoed in the Doctrina (and Barnabas) is obviously controlled by two opposing principles, our initial concern will be with the widespread imagery of two contrasting ways in apocryphal and pseudepigraphical writings (pp. 143-47). The dualistic schema, however, preeminently appears in the Two Spirits section of the Qumran Community Rule (1QS 3:13-4:26). It may be revealing to see how the sect modified an existing form of the Two Ways to fit their predestinarian views (pp. 147-55). But it is important to notice that, in comparison with the Qumran document, the Two Ways source (underlying the Doctrina and the Didache) shows particular interest in the Way of Life. The Way of Life is enriched by further ethical advice, whereas the Way of Death remains a mere list of sins. For this reason, the various traditions in the Way of Life segment (as far as retained in 1:1-3:6) will be examined next. We will discover many similarities with materials found in rabbinic literature and, especially, in Derekh Erets tracts (pp. 155-72). Themes and terminology show sufficient parallels which suggest that the early layer of Derekh Erets tracts and the rabbinic traditions representing a similar spiritual and ethic thought provide the most appropriate framework for understanding the Two Ways doctrine as a whole (pp. 172-79). This will finally enable us to trace the concrete life situations of the circles in which the Two Ways could emerge. It will appear, firstly, that the diverse units incorporated in the Two Ways must have been collected and preserved in the pious milieu of hassidic Sages who strived for absolute moral purity (pp. 180-82); and, secondly, that, in these circles, a sharing of property was practised which was not based on sectarian separatism but extended beyond narrow group boundaries (pp. 182-90). If these results are correct, this study will be relevant not only to the interpretation of the Two Ways but, conversely, may also contribute to our knowledge of the development of the Derekh Erets literature.

Yet, he acknowledges that the catalogue in the Way of Life is expanded considerably with additional materials. Berger also considers the conclusion in Did 6:1-3 as typical of the προτρεπτικὸς λόγος genre. In Chapter 7, however, we will see that the passage in Did 6:2-3 originally did not belong to the Two Ways.

[14] For the following, see also Alon, 'Ha-halakha ba-Torat 12 ha-Shelihim' (ET: 'The Halacha in the Teaching of the Twelve Apostles'); Flusser, 'Shte Derakhim Hen'; Id., 'Ezohi Derekh Yashara'; Id., 'The Didache and the Noachic Commandments'; Id., *Das essenische Abenteuer*, 79-96; Id., 'The Ten Commandments'; Id., 'A New Sensitivity in Judaism'; Id., 'Jesus' opinion about the Essenes'.

Any discussion of the problem of the genre and provenance of the Two Ways must take note of the materials belonging to the original document. It was established in Chap. 2 that the source used by Didache 1:1-3a; 2:2-6:1, which was taken over via a (later) revision in the Letter of Barnabas 18-21, was none other than the Greek original of the Latin text entitled "(De) Doctrina Apostolorum." Therefore Chap. 4 was focussed especially on the reconstruction of the Greek version of the Jewish Two Ways that the Latin Doctrina was based on. Because it is assumed here that this reconstruction represents the lost document of the Two Ways on which the writer of the Didache and the translation in the Doctrina drew, this (hypothetical) text – designated as the "Greek Two Ways" (GTW) – will be the basis for the discussion on the following pages.

The Dualistic Setting of the Two Ways

Above, it was established that the Hebrew Bible exhibits an abundance of examples of the Two Ways metaphor,[15] the most interesting of which are the passages in Deut 30:15 and 19. Although these two verses are not instances of the metaphor proper, they describe the choice God has given between "life and good" and "death and evil" (30:15), or "life and death" and "blessing and curse" (30:19). In rabbinic writings, especially in the Palestinian Targum tradition, the alternatives proposed here are associated with the two ways of life and death:

> See, I have set before you this day the way of life, by which the good reward for the just is fulfilled, and the way of death by which the evil reward for the wicked is fulfilled (TgPs-Yon on Deut 30:15)

and

> ... the way of life and the way of mortality have I provided for you, the blessing and the curses; and you shall choose the way of life, in order that you may live... (TgNeof on Deut 30:19).[16]

This interpretation was undoubtedly influenced by Jer 21:8, where the phrase 'to give before you' (נתן לפניכם), also occurring in Deut 30:15.19, is combined with the way of life (דרך החיים) and the way of death (דרך המות).[17] Other rabbinic instances linking the two ways theme with Deut 30 are DeutR 4,3, SifDeut (pisqa 53), and Pirqe R. El. 15.

It may be true that the above formulations in Deut 30 and related Jewish traditions have played a part in the development of the Two Ways tradition. On the other hand, it is difficult to imagine that the sharply dualistic construction of

---

[15] See Chap. 2, p. 58.

[16] For these and other Targumic versions, see Brock, 'The Two Ways', 140-41.

[17] Cf. also Michaelis, 'ὁδός κτλ.', 59.

the Two Ways in the Greek document should draw upon such wording.[18] In the opening words, the moral opposition of the Two Ways, introducing the lists of virtues and vices in chapters 2-5, is expressed in terms of light and darkness, a duality which is underscored by their characterization as being presided over by the angels of righteousness and evil. Certainly, on a biblical basis the Two Ways may have had a fixed place in popular imagery, but the presence of the antagonistic wording in our Greek Two Ways argues for a derivation from a strand of materials that functioned in a dualistic setting.

In our search for clear indications of origin, we thus have to look for background traditions in which the antithetical formulation of the Two Ways metaphor could have been transmitted within a dualistic pattern of thought, revealing two sets of opposing ethical characteristics or antagonistic groups of people. Essential features of contrary categories are found in the Apocrypha and Pseudepigrapha, writings which mostly date from the Second Temple period and which are somehow connected with the Bible. The earliest extant witness[19] to the 'Ways'-image used in a context of opposites or contrasts is found in Sir 33(36):7-15:

7) Why is one day more important than another,
   when the same sun lights up every day of the year?
8) By the Lord's knowledge they are kept distinct;
   among them he designates seasons and feasts.
9) Some he exalts and sanctifies,
   and others he lists as ordinary days.
10) So, too, all people are of clay,
   for from earth humankind was formed;
11) Yet in the fulness of his understanding the Lord makes people unlike:
   in different paths (ὁδούς) he has them walk.
12) Some he blesses and makes great,
   some he sanctifies and draws to himself.
   Others he curses and brings low,
   and expels them from their place.
13) Like clay in the hands of a potter,
   to be moulded according to his pleasure,
   So are people in the hands of their Maker,
   to be requited according as he judges them.

---

[18] Contrast Str-B 1, 460 where Deut 30:15 (and 11:16) is called the biblical basis of the metaphor because "im Anschluss an die Worte 'Ich lege euch vor Segen und Fluch', bezw. 'Leben u. Tod' sofort geredet wird von dem Wege oder den Wegen Gottes." Brock ('The Two Ways') refers to the combination of Jer 21:8 with Deut 30:15.19 as the starting point for our metaphor. He argues that a similar fusion of Deut 30:15.19 and Jer 21:8 is found in the Clementine Homilies XVIII.17.2; in Origen, De Principiis III.1.6 and in the Apostolic Constitutions VII.1.1. In these documents, then, we are supposed to have "three separate new witnesses to an earlier form of the Palestinian Targum tradition to Deut. 30.15 ..." (142). It is hard, however, to see in Deut 30:15.19 the direct antecedents to Doctr. 1:1 (or to Barn. 18:1 for that matter) and, in addition, it must be noted that these biblical places do not account for the elements of dualistic cosmology and angelology in the latter writings.

[19] For most of the following occurrences, see Wibbing, *Die Tugend- und Lasterkataloge*, 33-42. Cf. also Gammie, 'Spatial and Ethical Dualism', 375-80 and Flusser, 'Shte Derakhim Hen', 241.

14) As evil contrasts with good, and death with life,
   so are sinners in contrast with the just;
15) See now all the works of the Most High:
   they come in pairs, the one the opposite of the other.[20]

The poem might be directed against those who claim that all people, the pious and the wicked, are similar, just as all days seem to be identical because "the same sun lights up every day of the year" (33:7). According to the writer, however, days are to be perceived as disparate. God "makes people unlike" (11) in the same way as he designates certain days to be "seasons and feasts" while listing others as "ordinary" (8-9). Although all human beings have a common origin as they are formed "from earth" (10), God has caused them to walk in different ways. Like a potter who shapes the clay, he predetermines man's nature and destiny which is expressed here by contrasting the opposites of evil and good, death and life, and sinners and the just (13-15).[21] The wording shows a dualism between two types of human beings (the sinners and the just) to the extent that their fate is expressed in terms of a double predestination, assigning man's good and evil behaviour to the "works of the Most High."

In *T. Asher* 1:3-5, the duality of existence as a part of the created order is clearly connected with the Two Ways scheme:

God has given two ways (δύο ὁδούς) to the sons of men
and two dispositions and two kinds of action
and two modes of living and two ends.
Therefore, all things are by twos, one over against the other.
(There are) two ways (ὁδοὶ δύο), of good and evil,
and with them there are the two dispositions
in our breasts distinguishing between them.[22]

In 1 Enoch (or the Ethiopic Enoch) 91:18-19, a contrast is drawn between the ways of righteousness and the ways of wickedness:

And now I tell you, my children, and I show you the paths of righteousness[23] and the paths of wrong-doing;
I will show them to you again,
that you may know what will come to pass.

---

[20] ET: Skehan-Di Lella, *The Wisdom of Ben Sira*, 394. The Greek version of Sir 36[33]:10-11 runs: καὶ ἄνθρωποι πάντες ἀπὸ ἐδάφους, καὶ ἐκ γῆς ἐκτίσθη Αδαμ· ἐν πλήθει ἐπιστήμης κύριος διεχώρισεν αὐτοὺς καὶ ἠλλοίωσεν τὰς ὁδοὺς αὐτῶν·...; cf. Ziegler, *Sapientia Iesu Filii Sirach*.
[21] Cf. Skehan-Di Lella, *The Wisdom of Ben Sira*, 399-401 and Winter, 'Ben Sira and the teaching', 315-18.
[22] ET: Hollander-De Jonge, *The Testaments*, 341-42. For the Greek text, see De Jonge, *The Testaments of the Twelve Patriarchs* (1978), 135.
[23] For the expression "paths of righteousness" (cf. v. 19 – that is here: lines 6 and 7 – as well), see also the phrase in Matt 21:32 ("For John came to you in the way of righteousness [ἐν ὁδῷ δικαιοσύνης], ..."); cf. also the wording in 1QS 4:2 ("And these are their ways in the world: to illuminate the heart of man and to level before him all the ways of true righteousness [כול דרכי צדק אמת]; ..."), and the following quotation from 1 Enoch 94:1-4.

And now, hearken unto me, my children,
and walk in the paths of righteousness,
and walk not in the paths of wrong-doing;
for all who walk in the paths of oppression shall perish everlastingly.[24]

This theme is further elaborated in 1 Enoch 94:1-4:

And now I say unto you, my sons, love righteousness and walk therein;
for the paths of righteousness are worthy of acceptance,
but the paths of unrighteousness shall suddenly be destroyed and fail.
And to illustrious men of a generation to come shall the paths of wrong-doing and death
be revealed,
and they shall hold themselves afar from them,
and shall not follow them.
And now I say unto you, the righteous:
walk not in the paths of wickedness, nor in the paths of death,
and draw not nigh to them lest you be destroyed.
But seek and choose for yourselves righteousness, and a life of goodness,
and walk in the paths of peace,
that you may live and prosper.[25]

In the Book of Jubilees 7:26, it says:

... And behold, I see your deeds before me that you have not been ones who walked in
righteousness because you have begun to walk in the paths of corruption. ... .[26]

The sharpness of the opposition between the good and evil way also appears in 2
Enoch (or the Slavonic Apocalypse of Enoch) 30:15:

And I gave him (= Adam) his free will; and I pointed out to him the two ways – light and
darkness. And I said to him, 'This is good for you, but that is bad'; so that I might come
to know whether he has love toward me or abhorrence, and so that it might become plain
who among his race loves me.[27]

So far, we have seen the Two Ways metaphor couched within polar tendencies of
good and evil, moral and immoral qualities, and righteous and wicked people. This
dualism refers to a pattern of thought which expresses two mutually exclusive
categories and, as such, stresses the importance on the part of man of making a
fundamental choice between right and wrong. In this respect, these cases reflect
the Two Ways in our Greek document and the material is extensive enough to
suggest that the Two Ways instruction flourished in circles fostering these dualistic
traditions. Yet, in the above instances the points of agreement with the Greek Two
Ways are almost completely limited to the opening words of our document. They

---

[24] ET: Black, *The Book of Enoch*, 84.
[25] ET: Black, *The Book of Enoch*, 87.
[26] ET: Wintermute, 'Jubilees', 70.
[27] ET: Andersen, '2 (Slavonic Apocalypse of) Enoch', 152; for the Slavonic version (and French
translation), see 50:25-29 in Vaillant, *Le livre des secrets d'Hénoch*, 100-101. For a German translation
and commentary, see Böttrich, *Das slavische Henochbuch*, 919-21 and n. 15.

do not provide an unambiguous example of the metaphor serving as a framework upon which catalogues of virtues and vices are constructed.

The Two Ways in its Essene and pre-Essene Form

A first-hand view of how the dualistic Two Ways tradition developed into our Greek Two Ways instruction is provided by the famous Treatise of the Two Spirits of the Manual of Discipline (1QS 3:13-4:26). There is a consensus that both this Essene[28] doctrinal unit, representing dualism preeminently, and the Greek Two Ways reveal a similarity in pattern and theme. After a Prologue dealing with the predetermination of all things (3:15-18a), the first section of the Two Spirits Treatise records that two antagonistic heavenly spirits were alotted to man, the spirit of truth and the spirit of deceit, representing two opposing forces of light and darkness. These two spirits rule the sons of righteousness and of injustice, respectively. In the next section (4:2-14), the ethical manifestation of this cosmic dualism is found in two parallel passages containing lists of virtues and vices. The behaviour (and future destiny) of man depends on what spirit controls him. The two forces of evil are not said, however, to be independent of God. In the end (4:15-26), God will intervene in the continuing battle in which the spirits are involved, and will destroy the spirit of injustice.

Obviously, there are close affinities between the doctrinal passage of 1QS and the Greek Two Ways, since the general pattern in both passages includes the following elements:

1. a theological introduction (1QS 3:13-4:1 which is summarized in the Greek Two Ways 1:1);
2. a list of righteous attitudes and moral deeds (1QS 4:3-6 = GTW 1:2-3; 2:2-4:14);
3. a list of immoral deeds (1QS 4:9-11 = GTW 5);
4. man's share to the divisions of the two spirits (1QS 4:15-16, which is rephrased in the admonition of GTW 6:1).

The view that the Treatise of the Two Spirits in 1QS is closely connected with the Greek Two Ways is supported further by textual evidence. The following points of unique agreement may be noted: the reminiscence of creation at the beginning

---

[28] We assume, as is accepted by most scholars, that the sectarians of Qumran, known to us from the Dead Sea Scrolls, were Essenes. See for example Vermes, *The Dead Sea Scrolls*, 116-36; Id., *The Dead Sea Scrolls in English*, XV; Milik, *Ten Years of Discovery*, 44-98; Cross, *The Ancient Library of Qumran*, 37-79; VanderKam, *The Dead Sea Scrolls Today*, 71-92; Sanders, *Judaism. Practice and Belief*, 341-79. This consensus has come under attack in recent years by those who do not identify the Qumran sect with the Essenes themselves but with a schismatic group which separated from the Essenes. The defenders of this position include J. Murphy-O'Connor, 'The Essenes and Their History'; Id., 'The Damascus Document Re-visited'; García Martínez, 'The Origins of the Essene Movement'; Id., 'Qumran Origins and Early History'; Boccaccini, *Beyond the Essene Hypothesis*. This discussion does not seem relevant, however, to the issues we will be dealing with in this chapter.

of 1QS 3:17-18 ("He created the human for the dominion of the world"[29]) is paralleled in GTW 1:2 (ἀγαπήσεις τὸν θεὸν τὸν ποιήσαντά σε); the characterization of the spirits as the contrast between light-*versus*-darkness in 1QS 3:18-19 ("the spirits of truth and deceit. In a spring of light emanates the nature of thruth and from a well of darkness emerges the nature of deceit") corresponds with GTW 1:2 (μία τοῦ φωτὸς καὶ μία τοῦ σκότους ἐφ' ἧς μὲν γὰρ εἰσιν τετάγμενοι ἄγγελοι δύο, ὁ μὲν τῆς δικαιοσύνης ὁ δὲ τῆς ἀνομίας); the phrase in 1QS 4:2 ("and these are their ways in the world") governing the development of 1QS 4:2-14 has verbal links with the incipit of the Greek Two Ways (ὁδοὶ δύο εἰσίν ἐν κόσμῳ) which controls the whole exposition of the Two Ways.

When all the parallels mentioned above are combined together, the case for the influence of 1QS 3:13-4:26 (or a document closely related to this passage) on the Two Ways tradition in the Greek document seems very strong.[30] Both texts share a similar wording, mentioning the (Two) Ways in the world (1QS 4:2a and GTW 1:1) as they introduce the double catalogue of virtues and vices. Moreover, the possibility of literary interdependence is increased by the following observation. In 1QS 4:2-6, the ethical implications of the ways of the 'spirit of light' are enumerated and many of them parallel the items that are part of the Way of Life described in GTW 3:7-10. If we compare 1QS with the Greek Two Ways in this light the resultant pattern may be outlined as follows:

1QS 4:2b-4a   *GTW 3:7-8.10*

("to illuminate the heart of man and to level
before him all the ways of true righteousness")

ולפחד לבבו במשפטי אל   (καὶ τρέμων τοὺς λόγους διὰ
                                                  παντός, οὓς ἤκουσας)
ורוח ענוה   ἴσθι δὲ πραΰς, ἐπεὶ οἱ πραεῖς
                                                  κληρονομήσουσιν τὴν γῆν
ואורך אפים   γίνου μακρόθυμος
ורוב רחמים   καὶ ἐλεήμων
                                                  καὶ ἄκακος
וטוב עולמים   καὶ ἡσύχιος
                                                  καὶ ἀγαθός
ושכל
ובינה
וחכמת גבורה
                                                  τὰ συμβαίνοντά σοι ἐνεργήματα ὡς
מאמנת בכול מעשי אל ונשענה ברוב חסדו   ἀγαθὰ προσδέξῃ, εἰδὼς ὅτι ἄτερ
                                                  θεοῦ οὐδὲν γίνεται

---

[29] For our text and translation of the Two Spirits Treatise, see Qimron-Charlesworth, 'Rule of the Community',15-19.

[30] Audet thus has good grounds for arguing that there is a direct literary relationship between 1QS and the Doctrina text: "... ce ne sont pas seulement des métaphores et des idées qui sont identiques de part et d'autre, c'est un cadre littéraire qui commande le développement entier de deux écrits. Des faits aussi nettement définis sont inexplicables, si l'on n'admet pas une relation littéraire certaine entre le *Duae viae* et l'instruction morale du *Manuel de discipline*" ('Affinités littéraires', 235).

In this passage, the wording of 1QS and the Greek Two Ways is often identical (רוח ענוה / πραΰς; ואורך אפים / μακρόθυμος; ורוב רחמים / καὶ ἐλεήμων; וטוב עולמים / καὶ ἄκακος / καὶ ἀγαθός) or alike, while the text as a whole follows the same sequence.[31] The terms in the Qumran catalogue that do not match the Two Way's listing (שכל; ובינה and חכמת גבורה) represent "descriptions of the secret knowledge claimed by the sect, and which are characteristic of the Scrolls."[32] They are idiosyncratic to the Qumran teachings. The corresponding materials in 4:2a.2b-4a and the GTW 1:1; 3:7-8.10 are extensive enough so as to suggest a literary relationship between the two documents. On the face of it, we might thus reasonably hold that the Greek Two Ways depends on the doctrinal unit in 1QS or at least on certain parts of this passage. It is not likely, however, that our tractate derives from 1QS 3:13-4:26 as the text now stands. Instead, there is a rather good possibility that both documents share a common source which is almost entirely limited to the Two Ways ethic. A further remark on Qumran ideology will demonstrate this point.[33]

A pivotal teaching of the Dead Sea sect is the doctrine of the double predestination, i.e. the fact that it is divinely preordained who will be saved and who will be damned, because it was God who created the righteous and the sinner.[34] Other Qumran documents (including 1QH 1:7-8.18-20 and CD 2:7-

---

[31] The wording וטוב עולמים, though, might correspond to καὶ ἄκακος ("and without guile") in the parallel position in GTW 3:7-8 and, in addition, to the wording καὶ ἀγαθός ("and good") in the sixth position.

For this correspondence, see already Flusser ('The Dead Sea Sect' 249, n. 116), who erroneously attributed his observation to Audet, 'Affinités littéraires', 219-38. This mistake was corrected in the article's reprint in Id., *Judaism*, 57, n. 116. See also Id., 'Ezohi Derekh Yashara', 164-65.

[32] Draper, *A Commentary on the Didache*, 78.

[33] T. Elgvin has published two small fragments of 4Q473. He has entitled these segments '4QThe Two Ways' because the second fragment deals with this theme, as the translation of the first lines shows:

1.] [the way you will walk(?)]
2. upon. [   ]He sets [before you life and death(?)   before you are]
3. t[wo]ways, one goo[d and one evil. If you walk in the good way He will guard you(?)]
4. and bless you. But, if you walk in the [evil] way,[He will curse you and revile you(?), and evil] .....
(293)

Interestingly, the editor writes: "There are no clear markers of the structure of the *yahad* or sectarian theology in this composition" (290) and in the introduction he states that the "literary setting is that of Deuteronomy" (289; see also p. 290). Indeed, the passage clearly alludes to Deut 30:15.19 which is interpreted in a traditional way, namely (as observed above, p. 143) with the help of Jer 21:8. The whole fragment belongs to the Deuteronomic framework and the entire scroll probably was a parabiblical composition.

[34] With regard to the sect's doctrine of fate or predeterminism by comparison with the parties of the Pharisees and the Sadducees, Josephus states: "As for the Pharisees, they say that certain events are the work of Fate, but not all; as to other events, it depends upon ourselves whether they shall take place or not. The sect of the Essenes, however, declares that Fate is mistress of all things, and that nothing befalls men unless it be in accordance with her decree. But the Sadducees do away with Fate, holding that there is no such thing and that human actions are not achieved in accordance with her decree, but that all things lie within our own power, so that we ourselves are responsible for our well-being, while we suffer misfortune through our own thoughtlessness." (*Ant.* 13, 171-73). See also Dimant, 'Qumran Sectarian Literature', 536-38; Hengel, *Judentum und Hellenismus*, 397-98, n. 639; Flusser, 'The Dead

12) express the same view but the 'dogma' is fully developed in the doctrinal passage in 1QS 3:13-4:2b. God has predetermined everything that happens in the universe. Predestination is offered within a cosmological framework and has its bearing on creation, salvation, human responsibility, and ethics. All things take place in accordance with the plans which God has laid down in advance. In the sect's belief, men are forced to go one way or the other and are denied the freedom of choice between the opposite ways:

> In the hand of the Prince of Lights (is) the dominion of all the Sons of Righteousness; in the ways of light they walk. But in the hand of the Angel of Darkness (is) the dominion of the Sons of Deceit; and in the ways of darkness they walk (1QS 3:20-21).

The Essene concept of two spirits is closely connected with this notion of predetermination. There is no doubt that in the above quotation the Prince of Lights is synonymous with the Spirit of Truth and the Angel of Darkness is equivalent to the Spirit of Deceit. The function of the two spirits is to control all people for good and evil and men are assigned to one or the other spirit as a result of the will of God. In 1QS 3:13-4:26 it is not the Two Ways that are decisive but the two spirits. God

> has created the spirits of light and darkness, and upon them he founded every work, ... every action, and upon their ways (are) [al]l... (1QS 3:25-26).

The theme of the two spirits, between whom all humanity is divided, pervades the entire passage and the dualism determining every human to either good or evil is dominated by the two spirits. According to 1QS 3:17-18, man does not walk in one of the two ways but in one of the two spirits. God has appointed

> for him two spirits in which to walk until the appointed time for his visitation, namely the spirits of truth and of deceit (1QS 3:18-19).

On the other hand, these quotations demonstrate that the Ways imagery in the sense of "conduct", "manner of life" also plays a special role. The noun "way" and the verb "to walk" occur sixteen times in the Two Spirits Treatise.[35] The ways of God, the ways of truth, or the ways of light coincide with the ways of the Spirit of Truth just like the ways of darkness and the ways of evil match the ways of the Spirit of Deceit.[36] Sinners are said to "walk in the ways of darkness" (1QS 3:21 and 4:11) and the two opposing spirits are presented as those who have "their ways in the

---

Sea Sect', 23-35; Becker, *Das Heil Gottes*, 83-87.

[35] The term "way" and its varied use in the sense of "to walk" is found in the Two Spirits Treatise in the following places: 1QS 3:18 ("to walk").20.21.26; 4:1.2 (twice).6 ("to walk").10.11.12 ("to walk").15.17.18 ("to walk").19.21 (?).24 ("to walk").

[36] "Sachlich sind die Wege Gottes oder die Wege seiner Wahrheit gleich den Wegen *des Geistes* (oder der Geister) *der Wahrheit* 1QS 3,26; 4,2.15 (vgl. 3,18f) und auch den Wegen des Lichtes 1QS 3,3.20, auf denen diese Geister selbst und ihre Anhänger wandeln. Das Gegenteil sind die Wege der Finsternis 1 QS 3,21; 4,11, die Gott für immer hasst 4,1 (...);" cf. Nötscher, *Gotteswege und Menschenwege*, 78.

world" (4:2; see also 3:19-20 above). The vestiges of the Ways imagery are still evident but the ways have largely given way to the spirits.[37]

How is this situation to be explained? The presence of the ways and spirits side by side tends to support the suspicion that in Qumran the Two Ways are substituted by the two spirits as a consequence of predestinarian thought.[38] This suggestion is corroborated by other sources. Dualistic beliefs in terms of predetermination are found in various Jewish writings which, although not sectarian in character, probably belonged to the wider Essene movement such as Jub 10:1.9.11; 15:31b-32a; Sir 42:24-25; *T. Asher* 1:8-9; 3:3; 6:2, and 6:4-6. It was observed in the previous section, however, that almost all Two Ways metaphors (dualistic or otherwise) of the period presuppose man's free decision between the two alternative paths of conduct.[39] It is not by the Two Spirits that each man is led astray or aright but by his own free will. In the dualistic form of the Two Ways – underlying the Didache, Doctrina and Barnabas – this same idea is echoed. The Two Ways are really two paths open to man. One may thus argue with some assurance that in Qumran the emphasis might have been deliberately shifted from freedom of choice and moral responsibility, represented by the option on the part of man between the Two Ways, to man's incorporation into two cosmic and ethical domains ruled by the two spirits.[40]

On the one hand, the affinity between the Treatise of the Two Spirits in 1 QS and the Greek Two Ways argues for a strong correlation between the two documents, especially in view of the correspondence in thought pattern and linguistic parallels between lines 2a.2b-4 in 1QS col. 4 and the verses 1:1a; 3:7-8.10 in the Two Ways. On the other hand, one cannot deny that the doctrinal passage in 1QS is built upon the dogma of double predestination, while conventional Two Ways imagery and also the Greek Two Ways invited the reader to choose between the Two Ways. It is likely therefore – and this will be supported further in the discussion below – that an earlier pre-Essene form lies behind the present doctrinal

---

[37] "In Qumran wird die Gegensätzlichkeit innerhalb der Menschenwege nur durch Wahrheit und Bosheit, durch Geradheit und Verkehrtheit sowie durch Licht und Finsternis bestimmt. Ausgangspunkt und Ursache dieses Widerstreits sind nach dem 'dualistischen Abschnitt' aber gar nicht die zweierlei *Wege*, sondern die zweierlei *Geister*, die Geister des Lichtes und die Geister der Finsternis, die zugleich die Geister der Wahrheit und die Geister der Bosheit sind 1 QS 3,18f; ... ; cf. Nötscher, *Gotteswege und Menschenwege*, 92.

[38] Certainly, the double predestination is also found in other sectarian documents (1QH; CD; 1QM; etc.; see Besch, *Der Dualismus in den Kernschriften von Qumran*, 51-101) but an explicit and unambiguous doctrine of the 'two spirits' is missing there. Cf. also Stegemann, 'Zu Textbestand und Grundgedanken', 127.

[39] As far as can be ascertained, the belief in predestination is found in a direct context of a Two Ways metaphor in Sir 33[36]:7-15 only (see pp. 144-45), though here again without the catalogues of virtues and vices. For Ben Sira, cf. Hengel, *Judentum und Hellenismus*, 255-66.

[40] VanderKam in outlining the sect's thought and practice presents "The Two Ways" as a basic principle of its theology: "In God's predestined plan there are two ways: the way of light and the way of darkness, the way of good and the way of evil. There is no mediating option. The entire universe is involved in this duality, which is ultimately under God's firm control" (*The Dead Sea Scrolls Today*, 110).

passage in 1QS. This hypothetical source shared by 1QS and the Greek Two Ways was dualistic but did not fit the Essene doctrine of double predestination. As a result of the sect's deterministic ideas, it was deliberately modified or "essenized". The two spirits are the mediating powers implementing God's predestined plan. In the Qumran sect, man is no longer in a position to choose between the Way of Light and the Way of Darkness, but the elected righteous walk in the Spirit of Light, while the rejected sinners walk in the Spirit of Darkness.

There is thus a good possibility that the sect worked over a separate and independent traditional Two Ways manual, containing lists of virtues and vices by incorporating into it predestinarian ideas of their own. As a matter of fact, it has been demonstrated that the passage in 1QS 3:13-4:26, as it has been preserved, represents a self-contained literary section with features which in many respects are unique to this segment. Firstly, the terminology that shows a strong sense of in-group awareness and is present preeminently in the remainder of the document, is lacking here.[41] Moreover, the figure of Belial is not mentioned here in spite of the section's cosmological and ethical dualism and, finally, the covenant is realized only in the eschaton (cf. 1QS 4:22), while in other parts of 1QS (see e.g. 1QS 1:16) the community sees itself as the true covenant.[42] Consequently, the passage in 1QS 3:13-4:26, as it now stands, differs in general outlook and wording from its surrounding context. It provides indications that it once existed independently of its present context[43] and it may well be that the primary shape of the instruction originated in a pre-Essene milieu. This teaching might have circulated in both oral and written forms. In any case, it is likely that a written manual became known to the sectarians of Qumran who took it over, reworked it, and incorporated it into the Community Rule.

---

[41] "Tatsächlich ... fehlt hier nicht nur entsprechende Terminologie wie YHD, 'DH, QHL oder H'M völlig, sondern ebenso jegliche Perspektive solcher Art. Stets ist ausschliesslich ‹die Menschheit› in ihrer Gesamtheit im Blick;" cf. Stegemann, 'Zu Textbestand und Grundgedanken', 128, n. 90.

[42] For these and additional arguments, see Lange, 'Wisdom and Predestination', 346-47, n. 18 and Id., *Weisheit und Prädestination*, 127-28.

[43] Parts of the text of 1QS are preserved in 4QS[a-j] (= 4Q255-264). Metso (*The Textual Development*, 91) suggests that 1QS 3:20-25 may be paralleled in fragment 3 of 4QS[a] (cf. also p. 137) but the evidence presented is too slight to substantiate this assumption. Elsewhere the author is more cautious about the matter: "There is a slight possibility that fragment 3 forms a loose parallel to 1QS 3,20-25" (18). The single item among the 4QS[a-j] manuscripts which indeed provides fragments of the Two Spirits doctrine is 4QS[c] (cf. Metso, *The Textual Development*, 35-36).
Interestingly, remnants of the Two Spirits Treatise are also lacking in 4QS[b], the only 4QS manuscript containing fragments of the text of 1QS 1:1-3:13 and 1QS 5-11. (cf. Qimron-Charlesworth, 'Rule of the Community', 55-56; Metso, *The Textual Development*, 26-30). This tends to support the view that the doctrine represented by in 1QS 3:13-4:26 seems to have been a separate and independant treatise in an earlier stage of its history (see also Lange, *Weisheit und Prädestination*, 126; Besch, *Der Dualismus in den Kernschriften von Qumran*, 56).
For the separate units of 1QS, see also Licht, *The Rule Scroll*, 18-22. See also Id., 'An Analysis', 100, for the chiastic form of 1QS 3:13-4:26; cf. Guilbert, 'Le plan de la Règle', 328-29; Leaney, *The Rule of Qumran*, 145-46; Dimant, 'Qumran Sectarian Literature', 500-501. For an analysis of the structure of the Two Spirits Treatise, and particularly of the literary organization of the segment representing the ways and the visitation of the two spirits (4:2-14), see Duhaime, 'Les voies des deux esprits'.

It is not clear to what extent the pecularities of a traditional Two Ways doctrine were eliminated and systematically reworked on the basis of the theological ideas within the sect. Any attempt to reconstruct all the details of the source of 1QS 3:13-4:26 in its pre-Essene stage would therefore be conjectural. Nonetheless, by focussing on one particular theme and with the aid of other sources, we are in a position to demonstrate how the sectarians might have revised traditional materials. One of the main lines of the treatise is the following:

> He created the human for the dominion of the world, designing for him two spirits in which to walk ... (1QS 3:17b-18a)
>
> ...והואה ברא אנוש לממשלת תבל וישם לו[44] שתי רוחות להתהלך בם...

Since this clause refers to an endowment which God provided for newly created humankind or man, the concerns are close enough so as to allow a more detailed comparison with a midrash about Adam in various Jewish traditions. In the Mekhilta to Ex 14:29 the following explanation of Gen 3:22 is attributed to R. Akiva:

> And how do you interpret: 'Behold, the man is become as one of us ("mimmenu" / ממנו)?' It only means that God put before him two ways (שני דרכים), one of death and one of life, and he chose for himself the way of death.[45]

The passage in 2 Enoch 30:15 (already quoted above) is even more interesting since it is not the Ways of life and death but those of light and darkness which are mentioned here:

> And I gave him (= Adam) his free will; and I pointed out to him the two ways – light and darkness. And I said to him, 'This is good for you, but that is bad'; so that I might come to know whether he has love toward me or abhorrence, and so that it might become plain who among his race loves me.

It is of importance to note that, according to the midrash, the ability to distinguish between good and evil did not occur in consequence of the eating of the forbidden tree (as described in Gen 2:9.17; 3:5.22). Here the Two Ways, of life and death / light and darkness, had already been proposed to Adam before the Fall. He is blamed for not having used his freedom and ability to choose between good and

---

[44] The expression וישם לו in these lines excludes the idea, suggested in connection with 4:23, that man was created by God with a dual nature, with two spirits who fight a battle in the heart of man; so Wernberg-Møller, 'A Reconsideration of the Two Spirits', 422-23.428.432-33. The passage in 3:18 makes clear that the two spirits need not dwell in man exclusively, for God did not create the spirits in man (וישם בו), but that he allotted them unto man (וישם לו). The sectarian teaching is clearly different from the rabbinic doctrine of the two inclinations, which is not reflected in the Qumranic documents; cf. Charlesworth, 'A Critical Comparison', 396-97; see also May, 'Cosmological Reference in the Qumran Doctrine', 1-2; Von der Osten-Sacken, *Gott und Belial*, 141-142 (incl. n. 4); Licht, 'An Analysis of the Treatise', 91, n.13; Besch, *Der Dualismus in den Kernschriften von Qumran*, 57-61 and 182-83.

[45] Cf. Horovitz-Rabin, *Mekhilta d'Rabbi Ismael*, 112, 14-16; see also on the same verse Epstein-Melamed, *Mekhilta d'Rabbi Šim'on b. Jochai*, 68, 14-17 and Theodor-Albeck, *Midrash Bereshit Rabba* 1, 200 (= 21,5) and the note there. The suffix of ממנו is held here to be third person sing., rather than first person plural (as in modern translations). R. Akiva thus takes the word ממנו to indicate the source, i.e. one who is able, from his own capacity, to choose good or evil; see Bacher, *Die Agada der Tannaiten* 1, 318 and 319, n. 1.

evil. A similar thought may be expressed in Pseudo-Philo's Biblical Antiquities (13,8-9):

> '...But that man (Adam) transgressed my (God's) ways ('vias meas')... And then death was ordained for the generations of men'. And the Lord continued to show him the ways of paradise and said to him: 'These are the ways that men have lost by not walking in them, because they have sinned against me'.[46]

In the sectarian passage (1QS 3:17b-18a), God has "created the *human* (אנוש) for the dominion of the world, designing for him *two spirits* (שתי רוחות) in which to walk ...". According to the Scripture, however, God did not confer rule over the earth on some general man, the "human", but on Adam (cf. Gen 1:26.28; Ps 8:7; see also Jub 2:14). This observation raises the probability that the phrase in the version behind the present form of 1QS 3:17b-18a might reflect the content of the midrash. If that is the case, the pre-Essene source was not about "the human" and two spirits, but about *Adam* before whom God has set *two* opposite *ways*. Thus, the pre-sectarian reading of the clause could have run thus:

> He created Adam for the dominion of the world, designing for him two ways in which to walk ... (1QS 3:17b-18a)
>
> ....והואה ברא אדם לממשלת תבל וישם לו שתי דרכים להתהלך בם...

It remains to be seen in what sense the above discussion is relevant to our investigation. We have discovered the likelihood that the extant version of 1QS 3:13-4:26 is a revision of an earlier Two Ways instruction. Because our Greek Two Ways is closely related to the Treatise of the Two Spirits but does not show traces of the sect's predestination, its composer was probably familiar with this earlier pre-Essene stage of the passage. There can be little doubt that the two contrasting lists of 1QS 4:2-14 (or similar opposite catalogues) appeared in his source. Not only 1QS 4:2b-4a is reflected in GTW 3:7-8.10, but also the clause in 1QS 4:2a about "the ways in the world," which serves as a heading of the two subsequent lists, is resumed in the Greek Two Ways' introduction. Now, if we compare the two catalogues of virtues and vices in these documents more closely, it is obvious that the Way of Death in GTW 5:1 equals the mere list of vices or sins in 1QS 4:9-11. GTW and 1QS both essentially offer a similar account of the Way of Death.[47] On the other hand, the Way of Life in the Greek Two Ways has been greatly expanded to include a great deal of ethical instructions in 1:2-3; 2:2-4:14. Relying on the present form of 1QS, it is reasonable to hypothesize that most of these moral directives did not form part of the Way of Life in the pre-Essene source. What seems to emerge, then, is that the Treatise of the Two Spirits and the Greek Two Ways represent divergent

---

[46] ET: Harrington, 'Pseudo-Philo', 322. For the Latin text, see Harrington-Cazeaux, *Pseudo-Philon* 1, 134.

[47] "Der Lasterkatalog des Todesweges ist in der Form und auch in einzelnen Begriffen der Aufzählung des »Gefolges des Geistes der Übertretung« von 1QS IV,11-16 eng verwandt. Er ist eben, auch wenn einzelne Sünden ersetzt und neu angefügt werden, nicht im Mittelpunkt des Interesses und wird deswegen einfach tradiert;" cf. Kamlah, *Die Form der katalogischen Paränese*, 213. See also Draper, *A Commentary on the Didache*, 118.

trends from a common starting point. The Way of Life in the Greek Two Ways (behind the Doctrina, the Didache, and Barnabas) has been extensively expanded and worked over and, indeed, shows a marked tendency to teach what a man has to do and how he has to be once he has decided to walk the right way. In anticipation of the section on pp. 172-79 (below), it should be noted that concern with the Way of Life is also the first and foremost feature of the rabbinic Derekh Erets literature.

The Various Traditional Materials Preserved in the Greek Way of Life

The above comparison between the earlier form of the Two Ways underlying 1QS 3:13-4:26 with the Greek Two Ways has demonstrated that the latter document shows an increasing interest in the Way of Life. In this section, the specific components and concerns of the Way of Life will be discussed in an attempt to determine the nature of its divergent traditions. Attention will be restricted here, however, to the tradional units in GTW 1:1-3:6, since the individual positive and negative exhortations in 3:7-4:14 mainly reflect the practical wisdom of the early parts of the Derekh Erets tracts which will be dealt with in the following section. In the first part of the final section (pp. 180-82), then, the common trend that emerges from the whole of the materials constituting the Two Ways in our Greek document will be examined. One further preliminary point to be made is that the scope of the present section does not permit a discussion of all verses of the Way of Life in detail as our initial focus of interest lies with the traditional Jewish forms of these materials.

THE ESSENTIALS OF THE WAY OF LIFE (1:2)

The points of contact between 1QS and the sharply dualistic introduction of the Greek Two Ways prove that both documents preserve, each in their own way, traits of the pre-Essene source. There is little doubt that in this early source the "ways in the world," the two contrasting angels and the incompatibility between the ways were mentioned.[48] This is to say that the beginning of the Greek Two Ways not

---

[48]   The following scheme may help to understand the whole situation:

The beginning of GTW	*1QS*
There are two ways in the world,	(4:2) And these are their ways in the world
one of life, the other of death, one of light, the other of darkness; upon them two angels are appointed, one of righteousness, the other of iniquity,	(3:20-21) In the hand of the prince of lights (is) the dominion of all the sons of righteousness; in the ways of light they walk. But in the hand of the angel of darkness (is) the dominion of the sons of deceit / iniquity, and in the ways of darkness they walk.
and between the two ways there is a great difference.	(4:18) (for) they do not walk together.

It is remarkable that in the sectarian Qumran text the contrast between life and death is missing, while it is present not only in the Tenach (Jer 21:8; Deut 30:15-19), but also in the New Testament (Matt 7:14).

(only) reflects a general 'Two Ways' metaphor but first of all reflects a specific dualistic Jewish tradition. The opening of the Two Ways form in the Didache, however, is at variance with this tradition in that it lacks the antagonistic angelology and dualistic cosmology.

The Way of Life is defined by the double love command and the subsequent Golden Rule. In the following pages, we will examine separately the different components of this basic moral code.

The Double Love Commandment (1:2ab)

The double love commandment associates in midrash-fashion the two precepts occurring in Lev 19:18 (covering man's duties to his fellow man)[49] and Deut 6:5 (covering the commandments between man and God), each of which start with the word ואהבת ("you shall love"). The two commandments are quoted by Jesus in Matt 22:37-39; Mark 12:30-31, and Luke 10:27, but also belong together in other Jewish sources. The earliest document providing the combination of the two commandments is the Book of Jubilees. Here Isaac, addressing his twin sons Esau and Jacob before his death, makes them swear that they fear God and love one another:

> And now I will make you swear by the great oath ... that you will fear him (God) and worship him. And (that) each one will love his brother with compassion and righteousness ... (36:7-8).[50]

Apparently, no distinction is made here between serving God in love or in awe. In this testament of Isaac, the precept to love God is probably synonymous with the commandment in Deut 6:13: "You shall fear him, your God ...."[51] A similar equation of love and reverence for God is found in Sir 7:29-30:

This phenomenon brings about the uneasy feeling that the Qumran covenanters have consciously censured the dualistic pair "life-death." In the Latin Doctrina (1:1), the way of life and that of death is followed by the way of light and the way of darkness, while Barnabas mentions the way of light and that of the darkness only. We decided in our reconstruction to follow the Doctrina (see Chap. 4). The two angels are described as controlling the Ways in Clementine Homilies XX. 2,5; Pirqe R. El. 15 and *Herm. Man.* VI, 2 as well. For the latter occurrence, see Snyder, *The Apostolic Fathers* 6, 76-78 (English translation and commentary), Brox, *Der Hirt des Hermas*, 223-28 (German translation and commentary), Körtner-Leutzsch, *Papiasfragmente. Hirt des Hermas*, 210-13 (Greek text, German translation and notes). In the preceding passage, *Herm. Man.* VI, 1, a description of the Two Ways is found. See the excellent explanation by Dibelius, *Die Apostolischen Väter* 4, 520-21.

[49] For a study of the love commandment (Lev 19:18) in the Hebrew Bible, see Mathys, *Liebe deinen Nächsten*. For the New Testament Synoptics, see Ebersohn, *Das Nächstenliebegebot*.

[50] ET: Wintermute, 'Jubilees', 124; cf. ARN a 16 (= Schechter, *Aboth de Rabbi Nathan*, 32b) where R. Shimon ben Elazar is reported to have said: "Under solemn oath was this statement pronounced, 'But you shall love your neighbour as yourself': (for) I the Lord have created him – if you love him, I am faithful to reward you in large measure; but if not, I am the judge to punish." See also Ebersohn, *Das Nächstenliebegebot*, 113-15.

[51] Also in rabbinic literature, many references are found that compare the awe and the love of God as superior means of worship; cf. Büchler, *Studies in Sin and Atonement*, 122-30; cf. Moore, *Judaism* 2, 98-100.

With all your soul fear God, revere his priests. With all your strength love your Maker (ἐν ὅλη δυνάμει ἀγάπησον τὸν ποιήσαντά σε), neglect not his ministers ... .[52]

Because the clause (ἀγάπησον) τὸν ποιήσαντά σε in Sirach is verbally identical to the phrase in GTW 1:2 (ἀγαπήσεις τὸν θεὸν) τὸν ποιήσαντά σε (cf. "diliges deum aeternum qui te fecit" in Doctrina 1:2), this passage may have left its imprint on the double love commandment in the Greek Two Ways.[53]

Also in *T. Benj.* 3:3, deep respect for God is combined with "philanthropy": "Fear the Lord and love your neighbour" (φοβεῖσθε κύριον καὶ ἀγαπᾶτε τὸν πλησίον. Cf. *T. Jos.* 11:1).[54] This occurrence aside, the two love commandments appear side by side in more than one place of the Testaments of the Twelve Patriarchs: "But love the Lord and your neighbour, show mercy to the poor and the weak" (*T. Issa.* 5:2); "The Lord I loved (ἠγάπησα) with all my strength, likewise, I loved (ἠγάπησα) also every man as my children" (7:6); "Love the Lord in all your life and each other with a true heart" (*T. Dan* 5:3).[55] In the New Testament texts, the twofold love commandment is a characteristic and important teaching. It is said to be the great commandment in the Law:

> And one of them, a lawyer, asked him a question, to test him. 'Teacher, which is the great commandment in the law?' And he said to him, 'You shall love the Lord your God with all your heart, and with all your soul, and with all your mind. This is the great and first commandment. And a second is like it, You shall love your neighbour as yourself. On these two commandments depend all the law and the prophets (Matt 22:35-40; cf. Mark 12:28-31).[56]

---

[52] ET: Skehan-Di Lella, *The Wisdom of Ben Sira*, 203 and, for the Greek version, Ziegler, *Sapientia Iesu Filii Sirach*. Both phrases "with all your soul" and "with all your strength" are taken from Deut 6:5: "And you shall love the Lord your God with all your heart, and with all your soul, and with all your strength."
Strangely enough, these verses in Jub and Sir are not referred to in the evidence adduced by Ebersohn, *Das Nächstenliebegebot*, 96-105.

[53] The same expression is found in Barn. 19:2. About this addition to Deut 6:5, see Niederwimmer, *Die Didache*, 89, n. 7.

[54] In the opening chapter of the Hebrew Testament of Naphtali (a mediaeval translation of a variant version of *T. Naph.*), the reverence for God is linked with the Golden Rule: "He (Naphtali) said to them: 'I give you no command save in regard to the fear of the Lord: you shall serve him, and you shall cleave to him.' They said to him: 'What need has he of our service?' He said to them: 'It is not that he has need of any creature, but that all creatures of his world have need of him. But he has not created his world in vain, but that his creatures should fear him, and that none should do to his neighbour what he does not like for himself'" (1:5-6); cf. the translation of R.H. Charles, revised by A. van der Heide in Hollander-De Jonge, *The Testaments of the Twelve Patriarchs*, 446-50; esp. 446.

[55] The two commandments also occur separately. For the precept 'to love (fear) the Lord', cf. *T. Levi* 13:1; *T. Zeb.* 10:5; *T. Dan* 6:1 and the precept 'to love one's neighbour' is found in *T. Reub.* 6:9; *T. Sim.* 4:7; *T. Zeb.* 8:5; *T. Gad* 6:1.3; 7:7; *T. Jos.* 17:2 etc.; cf. Ebersohn, *Das Nächstenliebegebot*, 57-96.

[56] Jesus' reference to the resemblance of these two commandments amounts to the identical term ואהבת, introducing the two precepts in Deut 6:5 and Lev 19:18. For the clause "on these two commandments depend all the law (and the prophets)," see the beginning of the midrash Sifra Qedoshim where it says that the Holiness Code (Lev 19) was expounded to the community of Israel מפני שרוב גופי תורה תלוים בה (= Weiss, *Sifra d'Be Rab*, 86c); cf. Bacher, *Die exegetische Terminologie* 1, 12 and 198.

In the Testaments of the Twelve Patriarchs, the twofold commandment has special prominence as well. Its occurrence at the beginning or close of an exhortation (*T. Issa.* 5:2; *T. Benj.* 3:3; *T. Issa.* 7:6; *T. Dan* 5:3), shows that it could serve as a summary of precepts. Moreover, this juxtaposition is often found in a context which incites us to keep the Law or all commandments (cf. *T. Issa.* 5:1; *T. Benj.* 3:1; *T. Issa* 7:1-6).[57]

In conclusion, two points are relevant with respect to our Two Ways passage. It is reasonable to assume that the direct antecedents to the association between the love of God and the love of others are to be found in Palestinian Jewish tradition[58], the more so since this tradition is based on the two clauses of Lev 19:18 and Deut 6:5, both of which begin with "you shall love." Moreover, as implied in the *T. 12 Patr.* and as specified in the synoptic teaching of Jesus and in the Greek Two Ways, the combination of the two commandments was usually held to be a summary of the entire Law.

The Golden Rule (1:2c)

It is important to emphasize here that the Golden Rule and the second half of the Decalogue are also found in Jewish sources as summaries of the essentials of the Law. The significance of this observation is immediately clear if we realize that

---

[57]   See Klinghardt, *Gesetz und Volk Gottes*, 141.

[58]   Cf. also Audet, *La Didachè*, 259; Rordorf-Tuilier, *La Doctrine des douze Apôtres*, 28-29; 142-43, n. 2. According to Berger (*Die Gesetzesauslegung Jesu*, 38-42; 136-176) the double commandment originated in Jewish Hellenism. For a somewhat different view, see Hollander-De Jonge, *The Testaments of the Twelve Patriarchs*, 418.

In the New Testament passages (Matt 22:34-40; Mark 12:28-34 and Luke 10:25-28), no controversy is reported between Jesus and the rabbis concerning the double love commandment. It is therefore somewhat surprising that it is not found unambiguously in extant rabbinic sources. The two rules are combined in substance in SifDeut to Deut 32:29: "What did he (Jacob) say to them? Take upon you the kingdom of heaven, and subdue one another in the fear of heaven, and conduct yourselves one toward another in charity (בגמילות חסדים)" (= Finkelstein, *Siphre ad Deuteronomium*, 372). Also the tractate Avot teaches that one should "Love the Eternal, and love humankind" (mAv 6:1; cf. 6:6). Of course, we now have a mediaeval midrashic compilation where the two great rules from Lev 19:18 and Deut 6:5 are found side by side (cf. Urbach, *Pitron Torah*, 79-80). This compilation, however, might have been influenced by the New Testament. For the *Pitron Torah*, see Strack-Stemberger, *Einleitung in Talmud und Midrasch*, 321.

It has been argued that the juxtaposition of the two commandments in the Greek Two Ways within the numerical schema of πρῶτον....δεύτερον ("primo ... secundo") represents a Christianization of the Jewish tradition in the light of Jesus' teaching. However, the combination of these precepts does not necessarily prove its debt to the synoptic tradition. Compare Josephus, who referring to an Essene oath, mentions: πρῶτον μὲν εὐσεβήσειν τὸ θεῖον, ἔπειτα τὰ πρὸς ἀνθρώπους δίκαια φυλάξειν ... ("first that he will practise piety towards the Deity, next that he will observe justice towards men: ...;" *Bellum* 2,139) and the way in which the exhortations to honour God and parents are connected in Ps.-Phoc. 8: πρῶτα θεὸν τιμᾶν, μετέπειτα δὲ σεῖο γονῆας ("honour God first, and thereafter your parents"); see also Josephus, *c. Ap.* 2, 206 (γονέων τιμᾶν μετὰ τὴν πρὸς θεὸν δευτέραν ἔταξε), Sib III, 593-94; etc.

both items sequel the twofold love commandment in the Greek Two Ways. Let us first focus on the so-called Golden Rule. This directive ("do not yourself do to another what you would not want done to you") is not only reflected in GTW 1:2c but is frequently found throughout both Jewish, Christian, and Hellenistic sources.[59] In Judaism, the Golden Rule is based on the biblical imperative "you shall love your neighbour as yourself" (ואהבת לרעך כמוך in Lev 19:18) and was used interchangeably in a positive form as well as in a restrictive (negative) formulation. The positive form of the expression can already be found in Jub 20:2. According to this ancient work, Abraham instructed his children and his posterity

> To observe the way of the Lord, to act righteously, to love each his neighbour, and to behave towards all men as one treats oneself.

The commandment to love one's neighbour – which is taken together with the Golden Rule – is presented here as one of the prime essentials of "the way of the Lord."[60] According to Matt 7:12 (and Luke 6:31), Jesus too has phrased the Golden Rule in a positive form: "So whatever you wish that men would do to you, do so to them; for this is the law and the prophets." Judging by the extant sources, however, the negative form of the Golden Rule was widely preferred.[61] In his famous reply to the pagan who inquired about a pithy summary of Judaism, Hillel is reported to have answered: "Whatever is hateful to you, do it not unto your fellow. This is the whole Tora, all the rest is explanation (זו היא כל התורה כולה ואידך פירושה היא); now go and study" (bShab 31a). There is a strong possibility, however, that the relevant pericope in the Babylonian Talmud does not contain a historically reliable tradition in stating that Hillel himself really quoted the Golden Rule.[62]

Be that as it may, it is interesting to see that Jewish tradition has assigned two different sayings to R. Akiva, both of which reduce the Tora to its basic principles. The first is similar to the one quoted above, which is attributed to Hillel, and is qualified by Akiva as "the general rule of the Tora (כללה של תורה)."[63] The other one is found in his well-known comment on Lev. 19:18: "you shall love your neighbour as yourself." This biblical precept, according to R. Akiva, is "the great (general) principle (כלל גדול)" of the Tora."[64] Even though the term "the great

---

[59] About the so-called "Golden Rule," see Dihle, *Die Goldene Regel*; Alexander, 'Jesus and the Golden Rule'; Wengst, *Didache (Apostellehre)*, 67, n. 5 and Niederwimmer, *Die Didache*, 91-92. According to Dihle, the Golden Rule belongs to the "Vulgarethik", while according to John Locke it is the "most unshaken Rule of Morality, and Foundation of all social Virtue;" cf. *An Essay Concerning Human Understanding* I,3,4 = Clarendon Edition, 68.

[60] Even though the Ethiopic text is unclear. See Berger, *Das Buch des Jubiläen*, 426, n. 2.

[61] Cf. Niederwimmer, *Die Didache*, 91-92, esp. n. 14. The negative form of the Golden Rule closes the Apostolic Decree according to the Western text (Acts 15:20.29; for the Jewish roots of the Decree, see below, Chap. 7). This form predominates in early Christian usage (cf the listing in Dihle, *Die Goldene Regel*, 107).

[62] Alexander, 'Jesus and the Golden Rule', 364-69.

[63] ARN b 26 (= Schechter, *Aboth de Rabbi Nathan*, 27a).

[64] Sifra Qedoshim 2,12 (= Weiss, *Sifra d'Be Rab*, 89b) and yNed 9,41c.

principle" need not in and by itself, necessarily denote a 'summary of the Law', its meaning certainly comes close to it.[65] Love of a neighbour is also considered to be the broad general principle of the Tora in Paul's Epistle to the Galatians: "For the whole law is fulfilled in one word, 'You shall love your neighbour as yourself'" (5:14). In any event, R. Akiva is presented in rabbinic sources as having voiced both the biblical love command (Lev. 19:18) and the Golden Rule as the fundamental and essential rule of the Law. Apparently, then, the Golden Rule came to be understood as an alternative form of the biblical "you shall love your neighbour as yourself" (Lev. 19:18),[66] an assumption which is supported by the Aramaic Targum. In TgPs-Yon on Lev 19:18, the Golden Rule is attached to the altruistic love commandment by paraphrasing the comparative pronoun כמוך with the following clause: "so that what is hateful to you, you shall not do to him."[67]

A general maxim, common to gentiles and Jews, became a pivotal expression for human ethics, as prescribed by the religion both in Judaism and later in Christianity. One of the oldest witnesses for such a Jewish interpretation of the Golden Rule is without doubt Philo of Alexandria. He writes: "Besides these" (commandments in the written Law of Moses) "there is a host of other things which belong to unwritten customs and institutions or are contained in the laws themselves. What a man would hate to suffer he must not do himself to others."[68] In Philo's view, the list he adds containing rules from the oral law and tradition was deduced from the words of the Tora. With regard to the Golden Rule's significance, he has put this maxim at the top of the list,[69] as the Golden Rule was seen as the essence of the Mosaic Law.

THE EXPLANATION OF THE ESSENTIALS OF THE WAY OF LIFE
IN THE GREEK TWO WAYS 1:3A-3:6

As has been observed above, the definition of the right way of life in the Greek Two Ways includes love of God, love of one's neighbour, and the Golden Rule. This exhortation establishes the ethical guideline for the remainder of the text. Further, we have noticed that the latter two precepts of this triad in fact indicate a single governing principle appearing here in two forms, namely the verse in

---

[65] Alexander, 'Jesus and the Golden Rule', 384-87.

[66] See also Bacher (*Die Agada der Tannaiten* 1, 4): "Dieses Wort" (the Golden Rule) "ist nichts anderes, als die negative Ausdrucksweise für das biblische: 'Liebe deinen Nächsten wie dich selbst' (Lev. 19,18) ... ." See also Borgen, 'The Golden Rule', 101 and 110.

[67] The Hebrew ואהבת לו כמוך is explained in TgPs-Yon on Lev 19:34 the same way, that is, as a reference to the Golden Rule in its negative form. Also the presentation of the Golden Rule in the Hebrew form of Sir 31:15 comes close to Lev 19:18: דעה רעך כנפשך; cf. MS B in Beentjes, *The Book of Ben Sira in Hebrew*, 56. For the combination of the Golden Rule and neighbourly love, see also the instances in Berger, *Die Gesetzesauslegung Jesu*, 133-34.

[68] Philo, *Hypothetica* 7,6; cf. Colson, *Philo* (LCL 363), 426-427. See I. Heinemann, *Philo's griechische und jüdische Bildung*, 352-358 and Bernays, 'Philon's Hypothetika', 272-276.

[69] Bernays, 'Philon's Hypothetika', 274.

Leviticus and the subsequent Golden Rule.[70] For this reason, it was probably added to the definition of the Way of Life in 1:2.

The Term "Explanation" (1:3a)

After the quotation of the main principles of the Way of Life, the text in the Greek Two Ways proceeds to describe the explanation of this basic code. On this point the Christian Didache, however, offers the evangelical section, a catena of Jesus-sayings that is not paralleled in the Doctrina, Barnabas, or in other early recensions of the Two Ways.[71] In order to bridge the sudden switch from the primary materials to the incorporation of the secondary Jesus tradition, the Didache has additional clauses in 2:1 and 1:3a. In Did 2:1, after the Christian interpolation, the phrase "but the second commandment of the teaching" (δευτέρα δὲ ἐντολὴ τῆς διδαχῆς), facilitates the transition to the original Two Ways document.[72] In Did 1:3a, the interpolation is introduced as follows: "Here is the *teaching* [that flows] from these words" (τούτων δὲ τῶν λόγων ἡ διδαχή ἐστιν αὕτη).

The Latin translation of the Two Ways in the Doctrina, where the materials in 2:2-7 immediately follow 1:3, does not need such editorial devices. In the Doctrina, the secondary verse of 2:1 is lacking and in 1:3, right after the "Great Rules" of the Way of Life, it says the following: "Here is the *explanation* of these words" ("interpretatio autem horum verborum est"). It is not difficult to explain why the clause in 1:3a shows a difference with regard to the terms διδαχή in the Didache and "interpretatio" in the Doctrina. Owing to his insertion of the evangelical section, the composer of the Didache was aware that he had supplied a new interpretation of the preceding definition of the Way of Life. Therefore, although he takes over the list of precepts in 2:2-7 almost unchanged, he was not in a position to consider the materials in 1:3b-6 as the interpretation of the essentials of the Way of Life in 1:2. He was forced to substitute the original Greek equivalent to the Latin "interpretatio" (probably ἑρμηνεία) for the word διδαχή.

The transition from the basic standards of the Way of Life to the distinct commandments by means of the term "explanation" in the version of the Latin Doctrina ("interpretatio autem horum verborum est") in a sense echoes the above-mentioned rules ascribed to R. Akiva and Hillel. The latter is even more conspicuous as Hillel taught that the entire Tora is incapsulated in the Golden Rule, while the particular commandments spell out the details of that one general Rule:

---

[70] For the observation that the Golden Rule may be considered a kind of variant to the love for the neighbour, cf. Dihle, *Die Goldene Regel*, 106-110. Dihle is possibly right when he sees a tension between the Golden Rule and the precept to love the enemy. According to Luke 6:27, the meaning of this precept is: "Do good to those who hate you." This does not fit the Golden Rule.

[71] See Chaps. 1 (pp. 40-48) and 2 (passim).

[72] See Kloppenborg, 'The Transformation of Moral Exhortation', 91; Jefford, *The Sayings of Jesus*, 53 and Niederwimmer, *Die Didache*, 70; 114-15.

"This is the whole Tora, all the rest is explanation (פירושה)."[73] The word "explanation" in the Greek Two Ways may thus rest on the Aramaic equivalent פירוש which could be rendered ἑρμηνεία. In Hillel's view, the whole Law of Moses is a specification of the Golden Rule, while according to the Greek Two Ways, the description of the Way of Life (2:2-4:14) is a specification of the two Great Rules, in combination with the Golden Rule.

The Second Half of the Decalogue (2:2-7)

The subsequent section in the Greek Two Ways (2:2-7) contains a list of precepts which was clearly meant to cover the essentials of the second half of the Decalogue.[74] To be sure, in the Greek Two Ways teaching as a whole, the list of prohibitions revolving around the second table of the Ten Commandments is one of the chief components. A cursory glance at the text immediately reveals similar records in 3:2-6 and 5:1. Although the items do not completely match their parallels in the Tenach or LXX and are expanded by additional elements,[75] the Jewish reader would obviously have recognized its source.

In the above discussion it was established that the double love commandment and the single verse commanding one to love one's neighbour (or its variant version in the Golden Rule) was thought of as covering the whole Tora. The urge to present the principles of Judaism can also be clearly perceived in the emphasis given to Decalogue which served as a matrix and fundamental essence of Jewish teachings in the second Temple period.[76] We will limit ourselves to a few observations in order to demonstrate the honoured place of the Ten Commandments in Judaism until the end of the first century.[77] The Nash Papyrus (probably dating from the second century BCE) comprises a version of the Decalogue in combination with the *Shema*, which indicates a liturgical recitation. Josephus gives absolute priority

---

[73]   In those days, the word פרש also meant "giving the particulars;" on this verb (and the substantive פירוש) see Rabin, *The Zadokite Documents*, 8 (n. 1 to II,13) and esp. 24 (n. 2 to VI,14); Bacher, *Die exegetische Terminologie* 1, 154-160 and 2, 165-169. See also I. Heinemann, 'Development of the Technical Terms'. Both scholars, Bacher (2, 169) and Heinemann (111), rightly mention Hillel's answer to a future proselyte.

[74]   Cf. Bourgeault, *Décalogue et morale chrétienne*, 27-63; Jefford, *The Sayings of Jesus*, 54-55; Flusser, 'The Ten Commandments', 236.

[75]   The extension was probably introduced with the purpose of providing a more thorough outline of moral standards paralleling the common accusations made in Jewish literature against gentile society: abortion, exposure of infants and the killing of new-born babies, fornication and pederasty, magical practices, astrology and omens; cf. Audet, *La Didachè*, 286-89; Rordorf-Tuilier, *La Doctrine des douze Apôtres*, 149, n. 7; Rordorf, 'Un chapitre d'éthique', 118; Bourgeault, *Décalogue et morale chrétienne*, 51-53. It is worth mentioning, however, that magicians and sorcerers also existed amongst Israelites, both in Israel and abroad. See Alon, 'Ha-halakha ba-Torat 12 ha-Shelihim', 280-81(ET: 174-75).

[76]   Cf. Alon, 'Ha-halakha ba-Torat 12 ha-Shelihim', 278-79 (ET: 170-71).

[77]   For more information, see Vokes, 'The Ten Commandments'; Berger, *Die Gesetzesauslegung Jesu*, 258-361; Amir, 'Die Zehn Gebote bei Philon'; Niebuhr, *Gesetz und Paränese*, 63-66; Alon, 'Ha-halakha ba-Torat 12 ha-Shelihim', 278-79 (ET: 170-71).

to the Decalogue. Its holiness demanded that "the excellence of the spoken words might not be impaired by human tongue" (*Ant.* 3, 89). In chapters 11 and 44 of Pseudo-Philo's Biblical Antiquities, the Decalogue is described as the preeminent legislation. It is called a "lumen mundo," a "testamentum cum filiis hominum" (11,1), or a "lex testamenti sempiterni" (11,5), and is held to be a summary of all precepts. Philo too views the precepts in the Tora as detailed regulations of the Ten Commandments and classifies them accordingly.[78] There are no compelling reasons, however, to assume a Hellenistic Jewish provenance for the favourable position of the Decalogue. After all, in caves 1 and 8 of Qumran, phylacteries were found containing the Decalogue. Moreover, it was recited with the *Shema* in the Temple (mTam 5:1) and in the synagogues and it was dropped from the liturgy in view of the "resentment of the Minim."[79]

In addition, the second table of the Decalogue was also commonly seen as summarizing the essentials of the Law. We may refer to Pseudo-Phocylides, *Sentences* 3-7, a passage which includes injunctions against murder, adultery, theft, covetousness, and speaking falsely.[80] From Mark 10:17b.19, it can be inferred that Jesus regarded the socio-ethical commandments of the second half of the Decalogue as a recapitulation of the Tora:

> 'Good teacher, what must I do to inherit eternal life?' ...'You know the commandments: Do not kill, Do not commit adultery, Do not steal, Do not bear false witness, Do not defraud, Honour your father and mother.'

A similar enumeration of the prohibitions of the second table of the Decalogue is found in the parallel accounts of Matt 19:18-19 and Luke 18:20[81] although Matthew closes the list with the phrase "you shall love your neighbour as yourself." The latter expansion is significant.[82] In the various books of the New Testament, the quotation of the second half of the the Decalogue is usually linked with the

---

[78] *Decal.* 29,154: "Enough on this subject, but also we must not forget that the Ten Words (οἱ δέκα λόγοι) are summaries of the special laws which are recorded in the Sacred Books and run through the whole of the legislation." See also *Spec. Leg.* I, 1.

[79] bBer 12a; yBer 1,3c; 7,11a; SifDeut 34 to Deut 6:7 (= Finkelstein, *Siphre ad Deuteronomium*, 60-61); cf. Moore, *Judaism* 1, 291, n. 3 and 3, 95-96, n. 64.

[80] Van der Horst, *The Sentences of Pseudo-Phocylides*, 112 and Wilson, *The Mysteries of Righteousness*, 66-74.

[81] Even though the synoptic versions show some differences. In Luke the precepts "do not kill" and "do not commit adultery" occur in reversed order. Moreover, in Matthew and Luke the clause "Do not defraud," which does not belong to the Decalogue, is missing. Finally, the prohibition "you shall not covet..." is absent from these synoptic places.

In the three reports, the prohibition to "honour your father and mother" seems out of place as it belongs to the first table of the Decalogue. Apparently, there were traditional divisions which assigned this precept to the second table; cf. SER, Chap. 7 (= Friedmann, *Seder Eliahu Rabba*, 35) and Ps.-Phoc. vv. 3-8. Also elsewhere in Jewish and early Christian literature, catalogues of sins are found which show a close connection with the second half of the Decalogue; cf. the list of examples of "dekalogähnlichen Lasterkatalogen" in Berger, *Die Gesetzesauslegung Jesu*, 272-273.

[82] For the following, see Flusser, 'The Ten Commandments', 223-28.

commandment to love one's neighbour. Thus Paul in his Epistle to the Romans states:

> Owe no one anything, except to love one another; for he who loves his neighbour has fulfilled the law. The commandments, 'You shall not commit adultery, You shall not kill, You shall not steal, You shall not covet,' and any other commandment, are summed up in this sentence, 'You shall love your neighbour as yourself.' Love does no wrong to a neighbour; therefore love is the fulfilling of the law (Rom 13:8-10).[83]

The love of one's neighbour is perceived here as a general rule which is spelled out in the second half of the Decalogue. Also, the Letter of James relates the second half of the Decalogue to the single all-inclusive principle of loving one's neighbour:

> If you really fulfil the royal law, according to the scripture, 'You shall love your neighbour as yourself,' you do well. But if you show partiality, you commit sin, and are convicted by the law as transgressors. For whoever keeps the whole law but fails in one point has become guilty of all of it. For he who said, 'Do not commit adultery,' said also, 'Do not kill.' If you do not commit adultery but do kill, you have become a transgressor of the law (Jas 2:8-11).[84]

As a result, the tradition of expressing the second half of the Decalogue in condensed form through the altruistic love commandment is quite common in the New Testament.[85] Independent evidence – that is to say materials that are probably not derived from passages in the New Testament – for this tendency may be found in

---

[83] A similar exhortation to love probably also underlies the wording ἵνα τὸ δικαίωμα τοῦ νόμου πληρωθῇ ἐν ἡμῖν ("in order that the just requirement of the law might be fulfilled among us") in the first clause of Rom 8:4; see Van de Sandt, 'Research into Rom. 8,4a'; Id., 'An Explanation of Rom. 8,4a' and Horn, *Das Angeld des Geistes*, 372-74.

[84] In addition, the Jewish idea that violating one commandment amounts to violating them all (see for instance Dibelius, *Der Brief des Jakobus*, 179-80 and Baer, 'The Historical Foundations', 127-28) is applied here to the second half of the Decalogue. It is quite likely that this passage in James is based upon the midrash offered in MekhRSbY on Ex 20:14: "You might have thought that a person is not guilty unless he transgresses all these commandments; therefore does the Tora say: 'You shall not murder, You shall not commit adultery, You shall not steal, You shall not bear false witness, You shall not covet' (Ex 20:13), in order to make one liable for each commandment separately. That being so, why does Deuteronomy join all these commandments together, saying 'You shall not murder *and* you shall not commit adultery *and* you shall not steal *and* you shall not bear false witness *and* you shall not covet' (Deut 5:17)? It is to teach us that they are all interrelated. When a person breaks one of them, he will end up by breaking them all." (= Epstein-Melamed, *Mekhilta d'Rabbi Šim'on b. Jochai*, 154, 21-25); see further, Flusser, 'The Ten Commandments', 225-26.

[85] Apart from Matt 19:18-19; Rom 13:8-10 and Jas 2:8-11, also the antithetical section of the Sermon on the Mount in Matt 5:17-48 (cf. murder, adultery and lying / false swearing in 5:21-37) reflects the second half of the Decalogue. Moreover, while the Greek Two Ways offers the verse from Lev 19:18 ("you shall love your neighbour as yourself") in its opening words, the selfsame verse is cited and elaborated upon by Jesus at the conclusion of the literary unit in Matt 5:17-48. The correspondence between the Greek Two Ways (esp. 3:1-6) and the Matthean section will be dealt with in the next chapter of this book. For the present, it suffices to establish that the text in Matt 5:17-48 displays a close tie between the last half of the Ten Commandments and the biblical altruistic love command.

the Pseudo-Clementine writings. In these two works, which are revisions of a common ancestor, the commandment to love one's neighbour – represented here by the Golden Rule – is linked with the second half of the Decalogue. At the same time, the mention of God-fearing Jews in connection with the Golden Rule may be an indication that the entire passage in the common source was derived from a Jewish tradition.[86]

The idea that all the commandments of the Tora are embedded in the Ten Commandments probably resulted in the notion that the last five of these commandments, dealing with the relations between man and his fellow man, are concentrated in the command to love one's neighbour. In the Greek Two Ways, the second half of the Decalogue does not only explain the Golden Rule but the double love commandment as well. It is quite possible, therefore, that, during the second Temple Period, a type of homily existed which was based upon the last five of the Ten Commandments combined with the verse "you shall love your neighbour as yourself" or with the Golden Rule. This paradigm of exhortation was obviously the product of a specific religious approach fostered in circles close to Hillel the Elder and R. Akiva.

Light and Weighty Sins (3:1-6)

After the first description of the Way of Life in 2:2-7 and right before the various positive exhortations in 3:7-10, a distinctive literary unit occurs in 3:1-6 which closely reflects the Decalogue themes of the preceding chapter 2. Scholars have traditionally noted that the section shows indications of having been incorporated into the Two Ways from an independent source. It differs noticeably in style compared with context since the precepts are formulated here in terms of a warm encouragement. Furthermore, the unit consists of five small strophes, each of

---

[86] The text in Clementine Homilies VII,4,3-4 refers to one "unique saying," transmitted to "God-fearing Jews," quotes the Golden Rule in its positive form and then proceeds thus: "if you do not want to be killed, do not kill anybody; if you do not want your wife to be forced into adultery by anybody else, do not commit adultery with anyone else's wife; if you don't want anything of yours stolen, do not steal anything that belongs to someone else" (τὰ δὲ λοιπὰ ἐνὶ λόγῳ ὡς οἱ θεὸν σέβοντες ἤκουσαν Ἰουδαῖοι, καὶ ὑμεῖς ἀκούσατε ἅπαντες ἐν πολλοῖς σώμασιν μίαν γνώμην ἀναλαβόντες· Ἅπερ ἕκαστος ἑαυτῷ βούλεται καλά, τὰ αὐτὰ βουλευέσθω καὶ τῷ πλησίον. οὕτω δ᾽ ἂν ὑμῶν ἕκαστος νοήσειεν τὸ καλόν, εἰ ἑαυτῷ διαλεχθείη τὰ τοιαῦτα· Οὐ θέλεις φονευθῆναι, ἕτερον μὴ φονεύσῃς· οὐ θέλεις τὴν σὴν ὑφ᾽ ἑτέρου μοιχευθῆναι γυναῖκα, τὴν ἑτέρου μὴ μοίχευε γαμετήν· οὐ θέλεις τι τῶν σῶν κλαπῆναι, ἑτέρου μὴ κλέπτε μηδέν); cf. Rehm, *Die Pseudoklementinen* 1, 118. The text in Rec. VIII,56,7-8 quotes the Golden Rule in its negative version and goes on to explain it thus: "in the same way in which you don't want to be killed yourself, you must be careful not to kill anybody else; ... " etc. ("omnis enim propemodum actuum nostrorum in eo colligitur observantia, ut quod ipsi pati nolumus, ne hoc aliis inferamus; sicut enim ipse occidi non vis, caveas oportet ne alium occidas, et sicut tuum non vis violari matrimonium, nec tu alterius macules t[h]orum, furtum pati non vis nec ipse facias; et intra hanc regulam humanorum gestorum singula quaeque concurrunt"); cf. Rehm, *Die Pseudoklementinen* 2, 253.

which is structured according to the same distinctive, symmetrical pattern which is not revealed elsewhere in the Greek Two Ways.[87]

The separate strophes in 3:2-6 display a particular repetitive pattern in that each, in turn, is divided into two parallel halves. In the first half, a warning against a specific minor transgression is uttered because this light sin, so it says, "leads to" a major transgression. Then, in the second half, an admonishment is phrased against two or more lesser sins, for these too are considered to "engender" a major transgression. Unlike the variety of light transgressions in the two halves of the separate strophes, the same weighty offense is repeatedly retained in each of the two halves, with the exception of 3:3, where the weighty sin is expressed in two different words ("fornication" and "adultery"). The weighty transgressions or sins occurring in this section, then, are murder (3:2), fornication and adultery (3:3), idolatry (3:4), theft (3:5) and blasphemy (3:6). The connection with the commandments of the Decalogue is clear enough as the tresspasses of murder, adultery, and theft are easily associated with the second table of the Ten Commandments.

It is important to recall that in the Greek Two Ways, the second half of the Decalogue has come to occupy a position of greatest authority. Also, the Way of Life commences its specification with a list of vices which is clearly designed to include the Second Table (2:2-7), and the Way of Death starts the list of variegated nastinesses (5:1) with specific items that have been borrowed from the second half of the Decalogue.[88] Properly speaking, however, the list of the major prohibitions in 3:2-6 covers but a part of these laws, since the precepts of false witness and coveting are missing here. The presence of all five principal items is more easily explained if they are related to the fundamental laws mentioned in Sifra Lev 18:4 (and bYom 67b):[89]

> You shall do my ordinances (Lev 18:4): these are the words written in the Tora, which, if they were not written, they should by right be written and these are they: (the prohibitions of) robbery, sexual immorality,[90] idolatry, blasphemy and bloodshed.[91] If these were not written, they should by right be written.

The five major sins in the Greek Two Ways 3:2-6 are thus identical with a list of basic transgressions handed down as commandments which are indispensable to

---

[87] It is noteworthy that the Letter of Barnabas has left out this tradition for whatever reason. The Doctrina lacks a counterpart to Did 3:3-4a. If the five major sins in Did 3:1-6 are identical with the five "fundamental laws" (see below), the least that can be said is that Did 3:3 seems to have formed part of this section.

[88] Cf. Bourgeault, *Décalogue et morale chrétienne*, 46-55. 59-63; Jefford, *The Sayings of Jesus*, 53-58. 84; Niederwimmer, *Die Didache*, 116-23.148.

[89] We translate here Sifra, Aharei Moth 9,10, on Lev. 18:4 (= Weiss, *Sifra d'Be Rab*, 86a).

[90] We have rendered עריות (גלוי) with "sexual immorality." In the strict sense it concerns "incest", which, however, was "extended to comprehend all illegitimate intercourse between men and women and the various abuses or perversions of sexual instincts;" cf. Moore, *Judaism* 2, 267.

[91] The sequence in bYom 67b is different: idolatry, immorality, bloodshed, robbery, blasphemy. The Hebrew word for "robbery" in this period was taken to mean "theft".

the survival of humankind. In rabbinic tradition, they are counted among the seven Noachide precepts, i.e. the laws which were held valid for the entire human race.[92]

The preoccupation of this *teknon*-section in the Greek Two Ways is expressed in the introductory sentence: "my child, flee from all evil and from everything like it" (3:1). It is intended to highlight the avoidance of anything resembling evil because it leads to evil itself. A statement similar to the one in the Two Ways 3:1 occurs in the literature of the Sages[93] and is found preeminently in the refined ethics represented by the rabbinic Derekh Erets tractates. In these tractates, the ethical rule serves as a résumé of moral codes.[94] We will return to the subject of Derekh Erets later. For the present, it suffices to note that oral tracts with subjects concerning Derekh Erets existed as early as the second century CE and that part of these writings reflect the teachings of pious circles in the Tannaitic period on moral behaviour.[95]

A dictum which is strongly reminiscent of the saying in the Greek Two Ways 3:1 is found in the treatise Yir'at Het, which is a separate denotation of the tract Derekh Erets Zuta, chapters I-IV and IX. Chapters I-III from this tract represent an early segment, probably dating from Tannaitic times.[96] In Yir'at Het I,13, then,

---

[92] See Flusser-Safrai, 'Das Aposteldekret', 187; Novak, *The Image of the Non-Jew*, 31 and 49-50, n. 143; see also Str-B 3, 36 and Klein, *Die älteste christliche Katechismus*, 62-64.

[93] "For R. Eliezer did teach: 'one should always flee from what is hideous and from whatever seems hideous'" and : "But the Sages said: 'Keep distant from what is hideous and from whatever seems hideous;'"; cf. tHul 2:24 (= Zuckermandel, *Tosephta*, 503) and tYev 4:7 (= Lieberman, *Tosefta ki-Fshutah* – Nashim, 12 and Zuckermandel, *Tosephta*, 245), respectively.

[94] Cf. Klein, *Der älteste christliche Katechismus*, 69: "Die kürzeste Formel für *Derech erez* lautet: *Halte dich fern von der Sünde und von dem, was hässlich ist.*"

[95] Lerner, 'The External Tractates', 380. Safrai, 'Teaching of Pietists', 25-28; Id. 'Hasidim we-Anshei Maase'; Id., 'Jesus and the Hasidim'; Id. 'Jesus and the Hasidic Movement'.

[96] The early (Tannaitic) part of Yir'at Het is identical with Massechet Derekh Erets Zuta, Chaps. I-III (minus I,18-20), edited by Van Loopik, *The Ways*, 172-251 (with commentary) = Massekhet Derekh Erets, Chaps. I-II, edited by Higger, *The treatises Derek Erez*, 1, 55-96 (Hebr.) and 2, 33-42 (ET). Cf. Van Loopik, *The Ways*, 9 and 16-17.

In a note, Lerner ('The External Tractates', 383, n. 108) refers to Higger's Massekhet Derekh Erets I-II,7 (= *The treatises Derek Erez*, 55-93) as representing the earlier segment, which portion corresponds with Massekhet Derekh Erets Zuta I-III,15 in Van Loopik, *The Ways*, 172-246. See also Ginzberg, 'Derek Erez Zuta', 530; Krauss, 'Le traité talmudique', (36) 40-44 and (37) 58-64.

In 1929, Higger edited the *Minor Tractates (Massekhtot Ze'irot)*. In this work he published the following shorter selections from Derekh Erets literature: Massekhet Yir'at Het, Massekhet Derekh Erets Zeira (= Derekh Erets Zuta, Chaps. V-VIII), Massekhet Arayot (= Derekh Erets Rabba, Chap. I), Perek Maasim (= Derekh Erets Rabba, Chap. II), Perek Shalom and Perek Gadol ha-Shalom. Then, in 1935, he published a complete critical edition of all extant Derekh Erets texts with an English translation in *The treatises Derek Erez*. It is important to note, however, that the internal division of Higger's *The treatises Derek Erez* is not identical with the ordinary printed editions in the Babylonian Talmud, which contain the Massekhet Derekh Erets Zuta (ten chapters and a supplementary chapter entitled Perek ha-Shalom, i.e., 'The Chapter of Peace') and Derekh Erets Rabba (eleven chapters). The arrangement in Higger, *The treatises Derek Erez* is as follows:

1. Massekhet Derekh Erets   =   Derekh Erets Zuta (= DEZ) I-IX
2. Pirke Ben Azzai   =   Derekh Erets Rabba (= DER) III-IX
3. Tosefta Derek Erez   =   DEZ X-XI and DER I-II and X-XI

Van Loopik, *The Ways*, offers a new English translation of the tractates DEZ (based on "Ms. Oxford

it states: "Keep aloof from everything hideous and from whatever seems hideous (הרחק מן הכיעור ומן הדומה לו) lest others suspect you of transgression."[97] The rule of refraining from anything hideous[98] reflects a strongly ethical approach, an attitude that is inspired by a deeply rooted fear of sin. The urge to abstain from evil incited pietistic Sages to keep to not only the literal meaning of a commandment but also its broad intention, surpassing the scope of widely accepted precepts. The most pertinent parallel to the preamble in GTW 3:1 and the subsequent strophes in 3:2-6 is the following statement that occurs in Yir'at Het as well:

> Keep aloof from that which leads to transgression, keep aloof from everything hideous and from what even seems hideous. Shudder from committing a minor transgression (מחטא הקל), lest it lead you to commit a major transgression (לחטא חמור). Hurry to (perform) a minor precept (למצוה קלה), for this will lead you to (perform) a major precept (למצוה חמורה]).[99]

Bodleian [cat. A. Neubauer, no. 896];" cf. p. 12), DER (based on "Ms. New York, Jewish Th. Sem. [cat. E.N. Adler, no. 2237];" cf.ibid.), and Perek ha-Shalom (based on the same manuscript "cat. E.N. Adler, no. 2237;" cf. ibid.) together with a commentary. In the following, the arrangement of the materials and the translation are borrowed from Van Loopik's edition and the Hebrew text, as far as possible, from Higger's *The treatises Derek Erez*.

[97] Yir'at Het I,13 according to Van Loopik, *The Ways*, 194-97 (with commentary) = Massekhet Derekh Erets I,12 according to Higger, *The treatises Derek Erez* 1, 63 (Hebr.) and 2, 35 (ET). Compare also the following saying: "Keep aloof from anything hideous and (even) from whatever seems hideous;" cf. DEZ VIII,3 according to Van Loopik, *The Ways*, 290 = Massekhet Derekh Erets VII,2 according to Higger, *The treatises Derek Erez* 1, 126 (Hebr.) and 2, 50 (ET). Cf. further Massekhet Yir'at Het, version a, Chap. 2 in Higger, *Minor Tractates*, 76 (lines 3-5); and version b, Perek Yir'at Heta in Higger, *Minor Tractates*, 82 (line 22) -83 (line 1) and Massekhet Derekh Erets Zeira, Chap. 4, in Higger, *Minor Tractates,* 90 (lines 12-13). See also the references in Sperber, *Masechet Derech Eretz Zutta*, 81 (Hebr.).

[98] For the term כיעור ("ugliness") as ethically offensive, see the warning in Seder Eliahu Rabba, Chap. 2: "for ugly things that aren't fitting" (דברים מכוערים ודברים שאינן ראויין) (= Friedmann, *Seder Eliahu Rabba*, 13); cf. also SER, Chap. 25 (= Id., 139): "And keep yourself distant from a transgression and from anything ugly" (והרחק] עצמך מן העבירה ומדבר מכוער). With reference to Gen 25:27 ("and Jacob was an upright man [איש תם]"), it says in SER, Chap. 7 (= Id., 32) that Jacob kept himself distant from robbery (הגזל), from transgression (העבירה) and from anything ugly (דבר מכוער); for the same triad (הגזל, העבירה, דבר מכוערה), cf. SER, Chap. 14 (= Id., 67). In SER, Chap. 18, the saying of the Sages, "your deeds will bring you near, your deeds will remove you" (mEd 5:7), is explained as follows: "when man goes ugly ways (דרכים מכוערין) and does things which are not appropriate, his deeds remove him away from the Shechinah. ..." (= Id., 104). The same expression is found, for example, in bYom 86a, where it says: "But if someone studies Scripture and Mishnah, attends on the disciples of the wise, but is dishonest in business, and discourteous in his relations with people, what do people say about him? ... This man studied the Tora: Look, how corrupt are his deeds and how ugly his ways (וכמה מכוערין דרכיו) ...."

[99] Yir'at Het (or DEZ) II,16-17 according to Van Loopik, *The Ways*, 229-31 (with commentary) = Massekhet Derekh Erets I,26 according to Higger, *The treatises Derek Erez* 1, 78-79 (Hebr.) and 2, 38 (ET); and see Massekhet Yir'at Het, version a, Chap. 1, in Higger, *Minor Tractates*, 75 (lines 20-23) and version b, Perek Yir'at Heta in Higger, *Minor Tractates*, 83 (lines 23-25). Cf. also the references in Sperber, *Masechet Derech Eretz Zutta*, 98-99.

The saying shows that the popular apophthegm, to be as careful of an unimportant precept as of an important one,[100] in its original meaning was an alternative form of the counsel "my child, flee from all evil and from everything like it." Certain things, not forbidden by the Law, were taken in these pious circles to be actual transgressions and are referred to as light sins. On the other hand, the current halakhic norms were tightened to the extent that they became light commands in their own right. A similar dictum occurs in ARN a, chapter 2:

> It is stated here, 'None of you shall approach' and it is stated there, 'You shall not approach'; do not therefore approach to any conduct which may lead to transgression. Keep distant from anything hideous or from whatever seems hideous. Accordingly the Sages said: keep distant from a minor sin lest it lead you on to a major sin ...[101]

Although the statements with regard to light and weighty sins are not found in the Greek Two Ways, the section in 3:1-6 is related to these views. It explains the connection between a light sin and a weighty one as the transgression of a minor precept (anger, envy, irascibleness etc.) leading up to a transgression of a major one (murder etc.). Here again, rabbinic literature offers parallel places. The same idea occurs in the midrash to Deut 19:11 ("But if any man hates his neighbour, and lies in wait for him, and attacks him..."):

> Hence they said: when a human being has transgressed a light precept he will in the end transgress a weighty precept. Did he transgress (the precept): 'you shall love your neighbour as yourself' (Lev 19:18), he will eventually transgress (the precept): 'you shall not take vengeance or bear any grudge' (ibid.) and (the precept): 'you shall not hate your brother' (Lev 19:17) and (the precept): 'that your brother may live beside you' (Lev 25:36) until he comes to shed blood. Therefore it is said: But if any man hates his neighbour, and lies in wait for him, and attacks him.[102]

---

[100] Cf. Böhl, *Gebotserschwerung und Rechtsverzicht*, 59-63 and 85-109. I am obliged to Dr. Marcus van Loopik for drawing this book to my attention (HvdS).
See also the following instances: "Rabbi said: '... And be heedful of a light precept (במצוה קלה) as of a weighty one (כבחמורה) for you know not the recompense of reward of each precept; ...';" mAv 2:1; cf. bMen 44a, top; bNed 39b; yPe'a 1,15d. The midrash in SifDeut 79 (= Finkelstein, *Siphre ad Deuteronomium*, 145) states to Deut 12:28 ("all these words which I command you"): "that a light precept is as dear to you as a weighty precept" (שתהא מצוה קלה חביבה עליך כמצוה חמורה) and the same clause occurs in SifDeut 82 to Deut 13:1 (= Id., 148), and in SifDeut 96 to Deut 13:19 (= Id., 157). See also Bacher, *Die exegetische Terminologie* 1, 172-74. An echo of the rabbinic usage of "light" and "weighty" precepts is also found in the wording of Jesus: "... and you have neglected the weightier matters of the Law (βαρύτερα τοῦ νόμου), ..." (Matt 23:23b).
About the concept of the light commandment being as important as a weighty one, cf. Str.-B 1, 900-05; esp. 901-02; Urbach, *The Sages* 1, 345-50 and for this notion in Philo's writings, see I. Heinemann, *Philo's griechische und jüdische Bildung*, 478-80.
[101] Cf. Schechter, *Aboth de Rabbi Nathan*, 5a.
[102] SifDeut 186-87 to Deut 19:11 (= Finkelstein, *Siphre ad Deuteronomium*, 226). Cf. also SifNum 112 to Num 15:22: "Rabbi said: someone who has fulfilled one precept for its own sake should not rejoice over that precept for in the end it draws many precepts in its train; and someone who has committed one transgression should not grieve over that transgression for in the end it draws many transgressions in its train; for one precept draws another precept in its train, and one transgression draws another transgression in its train" (= Horovitz, *Siphre d'be Rab*, 120).

In the series of transgressions described here, the shedding of blood is considered to be the major sin. This explanation of Deut 19:11 is reflected in the following statement in the treatise Derekh Erets and is attributed to Rabbi Eliezer:

R. Eliezer says, 'One who hates his fellow, such a person belongs to the shedders of blood, for it is said: 'And if a man should hate his fellow and lie in wait for him, and smite him mortally that he die' (Deut 19:11).[103]

The original midrash is probably best preserved in this Derekh Erets tract.[104] As a result, there can be little question that the Greek Two Ways section in 3:1-6 draws upon traditions which flourished within the pious Jewish "Derekh Erets" groups. Because these views and ideas, however, are also reflected in other rabbinic writings, they seem to have diffused among the wider circles of the Sages as well.

Nevertheless, there remains the problem of how to account for the carefully structured form of the ethical instruction in the *teknon*-section of GTW 3:1-6. The following observations might be helpful. The above maxims in rabbinic literature against participation in any light sin are based on the severity of the weighty sins entailed by minor transgressions. The evaluation of a light sin as "leading (המביא) to transgression"[105] of a weighty one is formulated in grammatical terms by the causative hif'il of the verb בוא. In this light, it is interesting to note that the effects of a minor vice are expressed by the verb ὁδηγέω in the Greek Testaments of the Twelve Patriarchs:

"My children, love of money leads to (πρὸς ... ὁδηγεῖ) idols" (*T.Judah* 19:1)

and

"And now, my children, be not drunk with wine; for wine ... leads the eyes into (ὁδηγεῖ εἰς ...) error" (ibid. 14:1).

Accordingly, it has been argued that the rhetoric of our section in the Greek Two Ways shows affinities with that of the Testaments since "the idiomatic expression

---

[103] DER XI,15 according to Van Loopik, *The Ways*, 164 = Tosefta Derekh Erets VI (Perek Ha-Yotzee),13 according to Higger, *The treatises Derek Erez* 2, 312-13 (Hebr.) and 117 (ET)).

[104] Cf. Flusser, 'A Rabbinic Parallel', 501-02, n. 34. See Van Loopik's commentary on the above statement from DER XI,15: "It was characteristic of the circles of the D.E." (= Derekh Erets) "traditions that the very consideration and intention of harmful deeds were judged in terms of the most extreme consequences possible. Cf. also the atmosphere in Mat. 5:22 and Did. 3:1ff., in which anger and murder are directly linked with each other" (*The Ways*, 164).
The following statement of Ben Azzai belongs to the same pietistic ideology: "Ben Azzai said: Run to fulfil the lightest precept even as the weightiest and flee from transgression; for one precept draws another precept in its train, and one transgression draws another transgression in its train; for the reward of a precept (done) is a precept (to be done), and the reward of one transgression is (another) transgression" (mAv 4:2).

[105] "... do not therefore approach to any conduct which may lead (המביא) to transgression. Keep distant from anything hideous or from whatever seems hideous. Accordingly the Sages said: keep distant from a minor sin lest it lead you (שמא יביאך) on to a major sin ..." (ARN a, Chap. 2) and "... Shudder from committing a minor transgression, lest it lead you (שמא יביא) to commit a major transgression. Hurry to (perform) a minor precept, for this will lead you (שתביאך) to (perform) a major precept" (Yir'at Het II,16-17). For these and other instances, see the above references.

that 'x leads (ὁδηγεῖν) to y' may indeed come from the *Testaments*."[106] As observed above, every strophe of 3:2-6, in its extant form, is divided into two parallel parts but the earlier form of the tradition may have contained the first division of every strophe only. The stylistic pattern of these single phrases with the repeated stereotyped formula ὁδηγεῖ γὰρ ... πρός may be traced back to a Jewish tradition, which is mirrored in rabbinic literature and, especially, in the Testaments of the Twelve Patriarchs. Thus, we suggest that the wording of this pericope in its initial stage was as follows:

(3:1)   My child, flee from all evil and from everything like it.
(3:2)   Be not an angry person, for anger leads to (ὁδηγεῖ γὰρ ... πρὸς ...) murder.
(3:3)   My child, be not a person given to passion, for passion leads to adultery.[107]
(3:4)   My child, do not practise soothsaying, because this leads to idolatry.
(3:5)   My child, do not be a liar, because lying leads to theft.
(3:6)   My child, do not be a grumbler, because this leads to blasphemy.

---

[106] Kloppenborg, 'The Transformation of Moral Exhortation', 106. Cf. Niederwimmer, *Die Didache*, 125 and n. 9; Rordorf-Tuilier, *La Doctrine des douze Apôtres*, 153, n. 1 and see also Kraft, *Barnabas and the Didache*, 146: "The precise background of *3,1-6* is not clear, but the best parallels come from the Testaments: see *T. Judah* 14:1, ... or 19:1 ...."

[107] The first half of GTW 3:3 reads: "My child, be not a person given to passion, for passion leads to fornication." It is, however, hard to believe that the term "fornication" was used in the earlier layer of GTW 3:1-6. The word πορνεία commonly is a translation of the Hebrew term זנות or a related form, which is used as technical terminology for prostitution. In the Tora – both oral and written –, prostitution (זנות) is prohibited when sexual intercourse is involved with a cultic and / or commercial prostitute. There is no condemnation of sexual relations that do not violate the marriage bond. Pre-marital, non-commercial sexual intercourse between man and woman is not considered a moral crime in the Tora and contemporary Judaism (see, for example, Malina, 'Does *Porneia* mean Fornication?', 10-17). Although fornication (πορνεία) is presented as a weighty sin in 3:3a, it is difficult to believe that the passage's concern would be with cultic or commercial sexual relations. It is therefore likely that the term in the first layer of this unit was adultery (μοιχεία), which also occurs in the second half of the present admonition ("for from all of these [actions] flow adulteries"). A contemporary attestation for this stereotyped wording is found in the antithetical section of the Sermon on the Mount:

Matt 5		GTW 3	
5:17-20:	preamble: ...Do not set aside even the least of these commandments	3:1:	My child, flee from all evil and from everything like it
5:21-22:	Anger and murder	3:2:	Anger leads to murder
5:27-28:	One who looks at a woman lustfully has already committed adultery with her in his heart	3:3:	Lust leads to adultery

The affinity between the two passages, both in content and method of argumentation, is undeniable. They are probably based on the same type of admonition.

Combining these data, we end up with the conclusion that adultery is meant in the original pattern of GTW 3:1-6. It would seem, therefore, that the redactor, who in a later stage extensively expanded the separate warnings of the section's earlier form, substituted the word μοιχεία (retained in the second half of the strophe in 3:3) for πορνεία in the first half because he misapprehended the latter term in the light of non-Jewish judgment about sexual morality.

This (hypothetical) layer underlying the section of the Two Ways in 3:1-6 represents an adequate tradition, corresponding both in conceptual framework and in literary expression to the observed subject matter in rabbinic literature and the phraseology in the Testaments. The five weighty sins are identical with the "fundamental laws," laid down in Sifra and bYom as crucial for mankind.[108]

Traditional Derekh Erets Materials Preserved in the Whole of the Greek Two Ways

The preceding sections have made it clear that the Greek Two Ways is a composite work. Four kinds of parallel materials were especially helpful in the task of distinguishing various strands of traditions. In the first place, there is no doubt that the tractate of the Greek Two Ways betrays literary affinities with the Essene Treatise of the Two Spirits. This correspondence appeared to be an important witness to the use of a pre-Essene source in the literary unit of 1QS and in our Two Ways. The resemblance, however, is by no means restricted to Essene materials. We have noted that the *teknon*-section and the double love commandment in the Greek document is similar to the *T. 12 Patr.* in wording, spirit, and social message. It was further established that the Golden Rule, the term "explanation", and the commandment to love one's neighbour reflect a prevailing propensity in rabbinic literature. Finally, the ethics in the discussions of light and weighty commandments suggested the undeniable relationship of our Greek text with a particular type of rabbinic literature, called Derekh Erets.

The present section argues for a close affinity between Jewish ethics in the Greek Two Ways and in the rabbinic Derekh Erets tractates. The common and accepted connotation of the term "Derekh Erets" (ארץ דרך - "The Way on Earth") is desirable behaviour, good manners and politeness of a man toward his fellows.[109] In this sense, it is found in rabbinic traditions and in the two major compositions

---

[108]   If the above reconstruction of the earlier layer of GTW 3:1-6 is correct, it remains to ask why this pattern was changed and expanded to the extent that the five single-phrased prohibitions became twofold. It has been argued that, in the Second Temple period, a basic pattern of exhortation existed which can be found in *T.Judah* 23:1-4, in the Palestinian Targum to the second half of the Decalogue and in Did 3:1-6. For a detailed comparison, see Van de Sandt, 'Didache 3,1-6'.

It is difficult to decide whether the expansion should be attributed to the editor of the Greek Two Ways or to the editor of the earlier form of the unit underlying GTW 3:1-6. There is some evidence that the changes did not belong to an earlier separate tradition but were provided by the Two Ways editor. A comparison of our section in 3:1-6 with the beginning of the Way of Death in 5:1 reveals that many sins in these passages correspond with one another in wording and, to some extent, in sequence. Taking the beginning of the list in 5:1 as a point of departure, the following agreements are to be noticed: φόνοι (murders = 3:2), μοιχεῖαι (adulteries = 3:3b), ἐπιθυμίαι (passions = 3:3a), πορνεῖαι (fornications = 3:3a), κλοπαί (thefts = 3:5), εἰδωλολατρεῖαι (idolatries = 3:4), ..., ψευδομαρτυρίαι (false witnesses = 3:5a?), ..., αἰσχρολογία (obscene speech = 3:3b).

[109]   Schlesinger, 'Derekh Erez'; Higger, *The treatises Derek Erez* 2 (Introduction), 11-12; Safrai, 'Teaching of Pietists', 27-28; Lerner, 'The External Tractates', 379; Van Loopik, *The Ways*, 2-4.

dealing specifically with the subject of Derekh Erets, namely Derekh Erets Zuta and Derekh Erets Rabba. Originally, however, the expression probably had a broader meaning as it designated ethical behaviour, i.e. moral conduct on earth. This is apparent from chapters I-III in Derekh Erets Zuta. These chapters, referred to above, are part of Yir'at Het and represent an early stratum of instruction dating back to the Tannaitic period.[110] The pithy maxims and exhortations in this unit are, with a single exception (I,12),[111] anonymous and deal with humility, modesty, and morals preventing a person from indulging in sin. The early layer reflects a life style which is called "derekh hasidut," the way of the pious. It reveals the teaching of the early hassidim who "placed extreme stress on self-deprival and the performance of good deeds and acts of loving kindness in lieu of pure academic 'ivory tower' scholarship."[112]

In order to capture the spirit of the common ground in the Greek Two Ways and in the primitive kernel of the tractates Derekh Erets, we will quote a passage from Yir'at Het (or Derekh Erets Zuta) III,1-8. This is also the only passage in the early layer of the Derekh Erets literature mentioning the term "Derekh Erets" (in III,1) which may more properly refer to the concept's original meaning, i.e. ethical behaviour, moral conduct rather than to good manners:

Judge your words before they issue from your mouth and consider your deeds in accordance with the right ethics (*Derekh Erets*) and let a (Divine) reward be given for every step you take. Acknowledge the justice of (Divine) judgment over you and refrain from grumbling. Judge your neighbour turning the scale to the side of merit, and do not turn for him the scale to the side of guilt. Rejoice about your portion and enjoy the little you have, and do not hate him who rebukes you. Be small in your own eyes. Let your share be blessed for ever, a benevolent eye and a humble spirit. Accustom your tongue to say: 'I do not know', lest you be led to tell a falsehood and be apprehended. If you are negligent in (the performance of) one precept, you will be in the end negligent in (the performance of) another. And likewise, if you make light of one precept you will in the end make light of another. And you will not be rewarded for your trouble. And likewise if you transgress the words of the Tora intentionally you will be made to transgress them intentionally and unintentionally. If you take money which is not yours, they will also take yours.[113]

It must be admitted that the final redaction of the Massekhet Yir'at Het is of a late date (the second half of the eighth century) and some sayings doubtlessly have been

---

[110] See above, p. 167.
[111] Yir'at Het (or DEZ) I,12 according to Van Loopik, *The Ways*, 193-94 (with commentary) = Massekhet Derekh Erets I,11 according to Higger, *The treatises Derek Erez* 1, 63 (Hebr.) and 2, 34 (ET).
[112] Lerner, 'The External Tractates', 380.
[113] Yir'at Het (or DEZ) III,1-8 according to Van Loopik, *The Ways*, 237-42 (with commentary) = Massekhet Derekh Erets I,30-II,2 according to Higger, *The treatises Derek Erez* 1, 85-90 (Hebr.) and 2, 39-40 (ET). Van Loopik's translation of the clause in the lines 1-2 "... in accordance with 'derekh 'eretz' (good manners) and let a reward be given ..." (237) has been altered here.

added to the earlier segment of this tractate.[114] It is also true that many of the materials in the above mentioned tracts can be found as well in Seder Eliyahu Rabba and Zutta, which exhibit similar tendencies.[115] Moreover, views and ideas dealing with the subject of Derekh Erets are found in other rabbinic compositions which are not consistent with the general drift of the latter works. A great deal of these "outside" materials were doubtlessly drawn from extant Derekh Erets collections. On the other hand, it must be borne in mind that not all aspects of hassidic piety were the exclusive possession of distinct qualified groups. In fact, the pious Sages who produced these traditions, far from constituting a separate sect, were highly conscious of their attachment to rabbinic Judaism. In spite of the wide diffusion of their views and beliefs, however, there is little question that some specific features of Derekh Erets quantitatively prevail in the primitive kernel of the treatises under discussion and in many cases no parallels are available in the Talmud and Midrash. They are characteristic of the piety in the circles from which they originated, that is to say, early hassidim. They certainly formed a defined group within the society of Pharisees and rabbis, practising an austere interpretation of halakhoth, performing good deeds and showing a far-reaching trust in God and providence.[116]

It is difficult to come up with a neat correlation between the early layer of the Derekh Erets tractates and the Greek Two Ways. At first sight, one is inclined to some scepticism. While the antagonistic construction of the pattern in the Two Ways traditions strongly indicates a dualistic setting – as seen above in passages from the Apocrypha and Pseudepigrapha (pp. 143-47) and the Treatise of the Two Spirits (pp. 147-55) – the Derekh Erets exhortations seemingly stand in continuity with the Jewish sapiential stream serving the simple function of ethical instruction. Yet, while it is correct that the ethics of Derekh Erets merely deals with the right "Way on Earth" (that is the "Way of Life"), this teaching does not preclude a dualistic origin. The following discussion about two rabbinic sayings (in mAv 2:9 and 2:1) will demonstrate that a close connection appears to once have existed between the Two Ways instruction and the basic core of our Derekh Erets tracts.

The following saying, assigned to Rabban Yohanan ben Zakkai and his five disciples, is found in mAv 2:9:

> He said to them: Go forth and see which is the right way (איזוהי דרך ישרה) to which a man should cleave (שידבק בה האדם). R. Eliezer said, 'A good eye'. R. Yoshua said, 'A good friend'. R. Yose said, 'A good neighbour'. R. Shimon said, 'One that sees what will be'. R. Elazar said, 'A good heart'. He said to them: 'I prefer the words of Elazar b. Arakh for in his words your words are included.
>
> He said to them: Go forth and see which is the evil way which a man should shun (שיתרחק ממנה האדם). R. Eliezer said, 'An evil eye'. R. Yoshua said, 'A bad friend'.

---

[114] E.g. Yir'at Het (or DEZ) II,18-20 according to Van Loopik, *The Ways*, 202-205 = Massekhet Derekh Erets I,16-18 according to Higger, *The treatises Derek Erez* 1, 65-70 (Hebr.) and 2, 35-36 (ET). See Lerner, 'The External Tractates', 382 and n. 100 and Van Loopik, *The Ways*, 17.

[115] Klein, *Der älteste christliche Katechismus*, 66-79; Lerner, 'The External Tractates', 380.

[116] Cf. Safrai, 'Teaching of Pietists', 32-33; Id., 'Hasidim we-Anshei Maase', 144-54; Id., 'Jesus and the Hasidic Movement', 415; Büchler, *Types of Jewish-Palestinian Piety*, 68-127.

R. Yose said, 'A bad neighbour'. R. Shimon said, 'He that borrows and does not repay. ...'. R. Elazar said, 'An evil heart'. He said to them: 'I prefer the words of Elazar b. Arakh for in his words your words are included.

The problem considered here is that of choosing between the Two Ways. What is the good way for a man to follow and, secondly, what is the evil way a man should shun? In each case, the five most outstanding pupils of Rabban Yohanan are allowed to give their solutions before the master himself decides the question.

For our purposes, two observations are significant. Firstly, the passage demonstrates that a Two Ways doctrine, containing lists of virtues and vices, underlies this rabbinic tradition.[117] The dualistic understanding of the Two Ways concept not only appears from the two opposing catalogues but also from the contrasting terminology "to cleave" (דבק) to the good way and "to shun" (רחק) the evil one. The tradition in mAv 2:9 thus provides evidence of the preservation of a teaching among the Sages which is analogous to the pattern found in the Greek Two Ways. Secondly, in terms of contents, this tradition also shares a feature which is prominent in the Derekh Erets ethics. The series of concrete examples defining the "good way" comprises a list of qualities which is similar to the sets of moral records often mentioned in Derekh Erets tracts. In fact, the text of Yir'at Het begins with a specification of "the way of Sages:"

> The ways of scholars (sages) are to be: meek, humble of spirit, diligent and filled (with knowledge), forbearing and beloved by all, humble to the members of his household, in fear of transgression and judging a man according to his deeds.[118]

Certainly, it would be difficult to find in the rabbinic tractates of Derekh Erets the list with the negative qualities of the "evil way" which man should shun because the very essence and nature of this kind of literature is expressed in the focus on the "good way." In keeping with their objective, the composers of these rabbinic Derekh Erets tractates utterly renounced any description of the wrong way on earth. It is thus inherently unlikely that the Derekh Erets tracts would provide evidence of a concept of two contrary ways. Their purpose was to teach how an individual, once he has decided to walk "the right way on earth," was supposed to behave and live. The same trend is obvious in the Two Ways, in which the Way of Light is enhanced by the inclusion of ethical instructions which, as far as it can be established from the doctrinal passage in 1QS, surely did not form a part of the Way of Life in the pre-Essene source. The Way of Death, on the other hand, remained restricted to a mere list of sins.

Another rabbinic statement, probably presupposing a relationship between Derekh Erets and the Greek Two Ways, is found in mAv 2:1. The saying is introduced with a question ("which is the right way") that is verbally identical to the statement quoted above from mAv 2:9. The passage reads thus:

---

[117] According to Michaelis, 'ὁδός κτλ.', 60, the passage in mAv 2:9 "ist das erste Beispiel für eine solche inhaltliche Füllung der Gegensätzlichkeit der beiden Wege."

[118] Yir'at Het (or DEZ) I,1 according to Van Loopik, The Ways, 172 = Massekhet Derekh Erets I,1 according to Higger, The treatises Derek Erez 1, 55-56 (Hebr.) and 2, 33 (ET).

Rabbi said: 'Which is the right way (איזוהי דרך ישרה) that a man should choose? That which is an honour to him and gets him honour from men. And be heedful of a light precept as of a weighty one, for you know not the recompense of reward of each precept; and reckon the loss through (the fulfilling of) a precept against its reward, and the reward (that comes) from transgression against its loss. ...

As to the verbal form of this saying, it has been suggested, not improbably, that the first segment of the answer ("That which ... from men") pertains to the initial question.[119] If this is the case, then Rabbi Judah the Patriarch first asks a long and complicated question and the answer does not begin until the wording: "be heedful of a light precept as of a weighty one." This ethical rule, as seen above, is an expression of a rabbinic Jewish trend in which the Derekh Erets works were written. It emphasizes the original meaning of Derekh Erets, namely that one must choose the right way in order to avoid the way of sin. It can further be noted that an alternative phrase to the expression under discussion ("be heedful of a light precept as of a weighty one") is found in the introductory statement of the literary unit in TW 3:1: "my child, flee from all evil and from everything like it." This statement is not only the guiding principle of the literary unit of 3:1-6; it also expresses a distinct characteristic of Derekh Erets.

The affinity between the ideas and ethical principles in the sayings provided by mAv 2:9 and 2:1, both of which represent early Derekh Erets doctrine, and the views occurring in the Greek tractate of the Two Ways suggest that some kind of relationship between the two types of instruction may be assumed. Both traditions highlight similar notions. The right way that a man should choose is identified with high ethical qualities and with the exhortation to flee evil. At the same time, these qualities and exhortations explicitly (mAv 2:9) and implicitly (mAv 2:1) require a dualistic setting as the framework which enables the question about the right way to be asked.

The possibility of interdependence is increased by the following observation. Rather than scrupulously discussing the specificities of Tora, the Greek Two Ways and the early parts of Derekh Erets betray a practical wisdom through their high ethical rules which appeal to a universal morality. According to a rabbinic midrash, the concept of "Derekh Erets" embodies a general morality without being revealed on Mount Sinai to Israel exclusively:

R. Yishmael b. Nahman said: Derekh Erets preceded the Tora by twenty-six generations. This is (implied in) what is written: 'to keep the way to the tree of life' (Gen 3:24). (First Scripture mentions) 'the way' which means Derekh Erets, and afterwards (it mentions) 'the tree of life', which means the Tora.[120]

---

[119]   Cf. Epstein, *Mavo le-nosah ha-Mishna*, 1108-09; Sharvit, 'Traditions of Interpretations', 117-18.
[120]   LevR IX,3 (= Margulies, *Midrash Wayyikra Rabbah* 1, 179); cf. the anonymous statement in XXXV,6 (= Margulies, *Midrash Wayyikra Rabbah* 4, 824). See also the beginning of SER, Chap. 1 (= Friedmann, *Seder Eliahu Rabba*, 3) and YalShim to Gen 3 (= Hyman-Lerrer-Shiloni, *Yalqut Shim 'oni* 1, remez 35, p. 117, lines 10-11 and remez 36, p. 118, lines 21-22). Cf. Bacher, *Die Agada der palästinensischen Amoräer* 1, 484, n. 3: "Dieser in bemerkenswerther Weise die Priorität der allgemein menschlichen Sittlichkeit vor der an Israel offenbarten Lehre betonende Ausspruch steht auch an der

In the opinion of R. Yishmael b. Nahman, the clause "to keep the way to the tree of life" in Gen 3:24 refers to the concept of Derekh Erets which leads up to the tree of life, that is, the Tora. His statement that Derekh Erets preceded the Tora by twenty-six generations[121] explains that the world practised Derekh Erets in the period between the creation of the world and the giving of the Tora on Sinai.[122] The midrash illustrates that the term 'Derekh Erets' refers to the instruction of mankind by a sort of natural law which, rather than being the result of a Divine revelation, was immediately evident. The earlier generations did not yet keep Tora but, even so, practised refined principles of moral conduct which were understood in their own right. Admittedly, R. Yishmael b. Nahman's statement probably was enunciated on an occasion after the Tannaitic period. It nevertheless reflects a tendency which is paralleled in the early layer of Derekh Erets tracts. The primary parts of this literature do not demarcate a number of specifically biblical commandments but a purified general morality. No reference is made to such unique Jewish commandments as circumcision, dietary or clothing restrictions or the observance of Sabbath and festivals. It is not a strict legal approach to the Law but a moral, personal and ethical attitude to life that is emphasized. Derekh Erets stresses the avoidance of transgression expressed in the appeal to Yir'at Het (fear of transgression).

The analogy to the Greek Two Ways is noticeable in two respects. Firstly, the purport of the preamble of the *teknon*-unit in GTW 3:1-6 is expressed in the remainder of the passage illustrating the connection between a light sin and a weighty sin. It has already been established that the five weighty commandments represent general rules for mankind: "If these were not written, they should by right be written."[123] In content and purpose, Derekh Erets regulations are similar to these noachitic laws, the five fundamental laws and other universally ethical standards. Secondly, it is not by coincidence that the Greek Two Ways is lacking specific commandments attributed to the Tora of Moses aside from those passages which, in fact, define the essential scope of the Tora (i.e., the double love commandment and the second half of the Decalogue).

A final point of similarity between Derekh Erets and the Greek Two Ways is the ideal of piety. As was observed in above (pp. 147-55), the passage in GTW 3:7-10 depends on the list of moral qualities of 1QS 4:2b-4a in its pre-Essene stage. By comparison with the literary unit in 1QS 4:2b-6, it is noteworthy, however, that the original list of moral values has been reworked and greatly expanded in the

---

Spitze des späteren, besonders ethische Ermahnungen enthaltenden Tanna⁻dibê Elija, gleichsam als Wahlspruch."

[121] Although we cannot rule out the possibility that the Sage caused the Tora to be preceded by Derekh Erets on the basis of a provocative explanation of the clause: "and at the east (מקדם) of the garden of Eden he placed the cherubim ...."

[122] See Kadushin, *Worship and Ethics*, 50. It is possible that some connection once existed between our midrash and the view that two ways – "one of death and one of life" (Mekh to Ex 14:29) or "light and darkness" (2 Enoch 30:15) – were proposed to Adam before the Fall; see above, pp. 153-54.

[123] Sifra Lev. 18:4; see above, pp. 166-67.

exhortations in GTW 3:7-4:14. This section is governed by counsels about constructive social behaviour, submissive humbleness of mind, and a peaceful spirit. The various instructions concern an attitude of humility (3:7-10), ethical duties toward others (4:1-4), obligations toward the needy (4:5-8), family and household duties (4:9-11), and a final summary exhortation (4:12-14). The recommendations are in line with the *teknon*-section in 3:1-6 and establish a core association with the gnomic exhortations of the practical ethic reflected in the old kernel of Derekh Erets literature. It would be a mistake to think that a sin-fearing man in these tracts is one of only negative virtue. Prominent in their doctrine is the focus on good deeds in public life. The ultimate purpose of the Derekh Erets approach is to attain perfect moral purity to the degree that is possible. The fear of sin implies not merely passively refraining from transgressions but actively observing positive commandments as well. The chapters of Yir'at Het embody a refined human ethic and highlight acts of charity, modesty, humility and a gentle attitude toward one's fellow man by estimating the honour and the interests of the others higher than one's own.[124]

As a result, although the two literary genres seem to represent separate traditions and settings at first sight, closer investigation suggests an underlying interrelationship between their conceptual frameworks. There is more than one piece of evidence to support this view. The presence of the lists of ethical qualities defining the right way, the central moral preventative to avoid anything resembling evil and the refined sensitivity with regard to modesty, humility and altruistic love – all distinctive traits within Derekh Erets and the Greek Two Ways – argue for one particular type of literature. In one case, a literary affinity was located:

Yir'at Het II,16-17	*Two Ways* 3:1-6
"Keep aloof from that which leads to transgression,	----------------
keep aloof from everything hideous and from what even seems hideous.	verse 1
Shudder from committing a minor transgression, lest it lead you to commit a major transgression.	verses 2-6
Hurry to (perform) a minor precept, for this will lead you to (perform) a major precept" (above, p. 168).	----------------

One may reasonably argue that the urge to choose the right way is not simply derived by both works in common from references in earlier Jewish sapiential literature. It seems rather justified to assume that the Greek Two Ways instruction

---

[124] Cf. Van Loopik, *The Ways*, 16-17; Lerner, 'The External Tractates', 381; Safrai, 'Teaching of Pietists', 27-28.

belongs to a specific trend in early Jewish thought which calls on a new human, moral behaviour.[125]

One final point should be made here. As observed above, both Derekh Erets and the Greek Two Ways doctrine appear to reflect a considerable concern with the Way of Life. Interestingly, the Greek tractate of the Two Ways has unambiguously preserved the explicit dualistic schema but at the same time does not elaborate on the Way of Death. In the Derekh Erets tracts, although their teaching might have derived from a dualistic origin, the contrast between the Two Ways has yielded complete precedence to the Way of Life. The Way of Death has been omitted entirely. It is therefore likely that the Two Ways instruction represents a link in a developing process in which a Two Ways doctrine, known to the composer of 1QS, took the form which became known to us in the Derekh Erets tracts. The teaching within the Greek Two Ways may even have played some formative role in the emergence of Derekh Erets. The evidence, however, does not allow us to encourage the belief that the early Derekh Erets parts directly used (a version of) our Two Ways treatise. All that can be said is that our Two Ways document, although it was written in Greek, probably represents the oldest extant treatise pertaining to this type of literature. In terms of content, it is likely to exemplify the earliest stage in the history of the surviving materials dealing with Derekh Erets. The initial meaning, then, of the term "Derekh Erets" seems to be embedded in the opening words of the Greek Two Ways tractate: "There are two ways in the world, one of life and one of death, one of light and one of darkness" and the purport of the Derekh Erets tracts was to stress the right way which man must choose in this world to avoid the way of sinfulness.

The Tractate of the Greek Two Ways in its Jewish Setting

It is not easy to determine the date of the composition of the Two Ways. The document was incorporated in the Didache and Barnabas. Because the Christian Didache was written before the Epistle of Barnabas, around the year 100 CE, its Jewish source cannot have been composed later than that time. The form of the Two Ways in the Didache, however, shows indications of having been constructed at an earlier stage in history. There is widespread scholarly consensus that Did 6:2-3 is a later addition to the basic tradition of the Two Ways. Below, in Chapter 7, evidence will be provided that the appendix is an expression of a Jewish-Christian attitude opposing those people who claimed that 'perfection' could be reached without keeping the entire Tora. Admittedly, we do not know with certainty whether the composer of Did 6:2-3 was familiar with Paul's view on gentile

---

[125] Klein already dealt with the close relationship between the Didache and Derekh Erets. In his conclusion, he states among other things: "Andererseits erweisen die vorhandenen Fragmente, dass wir es in der Didache mit einem ursprünglich jüdischen Katechismus, einem Derech-erez-Traktate zu tun haben" (*Die älteste christliche Katechismus*, 244).

Christians observing the Tora. If this was the case, we would have a clear proof that the Jewish source was in existence in the first decades of Christianity. Another clue may be found in the works of Philo, who was possibly familiar with the Jewish teaching about the Two Ways. He writes that one has to "discriminate and distinguish (...), so that we can choose what we should choose and avoid the contrary, ... For the Way of Life is twofold, one branch leading to vice (ἐπὶ κακίαν), the other to virtue (ἐπ' ἀρετήν) and we must turn away from the one and never forsake the other."[126] One may also refer to the variety of lists of virtues and vices in early Jewish and Jewish-Christian texts, some of which resemble the lists in the Two Ways.[127] Unfortunately, these similarities do not settle the question and fix the exact date when the Greek tractate of the Two Ways was composed.

The materials in the Greek Two Ways, however, do permit some observations about origin and provenance if we assume that its present form represents the interests and beliefs of the circles in which it was produced. The next exposition will proceed in two phases. Firstly, an attempt will be made to provide an appropriate framework within contemporary Judaism for the intriguing parallels between the Greek Two Ways on the one hand and the Essene Treatise of the Two Spirits, the Testaments of the Twelve Patriarchs, the rabbinic literature and the Derekh Erets tracts, on the other. We will see that these similarities, rather than reflecting common places current in early Judaism, are due to the conceptual ambiance of the circles in which the doctrine of the Greek Two Ways was created and transmitted (pp. 180-82). Secondly, we hope to show that social welfare in these circles represents a form of radical charity and disbursement of possessions. Closer investigation will reveal, however, that at variance with Qumran doctrine and practice, the sharing of financial and material resources exceeds the limits of a closed sectarian community (pp. 182-90).

THE SPIRITUAL AND ETHICAL MILIEU OF THE GREEK TWO WAYS

Early Judaism exhibited great variety, and it is almost impossible to describe a comprehensive picture of the entire range of Jewish beliefs and religious groupings. Since it is also hazardous to infer the existence of groups or trends in a society from views expressed in particular texts, we have to proceed with caution. Still, there are serious indications that the Greek Two Ways originated in a trend which should be located on the border where the fringes of the Essene movement met the "left

---

[126] *Spec. Leg.* IV, 108. For text and translation, see Colson, *Philo* 8 (LCL 341), 73-75.

[127] In the transmission of a text, however, such lists are easily susceptible to modification. For the list of vices and virtues, see Wibbing, *Die Tugend- und Lasterkataloge*, passim. For representatives of the lists analogous to the catalogue of sins in the Two Ways, cf. especially Philo's *Conf. Ling.* 117 and the Book of Wisdom 14:25-27 (the latter records sixteen sins, nine of which appear in the Didache). See also the catalogue of thirteen sins in Mark 7:21-22 (par. Matt 15:19) and the lists of vices and virtues in Gal. 5:19-21a and 22-23, resp. (the latter verses contain a positive list close to the one in the Two Ways). Cf. Flusser, 'Shte derakhim hen', 239-40.

wing" of the Pharisaic circles. This assumption explains why the instruction is indebted to the pre-Essene form of the Treatise of the Two Spirits in the Manual of Discipline (1QS) on the one hand and why the Two Ways has important ties with Pharisaism, on the other. We have seen that there is even a literary connection between the Two Ways and the doctrinal passage in 1QS – evidently in its pre-Essene stage – and yet, it is also clear that the ethical approach to one's fellow men points to direct historical relations with such Pharisees who saw in the precept of love of one's neighbour the essence of the law.

The Greek Two Ways also suggested an apparent correspondence with the Testaments of the Twelve Patriarchs, and closer observation provides evidence that this composition is also the product of the same circles in which the Two Ways were created. At Qumran, several sources for some of the individual testaments have been discovered: a few (incomplete) copies of an Aramaic Levi Document, two fragmentary texts that have been labeled a Testament of Judah, another tiny Aramaic piece that has been identified with the Testament of Joseph, and a fragment of a Hebrew document that shares distinctive features with the Testament of Naphtali.[128] Moreover, the doctrines propagated in the *T. 12 Patr.* are related to the sect's teachings.[129] The writings express the same moral and spiritual dualism, and they presuppose a permanent struggle between God and the forces of evil in the world, commanded by their demonic leader Beliar.

It is important to notice, however, that the groups within which the *T. 12 Patr.* was preserved were not real Essenes but are to be located on the periphery of the movement. They did not accept the doctrine of predestination, so characteristic of the sect, but acknowledged that the constant danger of being influenced by Beliar had to be fought by man himself. Their dualism is anthropologically orientated in that they developed a very humane and humanistic doctrine of love.[130] They offer perhaps the greatest refinement of ethical dualism in advancing the virtues of compassion, humility, and kindness. Love of one's neighbour and the abolition of all hatred is of central importance in the *T. 12 Patr.*. The good man is characterized by compassion, integrity, and, above all, by an undivided love toward the rest of mankind. In this respect, the composition expresses the universalist doctrine of love fostered by the Pharisee school of Hillel.

The same ethical approach, combining ideas of marginal Essenes and pious Sages, is articulated in The Two Ways. A similar deep sympathy with the others is reflected here (2:7), the fear of God (4:9), meekness combined with a humble and peaceful spirit (3:9 and 4:3), simplicity of heart (2:4), and freedom from any

---

[128] Cf. García Martínez, *The Dead Sea Scrolls Translated*, XII and 265-71. See also Stone, 'The Dead Sea Scrolls', 279-82.

[129] For the unmistakable Essene features of the *T. 12 Patr.*, see e.g. Braun, 'Les Testaments des XII Patriarches', 518-20; Dupont-Sommer, *Les Ecrits esséniens*, 310-18; Dupont-Sommer et Philonenko, *Ecrits intertestamentaires*, LXXV-LXXVI; Flusser, 'Testaments of the Twelve Patriarchs', 184-86.

[130] Cf. Becker, *Untersuchungen zur Entstehungsgeschichte*, 377-401; Id., *Unterweisung in lehrhafter Form*, 27-28; Eppel, *Le piétisme Juif*, 143-188. The *T. Asher* which in contrast breathes a spirit of hatred, is an exception to the rule.

hypocrisy (4:12).[131] The precepts to love God and one's fellow men (1:2; also found in the teaching of Jesus) occur in juxtaposition in both the *T. 12 Patr.* and the Two Ways. We have discovered a similar attitude in the old kernels of the tractates "Derekh Erets." Moreover, like in the Derekh Erets literature and in the Two Ways, the exhortations of the Testaments represent a universal ethic. They do not provide special regulations of the Tora and are (almost) exclusively restricted to general ethical commands.[132] A fundamental feature prominent in all three strands of materials is their movement away from particular legal requirements toward all-encompassing moral rules and ideals.

The Greek Two Ways are a product of the circles from which both the *T. 12 Patr.* and the early portions of Derekh Erets literature emanated. The common atmosphere in these works represents a well-defined trend in early Judaism which met a definite local need in providing humane ethical principles. Apparently, this tendency was firmly rooted in the milieu of the hassidim, i.e., those pious Jewish groups responsible for the formation of the earliest kernel of Derekh Erets literature. In these circles, the dualistic pre-Essene materials underlying 1QS 3:13-4:26 were reorganized, extensively expanded, and ethically refined into the teaching of the Greek Two Ways. The document thus represents a stage in a Jewish historical trajectory of an increasing moral sensitivity in devout semi-Essene circles. In the next section, we will see that similar tenets are present in the doctrine of Jesus as presented by Matthew. It is possible that Jesus belonged to these hassidim. In any case, his moral views of life and humanity, especially his position in the Sermon on the Mount (cf. below, Chap. 6), are so closely related to the ethics of the Greek Two Ways (and to those of the *T. 12 Patr.* as well) that his approach seems to have evolved out of these very circles.

THE SOCIAL MILIEU OF THE GREEK TWO WAYS

The following remarks should be prefaced by the reservation that we cannot construct a coherent picture of the economic and social organization of the circles in which the Greek Two Ways were composed. Much must remain conjectural, but we can make out a certain feature of the social milieu by drawing attention to GTW 4:8. This verse, which is part of a series of specific instructions with regard to the poor (4:5-8), states:

> You shall not turn away anyone who is in need; on the contrary, you shall hold every-thing in common with (συγκοινωνήσεις) your brother, and you shall not say that anything is your own, for if you (pl.) are partners (κοινωνοί) in what is immortal,

---

[131] These and other qualities are spread throughout the whole of the *T. 12 Patr.* and are summed up in the exhortatory section of the last testament (*T. Benj.* 3-8).

[132] Hollander-De Jonge, *The Testaments of the Twelve Patriarchs*, 43-44.

(should you be not so) all the more in things that perish? For the Lord wants that one shall give to all from His own gracious gifts.[133]

Before moving on, it is to be noted that the last clause of 4:8 echoes a well known Jewish maxim: "Give to him" (to God) "what is his" (God's) "for you and what you have are his" (mAv 3:7; see also 5:13).[134] It is only natural that this understanding has a parallel in the Derekh Erets literature: "and do not say: 'I did good with my own (money)', but (say) 'From the good that one did to me.'"[135] The same idea seems to underlie Jesus' parable in Matt 20:1-16, where the landowner - God - says: "Am I not allowed to do what I choose with what belongs to me?" (20:15).

The passage in GTW 4:8 as a whole recalls the famous practice of the community of goods in Qumran, and if we take the verse at face value, it might indicate a dependence on the economic communism as reflected in the Scrolls.[136] After all, it has become clear that the teaching of the Greek Two Ways represents a thorough revision of the pre-Essene materials underlying the Treatise of the Two Spirits and, moreover, we noticed that the doctrine stems from pious groups or streams within Judaism that share features with the Qumran sectarian scrolls in other respects as well. If the Two Ways is ultimately derived from a pre-Essene writing that has been reworked and elaborated in pious circles close to the Dead Sea sect, it is tempting to ask whether Essene ideas may have affected their social pattern of life as described in our document. Let us, then, by way of introduction, briefly portray the sectarian understanding of *koinônia*.

When entering the sect, new members were required to surrender all their private belongings to the bursar, who administered the common property for the

---

[133] For the transference of the last clause "For the Lord wants etc." from Did 1:5 to its present position in GTW 4:8, see above Chap. 4, pp. 136-37. As to the following, see also Flusser, 'Jesus' opinion about the Essenes', 150-68 and Id, 'The Parable'.

[134] See also PesR 25 (= Friedmann, *Pesikta Rabbati*, 126a) and Canticum Zuta in Buber, *Midrasch suta*, 18. Cf. also Philo, *De Cherubim*, 123.

[135] See Yir'at Het II,26 according to Van Loopik, *The Ways*, 234 = Massekhet Derekh Erets I,29 according to Higger, *The treatises Derek Erez* 1, 82-83 (Hebr.) and 2, 39 (ET).

[136] Cf. Rordorf-Tuilier, *La Doctrine des douze Apôtres*, 161, n. 7. Also according to M. Del Verme, the *koinônia* understanding in the Didache reflects an Essenian practice. He differentiates between two varieties of Essene life. On the one hand, there were the brethren in the monastic settlement in the desert who practised common ownership and were focussed completely on the needs of their own members (cf. 1QS; Josephus, *Bellum* 2, 122). The organization of the Essenes in the villages and towns of Judaea (and the diaspora?), on the other hand, was completely different, as they were not required to surrender their property and provided help to needy strangers, that is, to individuals who were not members of the Essene movement (cf. CD 13:15-16; 14:12-16; Josephus, *Bellum* 2, 127.134). In the opinion of Del Verme, the *koinônia* in Did 4:8 reflects the latter type of Essenism; cf. 'Medio giudaismo e *Didaché*', 311-18. We do not think that the postulate of the two branches of the sectarian movement is necessary in order to explain GTW 4:8. In any event, because the Greek Two Ways teaching is grafted on the model of the Treatise of the Two Spirits (1QS 3:3-4:26) in circles close to Qumran, one might take the more radical form of *koinônia* for granted here.

benefit of all.[137] The emphasis on entirely shared resources was such that buying and selling with outsiders was restricted as much as possible:

> No one must be united with him in his duty or his property, lest he burden him (with) guilty iniquity. But he shall keep far away from him in everything, ... No one must either eat or drink anything of their property, or accept anything whatever from their hand without payment, ... For all those who are not accounted within his covenant, they and everything they have must be excluded. ..., and all their works are impure before him, and all their property is unclean. (1QS 5:14-20)

The Qumran Essenes had to separate themselves from the property of the people outside the community, and this economic separation was linked with their concern to preserve the ritual purity of the community.[138] It has already been noted above that 1QS manifests a powerfully dualistic outlook, especially in the teaching on the two spirits. The world is seen as irredeemably evil, and salvation depends upon complete withdrawal from the sons of darkness. The introversion of the community was manifested in a profound economic isolation from non-members, and from the general world.

Josephus too refers to the life of the Essene sect as a community, sharing material goods and prosperity:

> Riches they despise, and their community of goods (τὸ κοινωνικόν) is truly admirable; ... They have a law that new members on admission to the sect shall confiscate their property to the order, with the result that you will nowhere see either abject poverty or inordinate wealth; the individual's possessions join the common stock and all, like brothers, enjoy a single patrimony.[139]

A similar terminology, referring to communal ownership within the Essene sect as well, is found in Philo:

> ... Their clothes are held in common (κοιναί) and also their food (κοιναί δὲ τροφαί) through their institution of public meals. In no other community can we find the custom of sharing roof, life, and board more firmly established in actual practice. And that is no more than one would expect. For all the wages which they earn in the day's work they do not keep as their private property, but throw them into the common stock and allow the benefit (κοινὴν ... ὠφέλειαν) thus accruing to be shared by those who wish to use

---

[137] See 1QS 1:12-13; 5:2 (14); 6:22-23; 7:6.25; CD 13:11 (14:4) and Vermes, *The Dead Sea Scrolls*, 96.126 (who also stresses that members of the Essene organization in towns were not required to give up their property; cf. 105.128); VanderKam, *The Dead Sea Scrolls Today*, 172-73.

[138] See also Harrington, *The Impurity Systems*, 104. In addition, compare the following statements: "And let no man of the covenant of God trade with the sons of perdition except for cash. And let no man make a partnership for trade unless he informs the overseer in the camp and makes a written agreement" (CD 13:14-16);
"And (concerning) the property of the men of holiness who walk perfectly, it must not be merged with the property of the men of deceit who have not cleansed their way by separating themselves from deceit and walking with the perfect of the Way" (1QS 9:8-9).

[139] Josephus, *Bellum* 2, 122; for this translation and Greek text, see Thackeray, *Josephus* 2 (LCL 203), 368-71.

it. The sick are not neglected because they cannot provide anything, but have the cost of their treatment lying ready in the common stock (ἐκ τῶν κοινῶν), ...[140]

Interestingly, both Josephus and Philo labelled the community of goods with the κοινων-root and no doubt the usage of τὸ κοινωνικόν and its cognates[141] were current to designate this kind of economic communism.[142]

In comparing the passages from Josephus and Philo with GTW 4:8 one cannot fail to note the similarity between this word and the term κοινωνός and its compound συγκοινωνέω:

> You shall not turn away anyone who is in need; on the contrary, you shall hold everything in common with (συγκοινωνήσεις) your brother, and you shall not say that anything is your own, for if you are partners (κοινωνοί) in what is immortal, (should you be not so) all the more in things that perish? ...

This passage on sharing property may reflect the Qumran insistence that those entering the sect should surrender their possessions, but it is not necessarily so. For in GTW 4:8 it is not at all implied that this distribution is only to be practised for

---

[140] *Omn. prob. lib.*, 86-87; for the translation and Greek text, see Colson, *Philo* 9 (LCL 363), 58-61.

[141] See also the following statement: "Moreover, they hold their possessions in common (τὰ χρήματά τε κοινά ἐστιν αὐτοῖς), and the wealthy man receives no more enjoyment from his property than the man who possesses nothing;" Josephus, *Ant.* 18, 20; cf. Feldman, *Josephus* (LCL 433), 18-19.

[142] Cf. Braun, *Spätjüdisch-häretischer und frühchristlicher Radikalismus* 1, 77-80. According to Dombrowski ('היהד in 1QS and τὸ κοινόν', 296), the Qumran sect accepted the noun יהד(ה) as a self-designation and this term is almost equal to the Greek (τὸ) κοινόν.
Compare also the description in Acts (2:42-47; esp. 2:44 and 4:32-35; esp. 4:32) of the Christians in the early church of Jerusalem, who are said to have held all things in common (κοινά). For the New Testament term *koinōnia* and its Essene background, see, for example, Wilcox, *The Semitisms of Acts*, 93-100; Fitzmyer, 'Jewish Christianity in Acts', 283-88; Manzanera, '*Koinonia* en Hch 2:42', 319-21. The analogy between the early Christians and the Qumran community is such that one should reckon with a (modified) influence of the Qumran practices on the former (cf. Braun, *Qumran und das Neue Testament* 1, 143-49). The motivation for this common ownership, however, is never described as a fulfilment of the injunctions of Jesus ("... er hat wohl den Reichtum für gefährlich gehalten, hat aber kaum auf Gütergemeinschaft zielende Gemeindeordnungen initiiert oder gar, wie in den Acta-Summarien, eine Besitzablieferung allgemein-verbindlich gemacht;" cf. Braun, *Qumran und das Neue Testament* 1, 149), and in the following pages it will become clear that Jesus did not want his adherents to behave like the Essenes on this point. The form of communal ownership of property as pictured in Acts might therefore reflect a later stage in the history of the Christian community in Jerusalem. In the opinion of St. Giet, the practice described in Acts 2:44 and 4:32, was influenced by an ancient version of the Two Ways. The teaching of the Apostles, to which the believers who share all things are said to "devote themselves" in Acts 2:42, was nothing but a version of the Two Ways. At the time of Luke, this early recension was already ascribed to the authority of the apostles so as to provide the manual with a high status (*L'Énigme de la Didachè*, 165-66). A more conceivable alternative, however, is that Acts 2:42-47 and 4:32-35 constitute two summaries which were added to the main text in order to generalize and idealize individual cases of sharing property in the early church. See, however, Flusser, 'Ostracon from Qumran', 12-15.
See also Justin Martyr, *1 Apol.* 14:2: "(... We who loved above all else the ways of acquiring riches and possessions) now hand over to a community fund what we possess, and share it with every needy person" (νῦν καὶ ἃ ἔχομεν εἰς κοινὸν φέροντες καὶ παντὶ δεομένῳ κοινωνοῦντες); for the Greek text, cf. Marcovich, *Iustini Martyris Apologiae*, 52-53, lines 10-12.

the benefit of the members of a closed group, separated off into a secluded conventicle or ghetto. On the contrary, it rather seems that the separatistic sectarian understanding of *koinônia* is weakened. Evidence for the attenuation of the *koinônia* concept is found in the motivation used: "for if you are partners (κοινωνοί) in what is immortal, (should you be not so) all the more in things that perish?" This incentive was apparently apt to serve ideologies advocating the revision of a self-designed sharing of material goods, which becomes clear when we consider Paul's letter to the Romans.

It has been widely observed that in Romans a similar line of arguing is found. In the final part of the body of the letter, Paul stresses his desire to visit the Christian community in Rome. First, however, he has to take to Jerusalem the contributions made by the gentile Christians:

> For Macedonia and Achaia have been pleased to make some contribution (κοινωνίαν) for the poor among the saints at Jerusalem; they were pleased to do it, and indeed they are in debt to them, for if the gentiles have come to share (ἐκοινώνησαν) in their spiritual treasures, they ought also to be of service to them in material treasures. (Rom 15:26-27)

Because the *koinônia* concept is linked with a spiritual motivation, involving an extension to the gentiles, its scope is considerably broadened. The common sharing of spiritual wealth involves a moral obligation to make the needy a participant in material wealth as well. If the gentiles share in the spiritual blessings of the poor in Jerusalem, extending beyond the limits of the local church, they for their part ought all the more to share their material property with them. This understanding is also at the basis of Paul's statement in 1 Cor. 9:11: "If we have sown spiritual good among you, is it too much if we reap your material benefits?" but the principle is preeminently laid down in Rom 15:27. It is in this light that we must interpret the passage in GTW 4:8. The material possessions are not confined to a group that has effectively insulated itself from the dangers of the outside world. The admonition reflects a reorientation upon ideologies, such as the one found in Qumran, which, preoccupied with its own purity ideals, restricted the meaning of the word κοινωνία to sharing resources within their own community exclusively.

The similarities in Rom 15:26-27 and GTW 4:8 can scarcely be due to pure coincidence. In either case, the *argumentum a maiori ad minus*[143] shows that participation in spiritual goods involves a broader-minded approach to the surrounding world.[144] The spiritual motivation extends the community of goods to a

---

[143] Cf. GTW 4:8: "if you are partners (κοινωνοί) in what is immortal, *how much more* in things that perish? ...." In Did 4:8, the pair of terms is: ἐν τῷ ἀθανάτῳ – ἐν τοῖς θνητοῖς; in Barn. 19:8a ἐν τῷ ἀφθάρτῳ – ἐν τοῖς φθαρτοῖς; and in Rom 15:27 (cf. also 1 Cor 9:11) τὰ πνευματικά – τὰ σαρκικά. See also Niederwimmer, *Die Didache*, 141, nn. 69 and 70.

[144] This principle appears to have been so pervasive in Paul's thought that on many occasions he not only extended the meaning of κοινωνία and (συγ)κοινωνέω to include a wider community of possessions but also provided these terms of the κοινων-root with an additional, material meaning. In Rom 15:26, for instance, he substitutes the word κοινωνία for the current secular term λογία so as to

boundless distribution of possessions among needy brethren.[145] A characteristic emphasis in the teachings of Jesus as recorded by Luke may improve our understanding of the argument in its historical framework. In his comment on the parable of the dishonest steward (Luke 16:1-13), Jesus may well be polemizing against the economic exclusiveness of the Essenes.[146] Most of the material, namely vv. 1-7, which make up the story proper, and vv. 8-12, which are appended to the parable, are exclusive to Luke. Only v. 13, Jesus' saying about the slave of two masters, has a parallel in the Sermon on the Mount in Matt 6:24.

In Luke 16:8, the prudence of the steward is dealt with, and Jesus, although not approving of the method the steward used, recommends his disciples to show the same cleverness. He then goes on to explain this:

> for the sons of this world are more shrewd in dealing with their own generation than the sons of light. And I tell you, make friends for yourselves from ($\dot{\epsilon}\kappa$) the mammon of unrighteousness, so that when it fails they may receive you into the eternal habitations (8b-9).

The first points to be noted about this text is that the wording "sons of this world" probably reflects a Qumran expression for all humans outside the sect's community[147] while the "sons of light" is the favourite self-designation of the community.[148] Also the term "mammon (property) of unrighteousness" has close

---

describe the monetary collection for Jerusalem's poor. Because the churches of the Greeks of Macedonia and Achaia owe the spiritual wealth they enjoyed to that of Jerusalem, they could only repay the debt of participation in spiritual goods by material assistance (κοινωνίαν), i.e., their contribution. The *argumentum a maiori ad minus* is employed to express the unity of the church and, this way, to induce the gentile churches to feel responsibility for the poor Jewish Christians in Jerusalem. A similar usage of the term κοινωνία is found in 2 Cor 8:4; 9:13. On the basis of the participation in spiritual goods, one is obliged to make the other a fellow-sharer in the material possessions. Also the verbs (συγ)κοινωνέω, with the meaning "to contribute" in Gal 6:6; Phil 4:14-16, imply an exchange of material and spiritual riches; cf. Mc Dermott, 'The Biblical Doctrine of KOINΩNIA', 71-73 and 222-25; See also Panikulam, *Koinōnia in the New Testament*, 57; Hainz, *Koinonia. »Kirche«*, 62-205.

[145] The same atttitude is ascribed to John the Baptist in the New Testament. There are many scholars who have considered John the Baptist as being close to the Qumran sect but not quite identical with it. This also applies to the sharing of property as outlined by John in Luke 3:10-11: "And the multitudes asked him, 'What then shall we do?'. And he answered them, 'He who has two coats, let him share with him who has none; and he who has food, let him do likewise.'" The teaching is reminiscent of Qumran but, at the same time, shows important differences. In spite of the radical charity and distribution of property recommended here, it is indicated that one could still possess very basic clothing and food for oneself. Moreover, whereas the Essenes maintained the community of property in a closed sect, John the Baptist asked his adherents to share their goods with paupers. Thus, although John may have been deeply influenced by Essenism, he mitigated its harshness and rigid outlook. It is not impossible that an Essene dissident like John the Baptist belonged to the broader semi-Essene movement within which the Greek Two Ways was composed.

[146] Cf. Flusser, 'Jesus' opinion', 156-67; Id, 'The Parable', passim.

[147] Fitzmyer, *The Gospel According to Luke* 2, 1108.

[148] Cf. Fitzmyer, *The Gospel According to Luke* 2, 1108; Grundmann, *Das Evangelium nach Lukas*, 320; Krämer, *Das Rätsel der Parabel*, 153; Benoit, 'Qumrân et Le Nouveau Testament', 288-90.

parallels in Essene writings[149] and specifically denotes the property of the outside people, of aliens.[150] These facts seem to endorse an explanation of the Lukan passage that takes a reference to the Qumran community into account. The derogatory sense which the word acquired within the sect is still noticeable in Jesus' characterization of the mammon as 'unrighteous'. The sons of light in Qumran separated themselves from the property of the wicked external world and restricted economic contact as far as possible. In this light, the Greek preposition ἐκ, preceding "the mammon of unrighteousness," must be explained. Whereas the preposition is mostly interpreted as meaning "by means of,"[151] the signification "from" seems to be the most obvious one. The statement in Luke 16:8b-9 explains that the "sons of this world" are more prudent than the "sons of light," the Essenes, who avoid trading relations with non-sectarians. Jesus views the position of economic separatism nourished and fostered by the "sons of light" as a dangerous attitude and warns his disciples not to choose the path of sectarian isolation. He favours an association with non-believers so as to transact business with them.

The function of the parable is found in vv. 10-12, where it is applied to a specific case of economic trade between believers and non-believers. It might concern a loan or deposit that had been entrusted by non-believers to disciples of Jesus[152] and the implication, then, would be that Jesus warns his followers to be trustworthy with what belongs to a non-believer:

---

[149] Fitzmyer, *The Gospel According to Luke* 2, 1109-10.

[150] See, for example, 1QS 5:14-20; 9:8-9 (the latter instance is quoted above, in n. 138). In the Dead Sea Scrolls the term 'mammon' (ממון) is interchangeable with the usual word 'hon' (הון); cf. also Flusser, 'Jesus' opinion', 153-55 and Id., 'The Parable', 180-82.

[151] For the various interpretations, see Fitzmyer, *The Gospel According to Luke* 2, 1109. If the preposition ἐκ is taken to mean "by means of," the "friends" in v. 9 are usually identified as the poor who are to be helped by works of charity; cf. Krämer, *Das Rätsel der Parabel*, 105.219; Arndt, *The Gospel according to St. Luke*, 357; Descamps, 'La Composition littéraire', 50; Johnson, *The Literary Function*,157; Seccombe, *Possessions and the Poor*, 169; Grundmann, *Das Evangelium nach Lukas*, 321; Ireland, *Stewardship and the Kingdom*, 96-99; etc.

[152] This suggestion is consistent with indications in a source dating from the beginning of the second century. It concerns the well-known letter of Pliny the Younger to the emperor Trajan (Ep. Ad Traj. X, 96, 7), written about 112 in Bithynia. In this letter Pliny, talking about Christians who were examined by him, states (see also above, Chap. 3, p. 88): "They also declared that the sum total of their guilt or error amounted to no more than this: they had met regularly before dawn on a fixed day to chant verses alternately among themselves in honour of Christ as if to a god, and also to bind themselves by oath, not for any criminal purpose, but to abstain from theft, robbery and adultery, to commit no breach of trust and not to deny a deposit when called upon to restore it (...ne fidem fallerent, ne depositum adpellati abnegarent);" for the Latin text and the English translation, see Radice, *Pliny*, 289. The whole of this oath, as recorded in Pliny's Letter to Trajan, is very similar to the passage of Aristides of Athens who writes in his *Apology* that Christians were prohibited to acquire a deposit for themselves (15,4). See Geffcken, *Zwei griechische Apologeten*, 24 (lines 3-6) and see the commentary on pp. 87-88. The clause, however, forbidding Christians to appropriate a deposit for themselves, only appears in the Syriac translation. For this and additional material, see Flusser, 'Jesus' opinion', 160 and Id. 'The Parable', 185.

(10) He who is faithful (or: trustworthy = הנאמן) in a small matter can be trusted also in a major one; and he who is dishonest (or: untrustworthy[153]) in a minor matter is dishonest (or: untrustworthy) also in a great one.[154] (11) If then you have not been faithful (trustworthy) in the unrighteous mammon (or: the property of unrighteousness[155]), who will entrust to you the true riches? (12) And if you have not been faithful (trustworthy) in another's goods, who will give you that which is your own?

The verses form a chain linked together by three arguments of *a minori ad maius* and are constructed in a parallel manner.[156] The "small matter" in v. 10a corresponds with the "property of unrighteousness" in v. 11a and with "another's goods" in v. 12a. As mentioned above, the "property of unrighteousness" in Essene terminology refers to all property that is owned by those who are not members of the sect. This assumption is confirmed by the agreement between vv. 11a and 12a: the property belongs to "another". Having expressed a general principle in v. 10, Jesus then goes on to oppose the extreme sectarian attitude and asks his followers to remain trustworthy with the "property of unrighteousness," with the resources belonging to non-followers. Only thus will they be able to gain friends.

The affinity between Luke 16:10-12 and the passage found in GTW 4:8 (and Rom 15:25-27) is obvious as is illustrated by the following comparison:

GTW 4:8	*Luke 16:9a.11-12*
a) you shall hold everything in common with your brother,	9a) And I tell you, make friends for yourselves from the property of unrighteousness
b) for if you are partners in what is immortal,	11b) who will entrust to you the true riches, 12b) who will give you that which is your own
c) (should you be not so) all the more in things that perish?	11a) if you have not been trustworthy in the property of unrighteousness? 12a) if you have not been trustworthy in another's goods?

The "property of unrighteousness" belonging to others (Luke 16:11a and 12a) corresponds with the perishable things in GTW 4:8c, while "the true riches" matching "that which is your own" (Luke 16:11b and 12b) corresponds with the spiritual treasures that are immortal in GTW 4:8b. Moreover, the reasoning in all

---

[153] ἄδικος: "unjust", "dishonest", "untrustworthy"; cf. Bauer-Arndt-Gingrich-Danker, *A Greek-English Lexicon*.

[154] The correspondence with ExR 2,3 is important: "Another interpretation of 'Now Moses was keeping the flock': it says: 'Every word of God is tried' (Prov 30:5); before God confers greatness on a man He first tests him by a little thing and then promotes him to greatness. Here you have two great leaders whom God first proved by a little thing, found trustworthy (ונמצאו נאמנים), and then promoted to greatness. He tested David ...;" ET: S.M. Lehrman in Freedman-Simon, *The Midrash Rabbah* 2, 49-50. As to additional rabbinic parallels, see Str-B 1, 972; 2, 221-22 and 500-01.

[155] "Obviously this means the same as the μαμωνᾶ τῆς ἀδικίας, ...;" cf. Plummer, *A Critical and Exegetical Commentary*, 386.

[156] For the parallellism in Luke 16:10-12, cf. also Ireland, *Stewardship and the Kingdom of God*, 110-12.

three texts is built upon conditional clauses ("If ..."). The argument in GTW and Romans shows that there is a necessary connection between a community of goods and a community in spirit. If one shares in the immortal (or, according to Rom 15:26-27, in the spiritual) treasures, how much more ought one to share in things that are mortal (or, according to Romans in material treasures). In Luke, a similar connection between spiritual and material treasures is found, but the order of argumentation is reversed. Here the material level, the economic contacts with outsiders, will cause these aliens to trust the disciples on a higher spiritual level. Economic participation with non-followers will encourage and stimulate these non-believers to open their hearts to the message of Jesus. This is not to say, however, that the argument in Rom 15:26-27 and GTW 4:8 ultimately goes back to Jesus or a tradition of Jesus-sayings. On the contrary, the presence of the characteristic reasoning in both the instruction of Jesus, in Romans, and in the Greek Two Ways rather seems to reflect an underlying tradition.

In conclusion, the following points seem relevant with respect to the social milieu of the Greek Two Ways. The terminology in the appended verses of Luke 16:9-12 shows that Jesus, when applying the parable of the dishonest steward, has in mind the Essene exclusive economic ownership. Of course, like the Essenes, Jesus too regards all possessions as a threat to true piety (Luke 16:13; cf. Matt 6:24), but he rejects the idea of an exclusive esoteric and closed group that avoids contacts with outsiders. He repudiates the inner-directed way of sharing goods and recommends another, broader-minded approach to the surrounding world. We further discussed GTW 4:8. With the help of the evidence in Rom 15:26-27, it was established that the terms κοινωνία, τὸ κοινωνικόν have taken on a new meaning in GTW 4:8 when considered against their Essene background. Rather than pertaining to a restricted communism based on economic separatism, they imply a sharing of property with all. The parallels, then, between Luke 16:9-12 and GTW 4:8 are close. Jesus and the composer of the admonition in GTW not only exhibit a common conviction in social matters but also share a similar argumentation, interconnecting spiritual and economic levels. It is therefore reasonable to assume that both views go back to the milieu of the hassidim and reflect a social trend within the pious circles from which the Greek Two Ways issued.[157] Unlike the sectarian scrolls, there is no indication in the Greek Two Ways, in the Testaments of the Twelve Patriarchs, or in the (early) Derekh Erets literature of a marked division between the pious Sages and the outside world. There is no derogatory expression for outsiders and no invocation to segregate oneself economically from non-members of the community. Instead, these writings teach undivided love and solidarity with mankind. It is likely, then, that the sectarian concept of *koinônia*, denoting exclusive communal property, was transformed into an all-encompassing social concern under the influence of the existing hassidic position within semi-Essene streams.

---

[157] We have seen that the *argumentum a maiori ad minus* also occurs in Rom 15:26-27, but this does not mean that Pauline communities had any links with our Jewish circles. Paul himself adopted the argument and used it for his own purposes (see above, n. 144).

II The Didache's Place in

Early Judaism

and

Nascent Christianity

Chapter Six

The Two Ways and the Sermon on the Mount

No other section of the Bible has attracted more attention in theological discussion and in the life of the church at large than the Sermon on the Mount. For most of church history, the Sermon on the Mount has been an interesting curiosity, exercising a fascination far beyond denominational boundaries. Often the discussion focussed on the conflict between the authority attributed to the Sermon, which was considered to be the essence of the teaching of Jesus, and the realities of common church life. It is not the aim of this chapter to provide an exhaustive review of the wide range of opinions that the Sermon has provoked from scholars,[1] but rather to show how it relates to the Greek Two Ways (GTW).

Taken at the topic's face value, one might question the relevance of an investigation like this to a monography which is devoted to the Didache. Two points may be noted at this stage. First, the opening theme of the Didache introducing the Two Ways doctrine appears in Matt 7:13-14 as well. There an easy way is mentioned, which "leads to destruction" and a hard way, which "leads to life." The presence of the Two Ways motif in this Matthean passage has often led scholars to argue for Matt 7:13-14 as the source of Did 1:1.[2] Secondly, there is widespread recognition that elements in Matt 5:17-48 closely agree with items in the Two Ways of the Didache.[3] The latter view will be buttressed in the following pages. We will attempt to show that Jesus in formulating his instruction used traditional materials transmitted both in the Sermon on the Mount and in the Greek Two Ways. The earlier layer of the Sermon appears to be a basic ethical unit which finds its best explanation in the light of traditions which were current in Jewish hassidic circles.

---

[1] For a review and summary of recent Matthean scholarship, see Stanton, 'The Origin and Purpose of Matthew's Gospel'; Dumais, *Le Sermon sur la Montagne*. See also Loader, *Jesus' Attitude towards the Law*, 137-154.

[2] See Schaff, *The Oldest Church Manual*, 18 (on top); Muilenburg, *The Literary Relations*, 73; Vokes, *The Riddle of the Didache*, 19.

[3] Especially between Matt 5:17-48 and Did 3:1-6. Cf. Funk, *Doctrina duodecim Apostolorum*, 12; Goppelt, *Christentum und Judentum*, 187; Lilje, *Die Lehre der zwölf Apostel*, 51-52; Giet, *L'Énigme de la Didachè*, 158-60; Jefford, *The Sayings of Jesus*, 65-67; H.D. Betz, *The Sermon on the Mount*, 219; Bornkamm, 'Der Aufbau der Bergpredigt', 432; Flusser, 'A Rabbinic Parallel', 497-99. 504-505; Id., 'Die Tora in der Bergpredigt', 106-09 and nn. 11-12. See also below, pp. 225-34.

It has often been maintained that Jesus perceived his instruction about the reorientation of conduct in the Sermon on the Mount as deriving from the imminent or incipient kingdom of God, which Jesus himself would make manifest. Perhaps the eschatological character of Jesus' ministry led to certain claims and actions which went beyond the then current range of debate about the interpretation of the Tora. And, of course, Jesus' ethic must be understood from the perspective of a belief that the kingdom of heaven was nigh. Nevertheless, we cannot be sure to what extent this urgency actually determined Jesus' teaching on ethics. Jesus may well have believed that, through him, the age of the kingdom was being inaugurated, but that this era did not necessarily represent the endtime. It may also embody the period *before* the end of days. Jesus conceivably considered himself to be living in an intermediary period in which the righteous and the wicked were to coexist until the final "age to come."[4] Moreover, a direct relation to eschatological expectations can hardly be established in the section of the antitheses (5:17-48), the part of the Sermon on the Mount that will be especially studied here.[5]

Other grounds for caution should also be borne in mind in explaining the Sermon on the Mount and especially the discussion about the Law in Matt 5:17-48. Matthew's gospel is not an anthology of the teachings of Jesus and not every part of the Sermon can be traced back to the historical Jesus. Furthermore, Matthew's portrait of Jesus' attitude towards the Law must not be separated from Matthew's own attitude towards the Law and that of his community. We should constantly be aware that in exploring Jesus' attitude towards the Law, one is, in fact, investigating Jesus' attitude towards the Law according to Matthew.

Although the source and redactional-critical problems raised by the comparison of the Sermon on the Mount and the Sermon on the Plain (Luke 6:20-49) cannot be treated adequately here, the question is nonetheless vital to our understanding of the text, and we cannot avoid it altogether. The close agreement in order and in content between the two texts has led most scholars to conclude that the 'Q' source contained an earlier form of the sermon and, indeed, it seems safe to suggest that each of the two evangelists has reworked the nucleus sermon in his own way. Both evangelists may have "preserved here something from an extended sermon delivered by Jesus toward the beginning of his ministry."[6] Usually, however,

---

[4] Flusser, *Jesus* (1998) 258-75; Id., *Das Christentum – eine jüdische Religion*, 37-52.

[5] Contra Guelich, who – with reference to Matt 5:17.18d – emphasizes the eschatological dimension of the Law as the expression of God's will which was brought to its ultimate completion by the person of Jesus. On the other hand he urges that – according to Matt 5:18b.c. – the Law will continue in force in its entirety until "heaven and earth pass away," the final consummation; cf. Guelich, *The Sermon on the Mount*, 140-53.162-68. The blending of these assumptions, however, is taken by Stanton to be "a somewhat artificial straitjacket;" cf. 'The Origin and Purpose of Matthew's Gospel', 1936.

[6] Fitzmyer, *The Gospel According to Luke* 1, 627. For a deliberate support of the Q hypothesis, see also 73-82, which is a summary of his 'The Priority of Mark'.

It must be remembered, however, that also in cases where Matthew renders material of his own, he might have had access to traditions whose roots extend to Jesus' ministry. This is not to say, of course, that the section 5:17-48 simply derives from the historical Jesus, in the sense that Jesus is the author of all sayings in their present form and context.

Luke's version is considered to be very close to the original version in Q.[7] If one takes the traditions behind Luke 6:20-49 to reflect the sayings collection of Jesus, it is not hard to observe that Matthew must have considerably changed the extent and profile of the traditional Q sermon. And as far as Matt 5:17-48 is concerned, he probably had another source at his disposal with which he intertwined the materials from Q, especially the passage reflected in Luke 6:27-36.

In other areas of modern research into Matt 5:17-48, opinions are much divided. Even if a redaction-historical approach is employed, it is not easy to obtain scientifically justifiable criteria for delineating stages in the development of the materials. In this chapter, we intend to offer a way forward by recovering a source used by Matthew in 5:17-48. Before mapping out the different layers of that section, however, other aspects of the Sermon on the Mount as a whole will be discussed.

We will see in the first section (pp. 197-204) that the beginning and ending of the Sermon provide materials which are closely akin to the early layers of Derekh Erets literature and the Jewish Two Ways, repectively. They form a ring composition reflecting the religious and historical milieu in which the central division (5:17-7:12) becomes intelligible. In the succeeding section, we will focus on the statements of principle in 5:17-20 and the so-called antitheses in 5:21-48. It has often been postulated that these two literary units offer disparate or even contradictory assertions on Jesus' attitude to the Law. While Jesus is upholding the integrity of the Law in the first unit, he seems to be attacking Tora commandments in the subsequent section. In order to understand their relationship, these units will be examined separately (subsections on pp. 205-16 and 216-25). In seeking to discover the evangelist's aim for both sections, we will look for pivotal concepts and phrases and thematically related material. Every attempt is made to discuss each of the two units on the basis of the text of the gospel itself in order to avoid the impression that the meaning and function of the Two Ways are simply and arbitrarily imposed on the gospel of Matthew. The six antitheses in 5:21-48 contain a premise or thesis, mostly citing from or referring to commandments in the Tora, and an antithetical response to these commandments, introduced by the formula "But I say to you." The positions refuted by Jesus and Jesus' own positions fall within the range of the then current debate about Tora interpretation. They are in line with the agenda of first-century Judaism and are frequently cited in recent research to prove that Jesus' demands would not be unfamiliar to his hearers.[8]

---

[7] Cf. Stanton, *A Gospel for a New People*, 288.

[8] Cf. Broer, 'Anmerkungen zum Gesetzesverständnis', 131-33; H.D. Betz, *The Sermon on the Mount*, 277-85; Friedlander, *The Jewish Sources*, 40-53; Str-B 1, 276-82. 298-301; Montefiore, *Rabbinic Literature*, 38-56; Percy, *Die Botschaft Jesu*, 131-63. With respect to their antithetical pattern as distinctively pre-Matthean (see below), the historical contexts of the first, second and fourth antitheses are particularly relevant:

1st antithesis: For similar teaching on anger, see Sir 1:22; 22:24; *T. Dan* 1:7-8; 2:4; 3-5; *T. Sim.* 2:6-7.11; *T. Zeb.* 4:11; cf. also Arist 168; 4 Macc 2:1-23; Ps.-Phoc. 57-58; Pesiqta Hadta, Shavuoth, in Jellinek, *Bet ha-Midrasch* 6, 45; SifDeut 186-87 to Deut 19:11 (= Finkelstein, *Siphre ad Deuteronomium,* 226);

As to the underlying framework of Matt 5:17-48, however, one can find a multiplicity of viewpoints in contemporary scholarship. The failure to reach unanimity draws attention to the complexity of the material and to the difficulty of distinguishing tradition and redaction in this section. None of the parallels, most of which are from early Jewish sources, has so far provided any external evidence of a similar line of reasoning, a corresponding topical organization, and an analoguous elaboration of preceding commandments. In this respect, the comparison of the similarities between Matt 5:17-48 and GTW 3:1-6 turns out to be helpful. When one seriously takes the reconstructed text of the Greek Two Ways as given in Chapter 4 to represent a Jewish document, one is in a position to establish the traditional character of some of the antitheses (see the subsection on pp. 225-34, below). The long-standing and rather widespread view which assigns three of the

SifDeut 235 to Deut 22:13 (= Finkelstein, 267); DER XI,15 according to Van Loopik, *The Ways*, 164 = Tosefta Derekh Erets VI (Perek Ha-Yotzee),13 according to Higger, *The treatises Derek Erez* 2, 312-13 (Hebr.) and 117 (ET).

2nd antithesis: see Sir 26:9; *Pss. Sol.* 4:4-5; *T. Issa.* 4:4; 7:2; *T. Benj.* 8; Philo, *Spec. Leg.* 3, 177-78; other appropriate parallels are found in Str-B 1, 299-301; Montefiore, *Rabbinic Literature,* 41-43; Moore, *Judaism* 2, 268-69

4th antithesis: The text referred to in the thesis is not drawn verbatim from the written Hebrew text of the Bible but made up of a number of citations and allusions from the Tora (e.g. Exod 20:7.16; Lev 19:12; Num 30:2; Deut 5:20; 23:22), all intending to safeguard the sanctity of God's name. Since a prohibition of this sort is considered as belonging to the Tora in a wide range of mostly parenetic Jewish materials (1 Esdr. 1:46; Wisd 14:25; *T. Asher* 2:6; Ps.-Phoc. 16; Or. Sib 2,68; cf. also Sir 23:9-11; 2 Enoch 40:1-2), the decree may have been regarded in Matt 5:33 as a Tora prohibition (cf. H.D. Betz, *The Sermon on the Mount*, 263-64). Warnings against false and excessive swearing are common · in Greco-Roman and Jewish literature. The distinction between an oath (שבועה: a commitment to do or to avoid a certain thing) and a vow (נדר: the dedication of something to the divinity and thus forbidding to use it or to benefit from it), however, is not always clear because these terms were often used interchangeably. Both the Greek and the rabbinic literature testifies to the popularity and variety of oaths and vows throughout antiquity by all classes of people. The Sages expended much effort, esp. in the tractates mShevu'ot and mNedarim, to suppress false and unnecessary swearing; see also Lieberman, *Greek in Jewish Palestine*, 115-43. Cf. Str-B 1, 328-30; Montefiore, *Rabbinic Literature*, 48. The divine circumlocutions in the substitute oaths of Matt 5:34b-36 probably arose from a pious effort to avoid profaning the holy name (Exod 20:7) by reducing God to an object of human manipulation.

Philo recommended avoiding the use of oaths (*Spec. Leg.* 2, 2-17; 2, 224), except when absolutely necessary (cf. *Decal.* 84-86) and regarded an opposition to oaths as a testimony of the love for God (cf. *Omn. prob. lib.*, 84). Cf. also Philo *Spec. Leg.* 1, 235; 2, 26; 4, 40; Josephus, *Bellum* 1, 260; *Ant.* 4, 169-70; 8, 17-20.

The members of the Sect in Qumran apparently took an oath regarding the practice of piety and secrets of the group when entering the community (1QS 5:8; CD 15:1-5; Josephus, *Bellum* 2, 139-42) but are at the same time warned to avoid certain forms of God's name in taking oaths (CD 15:1). The latter document (CD 9:9-12, 15:3-5 and 16:7-12) and the Temple Scroll (11QTemple 53:9-54:7) regulate some cases of vows and thus appear to accept those on topics other than admission into the Sect; see, furthermore, H. Braun, *Qumran und das Neue Testament* vol. 1, 16 and vol. 2, 98-99.289.296. Josephus tells us of some Essenes, who having sworn oaths at initiation, then refused to take oaths altogether (*Bellum* 2,135). The complete abstention on the part of (some of) the Essenes may also explain why Herod acquitted them of the requirement to take an oath of loyalty (*Ant.* 15, 371-72). See also Str-B 1, 321-32; Friedlander, *The Jewish Sources*, 60-65; Sanders, *Jewish Law*, 51-57; Saldarini, *Matthew's Christian-Jewish Community*, 151-60.

antitheses to a pre-Matthean stage (5:21-22. 27-28. 33-34a) is supported by the striking recurrent patterns that can be observed between the two units.

The early stratum of Matt 5:17-20 and the format of the antitheses proper in paragraphs 1, 2, and 4 probably came from an earlier stage in the community's history and represent a form of argumentation that may have been available at the time and in the milieu of Jesus' ministry. The parallel part of this instruction in the Greek Two Ways, however, does not provide us with a full understanding of the Matthean Jesus. The question of why Jesus, in his antithetic counterstatements, modified at least two of the three minor sins as compared with the manner in which the minor sins are presented in the Two Ways is addressed in the last subsection (pp. 234-36). While in the Two Ways the vices of intense anger and a lustful glance are mentioned to prevent people from breaking major Decalogue sins, they have taken the shape of autonomous and isolated sins, cast in legally formulated phrases, in the antitheses.

The Preamble (Matt 5:3-16) and Conclusion (7:13-27) of the Sermon on the Mount

The Sermon on the Mount, bracketed by the ascent of and descent from the mountain in 5:1 and 8:1, is the first detailed portrayal in Matthew's gospel (5:3-7:27) of Jesus as a teacher. Let us consider the sermon's structure first. The discourse in Matthew, addressed first of all to Jesus' disciples and collaterally to the crowds (5:1; 7:28), falls into three main parts: the introduction (5:3-16), the main body of the sermon (5:17-7:12) and the last section representing concluding warnings (7:13-27). The introduction consists of two units: the so-called Beatitudes (Matt 5:3-12) and the similarly structured 'salt' and 'light' sayings (5:13-16). The Beatitudes are pervaded with a tone of promise but, at the same time, diffuse an atmosphere of exhortation and moral parenesis on appropriate attitudes and correct conduct. For our purpose, it is important to note that the positive qualities described in this segment are consistent with values hailed in the early layers of the Derekh Erets literature, studied in Chapter 5, pp. 172-74 above. God's blessing is promised to those disciples who exhibit attitudes of meekness, hungering and thirsting after righteousness, mercy, purity of heart, and peacemaking:

> Blessed are the meek, for they shall inherit the earth.[9]
> Blessed are those who hunger and thirst for righteousness, for they shall be satisfied.
> Blessed are the merciful, for they shall obtain mercy.
> Blessed are the pure in heart, for they shall see God.
> Blessed are the peacemakers, for they shall be called sons of God (Matt 5:5-9).

---

[9] For this phrase, see GTW 3:7; Did 3:7; Doctr. 3:7; cf. above, Chap. 4, pp. 134-35 and Jefford, *The Sayings of Jesus*, 73-81.

Matthew shares four Beatitudes with Luke (6:20-22) referring to the poor, the hungry, those who weep, and those who are persecuted. The additional five macarisms in his gospel, quoted above, show great interest in highly developed ethical behaviour, traits that seem synonymous with the Matthean concept of 'greater righteousness' or more righteous conduct, which is already stressed in 3:15; 5:6.10 and returns in 5:20; 6:1.33. This advanced standard of morality permeates the entire Sermon on the Mount. The disciples are called the "light of the world," an expression referring to their good deeds, which shine in the world so that mankind will glorify the heavenly Father (5:14-16). The correspondence between the values propagated in Matthew's Beatitudes and the particular emphases in the teaching of Derekh Erets are significant for our interpretation of the Sermon. For the present, it suffices to note that the outlook and practice promoted in the Sermon on the Mount is thoroughly Jewish as it reflects the traditions which were operative in hassidic Jewish circles.[10]

The central section of the sermon opens and closes with references to "the Law and the Prophets" (5:17 and 7:12). This section is in turn divided into two further divisions. The first is the unit in 5:17-48, presenting a collection of materials dealing with the Law. It begins with a unit containing a programmatic statement on the validity of the Tora in Matt 5:17-20. In the next segment (5:21-48), the so-called antitheses occur, each of which is made up of two parts including an initial quotation from the Law and, so it seems at first glance, Jesus' refutation of it. The second division (6:1-7:12) of this main section is only indirectly connected with issues of the Law and is somewhat loosely related to the other Sermon elements as well. The instructions in 6:1-18 contain three paragraphs on almsgiving, prayer, and fasting, all of which use similar formulations in condemning hypocrisy and urging behaviour which will earn God's reward (6:2-4. 5-6. 16-18). The ensuing three loosely knit clusters (6:19-7:11) deal with thrust, unjustifiable condemnation of others, and the effectiveness of prayer.

Finally, in 7:12, this middle section is brought to a close by the ethical maxim: "So whatever you wish that men would do to you, do so to them; for this is the law and the prophets." This saying is a positive formulation of the Golden Rule which – although its negative format is more common – is found in Luke 6:31 and in Jewish writings such as Jub 20:2[11], Arist 207, and 2 Enoch 61:1-2. In comparison to Luke 6:31, the occurrence of the Golden Rule in Matthew is noteworthy in two respects.

---

[10]   Cf. Hengel, 'Zur matthäischen Bergpredigt', 355-56: "Hier" (i.e. in Tosefta Derek Erez: Perek Ha-Minin 19-24 in Higger, *The treatises Derek Erez* 2, 287-89 [Hebr.] and 107-09 [ET] = Derekh Erets Rabba II, 19-24; cf. above, Chap. 5., n. 96) "erscheinen in etwas anderer Sprachform nahezu alle Motive der Preisungen des Mt, wobei eine Abhängigkeit des jüdischen Textes von Mt extrem unwahrscheinlich ist. Trotz des relativ späten Charakters der Sammlung befinden wir uns in einem ähnlichen, religiös-ethischen, »chassidischen«, man könnte auch sagen »pietistischen« Milieu, ..." (356); cf. also 379-80; and cf. Flusser, *Jesus* (1998) 96-97. For the ideological and literary affinity of the first three Beatitudes with the Dead Sea Scrolls, cf. Flusser, 'Blessed are the Poor in Spirit' and Id., 'Some Notes to the Beatitudes'. Further, see 4Q521, frag. 2 col. 2 and 4Q525, frag. 2 col 2.

[11]   See above, Chapter 5, p. 159.

In the first place, Matthew and Luke use the Golden Rule within differing contexts. It has been established that the versions of the Sermon in Matthew and Luke, as far as they share common materials, are in striking agreement in rendering the order of the traditions, except for the position of the Golden Rule.[12] In Luke 6:31, the Rule follows the examples of conduct illustrating love for one's enemy (6:29-30), and, in a context of verses dealing with behaviour to other people, this seems the more natural setting. This judgment is underscored by the observation that in Jewish and Christian tradition, the Golden Rule became understood as synonymous with the love command.[13] We thus might have expected this saying in the gospel of Matthew in a parallel position to Luke's passage, i.e., in Matt 5:43-48, where Jesus extends the command to love your neighbour (Lev 19:18) to include enemies. The omission of the statement within the comparable context suggests that Matthew dropped the Golden Rule from its Q setting to insert it at the end of the main body of the Sermon on the Mount, right before the final admonitions in 7:13-27.

The second reason to claim that Matthew's version of the Golden Rule is somewhat peculiar as compared with Luke is provided by the ensuing phrase in 7:12c, indicating that the Golden Rule can serve as an underlying principle of "the Law and the Prophets." The clause is missing in Luke 6:31 and may have been inserted by Matthew to create a deliberate link between the Golden Rule and the almost identical phrase[14] in 5:17. The vv. 5:17 and 7:12 then form a thematic inclusion around the core of the middle section, indicating that, rather than the Tora instruction in 5:17-48 only, it is the whole of the central section of the Sermon – also those kinds of teaching about almsgiving, praying, fasting and trust, topics which at first sight are unrelated to Tora – which represents extrapolation of Tora.[15]

The additional phrase in Matt 7:12, "for this is the law and the prophets," thus appears to be a juxtaposition provided by Matthew. This is not to deny, however, that the idea in 7:12 might be pre-Matthean, meaning that some form of the Golden Rule, being a summary of all provisions of the Tora, may have its ultimate roots in Jesus' ministry. The distribution of the evidence in the New Testament indicates that for Jesus the love commandment served as the center of Law (Matt 5:43-48;

---

[12] "The only *transposition* within the Q speech is the golden rule, which Matthew found in the section on enemy love and postponed to 7,12;" cf. Syreeni, *The Making of the Sermon*,159. Cf. also Stanton, *A Gospel for a New People*, 287.

[13] See above, Chap. 5, pp. 158-60. Cf. also Luz, *Das Evangelium nach Matthäus* 1, 387-91; Gnilka, *Das Matthäusevangelium* 1, 143-44; cf. also H.W. Kuhn, 'Das Liebesgebot Jesu', 205-07.

[14] One notes that the formula in 7:12c slightly differs from 5:17 in that the former has καί ("and") while the latter has ἤ ("or"). Of course, there is solid evidence that Scripture was referred to under the general heading of the 'Law and the Prophets' in first-century Judaism. Taken by itself, then, the phrase "the Law or / and the prophets" is traditional; cf. also Berger, *Die Gesetzesauslegung Jesu* 1, 209-27; esp. 224. The obvious reason for assuming the phrase "or/and the prophets" in 5:17 to be redactional is found in 5:18 where Jesus refers back to the Law alone. See Dumbrell, 'The Logic', 17. Cf. also Bergemann, *Q auf dem Prüfstand*, 137; Luz, *Das Evangelium nach Matthäus* 1, 387 and below, n. 103.

[15] See Loader, *Jesus' Attitude towards the Law*, 184

19:19; Mark 22:31 par.; Luke 6:27-36; cf. Rom 13:8-10; Gal 5:14).[16] Thus, although the precise formulation and location of the statement in 7:12 might be Matthew's, it hardly seems likely that it would not represent what Jesus actually taught.

Inserted at the end of the main body of the Sermon, the Golden Rule occupies a significant position. Matthew perceives the Golden Rule as an eminent summary and decisive climax of the preceding demands, prohibitions, and ethical discussion in 5:17-7:12.[17] The Golden Rule achieves programmatic importance as the culmination of the argument. In the final resolution, the Law is reaffirmed and joined with the principle of love of neighbour. We have seen that Jewish tradition attributes a negative form of this saying to Hillel who presents the Rule as the summation of the Law. At this point it is also important to note that the same phenomenon occurs in the rudimentary teaching of Didache 1-6 and the Doctrina. In the Greek Two Ways 1:2, the double love commandment, i.e., love of God and love of neighbour, and the Golden Rule serve as the essential components of the Way of Life.

The importance of the latter observation increases when one sees that Matthew – unlike Mark and Luke – places the Rule in close proximity to a statement on the Two Ways in 7:13-14:

> Enter by the narrow gate (εἰσέλθατε διὰ τῆς στενῆς πύλης); for the gate is wide and the way is easy, that leads to destruction (ἡ ὁδὸς ἡ ἀπάγουσα εἰς τὴν ἀπώλειαν), and those who enter by it are many. For the gate is narrow and the way is hard, that leads to life (ἡ ὁδὸς ἡ ἀπάγουσα εἰς τὴν ζωήν), and those who find it are few.

It is difficult to retrieve a coherent image of this logion presenting the motif of the Two Ways in combination with the theme of the Two Gates. As a matter of fact, the gates, being mentioned first, may characterize the beginning of the roads or ways, a passage on the roads, or the destination to which the roads lead.[18] The confusion can be explained, however, when we consider the Matthean logion to be the product of a developing process. The two divergent topics (the Two Ways and Two Gates) may represent two different stages in the history of our saying. This observation is reinforced further by the evidence in Luke 13:23-24:

> And someone said to him: 'Lord, will those who are saved be few?' And he said to them, 'Strive to enter by the narrow door (ἀγωνίζεσθε εἰσελθεῖν διὰ τῆς στενῆς θύρας); for many, I tell you, will seek to enter and will not be able.'

---

[16] See also Lührmann, 'Liebet eure Feinde'.

[17] Stanton, *A Gospel for a New People*, 303-04; Hengel, 'Zur matthäischen Bergpredigt', 394; Guelich, *The Sermon on the Mount*, 360-63. 379-81; H.D. Betz, *The Sermon on the Mount*, 518; Borgen, 'The Golden Rule', 105-06.

[18] Cf. H.D. Betz, *The Sermon on the Mount*, 523-24; Davies-Allison, *The Gospel according to Saint Matthew* 1, 696-98; Luz, *Das Evangelium nach Matthäus* 1, 395. For the problems caused by the combination of the motifs of 'the gate' and 'the way', see the textual emendations. Some witnesses omit 'the gate' but "On the whole it seemed best to follow the reading of the overwhelming weight of the external evidence, and to account for the absence of the word in one or both verses as a deliberate excision made by copyists who failed to understand that the picture is that of a roadway leading to a gate;" cf. B.M. Metzger, *A Textual Commentary*, 19.

Because these verses show close affinities to Matt 7:13-14, both Matthew and Luke might have drawn on the common Q source.[19] Many scholars even argue that this Q logion has been more faithfully preserved in Luke,[20] but one should not press this point too far since the passage in Matthew only approximately agrees with the Lukan counterpart and the discrepancy between the two texts is substantial. The disparity is signaled by several factors. The contexts of Luke 13:23-24 and Matt 7:13-14 reveal a different setting, the rhythmic character of the logion in Matthew varies from the Lukan shape of the logion, and, furthermore, the passage in Luke simply focusses on the limited size of the gate, while the Matthean text pairs this theme with the Two Ways. Together, these various considerations suggest that the text in Matthew is the result of a development independent of the Lukan version.[21] Yet, there might be some justification in the view that either statement in Luke and Matthew stems from one and the same tradition which is retained in a more authentic form in Luke 13:23-24.[22] Because the Two Ways motif appears to seriously interfere with the structural pattern of the statement on the gates, it may have been added to the logion in a later stage.[23] In that case, Matthew or his tradition has adapted and expanded the original gate saying[24] by the inclusion of the Two Ways emphasis.

Is the phraseology of the Two Ways addition to be assigned entirely to Matthean creativity? It does not seem likely. It is preferable to assume that Matthew supplemented his material from a special source. His dependence upon a tradition is supported by several factors: the lack of any specifically Matthean terminology in the formulation,[25] the omission of the explicit theme of the Two Ways elsewhere in his gospel, and the sudden interruption in the description of the gate (7:13a.b.d) by an account of the Way (7:13c).[26] Granting the traditional character of the Matthean Two Ways supplement, a second question begs consideration. Does it not make sense that the Two Ways metaphor, looked at in this way, might represent an echo of a well-known *topos* in antiquity? The answer must be negative since there are reasons to assume that the saying was part of a more elaborated Two Ways

---

[19] Denaux, 'Der Spruch von den zwei Wegen', 318; Strecker, *Die Bergpredigt*, 161; Luz, *Das Evangelium nach Matthäus* 1, 395-96; Manson, *The Sayings of Jesus*, 175; Streeter, *The Four Gospels*, 283-84; Kilpatrick, *The Origins of the Gospel*, 22-23.

[20] Manson, *The Sayings of Jesus*, 175; J. Dupont, *Les Béatitudes* 1, 95; Jeremias, *Neutestamentliche Theologie* 1, 28, n. 19; Id., 'πύλη, πυλών', 922-23; Mussner, 'Das "Gleichnis" vom gestrengten Mahlherrn', 131-132.

[21] Michaelis, 'ὁδός κτλ.', 71.

[22] Cf., in addition to the authors mentioned above (n. 19), Jefford, *The Sayings of Jesus*, 25-26 and his Appendix A (146-59), where a detailed examination of Matt 7:13-14 and Luke 13:23-24 – including the reconstruction of Q 13:23-24 – is found. See also Davies-Allison, *The Gospel according to Saint Matthew* 1, 696-98.

[23] Denaux, 'Der Spruch von den zwei Wegen', 322-23; Davies-Allison, *The Gospel according to Saint Matthew* 1, 696-98.

[24] Which was also a traditional theme in antiquity, where gates are associated with the entrance leading to the afterlife; cf. Jeremias, 'πύλη, πυλών', 920-27; Kratz, 'πύλη'.

[25] Davies-Allison, *The Gospel according to Saint Matthew* 1, 696-98.

[26] Jefford, *The Sayings of Jesus*, 25-26; Luz, *Das Evangelium nach Matthäus* 1, 396-97.

form circulating within Matthew's community. Before discussing the possibility whether this tradition reflects the ethical framework of the Greek Two Ways, some comments on the literary context are needed.

The Matthean Two Ways saying at the beginning of the final section of the Sermon on the Mount stands out because of the antithetical parallelism describing two roads. The easy way, "leading to destruction," and the hard way, "leading to life," confront the readers with an ultimatum. The choice is between these alternatives and there is no middle way. In the next units, the image of the Two Ways is maintained and explained with further alternatives. The admonition against false prophets (7:15-23) offers a contrast of good trees and virtuous fruit (good natures generating good deeds) with bad trees and evil fruit (bad natures producing bad deeds). The subject of false prophets continues through vv. 21-23 mentioning those people who do the will of the Father as opposed to those who do not. In the subsequent parable of the two builders (7:24-27), the antithesis is between those hearing and obeying to the words of Jesus and those hearing but not obeying them. What is of interest, however, is that the series of contrasts in the three sayings compositions (7:13-14. 15-23. 24-27) make the last section revolve around one main point, i.e., 'life' as the goal to be attained. Entering the narrow gate or going down the constricted way by means of bearing good fruit (7:17), performing the will of the Father (7:21) and complying with the words of Jesus (7:24) ultimately leads to a final state of blessedness. The right way is responding to the words of Jesus which, effectively, is his exposition of the Law (5:17 and 7:12), as it is delivered in the Sermon on the Mount.[27]

The presence of the Two Ways logion in Matt 7:13-14, apart from the "narrow gate" elements within the framework of this passage, might be due to the popularity of the theme in all of the ancient world[28] where a similar statement existed as an independent entity. On the other hand, there is also the possibility that the mention of the Two Ways in Matt 7:13-14 transcends the boundary of the mere motif or metaphor since its surrounding context includes items similar to those present in the GTW. Examining the Sermon on the Mount as a whole, one establishes that the Two Ways motif (7:13-14) appears close to the Golden Rule (7:12), which is the essential scope and climax of the preceding rules of conduct for believers. Furthermore, it was observed above that the macarisms in 5:3-12 embodied a type of norms and values which pious hassidic Jews strived for. The same elements are found in the Greek reconstruction of the Two Ways, albeit in an inverted position. There the metaphor of the Two Ways (1:1) is followed by the double love com-

---

[27] "Es wird sich jedoch empfehlen, vor allem, wenn man den Zusammenhang von Weg und Gebot im Alten Testament bedenkt und wenn man die abschliessende Art der Komposition für die Bergpredigt als Ganzes beachtet, eben in dem, was Jesus in der Bergpredigt nach der Darstellung des Matthäus lehrt, das Tor zur Gottesstadt und den Weg zum Königtum Gottes zu verstehen; sie enthüllt den Willen Gottes, von dem Jesus sagt, dass indem er getan wird, der Zugang zum Königtum Gottes gefunden wird (7,21);" cf. Grundmann, *Das Evangelium nach Matthäus*, 231; H.D. Betz, 'The Sermon on the Mount (Matt. 5:3-7:27)', 3; Davies-Allison, *The Gospel according to Saint Matthew* 1, 720.

[28] See above, Chap. 2, p. 58 and nn. 7 + 8.

mand and the Golden Rule as the fundamental principles underlying the further explanation of the Way of Life (1:2). This part of the Two Ways is concluded with a list of moral values in which counsels about social conduct, acquiescent meekness and a gentle heart prevail (3:7-4:14).

In terms of genre, the Sermon on the Mount represents ethical instruction or, rather, a catechetical unit. The text is framed by occurrences of the verb "to teach" (7:29 and 5:2) and concludes with the remark that these sayings (τοὺς λόγους τούτους) of Jesus constitute his "teaching" (διδαχή). The portions 5:3-12; 7:12, and 7:13-14 probably represent a reworking of pre-Matthean Q traditions which are also reflected in Luke 6:20-22.31 and 13:23-24. Matthew may have revised these passages under the influence of an ancient Jewish recension of the Two Ways doctrine reflected in the Doctrina and Didache.[29] Yet, although some important items of the early representatives of the genre in the Greek Two Ways (the list of moral values, the Golden Rule and Two Ways motif) are recognizable in the ring composition of Matt 5:3-12 and 7:12-14, it would be impossible to ascertain that the gospel of Matthew betrays knowledge of the precise form of the GTW as reconstructed in Chapter 4. The Greek Two Ways might have circulated in different recensions or, to mention another possibility, may have undergone minor revision or even major redaction after it became available to Matthew.

There are some additional features characterizing the nature of the pre-Matthean tradition of Matt 7:13-14. The first to be mentioned in this respect is that the angels/spirits dichotomy as well as the light-darkness contrast – both present in the Qumran structure of the Two Ways (see pp. 149-51 above) – are missing in the dualistic description of Matt 7:13-14. This phenomenon fits in well with a trend in early Derekh Erets circles. Within these pious Jewish circles, the dualism of the original Two Ways pattern was reshaped into the ethically advanced teaching of the Greek Two Ways.[30] Secondly, the passage focusses on "life" as the goal to be attained. It was observed above[31] that the GTW exhibits a considerable concern with the Way of Life as it takes up much a bigger part of the doctrine (Chaps. 1-4) than does the Way of Death (Chap. 5 only). A similar emphasis is found in Matt 7:13-14 since it challenges the reader to choose the road to life: "Enter by the narrow gate. ... For the gate is narrow and the way is hard, that leads to life,... ." Consequently, the very content of the Two Ways metaphor as well as its association with the Golden Rule, virtuous fruit-evil fruit and the Macarisms in the Sermon on the Mount suggest a familiarity with a setting of the Two Ways in the context

---

[29] "Es lässt sich wahrscheinlich sogar zeigen, dass in der mt Gemeinde der Gedanke der beiden Wege bekannt gewesen ist. Did 1,2-5,2 wird eine Zweiwegeparänese aufgenommen, die eindeutig traditionell und von Mt noch nicht beeinflusst ist. Da die Didache aus einer mt geprägten Gemeinde stammt, können wir vermuten, dass Mt das aus Q stammende Wort vom engen Tor durch einen in seiner eigenen Gemeinde geläufigen paränetischen Topos erweitert hat. Seine Redaktion wäre dann durchaus »traditionell«! Er hat den ihm literarisch vorgegeben Q-Text im Stil der seiner Gemeinde vertrauten Paränese erweitert;" cf. Luz, *Das Evangelium nach Matthäus* 1, 397.

[30] See above, Chap. 5, pp. 178-79.

[31] See Chaps. 4, p. 117 and 5, p. 179.

of Derekh Erets. In the following, we shall see that the wording in Matt 5:17-48 is so close to GTW 3:1-6 that some kind of literary relationship between the two texts must be assumed.

The Statements of Principle (Matt 5:17-20) and the so-called Antitheses (5:21-48)

Few issues in Matthean scholarship have been more keenly debated than the relationship between the statements of principle in Matt 5:17-20 and the subsequent exposition of the six so-called antitheses (5:21-48). The section begins with a prefatory statement in Matt 5:17-20 underlining the continuing validity of the Law. Every aspect of the Law is binding. In the next division, however, Jesus' demands seem to stand in contrast to the requirements of the Law, and many scholars have argued that he is presented here as setting the Law (or part of it) aside.

The six antitheses of the exposition report what Jesus, according to Matthew, taught about offenses like murder, adultery, divorce, perjury, retaliation, and hatred of one's enemy. They include a thesis, an antithesis and, with the exception of the third scenario, an illustration. The thesis in the premise usually contains a quotation from the Law, introduced by the formula "You have heard that it was said (to those of old)." This legal formulation is refuted by the ensuing antithesis, a seemingly contrary response on the part of Jesus, introduced by "But I say to you." Finally, each case, except for the issue of divorce in 5:31-32, is provided with examples to illustrate the significance of the saying (cf. 5:23-26 elaborating on 5:21-22; 5:29-30 on 5:27-28; 5:34b-37 on 5:33-34a; 5:39b-42 on 5:38-39a and 5:45-48 on 5:43-44). The latter elaborations sometimes reflect sayings of Jesus found elsewhere in the gospels and are sometimes later interpretations of the demands of Jesus. They seem to be extraneous materials which once circulated as independent sayings. Because these additions are likely to have been attached to the simple antitheses at a later stage, they will not be discussed here.[32]

Considering the particular arguments, many have taken the antithetical formulation – at least in some of the paragraphs – to express Jesus' negative attitude toward the Law.[33] The critical point, however, is the resultant shift in focus between the two blocks of material. If it is true that the antitheses annul the Law, this will have repercussions on the whole of 5:17-48 as a coherent line of thought. Any interpre-

---

[32] See also Meier, *Law and History in Matthew's Gospel*, 126.

[33] For example, the prohibition of oaths in 5:34.37 and the rejection of the 'lex talionis' are considered to contrast with the Tora by Räisanen, *Paul and the Law*, 87. According to Guelich "... three Antitheses live up to their name by clearly setting aside their corresponding premises: no divorce in 5:32 is set against divorce in 5:31; no retaliation in 5:39a is set against the *lex talionis* of 5:38; and love for one's enemy in 5:44 is set against hatred for same" (= some?) "in 5:43." (cf. *The Sermon on the Mount*, 177) and in the opinion of R. Mohrlang we must admit that "in some cases ... the actual effect of an antithesis *is* to annul a precept of Torah" (*Matthew and Paul*, 19). See also below, n. 38.

tation that suggests that Jesus contradicts the Tora in 5:21-48 must come to terms with the assertion in 5:17-20 claiming that the entire Law remains in force.

PRINCIPLES AND ANTITHESES (MATT 5:17-20. 21-48): TWO CONFLICTING LITERARY UNITS?

How do we reconcile the seemingly existing tensions in Matt 5:17-48 with respect to the Law? A possibility to consider here is the history of tradition underlying 5:17-20 and the extent to which these sayings do or do not represent Matthew's own understanding.[34] Before discussing the subject, it is worth mentioning that most scholars consider v. 20 to be redactional in view of its characteristic Matthean diction. This means that usually the instructions in vv. 17-19 (except for some modifications) are taken to represent an earlier stage in the tradition's history.

Some source-critical investigations of Matt 5:17-48 assume that the unit in 5:17-19 originally existed independently of 5:21-48. Because those verses embody a distinctive theology, unambiguously demanding obedience to the whole Tora, they are assigned to the Jewish-Christian stratum of the tradition. At the same time, the evangelist is portrayed as preserving this transmitted tradition, but disagreeing with it. Especially the verses in 5:18-19 would represent a Jewish-Christian layer that does not, at least in its original strict sense, reflect Matthew's own viewpoint. Though considered loyal to his tradition, Matthew is not depicted as merely preserving, passing on, and thus implicitly endorsing the strict Jewish-Christian view. In this perception, he has supplied additional verses (for example, the redactional verse 20) or clauses (for example, the phrase "until all things come to pass" in 5:18) to drastically modify the strict Jewish-Christian thrust of the tradition.[35]

---

[34] An alternative interpretation might be to view Matthew's divergent statements regarding the Law as the work of a writer who takes issue with two positions: (1) by defending the abiding validity of the Law, he opposes Christian antinomians who wish to abolish the Law (however, the evidence for a substantive antinomian tendency turns out to be rather thin and speculative!); (2) he also opposes the Pharisees in stressing the right interpretation of the Law. For this view, cf. e.g. Barth, 'Das Gesetzesverständnis'. See also Guelich, *The Sermon on the Mount*, 154-55.

[35] For this judgment, see Guelich, *The Sermon on the Mount*, 134-74; esp. 153-54; cf. also Trilling, *Das wahre Israel*, 179. 182-84; Hübner, *Das Gesetz*, 39; Schweizer, 'Matth. 5,17-20' (1963) 400-06; Hill, *The Gospel of Matthew*, 117-18; Green, *The Gospel according to Matthew*, 80-81.
It may be useful in this connection to point out that the gospel of Matthew contains some genuine anti-Jewish passages. From the passages in Luke comparable to those in Matthew (Matt 23:32-36 / Luke 11:49-51; Matt 7:21-22.23; 8:11-12 / Luke 6:46; 13:26-30; Matt 21:33-46 /Luke 20:9-19; Mk 12:1-12 and Matt 22:1-10 / Luke 14:16-24), it is obvious that Matthew manipulates his sources by small modifications so as to support the election of the gentile church over against Judaism. These montages showing the supersession of Judaism by gentile Christians may be explained by the assumption that Matthew was not a Jewish Christian but a gentile. Another possibility might be that these anti-Jewish features have come into the gospel in its final stage of editing by a separate channel, that is by the redaction of an unknown gentile reviser; cf. Flusser, 'Two Anti-Jewish Montages' and Id., 'Matthew's "Verus Israel"'.

However, it is doubtful, to say the least, whether this kind of eclectic approach is required for the text to communicate its real meaning. Rather than selecting some scattered elements in vv. 17-20 as an expression of what Matthew really thinks, it is preferable to determine the meaning of each verse within its present context and to ascertain the gist of the passage as a whole.[36] For it surely is legitimate to suppose that the final redactor intended the separate verses to be understood in relation to one another. Furthermore, in the above reconstructions, Matthew turns out to be contending the contrary of what he actually says.[37] The most natural reading of the unit in 5:17-19 is rather that Jesus was Tora observant and expected the same of his followers. The point of the present passage, then, can only be that the entire Law remains valid.

The alternative solution to the problem of the relationship between Matt 5:17-19 and 5:21-48 might be found in the meaning we attribute to the six antitheses in Matt 5:21-48. The six scenarios seem to set sayings of Jesus in opposition to Scripture and many scholars, in fact, hold that Jesus clearly abrogated commandments of the Law in this unit.[38] But, does the Matthean Jesus really take issue with the Law here? Just how antithetical are the antitheses? These are the questions requiring attention in the following pages. If closer investigation shows that none of the antitheses revokes, abrogates, or annuls the commands of the Law, then these verses do not contradict the statements in 5:17-19. It is not our purpose, though, to review here the massive work already done by a variety of modern scholars on each particular paragraph of the so-called antitheses. We only argue that the attempt to take the antitheses as representing a contrast between the word of God and the word of Jesus may be unfounded for several reasons which regard their context, content, and form.

Our first concern is with the Matthean context of the antitheses. Nothing in the narrative of the first gospel so far would suggest that Jesus intended to overturn Tora. It is even unlikely that the antithetical formulation would provide the essential clue to this attitude toward the Law since it is hard to find in Matthew any indication of Jesus abrogating, let alone rejecting, parts of the Tora. He much more presupposes the validity of private sacrifice (Matt 5:23-24), almsgiving, prayer, and fasting (6:1-18), provided their practice is not induced by hypocritical incentives. The same position applies to Sabbath observance and purity rites. Jesus complies with the current practice of Jewish law regarding these matters and there

---

[36] "Zudem ist die Annahme prinzipiell misslich, der Evangelist überliefere – und dann noch an so herausgehobener Stelle – einfach Material, zu dem er im Grunde genommen selbst nicht mehr stehen könne. Wir suchen also eine Interpretation, die V 18f ernst zu nehmen vermag;" cf. Luz, *Das Evangelium nach Matthäus* 1, 231.

[37] Cf. Snodgrass, 'Matthew and the Law', 545.

[38] Contending, for example, that the third, fifth and sixth antitheses abrogate the law, while the first, second and fourth deepen or intensify it; cf. Bultmann, *Die Geschichte*, 143-44 (ET:134-36); Schulz, *Die Stunde der Botschaft*, 186; Lohse, "'Ich aber sage euch'" (1970) 189-90; Sand, *Das Gesetz und die Propheten*, 52-53; Schweizer, *Das Evangelium nach Matthäus*, 66; (ET: 110-11); Carlston, 'The Things that Defile', 80-81, n. 6; Strecker, *Der Weg der Gerechtigkeit*, 146-47; Klostermann, *Das Matthäusevangelium*, 42; Guelich, *The Sermon on the Mount*, 268. See also above, n. 33.

is no incident in the synoptics of Jesus neglecting or even deliberately transgressing the Law.[39] In fact, Matt 23:2-3 and other statements such as 23:23 and 24:20 suggest a concern for a detailed observance of the Law. As a result, one is inclined to believe that the six-fold formulas show the Matthean Jesus as somehow support- ing and affirming the Tora commandments. Unfortunately, the term "antitheses" has become the traditional designation of this phraseology implying the conviction that Jesus contradicted the Law of Moses.[40] In any case, the remainder of the gospel does not suggest that Jesus' demands must be confused with abrogating or watering down the Jewish Law. On the contrary, in 5:17-19, Matthew offers the assurance that the antitheses are not intended to abolish but to carry forward the tendencies already implicit in them. He certainly has ruled out the possibility of an opposition to the Law.

Secondly, there exists a widespread scholarly consensus with regard to, at least, a part of the content of the antitheses. Even those who find the Tora – and, conse- quently, the unit in 5:17-20 as well – contradicted in 5:21-48 must concede that this possibility does certainly not apply to the first, second, and fourth antithesis. In these paragraphs (5:21-26. 27-30. 33-37), the counterstatement radicalizes, intensifies, and transcends the premise rather than revoking or changing it. The sayings concern anger and murder, lust and adultery, and the teaching about oaths. Not only must you not kill, you must not even reach that level of anger (5:21-22). Not only must you not commit adultery, you must not even look covetously at another man's wife (5:27-28). Not only must you keep the oaths sworn by God's name, you must not swear oaths at all (5:33-34a). In these antitheses, 1, 2, 4, Jesus' demands transcend or surpass the requirements of the Law rather than opposing them.[41]

---

[39] See e.g. Flusser, *Jesus*, 56-80.

[40] The second member of the antithesis, "but I say to you," is introduced by δέ instead of ἀλλά. The conjunction δέ must not be taken as a strong adversative and translated as if ἀλλά were used. The translation 'but' makes the contrast too strong and gives the impression that Jesus deliberately sets himself over against the Law; cf. Flusser, '«Den Alten ist gesagt»', 38; Gundry, *Matthew*, 83. See especially J. Levison who argues: "When one considers the alternatives open to Matthew by which he might express antithesis, and that the formula he chooses expresses affirmation and continuation of a preceding statement, then it is evident that the formula, *ego de lego hymin*, should *not* be translated, 'But (in contrast) I say to you,' but 'And I say to you;'" cf. 'A better Righteousness', 176. See also Davies-Allison, *The Gospel according to Saint Matthew* 1, 507 who would translate the antitheses this way: "You have heard that it was said (to the ancients) ... but I (in addition) say to you ...."

[41] Cf. above, n. 38. See also Davies-Allison, *The Gospel according to Saint Matthew* 1, 504-05; Eichholz, *Auslegung der Bergpredigt*, 70; Bultmann, *Die Geschichte*, 143-44; Kümmel, 'Jesus und der jüdische Traditionsgedanke', 125, n. 75; Davies, *The Setting of the Sermon*, 101; Merklein, *Die Gottesherrschaft*, 260; etc. As to the fourth antithesis, Jesus does not quote the Decalogue here, but see above, n. 8. He transcends the requirement that oaths must be performed. Not only 'false oaths' and 'unfulfilled oaths' are excluded, but all oaths. Cautioning against careless and thoughtless swearing, he prohibits swearing completely and demands that "yes" be "yes" and "no" be "no". Absolute honesty makes oaths meaningless.

The topics dealt with in the three remaining antitheses do not contradict the Law either. It has often been suggested that the third antithesis, treating divorce (Matt 5:31-32), opposes biblical Law,[42] but the thesis "Whoever divorces his wife, let him give her a certificate of divorce" is not an explicit quotation. It is rather a biased summary of the situation envisaged in Deut 24:1-4. In Matt 5:31-32, Jesus is not attacking the divorce provision in the Law, that is, the certificate of divorce command, but the liberal divorce practice based on the Deuteronomy passage.[43] The instructions being refuted in the fifth and sixth antitheses apparently are also not biblical commandments themselves, but their inadequate interpretation. Refutations of inadequate interpretations or misuse of the Law must not be confused with abolishing the Law. The controversial positions on Scripture passages developed within the range of Jewish discussion, in fact, were being handed down within first-century circles. In 5:38, the literal interpretation of the principle "An eye for an eye and a tooth for a tooth" stemming from Exod 21:24; Lev 24:20 and Deut 19:21 may reflect the view of Boethusian Sadducees.[44] It is unlikely that the Pharisees are addressed here since the issue mentioned is equal retribution, whereas rabbinical laws provide proportional compensation in terms of money for the injury or damage incurred. The refutation formulated in the thesis of the ensuing paragraph "You shall love your neighbour and hate your enemy" (v. 43b) may be directed against the same group. The verse claims to be the quotation of Lev. 19:18 but, in fact, is both quotation ("You shall love your neighbour") and provocative expansion. The same kind of retaliatory reasoning is likely to underlie the interpretation here since one's attitude toward another (loving one's neighbour and hating one's enemy) is conditioned by who the other is.[45] A command instructing you to hate your enemies is found neither in the Hebrew Bible nor in rabbinic teaching.

---

[42] E.g. Meier, *Law and History*, 140-47; Guelich, *The Sermon on the Mount*, 209.

[43] Cf. Loader, *Jesus' Attitude towards the Law*, 174-75; H.D. Betz, *The Sermon on the Mount*, 244; Moo, 'Jesus and the Authority', 19-21.

[44] According to *Megillat Ta'anit*, the 'Scroll of Fasting', the rabbis forbade fasting on the festive 14th of the month Tammuz because this day commemorates a Pharisaic victory over the Sadducees in the Second Temple period. At the same place it says that the Boethusian Sadducees took the principle "An eye for an eye and a tooth for a tooth" to imply equal retribution: הפיל אדם שן חברו יפיל את שנו
סמא עין חברו יסמא את עינו יהו שוים כאחד. ("If somebody strikes out his neighbour's tooth, he shall strike out his tooth; if somebody blinds his neighbour's eye, he shall blind his eye, and they will be equal"); cf. H. Lichtenstein, מגילת תענית, 331, lines 8-9; see also Flusser, 'Die Tora in der Bergpredigt', 103, n. 2. See also Broer, 'Das Ius Talionis'.
For the Scroll itself, see Moore, *Judaism* 1, 160; 2, 54; 3, 27.45-46; Schürer, *The History of the Jewish People* 1, 114-15.

[45] Cf. H.D. Betz, *The Sermon on the Mount*, 304; Guelich, *The Sermon on the Mount*, 325-27; Loader, *Jesus' Attitude towards the Law*, 177-78.
Other interpretations are possible too. Matt 5:43 may represent a more general understanding of the scriptural love command in Lev 19:18. "... the widespread attitude of non-love to outsiders was ostensibly grounded in an Old Testament regulation;" cf. Piper, *'Love your enemies'*, 91. On the other hand, this may also be a repudiation of the Qumran sect because love and hatred are often positioned side by side as a result of the dualism of Qumran ideology; cf. the references in H. Braun,

We will examine, thirdly, the form in which the antitheses are couched for they all follow more or less the same pattern: "You have heard that it was said (to the ancients)" ... "but I say to you." Because the six-fold – nearly standardized – formula has often given rise to the conviction that Jesus contradicts parts of the Law, this question will be considered here at some length. The pattern of juxtaposed formulas has no analogy elsewhere in Matthew, in the other gospels, or in early Christian literature. This is not to say that Matthew has framed the line of reasoning himself. He may have found the antithetical argument in one of his sources as it basically reflects a technical rabbinic שמע-type of argumentation. In its present form, the phrase "You have heard that it was said to the ancients" does not easily fit in the rabbinic framework and, as it stands now, the wording might represent a conflation of two originally independent basic statements, namely, the introductory formula "You have heard from the ancients" and the quotation formula "It was said."[46] In the following pages, the constituting elements of this introductory formula ("It was said," "you have heard," and "to the ancients") will be studied successively.

Let us deal with the phrase *"It was said"* first. Matthew often uses a form of "to say" (λέγω / εἴρω) to introduce biblical quotations, as is demonstrated by the following list of references to citations of Scripture, each of them peculiar to his gospel: 1:22; 2:15.17.23; 3:3; 4:14; 8:17; 12:17; 13:35; 21:4; 22:31; 24:15; 27:9.[47] In addition, the clause "It was said" (ἐρρέθη) reflects the passive equivalent נאמר, which is the most frequent introduction in rabbinic literature to a biblical quotation.[48] The six uses of the passive verb "it was said" – purposefully circumlocuting the name of God – thus almost certainly imply "it was said *by God*" in Scripture."

The precise form of the remaining part of the first opening formula, repeated at the beginning of each paragraph, differs in length from antithesis to antithesis. How is this phenomenon to be explained? As was observed above, the long formula "You have heard that it was said to the ancients" might have emerged from a fusion of the wording "It was said" with the statement "You have heard from the

---

Qumran und das Neue Testament 1, 17-18; Id., *Spätjüdisch-häretischer und frühchristlicher Radikalis--mus* 2, 57-58, n. 1; M. Smith, 'Mt. 5:43 "Hate Thine Enemy"'; Grundmann, *Das Evangelium nach Matthäus*, 176-77; Seitz, 'Love Your Enemies', 50-51.

There is no absolute need, however, to interpret the antithesis in vv. 43-44 polemically as directed against some group, since the saying might be a popular maxim or a "rhetoric counter-formulation" instead, suggested by Lev 19:18; cf. Luz, *Das Evangelium nach Matthäus* 1, 311: "V43b will also vermutlich nicht eine bestimmte Position oder Gruppe treffen, die Feindeshass vertritt, ... »Deinen Feind hassen« ist eine von Lev 19,18 angeregte rhetorische Gegenformulierung, ..." Cf. also Ebersohn, *Das Nächstenliebegebot*, 196-97. In view of the evidence that the antithesis in this paragraph probably represents Matthean redaction (see below), Matthew may simply have wished to construct an antithetical matrix for the command in 5:44; cf. Guelich, *The Sermon on the Mount*, 253.

[46] Cf. Flusser, «Den Alten ist gesagt», 37-38.

[47] "Without a single exception, Mt always uses the passive aorist of *eirō* for the words of God as recorded in Scripture;" cf. Meier, *Law and History*, 132.

[48] It is frequently found here, as is stated by W. Bacher: "Die passivische Ausdrucksweise נאמר 'es ist gesagt worden,' ist die häufigste Form der Citirung von Bibelstellen;" cf. *Die exegetische Terminologie* 1, 6. See also Fitzmyer, 'The Use of explicit Old Testament Quotations (1974) 15.

ancients." But even if the case applies, we are left with the question about the variation between the short formula "You have heard that it was said" and the long
formula adding "the ancients."[49] Rabbinic literature might provide the setting
required to solve this problem. The locution "*you have heard* (that it was said)"
is the first matter for consideration here. It may have developed from an anterior
rabbinic expression, namely שומע אני (literally, "I might hear" or "I might
understand").[50] This phraseology introduces an interpretation of Scripture which,
while conceivable, is rejected by the rabbis as an inappropriate deduction from the
verse at hand. Admittedly, the rabbinic examples are not entirely parallel and the
rabbinic form may have been altered to adapt it to the Matthean context. Nevertheless, this kind of argument is commonly found in similar rabbinic contexts on
contrasting viewpoints. The wording "You have heard" means "You have understood," assuming that differing interpretations of the Law are possible.[51] Against
its rabbinic background, the formula discredits an interpretation of the biblical verse
as inadequate or, at least, corrigible and suggests a contrary interpretation that is
to be accepted as accurate.

According to Daube, the rabbis closely associate the root "to hear," and "to
understand" with the literal interpretation, while the wording השומע ("he who
hears") is used to describe "he who sticks to the superficial, literal meaning of
Scripture." He, then, translates the preface to the first argumentative part of the
antithesis, the misconceived doctrine, by "Ye have literally understood" and "Ye
might understand literally."[52] It is assumed that the thesis being attacked is not the
commandment itself, given by God, but the literal interpretation of the text. Where
the Scripture quotation is left to stand without further comment, the incorrect
interpretation coincides with the literal, narrow understanding of the biblical
statement (5:27.38). The formula is used in midrashic discussions to introduce a
misunderstanding of a text due to an overliteral exegesis. In the antitheses, those
Scripture interpretations which are introduced by the formula "you have heard that
it was said" are refuted as false. Thus, Jesus is not contrasting his teaching against
a commandment of the Tora here but against a literal interpretation of a commandment.

---

[49]   The third antithesis in Matt 5:31-32, lacking the terminology "you have heard" as well as a further
expansion subsequent to Jesus' counterstatement, is not considered here. See also below, n. 67.
[50]   Cf. Daube, *The New Testament*, 55-62. The use of the term שמע as related to ἠκούσατε in the
antitheses has earlier been suggested by Schechter, 'The Rabbinic Conception of Holiness', 11, n. 3
and for the same suggestion, see his *Aspects of Rabbinic Theology*, 214, n. 1. Compare also Id., 'Some
Rabbinic Parallels', 427: "Put into modern language the formula means this: The words of the Scriptures
might be at the first glance (or first hearing) conceived to have this or that meaning, but if we consider
the context or the way in which the sentences are worded, we must arrive at a different conclusion. ...."
[51]   Cf. Schechter, 'Some Rabbinic parallels', 427-28; Montefiore, *The Synoptic Gospels* 2, 56; Daube,
The New Testament, 55-58; Davies, *The Setting of the Sermon*, 101-02; Sanders, *Jewish Law*, 93; H.D.
Betz, *The Sermon on the Mount*, 205-08.
[52]   Daube, *The New Testament*, 55-56; H.D. Betz, *The Sermon on the Mount*, 208.

The last element of the expression "You have heard that it was said to the ancients" still deserves further explanation. This addition, *"to the ancients,"* is found in the formula introducing the premise in 5:21 and 5:33 and may anticipate the interpretation of the subsequent Scripture citation in these verses. In order to understand it, let us examine more closely Matt 5:21. The verse includes an extended introductory formula (21a), then a quotation from Exod 20:13 ("You shall not kill"), and, finally, the clause: "and whoever kills shall be liable to judgment" (21c). The sanction referred to in the latter phrase is not found in the Bible, but there is a good possibility that the commandment against murder was taught in the synagogues this way. In the Mekhilta to Exod 20:13, it says that the penalty for murder is found in Gen 9:6.[53] According to the midrash, the instructions in Exod 20:13 (warning against murder) and Gen 9:6 (penalty for murder) constitute two elements of the same prohibition. Furthermore, in both Tgs. Onqelos and Pseudo-Yonatan, the text of Gen 9:6 is modified in the sense that the murderer is to be brought to judgment.[54]

Because the linkage between Exod 20:13 and Gen 9:6 appears to be presupposed in Matt 5:21b-c, the latter saying must reflect an accepted exegetical tradition. The sanction articulated by Jesus in Matt 5:21, therefore, is not borrowed from Scripture but probably points to a rabbinic viewpoint in his time.[55] By the same token, Matt 5:33c too may be labeled a traditional halakhic interpretation of a Scriptural prohibition, in this case, against the popular ancient custom of taking rash and hasty oaths (5:33a),[56] and thus probably reflects a contemporary rabbinic commandment. It is true that these two verses open with the formula "you have heard." But this does not necessarily preclude any further explication. In cases where the formula introduces a quotation provided with a comment, the implication is that the comment is on a par with the literal understanding.[57] Where no further interpretation is supplied, however, it is the quotation's literal understanding which is supposed to be erroneous. Thus, the conclusion to be drawn is that the designation "the ancients" in Matt 5:21.33 stands for the Pharisaic interpreters belonging to earlier generations, who developed and supplied the further interpretation of the preceding

---

[53] For the Hebrew text, see Horovitz, *Mechilta d'Rabbi Ismael*, 232: לא תרצח למה נאמר, לפי שנאמר שופך דם האדם, עונש שמענו אזהרה לא שמענו,ה'ללא הרצח. ET: "'You shall not murder'. Why is this said? Because it was said: 'Whosoever sheds man's blood' etc. (Gen 9:6). We have thus" (in Gen 9:6) "heard the penalty but have not heard the warning; therefore it says here:" (in Exod 20:13) "'You shall not murder.'"

[54] "Who sheds the blood of man with witnesses, according to the sentence of the judges, shall his blood be shed; because in the image of the Lord he made man" (TgOnq to Gen 9:6);
"Who sheds the blood of man with witnesses, the judges shall find him guilty of murder. And he who sheds (blood) without witnesses, the Lord of the world will call him to account on the Day of Great Judgment; because in the image of the Lord he made man" (TgPs-Yon to Gen 9:6).

[55] Cf. McNamara, *The New Testament*, 126-31; Ruzer, 'The Technique', 66-67.

[56] Cf. Flusser, '«Den Alten ist gesagt»', 37; Ruzer, 'The Technique', 72; see also above, n. 8.

[57] "In modern writing, we should mark off the comment by a phrase like *scilicet*. That was not necessary where the force of 'to hear' was properly appreciated;" cf. Daube, *The New Testament*, 56.

biblical quotation.[58] The addition of "the ancients" reveals that it is not the citations from Scripture and their verbatim understanding which is opposed by Jesus in these instances but the explanation that has been created, fostered, and taught by (some of) the Sages.[59]

The formulation *"But I say to you,"* introducing the antitheses proper, counters the preceding Scripture interpretations as being false. Several attempts have been made to provide an explanation for the statement's form but they are not all convincing. One is inclined to assume that Jesus uses an expression here that is customary in Jewish legal argumentation. Taken by itself, the clause has close parallels in contemporary Jewish sources but most of these counterparts are inappropriate since they occur in isolation, without taking into account the thesis stated beforehand: "You have heard that it was said (to the ancients)." In search of parallels, one has come up with some examples, exhibiting the formula "Rabbi so-and-so used to say ..., but (and) I say (ואני אומר) ..." These wordings are close to the form of the statements in Matthew because they introduce a legal opinion contradicting one that is generally accepted[60]. There is also some proof that the phrase "But I say to you" corresponds to the verb אמרת ("you say"), introducing the correct interpretation of Scripture in rabbinic texts which discredit inadequate understandings prefaced by שומע אני ("I might hear" or "I might understand").[61] The pronouncements of Jesus do not have precisely the same form as the rabbinic material, but the reasoning is very similar. While the phrase "you have heard that it was said" means: "you have understood a Scriptural passage in the following way," the second phrase "but I say to you" presents a different explanation that departs from the customary interpretation. The Scripture interpretations that were

---

[58] Because elsewhere in Matthew passive forms of the verb of speaking always take διά or ὑπό for the speaker, and, moreover, because the dative used with this verb in the passive voice always expresses the dative of indirect object, ἀρχαίοις cannot indicate the speakers ("You have heard that it was said by the ancients, ...") but refers to the ones addressed. Furthermore, in that case the phrase would introduce what the "ancients" rather than God said in a quotation of Scripture. See Schweizer, *Das Evangelium nach Matthäus*, 71; Guelich, *The Sermon on the Mount*, 179; Meier, *Law and History*, 132, n. 18; 133, n. 19.

[59] Although the addition "to the ancients" is not found in Matt 5:43, the instance deserves some attention here as well. See above, p. 208 and n. 45.

[60] SifNum 95 to Num 11:21-22 (= Horovitz, *Siphre d'be Rab*, 94-95) and SifDeut 31 to Deut 6:4 (= Finkelstein, *Siphre ad Deuteronomium*, 50). In the latter passage the expression ואני אומר is found several times. The usage of this terminology is not confined, however, to aggadic exegesis only, but also introduces halakhic innovations, as may be seen in instances like tBik 1:2; tMikw 3:4; tBekh 6:15. Cf. M. Smith, *Tannaitic Parallels to the Gospels*, 27-30; see also Lohse, "'Ich aber sage euch'", 193-196. The parallels still are not completely satisfactory yet as they do not set the second part of the argument over against an apodictic and unchanging law in the premise.

Someone as early as John Cameron (*Myrothecium Evangelium*, Geneva, 1632) refers to rabbinical writings in his comment on the antithetical formulation in Matt 5:22: "Sic loqui solent R.R. ואני אומר, cum alicujus sententiam corrigunt vel refellunt, aut in eam aliquid annotant" in: Pearson, *Critici Sacri* 6, 152. See also Kooyman, *The Jewish Context of Matthew 5:31-32*, 21 and n. 8.

[61] Daube, *The New Testament*, 57; cf. also Davies, *The Setting of the Sermon*, 101-02; H.D. Betz, *The Sermon on the Mount*, 208.

refuted as false from the very beginning by the formula "you have heard" are now contrasted with Jesus' own interpretation, introduced by the formula "but I say."

Thus far, we observed that neither the context, nor the content, nor the antagonistic structuring of the antitheses sets Jesus in competition with God. There is no discrepancy between the affirmation of Tora at 5:17-19 and the antitheses of 5:21-48. The terminology suggests that Jesus' teaching does not contain a new Law but another interpretation of the Law, in contrast to current interpretations of that Law. His criticism in 5:21-48 is not directed against the Law itself, but against an interpretation and practice of it. The essence of the contrast between thesis and antithesis is that it reflects the rabbinic midrashic argumentation to introduce a misunderstanding of a text and subsequently the correct interpretation. The antithetical form is thus designed to contrast erroneous beliefs which may not just be theoretical possibilities but may be interpretative traditions instead.

At variance with his rabbinic counterparts, however, the Matthean Jesus does not justify his position by reference to Scripture passages.[62] Instead, he seems to use his authority to expound the demands of Tora. Rather than the above rabbinic phrases contrasting the view of one scholar with another on the basis of a Scriptural authority, the frequent self-references "But I say to you" in Jesus' response demonstrate that the status of his antithetical statement is not just a second opinion in legal matters. His self-references express a high degree of self-awareness, the obvious implication being that the discussion is not academic here. There is no debate or dialectic exposition of the Law contrasting the views of one scholar with the alternative positions of another. The tone is final, definitive, and conclusive. Matthew does not give the impression that Jesus is merely another interpreter of Tora. The prominence of the first person singular and the peremptory ἐγώ brings out the centrality of the figure of Jesus.[63]

It is likely, however, that Matthew himself is responsible for the substitution of scholarly dialectics for authoritative declarations. Matthew's use of the antitheses correlates with his christological viewpoints elsewhere in the gospel, emphasizing Jesus' relationship with God, his high status, and divinely given knowledge. The Sermon on the Mount is part of an instruction by Jesus who has been portrayed by Matthew thus far as Israel's Messiah and the Son of God who will judge the world,[64] and it is in this authority that he has Jesus give his dis-

---

[62] Bacher, Die exegetische Terminologie 1, 189. Nevertheless, the segments in Matt 5:33-37 and 43-48 offer some justification for Jesus' demands.

[63] The particular emphasis of Matthew's redaction may also be derived from the fact that the personal pronoun ἐγώ is missing in the parallel passage in Luke 6:27a: ἀλλὰ ὑμῖν λέγω (τοῖς ἀκούουσιν).... . It is conceivable that Luke's antithetic statement represents the underlying Q tradition which, supposing this tradition reflects a Semitic substratum, may not have contained a parallel of the Greek pronoun ἐγώ either. The Greek pronoun is also lacking in the phrases λέγω γὰρ ὑμῖν, said by John the Baptist in Matt 3:9 (= Luke 3:8), and ἀμὴν γὰρ λέγω ὑμῖν, said by Jesus in Matt 5:18. These observations support our suggestion that the repeated self-references by means of the pronoun ἐγώ in our passage is an editiorial insertion and cannot be referred to Matthew's sources, much less to Jesus himself.

[64] Loader, Jesus' Attitude towards the Law, 165 (and n. 57). 255-60.

course. The expression "But I say to you" may therefore be a Matthean christological transformation or interpretation of an underlying rabbinic wording like
אמרת ("you say") or ואני אומר ("and I say"). We will see presently that he
developed this same christological concern in 5:17 and 18.

Now that it has become clear that the antithetical terminology does not represent
a refutation but an interpretation of the Law, we are in a position to understand
Matthew's christogical interest. The final redaction of his gospel did not take place
in a historical vacuum. It is possible that he exposes Jesus as the authoritative
teacher in this section in order to establish a binding interpretation of the Tora
against the views of a contending party. What Matthew's Jesus teaches in the
sermon seems thoroughly consistent with the variety of belief and practice in first-
century Judaism. The Matthean community was predominantly a Jewish Christian
sect within Judaism at the time Matthew wrote his gospel, and it is likely that the
community was encountering severe opposition from Jewish leaders, especially
from those belonging to emerging rabbinic Judaism. This tension, conflict, and
struggle probably concerned the interpretation and practice of Jewish Law.[65]
Matthew may have reshaped Jesus' counterstatement in the form of a powerful
declaration to meet the polemical needs of his Christian community against other
groups in his time.

If, in fact, the evidence points to Matthew as the one who has transformed these
formulas, the question arises as to what extent Matthew transmits the tradition he
received. After all, as observed above, Matthew did not write the Sermon on the
Mount as such but used other traditional materials and his own shaping of the
material as well. Does Matthew faithfully preserve and hand over a tradition
(genuine words of Jesus?) in 5:21-48 or is this antithetic section the result of
redactional activity? There is widespread agreement that the content of all antitheses is traditional. This does not extend to the formal composition, however. Most
commonly, the specific antithetical formulations of the first, second, and fourth
antitheses (Matt 5:21-22. 27-28. 33-34a) are considered pre-Matthean while the
antithetical pattern in the remainder of the series is assumed to be a secondary
arrangement on the basis of the earlier three. Thus, those antitheses, showing a
radicalization of the commandments rather than a direct opposite character, are
generally considered to have been received by Matthew in antithetical form. These
traditional or primary antitheses may belong to a pre-Matthean stage and even go
back to Jesus' own ministry, while the secondary antitheses (5:31-32. 38-39a. 43-
44) have taken this form because they have been inserted into a context where the
antithetic framework was the primitive one.

As was observed earlier, the opinion arguing for the redactional character of the
latter three antitheses does not rule out that their substance is traditional. Because
they present materials partially paralleled in Luke, their content is often assigned

---

[65] See e.g. Saldarini, *Matthew's Christian-Jewish Community*, 7-9 and passim; Overman, *Matthew's Gospel and Formative Judaism*, 86-90; Segal, 'Matthew's Jewish Voice', 32-37; Stanton, *A Gospel for a New People*, 113-45; Sim, *The Gospel of Matthew*, 109-213.

to the Q source. The third antithesis about divorce (Matt 5:32) parallels Luke 16:18; the fifth about retaliation (Matt 5:39b-43) corresponds with Luke 6:29-30, and the sixth about love of one's neighbour (Matt 5:44-48) parallels Luke 6:27-28. 33-36. Because the antithetical form of arguing in a pattern of juxtaposed contrasting formulas is lacking in the Lukan parallels, however, the antagonistic statements in these Matthean instances are generally regarded as secondary. There is widespread agreement that Matthew has patterned the materials he found in Q upon the formulations of the antitheses Nos. 1, 2, 4.[66] Moreover, the parallels in Luke enable us to ascertain that the Matthean units Nos. 5 and 6 were combined at the earlier stage of the tradition in Q.[67] It is Matthew who has separated them and who is responsible for the antithetical format of the two passages.

This observation leaves us with some new questions. If the actual background of the antithetical structure in the three primary antitheses comes particularly close to the rabbinic legal debate, and if it is not until the Matthean redaction that this tradition is christologically transformed by means of authoritative ἐγώ pronounce-

---

[66] In contemporary research there are three major positions with regard to the sources of the antithetic form in Matt 5:21-48. Most scholars subscribe to Bultmann's analysis that the first, second and fourth antitheses are traditional (pre-Matthean) while the other three (with Lukan parallels) are assigned to Matthew's redaction; cf. Bultmann, *Die Geschichte,* 143-44 (ET: 134-36); Luz, *Das Evangelium nach Matthäus* 1, 246 (though he is inclined to believe that the fourth antithesis is redactional too); Kümmel, 'Jesus und der jüdische Traditionsgedanke', 125 and n. 75; Eichholz, *Auslegung der Bergpredigt,* 69-70; Hummel, *Die Auseinandersetzung,* 67; Goppelt, 'Das Problem der Bergpredigt', 28-29; Strecker, *Die Bergpredigt,* 64-67; Klostermann, *Das Matthäusevangelium,* 42; Lohse, '"Ich aber sage euch"', 189-90; Lambrecht, *The Sermon on the Mount,* 94-95; Davies-Allison, *The Gospel according to Saint Matthew* 1, 504-05. This view has particularly been defended by Guelich, 'The Antitheses of Matthew' and Strecker, 'Die Antithesen der Bergpredigt', 39-47; Beare, *The Gospel according to Matthew,* 146. The second position, attributing the form of all six antitheses to pre-Matthean tradition, is defended by Wrege, *Die Überlieferungsgeschichte der Bergpredigt,* 56-57; Jeremias, *Neutestamentliche Theologie* 1, 240-41; Sand, *Das Gesetz und die Propheten,* 48; Lührmann, *Die Redaktion der Logienquelle,* 118; H.D. Betz, *The Sermon on the Mount,* 214. Other scholars, who take the third antithesis to be an insertion on the part of Matthew (see below, n. 67), believe that the remaining five are traditional. Criticism is offered by Luz, *Das Evangelium nach Matthäus* 1, 245-46.
A third position, assigning all antitheses to Matthean redaction, is expressed by Gundry, *Matthew,* 82-84; Suggs, 'The Antitheses as Redactional Products'; Id., *Wisdom, Christology and Law,* 110-115; Hasler, *Amen. Redaktionsgeschichtliche Untersuchung,* 79, n. 93 and 127-28; Broer, 'Die Antithesen', 54; Lührmann, 'Liebet euere Feinde', 413, n. 4. For a critique on this position, cf. Luz, *Das Evangelium nach Matthäus* 1, 246.
[67] Scholars have often concluded that the logion in Matt 5:31-32 is a later insertion. It appears in close proximity to the second antithesis and is related through the common verb "to commit adultery" (μοιχεύω) in 5:27-28.32. Moreover, rather than including the characteristic "you have heard" in the introductory formula and rendering a Scripture quotation, verse 31 moves directly to a summary of one element of Deut 24:1-4. Also the examples which were provided in the other cases to illustrate the point of the saying, are missing here. Thus, although its nucleus might be traditional (cf. Luke 16:18), the logion has all the marks of an appendix to the second antithesis and may be assigned to a later hand, probably to Matthew. See H.D. Betz, *The Sermon on the Mount,* 243; Guelich, *The Sermon on the Mount,* 197-98. See also Branscomb, *Jesus and the Law,* 234; Kilpatrick, *The Origins of the Gospel,* 85; Bacon, *Studies in Matthew,* 181; Manson, *The Sayings of Jesus,* 135-37; Davies, *The Setting of the Sermon,* 387-88; Schmahl, 'Die Antithesen der Bergpredigt', 290-91; Gnilka, *Das Matthäusevangelium,* 169-171; cf. also Luz, *Das Evangelium nach Matthäus* 1, 269-75.

ments, how did Jesus account for his counterposition in the earlier pre-Matthean layer of the discourse? For, in comparison with the usual pattern of rabbinic discussion consisting of juxtaposed formulas, the important biblical support from Scripture is lacking in the primary antitheses (except for the fourth one on oaths). Another related question is concerned with the disposition of the antitheses. How is the radical restatement of the Tora commandments in 5:21-22. 27-28 and 33-34a linked with the profound setting of Tora essentials in 5:18-19? In the next section, we will see that, in the Matthean gospel, Jesus bases his interpretation of the requirements in 5:21-48 on a significant hermeneutic principle stated in Matt 5:17-20.

PRINCIPLES AND ANTITHESES: TWO COMPLEMENTARY LITERARY UNITS

The passage in Matt 5:17-19/20 which has been scrutinized over the years by many commentators is notoriously difficult to interpret.[68] However, as observed above, there can be little doubt that neither the tradition underlying Matt 5:17-20, nor its Matthean redaction, considered Jesus as having "fulfilled" the Law by setting aside, abolishing, or breaking with the Law of Moses. This is also important for our understanding of Jesus' teaching in the six so-called antitheses. From the very beginning, the possibility is ruled out that the antithetical pattern was intended to attack the Law of Moses. On the other hand, in view of the radicalizing tendency in the three primary antitheses, the introduction in 5:17-20 can hardly have served to simply confirm the traditional teaching of the Law. How does the intensification of the Law's requirements dovetail into the framework of vv. 17-19/20? Is the more penetrating appreciation of – and obedience to – the Law in line with the introductory unit? It is not easy to answer these questions. The problem is made still more complicated by a gamut of possible interpretations of terms and expressions like "to fulfil," "iota or tittle," "until all is accomplished," the "least commandments," and the "least in the kingdom."

One of the most important issues in Matt 5:17-19/20 is how the Matthean Jesus has 'fulfilled' the Law or the prophets: "Think not that I have come to abolish the law or the prophets; I have come not to abolish them but to fulfil them" (5:17). The opening statement "Think not" must not lead us to believe that opponents have accused Jesus of abolishing or neglecting the Law and that the verse serves to clear

---

[68] See the investigations by a wide variety of modern scholars. For the more general question of Jesus and the Law, cf. e.g. Berger, *Die Gesetzesauslegung Jesu*; Hübner, *Das Gesetz in der synoptischen Tradition*; Banks, *Jesus and the Law*; Vouga, *Jésus et la Loi* and Loader, *Jesus' Attitude towards the Law*.

Apart from the investigations in the individual gospels of Mark, Luke and John, one finds a treatment of the theme in the gospel of Matthew in e.g. Barth, 'Das Gesetzesverständnis'; Sigal, *The Halaka of Jesus of Nazareth*; Overman, *Matthew's Gospel and Formative Judaism*; Saldarini, *Matthew's Christian-Jewish Community*; Meier, *Law and History*.

Jesus of such an accusation.[69] Similarly, behind the use of the terms "abolish" and "fulfil", there is no Jewish debate over whether Jesus was an observant Jew.[70] The following observations, relating to the immediate context, may shed light on the wording. Firstly, the clause "or the prophets" is likely to have been inserted into an earlier pre-Matthean tradition which had simply "the Law" as the object of "to fulfil." Although Jesus speaks here of "the Law and the Prophets," the teaching which follows is concerned with the Law only. This point is made by many scholars and, indeed, with regard to its repeated occurrence in Matt 7:12 and 22:40, one may well argue that the phrase belongs to Matthew's favorite diction.[71] Secondly, fulfilment of the Law does not mean replacement of the Law by Jesus, who completes the Law by bringing a new one which transcends the old, or abrogation of the details of the Law through the love commandment.[72] These explanations would come too close to meaning the opposite of 5:17. Moreover, if this were meant by the fulfilment of the Law in v. 17, continuity with 5:18-19 would be akward, leaving us with the question what the "jot" and "tittle" (v. 18) and "the least of these commandments" (v. 19) would signify. According to a wide consensus among scholars, the "fulfilment" of the Law "implies that Jesus modifies in some ways contemporary understandings of the Law."[73] How? We have seen that Jesus is portrayed in 5:21-48 as upholding the integrity of the Law by giving it (authoritative) interpretation. If this focus is applied to the introductory unit 5:17-20, the fulfilment of the Law appears to be determined by one's interpretation of the Law. What is essential here is the distinction between violating the Law and fulfilling it through a different interpretation. The purpose of the unit in 5:17-20 as a whole, and particularly of v. 17, is to refute the charge that Jesus was misinterpreting, and as a result, undermining the Law.

The words "to abolish" and "to fulfill" fit within this framework. The terms probably are the Greek equivalents for the semitic counterparts לבטל and לקיים

---

[69] The wording "Think not" in 5:17a is just a rhetorical figure of speech, uttered only to be repudiated so as to prepare the reader for the peremptory assertion in 5:17b; cf. both Strecker (*Die Bergpredigt*, 57) and Banks ('Matthew's Understanding of the Law', 226), who refer to a similar non-polemical use of the clause in Matt 10:34.

[70] "Jesus drückt da also nicht seine Treue zum jüdischen Gesetz aus, sondern er verteidigt sich gegen den möglichen Vorwurf, dass er in der folgenden Erklärung der Gesetzesworte durch gewagte Exegese ihren ursprünglichen Sinn aufhebe;" cf. Flusser, 'Die Tora in der Bergpredigt', 108; see also Gnilka, *Das Matthäusevangelium* 1, 143.

[71] Cf. Guelich, *The Sermon on the Mount*, 137-38. 142-43; Davies-Allison, *The Gospel according to Saint Matthew* 1, 484 and n. 7; Gundry, *Matthew*, 78-79; W.C. Allen, *Gospel according to S. Matthew*, 46; Descamps, 'Essai d'interprétation de Mt 5,17-48', 160-62. Above (p. 199) it has been observed that the expression νόμον ἢ τοὺς προφήτας forms an inclusion with 7:12 (see also below, n. 103).

[72] For the possible interpretations, see e.g. Davies-Allison, *The Gospel according to Saint Matthew* 1, 485-86 and Luz, *Das Evangelium nach Matthäus* 1, 232-36.

[73] Stanton, 'The Origin and Purpose of Matthew's Gospel', 1937. This does not solve all problems, however, since, as Stanton makes clear, some scholars have unconvincingly attempted to explain Jesus' attitude towards the Law in Matthew by appealing to the latter's christology or eschatology; cf. Id., 1934-37.

(אֵת הַתּוֹרָה), to "to annul" and "uphold" (the Tora),[74] and are used in a technical sense here. Whereas the first word means to undermine the Tora (by an incorrect exegesis), the latter stands for revealing (by means of proper interpretation) its true meaning. It is the same exegetical terminology which is reflected in Rom 3:31: νόμον οὖν καταργοῦμεν διὰ τῆς πίστεως; μὴ γένοιτο· ἀλλὰ νόμον ἱστάνομεν ("Do we then overthrow the law by this faith? By no means! On the contrary, we uphold the law").[75] It follows, therefore, that the correct understanding of the Law provides for its fulfilment. In Matt 5:17, however, rather than the word πληρῶσαι, one would have expected to find the verb ἱστάναι, στῆσαι or something similar as an equivalent of the Aramaic לְקַיֵּם – with the meaning "to uphold," "establish," "make valid," "bring into effect." Why did Matthew choose πληρῶσαι? To answer this question we refer to many other instances where Matthew uses this verb to emphasize the predictive function of Scriptures with regard to Jesus' ministry. He apparently takes the coming of Jesus Messiah to be the fulfilment of biblical prophecies. In this respect, the addition of the clause "or the prophets" in v. 17 is significant as well. In conjunction with the verb πληρῶσαι, the clause underpins the christological aspect, present in the fulfilment quotations. Although v. 17 originally might have been a pre-Matthean saying, the alterations of the tradition in v. 17 are such that they betray obvious Matthean traits. They show an interest that is consistent with his christological concerns, as observed above in the self-references (ἐγώ) of the counterstatements of the antitheses.[76]

Matthew's christological interpretation of the tradition in 5:17, however, does not contrast the authority of Jesus with the Law. The emphasis remains on the continuing obedience to commandments as long as the conditions of this transitory world persist: "For truly, I say to you, till (ἕως ἄν) heaven and earth pass away, not an iota, not a tittle, will pass from the law until (ἕως ἄν) all is accomplished"

---

[74] For the Hebrew and Aramaic counterpart, cf. Str-B 1, 241; Schlatter, *Der Evangelist Matthäus*, 153-54; Dalman, *Die Worte Jesu*, 52-57; Id., *Jesus – Jeshua*, 52-57; Fiebig, *Jesu Bergpredigt*, 27-28; Percy, *Die Botschaft Jesu*, 120; Hill, *The Gospel of Matthew*, 117; Branscomb, *Jesus and the Law*, 226-28. The objection to this suggestion that the verb πληρόω translates the verb *ml'* but never *qûm* in the LXX (see Guelich, *The Sermon on the Mount*, 139 and Davies-Allison, *The Gospel according to Saint Matthew* 1, 485, n. 3) will not wash. If our focus is on the reconstruction of the verb πληρόω in combination with νόμος, it is interesting to see that its equivalent is not found in the LXX, apocryphal and pseudepigraphical literature. Moreover, the combination *ml' torah*, and even the separate verb *ml'*, hardly ever occurs in the Qumran Scrolls and rabbinic literature. On the other hand, it is clear that the verb *ml'* in the Tenach (in the sense of 'to fulfil') is replaced usually by the pa'el of *qûm* in the targumim. Also other rabbinic writings (e.g. Mishna, Mekhilta de-R. Yishmael, Babylonian Talmud) often have the verb *qûm* (in the sense of 'to fulfil') and, depending on the Hebrew or Aramaic, in the pi'el and pa'el form respectively. For these and other observations, see Van de Sandt, 'An Explanation of Rom. 8,4a', 364-71.

[75] See the discussion in Flusser, 'An Early Jewish-Christian Document' (1988) 378-80; cf. also Id., 'A Rabbinic Parallel', 495; Id., 'Die Tora in der Bergpredigt', 107-08; Gerardsson, *Memory and Manuscript*, 287; Albright-Mann, *Matthew*, 58; Bacher, *Die exegetische Terminologie* 1, 170-72; 2, 186-89.

[76] Cf. Gnilka, *Das Matthäusevangelium* 1, 144.

(5:18). Not even the tiniest detail of the Law is to be changed "till heaven and earth pass away" (5:18b) and "until all is accomplished" (5:18d). No criticism is expressed in these clauses against the Law as being valid only within a limited time period. The emphasis on obedience to the commandments in the immediate context (5:17.19-20) precludes reading even one of these clauses as implying a time limit for the inviolability of Tora. Rather than suggesting its temporary validity,[77] the second temporal saying of v. 18d (beginning with ἕως ἂν as well) merely reiterates the sense of the first one in v. 18b. The phrase of v. 18b simply is a vivid way of saying "never",[78] the implication being that still a long period of time is to elapse before the Law passes away. No limitations are set to the Law's applicability; on the contrary, the perpetuity of the Law is stressed.[79]

The Tora is considered to be perpetually binding down to its shrimpy jot and tittle, i.e. to the details of its wording. Evidently, the written Law is meant here, which must be interpreted for the purpose of teaching. Interestingly, these tiniest minutiae, underscoring the immutability of the Tora thus far, come to serve as a metaphorical designation for the least important commands in 5:19: "Whoever then relaxes one of the least of these commandments and teaches men so, shall be called least in the kingdom of heaven; but he who does them and teaches them shall be called great in the kingdom of heaven." The reference of "one of the least of these commandments" or, better, "one of these least commandments" (μίαν τῶν ἐντολῶν τούτων τῶν ἐλαχίστων) is to the "iota or a tittle" in 5:18. The lack of a direct grammatical antecedent has led some to connect the pronoun "these" (τούτων) with the commandments of Jesus as presented in 5:21-48,[80] but this solution fails to take seriously enough the relationship of 5:19 to 5:18. The adjective "least" makes it clear that the demonstrative pronoun "these" adverts back to 5:18 and identifies the commandments in v. 19 with the jot and tittle mentioned in v. 18.[81] The iota and tittle represent both the smallest graphic elements of the Law in a literal (v. 18) and figurative (v. 19) sense.

---

[77] So e.g. Meier, *Law and History*, 58-65; Banks, *Jesus and the Law*, 213-17; Id., 'Matthew's Understanding of the Law', 235-37; R. Hamerton-Kelly, 'Attitudes to the Law'. See also Davies-Allison, *The Gospel according to Saint Matthew* 1, 494-95 (and 490).

[78] "... es ist zu fragen, worauf das Wort im Kontext den Akzent legt, darauf, dass einmal das Gesetz keine Gültigkeit mehr haben wird oder darauf, dass das Gesetz mit allen Häkchen in diesem Äon unwiderruflich gilt? Schon das Einzelwort dürfte, da es ja nicht einfach vom Gesetz, sondern von Jota und Häkchen des Gesetzes spricht, gerade nicht auf die dereinstige Ablösung des Gesetzes, sondern auf dessen Unauflöslichkeit in diesem Äon abgehoben haben. ...;" cf. Broer, *Freiheit vom Gesetz*, 43. See also Loader, *Jesus' Attitude towards the Law*, 169 and n. 73; Strecker, *Der Weg der Gerechtigkeit*, 143-44; Id., *Die Bergpredigt*, 58; Luz, *Das Evangelium nach Matthäus* 1, 236-37; W.C. Allen, *Gospel according to S. Matthew*, 46; Klostermann, *Das Matthäusevangelium*, 41.

[79] On the perpetuity of the Law, see Moore, *Judaism* 1, 263-80.

[80] See Lohmeyer, *Das Evangelium des Matthäus*, 110-12; Banks, *Jesus and the Law*, 223; Schweizer, *Das Evangelium nach Matthäus*, 65; H.D. Betz, *The Sermon on the Mount*, 187; Id. 'The Hermeneutical Principles' (1985) 48-49; Stanton, *A Gospel for a New People*, 300.

[81] Cf. Schürmann, '"Wer daher eines dieser geringsten Gebote auflöst ..."', 241; Luz, *Das Evangelium nach Matthäus* 1, 238; Davies-Allison, *The Gospel according to Saint Matthew* 1, 496; Guelich, *The Sermon on the Mount*, 151-52; Meier, *Law and History*, 91-92.

Whoever abrogates "the least of these commandments," according to v. 19, will be "the least in the kingdom," and whoever supports them will "be called great in the kingdom." Although the assumption was that all commands are kept (v. 18), this verse shows that comparative valuations were made among the different commands. Nowhere does the text mention what is meant by the expression "the least of these commandments." It is generally held by commentators, however, that the phrase reflects the discussion in Jewish sources about "light" and "heavy" commandments of the Law. Indeed, such a differentiation can be variously documented in postbiblical Jewish thought,[82] not least in rabbinic discussion.[83] One may note, for example,[84] the following saying:

> A man may not take the dam and her young even for the sake of cleansing the leper. If then of so light a precept (מצוה קלה) concerning what is worth but an issar the Law has said 'that it may go well with you, and that you may live long' (Deut 22:7), how much more [shall the like reward be given] for [the fulfilment of] the weightier precepts (חמורות מצות) of the Law (mHul 12:5).

Although obedience to all precepts was equally binding, the example shows an obvious consciousness of the existence of "light" and "heavy" precepts.[85] On the other hand, the light-heavy distinction is not clear-cut since there were no unanimous criteria to distinguish between the two categories of commandments. A great deal of room was given to one's subjective judgment and much depends upon the theme that is being treated as well: what seem to be light precepts in a given argument may take on the significance of heavy commandments in another line of reasoning.[86]

The emphasis on the light precept in the mishna quoted above corresponds with the gist of the argument in Matt 5:19. The basic logical tool of reasoning is a קל וחומר-assumption,[87] here an inference *a minori ad maius*, meaning that what is sure of the smallest letter in the Law must, by implication, be true of the rest of

---

[82]   Cf. 4 Macc 5:19-21, dismissing the suggestion that less weighty sins are less serious: "Accordingly, you must not regard it as a minor sin for us to eat unclean food (μὴ μικρὰν οὖν εἶναι νομίσῃς ταύτην, εἰ μιαροφαγήσαιμεν, ἁμαρτίαν); minor sins are just as weighty as great sins (τὸ γὰρ ἐπὶ μικροῖς καὶ μεγάλοις παρανομεῖν ἰσοδύναμόν ἐστιν), for in each case the Law is despised;" ET: Anderson, '4 Maccabees'.

[83]   About this concept, see already Wettstein, *Novum Testamentum* 1, 295-96; cf. also Str-B 1, 249.900-05; esp. 901-02; Abrahams, *Studies in Parisaism* 1, 18-29; Urbach, *The Sages* 1, 345-50. See also above, Chap. 5, pp. 165-72.

[84]   For additional instances, cf. Str-B 1, 900-05; esp. 902-03.

[85]   Contra Banks, *Jesus and the Law*, 170 who claims that Palestinian and Hellenistic Judaism never negated "the principle of the equivalence of commandments, according to which, whatever importance was attached to individual instructions, from the point of view of obedience all had the same status."

[86]   See Str-B 1, 901-02; Abrahams, *Studies in Parisaism*, 27-29; Flusser, 'A Rabbinic Parallel', 496 and 502-03.

[87]   "Name der exegetischen Regel, vermöge welcher vom Leichten aufs Schwere, vom minder Bedeutenden auf das Bedeutendere, oder auch umgekehrt vom Schweren aufs Leichte geschlossen wird, also der Schluss a minori ad majus oder a majori ad minus"; cf Bacher, *Die exegetische Terminologie* 1, 172; see also 2, 189-90.

the Law. The only difficulty is the disparity of language, since the common Hebrew terms are "light" and "heavy" precepts and not "least" and "great" precepts. Yet, in Matthew's gospel Jesus appears to be familiar with the rabbinic differentiating of the "light" and "weighty" precepts, as is shown by the usage of the term "weighty" in the saying: ".. and you have neglected the weightier matters of the Law (βαρύτερα τοῦ νόμου), ..." (Matt 23:23b).

Why is this exact sense obscured in the Greek text of Matt 5:19, which contrasts "small" with "great" precepts? A first explanation may be found in the characterization of the commandments as having the physical magnitude of the tiniest alphabetic details in v. 18. Secondly, the qualification "small" or its superlative "least" enables the Greek text to create a rhetorical juxtaposition by combining this clause with the next phrase in this verse: whoever abrogates the "least" command is the "least" person in the kingdom. This suggestion, for its part, is directly related to the problem of how to interpret the latter expression. Being the "least in the kingdom" is not likely to mean that someone ignoring the light commands was rewarded a position in the kingdom, be it the lowest. A concessional interpretation, allowing a place in the kingdom to a disloyal teacher who slackens the light precepts, would oppose the negative and discouraging purport of the statements in 5:17-20. It is hard to believe that, after the firm statement of v. 18, the passage would suddenly suggest a moderate sanction of having a very low place in the kingdom. Because a ranking in the kingdom apparently is out of the question here, the expression "least in the kingdom" must have been metaphorically used for exclusion from the kingdom. The phrase is a rhetorical way of saying that there will be no place in the kingdom for people demonstrating any laxity in observance of the Law.[88]

The main point in Matt 5:19, however, is not the difference between the commandments for their own sake, but the importance of the light commandment. Not the people teaching contempt for the weighty commandments would be made least in the kingdom, as one would expect (in Matt 23:23 the weighty things in the Law must be given precedence), but those people teaching contempt for the light commandments. Although the introductory passage in Matt 5:17-20 does not pursue this topic, Jesus in 5:19 merely seems to reconfirm an understanding with respect to the value of the light commandments. This is of particular interest to the problem under consideration, i.e. the explanation of the relationship between the units in 5:17-20 and 5:21-48. The unanticipated appeal in 5:19 leads one to assume that some widely recognized teaching about this theme lays behind its exhortation. As a matter of fact, a further elaboration on the topic is found in Philo and in rabbinic literature. For Philo, who probably was familiar with Palestinian tradi-

---

[88] See Luz, *Das Evangelium nach Matthäus* 1, 238; Hoppe, 'Vollkommenheit bei Matthäus', 149-50; Loader, *Jesus' Attitude towards the Law*, 171; Bonnard, *L'Évangile selon Saint Matthieu*, 62; Schweizer, *Das Evangelium nach Matthäus*, 62.

tions,[89] the observance of the light commandments is as essential as having no basic part removed or destroyed from a building:

> One nation only standing apart, the nation of the Jews, was suspected of intending opposition, since it was accustomed to accept death as willingly as if it were immortality, to save them from submitting to the destruction of any of their ancestral traditions, even the smallest, because as with buildings if a single piece is taken from the base, the parts that up to then seemed firm are loosened and slip away and collapse into the void thus made[90]

An equally strict or even more rigorous attitude is found in rabbinic sources:

> Ben Azzai said: Run to fulfil the lightest precept even as the weightiest and flee from transgression; for one precept draws another precept in its train, and one transgression draws another transgression in its train; for the reward of a precept (done) is a precept (to be done), and the reward of one transgression is (another) transgression (mAv 4:2)[91].

The focus on the light commandments also occurs in other general instances of rabbinic literature[92] but is found preeminently in that strain of tradition reflecting the ethics of the hassidic circles:

> Rabbi said: '... And be heedful of a light precept (במצוה קלה) as of a weighty one (כבחמורה) for you know not the recompense of reward of each precept; ...' (mAv 2:1).[93]

In chapter 5 we have seen that the maxim "be heedful of a light precept as of a weighty one" serves as a recapitulation of morality found in the refined ethics represented by the Derekh Erets tracts. It was the quintessence of pious ethics. Such warnings appear throughout in the early stratum of Derekh Erets materials which stem from the hassidim in the Tannaitic period. Prominent in their doctrine is a rigorous attitude towards the prevailing halakha and the propensity for good deeds in public life, such as the redemption of captives, the restoration of property, the consolation of the mourners, the giving of alms etc. As noticed in Chapter 5 (pp. 172-74), above, the chapters of Yir'at Het, an early layer of Derekh Erets literature, appeared to embody a refined human ethic highlighting acts of charity, modesty, humility. Especially the following statement occurring in Yir'at Het II,16-17, is significant:

---

[89]   See Alon, 'On Philo's Halakha'; Borgen, 'Philo of Alexandria', 258-59; Schürer, *The History of the Jewish People* 3/2, 873-76.

[90]   *Legat.*, 117; cf. Colson, *Philo* 10 (LCL 379) 58-59; cf. also Philo's *Legum allegoria* III, 241; cf. Colson, *Philo* 1 (LCL 226) 462-65; see also I. Heinemann, *Philo's griechische und jüdische Bildung*, 478-80.

[91]   Cf. above, Chap. 5, n. 104 and Moore, *Judaism* 1, 470-71.

[92]   The midrash in SifDeut 79 (= Finkelstein, *Siphre ad Deuteronomium*, 145) states to Deut 12:28 ("all these words which I command you"): "that a light precept is as dear to you as a weighty precept" (שהוא מצוה קלה חביבה עליך כמצוה חמורה), a clause that in the same form occurs in SifDeut 82 to Deut 13:1 (= Id., 148) and in SifDeut 96 to Deut 13:19 (= Id., 157). See above, Chap. 5, n. 100 and also Schlatter, *Der Evangelist Matthäus*, 679.

[93]   See above, Chap. 5, p. 176 and n. 100; cf. also bMen 44a, top; bNed 39b; yPe'a 1,15d.

Keep aloof from that which leads to transgression, keep aloof from everything hideous and from what even seems hideous. Shudder from committing a minor transgression (מחטא הקל), lest it lead you to commit a major transgression (לחטא חמור). Hurry to (perform) a minor precept (למצוה קלה), for this will lead you to (perform) a major precept (למצוה] חמורה[)[94]

The saying shows that the popular apophthegm, to be as careful about an unimportant precept as about an important one, in its original meaning was a collateral form of the exhortation in actual writings like the Didache and the Doctrina. As is demonstrated in the same chapter, above, these two versions are dependent on a common Jewish ancestor, designated above as the Greek Two Ways:

my child, flee from all evil and from everything like it (3:1)

The agreement between the two maxims is not surprising, since we have established that an affinity exists between the ideas and ethical principles in the early Derekh Erets doctrine, on the one hand, and the views occurring in the Greek tractate of the Two Ways on the other. Both types of ethical teaching, being preserved and transmitted in common pious circles, constitute a definite current in early halakha.

It is not difficult to envisage that the sayings in Matt 5:19 and GTW 3:1 belong to the same particular strand of Jewish tradition: "Whoever then relaxes one of the least of these commandments and teaches men so, shall be called least in the kingdom of heaven; but he who does them and teaches them shall be called great in the kingdom of heaven". In our treatment of the Two Ways as a Jewish manual, the verse GTW 3:1 turned out to serve a governing function in the *teknon*-section (3:1-6). The preoccupation of this *teknon*-section, with its repetitive use of the phrase τέκνον μου, is expressed in the introductory sentence: "my child, flee from all evil and from everything like it" (3:1). It is intended to highlight the avoidance of anything resembling evil because it leads to evil itself. The tradition is the basis upon which the hassidically-oriented materials have been formulated as a moral guide for Derekh Erets. The opening unit in Matt 5:17-19 has the programmatic significance of supplying the reader with a clue as to the right interpretation of the Scripture quotations in the subsequent antitheses.

In Matt 5:17-20, we face the transparent principles of hermeneutics which are applied to the traditional commandments of the Scripture in 5:21-48. If you transgress a light precept, you will end up committing a grave sin. It is this distinct characteristic which makes the introductory unit 5:17-20 and the succeeding antitheses a coherent whole. While the pivotal principles of rabbinic and semi-Essene Judaism are reflected in the double love commandment, in the Golden Rule and in the emphasis given to the (second part of the) Decalogue, the fundamental essence of Jewish Derekh Erets teachings is represented particularly in the saying that a light commandment is as important as a weighty one. In other words, the

---

[94]   Yir'at Het (or DEZ); further, see Chap. 5, pp. 168-69 (and n. 99).

Scripture texts in the antitheses, if interpreted by this principle, must lead to the interpretation given by Jesus.

Before expanding on this subject further, v. 20 deserves some separate discussion. The verse serves as a pivot between 5:17-19, stating the principles for the correct interpretation of Scripture, and 5:21-48, a series of sayings expressing the intention of biblical demands for those aspiring to enter the Kingdom: "For I tell you, unless your righteousness exceeds that of the scribes and Pharisees, you will never enter the kingdom of heaven." Because it is characteristic Matthean terms that constitute its content, the verse is likely to be redactional.[95] The Matthean features become particularly clear in the clause "the scribes and Pharisees," which certainly exhibits Matthew's favourite diction.[96] On the other hand, the mention of both groups in relation to the term 'righteousness' shows that 'righteousness' is not referred to as God's gift but as ethical conduct, as a capacity enabling one to enter the kingdom of heaven.[97] If Matt 5:20 has any historical value, we might deduce from it that the light precepts, expounded in the next verses, rather than being commonly accepted, were popular only in the pious circles referred to above.

Examples of what it entails to abide by a 'greater righteousness' are given in 5:21-48, but the hermeneutic key to this program is offered in 5:17-19. The section, Matt 5:17-48, does not contain disparate material loosely strung together. When Matthew has Jesus in v. 20 demand that the disciples' righteousness must exceed that of the scribes and Pharisees, he not just validates the continuance of the Tora (v. 18) but also the keeping of the "least of these commandments" (v. 19). Furthermore, the inferential particle "For" (γάρ) denotes a connecting link between this verse and the preceding materials. Finally, the expression about "righteousness" being "greater" (πλεῖον) than that of the scribes and Pharisees is echoed in 5:48:

[95]   Cf. Guelich, *The Sermon on the Mount*, 135. 156; Luz, *Das Evangelium nach Matthäus* 1, 230; H. Braun, *Spätjüdisch-häretischer und frühchristlicher Radikalismus* 2, 7-10; Id., *Qumran und das Neue Testament* 1, 15; Descamps, 'Essai d'interprétation de Mt 5,17-48', 163; J. Dupont, *Les Béatitudes* 3, 251, n. 2; Meier, *Law and History*, 116-119; Davies-Allison, *The Gospel according to Saint Matthew* 1, 501.

[96]   See also Matt 23, where Matthew levels against the "scribes and Pharisees" the usual charge of hypocrisy (vv 4-7) and attacks the Jewish community leadership (of his own post CE 70 situation?) in seven woe oracles, in which Jesus condemns the "scribes and Pharisees" seven times.

[97]   There is a scholarly consensus that the concept of 'righteousness' is important in the gospel of Matthew, but it should be emphasized here that the Matthean and Pauline concepts certainly do not agree. Strecker has established that the term 'righteousness', found at seven key passages in the Matthean gospel (3:15; 5:6.10.20; 6:1.33; 21:32) reflects a particular redactional emphasis (*Der Weg der Gerechtigkeit*, 149-58. 179-81. 187); cf. Hill, *Greek Words*, 124-28. It is not 'righteousness' seen as a gift of God, but as a demand upon man and, accordingly, it is the ethical interpretation which is correct. B. Przybylski has made clear that Matthew uses the concept of righteousness in a way that directly reflects the usage of the Tannaitic literature and the Dead Sea Scrolls. "By using the concept of righteousness Matthew found a point of contact between the religious understanding of first-century Palestinian Jews and the teaching of Jesus. Matthew could point out that just as Judaism required righteousness, so the teaching of Jesus required righteousness, that is, proper conduct according to the law" (*Righteousness in Matthew*, 121). This view was accepted by Luz, *Das Evangelium nach Matthäus* 1, 240 and Davies-Allison, *The Gospel according to Saint Matthew* 1, 327.

"You, therefore, must be perfect (τέλειοι), as your heavenly Father is perfect (τέλειός)." The greater righteousness is resumed in the idea of perfection in 5:48 and both verses 5:20 and 48 act like a frame for the six antitheses in 5:21-47.

Perfection in v. 48 is understood in a quantitative sense because it is directly linked with the preceding verse: "And if you salute only your brethren, what more (περισσόν) are you doing than others? Do not even the gentiles do the same?" (5:47). Being perfect involves doing more than others. Interestingly, the term (περισσόν) reflects the verb περισσεύσῃ in v. 20 which further corroborates the assumption that obviously a sense of quantity is implied here. This quantitative bracketing denotes a righteousness measurable in terms of magnitude and at least a rigorous observance of all commandments.[98] It is undeniable that v. 20 presumes a high degree of concern about fulfilment of the Law on the part of the Pharisees and scribes. They have righteousness insofar as they live according to the demands of the Law. The greater righteousness, however, implies a life-style which is not according to a different Law but according to a different interpretation of the Law. It involves a surpassing of the bounds of legal requirements of the Tora to the extent that also additional norms, not explicitly mentioned among the biblical commandments, are stringently applied.

PRINCIPLES AND PRIMARY ANTITHESES:

A REFLECTION OF AN INTEGRAL JEWISH TRADITION (GTW 3:1-6)

When all the above considerations are taken in combination, the general case for the literary unity of 5:17-20 and 21-48 seems very strong. The ethical code transmitted in the preamble and the subsequent antitheses mutually illuminate one another, imposing higher standards for the halakhic way of life proposed by Jesus. The direct aim of the following pages is to corroborate by external evidence the foregoing internal indications that the two blocks are intrinsically an integral whole.

---

[98] Cf. Przybylski, *Righteousness in Matthew*, 85-87. Differently: Gnilka, *Das Matthäusevangelium* 1, 147: "Es lässt sich nicht leugnen, dass die griechische Formulierung ein quantitatives Verständnis dieses Übermasses nahelegt. Es wäre aber absurd zu meinen, dass dieses quantitative Übermass sich auf die Erfüllung der eben erwähnten geringsten Gebote erstreckt, so dass diese zum Kriterium für die echte und falsche Gerechtigkeit würden".

Luz understands 'righteousness' in a quantitative sense from the perspective of 5:17-19 and in a qualitative sense in the light of the love commandment: "Der Komparativ περισσεύειν ... πλεῖον fällt auf; gebräuchlicher wäre μᾶλλον. Πλεῖον legt eine quantitative Deutung nahe: Wenn eure Gerechtigkeit nicht in messbar höherem Mass reichlicher vorhanden ist als die der Schriftgelehrten und Pharisäer, werdet ihr nicht ins Himmelreich kommen. .... Die bessere Gerechtigkeit der Jünger bedeutet also, von V17-19 her gelesen, zunächst ein quantitatives Mehr an Toraerfüllung. ... Von den Antithesen her bedeutete die bessere Gerechtigkeit der Jünger nicht nur eine – an der Tora gemessene – quantitative Steigerung der Gesetzeserfüllung, sondern vor allem eine – an der Liebe gemessene – qualitative Intensivierung des Lebens vor Gott"; Luz, *Das Evangelium nach Matthäus* 1, 240-41; similarly Davies-Allison, *The Gospel according to Saint Matthew* 1, 500. Below, in the Conclusion of this chapter, the relation between the better righteousness, illustrated in the antitheses, and the love commandment will be discussed briefly.

The primary set of materials to consider in this respect is once again the separate section in GTW 3:1-6.

A number of scholars have found important links between Matthew 5:21-48 and Did 3:2-6.[99] In order to prove the relevance of the Two Ways section to our part of the Sermon on the Mount, our initial concern must be to establish such definitive connections. The following discussion will show that, when considered together, the parallels are extensive enough to establish an undeniable relationship between the two sections. The specific elements under consideration are as follows:

1) Both sections share the focus on minor vices and precepts as their leading principle;
2) Both sections presuppose a Decalogue background;
3) Both sections have a common structure as far as the preamble and the first two paragraphs are concerned (the sixth and seventh commandments);
4) Both sections draw the same conclusions from the sixth and seventh commandment, along the same line of reasoning;
5) Both sections belong to an all-embracing Two Ways doctrine.

1) Above, it was observed that the maxim of the first sentence in GTW 3:1 closely corresponds to the ethical doctrine in the preamble of Matt 5:17-20. The opening units express the fundamental principle which is expounded in the remainder of the passage by showing the connection between a light sin and a weighty one, and a light commandment and a weighty one. As the parallel verse in GTW 3:1 was largely indicative of the *Sitz im Leben* of the unit 3:1-6 as a whole,[100] so the idea in the preamble of Matt 5:17-20 might hold the clue to the setting of the early layer of 5:17-48, that is, before it was introduced into its present context.

2) Each of the two units, GTW 3:1-6 and Matt 5:17-48, are linked up by treating the sixth and the seventh commandments of the Decalogue as the first two weighty commandments (murder and adultery). The second half of the Decalogue is even more likely to stand in the background of Matt 5:21-48 since the last unit (5:43-48) stresses the love of one's neighbour which, as we have seen, is often used in early Judaism to express in crystalized form the second table of the Decalogue.[101] Rather interestingly, the items "murder" and "adultery" (in this order) also head the rather long catalogue of prohibitions in GTW 2:1-7 and again the list of vices that serves as an explication of the Way of Death in GTW 5. Altogether, it does not seem unreasonable to suppose that the first two items in the arrangement of the lists, which are modelled after the second tablet

---

[99] See above, n. 3.
[100] Cf. Chap. 5, pp. 167-69, above.
[101] Cf. Chap. 5, pp. 163-65, above.

of the Decalogue, are more tightly strung together by tradition than the remainder, which rather seems a haphazard and free adaptation in the various lists.[102]

3) Both GTW 3:1-3 and Matt 5:17-19. 21-22. 27-28 have structural elements in common. The chart below shows the points of unique agreement:

Matt 5		GTW 3	
5:17-20:	preamble: ... Do not set aside even the least of these commandments	3:1:	My child, flee from all evil and from everything like it
5:21-22:	Anger (...) (equals) murder (...)	3:2:	Anger (...) leads to murder (...)
5:27-28:	Lust (...) equals adultery (...)	3:3:	Lust (...) leads to adultery (...)

4) GTW 3:1-6 and Matt 5:17-19. 21-22. 27-28. 33-34a share the method of applying the principle laid down in the preamble. To prevent people from ignoring light commandments or committing light sins, the linkage of these minor items with the weighty ones is elucidated. In GTW the minor sin is repeatedly said to lead to a major one. Being bad-tempered or angry yields murder, and a lustful person is likely to end up committing adultery. The kind of argumentation used here is *a minori ad maius* (קל וחומר), presupposing that what is known about something 'light' can be known "all the more so" about something 'heavy'. One can hardly doubt that the first, second and fourth antitheses in Matthew presuppose the same logical method. Matthew has Jesus explain that the original intention of the prohibition of murder, adultery and oaths is to include all attitudes and actions which potentially lead to such acts. The disposition of such explanations is clearly from the light to the weighty demands, from the lesser to the greater.

5) Both textual units, GTW 3:1-6 and Matt 5:17-48, are part of a larger overarching compositional framework of the Two Ways. It is important to note that the GTW not only places the precepts in 3:2-6, but the additional materials in 1:3-2:7 and the refined human ethic in 3:7-4:14 as well, under the headings of neighbourly love and the Golden Rule in 1:2 as a further explicitation of the Way of Life. A similar procedure is found in Matthew but arranged in reversed order. The outline below shows that, in spite of their inverted positions, the constitutive elements of the two versions agree strikingly:

---

[102] The traditional list of antitheses in Matt 5:21-48 offers the two offenses, murder and adultery (5:21-22. 27-28), and the other offense – despite the fact that the Decalogue is not cited here – refers to the third commandment: "for the Lord will not hold him guiltless that taketh His name in vain" (Exod 20:7; cf. Lev 19:12. Either instance forbids abuse of God's name for unworthy purposes); cf. Friedlander, *The Jewish Sources*, 61-65; H.D. Betz, *The Sermon on the Mount*, 262; Gnilka, *Das Matthäusevangelium* 1, 174; Guelich, *The Sermon on the Mount*, 212; see also Ruzer, 'The Technique, 72-74.

Matt 5-7		*GTW*	
7:13-14	The Two Ways	1:1	The Two Ways
7:13a	The invitation to enter the narrow gate with the Way to Life	1:2a	The Way of Life
7:12	The Golden Rule as a summary of the "Law and the Prophets" in 5:17-7:11	1:2b-c	The double love commandment and the Golden Rule which is explained in 2:2-4:14
6:1-7:11	....	1:3-2:7	....
5:17-48	(Fulfilment of "the Law and the Prophets"). Admonition to observe the minor commandments and the elaboration on this instruction	3:1-6	Admonition to keep far from a minor transgression and the elaboration on this instruction
5:3-12	Admonition governing a refined ethic	3:7-4:14	Admonition governing a refined ethic

The comparison requires some explanation. We have seen that the love commandment and the Golden Rule are taken in Jewish sources to be ways of summarizing the essentials of the Tora. Now, all materials in Chaps. 1-4 of the Two Ways – this is the whole Way of Life and not just 3:1-6 – are said in 1:3a to be the interpretation of the love commandment as formulated in GTW 1:2. The same understanding applies to the middle section of the Sermon on the Mount, which begins with a redactional reference to Jesus fulfilling the Law and the Prophets and concludes with another redactional reference to the Law and the Prophets. This means that, according to Matthew, not only the concerns dealt with in 5:17-48 but also the instructions of 6:1-7:11 are related to the Tora. The Golden Rule in Matt 7:12 includes all the materials intervening between the "Law and the Prophets" of 5:17 and its duplicate formula in 7:12.[103]

Why did Matthew link up the Two Ways topic with precisely the final part of the Sermon on the Mount? The Q tradition supplies some evidence. The Sermon in Q probably concluded with two units which Matthew has taken up in his closing section. The first passage concerned good and bad fruit (cf. Luke 6:43-44), a pair of opposites which Matthew creatively incorporated into his warning about false prophets (Matt 7:15-23). The second and final unit dealt with the wise and the foolish builders, which is reflected in Luke 6:47-49 and was retained, albeit in an adapted form, in Matt 7:24-27. Thus, in both Luke and Matthew, as probably did Q, a series of counterbalancing alternatives terminate the sermon of the instructions

---

[103] Cf. Loader, *Jesus' Attitude towards the Law*, 184 and Luz, *Das Evangelium nach Matthäus* 1: "7,12 ist als zweiter Teil der Klammer um die Bergpredigt besonders wichtig" (236, n. 67). Matt 22:40 gives the love commandment as the summary of the Law as well. The presence of the disjunctive ἤ ("or") instead of the more usual conjunctive καί ("and") in Matthew's pairing of Law and Prophets might either be due to his favourite vocabulary (Gundry, *Matthew*, 79; Guelich, *The Sermon on the Mount*, 137-38), or to the negative form of the sentence (Davies-Allison, *The Gospel according to Saint Matthew* 1, 484). In either case, however, both "or" and "and" are justifiable as translations; cf. Blass-Debrunner-Rehkopf, *Grammatik*, 376 (= Section 446, 1b, n. 2).

by Jesus. Matthew opens this general drift of two opposing paradigms by presenting the Two Ways (7:13-14), contrasting the gate and the way which lead to destruction with the gate and the way which lead to life. He seems to elaborate here upon the theme present in the Q sermon, for the ways correlate with the positive and negative examples of the concluding units.

One of the developments within Matthew not paralleled within the GTW (and Doctrina, Didache, Barnabas or other versions) is the function of the Two Ways topic. Indeed, it is still part of a traditional Two Ways doctrine but, instead of introducing the actual implications of the Way of Life and the Way of Death, it is being used explicitly now as an ethical invitation or a moral appeal. The Two Ways theme in 7:13-14 sets the stage for the cautions that follow in the final section (7:13-27) of the Sermon urging the hearers to approvingly accept Jesus' words.[104] By referring to the preceding Sermon on the Mount as "my words" and "these words" (μου·τοὺς λόγους τούτους) twice over (7:24.26), the 'narrow gate' (or the 'hard way') is identified with obedience to the antecedent sayings of Jesus. The subject of the Two Ways (7:13-14), in fact, brings the Sermon to its conclusion by an appeal to respond positively to Jesus' life-bringing words in Matt 5-7.

So far our investigation has revealed close associations between GTW 3:1-6 and Matt 5:17-48. At the same time, it is difficult to differentiate the evangelist's own modifications from the sources on which he drew. The similarities and differences between the two texts are evidence that in some way or other the material derived from a common source. Yet, here again lies a riddle which is not easy to solve. Both units, Matt 5:17-48 and GTW 3:1-6, may be part of a common all-embracing Two Ways schema, but it is also possible that the tradition behind these units is merely confined to an account identical with, or similar to, the source of the individual *teknon*-passage. For, as was seen in Chap. 5, the carefully structured pericope in GTW 3:1-6 originally made up an independent tradition and did not belong, initially, to the Two Ways. The section of Matt 5:17-48 may thus have been derived from a form of the *teknon*-passage[105] which was either part of a Two Ways schema, or was limited to the block in 3:1-6 which circulated as a separate unit.

There is some evidence to support the last alternative. We have seen that the place and form of Two Ways elements in the Sermon on the Mount other than the *teknon*-passage (like the Golden Rule in 7:12 and the Two Ways metaphor in 7:13-14) probably result from an extensive relocation, adaptation and elaboration on the part of Matthew. There is a good possibility, then, that Matthew's source passed on only a separate *teknon*-tradition while Matthew himself may have drawn on a

---

[104] "In comparison with the presentation of the ways in Did 1-6 and Barn. 18-20/21, we see that Mt 7,13-14 does not exemplify the alternatives but only urges one to choose the way that leads to life. The reason for this difference is plain: the parenesis corresponding to the teaching of the two ways is found already in the preceding sections of Matthew's Sermon, that is, in 5,17-7,12." Cf., also for Matthew's handling of the verses at the close of the Q block, Syreeni, *The Making of the Sermon*, 178.

[105] The twofold prohibitions in every strophe of GTW 3:2-6 may originally have consisted of single phrases repeatedly presenting the same stereotyped formulas; see Chap 5, pp. 171-72, above.

Two Ways tradition in which the *teknon*-passage was transmitted as a part of this doctrine. Because the common tradition behind GTW 3:1-6 conceivably circulated in connection with the Two Ways schema in his community, there is a good possibility that Matthew himself incorporated the Golden Rule and the Two Ways metaphor into the Sermon. The supposed *Sitz-im-Leben* of the Two Ways tradition used by Matthew, that is the setting of the Two Ways before it was introduced into the present context of the gospel, was a situation of a catechetical nature, perhaps even an instruction for neophytes.[106]

Thus, while it is possible that Jesus used a separate tradition similar to our *teknon*-passage, Matthew may have supplemented this tradition with some additional elements, like the Golden Rule, the Two Ways metaphor, and the higly-developed ethic as reflected in the macarisms (5:3-12). The items may have been transmitted in his community as a traditional part of the Two Ways catechism. It is tempting to speculate, moreover, that some form of the instructions on alms-giving, prayer and fasting, now incorporated in Matt 6:1-18, and some form of the prohibitions concerning wealth, judgment of others and perverted zeal, now in Matt 6:19-7:6, appeared in this catechetical source as well. Because the present evidence is insufficient, however, we have no real way of telling whether the Two Ways items conflated with the underlying framework of the Sermon merely in the final stage of the editing of the gospel, or whether the fusion was a long-lasting process that had already started at some stage before the doctrine came to Matthew. It would be even more conjectural to restore the form itself of the Two Ways which guided Matthew in systematizing his material for the gospel. The version we have reconstructed in Chapter 4 is hypothetical and, if it is close to the authentic reading, the tradition might even have undergone revision once it became available to Matthew's community. After all, the genre of catechesis is fundamentally open to transformation, revision, and emendation of individual parts.

Having established that the congruities of Matt 5:17-48 with GTW 3:1-6 are likely to reflect an early stage in the transmission process, we are now in a position to evaluate the above evidence with respect to the interpretation of Matt 5:17-48. As noted before, the statement in GTW 3:1, the guiding principle of the literary unit of 3:1-6, has played a formative role in a particular type of rabbinic Judaism. It is true, the view expressed in this maxim was also spread in wider circles of

---

[106] With regard to the additional five Matthean Beatitudes, as compared with those in Luke 6:20-22, baptism was suggested as its real-life context by Braumann, 'Zum Traditionsgeschichtlichen Problem', 259-60. This view is supported and broadened by W. Popkes: "Offensichtlich wurde die alte »Rede«, die in der Feldrede Lk 6 noch in einem traditionsgeschichtlich früheren Stadium steht und von Hause aus eher eine prophetische als eine katechetische Rede darstellte, zum Zweck der Anfängerunterweisung von der Neophytentradition her ebenso strukturiert wie kommentiert, vermutlich bereits vor Matthäus, aber doch durchaus noch bis in die Endredaktion hinein, ..." ; cf. 'Die Gerechtigkeitstradition', 17. Popkes argues that the real-life context for the 'righteousness'-tradition in the Sermon on the Mount is found in a pre-baptismal catechetical instruction or in the instruction for neophytes. See also Syreeni, *The Making of the Sermon*, 99 and Draper, 'Torah and troublesome Apostles' (1996) 350-51. For arguments in support of the early usage of the Two Ways doctrine as an initiation instruction before the ritual of Baptism, see Did 7:1 and above, Chapter 3, pp. 86-89.

rabbinic teachers, but essentially it is an adage representing the characteristic feature of the early layer in the Derekh Erets compositions.[107] This, in turn, indicates that the tradition underlying the antitheses and their preamble should be read along with this hassidic literature of the time. Let us consider the literary affinity between the apophthegm in Yir'at Het II,16-17 and GTW and Matt 5:17-48 once again:

> ... keep aloof from everything hideous and from what even seems hideous. Shudder from committing a light transgression (מחטא הקל), lest it lead you to commit a weighty transgression (לחטא חמור).

The saying provides the critical principle by which the Law is to be read, interpreted and evaluated within the early milieu of Derekh Erets and, as has become clear, within the circles in which the Two Ways and Matt 5:17-48 originally were kept alive. Within pious Jewish circles in the Tannaitic period, the belief was prevalent that fulfilment of explicit halakhic duty did not exhaust clearly felt moral responsibility. The interpretative tradition in the first part of the antitheses to which Jesus takes an opposing stand, appears to restrict moral responsibility to the mere performance or omission of a particular act. Only a person who really murders must be brought to trial, only actual adultery must be avoided and with regard to perjury, it is only required that you keep your oaths sworn before God. As observed above, the early layer of Derekh Erets presents a life style which is known as the "Mishnat Hassidim", the teaching of the pious.[108] These pious constituted a concrete group within the society of the Sages, practising charities, performing deeds of loving-kindness, and possessing virtues of dedication to humility and modesty. Because they believed that a literal interpretation of the commandments resulted from a lack of positive motivation, they did more than the Law required. Such extra-pious deeds were called commandments "beyond the line of the law" (לפנים משורת הדין).[109]

That their morals were meant to prevent a person from indulging in sin is reflected in the title of the treatise Yir'at Het, which for the most part represents an early layer of the Derekh Erets literature. As observed above, the instruction of individual moral precepts in GTW 3:1-6 and the relevant maxims in the early stratum of Derekh Erets elucidate the link between attitude and behaviour. The risk of acquiring settled traits of character will make someone prone to major sins. The

---

[107] Cf. G. Klein, *Der älteste Christliche Katechismus*, 69: "Die kürzeste Formel für *Derech erez* lautet: *Halte dich fern von der Sünde und von dem, was hässlich ist*".

[108] Cf. above, chapter 5, pp. 172-74. See further Safrai, 'Teaching of Pietists', 25-26 (about the expression "Mishnat Hassidim") and 32-33; see also Id., "Hasidim we-Anshei Maase", 144-54; Id., 'Jesus and the Hasidic Movement', 415.

[109] Or: "lifnim mishurat hadin"; cf. Urbach, *The Sages*, 330-33; Berman, 'Law and Morality'; A. Lichtenstein, 'Does Jewish Tradition Recognize An Ethic', 107-116. For this principle of "lifnim mishurat hadin" (translated as "[das Handeln] innerhalb der Rechtslinie"), see Böhl, *Gebotserschwerung und Rechtsverzicht*, 59-60 and (for the functioning of this fundamental notion within hassidic circles) 85-109. With regard to Matthew, see also Montefiore, *The Synoptic Gospels* 2, 499 and Luz, *Das Evangelium nach Matthäus* 1, 255, n. 34.

ethical demand is preventive in that it promotes a behaviour that gains control over anger, lust and dishonesty, thereby eliminating the root cause of murder, adultery and using the Lord's name falsely (even perjury), respectively.[110] Certain things permissible in the Law were considered to be transgressions and were referred to as light sins.[111] Conversely, the halakhic rules, not being legally mandatory but actively observed, were referred to as light commands. An explanation of the concept of "beyond the line of the Law" on the basis of Scripture is attributed to R. Elazar of Modiim (a "Tanna" at the end of the first and the beginning of the second centuries CE) in the Mekhilta of R. Yishmael. R. Elazar learnt from Scripture that it was his duty to act beyond the strict requirements of the Law and to perform good deeds. The discussion is focussed here on the second part of the verse in Exod 18:20: "and you shall teach them the statutes and the decisions, and you shall make them know the way in which they must walk and the work they must do:"

> 'and you shall make them know the way in which they must walk' – meaning the study of Tora; 'and the work they must do' – meaning good deeds; these are the words of R. Yoshua. R. Elazar of Modiim says: 'and you shall make them know' – make them know how to live; 'the way' – this refers to visiting the sick; 'they must walk' – refers to burying the dead; 'in which' – refers to the giving of kindnesses; 'and the work' – this means the line (of the strict letter) of the Law (זו שורת הדין); 'they must do' – beyond the line (of the strict letter) of the Law (זה לפנים משורת הדין).[112]

By comparing Matt 5:17-48 with GTW 3:1-6 and Yir'at Het II,16-17, several pertinent issues in the antithetic doctrine of the Sermon on the Mount are elucidated. The first thing that becomes clear is that the argument *a minori ad maius*, from the lesser to the greater or קל וחומר, provides the essential clue to Jesus' attitude toward the Law in the Sermon on the Mount. This way of reasoning, clearly applied in GTW 3:1-6 and Yir'at Het II,16-17, is not made explicit in Matt 5:17-48 but it is obviously presupposed in the more stringent application of the weighty commandments. The argumentative strategy in GTW 3:1-6 and Yir'at Het II,16-17 explains why in Matt 5:21-22. 27-28 the sin of 'murder' is replaced by 'anger' and why the sin of 'adultery' is redefined by the 'covetous look'. Gaining control over lesser offences like anger and an adulterous desire are preventive measures to protect oneself from transgressing the major commandments of murder and adultery. The expression in Yir'at Het not only formulates the basic doctrine, warning as it does against a light transgression or promoting the light commandments, but it also provides us with the justification behind this admonition. Im-

---

[110] See also the excellent observations in H.D. Betz, *The Sermon on the Mount*, 220.

[111] See above, Chap. 5, p. 169 and cf. Van Loopik, *The Ways*, 196.

[112] *Massekhta da-'Amalek, Yitro* 2 (= Horovitz-Rabin, *Mechilta d'Rabbi Ismael*, 198); cf MekhRSbY to Exod 18:20 (= Epstein-Melamed, *Mekhilta d'Rabbi Šim'on b. Jochai*, 133). The exegesis of R. Elazar is quoted by Rav Yoseph in bBK 99b-100a and in bBM 30b. Examples are found in stories, as in e.g. bBK 99b-100a; bBM 24b; 30b and 83a; bBer 45b; bKet 50b and 97a. These show that "acts beyond the line (of the strict letter) of the Law" are not imposed by the Law. See also Böhl, *Gebotserschwerung und Rechtsverzicht*, 60-63.

proper conduct, though not sin itself, causes a person to slip into sin. The rule articulates a preventive measure to protect one from transgressing the weighty commandments,[113] and the same explanation for the minor vices to be avoided is found in each paragraph of GTW 3:2-6. The root of the problem, the beginning of major transgressions, is reflected in one's specific attitude toward minor precepts. Jesus' teachings lay bare the true meaning of the requirements of the Law as seen through the eyes of pious Jewish Sages.

A second result of the comparison is that the tradition underlying the present section of Matt 5:17-48 is likely to have originally contained some form of the introduction and the three primary antitheses. The blocks of Matt 5:17-19 on the one hand, and of 5:21-22. 27-28. 33-34a on the other, were not transmitted in isolation from one another but as one integral, organic and intrinsic cluster of sayings.[114] Jesus carries forward the teaching already implicit in the weighty commandments by expounding them within the parameters of the maxim that a light commandment is as important as a weighty one. Already in its pre-Matthean Jewish stage, the preamble was united with the remainder of the passage, showing an argumentative structure which is perceptible in the passages 5:17-19 and 21-22. 27-28. 33-34a of the present text. In fact, these materials constitute a traditional unit which can be explained as a rendering of viewpoints expressed and considered important in hassidic circles. The manner in which these primary antitheses, or in all probability Jesus himself, interpret the Tora is based on the leading principle that a light precept or sin is as important as a weighty one.

One question needs consideration yet. In his treatment of the minor sins, Jesus' argument in Matthew seems rather more rigorous than the line of reasoning in the Two Ways or in the early stratum of Derekh Erets. Although the loss of temper, a lustful look, or the taking of an oath do not replace the acts of murder, infidelity

---

[113] For additional instances, cf. Chap. 5, pp. 167-70; see also Moore, *Judaism* 2, 269.

[114] A similar conclusion was already formulated by M. Albertz (*Die Synoptischen Streitgespräche*, 146-51), although he failed to take the obviously Jewish character of the "least command" in Matt 5:(18)-19 sufficiently into account. He reconstructed a source containing Matt 5:17.21-22a.27-28.33-34a.37: "... zwar wird jedesmal das alte Gebot durch Rückgang auf die Gesinnung unerhört erweitert. So wird in der ersten dem Mord der Zorn 5,21.22a, in der zweiten dem Ehebruch das sündige Begehren 5,27.28 gleichgestellt, in der vierten das Verbot des Meineids zum Verbot jedes Schwörens 5,33.34a erweitert. Dem kurzen Gotteswort der Alten wird eine prägnante Forderung des neuen Gesetzesinterpreten entgegengestellt, jedoch so, dass das alte Wort nicht aufgehoben, sondern in seiner Anwendung zur Vervollkommnung geführt wird." (146) ... "Die drei Antithesen in ihrer Urgestalt geben eine treffende Illustration zu dem Programm Mt 5,17. Keins von den drei grossen Mosesgeboten wird für ungültig erklärt und doch jedes einer ungeahnten Vervollkommnung entgegengeführt. Dagegen bieten die drei von Mt hergestellten Antithesen das entgegengesetzte Bild: 5,31f. Mose gestattet die Ehescheidung, Jesus erklärt sie für Ehebruch. 5,38f.: Das alte Gebot gebietet das jus talionis, Jesus hebt es auf und verbietet den Widerstand gegen das Böse. 5,43f.: Das alte Gebot gebietet den Feindeshass, Jesus die Feindesliebe. Der Widerspruch dieser Antithesen ist formell demnach viel schärfer. Da nun diese von späterer Hand sind, so liegt es nahe, zu vermuten, dass Mt 5,17 mit der ersten, zweiten und vierten Antithese aus derselben Quelle geflossen sind" (148). This position is largely supported by V. Taylor, *The Formation*, 94-100 and Davies-Allison, *The Gospel according to Saint Matthew* 1, 505, n. 1.

and perjury, they are valued in the Sermon on the Mount as sins in their own right, incurring the same penalty as murder or adultery. The view that anger *equals* murder and that lust *equals* adultery, is toned down in GTW 3:1-6 (and in, say, Yir'at Het II,16-17 as well). The passage in GTW 3:1-3 objects to aggression and lust because they lead to real sin. These teachings appear largely to represent preventive measures to protect someone from transgressing weighty commandments. A bad-tempered or lustful person runs the risk of ending up committing murder and adultery. The attention does not seem focussed here on the minor sins of infuriation or desire, but on the perils of the grave sins of murder and adultery. In the Sermon on the Mount, however, Jesus almost substitutes anger against the brother for murder, lust for adultery, etc. How is one to understand this rigorous tendency in Matthew?

THE RIGOROUS FORMULATION OF THE MINOR SINS IN THE PRIMARY ANTITHESES AS A FURTHER RADICALIZATION OF THE UNDERLYING JEWISH TRADITION

The concept of acting "beyond the line of the law" is equated in essence with the virtue of *hesed* and these deeds are traced back to the halakhic teaching, represented by the current of the hassidim. Since a mere compliance with the written statutes of Law represents a lower standard of righteousness, one cannot regard such conduct as morally and ethically adequate. "Additional" deeds are needed. Within this framework of pious Jewish thought, the structure and themes of the teaching in Matt 5:17-48 can be accounted for in a meaningful way. The logion of Matt 5:20, after mentioning that entering the kingdom of heaven requires someone to "add to righteousness", introduces the heightening of the commandments in 5:21-48. Jesus rejects a minimalistic understanding of the weighty commandments. The "entrance saying" makes clear that doing the will of God or going the Way to Life implies a strict observance not only of the major commandments but of the minor ones as well. Jesus based his interpretation of Scripture on the theological insight current within hassidic circles into the basic intention of the Legislator.

There is little question, however, that the tenor of the Sermon on the Mount is even more rigorous than the supralegal conduct prevalent in the pious environment of the hassidim. Firstly, Matthew's Jesus does not explicitly highlight here the active observance of light commands with a view to avoiding the major ones. In 5:21-22. 27-28. 33-34a he attaches an equal moral significance to being angry with your brother *and* to killing him, to looking lustfully at a woman *and* to committing adultery with her, to taking oaths *and* perjury. These sayings give the impression as if the biblical commandment has been replaced by its moral complement. This, however, is not likely. Instead, Jesus made a higher standard of enforcement and liability felt to his audience by equating the gravity of obviously more innocent and minor offenses with the major legal transgressions. This way he was in a position to set even more store by the minor commandments than was accepted in the early Derekh Erets circles. The emphasis has been preserved by Matthew. Jesus' spiritual re-orientation of the halakha, though in line with the hassidim, is clearly perceptible in the preface of 5:17-19, when he urges his disciples to carry out the Law in their ethical conduct to the very extent of the jot and tittle.

Secondly, there is the judicial setting of the second part of the antitheses, which attests to a greater gravity of light sins in the Sermon on the Mount as compared with the instructions of the Greek Two Ways and the early stratum of Derekh Erets. It is noteworthy, indeed, that Jesus, in opposing the inadequate interpretative tradition of the first half of the antitheses, subsequently formulates his own moral position in legal terms as well.[115] The second part of each antithesis continues the legal form of the first part. This appears in the recurring introductory statements which, as observed above, correspond to the terminology in legal debate of the rabbinic tradition. Like their technical parallels in the literature of the Sages, the words "But I say to you" introduce a legal opinion contradicting the generally accepted one. Jesus thus uses an expression customary in Jewish legal argumentation.

In addition to the legal format of the introduction formulas, also the general phraseology of Matt 5:21-22 and 5:27-28 may indicate the juridical scope of these instances. In 5:21, Jesus quotes the sixth commandment "You shall not kill" and repeats the current interpretation by announcing the penalty in response to the crime of murder. In the following verse, Jesus offers his alternative explanation of the commandment: "But I say to you that every one who is angry with his brother shall be liable to judgment". The structure runs parallel to the preceding legal stipulation. He exactly repeats the punishment of verse 21 ("shall be liable to judgment") but substitutes a different condition ("every one who is angry with his brother"). The legal form of the ordinance is corroborated by the use of "every one" ($\pi\tilde{\alpha}\varsigma$) and a present participle in the protasis that states the crime again, followed by a future apodosis that mentions the penalty. An analogous case of legal setting is found in 5:27-28. The first part of the antithesis renders the seventh commandment "You shall not commit adultery", while the second part, refuting the implied restriction by a literal interpretation of that commandment, redefines the term 'adultery'. Adultery is not only the physical act of intercourse but also the covetous look: "But I say to you that every one ($\pi\tilde{\alpha}\varsigma$) who looks at a woman lustfully has already committed adultery with her in his heart" (v. 28). Here again, both the presence of the element "every one" in conjunction with a present participle in the protasis and the aorist construction in the apodosis indicate a legal ordinance.

Why does the Matthean Jesus set his demands about anger, sexual desire (and perfidy) in the form of a legal ordinance, irrespective of the fact that thoughts and feelings hardly accommodate themselves to legislation and enactment? For, in contrast to legal ordinances, moral and ethical norms cannot be enforced by

---

[115] "Vor allem kleidet er seine Mahnung in die Gestalt eines Rechtssatzes. So hebt er ihren absolut verpflichtenden Charakter heraus;" Luz, *Das Evangelium nach Matthäus* 1, 255; see, also for the following, Guelich, *The Sermon on the Mount*, 186.193; Gnilka, *Das Matthäusevangelium* 1, 160.

sanctions of the courts. One could prosecute murder, adultery and perjury but it escapes the bounds of legal practice to guarantee the prohibitions of anger, lust and insincere speech. For what reason, then, have moral attitudes and actions, characteristic of the above-mentioned pious Jewish circles, become legal imperatives in the teachings of Jesus? The very use of legal terminology in formulating his moral position may have been particularly motivated by the desire to expand the scope of enforcement. While formal legislation was basically absent and Jesus' interpretation did not really involve the creation of new laws, such juridical wording bolstered the moral pronouncements which in themselves resonate with the attitude and acts of the above-mentioned pious Jewish circles. The legal formulation confers the status of a normative duty on a behaviour which is morally desirable. It underlines the degree of obligation, incumbent upon everyone, to act according to the pietist rule "beyond the line of the law".

Conclusion

A radicalization of the Tora commandments similar to the one found in Matt 5:17-48 occurs in GTW 3:1-6 as well, the implication being that Jesus probably was not the first to introduce such a deepening of the Law. Of course, the individual sayings of the Sermon are primarily presented as an interpretation of biblical commandments, as a Jewish *derasha*, whereas those in GTW 3:1-6 belong to a moral instruction formulated independently of Scripture. They may represent a basic teaching of Jesus but because the instruction itself reflects the ethical sensitivity current in pious Jewish circles, Jesus' demands in the Sermon are preceded or prepared in the history of this hassidic milieu. Nevertheless, the legal formulation of moral principles and the seeming identification of light sins with heavy sins may have represented a new step at that time. Implicitly appealing to the programmatic statement in 5:18-19 containing the hermeneutic key which is to be used, Jesus declared his decisions, exposed in the so-called antitheses, to be binding for his followers. The main aim of the moral approach that the light sin is as important as the weighty one is to avoid sin and, as far as possible, to attain moral perfection (Matt 5:48).

It thus needs hardly be mentioned that these prohibitions were meant to be followed literally. On the other hand, it has been established above that the 'great commandment' of love in Lev 19:18 is the foremost commandment. It is used to form the conclusion of the discourse in 5:43-48 and evidently summarizes the second half of the Decalogue here. Also in Matt 7:12 and GTW 1:2 – in the passages recapitulating the Sermon in Matt 5:17-7:12 and the Way of Life in the GTW 1:2-4:14 –, the original intent of the divine legislator concerns the basic principle of the love command. The diverse laws are organized by and subsumed under the love command. It is the commandment on which the whole of the Law hinges (Matt 22:40) and, in the previous chapter, we also found evidence of the love commandment being the moral essence of Law in rabbinic sayings attributed to Hillel and Akiva. Furthermore, in the opinion of the hassidim, a sin-fearing man is not merely passively refraining from transgressions. He is someone who also practises loving-kindness, charity and other highly esteemed acts of benevolence toward his fellow men. Love of one's neighbour and abolition of all hatred was of central importance for them. How, then, does the love commandment in the closing antithesis relate to the injunctions in the remaining antitheses? In what sense are these radicalized demands of the antitheses, representing the "jots and tittles" of the Tora in 5:18-19, related to the love commandment?

Jesus' teaching in the primary antitheses essentially is an exposition of verses taken from the Pentateuch. Crucial for understanding the section of Matt 5:17-20 is that the fulfilling of the Law is determined by one's interpretation of the Law. The stricter interpretation of the weighty commandments as observed within hassidic circles (and required in the Sermon on the Mount, the Two Ways, and Derekh Erets) presents an attitude towards life that is beneficial to one's neighbour and emphasizes a more generous, positive attitude towards people throughout. Faithful adherence to the light commandments implies a definite shift in moral focus and a transformation of social relations. "Purely legal norms, such as those cited in Matt 5. 21, 27, 31, 33, 38, and 43, can never convey how life is to be lived by those who are genuinely poor in spirit, pure in heart, and full of mercy (5, 3. 7. 8)."[116] The light commandments occurring in the antitheses of 5:21-48, however, are crystallizations of neighbourly love, the neighbours being the concrete victims of anger, sexual desire, disloyalty. Jesus' instruction is an elaboration of the love commandments within a basically halakhic framework. The substance of love must be outlined with minor commandments which are not meant to limit but, on the contrary, to reinforce the law of love.

---

[116] Stanton (*A Gospel for a New People*, 302), quoting Davies-Allison, *The Gospel according to Saint Matthew* 1, 509f. We were unable, however, to trace this observation on the pages of the latter work referred to by Stanton.

Chapter Seven

A Jewish-Christian Addition to
the Two Ways: Did 6:2-3

The statement in Did 6:2-3 represents a considerable shift in focus compared with the ethics and values that were exhibited in the preceding section. After the sharp warning to preserve the aforesaid prescriptions in their integrity in Did 6:1, the two subsequent verses are pervaded with an atmosphere of concession and tolerance:

> 1. See to it that no one leads you astray from this way of the doctrine, since [the person who would do so] teaches apart from God. 2. For if you can bear the entire yoke of the Lord, you will be perfect, but if you cannot, do what you can. 3. As for food, bear what you can, but be very much on your guard against food offered to idols, for it is worship of dead gods.

Whereas the prohibitions in Chapters 1-5 (and the verse in 6:1 as well) suggest a morality which applies to a community within the boundaries of Judaism proper, Did 6:2-3 has all the markings of an address to non-Jewish Christians. The passage represents an adjustment to the perspective of gentile believers who are not capable of bearing the entire "yoke of the Lord" and may have difficulties in observing Jewish dietary laws. An observant Jew does not have the choice mentioned here. Thus, there is a strong possibility – and this position reflects a broad scholarly consensus – that these two verses originally did not belong to the teaching of the Two Ways.

Only with great effort and more than a little imagination can a balanced interpretation be achieved of such a brief notice as that found in Did 6:2-3. The content of the present chapter focusses on three aspects. After a short discussion of recent studies on Did 6:2-3 (pp. 239-42), the relationship between the passage and the Apostolic Decree will be discussed. There is strong evidence that the materials in Did 6:2-3 reflect a separate tradition of the Decree which is found in Acts 15:20.29; 21:25 and in Rev 2:14.20 as well. Since the Decree is edited explicitly in Acts, this study attempts to first reconstruct the original prohibitions of the decision as rendered in Acts. In search of its authentic form in Acts, special notice will be taken of the Noachide laws and their pre-rabbinic equivalents which, as will become clear, are the most appropriate framework for understanding and appreciating the Decree (pp. 243-53). Next, attention is drawn to the particular wording in the other two first-century sources that echo the Decree, namely Rev 2:14.20 and Did 6:2-3. Although the statements mentioned here have clearly been influenced by the Decree, it is their specific forms which demand further explanation because they reveal a variety in the number of requirements. This examination enables us to further uncover some additional materials which might have been attached to the Decree's prohibitions in its earliest form. Next, we go on to discuss the markedly Jewish character of the final clause of Did 6:3 that substantiates the idol food prohibition (pp. 254-65). The final section will explore the type of phraseology used in Did 6:2. In this and in other scattered references (Acts 15 and 21; Rev 2:14.20), the Decree represents a minimum of laws for believing gentiles. This halakhic position conflicted with Paul's view. Rather than interpreting the Apostolic Decree as a minimum, Paul evidently considered these three precepts as the upper limit on the obligations of gentile Christians. Both attitudes, however, may echo contemporary Jewish views (pp. 265-69). In our conclusion, we will suggest that the specific emphasis on the "whole yoke of the Lord" in Did 6:2 may have been intended to discredit those people who, like Paul, taught that one can be perfect without keeping to the Tora to its full extent (pp. 269-70).

Introduction

If Did 6:2-3 is a supplement to the original Two Ways teaching, the question arises what it means and where it comes from. With respect to its content, several explanations have been offered. One suggestion is that asceticism is the issue here.[1] This opinion seems to be corroborated by the Ps.-Cyprian treatise *De centesima, sexagesima, tricesima* which distinguishes three classes of Christians, yielding different quantities of fruit ("hundred-fold", "sixty-fold" and "thirty-fold") and, in support of this view, almost literally quotes (as "Scripture") Did 6:2.[2] Our passage thus underlies a doctrine of asceticism in this fourth (?) century document[3] which divides Christians into the elect few who live a life of moral perfection and others who do the best they can. It would be wrong, however, to suggest that, as a result, the text of Did 6:2-3 itself also reflects an ascetic tradition. For although these verses came to be used this way in a later document, it does not follow that this was their original meaning. First of all, the remainder of the Didache does not focus any real attention on an austere life-style. Moreover, the exhortation concerning "food" in Did 6:2-3, which the reader is challenged to accept to whatever degree he is able, does not refer to fasting but to Jewish dietary laws. Finally, there is no example

---

[1]   For this explanation, especially with regard to sexual abstinence, see Von Harnack, *Lehre der zwölf Apostel*, 19-22; Knopf, *Die Lehre der zwölf Apostel*, 20-21.
[2]   "... et alio in loco scriptura haec testatur et admonet dicens: 'Si potes quidem, fili, omnia praecepta domini facere, eris consummatus; sin autem, uel duo praecepta, amare dominum ex totis preacordiis et similem tibi quasi ‹te ipsum›.;'" cf. Reitzenstein, 'Eine frühchristliche Schrift', 74-90 (text of the treatise), esp. 79, lines 132-35; cf. also Daniélou, 'Le traité De centesima, sexagesima, tricesima', 173. See also Rordorf who believes that Did 6 might reflect the same ascetic tradition: 'Un chapitre d'éthique' (1986) 171-72.
[3]   According to A.P. Orbán, the treatise was composed at some point in the period between 251-7 and ca 383 CE; cf. 'Die Frage der ersten Zeugnisse', 234-35; see also Quasten, *Patrology* 2, 372; Altaner-Stuiber, *Patrologie*, 178. However, the third and second centuries too have been suggested as dates of origin; see Rordorf, 'Un chapitre d'éthique' (1986) 172, n. 79.

in other Christian sources associating the clause "yoke of the Lord" with ascetism. As a matter of fact, the strict observance of the Jewish Law by those who could "bear the yoke" and those who could "bear the yoke" only in part, has been replaced in the ascetic view by the double standard for Christians representing a two tier ethic of perfection and mediocrity.[4]

Other interpreters have drawn attention to the close correspondence between the clause τέλειος ἔσῃ in Did 6:2 and the wording of (καὶ) ἔσῃ τέλειος in 1:4b. This correspondence suggests the same redactional hand and, as such, represents a contribution by the Didachist himself. Although opinions differ as to whether the passage of Did 6:2-3 has to be contributed to the Didachist in its entirety[5] or only with respect to this specific clause,[6] the close relationship between these phrases is believed to indicate a Christian understanding of Did 6:2-3. By repeating the clause of 1:4b in 6:2, the Didachist remembers the special laws of the Lord which are based upon the Sermon on the Mount. The "yoke of the Lord" in Did 6:2, then, is the yoke of Jesus and "perfection" refers to the fulfilment of the radical ethical demands of Jesus as summarized in 1:3-6. Upon closer observation, this understanding is also somewhat strained, since the "yoke of the Lord" in 6:2 is not explicitly said to be a *nova lex Christi*. Further, if the "yoke of the Lord" in 6:2 refers to the requirements of Jesus in his Sermon on the Mount, as reflected in Did 1:3-6, it would be difficult to uphold the coherence between Did 6:2 and 6:3.[7] The Christian interpretation would be very loosely connected with the subsequent, undoubtedly Jewish, admonition.

Would Did 6:2-3, then, represent an appendix of Jewish origin? This view has been proposed by A. Stuiber.[8] He suggests that our passage might have originated within Jewish circles to appeal to "those who fear the Lord," i.e., non-Jewish adherents to the synagogue who did not embrace Judaism in its entirety. Because the Tora was given to Israel, only Jews were strictly charged to keep the Law while, for the Godfearing gentiles, only some (Noachide) commandments were sufficient. Stuiber believes that Did 6:2-3 reflects the hope in Jewish circles that these gentiles would observe, as much as they could, the ritual commandments of the Law as a step to full conversion in the end. The reference to the Jewish Law

---

[4] See, also for other arguments, Stuiber, "'Das ganze Joch'", 325-26; Kretschmar, 'Ein Beitrag zur Frage' (1975) 172-73.

[5] "Ist diese Deutung richtig, dann scheint es mir konsequent, 6,2 (ebenso wie das Folgende 6,3) zur Gänze der didachistischen Redaktion zuzuschreiben;" cf. Niederwimmer, *Die Didache*, 156.

[6] Rordorf-Tuilier agree with Stuiber that these verses are Jewish in origin but wonder what sense was conveyed once this instruction was inserted in the Didache. "En revanche, dans la *Didachè*, ce joug doit être celui du Seigneur Jésus (cf. *Matth.* 11,29-30), tel qu'il est exprimé dans le Sermon sur la montagne. Nous pouvons l'affirmer avec certitude, puisque la formule – καὶ ἔσῃ τέλειος – qui apparaît à cet endroit (*Did.* 6,2), trahit la main du rédacteur qui a précédemment inséré cette expression dans la ‹section évangélique› du texte (1,4);" cf. *La Doctrine des douze apôtres*, 32-33; cf. 92.

[7] Cf. Wengst, *Didache (Apostellehre)*, 96, n. 52.

[8] Stuiber, "'Das ganze Joch'", 327-29.

as a yoke is well attested in rabbinic Literature,[9] and thus may support this point of view.

Below, the possibility will be discussed, however, that the section under consideration originated and survived in a Jewish-Chistian milieu where the Tora was still faithfully observed by Christians of Jewish origin. In the passage, they directly appeal to gentile Christians to observe the Mosaic Law as far as they can. It is not easy to determine when and where this appendix was added. Yet, one thing is clear. It is not the type of Christianity which is subscribed to by the Didachist. On the contrary, the part of the Didache subsequent to the Two Ways section exhibits an apparent hostility against Judaism. In 8:1-2, the community is cautioned not to have their days of fasting coincide with those of the "hypocrites", nor to pray as the "hypocrites" do.[10] These obvious features of enmity indicate that the appendix can hardly be explained as an original contribution by the final author-editor of the Didache.

Presumably, the supplement in Did 6:2-3 existed in the copy of the Two Ways treatise used by the Didachist.[11] He may have accepted and retained the passage in his final version of the Didache because he did not notice its Jewish character.[12] In accordance with other early Christian authors (cf. Matt 11:29-30; *1 Clem.* 16:17; *Odes Sol.* 42:7.8; *Gos.Thom.* 90; Justin, *Dialogue* 53:1), he probably interpreted the "yoke of the Lord" as the yoke of Christ and understood this expression as referring to Christian duties in general. In this perception, the strict observance of the Mosaic Law ceased to be the content of perfection. With regard to the admonition in Did 6:3, he, of course, abhorred food offered to idols, an attitude which persisted in the primitive church for centuries. This observation, however, provides an additional reason why the final redactor may have left the verses of Did 6:2-3 untouched. There is a strong possibility that he recognized in this short exhortation

---

[9] Rabbinic texts which speak of the "yoke of the Law," yoke of the Kingdom" etc. are conveniently gathered by Str-B 1, 608-10 and 176-77.

[10] Also, the admonition in Did 14:1 to celebrate the Eucharist on Sunday might indicate this unfriendly attitude; cf. below, Chap. 9, pp. 350-51 (and Chap. 8, n. 99).

[11] It is even possible that an expanded form of the Two Ways (i.e. including some form of Did 6:2-3) was known to the author of the Letter of Barnabas as well. For, although he does not present a parallel text of Did 6:2-3, he is attacking the Mosaic Law and Jewish dietary laws. The Law, being characterized as a "yoke of necessity" (ζυγοῦ ἀνάγκης), is repudiated in favour of the "new law of our Lord Jesus Christ" (2:6), while the ritual food laws are rejected and interpreted metaphorically in Chap. 10. It is interesting to see that even the wording in Did 6:2-3 closely corresponds with a clause in Barn. 10:10: ἔχετε τελείως καὶ περὶ τῆς βρώσεως.

[12] Stuiber, advocating the Jewish origin of Did 6:2-3, ultimately refers to the carelessness of the redactor: "Warum wurde dieser Nachtrag nicht beseitigt, da er doch für Christen ohne Bedeutung war, ja sogar Anstoss erregen konnte? Wirkliche Schwierigkeiten enthält nur *Did.* 6,2, während *Did.* 6,3 mit dem Verbot des Opferfleischessens auch ein für Christen wichtiges Anliegen vertritt, so dass man wegen dieses Satzes auch die weniger brauchbaren Sätze von 6,2-3 übernehmen konnte. Vielleicht handelt es sich aber auch nur um die Sorglosigkeit des christlichen Kompilators, der seinen Text im einzelnen nicht immer genau geprüft, sondern als Ganzes übernommen hat" ("'Das ganze Joch'", 328). Niederwimmer, however, calls the "Sorglosigkeit des christlichen Kompilators" into question and states that this solution "doch eher einer Verlegenheitsauskunft gleichkommt" (*Die Didache*, 155).

some form of a common, widespread, and authoritative instruction, circulating in early Christian communities. Such a statement occurs in Acts 15 as well and is known as the Apostolic Decree.

Did 6:2-3 in a Wider Perspective

Did 6:2-3 sets forth an issue that appears to be debated in the Acts 15 as well,[13] namely, the imposition of the Tora on gentile converts. What is the situation recorded in Acts 15? Some Christians from Judea had come to Antioch (14:26) and argued that, unless someone observed the Mosaic Law, he could not be saved. At issue is the halakhic status of the gentiles and the question that is disputed is what they must do to be saved. Acts next describes the conference in Jerusalem on this matter attended by the apostles and elders. Peter, referring to the members of the household of Cornelius who have been saved, claims that there is no need for gentiles to fully observe the commandments of the Tora. James sustains Peter's argument and proposes a regulation, the so-called Apostolic Decree, which was then accepted by the assembly. It was decided that certain minimum requirements were to be imposed on the gentiles. These are mentioned in 15:20 and again in 15:29 and 21:25.

It is noteworthy that the problem and solution described in Acts 15 are substantially the same as the ones mentioned in Did 6:2-3. While Jews remain bound to observe the whole Mosaic Law, both texts present a compromise for the gentile followers of Jesus. Moreover, it cannot escape our attention that the terminology of the two accounts is strikingly similar in some cases. In Did 6:2, the observance of the Law is referred to as "to be able to bear the whole yoke" (δύνασαι βαστάσαι ὅλον τὸν ζυγόν) which, like the repeated βάστασον in 6:3, implies that the Law is burdensome to the extent that not all are able to "bear the yoke" of the Tora.[14] A similar combination of words "a yoke ... which ... we have been able to bear..." (ζυγὸν ... ὃν ... ἰσχύσαμεν βαστάσαι) is found in Acts 15:10 and the connotation is also the same. In Acts 15, the implication that the Law is a burden is still corroborated by the term βάρος ("weight"), right before the second formulation of the decree: "To lay upon you no greater burden (μηδὲν πλέον ἐπιτίθεσθαι ὑμῖν βάρος) than these necessary things: ..." (15:28). An additional verbal identity appears in the occurrence of the necessary requirement applied to

---

[13] For the close relationship between Acts 15 and Did 6:2-3, see e.g.: C. Taylor, *The Teaching of the Twelve Apostles*, 46-48; Vokes, *The Riddle of the Didache*, 95-96; Kraft, *Barnabas and the Didache*, 163; Rordorf-Tuilier, *La Doctrine des douze apôtres*, 33-34. 168-69; Jefford, *The Sayings of Jesus*, 96-98; Draper, 'Torah and troublesome Apostles' (1991) 363; Flusser, 'Paul's Jewish-Christian Opponents', passim; Tomson, *Paul and the Jewish Law*, 180.

[14] According to some interpreters, the motif "the yoke of the Lord" in Did 6:2 might be dependent on the saying in Matt 11:28-30. However, whereas it says in Matthew that this yoke is light and thus can be carried with ease, the text of the Didache suggests that the yoke is so burdensome that only "perfect" Christians are able to bear it. See Jefford, *The Sayings of Jesus*, 94-95.

gentile converts in Acts 15:(20).29; 21:25 and Did 6:3, namely in the prohibition of "food sacrificed to idols" (εἰδωλόθυτον).

A final indication supporting the association of Did 6:2-3 with the Apostolic Decree in Acts, may be provided by the Ethiopian Church Order or the Ethiopic version of the Canones Ecclesiastici. Above, in Chapter 1, it was established that this church manual contains an interpolated section in the canons 49-52. In can. 52 some portions of the Didache appear, namely Did 11:3-13:7 which are followed directly by Did 8:1-2a. For our purpose, it is of importance to note that the same canon displays a passage which strongly echoes the restrictions of the Apostolic decree in Acts 15 and 21. It admonishes the reader to avoid idolatry, corpses (of animals), blood, things (i.e. animals) strangled, and broken bones: "But keep yourselves from the religion of demons and from gods, and from dead things keep, and from blood and things strangled, and further, a bone shall not be broken."[15] Because this section immediately precedes the two distinct extracts of Did 11:3-13:7 and Did 8:1-2a, it presumably was incorporated here in association with Did 6:2-3.[16] There is a strong possibility, then, that the translator of the Didache or the tradition which preserved Did 6:2-3 until its translation into Ethiopic, has connected this passage with the wording of the Decree in Acts 15.

THE APOSTOLIC DECREE IN ACTS AND THE NOACHIDE LAWS

In both the Decree and Did 6:2-3, we have witnesses to an agreement in the early church about certain moral and religious obligations for gentiles who are not full members of the Jewish community. Why were these moral codes created? Or, to limit ourselves to the account in Acts, on what grounds did the Jerusalem church define a minimum of practice for new gentile Christians? Peter and James were observant Jews whose aim was certainly not to discourage gentiles from becoming full converts to Judaism, thereby becoming Jewish Christians. What, then, was the rationale behind the concrete ethical instructions? Before these issues[17] are explored further, it is necessary first to look more closely at the actual terms of the decree.

There has been considerable debate about the original version of the code of laws drawn up for gentile converts to Christianity in Acts 15:20.29 and 21:25. In the majority Eastern reading, the Decree forbids four things: "things sacrificed to idols" (εἰδωλόθυτα), "blood" (αἷμα), "things strangled" (πνικτά), and "fornication" (πορνεία), while the minority Western reading omits "things strangled"

---

[15] Horner, *The Statutes*, 193,3-6. The text then links up with Did 11:3: "But concerning Apostles and Prophets according to the ordinance of the Gospel thus do ye" (193,7).

[16] See Audet, *La Didachè*, 35.

[17] Other problems, indirectly related to our discussion, are for example: was the Decree originally intended for a limited number of mixed congregations? Was Paul absent when the Decree was devised? Was the Decree promulgated at the conference Paul describes in Gal 2:1-10?

(πνικτά) in all three occurrences.[18] The difference between the two lists is not without implications.[19] The Eastern version, including πνικτά (denoting the meat which is provided by the strangling of an animal), represents an understanding of the Decree in which the dietary aspect is predominant. The commandment at issue here mainly pertains to the consumption of unacceptable meat. In the three-clause version reflected in the Western text, however, the ethical interpretation prevails as the most natural references of this listing would be to idolatry,[20] the shedding of blood (i.e., murder), and fornication. It is difficult to retrieve precisely the authentic version but the number and the weight of the manuscripts[21] seem to favour the fourfold prohibition. If the Eastern text embodied the authentic form of the Decree, it must have been transformed into a threefold (mainly moralizing) Decree at some stage of its transmission.

On the other hand, one may ask whether, in this particular case, the significance and number of manuscripts really settles the question. In the first place, the three-fold form is found in early church Fathers, like Tertullian, Irenaeus, Cyprian, Ambrosiaster, and Augustine.[22] This means that, in the West, the threefold Decree enjoyed at least some popularity in the third and fourth centuries. Moreover, the Decree was probably apostolic in origin and because of this particular status it must have had a strong impact on the everyday life-style of the early gentile Christians. The wide diffusion of the decree in the first and second centuries CE is attested

---

[18] In all three passages, the reference to things strangled (τοῦ πνικτοῦ / πνικτῶν / πνικτόν) is omitted in the Western text (D) and it is missing in the Old Latin codex gigas in 15:20 and 21:25 as well. The Golden Rule, in its negative version, appears in two of the three occurrences (except for 21:25). Because Tertullian (*De Pudicitia* 12,4) supports the Bezan text by omitting πνικτός but leaves out the Golden Rule, the latter may represent a later addition and will not be discussed here.

[19] Among the advocates of the originality of the Western text (the three-clause version) are e.g. Hilgenfeld, 'Das Apostel-Concil'; Resch, *Das Aposteldecret*; Von Harnack, *Beiträge zur Einleitung* 3, 188-98; and his later position in 4, 22-23; D. Smith, *The Life and Letters of St. Paul*, 671-74; Clark, *The Acts of the Apostles*, 95.97.360-61; Lake *The Acts of the Apostles*, 204-209; Ropes, *The Text of Acts*, 265-69; Boman, 'Das textkritische Problem', 26-30; Flusser-Safrai, 'Das Aposteldekret', 174-84.
The priority of the Eastern text (the four-clause version) has (among others) been defended by Zahn, *Die Apostelgeschichte des Lucas*, 523ff; Jacquier, *Les Actes des Apôtres*, 455-58; Brun, 'Apostelkoncil und Aposteldekret'; Von Harnack, 'Das Aposteldekret (Act. 15,29)', reflecting his earlier position; Lietzmann, 'Der Sinn des Aposteldekrets'; Haenchen, *Die Apostelgeschichte*, 390 and n. 5; Kümmel, 'Die älteste Form des Aposteldekrets' (for further references, see n. 4); Simon, 'The Apostolic Decree', 438-39; Catchpole, 'Paul, James and the Apostolic Decree', 430.

[20] The clause ἀλισγήματα τῶν εἰδώλων in Acts 15:20 paralleling the εἰδωλόθυτα of 15:29 and 21:25, possibly a reformulation of the text proper, refers to the pollution by idols (cf. mShab 9:1) and cannot be narrowed down to idol food.

[21] Cf. the surveys in Hurd, *The Origin of 1 Corinthians*, 247-48 and G. Schneider, *Die Apostelgeschichte* 2, 192.

[22] With regard to the church Fathers, the following attestations may be mentioned:
• the clause καὶ τοῦ πνικτοῦ (15:20) is omitted in Irenaeus (Latin translation), Ephrem and Augustine;
• καὶ πνικτῶν (15:29) is not found in Irenaeus (Latin translation), Ephrem, Tertullian, Cyprian, Jerome, Ambrosiaster, Augustine and Pacian of Barcelona (died between 379 and 392 CE) and Fulgentius;
• καὶ πνικτόν (21:25) is omitted in Augustine.

by several witnesses. The book of Revelation issues a condemnation of those who teach Christians to "eat food sacrificed to idols and practise fornication" (φαγεῖν εἰδωλόθυτα καὶ πορνεῦσαι) or to "practise fornication and to eat food sacrificed to idols" (πορνεῦσαι καὶ φαγεῖν εἰδωλόθυτα) in 2:14 and 20, respectively. These terms, admonishing the Christian communities of Pergamum and Thyatira, seem to evoke the minimum requirements of the Apostolic decree.[23] This assumption is underscored by the assurance to the church of Thyatira in 2:24 that "I do not lay upon you any other burden" (οὐ βάλλω ἐφ'ὑμᾶς ἄλλο βάρος), which may well echo Acts 15:28. Another occurrence reflecting some form of the Decree is found in Justin, *Dialogue*, 34, where is said that "the gentiles, who know God, ..., would rather endure every torture and pain, even death itself, than worship idols, or eat meat sacrificed to idols" (περὶ τοῦ μήτε εἰδωλολατρῆσαι μήτε εἰδωλόθυτα φαγεῖν).[24] Furthermore, we have seen that the Decree is also referred to in Did 6:3 and, finally, it is probable that Paul too knew and accepted some form of the Decree.[25] It is thus safe to say that the Decree belongs to a pre-Lukan tradition and was considered, at least by Luke, as appropriate to all gentiles (Acts 16:4). In some form, it must have circulated in Christian communities from an early stage and apparently Luke was not the only one to record it. Because the Decree was preserved independently of Acts in other early Christian texts as well, it is questionable whether, in this specific case, the normal textual-critical rules are suitable standards for evaluating its proper reading.[26] The following discussion will reveal that the Western text might very well represent an earlier phase in the history of the Decree than the form displayed in the Eastern text.

In order to fully appreciate the Western form of the Decree, we need to broaden our search for clues. An important thing to note is the fact that the Decree has a parallel in the Jewish Noachide laws. These laws represent a trend in rabbinic Judaism to codify the behaviour of non-Jews. They offer a perspective of what halakha, according to the Sages, requires of righteous gentiles. By observing this minimum level of morality, such gentiles would win divine favour and a share in the world to come. The relevance of this doctrine becomes clear when we ascertain that, within the Greco-Roman world, Judaism held a fascination for outsiders who were attracted by its spirituality and high ethical values. These partial adherents to the synagogue were called Godfearers (שמים אלהים / ירא, σεβόμενοι τὸν θεόν, φοβούμενοι τὸν θεόν or θεοσεβεῖς or metuentes)[27]. Many accreted to

---

[23] Cf. S.G. Wilson, *Luke and the Law*, 77-78; Syreeni, 'Matthew, Luke, and the Law', 139-41 and n. 28.

[24] ET: Falls, *Saint Justin Martyr*, 199-200.

[25] See below, pp. 259-60.

[26] See S.G. Wilson, *Luke and the Law*, 77-78.

[27] Cf. Guttmann, *Das Judentum und seine Umwelt*, 67-69. 98-114; Bamberger, *Proselytism in the Talmudic Period*, 135-38; Lieberman, *Greek in Jewish Palestine*, 77-82; Moore, *Judaism* 1, 325-26; Siegert, 'Gottesfürchtige und Sympathisanten'; Stern, 'The Jews in Greek and Latin Literature', 1158-59, n. 1; Simon, 'Gottesfürchtiger'; Schürer, *The History of the Jewish People* 3/1, 165-173; Van der

Jewish communities in all sorts of loose ways, without taking the final step in the process of Judaization so as to become full converts. Evidence of the powerful influence of a Jewish community upon Godfearers is provided by the recent discovery of a major inscription from the beginning of the third century CE during the excavation of the city of Aphrodisias in ancient Caria. This inscription records the names of a relatively large number of local gentiles, who are explicitly called Godfearers and appear to have been contributors to an institution of the synagogue in Aphrodisias.[28]

The Noachide laws were designed to establish a minimum of obligations for the Godfearers so they could be saved with the Jews who were required to strictly keep to the whole Law of Moses. It has been established that Jews in antiquity were not active proselytizers and Judaism neither wished nor required that all gentile Godfearers should become full converts.[29] The biblical basis for the Noachide laws was found in the commandments given to Noah before the flood. In the rabbinic writings, an early listing of these laws is found in an anonymous tradition which probably stems from the mid-second century CE. It comprises one requirement and six prohibitions:

> Seven commandments were given to the children of Noah: regarding the establishment of courts of justice, idolatry, blasphemy, fornication, bloodshed, theft (and the torn limb)... (tAvoda Zara 8:4).[30]

The Noachide laws are often mentioned in the rabbinic writings and the prevailing opinion limited them to these seven. It is noteworthy, however, that the number and content of the indispensable laws for gentiles was never determined in a conclusive way and variations are discussed in many different contexts of rabbinic

---

Horst, 'Gottesfürchtige'. For a recent study about the specific terminologies, see Wander, *Gottesfürchtige und Sympathisanten*, 228-34.

[28] Face b (Col. II), lines 34-60, of this inscription records the names of fifty-two θεοσεβεῖς while on face a (Col. I), lines 19-20, two additional ones are named; cf. Reynolds-Tannenbaum, *Jews and Godfearers at Aphrodisias*, 6.11-12 and 5.9, respectively. For their discussion about sources and modern studies concerning the subject of Godfearers, cf. pp. 48-66 and pp. 72-77, notes 167-289. See also Van der Horst, 'Jews and Christians in Aphrodisias', 109-110. For this and other evidence supporting the existence of Godfearers, see also Levinskaya, *The Book of Acts*, 51-82.

[29] See the discussion of the epigraphic evidence and of the sources in gentile, Jewish, and Christian literature in Levinskaya, *The Book of Acts*, 19-49. Further see Goodman, 'Jewish Proselytizing in the First Century'; Id., *Mission and Conversion*; Cohen, 'Was Judaism in Antiquity a Missionary Religion'; McKnight, *A Light among the Gentiles*, 30-48; Will-Orrieux, *Prosélytisme juif?*; Kraabel, 'Immigrants, Exiles'; Riesner, 'A Pre-Christian Jewish Mission?'.
This is not to say, however, that individual Jews could not make efforts to spread Judaism; cf. Paget, 'Jewish Proselytism', 101. Moreover, it is of importance to distinguish between an "informative, educational, apologetic, proselyting mission" (Goodman, *Mission and Conversion*, 5). Only the latter type tends towards a systematic proselytizing of the later Christian type.

[30] Cf. Zuckermandel, *Tosephta*, 473. These are also listed in a different order in a Baraita in bSan 56b. For other Tannaitic versions, see e.g. SifDeut 343 (= Finkelstein, *Siphre ad Deuteronomium*, 396) and Mekh *Bahodesh, Yitro* 5 (= Horovitz-Rabin, *Mechilta d'Rabbi Ismael*, 221).

literature.[31] On the other hand, the Sages do not debate the concept of such a code in itself. The principle that gentiles could be righteous without conversion might thus have been generally accepted by the Sages in the Tannaitic period.

Early material evidence for the idea that God had given certain pre-Sinaitic laws to all mankind is found in Jub. 7:20-21a (second century BCE):

> And in the twenty-eighth jubilee Noah began to command his grandsons with ordinances and commandments and all of the judgments which he knew. And he bore witness to his sons so that they might do justice and cover the shame of their flesh and bless the one who created them and honour father and mother, and each one love his neighbour and preserve themselves from fornication and pollution and from all injustice. For on account of these three the flood came upon the earth.[32]

This is the earliest extant text which links the figure of Noah to a universal ethic that is obligatory for the children of Noah. It is only fair to say, however, that the Noachide commandments are included here for a negative reason, namely to guarantee that the gentiles would not keep these laws and, consequently, were not capable of righteousness. This position, which, of course, is typical of the strongly separatistic Book of Jubilees, is found within the mainstream of rabbinic Judaism as well.[33] Nevertheless, in non-sectarian communities, more lenient views are also expressed, which tend to allow that some gentiles conform to a minimum level of morality and might be considered righteous.

There is a rabbinic tradition which holds that a Noachide is executed for three of the Noachide laws: blasphemy or idolatry, bloodshed, and fornication.[34] These crimes are considered to be the three primary sins of the gentiles and it is important to establish that this triad of prohibitions is also included in the extant seven Noachide laws. The particular listing of these three offences עבודה זרה גילוי, עריות, שפיכות דמים is often found in rabbinic literature. In tShab 16:17, it is suggested that the Sabbath may be discarded in order to save life, with the exclusion of three particular cases:

> There is nothing that stands before the duty of saving life except three things: idolatry, fornication, and bloodshed.[35]

Another example reads thus:

> When Rabin came he said in the name of R. Yohanan, 'With all things it is permitted to cure oneself except by means of idolatry, and fornication and the shedding of blood' (bPes 25a).

---

[31] Cf. Bockmuehl, 'The Noachide Commandments', 89 and Flusser-Safrai, 'Das Aposteldekret', 187-191.

[32] ET: Wintermute, 'Jubilees', 35-142; esp. 69-70.

[33] See below, pp. 267-68.

[34] bSan 57a (idolatry is added here by R. Sheshet); cf. Bockmuehl, 'The Noachide Commandments', 90, n. 62.

[35] Cf. Lieberman, *Tosefta ki-Fshutah* – Moed, 75 and Zuckermandel, *Tosephta*, 134. This saying is repeated in bKet 19a and bYom 82a.

These prohibitions were also current as a threefold formula of capital sins:

> When Rabban Shimon ben Gamliel and Rabbi Yishmael were taken off to be slain, Rabbi Shimon ben Gamliel kept turning the matter over in his mind, saying: 'Woe unto us that we are being slain like Sabbath breakers, like idol worshipers, like the fornicators, and like bloodshedders!'[36]

A further instance:

> As to Jerusalem's first building, on what account was it destroyed? Because of idolatry and fornication and bloodshed which was in it.[37]

As a last example, we quote the following statement:

> For these things they punish a man in this world while the (eternal) punishment is laid aside for the world to come: for idolatry and for fornication and for murder and for gossip which is worse than all of them.[38]

In this light, the following rabbinic decision is particularly important. During the Hadrianic persecution (ca. 135 CE), the rabbis defined at Lydda a minimum of three indispensable laws which no Jew can violate even if his life were at stake:

> R. Yohanan said in the name of R. Shimon ben Yehotsadak: By a majority vote, it was resolved in the upper room of the house of Nitza in Lydda that in every [other] law of the Tora, if a man is commanded: 'Transgress and suffer not death' he may transgress and not suffer death, – except for idolatry, fornication and bloodshed.[39]

Under extreme duress, the Mosaic Law could be ignored, with the exception of the prohibitions of idolatry, fornication, and murder. These three "fundamental laws" apparently were taken to be the heart of Jewish ethics in that they succinctly express what Judaism condemns strongly and always shuns. No reference is made to the special provisions of the Jewish Tora, such as circumcision, food laws, or the observance of Sabbath and festivals. Although these regulations were not denied as dispensable, they are not regarded here as the most important dimension

---

[36] ARN a 38; cf. b 41 (= Schechter, *Aboth de Rabbi Nathan*, 57b).

[37] tMen 13:22 (= Zuckermandel, *Tosephta*, 533-34). Cf. bYom 9b: "On what account was the first temple destroyed? On account of three things in it: idolatry, fornication and bloodshed;" cf also yYom 1,38c. See also mAv 5:9: "Exile comes upon the world because of idolatry (על עובדי עבודה זרה) and fornication (ועל גלוי עריות) and bloodshed (ועל שפיכה דמים); and because of (neglect of the year of) the release of the land."

[38] tPea 1:2 (= Zuckermandel, *Tosephta*, 18); cf. bAr 15b. For additional instances, see e.g. bShevu 7b; ARN a 40 (= Schechter, *Aboth de Rabbi Nathan*, 60b); yBM 5,10d (cf. tBM 6:17 = Zuckermandel, *Tosephta*, 384-85); yHag 1,76c; SifDeut 254 (= Finkelstein, *Siphre ad Deuteronomium*, 280); Mekh *Bahodesh, Yitro* 9 (= Horovitz-Rabin, *Mechilta d'Rabbi Ismael*, 238). For a survey of some of these and other places, cf. Hunkin, 'The Prohibitions of the Council', 273-77; Dietrich, 'Die "Religion Noahs"', 305; Sjöberg, *Gott und die Sünder*, 65, n. 2 and particularly Strothotte, *Das Apostelkonzil*, 10-62. For the same triad of sins, cf. also TgNeof Gen 24:31 (Marg); TgPs-Yon Gen 28:20 and Deut 23:10.

[39] bSan 74a; the same occasion is referred to in ySan 3,21b; SifDeut 41 (= Finkelstein, *Siphre ad Deuteronomium*, 85); bKid 40b; see also Str-B 1, 221-224; Dalman, *Die Worte Jesu* 1, 306-07; Müller, *Tora für die Völker*, 51-59.

of Jewish practice. The definition of what is essential for Jews necessarily intimates what is essential for the gentiles. The universality of the three laws is reflected in two separate haggadic treatments of the misconduct of Ismael and Esau, both pre-Sinaitic Noachides, who are condemned for having violated these principal prohibitions. The same judgment is passed on the inhabitants of Sodom, who were non-Jews as well.[40]

Interestingly, the early church came to apply the same list of offences for its own discipline. After baptism, which was believed to absolve all sins that had been committed before it was administrated, the Christians were supposed not to lapse into immoral acts again. On account of the vows and the rejection of sin performed during the baptismal ritual, a radical refrainment from evil was required. However, practical experience was different and the question arose whether some post-baptismal offences were not too grave to be remitted by the church. In sources dating from circa 200 CE, the above triadic list reemerges, enumerating the offences which were regarded as unforgivable: apostasy, fornication, and bloodshed. This catalogue, at least since Tertullian, Hippolytus of Rome, and Origen,[41] was known in the early church, and has played an important part in the evolution of the penitential discipline in the church.[42] Tertullian distinguishes *peccata remissibilia* and *irremissibilia*. In his opinion, it is not the church but only the almighty God Himself who has the power to forgive the last group of the three

---

[40] GenR 63,12 (= Theodor-Albeck, *Midrash Bereshit Rabba* 2, 694-95); SifDeut 31(= Finkelstein, *Siphre ad Deuteronomium*, 50) and bBB 16b; for Yishmael, cf. tSot 6:6 (= Lieberman, *Tosefta ki-Fshutah* – Nashim, 184-86 and Zuckermandel, *Tosephta*, 304); for Sodom, cf. tSan 13:8 (= Zuckerman-del, *Tosephta*, 435).

[41] Maybe Irenaeus should be included in this list. Against the doctrine of heretics he declares that the unjust, idolators, and fornicators would be thrown in the everlasting fire: "Et quemadmodum ibi injusti et idolatres et fornicatores vitam perdiderunt, sic et hic, et Domino quidem praedicante in ignem aeternum mitti tales ...;" cf. *Adversus Haereses* IV, 27, 4; Rousseau, *Irénée de Lyon*, 748, lines 159-62.

[42] Cf. Karpp, *Die Busse*, IX-XXIX; esp. XIV-XV.XVII.XXVIII-XXIX.

Also in the fourth and fifth century CE this triad is explicitly attested to:

- Pacian of Barcelona in his *Paraenesis ad Poenitentiam* 4 refers to the three items of the Decree in Acts 15:29 and continues: "Haec est novi Testamenti tota conclusio. ... Reliqua peccata meliorum operum compensatione curantur: haec vero tria crimina, ..., metuenda sunt.... Quid vero faciet contemptor Dei? Quid aget sanguinarius? Quid remedium capiet fornicator? ... Ista sunt capitalia, fratres; ista mortalia." (*PL* 13, 1083-84).

- Pope Leo I writes to Rusticus, bishop of Narbonne, that those who have partaken of gentile banquets can be purged by fasting and the laying on of hands. But he mentions three cases in which they must not be admitted to communion except through public penance: "Si autem aut idola adoraverunt, aut homicidiis vel fornicationibus contaminati sunt... ." (*Epistola* 167, ad Rusticum; Inquis. 19 in *PL* 54, 1209).

- A note in Augustine provides documentation of a wider knowledge of this triad of cardinal sins. In his *De Scriptura Sacra Speculum* 29 (*PL* 34, 994) he writes that "nonnulli putant tria tantum crimina esse mortifera, idololatriam, et homicidium, et fornicationem." (*PL* 34, 994). Similar information is found in his *De Fide et Operibus* 19,34. He states that there are people who think that all sins are easily compensated by charity except for three: "... tria tamen mortifera esse non dubitant et excommunicationibus punienda, donec poenitentia humiliore sanentur, impudicitiam, idololatriam, homicidium." (*PL* 40, 220 and Madec-Pegon, *Oeuvres de Saint Augustin* 8, 431).

capital sins: idololatria, moechia / fornicatio, and homicidium.[43] Hippolytus mentions the three deadly offences in a fragment of his commentary on Proverbs 30:15.[44] Origen, finally, refers to the officiating priests in the Jerusalem temple (the "priests in the Law") who did not sacrifice burnt-offerings and sin-offerings to gain forgiveness for the transgressions of "adultery, deliberate murder, or any other graver fault." Some lines further down in his discussion he wonders why some people boast that they are able to forgive "even idolatry and to pardon adultery and fornication, supposing that the prayer they say for those who have ventured these crimes were even to wipe out mortal sin."[45] As a matter of fact, the connection between the traditional deadly sins of fornication, apostasy, and bloodshed, and the triadic list in rabbinic literature has been noted before.[46] It is possible that Christians were particularly strict in the observance of these rules because they were aware that, from a Jewish halakhic viewpoint, these rigorous standards guaranteed that a large section of the church would be saved as gentiles. Be that as it may, at the Synod of Elvira in ca. 306 CE,[47] it was decided that a number of severe sins (among which the above triad is mentioned separately), if indulged in

---

[43] "'Visum est', inquiunt, 'Spiritui sancto et nobis nullum amplius uobis adicere pondus quam eorum a quibus necesse est abstineri, a sacrificiis et a fornicationibus et sanguine. A quibus observando recte agetis uetante uos Spiritu sancto.'" After this quotation from Acts 15:28-29 (D) he continues as follows: "Sufficit et hic seruatum esse moechiae et fornicationi locum honoris sui inter idololatriam et homicidium ... Lucrati sumus multa, ut aliqua praestemus. Compensatio autem reuocabilis non est, nisi denique reuocabitur iteratione moechiae utique et sanguinis et idololatriae;" De Pudicitia 12,4-5 and 8, respectively. Cf. Micaelli-Munier, Tertullien, La Pudicité (De pudicitia) 1, 204. See also Goldhahn-Müller, Die Grenze der Gemeinde, 374-78; Quasten, Patrology 2, 312-25; Altaner-Stuiber, Patrologie, 162-63.

[44] Τῇ Βδέλλῃ· τῇ ἁμαρτίᾳ· θυγατέρες· πορνεία, φόνος, εἰδωλολατρεία. Καὶ οὐκ ἐνεπίμπλασαν αὐτήν, οὐ γὰρ πίμπλαται αὕτη ἀεὶ διὰ τούτων τῶν πράξεων, νεκροῦσα ἡ ἁμαρτία τὸν ἄνθρωπον μηδέποτε ἠλλοιωμένη, ἀλλὰ πάντοτε ἐπαύξουσα...; In Prouerbia Fragmentum XXI. See also Hippolytus' controversy with Pope Callistus over the remission of sins when he charges the latter with teaching and inculcating adultery and murder: Ὁρᾶτε εἰς ὅσην ἀσέβειαν ἐχώρησεν ὁ ἄνομος μοιχείαν καὶ φόνον ἐν τῷ αὐτῷ διδάσκων; Refutatio omnium haeresium IX, 12, 25; cf. Karpp, Die Busse, nr. 140 (p. 224) and 124, lines 32-33 (p. 160), respectively. See also Altaner-Stuiber, Patrologie, 169.

[45] Οἱ κατὰ νόμον ἱερεῖς κωλύονται περί τινων προσφέρειν ἁμαρτημάτων θυσίαν, ἵνα ἀφεθῇ τοῖς περὶ ὧν αἱ θυσίαι τὰ πλημμελήματα. Καὶ οὐ δή που τὴν περί τινων ἐξουσίαν ὁ ἱερεὺς ἀκουσίων ἢ πλημμελημάτων ἀναφορὰν ἔχων ἤδη καὶ περὶ μοιχείας ἢ ἑκουσίου φόνου ἤ τινος ἄλλου χαλεπωτέρου πταίσματος προσφέρει ὁλοκαύτωμα καὶ περὶ ἁμαρτίας. ... Οὐκ οἶδ᾽ ὅπως ἑαυτοῖς τινες ... αὐχοῦσιν ὡς δυνάμενοι καὶ εἰδωλολατρείας συγχωρεῖν μοιχείας τε καὶ πορνείας ἀφιέναι, ὡς διὰ τῆς εὐχῆς αὐτῶν περὶ τῶν ταῦτα τετολμηκότων λυομένης καὶ τῆς πρὸς θάνατον ἁμαρτίας· ...; De Oratione XXVIII, 9 and 10; cf. Karpp, Die Busse, nr. 143, lines 19-24 and 35-39 (p. 228), respectively.

[46] By Frend, Martyrdom and Persecution, 56-57 and 374. See also Flusser-Safrai, 'Das Aposteldekret', 180.

[47] For this date, cf. Orlandis and Ramos-Lisson, Die Synoden, 6.

after the rite of Baptism was administered, was to exclude the sinner from the church once and for all.[48]

So far, we have seen that a short catalogue of commandments for Noah's descendants existed as early as the second century BCE (Jub. 7:20-21a), whereas the versions of the seven (rabbinic) Noachide laws and the three pre-rabbinic Noachide principles are not attested before the second century CE. The question, then, that arises is what specific Noachide laws were in force in first-century Judaism? In the above quotation from Jub. 7:20-21a, the laws applying to the Noachides is limited to fornication, pollution, and injustice. Because here and elsewhere in the Book of Jubilees (20:5-6; 23:14.17) the number of sins causing the flood amounts to three, this triadic listing may have been the usual form of the Noachide laws from the outset.[49] With respect to the distinct items of the pre-rabbinic catalogue, the version of the three cardinal sins as reported in rabbinic sources (idolatry, fornication and bloodshed) is particularly relevant. This brief list, representing a triadic cluster of sins as well, is amazingly constant, in spite of the different situation in which it is used. The same catalogue is found in many instances in rabbinic literature referring to capital sins. Moreover, it is part of the extant seven Noachide laws. It is further recorded as the rabbinic decision in Lydda and, in addition, it is taken to apply to all mankind in some Jewish sources. Finally, it is precisely this short list of offences that was adopted by the early church – which was predominantly composed of gentile members – as the triad of mortal sins. If all these data are considered in combination, it becomes clear that this threefold prohibition must have been widely known in ancient times. Because this enumeration of "idolatry, fornication and bloodshed" appears to have been a fixed formula as early as in the second century, we should probably not go far wrong in supposing that this triad may well reflect an earlier Jewish tradition.

---

[48] The first of the 81 canons of the Synod strongly opposes idolatry which obviously was held to be the most grievous sin. Christians having committed this "crimen capitale" remained excluded from communion with the church until death. The second canon demands that priests, who were in special service of the Roman and imperial cult (the so-called "flamines") but had adopted Christian faith, were to be excommunicated until death when, in addition to idolatry, they also committed homicide and adultery: "Flamines, qui post fidem lavacri et regenerationis sacrificaverunt, eo quod geminaverint scelera accedente homicidio vel triplicaverint facinus cohaerente moechia, placuit nec in finem accipere communionem;" cf., also for a commentary on the separate canons, Reichert, *Die Canones der Synode*, 75-83; see also Orlandis and Ramos-Lisson, *Die Synoden*, 9-14. For a more general outline, see Poschmann, 'Busse', 807-08.

[49] See also the Damascus Document (CD 4:13-19), a writing which originated in a milieu which was closely related to the Qumran community. In 4:17-18 the text mentions "three kinds of righteousness," that is, what evildoers considered to be the right way of life: "the first is fornication, the second property, the third defiling the sanctuary" (For the translation and explanation, cf. Kosmala, 'The three Nets of Belial', 92 and 95; see also Wacholder, *The Dawn of Qumran*, 119-24). At first sight this example of three basic sins occurring in the Sectarian document seems to be of a quite different type than the above short list recorded in rabbinic literature. Upon closer consideration, however, these succinct catalogues are more akin than the formulation of their distinct items demonstrates; cf. Sahlin, 'Die drei Kardinalsünden', 93-95; see also Flusser-Safrai, 'Das Aposteldekret', 183.

The main point of the present discussion, however, is that the same ethical principles are applied to the gentiles in the Western version of the Apostolic Decree which refers to idolatry, the shedding of blood, and fornication. In the light of the above evidence, the Western text appears to render the current version of the pre-rabbinic Noachide laws in the first century CE.[50] In fact, there was nothing new in laying down such rules as the basic moral code for gentile believers. The Decree is thoroughly traditional in prescribing for Christian gentiles the code of conduct which non-Christian Judaism prescribed for non-Christian gentiles.[51]

Although the case for the originality of the Western text seems very strong, our discussion has left some serious problems unresolved. For one thing, there is the question of the fourfold prohibition in the Eastern version. Furthermore, the items in other first-century sources echoing the apostolic decision (Rev 2:14.20; Did 6:3) also show an obvious dissimilarity, compared with the three-clause version of the Western Decree. How can these differences be accounted for? Because the latter problem will come up for discussion in the next section, we will limit ourselves now to the first issue. If the Western text derives from an earlier Jewish form of the Noachide laws, we have to assume that, at some stage, πνικτόν (strangled meat) was added to the original threefold decree. However, this injunction, instead of reflecting a strictly Christian concern, is closely related to Jewish tradition as well. The regulation appears to be connected with the biblical commandments about נבלה (an animal which dies of itself) and טרפה (an animal torn by beasts) in Lev 17:15 (cf. Deut 12:16.23), and the meaning of these two terms is extended and developed in rabbinic Law. The biblical injunctions regarding נבלה and טרפה, for their part, are based on the ancient prohibition in Gen 9:4 which is addressed to Noah, the patriarch of the gentiles: "Only you shall not eat flesh with its life, that is, its blood" (cf. Lev 17:14). Consequently, if an animal was not killed by pouring out its blood (such as in cases of נבלה and טרפה) it would "choke" because in that situation the life seated in the blood remains in the body.[52] If the πνικτόν item was

---

[50] Cf. Guttmann, *Das Judentum und seine Umwelt*, 118; Alon, 'Ha-halakha ba-Torat 12 ha-Shelihim', 277-78 (ET:165-94).

[51] It has been noted above that this threefold prohibition came also to be used in the early church. It is even possible that the Western text of the Decree stands behind the list of sins mentioned in Rev 22:15 where it says: "Outside are the dogs and sorcerers and fornicators and murderers and idolaters, and every one who loves and practises falsehood" (cf. 21:8). The "dogs" probably refers to the apostates and false teachers. The text suggest the disciplinary measure of excluding false teachers and those who commit the most grievous sins (the sorcerers, fornicators, murderers and idolaters) from the rites (esp. the Eucharist) of the church; cf. Kraft, *Die Offenbarung des Johannes*, 279-80. See also Müller, *Tora für die Völker*, 192-93. A section in the comment of O. Böcher is especially relevant here: "Auch an anderer Stelle verrät die Apokalypse Bekanntschaft mit dem Aposteldekret oder einer inhaltlichen gleichlauten-den Vorschrift: in drei kurzen Lasterkatalogen (Apk 9,20f; 21,8; 22,15). Nach Abzug sekundärer Erweiterungen (Diebstahl, Feigheit, Treulosigkeit) und Rubrizierungen (Lügner, Befleckte, Hunde) bleibt als Grundbestand die Tetras Götzendienst, Mord, Zauberei und Unzucht. Da Zauberei nach altjüdischer Vorstellung zum Götzendienst gehört, während das Verbot ungeschächteten Fleisches fehlt, ist an die "westliche" Variante des Aposteldekrets zu denken;" cf. 'Das sogenannte Aposteldekret', 334 (and 329).

[52] Cf. Bietenhard, 'πνίγω κτλ.', 455; see also Str-B 2, 730.

included in the authentic form of the Decree, the prohibition of αἷμα (blood) too may have been understood differently from the outset. In line with the commandment of the strangled meat, the αἷμα item would refer to the consumption of blood, rather than to homicide. This prohibition is also frequently found in Jewish sources.[53]

The above evidence supports the view that the prescriptions in the Eastern text of the Decree depend on biblical sources which have been preserved and developed through rabbinic traditions. In consequence, the existence of Jewish materials paralleling the prohibitions of both the Western and Eastern text would seem to suggest that either version might represent the original text of the Decree. Yet, we are probably not wrong to decide in favour of the Western text. The triad of items, reminiscent of the recurring principal prohibitions and cardinal sins in Jewish and Christian sources, provide sufficient indication to assume the priority of the Western form. It is likely that this three-clause tradition was widely diffused in Judaism of the pre-rabbinic period and probably also represents the established practice in Jerusalem, the center of halakhic Judaism. If the apostles and elders in Jerusalem hoped to preserve continuity with Judaism – which is without any doubt correct – it is only logical to suppose that the Apostolic church accepted the view of the Synagogue in this matter. Peter and James were observant Jews themselves, who by promulgating the laws incumbent on the children of Noah proved themselves to be loyal to the prevailing conventions. A sudden innovation of customary ideas with regard to the acceptance of gentile Godfearers would be rather difficult to explain. On the basis of these observations, then, we reach a different assessment of the fourfold Decree as represented by the Eastern version of Acts. This text may very well reflect a variant form of pre-rabbinic Noachide injunctions which might have been current elsewhere. It is perfectly understandable that the basic tradition of the Decree, reflected in the Western text, came to be expanded by the addition of πνικτόν, under the influence of prevailing local Jewish practice.

One problem has been left aside so far. It must be admitted that the term εἰδωλόθυτον (or the plural εἰδωλόθυτα) is not a real synonym for the sin of εἰδωλολατρεία (idolatry) that is referred to in the Noachide formulation for gentile conduct. The term occurs in both the Eastern and Western text of the Decree and in all instances within early Christian writings referring to the Decree (Rev 2:14.20; Acts 15:29; 21:25; Did 6:3). Furthermore, the expression is discussed at some length by Paul (1 Cor 8:1.4.7.10; 10:19). We will return to this problem later. Suffice it to note at this stage that the term points to an offence within the realm of the practically unforgivable sin of idolatry.

---

[53] Cf. Jub. 6:7.12ff.; 1 Enoch 98:11; 7:5; Josephus, *Ant.* 3, 260; for the rabbinic references, cf. Str-B 2, 734-738; for this commandment as a Noachide law, cf. Jub. 7:28-32; tAZ 8:4-8 (= Zuckermandel, *Tosephta*, 473-74).

254

THE FORMS OF THE APOSTOLIC DECREE IN REV 2:24.20 AND DID 6:2-3

It has been pointed out above that Did 6:2-3 and Rev 2:14.20 probably echo the Decree which was promulgated by the apostles and elders in Jerusalem. We are, however, faced with the problem that the lists of commandments in Revelation and the Didache vary in number. Whereas the Lukan version in Acts mentions three requirements (or even four in the Eastern text), Revelation forbids only two things while Did 6:2-3 merely shows one single concern. How do we account for these dissimilarities? Our investigation begins with the book of Revelation. In Rev 2:14 and 20, the consumption of εἰδωλόθυτα is found in a recurrent juxtaposition with fornication (πορνεῦσαι).

With regard to the conjunction of fornication or unchastity (πορνεία) with idol food (εἰδωλόθυτα), a particularly significant section is found in the Baal-Peor episode of Num 25:1-18. The narrative is a sequel to the Balaam oracles in the preceding chapters and begins by recounting how Israel sexually abused Moabite women and ate from their idol food:

> While Israel dwelt in Shittim the people began to play the harlot (לִזְנוֹת / ἐκπορνεῦσαι) with the daughters of Moab. These invited the people to the sacrifices of their gods, and the people ate (וַתִּקְרֶאןָ לָעָם לְזִבְחֵי אֱלֹהֵיהֶן וַיֹּאכַל הָעָם / καὶ ἐκάλεσαν αὐτοὺς ἐπὶ ταῖς θυσίαις τῶν εἰδώλων αὐτῶν, καὶ ἔφαγεν ὁ λαὸς τῶν θυσιῶν αὐτῶν), and bowed down to their gods. So Israel yoked himself to Baal of Peor. And the anger of the Lord was kindled against Israel (Num 25:1-3).

The story next mentions how the Lord orders Moses to hang Israel's leaders. The subsequent scene (vv. 6-15), loosely connected with the previous one, focusses on a Midianite woman who is brought by an Israelite man to his family in the camp quite openly. This ostentatious show incites Phinehas to kill both the Israelite and the Midianite and this action causes the wrath of the Lord to stop the plague by which twenty-four thousand people had already been killed. As a reward for Phinehas' initiative, God grants him and his descendants an everlasting priesthood and the Midianites are punished for their seductive cheat. The story shows that sexual relations with non-Israelite women lure men into pagan cults (Hos 9:10). Illicit sexuality or unchastity leads to idolatry. The experience in Shittim is at the background of the text in Ps 106:28-31, a passage which presently will be of interest to our examination.[54]

According to Num 31:16, it is Balaam who is to blame for the apostasy in Shittim and, although the account in Num 25:1-16 does not say a word about such a counsel of Balaam, his supposed responsibility has been considerably expanded in later Jewish traditions as recorded in Philo, Josephus, and rabbinic passages. The theme has developed here in a cautionary legend mentioning how Balaam advised Balak how Israel was to be seduced in order to make it commit idolatry and

[54] See below, pp. 262-63. The account of Num 25 is also referred to in Deut 3:29-4:4 where it serves as a proof of the assertion that obedience to the Law brings life with it.

apostate.[55] The activity of Balaam is also briefly mentioned in 2 Pet 2:15-16 and Jude 11.[56] In 1 Cor 10:8, the punishment of the twenty-four thousand (here: twenty-three thousand) in the Baal-Peor account is used in the warning against fornication (πορνεία). A text which is very close to that in Num 31:16 and recalls the above mentioned Jewish interpretation of the role of Balaam with regard to the apostasy in Shittim is found in Rev 2:14. The passage, moreover, not only exemplifies the direct connection between fornication and idolatry in general but, like the instance in Num 25:1-2, also in particular between fornication and the eating of idol food (εἰδωλόθυτα). In the letter to Pergamum (Rev 2:12-17), condemnation is pronounced on those

> who hold the teaching of Balaam, who taught Balak to put a stumbling block before the sons of Israel, that they might eat food sacrificed to idols and practise fornication (φαγεῖν εἰδωλόθυτα καὶ πορνεῦσαι) (Rev 2:14).

The charges in the letter to Thyatira (Rev 2:18-29) closely resemble the accusation against the adherents of the teaching of Balaam at Pergamum:

> But I have this against you, that you tolerate the woman Jezebel, who calls herself a prophetess and is teaching and beguiling my servants to practise fornication and to eat food sacrificed to idols (πορνεῦσαι και φαγεῖν εἰδωλόθυτα) (Rev 2:20).

Both letters clearly manifest a concern with idolatry and because the accusations against the leaders (Balaam and Jezebel) are substantially alike, they may refer to one and the same movement in Pergamum and Thyatira. They seem to suggest that, within these local churches, a movement of (gnostic) libertine Nicolaitans[57] wished to maintain a peaceful coexistence with paganism. In order to strengthen these relations, so it appears, they were prepared to eat food that was sacrificed to idols (φαγεῖν εἰδωλόθυτα). In the Greco-Roman world, food offered to idols might have included grain, oil, wine, and honey, as well as many sorts of animals.[58] It was offered in sacred rites of a pagan cult and eaten by the priest and worshippers in the sanctuary or taken outside the sanctuary for consumption elsewhere. On many occasions, this food was eaten in private homes by hosts and guests. However, hallowed food did not always presuppose a history of sacred use in sanctuaries. On socially significant occasions (weddings, funerals, birthdays, reunion of friends, etc.) sacrificial rites in honour of a god were performed in private homes before

---

[55] Cf. Philo, *Vita Mosis* I, 294-304; cf. also *Virt.*, 34-42; Josephus, *Ant.* 4, 126-130; Pseudo-Philo, *Antiq. Bibl.*, 18,13; TgPs-Yon (= TgYer) to Num 24:14; Frg.Tg to Num 24:14 (= M.L. Klein, *The Fragment-Targums* 1,105 and 203) and ySan 10,28cd; SifNum 131 to Num 25:1 and 157 to Num 31:8-17 (= Horovitz, *Siphre d'be Rab*, 169-171 and 210-12, respectively); bSan 106a; NumR 20,23 (= Mirkin, *Midrash Rabbah* 10, 272) etc.

See also Van Unnik, 'Josephus' Account'. For a comparison of the various traditions, see Vermes, *Scripture and Tradition*, 127-177; esp. 162-77.

[56] See also Origen, *In Numeros Homilia* 20,1.4; cf. Baehrens, *Origenes Werke*, 132. 185-98.

[57] Cf. Prigent, *L'Apocalypse*, 38.52.57; Charles, *The Revelation of St. John* 1, 64 and see, also for the following, Caird, *The Revelation*, 37-44.

[58] See, also for the following, Gooch, *Dangerous Food*, 15-46.

and during the meals. These shared meals were a central feature in Greco-Roman culture. In the light of these data, it may well be the case that movements within the local communities of Pergamum and Thyatira, fostering the maintenance of social relationship with gentiles, propagated Christian participation in pagan meals, regardless of the fact that sacred food would be served.

The term "to fornicate" (πορνεῦσαι) is perhaps used in a double sense in Rev 2:14, referring literally to illicit sexual activities and figuratively also to idolatry as a form of religious infidelity. The latter meaning is preferable, however, because in Jewish tradition, the word has a long history as a metaphor for participation in idolatrous worship (e.g. Exod 34:15-16; Num 14:33; Jer 3:1-9; Ezek 16:15; Hos 6:10; Mic 1:7; Wis 14:2), and Revelation commonly (with one exception) uses the noun πορνεία and the verb πορνεύω in a figurative sense. The consumption of idol food, then, appears to be the basic accusation. There is even less doubt about its metaphorical significance in the letter to Thyatira. The alleged profetess Jezebel, who according to Rev 2:20 teaches the local Christians harlotry (πορνεῦσαι) and the eating of εἰδωλόθυτα, replaces the figure of Balaam (of Pergamum) here. There is a strong possibility that the name Jezebel was attributed to her in an attempt to undermine her influence in Thyatira. Ahab's wife was also called Jezebel and she was accused of harlotry (2 Kgs 9:22), since she led her husband into idolatry (1 Kgs 16:31; 21:25-26).[59]

This also raises questions with regard to the name of Balaam in the letter to Pergamum because it is unlikely that the Nicolaitans, attacked in Rev 2:12-29, would have claimed to be followers of Balaam, considering his mean role in the Baal-Peor incident. The name takes the reader's mind back to the figure of Balaam in the Baal-Peor event of Num 25 and was probably transferred to the Nicolaitans in Pergamum by the author of Revelation. Like Balaam seduced the Israelites to licentiousness and to the consumption of idol food, so the Nicolaitans enticed the churches by their teaching to be unfaithful to God and to eat idol food. At this point two things in the letters to Pergamum and Thyatira should be considered more closely. The warning against idol food in Rev 2:14.20 (φαγεῖν εἰδωλόθυτα) is not phrased in the wording of Num 25:2 (θυσίας τῶν εἰδώλων) but seems to refer to the Apostolic Decree. Furthermore, as is noted above, the clause in Rev 2:24 ("I do not lay upon you any other burden") echoes the formulation of Acts 15:28 that introduces the particular items of the Decree in the next verse.

It would appear, then, that the charge in Rev 2:14.20 as far as its content is concerned, is linked to the offences mentioned in Num 25:1-2. The choice of the specific wording, on the other hand, is in agreement with the formulation of the requirements of the Decree. The letters of Revelation have deliberately shaped the two capital sins at Shittim into the standardized terms of the Decree. They recall the communities of Pergamum and Thyatira to the relevant precepts of the Decree as the legal warrant for regulating Christian practice. By the time the book of Revelation was written, the commandments which Christianity adopted from Jewish

---

[59] Cf. Caird, *The Revelation*, 39; see also Prigent, *L'Apocalypse*, 57.

Noachide laws for sympathizing gentiles had apparently acquired a position of unchallenged authority in Asia Minor. The Decree served as a distinguishing feature for Christian self-understanding vis-à-vis the gentile world. At the same time, the influence of biblical and Jewish Balaam traditions is clearly noticeable in the curtailed formulation of the Decree, only enumerating the two commandments of εἰδωλόθυτα and πορνεία.

Let us turn now to Did 6:2-3. The agreements with the Apostolic Decree in Acts 15 suggest that this passage is a reflection of some form of the decree as it was known and circulated in early Christian communities. For the present subject, we draw attention to Did 6:3:

> As for food, bear what you can, but be very much on your guard against food offered to idols (τοῦ εἰδωλοθύτου), for it is worship of dead gods (λατρεία γάρ ἐστι θεῶν νεκρῶν) (Did 6:3).

Two things call for comment here. First, the three (or four-) fold prohibition is reduced to the mere item of εἰδωλόθυτον and, secondly, this single prohibition is expanded with the explicative clause "for it is worship of dead gods." To begin with the exclusive mention of εἰδωλόθυτον, the word is an equivalent of the ordinary Greek θεόθυτον or ἱερόθυτον and appears to have a derogatory connotation. It literally means "something offered to idols" and refers to food which has been offered in heathen worship as a sacrifice.[60] The term is rare in secular Greek and has an extremely meager documentation in Hellenistic-Jewish writings. It is found for the first time in 4 Macc 5:2 which indicates that it might have been current in some Hellenistic-Jewish circles. In this verse, which belongs to the account of the martyrdom of Eleazar (chs. 5-7), the king Antiochus commands his spearbearers "to seize every one of the Hebrews and to compel them to taste swine's flesh, and things offered to idols" (καὶ κρέων ὑείων καὶ εἰδωλοθύτων ἀναγκάζειν ἀπογεύεσθαι). The verse indicates that compelling a Jew to eat idol meat amounts to the brutal deed of enforcing apostasy. In some Hellenistic-Jewish circles, the prohibition against idol food apparently served as a rule of conduct which no Jew might transgress even at the risk of his own life. It is difficult, however, to assess the extent to which 4 Maccabees, which may have been written in the mid-first century CE, represents views generally held in Hellenistic Judaism at the time.[61]

---

[60] Büchsel, 'εἰδωλόθυτον'. As it has been noted above, it need not always refer to a meat sacrifice because all sorts of foodstuffs were offered to the gods, including grain, honey, cheese, liquids, etc; cf also Tomson, Paul and the Jewish Law, 189.

[61] The book of 4 Maccabees might have been composed in Antioch in Syria. Because in 5:1 the Seleucid king Antiochus is mentioned to be present at the tortures, the Seleucid capital presumably is the scene of the action (cf. Hadas, The Third and Fourth Books of Maccabees, 109-113 although "this may be only a dramatic convention;" cf. Schürer, The History of the Jewish People 3/1, 590). If Did 6:2-3 equally originated in the region of Syria-Palestine (which we don't know for sure), the passage might reflect contemporary local thought. In that case the understanding of εἰδωλόθυτον as a fundamental Jewish law against pagan cult, like it is reflected in 4 Macc 5:2, might have provided the formative influence for a stricter definition of a minimum code of conduct in Did 6:2-3 than the standard requirements found in the Decree.

It is thus problematic to say definitely when and where the Greek term εἰδωλόθυτον originated. The evidence in 4 Macc 5:2 indicates early Jewish usage. Greek speaking Christians may have adopted the word from Jewish circles although it is fair to say that, aside from the usage in 4 Macc 5:2, there are no additional precedents in Hellenistic-Jewish literature.[62] It is also conceivable that they coined it themselves, in ignorance of the rare Greek uses of it. In any event, because the term is found in the two versions of the Decree in Acts and in texts related to the Decree (Rev 2:14.20; Did 6:3), the Greek word must have become a constituent part of the distinctively Christian code for believing gentiles as early as the middle of the first century.[63] It is not unreasonable, therefore, to assume that the word εἰδωλόθυτον (or its Semitic equivalent) came into existence at the Jerusalem conference. The participants in that meeting changed one of the three pre-rabbinic Noachide laws by altering the traditional ban on idolatry into the specific Jewish prohibition of idol food. They appear to have radicalized the general injunction by extending it to the consumption of any food which was contaminated with idolatry.[64]

The evidence so far allows us to draw some conclusions about the diffusion of the Apostolic Decree. We have noted the numerical variations in the rendering of the Decree. The author of Did 6:2-3 uses the single injunction against idol food (εἰδωλόθυτον) as a criterion to value gentile morality while the composer of Revelation leveled two charges (πορνεῦσαι and φαγεῖν εἰδωλόθυτα) against the communities of Pergamum and Thyatira. On the other hand, the admonitions in Revelation and the Didache share some essential features with the threefold Apostolic Decree in that they firstly include the idol food prohibition and, secondly, preserve some stereotyped wording. It is difficult to admit that so close a parallelism and such a striking verbal analogy is merely fortuitous. As has been indicated above,[65] the differences and similarities in the reproduction of the Decree in the three writings rather suggest that at one time it existed apart from its presence in Acts. The independent tradition retaining the Decree included the list of the three pre-rabbinic Noachide provisions in combination with some sort of reference – in terms of "bearing the yoke" (βαστάσαι τὸν ζυγόν) and the "burden" (βάρος) –

---

[62] The term is also present in (only) one ms. of the Sibylline Oracles: αἷμα δὲ μὴ φαγέειν, εἰδωλοθύτων δ᾽ ἀπέχεσθαι (2,96; cf. Geffcken, *Die Oracula Sibyllina*, 31). This phrase, however, may be borrowed from Ps.-Phoc. 31, where an almost verbally identical clause is found which, in its turn, is generally regarded as an interpolation derived from Acts 15:29 (cf. 21:25; cf. Young, *Theognis, Ps-Pythagoras, Ps-Phocylides*, 100 and Van der Horst, *The Sentences of Pseudo-Phocylides*, 135-36. See also Gauger, *Sibyllinische Weissagungen*, 46-47 and 485.

[63] In the course of history, the εἰδωλόθυτον prohibition continued to enjoy wide acceptance in the in the Eastern and Western church. In its struggle against persisting pagan cults within the Greco-Roman world, the church maintained the abstention from idol food through the fourth and fifth centuries, while those who did not accept this restriction were dismissed as false teachers (cf. Justin, *Dialogue*, 34-35). For a survey, cf. Tomson, *Paul and the Jewish Law*, 180-85 who relies on Böckenhoff, *Das apostolische Speisegesetz*.

[64] Cf. Flusser-Safrai, 'Das Aposteldekret', 181.

[65] See p. 245.

to the incapability of gentiles to carry the burden of the Tora. This basic form undoubtedly has been widely known within Christian communities, although we cannot exclude the possibility that other versions may have been popular in some place or other.[66] The author of Acts incorporated the instruction into his composition, although not without blending it with certain theological ideas of his own. The composer of Did 6:2-3 shaped the fundamental Jewish law against pagan cult, reflecting the historical situation and values of his community, into standard expressions of the widely accepted and recognized Decree so as to provide it with undisputed authority. Finally, the book of Revelation likewise adapted the two offences mentioned in Numbers 25:1-2 to the Decree in order to enforce the warning against idol food.

One additional point needs some further elaboration here. The present study has assumed from the outset that Paul knew the Decree when he composed 1 Cor 8-10. According to the narrative in Acts 15, Paul was a participant in the Jerusalem conference that produced the Decree. It further relates that he was included in the delegation that delivered the letter containing the decision to the churches in Antioch, Syria, and Cilicia (15:22-23). It is not certain, however, whether the report in Acts is sufficient to reconstruct a historically balanced picture, since it conflicts to some extent with the information in Paul's own letters.[67] As a matter of fact, there has been considerable debate whether or not Paul knew of the Decree when he wrote his first letter to the Corinthians.[68] With regard to the latter issue, this much may be said here. It is true that Paul does not explicitly mention the Apostolic decision in the letters which survive, but it is difficult to admit that he did not know some form of the Decree.[69] His exhortations in 1 Corinthians 5-10 deal with two major concerns of the Decree. The topics that come up for discussion in 1 Cor 5-7 are unchastity, marriage, and sexuality, while idol food is the central concern in the subsequent Chapters 8-10. The interconnection between Chapters 5-7 and 8-10 is buttressed by the correspondence between the succinct warnings in 1 Cor 6:18 ("Shun fornication / φεύγετε τὴν πορνείαν"), and 10:14 ("... shun the worship of

---

[66] See, for example, the four-clause listing of the Decree in the Eastern version of Acts.

[67] On the basis of these letters many scholars have, in fact, concluded that Paul could not have been present when the Decree was formulated; see the views mentioned in Hurd, *The Origin of 1 Corinthians*, 255, n. 4; cf. also Nickle, *The Collection*, 54-55, n. 39; Catchpole, 'Paul, James and the Apostolic Decree', 431; J.A. Fischer, 'Das sogenannte Apostelkonzil', 13-15; Achtemeier, 'An Elusive Unity', 20-21 etc.

[68] See the review in Hurd, *The Origin of 1 Corinthians*, 254-59.

[69] Among others the following authors have supported Paul's familiarity with the Decree: Lake, *The Earlier Epistles of St. Paul*, 202; Burkitt, *Christian Beginnings*, 116-29; Knox, *St. Paul*, 234-36, n. 41; 316 and 326, n. 31; Grant, *A Historical Introduction*, 395; Simon, 'The Apostolic Decree', 452-54; Hurd, *The Origin of 1 Corinthians*, 259-260; Meeks, *The Moral World*, 132-33; Flusser, 'Paul's Jewish-Christian Opponents', 80-81; Tomson, *Paul and the Jewish Law*, 270-74; Witherington, 'Not so idle Thoughts', 237-54; Müller, *Tora für die Völker*, 174-86; Wehnert, *Die Reinheit des »christlichen Gottesvolkes«*, 128-43.

idols / φεύγετε ἀπὸ τῆς εἰδωλολατρίας").[70] It is further worthwile to recall that the uncommon term εἰδωλόθυτον /– τα is used in Chapters 8-10 as often as five times (8:1.4.7.10; 10:19). The prohibition of bloodshed, however, is not found in these chapters, presumably because an admonition on this point was not needed with regard to the problems at hand within the Corinthian church. Instead, Paul speaks at length on the issues of sexual misconduct and idol food and appears to have considered these problems in the light of the Decree as two related problems.[71]

Immorality and idol food are so closely connected that the two seem to underlie Paul's argument in 1 Cor 5-10. He explains his position about the Tora in a principle regulating the line of conduct for all churches in 1 Cor 7:17-24:

> Only, let every one lead the life which the Lord has assigned to him, and in which God has called him. This is my rule in all the churches. Was any one at the time of his call already circumcised? Let him not seek to remove the marks of circumcision. Was any one at the time of his call uncircumcised? Let him not seek circumcision. For neither circumcision counts for anything nor uncircumcision, but keeping the commandments of God. Every one should remain in the state in which he was called ... (7:17-20).

Both Jews and gentiles are obliged to obey the commandments of God, that is, for Jews (and Jewish-Christians) to keep the Tora (cf. also 1 Cor 9:19-21; Gal 5:3) and for gentiles that which they were supposed to observe before they became Christians: the three Noachide laws.[72]

The riddle that remains to be solved is the validation of the idol food prohibition in the final clause of Did 6:3: "for it is worship of dead gods." The most appropriate setting for understanding and appreciating this clause is rabbinic Judaism. In rabbinic writings, the clause "sacrifices of the dead" (זבחי מתים) is used as an argument against idol food. Of particular interest are the following

---

[70] For other structural similarities between 1 Cor 6:12-20 and 10:14-22, see Tomson, *Paul and the Jewish Law*, 201. See also Fee, 'Εἰδωλόθυτα Once Again', 186-87.

[71] For the question why Paul, when dealing with immorality and idol food, did not call upon the authority of the Apostolic Decree, see e.g. Hurd, *The Origin of 1 Corinthians*, 262-69 (and, for other views, 254-59).

[72] Flusser, 'Paul's Jewish-Christian Opponents', 81; Tomson, *Paul and the Jewish Law*, 270-73; Bockmuehl, 'The Noachide Commandments', 98-99; Müller, *Tora für die Völker*, 174-86.
In this context, the view of John Toland (1670-1722) might be relevant, although he probably was familiar with the canonical text of Acts (and thus with the four precepts) only. In 1718 (London) he published his *Nazarenus: or Jewish, Gentile, and Mahometan Christianity*. In his view, the original goal of Christianity was a community in which Jewish Christians and gentile Christians were supposed to live together. This was, what he called, "the original plan of Christianity." According to Toland, the Jews, whether they became Christians or not, were forever bound to the Law of Moses, whereas the gentiles, and the Christians of gentile origin, were enjoined to observe the Noachic precepts mentioned in the Apostolic Decree (cf. *Nazarenus*, 43-51; 65); see Flusser, 'John Toland'; Müller, *Tora für die Völker*, 228-31; Palmer, *Ein Freispruch für Paulus*, 73-93.

examples, probably dating from Tannaitic times,[73] the first two of which are found in the Mishna:

> These things that belong to idolaters (= gentiles) are forbidden (for Jews), and it is forbidden to have any benefit from them: wine, or the idolater's vinegar that was at first wine ... Flesh that is going into (a place) for idol worship is permitted, but what comes out is forbidden, for it is as sacrifices to the dead (מפני שהוא כזבחי מתים); the words of R. Akiva (mAZ 2:3; cf. yAZ 2,40b; bAZ 29b. 32b).

Using and trading gentile wine was forbidden because, even without specific proof, the general assumption was that it might have been used for a libation and thus sacrificed to an idol. In fact, all gentile wine was a primary source of impurity because it bore the taint of "dedicated" wine.[74] With respect to meat, the attitude toward the gentiles was less strict. In the above quotation from the Mishna, R. Akiva, who belongs to the more moderate Hillelite tradition, allows meat obtained directly from gentiles to be eaten, even though he too prescribes that the consumption of meat that has been dedicated in the temple is forbidden.

In mAv 3:3 R. Shimon ben Yohai is cited as saying:

> If three have eaten at one table and have not spoken over it words of the Tora, it is as if they had eaten sacrifices of the dead (כאלו אכלו מזבחי מתים), for it is written: 'For all tables are full of vomit and filthiness without (the) Place (מקום)' (Isa 28:8). But if three have eaten at one table and have spoken over it words of the Tora, it is as if they had eaten from the table of the Holy one (שלמקום), blessed be He, for it is written: 'and he said to me, This is the table which is before the Lord (Ezek 41:22).'

The association of "sacrifices of the dead" with idolatry appears from the subsequent quotation from Isa 28:8. Because the noun "place" (מקום) is a frequent designation of God in rabbinic literature (as becomes even clear in the next sentence), the clause "filthiness without place" (צאה בלי מקום) seems to be understood as referring to the impurity of idol food here. On the other hand, the table "they have spoken over words of the Tora" is as a sacrifice that attends to the Lord.

The following two examples concerning the "sacrifices of the dead" condemn eating with gentiles. In order to avoid food tainted by idolatry, the Sages sometimes advise against dining with gentiles altogether. R. Shimon ben Elazar at least appears to propose total abstinence in the company of gentiles:

> R. Shimon ben Elazar says: Israel(ites) outside the land worship idols in purity. Now, how so? If a gentile prepared a banquet in honour of his son and sent for and invited all the Jews in his city – although they eat and drink of their own (food and wine) and their

---

[73] Additional instances are found in yShab 9,11d; ySan 7,25d; yAZ 2,40b; 3,43a; bAZ 8a; 29b; 32b; 42b; 48b; 50a; bHul 13b; 39b; 40a. In places where the expression "sacrifices of the dead" is mentioned within a quotation from Ps 106:28, it comes to be used as a reference to corpse-uncleanness, contracted by being under the same roof with a corpse (Num 19:14). In these cases it is argued that as a dead body communicates defilement in a space which is covered over, so does an idolatrous sacrifice (cf. yShab 9,11d; yAZ 3,43a; bAZ 32b; 48b; 50a; bHul 13b).

[74] For a discussion about laws relating to gentile food, cf. Tomson, *Paul and the Jewish Law*, 151-177; cf. also Segal, *Paul the Convert*, 231-33 and Novak, *The Image of the Non-Jew*, 108-117.

own servant stands by and pours for them – Scripture accounts it to them as if they had eaten of the sacrifices of the dead (כאלו אכלו מזבחי מתים), as it is said '(lest you make a covenant with the inhabitants of the land, and when they play the harlot after their gods and sacrifice to their gods) and one invites you, you eat of his sacrifice (Exod 34:15).'[75]

A similar view is expressed by an anonymous tradition:

> ... Thus they said: anyone who eats with a gentile at table, worships idols and eats sacrifices of the dead (ואוכל זבחי מתים).[76]

Gentile meats and wine were deemed impure since they were "sacrifices of the dead" and proper Jewish behaviour, according to the latter two traditions, necessitates total refrainment from gentile tables.

For the Tannaitic Sages, the expression "sacrifices of the dead" was obviously a standard reason to reject food sacrificed to idols. The latter instance shows that the association is so close that sometimes the phrase itself is used to indicate idol food (cf. also ySan 7,25d and bAZ 42b). Against this background, it is something of a surprise to discover a similar argument in the final clause of Did 6:3: "for it is worship of dead gods," the more so since idol food is a prominent issue here. In order to reveal the nature of the expression "for it is worship of dead gods," we have to ask first how the rabbinic saying "sacrifices of the dead" (זבחי מתים) may be understood. The wording is found for the first time in Psalm 106, which probably stems from exilic or from post-exilic times.[77] Verses 28-31 of this psalm are relevant to our subject. They comment upon the Baal-Peor episode in Num 25, mentioned above, and comprise the following issues: the consumption of pagan sacrifices (28), the plague as a punishment of the Lord (29), its termination through the intervention of Phinehas (30), and his reward (31). Particularly instructive for our investigation, however, is the verse which refers to Num 25:1-3a:

> Then they attached themselves (ויצמדו) to the Baal of Peor and ate sacrifices of the dead (זבחי מתים/ θυσίας νεκρῶν) (Ps 106:28)

The similarity between the first phrase of Ps 106:28 with Num 25:3a.5 is easily noticed since Israel is said to have attached itself to Baal-Peor. The affinity between the two texts becomes even more obvious when we establish that the verb "to bind (or yoke) oneself" (צמד) appears only twice in the Hebrew Bible: here and in Num 25:3.5. There are, however, also significant deviations from the text of Num 25: the sin of adultery (Num 25:1) is not mentioned here and the "sacrifices of their gods" (זבחי אלהיהן in Num 25:2) have become "sacrifices of the

---

[75] ARN a 26 (= Schechter, *Aboth de Rabbi Nathan*, 41b); see also bAZ 8a and tAZ 4:6 (although the typical phrase "sacrifices of the dead" is missing here). For a discussion about this and the following saying, see especially Tomson, *Paul and the Jewish Law*, 233-35.

[76] SER 9 (8) (= Friedmann, *Pseudo-Seder Eliahu zuta*, 48).

[77] Cf. Kraus, *Psalmen*, 728: "B. Duhm vermutet mit Recht, dass unser Psalm in den in Sach 7 und 8 erwähnten Klagefeiern der exilischen oder nachexilischen Gemeinde seinen "Sitz" gehabt haben könnte;" L.C. Allen, *Psalms 101-150*, 52: "Probably the origin of the psalm is to be set in the exilic period ...."

dead" (זבחי מתים). Our present concern is with the latter deviation. In Num 25:1-3a, the people are said to apostate by committing sexual immorality and eating idol food. In describing the cult of Baal-Peor as the eating of sacrifices for the dead, Ps 106:28 applies an expression to these offences which first of all reflects contemporary practice of funeral ceremonies. At the time when this psalm verse was created, the idiom "sacrifices of the dead" probably referred to funeral banquets which were held in both mourning and exuberant festivity for the dead. These funeral cults, involving ritual eating, drinking, music, song, and sexual activities, were in fashion in the ancient world from early times onward.[78] By equating זבחי אלהיהן (the sacrifices of their gods) with זבחי מתים (the sacrifices of the dead), the sin in the Baal-Peor episode is taken to be ancestor worship and the deification of the dead.[79]

Another early text presenting the sacrifices for the dead is found in Jub. 22:17a. The readers are enjoined here not to eat with gentiles:

(16. Separate yourself from the gentiles. And do not eat with them, and do not perform deeds like theirs. And do not become associates of theirs. Because their deeds are defiled, and all of their ways are contaminated, and despicable, and abominable.) 17. They slaughter their sacrifices to the dead, and to demons they bow down, and they eat in tombs ...

The expression "sacrifices to the dead" indicates that the author has drawn upon Ps 106:28, while the connection with the eating in tombs obviously refers to mortuary meals, held on the graves of the dead. Because the clause "and to demons they bow down" probably echoes the phrase "and (they) bowed down to their gods" in Num 25:2, the reference in the Jubilee text presumably attests to a similar understanding of the people's offence at Shittim as indicated in Ps 106:28.

The offence at Shittim as described in Ps 106:28, referring to idolatry by eating pagan food, thus stands behind the standard expression "the sacrifices of the dead" in Jubilees and rabbinic literature. In rabbinic writings, the expression probably reflects the negative attitude of the Sages toward contemporary offerings to ancestors still persisting in their times.[80] The connotation of disapproval was apparently widely recognized. In the cases covered above, at least, the wording seems merely to confirm a disparaging understanding that did not necessitate any further elaboration.

To turn now again to Did 6:3, we see that the term εἰδωλόθυτον occurs in combination with a clear allusion to the phrase "sacrifices of the dead." After the exhortation to observe as many dietary laws as possible, the verse continues thus:

but be very much on your guard against food offered to idols (τοῦ εἰδωλοθύτου), for it is worship of dead gods (λατρεία γάρ ἐστι θεῶν νεκρῶν).

---

[78] See Pope, *Song of Songs*, 210-229; cf also Gill, '*Trapezomata*', 121 and 122.
[79] Cf. Pope, *Song of Songs*, 217 and Dahood, *Psalms III: 101-150*, 73-74.
[80] See Pope, *Song of Songs*, 217-228 and Segal, *Paul the Convert*, 232.

The Greek εἰδωλόθυτον may have prompted the implicit reference to the Hebrew זבחי מתים since the similarity in terminology is most remarkable. The juxtaposition of the Greek noun and the subsequent substantiating clause suggests that the prohibition against idol food with the caution referring to sacrifices of the dead was also current in the Jewish-Christian milieu where Did 6:2-3 was composed.

At first sight, it is remarkable that Did 6:3 does not translate the basic Hebrew clause appendant to the idol food prohibition into a phrase like θυσίαι γάρ εἰσι νεκρῶν, but transforms it by rendering λατρεία γάρ ἐστι θεῶν νεκρῶν. The danger of idol food is not associated with sacrifices offered to the dead who are considered to be gods but with worship of gods who are considered to be dead. Within a Christian setting, however, the inversion of this traditional expression is understandable. The argument involving a sacred veneration for the dead might easily boil down to a self-accusation, since Christians were worshipping a crucified messiah as Lord. The composer of Did 6:2-3, therefore, rephrases the recurring wording in accordance with a tradition of polemic against pagan gods. The λατρεία ... θεῶν νεκρῶν represents worship of idols who are non-existent. An atttitude which derides the idols as lifeless gods because they are as dead as their images, is portrayed in Deut 4:28; Jer 10:3-5 and figures prominently in Deutero-Isaiah. This tradition is continued in Hellenistic Jewish literature, where it is found in Wis 13-15, in Philo, *Decal.* 52-82 and *Vit. Cont.* 3-9.[81] The argument also occurs in *Diogn.* 2:4-5; *2 Clem.* 3:1 and, more interestingly, in Paul's discussion with Corinthian dissidents on idol food in 1 Cor 8:4 and 10:19.[82] It is this established

---

[81] Cf. Horsley, 'Gnosis in Corinth', 38-39. Horsley suggests that two different attitudes to pagan religion are recorded within Judaism. The first ridicules these idols as lifeless gods and is found in rabbinic and Hellenistic Jewish literature, in Wisdom and in Philo. The second line, although it agrees that idols are "nothings", sees in idolatry the service or influence of demons. This tradition is represented by writings which are close to Essenism and apocalyptic literature; see also Tomson, *Paul and the Jewish Law*, 156-57.

[82] The warning against sacrificed food in Did 6:3 agrees with the first argument against idol food advanced in 1 Cor 8-10. The passage in 1 Cor 8:4-6 opens with the same wording as does Did 6:3 (περὶ δὲ τῆς βρώσεως): "Hence, as to the eating of food offered to idols (περὶ τῆς βρώσεως οὖν τῶν εἰδωλοθύτων), we know that there is no idol in the cosmos, and that there is no God but one. For although there may be so-called gods in heaven or on earth – as indeed there are many gods and many lords – yet for us there is one God, ..." Paul believes that "gods" do not really exist though he does accept "so-called gods" (λεγόμενοι θεοί) who, in fact, are demonic powers. He resumes this argument in 10:19, a verse which belongs to the unit 10:14-22 and is explicit in the denunciation of idol food. Aside from the occurrence of the term εἰδωλόθυτον in 1 Cor 8:4 (and three additional times in 8:1.7.10) it is found one further time in the rhetorical question of 10:19: "What do I imply then? That food offered to idols is anything, or that an idol is anything?" The expected answer is of course negative. It thus appears that Paul in his rejection of gods or idols and idol food draws on a distinct traditional polemic against false gods as non-existent. See Fee, 'Εἰδωλόθυτα Once Again', 188; Tomson, *Paul and the Jewish Law*, 202-03; Smit, '1 Cor 8,1-6: A Rhetorical *Partitio*', 584-85; Dawes, 'The Danger of Idolatry', 91-92.

K. Böckenhoff (by quoting J.G. Sommer, *Das Aposteldekret*, 175-228; esp. 184) argues that the admonition against idol food in Did 6:3 is based on the danger of entering into a partnership with demons (κοινωνία τῶν δαιμονίων) as proposed by Paul in 1 Cor 10:20: "... vielmehr steht es" (i.e. das Verbot von Götzenopfer) "hier" (i.e. in Did 6:3) "als selbständiges Glied christlicher Anforderungen

view which also underlies the modified presentation of the fixed Jewish expression "sacrifices of the dead" in Did 6:3. The abhorrence of idol food is no longer connected with the practice of deifying the dead, but comes to be embedded in an established tradition of idol-critique.

TWO EARLY INTERPRETATIONS OF THE APOSTOLIC DECREE: DID 6:2-3 AND PAUL

In this section we would like to draw attention to the fact that the Apostolic Decree raised conflicting opinions regarding the status of the believing gentiles toward Judaism.[83] Two views found in non-Pauline and Pauline writings will be discussed. The first one is the belief that gentiles are allowed to exceed the fixed number of universal Noachide laws and, even more so, that they are invited to obey additional Jewish commandments as well. The occurrence of the few Noachide prescriptions in Acts 15; Rev 2:14.20 and Did 6:2-3, in connection with a reference to the burden of the Tora, seems to indicate that the Decree must have circulated in an early stage as a concession to gentile Christians who were unable to fulfil all the Mosaic commandments. In Acts 15, James states "that we should not trouble those of the gentiles who turn to God" but he certainly does not forbid seeking additional ethical perfection. Although it was decided to lay no burden upon the gentile believers beyond the Noachide precepts, there was no objection to their voluntarily observing more than the essential ones.

The admonition in Did 6:2-3 even extends beyond this scope and appears to imply that "perfect" Christians will attempt to bear the burden of the yoke as they are able. In addition to the basic moral code, gentile Christians are recommended to fully observe the Tora. The fragmentary evidence in the sources seems to indicate that this was the predominant attitude in the early church. And this position is taken up with reason. For observance of the Jewish Law to the highest degree attainable would certainly strengthen the ties between the Jewish and gentile members of the church. In this way, the pagan brethren would be drawn nearer to the Jewish Christians and their differences would be reduced to a minimum.

On the other hand, Paul always warns gentiles not to keep Jewish commandments and strongly opposes those fellow Christians who recommend to gentile

---

wie im Korintherbriefe, wo auch die gleiche Begründung des Verbotes gegeben ist, dort der Hinweis auf die κοινωνία τῶν δαιμόνων (I. Kor. 10,20), hier die λατρεία θεῶν νεκρῶν." (*Das apostolische Speisegesetz*, 23). It is unlikely, however, that the reason given in the Didache accords with the Pauline reference to the partnership with demons. In fact, subsequent to the first argument against idol food, referring to lifenessness and nothingness of gods or idols, "verse 20 of chap. 10 ... introduces a new consideration: what is offered to idols is in fact offered to demons. In other words, in 10:14-22 the apostle takes up the point made in chapter 8 (where he agrees with those "having knowledge" that pagan gods are nothing), but here he carries the argument further by introducing another fact which they have failed to take into account, that of the danger of fellowship with demons;" cf. Dawes, 'The Danger of Idolatry', 92.

[83] For the following, see especially Flusser, 'Paul's Jewish-Christian Opponents', 78-90.

believers the observance of sacred days, circumcision, or other Jewish commandments (Gal 3-5; Phil 3:2-21; Col 2:16-23). In the following pages, these two
opinions will be examined successively in the light of various trends within (later)
rabbinic sources, although it is worth noting that the Sages deal with the gentiles
only sporadically. We will see that the latter position, the view defended by Paul,
may be understood as a different interpretation of the Apostolic Decree.

Rabbinic Sages teaching from the second century CE onward, at a time when
the (pre-rabbinic) Noachide laws are likely to have been accepted in Judaism,
differ on the question whether or not the duties of Godfearing gentiles are restricted
to the observance of these laws. The first trend to be noted here considers the
prohibitions for righteous gentiles as an absolute minimum. In the Tannaitic
Midrash Sifra[84] on Lev 18:5 and in parallel texts (bAZ 3a; bBK 38a and bSan 59a),
a statement is found which recommends gentile sympathizers to fulfil more commandments of the Tora than the minimal moral standards required by the Noachide
laws:

> Whence do we know that even a gentile (גוי) who does the Law (וְעוֹשֶׂה אֶת הַתּוֹרָה) is
> like the high priest, Scripture teaches: 'Which, if a man (הָאָדָם) do, he shall live by them'
> (Lev 18:5). And again it does not say, 'this is the Law of priests and Levites and Israel-
> ites' but 'this is the Law of man (הָאָדָם), Lord God' (2 Sam 7:19). And again it does not
> say, 'open the gates that there may enter priests, Levites and Israelites' but 'that the
> righteous gentile (גוי צדיק) which keeps faith may enter in' (Isa 26:2). And further, 'this
> is the gate of the Lord'; it does not say, 'priests, Levites, Israelites (shall enter by it)' but
> 'the righteous shall enter by it' (Ps 118:20). And again, not 'rejoice, priests and Levites
> and Israelites', but, 'rejoice, you righteous, in the Lord' (Ps 33:1). Not, 'do good, O Lord,
> to the priests, Levites and Israelites, but 'do good, O Lord, to the good' (Ps 125:4). Hence
> it follows that even a gentile who does the Law is like the high priest.

A gentile who practises Tora[85] is considered to be equal to the High Priest. It must
be emphasized that this statement does not refer to proselytization. The requirements for converts to Judaism are not degraded to a more moderate level so as to
increase the number of gentile converts.[86] In fact, it would hardly have been a sound
strategy to adopt an expansionist drive in an attempt to win proselytes, on the one

---

[84] Sifra, Aharei Moth, 13.13 (= Weiss, *Sifra d'Be Rab*, 86b). The saying is cited here in the name of
R. Yeremia, a Sage of the school of R. Yishmael who is seldom mentioned. This may have been a
mistake for R. Meir (second century CE), who is named in the parallel texts (bAZ 3a; bBK 38a and bSan
59a); cf. Bacher, *Die Agada der Tannaiten* 2, 31, n. 2 and Flusser, 'Paul's Jewish-Christian Opponents',
82, n. 19. For the passage, see also Urbach, *The Sages* 1, 544.

[85] Whereas the gentile is described here in accordance with the scriptural text in Lev 18:5 (אֲשֶׁר יַעֲשֶׂה
אוֹתָם הָאָדָם) as doing the Tora (for the Jewish expression "to do the Law," cf. Flusser, 'Paul's Jewish-
Christian Opponents', 82, n. 20), parallel versions present him as studying the Tora (הָעוֹסֵק בַּתּוֹרָה: bAZ
3a; bBK 38a and bSan 59a; see Urbach, *The Sages* 2, 932, n. 71). It seems appropriate, however, to
suppose that study includes observance.

[86] It is of importance to recall here that Judaism was and is not a missionary religion engaged in an
active pursuit of gentile converts. Admittedly, in the Second Temple Period it mostly welcomed
proselytes but the evidence for an 'aggressive' Jewish missionary or proselytizing movement is scanty.
See above, p. 246.

hand, and to enforce the Noachide laws, implying that Godfearing gentiles could be saved while remaining gentiles, on the other. After all, requirements like the Noachide laws would tend to make conversion to Judaism irrelevant. The gentiles referred to in the above passage in Midrash Sifra therefore are Godfearers, who accepted the Noachide laws, rather than proselytes. Within the Jewish circles where this saying originated, it apparently was commendable for individual gentiles to fulfil more commandments than just the Noachide laws. With this suggestion, the Sages expressed their belief in the universal validity of the Tora as being intended for all mankind.

Aside from the Jewish religious leaders who advocated the lenient view, there were other Sages who took a more negative line. Not all of them subscribed to the liberal idea that there are righteous people among the gentiles who were capable of keeping to some basic moral laws.[87] Some rabbis were even of the opinion that they would not have a share in the world to come.[88] These feelings were often reinforced by historical circumstances and may reflect individual experiences as well. In the days of the revolt against the Romans, the destruction of the temple, and the Bar Kokhba rebellion, it was difficult to count on a Godfearer as he might endanger the lives of the people by joining the enemy or by becoming an informer. The prospective threats from gentiles mitigated Jewish enthusiasm for gentile sympathizers who observed the Noachide laws without embracing Judaism in its entirety. These historical circumstances sometimes moved the Sages to harbour suspicions against gentiles, who were drawn towards Judaism. It is not surprising, then, that in days of adversity, the Sages considered it their task to delineate more precisely who was and who was not Jewish and it might well be that in these circumstances the Noachide laws came to function as a boundary between the Jews and gentiles. Evidence of such an attitude is found in the *Gemara* of the Babylonian Talmud (bSan 58b-59a) on the rulings of two third-century Palestinian Amoraim, R. Yohanan ben Nappaha and R. Shimon ben Lakish:

> Resh Lakish said: A gentile who keeps a day of rest (the Sabbath), deserves death, for it is written, 'Day and night they shall not cease' (Gen 8:22). ... R. Yohanan said: A gentile who studies the Tora deserves death, for it is written, 'Moses commanded us a Law for an inheritance' (Deut 33:4); it is our inheritance, not theirs. ... An objection is raised: R. Meir used to say, Whence do we know that even a gentile who studies the Tora is as a High Priest? From the verse '(You shall therefore keep my statutes and my ordinances) which, if a man do, he shall live by them' (Lev 18:5). Priests, Levites and Israelites are not mentioned, but men: hence you may learn that even a gentile who studies the Tora is a high priest. – That refers to their own seven laws.

---

[87] See e.g. SifDeut 343 (= Finkelstein, *Siphre ad Deuteronomium*, 396) and Mekh *Bahodesh, Yitro* 5 (above, n. 30); bBK 38a; cf. also bBB 10b (on Prov 14:34). For the opposite attitudes towards gentiles between representatives of the liberal Hillelite strand and those who defended a stricter view related to the school of Shammai, cf. Tomson, *Paul and the Jewish Law*, 234-35.

[88] Famous in this respect is the early second-century debate between R. Eliezer ben Hyrcanus and R. Yoshua ben Hananyah in tSan 13:2. In this tradition, R. Eliezer maintains the view that the gentiles as a group are excluded from the world to come.

The opinions of Resh Lakish and R. Yohanan reflect a tendency to no longer recognize quasi-Jews. The Sabbath and Tora, needless to say, were two cardinal features of Jewish life. The *Gemara*, however, objects to R. Yohanan's dictum, condemning gentiles who observe precepts of the Tora, because the statement contradicts the liberal baraita of R. Meir (also quoted above from Midrash Sifra on Lev 18:5) which regards the gentile who studies and practises Tora as comparable to the High Priest. The contradiction is resolved by restricting the scope of R. Meir's dictum. It is meritorious for the gentiles to study and to observe the laws which pertain to them, whereas Jews are supposed to study and keep the entire Mosaic Tora.[89] In this case, the Noachide commandments ("their own seven laws") thus serve as a strict demarcation between Jews and non-Jews. Also, in other statements the Sages testify that Israel was bound to observe special obligations which did not fall on the gentiles,[90] probably suggesting thereby that the gentiles are recommended to confine themselves only to those prescriptions which are indispensable for them to be saved.

It is true that these statements are attributed to Sages living after the destruction of the temple but they may reflect tendencies that existed before the destruction. For gentile 'Judaizers' became not only undesirable for rabbinic (and present-day) Judaism but, as noted above, also for Paul.[91] Both Paul and some of the Sages wanted to reinforce the barrier separating Jews from non-Jews and it is precisely the Noachide laws which made it possible to mark this distinction in kind.[92] The current Jewish position was that a gentile should either become a full convert and accept all the commandments of Moses or remain with the Noachide precepts. Paul's view was basically not dissimilar. He urges every one to "lead the life which the Lord has assigned to him, and in which God has called him" (1 Cor 7:17) and inculcates every Christian to "remain in the state in which he was called" (1 Cor 7:20). There is nothing more desastrous in achieving the full separation between Jews and non-Jews than gentiles who begin to fulfil, even partially, the Jewish Law. Such a practice would imply that the doctrine of the Noachide laws represents a mere difference in degree between Jews and non-Jews.

---

[89]   Cf. Novak, *The Image of the Non-Jew*, 27.

[90]   bHag 13a: "R. Ammi said: The teachings of the Tora are not to be transmitted to a gentile, for it is said: 'He has not dealt thus with any other nation; they do not know his ordinances'" (Ps 147:20). In SifDeut 345 (= Finkelstein, *Siphre ad Deuteronomium*, 402) the Scriptural passage "Moses commanded us the Law" is explained as "This commanding (of the Tora) is only for us and for our sake." With regard to the prohibition for non-Jews to keep the Sabbath, see also DeutR 1,21 (= Mirkin, *Midrash Rabbah* 11, 23).

[91]   And this approach is continued in the attempts of early church fathers who strongly emphasize the differences between Christianity and Judaism (Ignatius of Antioch, the author of the Letter of Barnabas and Justin Martyr) and discourage Christians to adopt Jewish practices (Ignatius); see Stanton, 'Other early Christian writings', 176-189; for Ignatius, cf. also Lieu, 'History and Theology', 92-94.

[92]   Cf. Novak, *The Image of the Non-Jew*, 25-28. We have noted above that the explicit "Noachide laws" do not predate the second century CE. But the concept and underlying ideas are clearly present in sources of the Second Temple period. With respect to Paul this designation, of course, refers to the three laws underlying (pre-rabbinic) moral principles.

Admittedly, it is impossible to prove that the rabbinic statements quoted above from Midrash Sifra and the Babylonian Talmud reflect first century trends. For that matter, the explanatory model proposed here does not transcend the level of a hypothesis. If the presuppositions apply, however, Paul's admonitions to the gentile Christians against observing the Tora may be explained from his Pharisaic past. Of course, we have to judge Paul's insights on their own merits. His conception of the gentile mission entailed the incorporation of non-Jews into the people of God without requiring their submission to the Tora. If pagan converts would accept Israel's legal obligations the sufficiency of Christ for human salvation would be endangered. On the other hand, in developing this component of his theology, he was probably indebted to his Pharisaic Jewish heritage. He might have argued that if keeping the Noachide laws was all that gentiles had to do to be considered virtuous, any encouragement to seek further Judaization would be unnecessary. In his eyes, this was even hazardous. Instead of being saved as converted Jews, gentile Christians are to be considered worthy while remaining gentiles. Thus, both the Sages and Paul show interest in the more precise boundaries of their communities to the extent that they no longer allowed the status of judaizing gentiles to be ambiguous. In this process of demarcation and separation, the Noachide commandments represent the maximum of rules to be kept by gentile Godfearers while the observance of the Tora was reserved for Jews only.

Conclusion: Did 6:2-3

After the Jerusalem church adopted the three pre-rabbinic Noachide laws as a code of conduct for gentile believers, the Decree circulated separately in the early Christian communities in an oral and/or written form.[93] It was probably known to the community in which Did 6:2-3 was created and it is likely that the prohibition of idol food was worded in terms of the Decree in order to confer on this basic obligation the undisputed status which the apostolic decision widely enjoyed. The reduction of the number of basic obligations to the mere rejection of idol food indicates that this commandment was the primary issue for the author of Did 6:2-3 and for his community. Yet, it is obvious that this prohibition represented the minimum standard. The real way to "perfection" is to submit to the whole Law, including the specifically Jewish precepts such as the observance of food laws, sabbaths, and festivals. The composer of Did 6:2-3 was an exponent of a group of Jewish-Christians who remained within the ambit of Tora-observance. Compliance with the entire Tora is the ideal but the text shows a tolerant attitude to those who are not capable of bearing "the whole yoke of the Lord."

The position of Did 6:2-3 clashes with the Pauline position. Paul uses the word "yoke" (ζυγόν), which is found in Did 6:2, only once. In a polemical response to

---

[93] We have attempted to show that there was one traditional and widespread version which in individual cases was used to implement values of a particular author or Christian community.

Jewish Christians or Judaizers, who attempted to persuade gentiles in Paul's communities to keep the Tora, he warns his readers in Gal 5:1 to stand fast "and do not submit again to a yoke of slavery" (καὶ μὴ πάλιν ζυγῷ δουλείας ἐνέχεσθε).[94] Our passage, in fact, discusses the observance of the Law from the non-Pauline side. We do not know whether the composer of Did 6:2-3 had any knowledge of the Pauline position, but he may well make a stand against people who teach that one can be perfect without the full observation of the Tora.[95] The verse concluding the Two Ways teaching, which precedes our passage, warns against those who teach "apart from God." Because Did 6:2-3 is related to this verse by the causal conjunction "for" (γάρ), the implication is that those people who assert that perfection can be attained without taking on the whole yoke of the Tora are false teachers:

> (1) See to it that no one leads you astray from this way of the doctrine, since [the person who would do so] teaches apart from God. (2) For if you can bear the entire yoke of the Lord, you will be perfect, but if you cannot, do what you can...

In the eyes of Christians who observed the Law to its full extent, any announcement involving a depreciation of legal obligations was tantamount to betraying the ancestral customs and the Jewish roots of Christian faith.

---

[94] For Paul's argumentation against Judaizers in Galatians, see Watson, *Paul*, 61-72.
[95] For the following, see Draper, 'Torah and Troublesome Apostles', 367.

Chapter Eight

The Didache's Ritual: Jewish and Early Christian Tradition (Did 7-10)

In this chapter, we will primarily be looking for antecedent and contemporary elements in Jewish worship with regard to the rituals in Chapters 7 to 10 in the Didache. It will become clear that the traditions concerning baptism (Did 7), the Lord's Prayer (Did 8) and the eucharistic meal (Did 9-10) present close parallels to Jewish liturgy in the Second Temple Period. This, of course, is not surprising since the pattern of Christian worship in general was undoubtedly very strongly influenced by Jewish worship, from which it issued. Another related element is more important and deserves particular consideration in this respect. It has become quite evident in the last few decades that Jewish liturgical traditions of Temple times were not so fixed and uniform as was once supposed. Especially J. Heinemann, in a study published in Hebrew in 1964 and in a slightly revised form in English in 1977, has emphasized the variety and flexibility of Jewish liturgical practices in the first century CE.[1] He attempted to show that Jewish prayers from the first were oral texts and fixation of this material occurred at a later stage in the transmission of these texts. Because all Jewish prayers originated in the oral tradition of liturgical life, the different recensions of a prayer in the various manuscripts may well represent variations of the prayer in this oral tradition. Certainly, in Heinemann's opinion, the basic forms and thematic structures are to be traced back to the time of the Second Temple, but not fixed texts. Jewish liturgy emerged gradually while the loss of the temple was the impetus to its institutionalization. When the oral prayers were written down, these variant forms became textually fixed.

This description of the origins of prayer needs some correction, though, since in 1977 – and even less in 1964 – the evidence of the Dead Sea Scrolls was not yet fully integrated into an all-encompassing study of Jewish liturgy. Heinemann, for example, did not have access to the collections of liturgical texts published in 1982, the cycle of Sabbath songs edited in 1985, and the non-canonical hymns from the fourth cave which appeared in 1986.[2] These and other publications show that at least the wording of a number of written prayers, and maybe the formulation of

---

[1] *Prayer in the Talmud*, 43.
[2] Respectively: Baillet, *Qumrân Grotte 4* (1982); Newsom, *Songs of Sabbath Sacrifice* (1985); cf. Id., 'Shirot 'Olat Hashabbat' (1998); Schuller, *Non-Canonical Psalms from Qumran* (1986); cf. Id., 'Hodayot' (1999).

those which were transmitted orally as well, were fixed. At the same time, it is of importance to realize that the Qumran prayers do not merely represent materials provided by an isolated separatist sect. They often parallel other known prayers in the Bible, the Apocrypha and rabbinic sources.[3] Furthermore, scholars have argued with good evidence that some of the prayer texts found in Qumran have originated outside of the secluded sect and thus are sources of information about practices within a broader Jewish context.[4] Those prayers which represent broader liturgical practice and those which do not show evidence of sectarian provenance may be considered witnesses to the wider development of the early pre-rabbinic history in Jewish liturgy. They attest to the fact that practice of prayers and blessings in mainstream Judaism was already on its way towards shaping a fixed form of divine worship in the Second Temple period.[5] In sectarian as well as in non-sectarian circles, the principle of fixity began to be applied both to the contents of prayer and to the form of its recitation. Admittedly, the loss of the Temple was an extra impulse to the further development of an institutionalized and fixed prayer and the process of crystallization of prayer, therefore, certainly reached its peak during the Tannaitic period.

In the field of Christian worship, a somewhat similar phenomenon is found. It may be helpful in studying the Didache's rituals to realize that first-century Christian worship was not nearly as established and homogeneous in doctrine and practice as was once assumed. The references to a variety of rites in the New Testament, such as baptism (Mark 1:9; Matt 3:16; Luke 3:21; John 3:22-23; 4:1-2; Matt 28:19), fasts (Matt 6:16-18), the Lord's Prayer (Matt 6:9-13; Luke 11:2-4) and the Last Supper (Matt 26:26-28; Mark 14:22-24; Luke 22:17-20; 1 Cor 11:23-25) may be treated as instructions given by Jesus. The surface implication is that the words and deeds of Jesus are faithfully preserved and transmitted in the New Testament gospels. At the same time, one should not ignore the creativity of the early church. The accounts of baptism, fasting, the Lord's Prayer and the Last Supper in the gospels may, of course, contain a definite and secure historical kernel

---

[3]   See Nitzan, *Qumran Prayer and Religious Poetry*, 1-115; Weinfeld, 'Traces of Kedushat Yotzer'; Id., 'The Morning Prayers; Id., 'The Prayers for Knowledge'.
Weinfeld has reconstructed 4Q434 fragm. 2 from two smaller fragments (cf. Chazon-Elgvin-Eshel *et alii, Qumran Cave 4,* 20, 262-63.279-81). In his opinion, the text represents an early form of the Grace after meals for Mourners known in the rabbinic tradition (see his 'Grace After Meals at the Mourner's House' and Id., 'Grace After Meals in Qumran'). It is doubtful, however, whether these smaller fragments really prove the existence of the Grace after meals at Qumran. According to Falk, *Daily, Sabbath, and Festival Prayers* (217, n.1) the fragments contain "rather a psalm about God's future consolation of Jerusalem's afflicted based on Isaiah 61:10-16. They are best understood," so Falk believes, "as a song of Zion (cf. Ps. 48; 11QPsᵃ *Hymn to Zion*; 4Q380 1-2) ...." If this view is correct, it is important to note that "no texts of meal prayers turned up at Qumran" (ibid.).
[4]   See Chazon, 'Prayers from Qumran', 271-73.283-84; Schuller, 'Prayer, Hymnic and Liturgical Texts'. For a recent discussion of the criteria to establish the provenance of the prayers found in the Qumran caves, see also Falk, *Daily, Sabbath, and Festival Prayers,* 9-16.
[5]   Nitzan, *Qumran Prayer and Religious Poetry,* 40-45; Falk, *Daily, Sabbath, and Festival Prayers,* 8.

but these reports certainly were also influenced by liturgical practices of later generations of Christians. We have to distinguish between the presumed origin of a tradition and the use to which it was put in the beginning. The accounts in the gospels represent a primitive instruction of Jesus to his disciples or an actual historical event on the one hand, and are stamped by the liturgical needs and preferences of the first Christians on the other. The New Testament itself shows primitive Christianity in general to be a marked variety in the way the different communities understood Christ, the Spirit and various aspects of Christian life. This diversity is reflected in the considerable variation of the theological emphases within the different liturgical traditions inside and outside the New Testament. As they are taken from their respective church traditions, the varying liturgical texts reflect primitive local practices.

Baptism (Did 7)

It has come to be widely accepted in our days that the ultimate roots of Christian baptism lay in Jewish immersion practices. Although we do not intend to reconstruct the general line of development of baptism in this section, some historical outline certainly is relevant to a better understanding of the text of Did 7. So our first step will be to shed light on the roots of Christian baptism (pp. 273-78). It is impossible, however, to correctly describe the provenance of baptism without anticipating details in the Didache as well. Some features in Did 7:1-4 undoubtedly contain traces from an earlier stage of the history of baptism and reflect characteristics which were operative in the earliest period. In a subsequent section (pp. 278-86), it will become clear that the themes and terminology of Did 7:1-4 show sufficient parallels to suggest that Christian baptism did not proceed unilaterally from the baptism of John. It is ultimately derived from a fusion of pre-Christian immersions in John's baptism and proselyte baptism, although it should be noted that after this fusion the pre-Christian elements were subject to some essential transformations. In a final section (pp. 286-91), we will investigate the provenance of baptism in the name of the Trinity, found twice in Did 7. Since the evidence appears to be against the hypothesis that the trinitarian formula has been borrowed from Matt 28:19, we must ask ourselves where it came from.

THE JEWISH ORIGINS OF BAPTISM

The origin of Christian baptism still is a matter of dispute. The traditional view is that the practice of baptism in the early church was the result of the command of the risen Lord, reported in the gospel of Matthew 28:18-20. It will become clear below, however, that there are difficulties in accepting this passage as an authentic saying of Jesus. In our search for the origin and background of Christian baptism, two phenomena have a firm claim to our consideration, i.e. the baptism of John (with an immediate antecedent in the Qumran washings) and proselyte baptism.

It is generally acknowledged that the direct background of Christian baptism is the baptism of John. There are two primary sources for investigating John the Baptist: the New Testament gospels and a short section of Josephus (*Ant* 18,117). The latter of these reads as follows:

> For Herod had put him to death, though he was a good man and had exhorted the Jews to lead righteous lives, to practise justice towards their fellows and piety towards God, and so doing to join in baptism. In his view this was a necessary preliminary if baptism was to be acceptable to God. They must not employ it to gain pardon for whatever sins they committed, but as a consecration of the body implying that the soul was already thoroughly cleansed by right behaviour.[6]

The baptism to which John called the Jewish people was a baptism of repentance, the individual's turning from sin to God. Both Matthew (3:2; cf. Mark 1:4) and Josephus present John the Baptist as a preacher of repentance. Only the sincere repentant is allowed to come to his baptism since moral purity is a necessary condition for ritual purity.[7] In the 'Q' source (Matt 3:7-10 and Luke 3:7-9), John contemptuously and bitterly castigates an unrepentant audience, those who do not practise deeds to match their 'repentance'.

One issue strongly debated among scholars is where John got his ideas for baptism. The nearest place to look would be in the area where John conducted his ministry. According to Matt 3:1 ("the wilderness of Judea") and Luke 3:3 ("region about the Jordan"), his location might have been in the vicinity (some 10 kilometres away?) of the Qumran community. Generally the scene of John's ministry is depicted as the range of hot desolate hills along the west bank of the Dead Sea. It is likely, then, that he knew about the sectarians' existence and was familiar with their beliefs. It is true that in itself this geographical proximity does not require influence or connection. Many scholars have noticed, however, the similarity between the ideas of John the Baptist and the Qumran community and, indeed, there are intriguing parallels between John and the Sect.[8] In view of John's thorough acquaintance with Essene thought, it is not at all improbable that the immediate antecedents to his baptism are to be found in the ablutions of the Essene community of Qumran.[9]

---

[6] ET: Feldman, *Josephus in Ten Volumes* 9 (LCL 433), 81-83. The authenticity of this passage is commonly accepted now; cf. J.E. Taylor, 'John the Baptist', 279, n. 68; Webb, *John the Baptizer*, 40-41.

[7] Cf. Flusser, 'The Dead Sea Sect and Pre-Pauline Christianity' (1988) 50-54; Beasley-Murray, *Baptism in the New Testament* (1972) 34-35.

[8] See for example: VanderKam, *The Dead Sea Scrolls Today*, 168-71; D.R. Schwartz, *Studies in the Jewish Background*, 3; Scobie, *John the Baptist*, 102-16; Thiering, 'Qumran Initiation'; Badia, *The Qumran Baptism*; Lieberman, 'The Discipline'; Rabin, *Qumran Studies*, 1-21; O. Betz, 'Die Proselytentaufe der Qumransekte'; Flusser, 'Tevilat Yohanan we-kat midbar Yehudah'; Brownlee, 'John the Baptist'; Id., 'A Comparison'.

[9] Cf. also Thiering, 'Inner and Outer Cleansing'; D. Smith, 'Jewish Proselyte Baptism', 27-32; Webb, *John the Baptizer*, 209-13; Beasley-Murray, *Baptism*, 39-40. Some scholars have even suggested that John the Baptist himself at one time might have been a member of the Sect; see, for example, O. Betz, 'Was John the Baptist an Essene?'; J.A.T. Robinson, 'The Baptism of John'; Geyser, 'The Youth of John the Baptist'; Brownlee, 'John the Baptist', 35.

Like John, the Sect attributed a double significance to baptism (טבילה), namely ritual purity and atonement or deliverance from sin. According to the Sect's ideology, a Jew who was not part of the community at Qumran was unclean (1QS 3:3-6). He was in need of a purification but an immersion would only be effective in the case of a person's humble submission to all the precepts of God (1QS 3:6-9). The purificatory rites were thought to have no effect unless accompanied by the appropriate inner disposition. The belief that only repentance and the practice of righteousness make the immersion effective is also found in 1QS 5:7-15. The point of contact between John's baptism and the initial immersion in Qumran is the view that immersion is pointless unless one repents of one's wicked deeds and practises righteousness. Both the Qumran sectarians and John believed that wholehearted repentance combined with deeds of righteousness caused their lustrations to be effective, i.e., that washings are an instrument of moral cleansing (deliverance from sin) and purification of the body so as to be "acceptable to God" (cf. the above quotation from Josephus, *Ant.* 18,117). This understanding was accepted by Christianity in general but the idea of ritual purity gradually vanished in a milieu which came to be dominated by gentile Christians.[10]

Does the Christian custom of baptizing new converts including gentiles derive from John the Baptist, and thus indirectly, from Qumran, or has the baptism of John been influenced by the practice of baptizing new converts to Judaism? As a matter of fact, some scholars have argued that the immersion rite required by the Qumran community may be viewed as a ceremony of admission.[11] It is hard to believe, however, that John regarded all Jews as virtual gentiles or that he had abandoned every hope for the nation. People needed repentance but John did not convert people with the purpose of having them give up one religion for another. Repentance is the return to a state they should have been in all along, namely the awareness and recognition of being a people of God.[12] Furthermore, with regard to the Qumran documents, they usually refer to washings that were repeated at intervals and practised by the group. The Qumran ablutions were doubtless more frequent. Even the initial immersion mentioned in 1QS 5:7-15 can hardly be qualified as initiatory since it was not the decisive step towards inclusion in the community. At least, there is no unmistakable statement that it had the character

---

J.E. Taylor, however, attempts to show that John did not have a clear and direct relationship with the Qumran group. He argues that the most significant evidence for their connection is to be found in their use of Isa 40:3, but that it cannot be assumed that John himself employed the verse. Instead, so he suggests, Christians may have had their own specific purposes for connecting the verse with John; cf.'John the Baptist' and Id., *The Immerser: John the Baptist*, 22-48. H. Stegemann, likewise, believes that "John the Baptist was neither an Essene nor a spiritual pupil of the Essenes. Were he ever to have made the effort to walk over to Qumran, as a non-Essene he would have been denied entry, and at best provided with enough food and drink for the long walk back;" see his *The Library of Qumran*, 225.

[10] See Taylor, 'John the Baptist', 278-79.

[11] Brownlee, 'John the Baptist', 38-39. For a discussion of this issue, see Gnilka, 'Die essenischen Tauchbäder und die Johannestaufe'.

[12] See Beasley-Murray, *Baptism*, 41-42.

of an initiatory rite. Nevertheless, a basic, fundamental meaning of the ritual of Christian baptism with regard to the cleansing of sins probably originated with John the Baptist and his immediate Qumran background.

John's baptism cannot be considered the exclusive channel, however, through which the ritual was mediated to Christianity. Of course, some elements in the ministry of Jesus himself may well have induced early Christians to adopt baptism but it is difficult to resolve whether the Christian adoption of baptism began with Jesus or at a later stage in the church. It is quite possible that early on, Christian baptism also developed connotations of initiation under the influence of another ritual. In uncovering this line of development, the Didache has been an essential factor. The striking resemblances between the baptismal instructions of the Didache and the Jewish proselyte baptism will be displayed in detail in the next section.[13] These parallels, however, not only bear witness to later developments but also acquaint us with the actual historical roots of Christian baptism and its Jewish antecedents. The various types of water with regard to the immersion bath in Did 7 indicate that ritual purity was considered to be of great importance.

Admittedly, in rabbinic writings the term טבילה is used in different ways. The term may point to Jewish lustrations in general but also to the bath that was part of the initiation of proselytes. Moreover, many regulations governing proselyte baptism – such as the directives for the quantity and quality of water, the injunction to remove clothing and ornaments and letting down the hair – reflect the basic procedure in ordinary ritual baths. In rabbinic texts, there is often nothing which would differentiate these washings from those applied to gentiles who were eager to become Jews. The usual ritual baths consequently might have influenced Christian practice without involving the intermediate step of proselyte baptism. An additional problem is the date of proselyte baptism. Since there is no explicit testimony to proselyte baptism in the Apocrypha, Josephus, Philo, and the New Testament, its origin has been much discussed and it is difficult to prove that the practice of proselyte baptism actually existed before the end of the first century.

Let us first consider the background of the practice itself. The policy of baptizing new converts to Judaism was based on the assumption that a gentile was unclean and had to be immersed upon conversion to Judaism. According to the halakhic system, ritual impurity or uncleanness pertains to the Temple and its holy things, and the laws in Lev 11:24-40; 13; 15 and Num 19:14-22 state the substances considered to be defiling. Some of these were regarded more defiling than others and each level of defilement has its own standard purification. While ritual purity was one of the priorities of the Essenes, the purity laws were also widely observed in the remainder of Jewish Palestine. Some of the Pharisees undertook a voluntary programme of ritual purity and advocated such a state for all Israel since they attempted to raise every-day Jewish life to the same level of sacredness as the priests. Of course, there were also many Israelites who remained unclean most of the time and did not worry about becoming ritually pure unless they wanted to enter

[13] This has been shown as early as 1953 by Benoit, *Le Baptême Chrétien*, 12-27.

the holy area of the temple or eat any holy food. In general, the greatest care was taken to achieve ritual cleanness on the arrival of the Sabbath or a feast-day. In these cases, cleanness could be achieved by the prescribed ablution (טבילה), i.e., an immersion in rainwater, water from a spring, from a river or in a specially constructed pool (מקוה). In contrast to the voluntary undertaking of a ritual bath in general, the immersion that was part of the initiation of proselytes was a precept and a duty. The ablution was imposed on gentiles and became a requirement because the uncleanness of a convert was thought to derive from his connection with paganism and idol defilement.[14] It was a once and for all ritual and seems to have developed only gradually as an essential part of initiation into Judaism.

Although a clear testimony to proselyte baptism is lacking in pre-Christian writings, there are some references which merit closer attention.[15] In the first instance, there is an exhortation in the fourth book of the Sibylline Oracles, which in its present form dates from the late first century CE. In vv. 161-77, we read what people must do to prevent the final destruction. It is interesting to see that a pivotal role is attributed to baptism to preclude the eschatological wrath of God and the disaster coming with it. The immersion "in perennial rivers" is linked with changing one's behaviour from a wicked conduct to piety:

> Wash (λούσασθε) your whole bodies in perennial rivers. Stretch out your hands to heaven and ask forgiveness for your previous deeds and atone with words of praise for bitter impiety; God will regret and will not destroy; .... (vss. 165-169)[16]

Secondly, Arrian has preserved a saying of Epictetus, *Diss.* II,9,20, stemming from about 108 CE:

> Do you not see in what sense men are severally called Jew, Syrian, or Egyptian? For example, whenever we see a man halting between two faiths, we are in the habit of saying, "He is not a Jew, he is only acting the part." But when he adopts the attitude of mind of the man who has been baptized (τοῦ βεβαμμένου) and has made his choice, then he both is a Jew in fact and is also called one.[17]

---

[14] Cf. Alon, 'The Levitical Uncleanness of Gentiles', 174, n. 52. H.K. Harrington, largely supporting Alon's claim, believes, however, that the number of Sages taking the gentiles to be inherently impure was limited: "However, from the substantial contact known to exist between Jew and gentile, and the laws of the Talmud encouraging this to a certain extent, it must be the case that this notion was not upheld by the majority of the Sages;" cf. *The Impurity Systems*, 106. See also Safrai, 'Religion in Everyday Life', 828-32 and Tomson, *Paul and the Jewish Law*, 166-77. For early witnesses to the uncleanness attributed to gentiles, see, for example, Josephus, *Bellum* 2,150; id., *Ant.* 18,90; mPes 8:8; mShek 8:1; tYom 4:20; John 18:28; Acts 10:28.

[15] For these (and additional) references, see A.Y. Collins, 'The Origin of Christian Baptism', 32-35; Smith, 'Jewish Proselyte Baptism', 19-21; Abrahams, *Studies in Pharisaism*, 36-46.

[16] For the date (late first century CE), see J.J. Collins, 'The Sibylline Oracles', 363. For the Greek text, see Gauger, *Sibyllinische Weissagungen*, 122.

[17] Cf. Stern, *Greek and Latin Authors* 1, 541-44. Stern emphasizes the impossibility of Epictetus having confused Judaism with Christianity here (cf. 541 and 543, commentary).

Thirdly, instances in rabbinic literature (mPes 8:8 and mEd 5:2) provide us with a dispute between the schools of Hillel and Shammai describing a situation where the paschal lamb was still being sacrificed. In this period, i.e., when the Temple was not yet destroyed, proselyte baptism apparently is assumed to be obligatory for conversion.[18]

It is clear that in these cases the evidence does not refer to the ordinary bath of purification before the festival but to an ablution with the character of an initiatory rite. Because the sources observed are from around the end of the first century, we still do not have direct proof that proselytes were baptized before the earliest stage of Christian baptism. On the other hand, the probability is greatly increased by this historical record. For one may argue that Epictetus, the fourth book of the Sibylline Oracles, and the rabbinic sources reflect established practice that must have existed for some time. The notion and practice of proselyte baptism seems to have evolved gradually rather than suddenly jumped into being. Therefore, although it remains unclear when the phenomenon first originated, it must have been a widely accepted part of the process of proselyte initiation to Judaism in Second Temple Period.[19]

JEWISH FEATURES OF BAPTISM IN DID 7:1-4

We have recognized the probability that proselyte baptism was being practised prior to the time of Christian baptism. Moreover, continuity has been established between the baptism of John and Christian baptism. There may have been links between the practices of proselyte baptism and the initiatory ceremony carried out by John. Possibly, the custom of baptizing new gentile converts to Christianity (טבילה) has derived from a fusion of the baptism of John with the baptism of proselytes.[20] This view does not seem far-fetched since either form of baptism

---

[18]   The statements in mPes 8:8 and mEd 5:2 are essentially the same:

  The School of Shammai say: If a man became a proselyte on the day before Passover he may'
  immerse himself and consume his Passover-offering in the evening. And the School of Hillel say:

  He that separates himself from his uncircumcision is as one that separates himself from the grave.
The latter sentence expresses the position of the School of Hillel: on a new proselyte who has just been circumcised the day before, rests the uncleanness of seven days. Compare also the views of R. Eliezer and R. Yoshua in bYev 46a. Also the statements in tPes 7:13 (= Zuckermandel, 167) and yPes 8, last lines, are interesting. Both traditions mention Roman soldiers guarding the gates of Jerusalem who were immersed prior to eating their Passover meal. For the example in mPes 8:8 and for other early Jewish sources, see also Alon, 'The Levitical Uncleanness of Gentiles', 149-54. Compare the treatise Gerim 1:1-7 as well (= Higger, *Seven Minor Treatises*, 68-70 [Hebr.] and 47-49 [ET]).

[19]   Support for an early date of proselyte baptism (as a widespread practice prior to John the Baptist) is found in Schürer, *The History of the Jewish People* 3/1, 173; Jeremias, *Infant Baptism*, 24-37; Leipoldt, *Die urchristliche Taufe*, 1-25; Daube, *The New Testament and Rabbinic Judaism*, 106-13; Torrance, 'Proselyte Baptism'; Schiffman, *Who was a Jew?*; Abrahams, *Studies in Pharisaism*, 36-46; Rowley, 'Jewish Proselyte Baptism'.

[20]   Of course, circumcision prior to Baptism remains a *conditio sine qua non*, since its omission would be opposed to the Law (cf. Exod 12:48). For the admission of proselytes into the Jewish community, the rabbinic literature demands the gentiles to be circumcised, perform an immersion in water and offer

differs fundamentally from the usual ablutions in that these rituals are administered and not performed by the subject itself or, to say the least, in the fact that the presence of witnesses is required.[21] Temporal priority, however, does not necessarily entail influence and dependence and, as yet, we have not found that Jewish proselyte baptism exercised a decisive influence on Christian baptism. However, as will be supported further in the discussion below, in the passage of Did 7:1-3 ✓ a regulation is laid down with regard to three matters (pre-baptismal instruction, baptismal water and baptismal formula), all of which clearly reflect elements present in Jewish proselyte baptism.

Pre-baptismal Fasting

Yet, before we study the directives of Did 7:1-3 also the final verse of that chapter (7:4) calls for comment. It concerns the instruction regarding pre-baptismal fasting:

> Before the baptism, let the person baptizing and the person being baptized – and others who are able – fast; tell the one being baptized to fast one or two [days] before.

A pre-baptismal fast is obligatorily imposed here upon the candidate and the officiant, i.e. the person to be baptized and the one designated to perform the rite of baptism. Moreover, the amount of time involved in the fast is specified. Finally, others are invited to join in their fast, a custom documented also in other early Christian sources. As early as 150 CE, Justin Martyr mentions a fast preparatory to baptism:

> Those who are persuaded and believe the things we teach and say are true, and promise that they can live accordingly, are instructed to pray and beseech God with fasting for the remission of their past sins, while we pray and fast along with them (ἡμῶν συνευχομένων καὶ συννηστευόντων αὐτοῖς). Then they are brought by us to where there is water, and are reborn by the same manner of rebirth by which we ourselves were reborn ... . (1 Apol. 61:2-3a)[22]

---

a sacrifice in the temple; cf. SifNum 108 to Num 15:14 (= Horovitz, Siphre d'be Rab, 112); bKer 9a; bYev 46a-47b. See Schürer, The History of the Jewish People 3/1, 173; Moore, Judaism 1, 331-333; Rowley, 'Jewish Proselyte Baptism', 327.

[21] Moore, Judaism 1, 332-33; Collins, 'The Origin of Christian Baptism', 32-35.

[22] ET: C.C. Richardson, Early Christian Fathers, 282. For the Greek text, see Marcovich, Iustini Martyris Apologiae, 118, lines 3-9. For other testimonies, see Niederwimmer, Die Didache, 164; Wengst, Didache (Apostellehre), 97, n. 62; Rordorf-Tuilier, La Doctrine des douze Apôtres, 172, n. 3. The practice of fasting involving (part of) the congregation disappears very early. We do not find a similar requirement in sources dating from the beginning of the second century or later; see Vööbus, Liturgical Traditions, 20-21. The commentary to the passage in Did 7:4 in Apostolic Constitutions, VII, 22,4-5 is instructive in this respect: πρὸ δὲ τοῦ βαπτίσματος νηστευσάτω ὁ βαπτιζόμενος· καὶ γὰρ ὁ κύριος πρῶτον βαπτισθεὶς ὑπὸ Ἰωάννου ... ἐβαπτίσθη δὲ καὶ ἐνήστευσεν οὐκ αὐτὸς ἀπορυπώσεως ἢ νηστείας χρείαν ἔχων ... ἀλλ' ἵνα καὶ Ἰωάννῃ ἀλήθειαν προσμαρτυρήσῃ καὶ ἡμῖν ὑπογραμμὸν παράσχηται ("Let the one who is baptized fast before the baptism: since also the Lord was first baptized by John ... He was baptized and fasted, not because he needed an ablution or

Nothing is said about the purpose of this practice but without doubt the directive teaches something substantial about the religious content of early Christian baptism. Because the fasting before and after the baptism evidently involves repentance and remission of (previous) sins,[23] this characteristic might derive somehow from the baptism of John. The Didache probably shows a stage in the development of this ritual. John's 'baptism of repentance' may have come to be understood as a baptism of contrition or penitence, dominated by feelings of remorse because of one's sins. And, as early as biblical times, it was common practice in Israel to identify this type of repentance with rituals like sackcloth, ashes and, of course, fasting.[24]

Pre-baptismal Instruction

The introductory clause of the instruction with regard to the proper wording and correct practice for the ritual of baptism ("Having said all this beforehand") is likely to indicate that the previous Two Ways teaching was used as a catechetical instruction preceding Christian baptism.[25] We can no longer say with certainty,[26] however, whether the Two Ways in Did 1-6 were meant to be recited verbatim before the rite of baptism[27] or whether these chapters represent a (larger) block of catechetical instruction designed to be taught to converts to the Christian community prior to the rite. The instruction may well have been part and parcel of the baptismal liturgy itself and have served within the context of ceremonial action as a kind of formal admonition containing a recitation of the Two-Ways moral

---

a fast ... but in order that he would witness the truth to John and provide us with an example"); see Funk, *Didascalia et Constitutiones*, 406, lines 12-18 and 407, n. 4.

[23] See Dölger,·*Der Exorzismus im altchristlichen Taufritual*, 80-86 and Schümmer, *Die altchristliche Fastenpraxis*, 175.

[24] See Behm-Würthwein, 'μετανοέω, μετάνοια κτλ.', 976-80.

[25] The possibility that this formula was used twice (7:1 and 11:1) by the redactor as a stylistic help, is very improbable; Rordorf-Tuilier, *La Doctrine des douze Apôtres*, 30-32; and Wengst, *Didache (Apostellehre)*,16-17 and note 54 there.
As has been shown above, in Chapter 3, the Two Ways instruction appears to have been rather popular in early Christianity since it is often referred to as a standard type of catechetical instruction in the church all through Carolingian times. In fourth-century Egypt, the Two-Ways manual served as a pre-baptismal teaching; Athanasius of Alexandria mentions that its use as a basic instruction to catechumens was ancient. In the same chapter, it was further suggested that a similar document containing baptismal instruction underlied a section of the Merovingian monastic codes, called the Rule of Benedict and the Rule of the Master (pp. 90-95). Moreover, also the Fifteenth Sermon of Ps.-Boniface, reminding converted Christians of their promises at baptism, indicates a special dependency on a version of the Two Ways (pp. 95-107). And finally, the persistence of the Two-Ways tradition appears from the Second Catechesis of the Ratio de Cathecizandis Rudibus (written in ca. 800), which – again – is concerned with pre-baptismal teaching (pp. 107-11).

[26] See Knopf, *Die Lehre der zwölf Apostel*, 21.

[27] Cf. Von Harnack, *Die Apostellehre*, 2 and Greiff, *Das älteste Paschariturale*, 121-26.

teachings. Jewish sources dealing with proselyte baptism display evidence that a baptismal instruction was offered to the convert when entering the water:

> after he [the future proselyte] has taken upon himself to accept Judaism, he is taken to the immersion-house. Having covered his nakedness with water, they instruct him in some of the details of the commands.... . Just as they instruct a man, so do they instruct a woman, ... After the immersion, they speak to him words of welcome, words of comfort: ....[28].

Yet, it goes without saying that candidates must have been informed and trained beforehand as well. There is no doubt that pre-baptismal instruction was given to adults before the actual rite of baptism[29] and the same procedure applied to Jewish immersions of proselytes.[30] Perhaps it suffices to conclude that the later lines of demarcation between catechetical instruction and liturgical celebration were not drawn so sharply in the first century.[31]

Baptismal Water

The directives in Did 7:1c-3a with regard to the kinds of water to be used in baptism are clearly borrowed from Judaism:

> (As for the baptism, baptize this way. Having said all this beforehand, baptize in the name of ...) in running water (ὕδωρ ζῶν). If you do not have running water, however, baptize in another kind of water (ἄλλο ὕδωρ); if you cannot [do so] in cold [water] (ψυχρῷ), then [do so] in warm [water] (θερμῷ). But if you have neither, pour water on the head thrice ...

We have seen above (pp. 276-77) that proselyte baptism was customary in order to purify converts to Judaism from gentile uncleanness. In Did 7:1c, the interest in ritual purity is still paramount since it reflects the central concern that one should use the most appropriate water available for baptism. Various types of water are mentioned in a descending order from the best water (ὕδωρ ζῶν), which is running water from a spring or river, to less and less good. "Living water" has long been highly valued in Israel (cf. Lev 14:5.50.52; Num 19:17) and in the Hellenistic-Roman world.[32]

Our text may reflect a development that abandoned an originally strict practice. At an earlier stage, it just might have been the "living water" (מים חיים) exclu-

---

[28] Cf. the treatise Gerim 1:1 (= Higger, *Seven Minor Treatises*, 68-69 (Hebr.) and 47 (ET). See also Hildesheimer, *Sefer Halakhot Gedolot*, 219-20, lines 60-70.

[29] This also fits the baptism of John the Baptist. According to both the gospels (Matt 3:7-10 and Luke 3:7-9) and Josephus (*Ant.* 18, 117), John said to the multitudes which came out to be baptized by him that their baptism would be valid only after they had their soul thoroughly cleansed by right behaviour.

[30] See the detailed description in the instruction prior to circumcision and the subsequent baptism in the Baraita of bYev 47a-b; cf. also Alon, *Jews, Judaism*, 174, n. 51.

[31] Cf. Benoit, *Le Baptême Chrétien*, 14.

[32] Klauser, 'Taufet in Lebendigem Wasser!', 177.180-82.

sively which was called for as necessary for the performance of Christian baptism – and possibly for the initiatory Jewish proselyte baptism as well. This kind of water was probably considered the best and most effective kind of water and was supposed to have the indispensable potential to ceremonially purify gentiles. John the Baptist baptized in the Jordan (Matt 3:6; Mark 1:5), and also from other early sources, we get the impression that the instruction to baptize in "living water" in Did 7:1 is archaic and goes back to the beginnings of the Christian mission (cf. Acts 8:36; 16:13). The earliest form of baptism seems to have been performed on the banks of a river, at a well or on the seashore.

The Didache, however, embodies a concession toward this formerly strict practice. Should circumstances so demand, it permits performance of the rite of baptism "in another kind of water." Interestingly, the directives in Did 7 seem to have their parallels in Jewish halakhic instructions about water for ritual washings. The normal condition of the water found in the rite of Christian baptism is indicated by the phrase 'living water" (ὕδωρ ζῶν), and also in the Mishnah it has the highest rank within the classification of kinds of water. In mMikw 1:1-8 a list is given classifying six kinds of water in an ascending order of value:

> (1:1) There are six grades among pools of water, one more excellent than another (זו למעלה מזו). The water in ponds (מי גבאים) .... (1:6) More excellent (למעלה מהן) is the water of a rain-pond (מי המצירות) before the rain-stream has stopped. ... (1:7) More excellent (למעלה מהן) is a pool of water (מקוה) containing forty seahs ... More excellent (למעלה מהן) is a well (מעין) whose own water is little in quantity and which is increased by a greater part of drawn water ... (1:8) More excellent (למעלה מהן) are smitten waters (מים מכין) which render clean such time as they are flowing water. More excellent than they (למעלה מהן) are living waters (מים חיים) ... .[33]

The list begins with the lower qualities of water and proceeds to the higher ones: the water of pits and pools, the water of rain drops, a pool of water containing 40 seahs,[34] a fountain, "smitten" water (i.e., salty water or hot water from a spring) and, finally, living water.[35] The categories do not accord in detail with the ones in Did 7 but, clearly, the regulation and discussion about water to be used in religious ablutions are much like the guidelines in our Didache passage. When running water is not available, so Did 7:2 says, baptize in 'other water' (or 'another kind of water' – ἄλλο ὕδωρ). This latter clause seems to include the subsequent kinds of water which, although not running, are allowed in Christian baptism; first, cold water (ψυχρῷ), probably referring to water that is borrowed from a spring or river and, second, warm water (θερμῷ) which may well characterize water in pools, cisterns and reservoirs. The warm water is likely to suggest 'still water' which standing in

---

[33] ET: Danby, *The Mishnah*, 732-33.

[34] On the types of *mikwaot*, see Sanders, *Jewish Law*, 214-227. See also Gavin, *The Jewish Antecedents*, 37.

[35] Cf. also bHul 106a. With regard to Qumran, cf. CD 10:10-13 and 1QS 3:4-5. See also Str-B 1, 108-9; 2, 436.

the sun no longer has its fresh temperature.[36] Finally, in the event that there is no access to living water or the other 'kind of water' in sufficient quantity for immersion, the water is to be poured three times over the head.

These regulations apparently reflect some minimum of adherence to Jewish halakhot governing ritual purity and a similar position is still conspicuous in the *Traditio Apostolica* ascribed to Hippolytus:

> It must be water flowing from a source, or flowing from above. Let it be done in this fashion, unless there be some other need. If, however, there is some continuing and pressing need, use whatever water you find.[37]

We have before us traditions on the way to a stage when the importance of the quality of the water for the ritual of baptism is evaporating. Should circumstances make it necessary, the neophyte could be baptized by affusion (*'per infusionem'*).[38] Even this aspect of the administration of baptism, the pouring of water over somebody, appears to be in consonance with ideas of early Jewish Sages, as becomes clear in the *Baraita* in bBer 22a.[39] Indeed, the affusion is still accredited legal status here but at the same time we see a further concession to the rigorous standards regarding the water for baptism. A century later, gentile Christianity will no longer experience any problem in liberalizing the former strict code:

> ... there is no difference whether one uses for lustrations ocean water or standing water, a river or a fountain, a lake or a spring.[40]

Because the rules which govern ritual purity had lost their significance near the end of the second century CE, the discussion about the most appropriate water for the performance of the ritual of baptism has faded away.

The Baptismal Clause: "in the Name of ..."

According to Did 7:1 the convert is baptized "in the name of the Father and of the Son and of the Holy Spirit" (εἰς τὸ ὄνομα τοῦ πατρὸς καὶ τοῦ υἱοῦ καὶ τοῦ

---

[36] See Vööbus, *Liturgical Traditions*, 24 and nn. 50. 51; Niederwimmer, *Die Didache*, 162; Ascough, 'An Analysis of the Baptismal Ritual', 208 and 211-12.

[37] "Sit aqua fluens in fonte (κολυμβήθρα) vel fluens de alto. Fiat autem hoc modo, nisi sit aliqua necessitas (ἀνάγκη). Si autem necessitas (ἀνάγκη) est permanens et urgens, utere (χρῆσθαι) aquam quam invenis;" cf. the beginning of Chap. 21 (Sahidic transl.) in Botte, *La Tradition Apostolique*, 80; see also (Schöllgen)-Geerlings, *Traditio Apostolica*, 256.

[38] Cf. Rordorf, 'Le Baptême selon la *Didachè*', 182 and n. 41 = ET: 219 and n. 41: "One must in fact avoid the term "by affusion" which leads to confusion."

[39] "You pour nine portions of pure water over the one having nocturnal pollution; Nahum of Gimzo whispered" (the "whisper" refers to a permission under constraint) "to R. Akiva who whispered to Ben Azzai and Ben Azzai withdrew and there was hatred towards his disciples in the market;" cf. Alon, 'Hahalakha ba-Torat 12 ha-Shelihim', 292; (ET: 190). See also mMikw 3:4; yBer 3, 6c. Compare also Ginzberg, *A Commentary on the Palestinian Talmud* 1, 217-222.

[40] "... nulla distinctio est, mari quis an stagno, flumine an fonte, lacu an alveo diluantur;" cf. Tertullianus, De Baptismo IV, 3 in Dekkers, *Tertulliani Opera* 1, 280.

ἁγίου πνεύματος). This formula is repeated in 7:3 (albeit without the articles!) so as to instruct the reader that it should not only be recited verbatim in the case of immersions practised as part of baptismal liturgy, but also in the case of affusion, i.e. when the officiant is to pour water on the convert's head thrice. The threefold baptismal phrase is identical with the words found in the Missionary Commission presented at the end of the gospel of Matthew (28:19). In the next section, we will establish that the wording of Matt 28:19 probably is secondary with respect to the instances of Did 7:1 and 3, which might stand for the oldest attestation. For now, it may suffice to note that we endorse the dominant scholarly view that it is definitely not the three-member formula ("in the name of the Father and of the Son and of the Holy Spirit") but the short clause "in the name of the Lord" (εἰς ὄνομα κυρίου) which is the oldest baptismal formula; only later did Christian baptism become connected with the trinitarian phrase.

The pre-triadic formula is even preserved by the Didache itself: "Let no one eat or drink of your eucharist save those who have been baptized in the name of the Lord" (εἰς ὄνομα κυρίου)..." (9:5). The formula probably was unintentionally included in this section dealing with other liturgical matters pertaining to the eucharistic celebration. This explains how this older, simpler formula managed to escape a later process that caused the trinitarian phrase to be accepted widely in the baptismal ritual. At the beginning of Christianity, baptism took place "in the name of the Lord" or "in the name of (the Lord) Jesus." In the New Testament, many instances of baptismal formulas are found consisting of the same or a similar member (Acts 2:38; 8:16; 10:48; 19:5; Rom 6:3; 1 Cor 1:13;[41] Gal 3:27).[42]

What is the significance of the phrase 'in the name of'? The terminology might well be a translation of the well-known Hebrew-Aramaic formula לשם (l'shem / l'shum). If one admits that Matt 28:19 does not render a word of Jesus himself, one could conclude that the expression does not go back to an Aramaic but to a Greek original. Some, indeed, have considered the formula 'in the name of' to be of Greek provenance and regarded it as a technical term in Hellenistic commerce.[43] But if this supposition is correct, how then is one to explain the variation in the Greek wording of phrases like ἐπὶ τῷ ὀνόματι in Acts 2:38, εἰς τὸ ὄνομα in 8:16; 19:5; 1 Cor 1:13 and ἐν τῷ ὀνόματι in Acts 10:48? The obvious reason must be that the expression εἰς τὸ ὄνομα was not yet current in Hellenistic-Jewish circles as an established rendering of the Semitic equivalent לשם. The various Greek forms reflect different translations of the Semitic phrase involved.

---

[41] For this instance, see Conzelmann, Der erste Brief an die Korinther, 49-50, 195.

[42] Cf. also Herm. Vis. III, 7,3. See Rordorf-Tuilier, La Doctrine des douze Apôtres, 170, n. 4; Rordorf, 'Le Baptême selon la Didachè', 180-81 (ET: 217); Vööbus, Liturgical Traditions, 35-39; Benoit, Le Baptême Chrétien, 15; Mitchell, 'Baptism in the Didache', 253; Contra: Niederwimmer, Die Didache, 160, n. 8.

[43] Cf. Oepke (following A. Deissmann and W. Heitmüller), 'βάπτω, βαπτίζω κτλ.', 537 and n. 51.

Indeed, the expression לשם, which is best translated as εἰς τὸ ὄνομα ("into the name"), is a Jewish technical term[44] which means: 'for the purpose of', 'for the sake of', 'with reference to'. One of the best-known uses of this Hebrew phrase is found in the expression: "For the sake of Heaven (God)." This phrase is commonly used to denote the proper religious motive for a particular action, e.g., "Any assembling together that is for the sake of Heaven (לשם שמים) will in the end endure, but any that is not for the sake of Heaven will not in the end endure" (mAv 4:11; cf. 5:17). The term is found also in rabbinic sources dealing with some form of initiation. It refers to the Samaritan circumcision in a tradition which allows Israelites to circumcise Samaritans but prohibits the reverse taking place. A Samaritan must not circumcise an Israelite because the Samaritans circumcise "into (לשם) the name of Mount Gerizim" (tAZ 3:13). The meaning fitting the drift of the passage regards the inner motives when one enters into a relationship: the idea of dedication, submission, belonging. Pagan slaves on their entry into a Jewish house were forced to be immersed "in the name of slavery" (לשם שפחות), i.e., to become slaves. But on their being set free, they were rebaptized and this slave baptism was termed a baptism "in the name of freedom" (לשם בן חורין or לשם שחרור).[45] By means of baptism a human being thus enters into that relationship which one has 'in mind' when performing the ritual.

In sum, the Semitic expression לשם and its Greek rendering εἰς τὸ ὄνομα ("into the name of") expresses the intention of the cultic action. A New Testament instance may show a trend of development of the basic meaning of the expression "into the name of Jesus" within the context of Christian baptism. In Acts 19:2-5, it is reported that Paul encounters some believing disciples in Ephesus who were baptized "into John's (i.e., the Baptist's) baptism." Apparently John's ministry and baptism and his disciples continued to have an influence in the early church.[46] Once the Ephesian disciples appear to be ignorant of the idea of the Holy Spirit, they are instructed about the particular character of John's baptism and are baptized next "into the name of the Lord Jesus" (v. 5). An important point emerging from this story is that the expression "into the name (לשם) of Jesus" defines the specific intention of this kind of baptism as distinct from other (Jewish) baptisms and immersions - even from that of John.[47] It may originally have been a definition

---

[44] See Flusser, "'I am in the Midst of Them'", 516-517 and nn. 9-10; Sievers, "'Where Two or Three ...'" ,177; Moore, *Judaism* 1, 338 and 2, 98; Benoit, *Le Baptême Chrétien*, 15; Bietenhard, 'ὄνομα, ὀνομάζω κτλ.', 274-75; Kretschmar, 'Die Geschichte des Taufgottesdienstes', 32.

[45] Cf. bYev 45b and 47b (last lines) and see also Str-B 1, 1055 and Abrahams, *Studies in Pharisaism*, 36-46; esp. 45-46. For additional examples, see Hartman, *"Auf den Namen"*, 44.

[46] For the ongoing Baptist movement, see Scobie, *John the Baptist*, 187-202; Webb, *John the Baptizer*, 273-74.354, n. 9. On possible polemics of Christianity against the Baptist movement, cf. Lichtenberger, 'Taufergemeinden und frühchristliche Tauferpolemik'.

[47] See Hartman, 'Into the Name of Jesus', 440. This meaning enables Paul to say metaphorically that those who under Moses passed through the Red Sea "were all baptized into Moses in the cloud and in the sea" (1 Cor 10:2).

mentioning Jesus as the fundamental reference of Christian baptism and distinguishing it from other rites.

Was it then, in early Christian baptism, said by the baptizer in so many words that the baptism would be performed "into the name of Jesus"? It is not improbable, as contemporary evidence shows the elevation of the name of Jesus in the early church. In Phil 2:6-11, generally considered a traditional hymn which might have been composed within Jewish Christian circles,[48] it says: "Therefore God has highly exalted him (Jesus) and bestowed on him the name which is above every name, that at the name of Jesus every knee should bow, in heaven and on earth and under the earth, ..." (2:10-11). The phrase "name which is above every name" elaborates on God's glorification of Jesus to the highest rank. Another example of the prominence of Jesus' name is found in Mark 9:38-41. Here John complains to Jesus about an exorcist who is casting out demons in the name of Jesus without being a disciple of Jesus: "Teacher, we saw a man casting out demons in your name ..." (Mark 9:38; cf. Luke 9:49).[49]

ORIGIN OF THE TRINITARIAN BAPTISMAL FORMULA (DID 7:1.3)

As observed above, it is not the trinitarian phrase in Did 7:1.3 but the one-member clause in 9:5 which probably represents the most ancient baptismal formula. If this is correct, the question inevitably arises when the trinitarian phrase made its appearance in this context. It is true, the trinitarian formula also implies the notion of baptism in Matt 28:18-20 and at first sight one might take Did 7:1 to depend upon Matthew in this instance. However, the Didache does not reveal anything permitting a safe inference about the relationship to the extant gospel of Matthew, and there is no evidence that the Didache used the text of Matthew as we have it today. Furthermore, there are problems with the assumption that the Matthean passage itself is authentic. We will say more about this shortly. The use of the trinitarian formula in a ritual of initiation that is framed within a context of prevailing Jewish terminology would suggest the triad to be a mere gloss in Did 7. In the following we will see, however, that this is not necessarily so.

Let us first consider the separate trinitarian formula. Evidence for the fact that there was a notion of the Trinity in the first century CE, detached from any baptismal context, is provided by some New Testament passages.[50] The text in 2 Cor 13:13 reads: "The grace of the Lord Jesus Christ and the love of God and the fellowship of the Holy Spirit be with you all" while, at the beginning of 1 Peter, the author addresses his readers by saying about them that they are "chosen and

---

[48] See e.g. Longenecker, *The Christology*, 58-62; 125-27; Hofius, *Der Christushymnus*; Stroumsa, 'Form(s) of God'; Martin, *Carmen Christi*, xxxiv.
[49] About healings in Jesus' name in rabbinic sources, see Str-B 1, 36 and 38; Travers Herford, *Christianity in Talmud and Midrash*, 103-111.
[50] See Selwyn, *The First Epistle of St. Peter*, 247-50 and especially Windisch, *Der zweite Korintherbrief*, 429-431.

destined by God the Father and sanctified by the Spirit for obedience to Jesus Christ and for sprinkling with his blood" (1:2). In the opening of this letter (and in the conclusion as well), the writer might have fallen back on the more prevalent concepts among his readers. It is thus worthwhile to establish that these and other passages in which God, the Lord or Jesus, and the Spirit are fairly closely associated (1 Cor 12:4-7; 2 Thess 2:13-14) make it clear that the use of such formulations was rather widespread in the early church. It is also true, on the other hand, that there was not a conscious, full-blown developed doctrine of the Trinity as it was later defined. These phrases need not correlate with a metaphysical understanding of oneness of essence and substance.

Besides Did 7:1.3, the text in Matt 28:19 is the earliest instance of a trinitarian formula in the rite of baptism:

> And Jesus came and said to them [his disciples], 'All authority in heaven and on earth has been given to me. Go therefore and make disciples of all nations, baptizing them in the name of the Father and of the Son and of the Holy Spirit, teaching them to observe all that I have commanded you; and lo, I am with you always, to the close of the age' (Matt 28:18-20)

According to all extant gospel manuscripts, Jesus commanded his disciples to baptize all nations "in the name of the Father and of the Son and of the Holy Spirit." More than seventy years ago, F.C. Conybeare discovered that a patristic author, Eusebius of Caesarea (ca. 263-ca. 340), quotes this text of the great commission sixteen times omitting both the baptismal command and the trinitarian formula. Eusebius' text of Matt 28:19, usually called 'the shorter reading', runs as follows: "go and make disciples of all nations in my name."[51] Conybeare noted that the shorter reading appears only in the writings of Eusebius composed before the Council of Nicaea (325) and the longer ones only afterward. Eusebius might have found this form of the text in the codices of the famous library in Caesarea, and it is quite possible that the shorter reading is the original one while the longer one, referring to baptism and the trinitarian formula, was created in order to make the gospel text conform to liturgical practice.[52]

---

[51] See Conybeare, 'The Eusebian form of the Text Matth. 28,19'.

[52] Criticism of the originality of the shorter Eusebian reading of Matt 28:19 is found, for example, in Riggenbach, *Der trinitarische Taufbefehl*; Leipoldt, *Die urchristliche Taufe*, 33; Cuneo, *The Lord's Command to Baptize*; Gnilka, 'Der Missionsauftrag des Herrn', 5-6; Kertelge, 'Der sogenannte Taufbefehl Jesu'; Kingsbury, 'The Composition and Christology of Matt. 28,16-20', 577; Barth, *Die Taufe in Frühchristliche Zeit*, 13-17; Wengst, *Didache (Apostellehre)*, 29 ("zweifelhaft"). But others claim that the shorter reading found in Eusebius preserves the earlier form of the text; cf., for example, Barnikol, 'Die triadische Taufformel'; Lohmeyer, '"Mir ist gegeben alle Gewalt!"'; Bultmann, *Theologie des Neuen Testaments*, 136; J. Schneider, *Die Taufe im Neuen Testament*, 31; Von Campenhausen, 'Taufen auf den Namen Jesu?', 208, n. 48; Kosmala, 'The Conclusion of Matthew'; Vööbus, *Liturgical Traditions*, 36-39; Flusser, 'The Conclusion of Matthew'; Green, 'The Commandment to Baptize'; Kasting, *Die Anfänge der urchristlichen Mission*, 34; Meyer, *Ursprung und Anfänge des Christentums*, 15, n. 1. See also Köster, *Synoptische Überlieferung*, 191: "Die Taufanweisungen, die sich in Did. 7 noch im Zusammenhang mit der Erwähnung der trinitarischen Taufformel finden, weisen uns auf eine ganz andere Quelle, aus der die Did. hier schöpft, nämlich die liturgische Praxis

It is true, the lack of manuscript evidence for the shorter reading of Matt 28:19 and of patristic evidence (aside from Eusebius) are serious objections to its acceptance. On the other hand, there are good grounds for arguing that the trinitarian formula was once absent from the Matthean gospel.[53] Firstly, in addition to the Eusebian evidence, vestiges of the shorter version of Matt 28:19 are still to be found in various documents, including a Jewish-Christian source,[54] a Coptic text,[55] and an ancient Sibylline prophecy.[56] These independent witnesses to the 'Eusebian' conclusion of Matthew are substantial enough to at least suggest that this form

der Gemeinde. Was liegt näher als die Annahme, Did. habe auch die trinitarische Taufformel aus der Praxis der Gemeinde übernommen! Hier war die trinitarische Taufformel sicher schon längst im Gebrauch, ehe sie in das Mt.-Evangelium Aufnahme fand. ..."

[53] The reason why there is no manuscript evidence for the shorter reading of Matt 28:19 may be due to dogmatic developments within the church. In the beginning of the fourth century CE, the doctrine of the Holy Trinity was considered to be so important that the original text in extant manuscripts and codices was revised and redacted by the prevailing orthodoxy in the church to reflect its trinitarian theology. Eusebius belongs to the long series of Christian scholars who are better philologists and historians than theologians and dogmatists (see Altaner-Stuiber, *Patrologie* 218; Quasten, *Patrology* 3, 310-11; Bardenhewer, *Geschichte der altkirchlichen Literatur* 3, 241-243). To say it in an anachronistic way: being a devout partisan of Constantine the Great, he was a far better Stalinist than Marxist-Leninist. Especially with regard to his doctrine of the Holy Trinity, he met with sharp criticism from the orthodox majority in the church. So – after Nicaea – it was evidently safer to renounce the better version and to subsequently quote the longer reading from the *Textus Receptus* instead.

[54] See Pines, 'The Jewish Christians', 261:
> He (Jesus) and his companions behaved constantly in this manner (i.e., they observed the commandments of the Mosaic Law), until he left the world. He said to his companions: 'Act as you have seen me act, instruct people in accordance with instructions I have given you, and be for them what I have been for you'. His companions behaved constantly in this manner and in accordance with this (70a).

For the evaluation of this evidence, see Flusser, 'The Conclusion of Matthew', 112-116. Compare also the criticism on the latter's view by Hubbard, *The Matthean Redaction*, 164.

[55] The document is called 'The Discourse on Mary Theotokos by Cyril, Archbishop of Jerusalem, describing her human origin and death'. The part of this text relevant to our subject concerns a controversy between the Patriarch Cyril of Jerusalem and an heretical monk:
> And the Patriarch Cyril said unto the monk, 'Who sent thee about to teach these things?' And that monk said unto him, 'The Christ said, Go ye forth into all the world, and teach ye all the nations in My Name, in every place' (Fol. 12 a-b).

Cf. Budge, *Miscellaneous Coptic Texts*, 637 (ET) and 60 (Coptic text).

[56] Namely the Tiburtine Sibyl, containing the interpretation of a dream of a hundred Roman senators who have seen nine suns, i.e., nine generations from the beginning of mankind to the end of days. The text which is of interest to us regards the fifth sun, that is the fifth generation when
> Jesus will select two fishermen from Galilee and will teach them (his) own law and say (to them): 'Go forth and the teaching which you have received from me, teach it to all the peoples and subdue all the nations through seventy-two writing tables (Latin: "lignas"; but one should probably read "linguas" – languages).

See Gauger, *Sibyllinische Weissagungen*, 316. Scholarly opinion is divided over the date of composition but it is almost certain that recensions of the work stem from the fourth century. The earliest layer underlying these recensions may even go back to a Jewish-Christian oracle of the late first century CE; so Flusser, 'An early Jewish-Christian Document', 374-75 and 382-84. For a critique of this proposal, see McGinn, '*Teste David cum Sibylla*', 27-28.

enjoyed some popularity. In view of the occurrences in these documents, the original form of Matt 28:19-20 may have run as follows:

> Go forth and make disciples of all nations in my name, teaching them to observe all that I have commanded you.

Secondly, this shorter reading is particularly close to several examples of rabbinic debate. The rabbinic expression בשם ('in the name of') is commonly used in the context of handing down a teaching. The clause "Rabbi X says in the name of Rabbi Y" means that the tradent brings a doctrine of a predecessor (his teacher): "He who relates a thing in the name of him who said it, brings deliverance to the world" (mAv 6:6). The Jewish understanding of the terminology "in the name of" is adopted by New Testament writers as well. In many passages of the New Testament, the apostles are reported to have spoken, preached and taught in the name of Jesus (Acts 4:17-18; 5:28.40; 9:27-29). Focussing on Matt 28:19-20, the rabbinic idiom corroborates the wording of the earlier form proposed above. The sentence is clear and self-evident since the instruction "to observe all that I have commanded you" is an explanation of "Go forth and make disciples of all nations *in my name*." The resurrected Jesus is said to have commanded his disciples to instruct all nations *in his name*, which means that the disciples should teach the doctrine of their master (all that he has commanded) after his death.[57]

Thirdly, the text is complete and coherent in the short form only. When one considers the present form of Matt 28:18-20, it is easy to perceive its asymmetrical structure, since the opening declaration requires not a trinitarian but a Christological statement to follow it. As a matter of fact, the extant passage in Matthew has all the marks of having been modified from a Christological to a trinitarian formula in order to suit to a liturgical tradition current in early days. The gospel must have received the tradition from the baptismal practice of a community like the one reflected in the Didache.

If the gospel of Matthew does not provide a credible context for the origin of baptism in the name of the Trinity, perhaps Did 7 provides the key. And indeed, one cannot completely exclude the possibility that Matt 28:19 was modified into its present form under the influence of Did 7:1 (and 3). In order to clarify the facts, let us first consider the second mention of the Trinity in Did 7:3: "But if you have neither, pour water on the head *thrice*, into the name of Father and Son and Holy Spirit." Is the mention of the *three* pourings and the three persons of the Holy Trinity a coincidence? Or does the same procedure of immersing three times also

---

[57] This is similar to what already a long time before, the biblical Joshua could affirm: "You have observed all that Moses the servant of the Lord commanded you, and have obeyed my voice in all that I have commanded you" (Josh 22:2 and see Deut 34:9). Thus the original saying in Matt 28:19 is in agreement with an old concept in Judaism.

apply to Did 7:1, where the trinitarian formula is found as well? In the discussion below, we will attempt to prove that the anwer is affirmative.[58]

According to the 'Apostolic Tradition' attributed to Hippolytus of Rome, baptism includes three immersions. While being immersed for the first time, the person to be baptized confesses his belief in God the Father; during the second bathing, he confesses his belief in Jesus Christ, the Son of God, and on the occasion of his third immersion the baptizand confesses his belief in the Holy Spirit.[59] A similar practice of three separate immersions each relating to a person of the Trinity is found in a writing of Tertullian: "We baptize not all at once but three times, for each of the names of each of the persons (of the Trinity)."[60] The conclusion to be drawn from this evidence is that the threefold affusion on the head of the baptized in Did 7:3b probably presupposes three distinct acts of immersion in 7:1 as well, each referring to one singular name of the three-membered trinitarian formula.[61]

We have already seen early witnesses to a separate circulation of trinitarian formulas, be it still in an undeveloped stage. In this light, the obvious question arises whether the three immersions in baptism were caused by the mention of the Holy Trinity in baptism or, conversely, whether the three immersions attracted the use of a trinitarian formula. In view of the Jewish provenance of baptism, the second possibility is preferable. It has been observed that, in the Jewish tradition, "according to law one immersion is sufficient, but three have become customary."[62] This practice is attested to in two rabbinic sources from the twelfth century, one called *Sefer Hamanhig*[63] and the other entitled *Sefer Hasidim*.[64] Admittedly, the attestation is late but this does not necessarily mean that the custom is late, as

---

[58]   See also the following statement: "Der Brauch, am Täufling nicht nur eine, sondern drei Taufhand-lungen zu vollziehen, sei es Untertauchen oder Übergiessen, den schon die Didache belegt, hängt nicht notwendig an der triadischen Formel, ... Aber beides zu verbinden, wird sich doch früh nahegelegt haben;" Kretschmar, 'Die Geschichte des Taufgottesdienstes', 36.

[59]   Cf. Chap. 21 (Sahidic transl.) in Botte, *La Tradition Apostolique*, 85-87; see also (Schöllgen)-Geerlings, *Traditio Apostolica*, 261-63.

[60]   "Nam nec semel sed ter ad singula nomina in personas singulas tinguimur;" cf. Tertullian, *Adversus Praxean* 26,9 in Gerlo, *Tertulliani Opera*, 1198, lines 59-60; cf. Niederwimmer, *Die Didache*, 162. For another witness to this custom, cf. the *Testamentum Domini nostri Jesus Christi* (which probably draws upon the church order ascribed to Hippolytus) in Fendt, *Einführung in die Liturgiewissenschaft*, 107. It is an interesting fact that also Martin from Braga (died in 580) defended this threefold practice of immersion or affusion in his "Epistola ad Bonifacium episcopum"; cf. Fendt, *Einführung in die Liturgiewissenschaft*, 126.

[61]   This type of baptism, which originated in the sub-apostolic period, survived in the West at least until the Carolingian age. Mediaeval texts evidencing three immersions related to the mention of one of the three persons of the Trinity in each case, run like this: "«Et ego te baptizo in nomine Patris» (et mergat semel). «Et Filii» (et mergat iterum). «Et Spiritus Sancti» (et mergat tertio);" see Fendt, *Einführung in die Liturgiewissenschaft*, 141-142; cf. also 139 and 143.144.

[62]   Posner, 'ablution', 82.

[63]   Raphael, *Sefer Hamanhig*, 567, line 30: ‏וזהו שנהגו הנשים לשקוע עצמן ג׳ פעמים במים‎....

[64]   The *Sefer Hasidim* is extant in two versions. One was edited by R. Margulies (Lwow 1929), and see there, p. 220. The other version was edited by J. Wistinetzki (Berlin 1891); see there, pp. 396-397, and the additional note: ‏ונשים רגילות ג׳ פעמים ... ולכן הטובל בערב יום הכפורים יכנים את‎ אח ‏ראשו ג׳ פעמים‎.

parallels in rabbinic sources may often be older than the first citation in which they are now found. Although it is impossible to say with certainty how the formula was given its present three-part form, it might be appropriate, therefore, to assume that the threefold immersion was the main cause why the baptism "into the name of Jesus" was modified into the trinitarian baptism which lasts until the present day. In that case, the fixed and tenacious liturgical form of the baptismal ceremony, which was a central experience in Christian life, may have helped to corroborate the belief in the Holy Trinity among Christians. This same ritual custom is found in another early tradition: "In the name of God, the Father and Lord of all, and of our Saviour Jesus Christ and of the Holy Spirit, they then perform the washing in the water."[65] Summing up, it has become quite likely that the text in the present form of Matt 28:19 is a retouche, an instance of the gospel tradition being affected either indirectly by liturgical or ritual revision, or directly by the wording of the Didache.

Fasting and the Lord's Prayer (Did 8)

The mention of the baptismal fast brings up the topic of the so-called stationary fast in 8:1. The reader is surprised, however, by the sudden introduction of the 'hypocrites'. While the text in Did 7 still shows the closeness of the rulings of the Didache to its Jewish roots, the instructions in 8:1-3 reveal a process of setting apart the community from its Jewish environment. The polemics against the ὑποκριταί seriously break in on the pattern of the solidarity that has so far existed with other Jewish groups and apparently manifest the necessity to distinguish oneself from Jewish practice. Christians are required to deviate from the ὑποκριταί by different days of fasting and divergent customs of prayer.

FASTING

Both fasting and praying are addressed in the context of avoiding the practice of the 'hypocrites'. First the fasts:

> Let your fasts not [coincide] with [those of] the hypocrites. They fast on Monday and Thursday; you, though, should fast on Wednesday and Friday (Did 8:1)

Does the expression 'hypocrites' in the Didache mean the Pharisees in particular? The wording surely reminds us of the New Testament and, it is true, the accusation of hypocrisy against Pharisees in Matthew and elsewhere in the gospels (cf. Luke 12:56 and 13:15) is rooted in Jewish tradition. More specifically, when the gospel

---

[65] Justin, *1 Apol.* 61:3b (= Marcovich, *Iustini Martyris Apologiae*, 118, lines 9-12); see also 61:10.13 (= id., 119, lines 31.36-37).

of Matthew records the sayings of Jesus about the fasts of the hypocrites (6:16-18), there is no doubt that the hypocrites refer to the Pharisees (cf. Matt 23). A similar situation obtains with respect to the writings of the Qumran sect, charging Pharisees with hypocrisy.[66] What is more, the Pharisees themselves admitted hypocrisy to be a real problem in their midst. They acknowledged that the discrepancy between social reality and the tougher standards of their elevated ethics created various types of hypocrites within their ranks.[67]

However, the gap between the facts of life and high moral codes was narrowed once the Pharisaic influence became stronger and the Jewish community accepted the leadership of Pharisaic rabbinism from the Yavne period onward. So, if the term 'hypocrites' in Did 8:1.2 characterizes the behaviour of the Pharisees in the generation following the destruction of the temple, its use might at least be somewhat anachronistic. Also for another reason it would be unjustified to associate the 'hypocrites' in Did 8:1 with the Pharisees of the gospels.[68] In Matt 6:16, Pharisees are attacked because they fasted for the sake of a pious external show only. Since they are not inwardly what is displayed outwardly, they are required to fast in secret. No such directive to secrecy, however, appears in Did 8:1. Because the Didache does not criticize the type but the time of fasting,[69] there is no need to see this expression as intended for Pharisees in particular.

The ὑποκριταί in Did 8:1 probably is a general reference to (pious) Jews.[70] During a period of national calamity, especially in times of drought affecting the agrarian society, the religious leaders requested a public fast.[71] There may have been one or more regular fasts in addition to Yom Kippur or the Day of Atonement in the first century CE, but in time of need, such as the shortage of rain in the autumn, special fast-days were added. Mondays and Thursdays were market days, and because the villagers used to gather in town on these days, they offered a good opportunity for Scripture reading and tribunal sessions. Fasts were connected with the public assemblies and this custom was almost certainly in existence before 70 CE.[72]

---

[66] Cf. Weinfeld, 'The Charge of Hypocrisy'.

[67] Cf. Flusser, "'Miqtsat maase ha-Tora'", 361-63.

[68] An interesting suggestion, namely that the hypocrites were judaizing Christian dissidents, is mentioned in Rordorf-Tuilier, *La Doctrine des douze Apôtres*, 36-37 for the following reason: "Mais il serait surprenant qu'un écrit comme la *Didachè*, qui doit tant à la tradition judaïque, s'exprime d'une manière aussi violente à l'égard des Juifs" (37). It is quite unlikely that judaizing Christians are attacked here, because the term "hypocrite" was coined against the Pharisees (the passage in Gal 2:13, adduced by Rordorf-Tuilier, *La Doctrine des douze Apôtres*, 37, n. 2, is not decisive here). For additional arguments, see also Wengst, *Didache (Apostellehre)*, 29-30, n. 109.

[69] See Niederwimmer, *Die Didache*, 166, n. 4 and Draper, 'Christian Self-Definition', 233-35.

[70] See Von Harnack, *Lehre der zwölf Apostel*, 24-25; Audet, *La Didachè*, 367-68; Wengst, *Didache (Apostellehre)*, 29-30; Niederwimmer, *Die Didache*, 166, n. 4. According to Draper ('Christian Self-Definition', 233), however, the term refers to "Pharisees in particular."

[71] For the following, see Alon, 'Le-jeshuva shel baraita achat'; Safrai, 'Religion in Everyday Life', 814-16; Abrahams, *Studies in Parisaism*, 121-28; Schürer, *The History of the Jewish People* 2, 483-84.

[72] Safrai, 'The Synagogue', 919; and cf. Moore, *Judaism* 2, 260. See also mTaan 1:6; 2:9.

Besides public fasts that were obligatory for all,[73] there were also individual private days of fasting. In Luke 18:12, a Pharisee fasts twice a week, but it is not clear whether the days referred to are Monday and Thursday. From evidence in other sources, however, one may draw the conclusion that, also for private fasts, Mondays and Thursdays were the favoured days.[74] Yet, the example in Luke 18:12 raises another question. Did an average Pharisee or, generally, a Jew fast twice a week? Indeed, there were "proto-rabbinic" Jews who individually fasted and valued this religious practice (Matt 9:14; Mark 2:18; Luke 5:33) but this custom never became a legal prescription. Certainly, there was "a great deal of voluntary individual fasting" and "some strict ascetics"[75] fasted on these days throughout the year. But the custom to fast twice a week is by no means characteristic of the Pharisees (or the Jews) as a whole. The instruction in Did 8:1 does not seem to presuppose a situation in which Jews and Christians fasted two days every week but rather implies a discussion as to which two days are preferable once an individual or a community had indeed decided to fast.

Why were the Wednesdays and Fridays chosen in the Didache? It may well be that the Didache instruction is directed against some Christians, who in solidarity with Jewish groups, fasted on Mondays and Thursdays. The manual remains silent, though, on the reasoning behind the change from Mondays / Thursdays to Wednesdays / Fridays. It has often been assumed that Christians merely picked these days at random, just to differentiate between the Christian community and the Jews. On the other hand, the choice of the primitive church may also have been influenced by the use of the solar calendar among the Jewish sect of Qumran. In this calendar, Wednesday and Friday had a certain prominence.[76] If early Christians were familiar with this sectarian time schedule and the significant position of these days, they may have transferred the fasting to Wednesday and Friday in the light of their polemic against the ὑποκριταί.

PRAYER

When it comes to praying, the Didache takes great pains to present well-defined formulae in the interest of disassociating his readers from the 'hypocrites':

---

[73] Str-B 2,241-44; 4/1,77-(78)-114 etc.; Draper, 'Christian Self-Definition', 233-35.
[74] Cf. mMeg 3:6; 4:1; Schürer, *The History of the Jewish People* 2, 483-84; Sanders, *Jewish Law*, 81-84.
[75] Schürer, *The History of the Jewish People* 2, 483-84. See also Alon, 'Ha-halakha ba-Torat 12 ha-Shelihim', 291 (= ET: 189); Str-B 2, 241-246; 4/1, 77-79.
[76] See Jaubert, 'Jésus et le calendrier', 1-11.27-28 and id., *La Date de la Cène*, 27.60-75; Blinzler, 'Qumran-Kalender und Passionschronologie', 242-46; Bradshaw, *Daily Prayer in the Early Church*, 40-41; Rordorf-Tuilier, *La Doctrine des douze Apôtres*, 37 and n. 3. Niederwimmer, however, qualifies the view that the Christian choice of these particular days might have been influenced by the solar calendar of Qumran as "Alles sehr unwahrscheinlich" (*Die Didache*, 167, n. 16).

> And do not pray as the hypocrites [do]; pray instead this way, as the Lord directed in his
> gospel (and the text goes on to present a version of the Lord's Prayer which is succeeded
> by the following final clause):
> Pray this way thrice daily (Did 8:2-3).

The distinction from pious Jews is accomplished in this passage by means of the
rejection of the regular Jewish prayer. Prayer (private or public) in Tannaitic
tradition always refers to the *tefilla* (= Shemoneh Esreh or Amidah) but there is
no evidence that exactly the same version, the same order and the same number
of the eighteen benedictions was recited in every place. While the *tefilla*'s main
outline was probably already fixed in the Second Temple period, the prayer was
given the set form and exact wording – in which it was recited three times a day
– during the Yavne period. There are indications, however, that the custom of
threefold daily prayer was already well established in earlier Judaism. The halakhic
instruction in 8:3, in any event, clearly associates the Lord's Prayer with the regular
Jewish *tefilla* because, like the *tefilla*,[77] it had to be said three times a day. Like the
Jew, the Christian is to follow the three-a-day rule but the prayer adopted considerably deviated from conventional Jewish worship.

Although the introduction and the text of the Lord's Prayer in Did 8:2-3 and Matt
6:5-13 match closely, it is unwarranted to assume literary dependence. Let us first
turn to the text of the prayer in Did 8:3. It is hard to accept that the Didache quotes
directly from the text of Matthew's gospel since the Lord's Prayer in its earliest
stage was an oral text. It was a regular communal prayer said aloud in Christian
services. Interestingly, the doxology at the end of the prayer ("for the power and
glory are yours forever") reveals the liturgical use of this prayer in the Didache.[78]
The doxology is lacking in the Lukan version of the Lord's prayer. With regard
to Matthew, it is absent in the best and oldest manuscripts, and the earliest patristic
commentaries on the Lord's Prayer (Tertullian, Origen and Cyprian) do not know
it. This clearly indicates that the doxology was originally not part of the Lord's Prayer
in Matthew and the reason for its absence may be simple. When the original function
of the doxology in the Lord's prayer was that of response by the worshipping
congregation, it might have been taken as not belonging to the Lord's Prayer itself
and was, consequently, not incorporated in the gospel. As a result, there is no need
to assume that the Didache is dependent on the gospel of Matthew, for it is most

---

[77] Cf. Dan 6:11; 2 Enoch 51:4; mBer 4:1 (and 4:3.7). See also Safrai, 'The Synagogue', 918; Bradshaw,
The Search for the Origins, 19.

[78] Many scholars believe that this doxology draws upon the Davidic praise in 1 Chr 29:11-12. The
doxology of the Lord's Prayer reappears in the Eucharist benedictions of Did 9-10 in a similar long
formula containing two members ('power' and 'glory' in 9:4 and 10:5) and in a short formula containing
just one member ('glory' in 9:2.3; 10:2.4). Cf. Niederwimmer, *Die Didache*, 172 and Rordorf-Tuilier,
La Doctrine des douze Apôtres, 174-75, n. 3. Surprisingly, in each of these Didache formulae the
mention of 'kingdom' is missing, while in 1 Chr 29:11-12 it is precisely three things that are connected,
namely the kingdom, power and glory. The same triad also emerges in the secondary addition to Matt
6:13 of the Mss. K L W Δ Θ Π *f*[13] and the 'majority text'. These doxologies indicate that both Did 8:2
and the secondary addition in Matt 6:13 reflect an ancient use of the Lord's prayer in Christian liturgy.

unlikely that the (Christian) editor of this unit in the Didache would have needed Matthew's text in order to reproduce the prayer. On the contrary, it makes more sense to assume that he is citing the liturgical, that is, the oral form of public prayer. Both the redactor of Did 8:1-3 and Matthew knew the prayer from its regular use in their respective church traditions. The agreements between Matthew and the Didache are to be assigned, then, to the liturgical tradition they have in common.[79]

The introduction to the Lord's Prayer in Did 8:2 recalls the preamble of the prayer in Matthew but, at the same time, considerably differs from its Matthean counterpart:

> And when you pray, you must not be like the hypocrites; for they love to stand and pray in the synagogues and at the street corners, that they may be seen by men. ... But when you pray, go into your room and shut the door ...And in praying do not heap up empty phrases ... (Matt 6:5-8).

In spite of the phrase "as the Lord directed in his gospel" (Did 8:2), there is no evidence that the Didache used the present text of Matthew. True, the word ὑποκριταί occurs in both texts. But the directive in the Didache is very unlike the one quoted above from the gospel of Matthew as the manual does not seem to be using the word ὑποκριταί with a focus on pretending. What is wrong with the hypocrites' prayer in the Didache is not that it is insincere, ostentatious, or needlessly loquacious (Matt 6:5-8), but that it does not fit the ritual of the Didache community. It is highly improbable that the Didache intended the Lord's prayer to be included in a longer act of prayer within the traditional Jewish liturgy.[80] On the contrary, it appears to be directed first of all against individual Christians who not only fasted on the 'wrong' days but also used Jewish daily prayers as well. Although there is no reason to think that Jesus meant the disciples to pray only the prayer which he taught them, in the Didache the Lord's Prayer turns out to be a self-sufficient and independent prayer, substituting for the daily Jewish *tefilla*. It is the Jewish prayer ritual which is rejected here and it seems that this message is directed first of all at Christian converts of gentile provenance. The Lord's Prayer is imposed on Christians with the purpose of replacing the recitation of the *tefilla* said by the 'hypocrites'.

The sharp polemics against the ὑποκριταί seem to reflect the emergence of tensions between the Didache community and Judaism. The necessity of distinguishing oneself from the fasting and worshipping practice by choosing other fast

---

[79] Betz, *The Sermon on the Mount*, 371.

[80] Such an attitude toward Jewish prayers will emerge in the later (third-century) Apostolic Constitutions. (Gentile) Christians were prepared to include several Jewish prayers in Christian liturgy after these were thoroughly Christianized only. The Didache was used by the compiler of the Apostolic Constitutions in VII,1-32 (see above, Chap 1, p. 27). In VII, 33-38, hence immediately after the (expanded) rendering of the Didache, the writing must have benefited from another source, a Jewish Greek version of several Jewish synagogal prayers. The corresponding text in the Apostolic Constitutions, however, clearly shows a heavy-handed editorial activity in, amongst other things, adding material containing peculiarly Christian elements, that is, references to Christ and to Christian and New Testament quotations; cf. Fiensy, *Prayers Alleged to be Jewish*, 129-34;165-87.

days and a different prayer, respectively, presupposes a continuing, close contact of the community with its Jewish environment. The world of ὑποκριταί apparently was fascinating enough to members of the Didache community to justify this kind of assault. Presumably, an important minority within the community continued to adhere to current Jewish practices. On the other hand, the wording ὑποκριταί is extremely derogatory and contemptuous. The text does not show any urge to prove the accusation of hypocrisy, which may indicate that the Didache community, or at least the redactor of Did 8:1-3, was in a irreversible process of moving away from its Jewish roots. Initially the community was composed of Jews who believed in Jesus, or Christian Jews whose religious views remained close to their Jewish roots. At some stage in the redaction of their old traditions, maybe when the interest in gentile converts increased, the manual took on some characteristics so as to prevent the community to fall apart. The whole section, in sum, reflects an attitude of animosity to Jews and Judaism; the unsubstantiated disparagement of the 'hypocrites' does not seem to leave open any possibilities of reconciliation.[81]

Eucharist (Did 9-10)

Did 9-10 contains prayers for what it describes as *eucharistia*, and indeed, there is an obvious reason to believe that the ritual meal concerned points to a celebration of the Lord's Supper. The Didache ritual shares important characteristics with the actual Eucharist in the New Testament. The verb εὐχαριστεῖν, which belonged from the beginning to the liturgy of the Eucharist, is found in the prayer to be said over the cup (9:2), the bread (9:3) and twice in the lengthy prayer of thanksgiving after the meal (10:2.4). Moreover, the celebration revolves around bread and cup. Both of these elements are brought into particular connection with Jesus and both are valued as holy and spiritual. Nevertheless, there are some salient features which considerably differ from the New Testament accounts of the Eucharist.[82] First, the ritual does not include the words of institution. The prayers do not refer to the body and blood of Christ nor do they show any awareness that the sacred ritual is related to the tradition of the Last Supper. And second, the prayer before the meal begins with the blessing over the wine (9:2) and only then follows the blessing over the bread (9:3-4). Unlike the canonical form of the celebration of the Eucharist, the blessing over the cup precedes the blessing over the bread.

Because the data about the ritual meal provided by the Didache do not harmonize with the evidence of the New Testament traditions, these chapters have often been taken as referring to any communal meal but a eucharistic one. The service

---

[81] See Draper, 'Christian Self-Definition', 243. For a different assessment of the facts, see Tomson, *'If this be from Heaven...'*, 380-91, who considers the whole of Did 1-13 to reflect the doctrine and practice of a Jewish-Christian group.
[82] For the following, see Vööbus, *Liturgical Traditions*, 133-34; Niederwimmer, *Die Didache*, 176; J. Betz, 'The Eucharist in the Didache', 248-49.

has been interpreted as an *agape* (a meal proper),[83] or as a combination, that is an *agape* followed by the Eucharist,[84] or as the Eucharist celebrated before the *agape*,[85] or as a full-course meal consisting of bread and wine.[86] Considering these divergent opinions, it is not immediately evident that it is the Lord's Supper which is meant when the Didache speaks of 'eucharist'. In the following pages, our interest will center upon the question concerning the kind of meal framed by the prayers in Did 9-10. Do these chapters include a meal that can be defined as the Lord's Supper? For this purpose, the extant text referring to the meal in Did 9-10 and the passage in Did 14 will be examined first. It will be established that the words εὐχαριστεῖν and εὐχαριστία in the Didache are technical terms referring to a Eucharist in the proper sense (pp. 298-304). In a subsequent section, we will look for materials comparable to the ritual in Did 9-10, for we need not assume that the Eucharist took the shape of the usual institution accounts everywhere. What may seem exceptional and unique in the Didache are the vestigial remains of a more common phenomenon in the early church (pp. 304-09). In a third section (pp. 309-29), it will become clear that the specific nature of the Eucharist in the Didache is related to its history. The prayers in Did 9-10 are shaped after Jewish models. They can best be explained by assuming that they represent a historical process of transforming the original Jewish Grace after meals via a Hellenistic Jewish reworking and rephrasing into a (gentile) Christian Eucharist. Ultimately and in its earliest stage of the development of the Christian Eucharist, the ritual in Did 10 is derived from the Birkat Ha-Mazon. When these benedictions were adopted by the Jewish Greek-speaking synagogue, they maintained their proper Jewish character (stage 2), but once they were taken up by non-Jewish Christians, these benedictions, though still broadly grounded upon Jewish tradition, moved away from their Jewish roots (stage 3).

---

[83] E.g. Vokes, *The Riddle of the Didache*,197-207; Dix, *The Shape of the Liturgy*, 90-95. For this interpretation and the following ones, see also Niederwimmer, *Die Didache*, 176-79.

[84] Did 10:6 is often interpreted as a transition from the proper meal to the Eucharist; cf., for example, J. Betz, 'The Eucharist in the Didache', 248; Rordorf, 'L'Eucharistie des premiers chrétiens', 198; Rordorf-Tuilier, *La Doctrine des douze Apôtres*, 41 and n. 2; Rordorf, 'Die Mahlgebete', 233-42; Niederwimmer, *Die Didache,* 179; but cf. the criticism of Wengst, *Didache (Apostellehre)*, 45 and n. 154.

[85] Cf. Lietzmann who readjusts the text through the specific deposition of 10:6 to 9:2-4 in his *Messe und Herrenmahl*, 233-37. See below, n. 89.

[86] Wengst, *Didache (Apostellehre)*, 43-57.

THE CHARACTER OF THE RITUAL MEAL IN THE EXTANT TEXT OF THE DIDACHE:
A EUCHARIST

If we consider the text of Did 9-10 as an isolated unit, in terms of wording and content, the prayers before and after the meal are to some extent parallel:[87]

---

[87] For a similar illustration of the resemblance between Chaps. 9 and 10, see Niederwimmer, *Die Didache*, 174-75 and Clerici, *Einsammlung der Zerstreuten*, 5-6; for our rendering, see especially Sandelin, *Wisdom as Nourisher*, 186-89.

With respect to the text offered here, some commentary is necessary:

- 9:1.5: the noun "eucharist" deviates from the translation by A. Cody ('The *Didache*: An English Translation') which we follow on the whole. In 9:1.5, the noun 'eucharist' replaces his 'thanksgiving', since the ritual meal described here is a celebration of the Eucharist (see below).

- 9:3.4: "with regard to the fragment:" Cody, basing his translation on the edition of the Greek text by Rordorf-Tuilier (*La Doctrine des douze Apôtres*, 141-199), here renders "fragment" (κλάσμα). This word is found in Did 9:3 (in genitive) and 9:4 in the Jerusalem Ms. (H) but is considered secondary by many contemporary scholars, who believe the original text reads ἄρτος; cf. Peterson, 'Über einige Probleme', 169; Vööbus, *Liturgical Traditions*, 146-48; Niederwimmer, 'Textprobleme der Didache', 124-25; Id, *Die Didache*, 185-86.188; Wengst, *Didache (Apostellehre)*, 78.97-98. Certainly, especially with regard to 9:4, where H has τοῦτο κλάσμα, parallels from later liturgies give ἄρτος. These (mostly eucharistic) texts, however, may have been affected by the New Testament. Moreover, we have to face up to the demands of the text-critical principle of the *lectio difficilior*. This is to say that a development of the term κλάσμα into ἄρτος is entirely intelligible, but the reverse is not. Furthermore, the descriptions in Did 9-10 and Did 14 are likely to refer to one and the same ritual (see below, pp. 303-4). The separate wordings κλάσμα in 9:3.4 and εὐχαριστεῖν in Did 9:1.2.3; 10:1.2.3.4 seem to have triggered the expressions in Did 14 to "break bread and give thanks" (κλάσατε ἄρτον καὶ εὐχαριστήσατε). Finally, the term κλάσμα might simply be a translation of the Hebrew equivalent פת as this is mostly rendered in the LXX by κλάσμα. This background seems to be corroborated in mBer 6:1, where specific blessings are listed: "What benediction do they say over fruit? Over the fruit of trees one says: .... except for the bread, for over the bread (הפת שעל ,הפת מן חוץ) one says: 'Who brings forth bread (לחם) from the earth'" and another example in 6:5: "If one said a benediction over the bread (הפת על ברך) he need not say it over the savoury; but if one said it over the savoury he is not exempt from saying it over the bread (הפת את פטר לא);" see also Sandelin, *Wisdom as Nourisher*, 206.198-99; Rordorf-Tuilier, *La Doctrine des douze Apôtres*, 46, n. 4; Kollmann, *Ursprung und Gestalten*, 82, n. 20.

- 10:4: the variant "for all things (περὶ πάντων)" of the Coptic translation is to be preferred to "above all (πρὸ πάντων)" in the Jerusalem Ms. (For the Coptic version, see Jones-Mirecki, 'Considerations on the Coptic Papyrus', 52-57; esp. 52-53, column 1, lines 4-6). The reading πρὸ πάντων is still found in Rordorf-Tuilier (*La Doctrine des douze Apôtres*, 180) and was supported by Cody ('The *Didache*: An English Translation', 3). Nevertheless, the reading in the Coptic translation probably reflects an early Jewish layer of the Grace after the meal (see below!): "for all these things we thank you" (לך מודים אנו כלם ועל). See Wengst, *Didache (Apostellehre)*, 80; Niederwimmer, 'Textprobleme', 125-26; id, *Die Didache*, 198.

- 10:5: according to Vööbus (*Liturgical Traditions*, 93) the appositional phrase "once it is sanctified" (τὴν ἁγιασθεῖσαν) is "precisely the kind of accretion which abounds in the transmission of any text." The reading is attested to in the Jerusalem Ms. but is lacking in the Coptic text. The latter absence, however, does not justify the assumption that the

Did 9

1. As for the eucharist [thanksgiving], give thanks this way. (οὕτως εὐχαριστήσατε·)
2. First, with regard to the cup: we thank you, our Father, for the holy vine of David (Εὐχαριστοῦμέν σοι, πάτερ ἡμῶν, ὑπὲρ τῆς ἁγίας ἀμπέλου Δαυὶδ) your servant which you made known to us through Jesus your servant. To you be glory forever.
3. And with regard to the fragment: We thank you, our Father, for the life and knowledge which you made known to us through Jesus your servant. To you be glory forever (ὑπὲρ τῆς ζωῆς καὶ γνώσεως, ἧς ἐγνώρισας ἡμῖν διὰ Ἰησοῦ τοῦ παιδός σου· σοὶ ἡ δόξα εἰς τοὺς αἰῶνας).

Did 10

1. When you have had your fill, give thanks this way: (οὕτως εὐχαριστήσατε·)

2. We thank you, holy Father, for your holy name (Εὐχαριστοῦμέν σοι, πάτερ ἅγιε, ὑπὲρ τοῦ ἁγίου ὀνόματός σου), which you made dwell in our hearts, and

for the knowledge and faith and immortality, which you made known to us through Jesus your servant. To you be glory forever (καὶ ὑπὲρ τῆς γνώσεως καὶ πίστεως καὶ ἀθανασίας, ἧς ἐγνώρισας ἡμῖν διὰ Ἰησοῦ τοῦ παιδός σου· σοὶ ἡ δόξα εἰς τοὺς αἰῶνας).

3. You, almighty Lord, created all things

phrase is an added gloss, since the people of God too is sanctified in the Bible (Exod 31:13; Lev 11:44; 20:8; 22:32; Ezek 20:12; 37:28); and see also Wis 17:2 and Philo, *Praem*, 123.

- 10:8:   the final variant to be discussed is the so-called μύρον prayer which, besides being found in the Apostolic Constitutions VII, 27,1-2 in a later form, occurs in the Coptic translation: "But concerning the saying for the ointment, give thanks just as you say, 'We give thanks to you Father concerning the ointment which you showed us, through Jesus your Son. Yours is the glory forever! Amen'" (Jones-Mirecki, 'Considerations on the Coptic Papyrus', 52-57; esp. 52-53, column 1, lines 15-20). The originality of this strophe has been discussed at great length and, indeed, the prayer itself gives the impression of antiquity. For also in the early church (Mark 6:13; Jas 5:14-15) and in Jewish sources (Apoc.Mos. 9; cf. also Str-B 1, 428-29) the oil is used to cure the sick (cf. Wengst, *Didache [Apostellehre]*, 59). On the other hand, there are also reasons to suggest that this 'Coptic' prayer could be a later emendation. Firstly, it remains difficult to explain the omission of this passage in Ms. H. Secondly, while the eucharistic prayers of the Didache offer thanksgiving for spiritual gifts ("life and knowledge," "knowledge, faith and immortality," "spiritual food and drink and eternal life"), the ointment prayer gives thanks for the physical oil of anointing itself (see Vööbus, *Liturgical Traditions*, 56-57). Thirdly, two later church orders also have a prayer over the oil of anointing subsequent to the eucharistic formula, which may betray the tendency of positioning this kind of prayer precisely here. It is thus quite possible that in the original text of the Didache this *myron* prayer was missing and that it was inserted at a relatively early time (Audet, *La Didachè*, 67-70; Vööbus, *Liturgical Traditions*, 51-60; Rordorf-Tuilier, *La Doctrine des douze Apôtres*, 48; Niederwimmer, 'Textprobleme', 121; Id, *Die Didache*, 209; Dehandschutter, 'The Text of the *Didache*, 44-45). An alternative solution might be that this prayer has been misplaced somehow (Alon, 'Ha-halakha ba-Torat 12 ha-Shelihim', 291 (ET: 188-89).

for the sake of your name, and you
gave food and drink to human beings
for enjoyment, so that they would
thank you; but you graced us with
spiritual food and drink and eternal life
through ‹Jesus› your servant.

4. For all things we thank you, Lord, because you are powerful. To you be
glory forever.

4. Just as this fragment lay scattered upon
the mountains and became a single
[fragment] when it had been gathered,

so may your church be gathered
from the ends of the earth
into your kingdom.

5. Be mindful, Lord, of your church, to
preserve it from all evil [or, from every
evil being] and to perfect it in your
love. And, once it is sanctified,
gather it
from the four winds,
into the kingdom which you have prepared for it.

For glory and power are yours, through
Jesus Christ, forever
(οὕτω συναχθήτω σου ἡ ἐκκλησία
ἀπὸ τῶν περάτων τῆς γῆς εἰς τὴν

σὴν βασιλείαν·
ὅτι σοῦ ἐστιν ἡ δόξα καὶ ἡ δύναμις
διὰ Ἰησοῦ Χριστοῦ εἰς τοὺς
αἰῶνας) .

For power and glory are yours forever

(καὶ σύναξον αὐτὴν ἀπὸ τῶν
τεσσάρων ἀνέμων, τὴν
ἁγιασθεῖσαν, εἰς τὴν σὴν
βασιλείαν, ἣν ἡτοίμασας αὐτῇ·
ὅτι σοῦ ἐστιν ἡ δύναμις καὶ ἡ δόξα
εἰς τοὺς αἰῶνας).

6. May favour [or, grace] come, and may
this world pass by. Hosanna to the God
of David!
If anyone is holy, let him come (εἴ τις
ἅγιός ἐστιν, ἐρχέσθω). If anyone is
not, let him repent. Our Lord, come!
Amen.

5. Let no one eat or drink of your eucharist save those who have been baptized
in the name of the Lord, since the Lord
has said, "Do not give to dogs what is
holy (Μὴ δῶτε τὸ ἅγιον τοῖς
κυσί)."

7. Allow the prophets, though, to give
thanks as much as they like.

Both prayers, the Grace before and after the meal, begin with an expression of
thanksgiving addressed to God in nearly identical wording, and when we read these
prayers side by side throughout, the resemblances of phraseology and content will
become quite obvious. The composition suggests that the subject of the prayers
in these two chapters must be eucharistic. Because their likeness is not restricted
to a casual analogy but appears to pervade the whole pattern of the two prayers,
certain phrases which at first sight do not seem to share similar content may
nevertheless clarify one another. We cannot leave the first prayer hanging in the
air precisely because it is parallel to the second. This, of course, applies first of all

to the doublet in 9:4 and 10:5 that speaks about the gathering of the dispersed church into the kingdom of God. We will say more about this shortly. For now, it is of importance to stress that the parallelism in structure and content between the benedictions in Did 9 and 10 suggest that these prayers refer to a single meal. They encircle the actions which occur between them. Rather than representing two different kinds of meals (first a Eucharist and then an *agape*, or first an *agape* and then a Eucharist), the prayers apparently frame a satiating meal. This supper, including the prayers, is called the 'Eucharist'.[88]

Theories to the effect that different types of meals are referred to in this part of the Didache are usually based on Did 10:6, a passage which still is a crux interpretum in view of its precise meaning and function. After the words in 9:2-10:5, considered to be referring to a proper meal, this verse is often understood as a rite of transition to the full eucharistic sacrament. There is a rapid shift in diction and phraseology here because this verse, like an abrupt chain of short and apparently loosely connected sentences, intrudes stylistically into the context. Did 10:6 displays a different type of discourse than the preceding verses, but the "amen" at the end of this passage seems to assign these lines to the foregoing liturgical portion. Moreover, according to H. Lietzmann this verse should be read as a liturgical dialogue between the celebrant and the congregation.[89] The clauses of 10:6b ("If anyone is holy, let him come. If anyone is not, let him repent") are understood generally as an invitation and caution. The celebrant bids the participants to leave their seats in order to take part in the Lord's Supper which follows immediately thereafter and, at the same time, warns against unworthy attendance.[90] This command would be meaningless unless it is spoken at the beginning of the Eucharist. At first sight, then, the clauses create the impression of presenting the most sacred part, the Eucharist proper, as happening only now, not as already having happened. In that case, however, the account of institution (like a sequel of the prayers), would have been omitted in the extant text.[91]

It is true, the exclamations in the first two sentences ("May favour [or, grace] come, and may this world pass by. Hosanna to the God of David!") and the last two words μαραναθά. ἀμήν may be seen as the conclusion of the eucharistic prayers in their Christian form. The clauses of 10:6b ("If anyone is holy, let him

---

[88]   Cf. among others: Sandelin, *Wisdom as Nourisher*, 224; Middleton, 'The Eucharistic Prayers', 259-63; Creed, 'The Didache', 386-87; Mazza, *The Origins of the Eucharistic Prayer*, 16-30; Kollmann, *Ursprung und Gestalten*, 91-98; Klinghardt, *Gemeinschaftsmahl und Mahlgemeinschaft*, 379-86.

[89]   But he also – rather unconvincingly – suggested that the sentences of this dialogue in 10:6 had been misplaced and should be transferred to their original position after Did 9:5; cf. Lietzmann, *Messe und Herrenmahl*, 236-37.

[90]   "... wir haben hier in εἴ τις ἅγιός ἐστιν ... die Einladung zur Kommunion und im folgenden die Warnung vor unwürdiger Teilnahme an ihr vor uns. – Mit dem Übergang zur sakramentalen Kommunion erfährt die Feier in den Kultrufen eine letzte Steigerung;" cf. Niederwimmer, *Die Didache*, 202; cf. also 179.

[91]   By deliberate suppression (cf. Rordorf-Tuilier, *La Doctrine des douze Apôtres*, 40, n. 2) or by allusion to the so-called arcane discipline (cf. Jeremias, *Die Abendmahlsworte Jesu*, 127-28 [ET: 86-87]; but see Niederwimmer, *Die Didache*, 180 and n. 54).

come"), however, are hardly meant to be an invitation to participate in the Lord's Supper. If the instruction "let him come" really implied the connotation "to come forward," the Greek text probably would require the compound verb προσερχέσθω, rather than just ἐρχέσθω.[92] The latter verb is an invitation to come but without saying where. Maybe it makes more sense to interpret the phrases "If anyone is holy, let him come. If anyone is not, let him repent" in the light of 9:5. In that case, we rely on the intrinsic evidence provided by the document itself, that in inner structure the two prayers in Did 9-10 run parallel.[93] Both phrases (9:5 and 10:6b) are not articulated by the celebrant but must be considered as rubrical instructions. For it is far more likely that these passages embody an admonition added at a later date by the final editor of the Didache for the purpose of instruction of his community.[94] He supplemented these two short phrases as a non-liturgical injunction when he integrated the two chapters in the body of the work. It is a general admonition to the readers of the manual reminding them to repent and be prepared. Since the ἅγιός ('holy') in Did 10:6 refers to the baptized person of 9:5, a verse which likewise gives an appended explanatory commentary, it is only the baptized that may eat from the Eucharist.[95] As we will see below, this explanation does justice to the eucharistic nature of the meal in accordance with Did 9:1.5. Since those who are called "holy" in 10:6 are those who have been baptized in 9:5, the order "let him repent" in the very same verse implies "let him be baptized." The instruction concerning the Eucharist occurs where one would expect the Eucharist to be dealt with: after the instruction on baptism. In liturgical practice as well in church orders, the celebration of the Eucharist follows baptism.

   A fundamental impediment to the view that Didache would picture here any-thing but a Eucharist is the definite statement in 9:1 and 9:5. The word *agape* does not occur, probably because in the Didachist's milieu a common religous meal that was not a Eucharist did not occur. The noun 'eucharist' (εὐχαριστία) is introduced in 9:1 with the article and in 9:5 the word reappears with the article. The phrase Περὶ δὲ τῆς εὐχαριστίας ("as for thanksgiving") in 9:1 has exactly the same pattern as the clause in Did 7:1 Περὶ δὲ τοῦ βαπτίσματος ("As for Baptism"), thus indicating that we are dealing with a rule for the conduct of church ceremo-nial. While a greater freedom is claimed for the prophets (see 10:7), other members

---

[92] "En outre, lorsqu'il interprète le εἴ τις ἅγιός ἐστιν, ἐρχέσθω, Lietzmann lit bien ἐρχέσθω, mais il entend προσερχέσθω, et dans le sens des liturgies postérieures. C'est l'invitation à «s'approcher» pour la communion;" cf. Audet, *La Didachè*, 413.

[93] See Draper, 'Ritual Process and Ritual Symbol', 134 and 141. "The common interpretation of 10:6 as providing a transition (...) to 'the sacrament proper' ... seems to be misplaced and based solely on the presupposition that a eucharist must contain the Words of Institution found in the Western eucharist-ic tradition. The second prohibition in 10:6 is a recapitulation and further development of the first in 9:5." (142).

[94] Cf. Riggs, 'The Sacred Food', 277-78; Vööbus, *Liturgical Traditions*, 70-74.

[95] See also Verheul, 'La prière eucharistique', 341.

We thus consider the isolated and disconnected clauses of Did 10:6 to have survived here as a conglom-erate of mere splinters of both liturgical and exhortative formulations; cf. Vööbus, *Liturgical Traditions*, 102; Knopf, *Die Lehre der zwölf Apostel*, 29; Sandelin, *Wisdom as Nourisher*, 226.

of the Christian community addressed in the Didache – apparently those without the charisma of spirit – were provided with rubrical instructions and model prayers for the ritual of the meal. The passage in 9:5 is even more interesting. The term εὐχαριστία here not only refers to the utterance of the thanksgiving prayers (Did 9:2-4; 10:2-5) but to what is revered thereby as well, namely the eucharistic food. Since the prayers do not give any explanation for this nomenclature, one may assume the term to have been perceived that way in the community of the Didache. The occurrence in 9:5 therefore seems to represent a technical use of the term.[96] The meal is not understood as an ordinary meal but as something special.

The food was holy and set aside for baptized members of the community only while the non-baptized are prohibited from taking part in 'the Eucharist'. Also by other early Christian writers like Ignatius of Antioch (*Smyrn.* 7:1 and *Rom.* 7:3; cf *Eph.* 20:2) and Justin Martyr (*1 Apol.* 66:1-2), the noun is used for eucharistic food.[97] The obvious solution to the problem that the words of institution are lacking in Did 9-10 is to put aside one's prejudice that the words are a necessary part of the ritual of the Eucharist in the first century. For the evidence seems to indicate that the food and drink are called 'eucharist' because they are blessed, 'eucharisti-fied' by the meal prayers (cf. 9:1: οὕτως εὐχαριστήσατε).[98] The term 'eucharist' in 9:1 therefore refers to the entire ritual of a meal which is truly *the* Eucharist, and every claim which presses for a non-eucharistic interpretation in Did 9-10 stands in patent contradiction to everything these prayers want to say.

In this context, the question whether Did 9-10 and Did 14 envisage one and the same rite is of importance as well. Did 14 deals with the assemblies on the day of the Lord[99] and requires of the community that they "break bread and give thanks" (κλάσατε ἄρτον καὶ εὐχαριστήσατε), expressions which exactly correspond to the wordings κλάσμα in 9:3.4 and εὐχαριστεῖν in Did 9:1.2.3; 10:1.2.3.4. The two expressions, accordingly, appear to represent a *hendiadys*, denoting a single rite of 'breaking the bread with thanksgiving;' Did 14, therefore, obviously refers to the same reality as that described in Did 9-10. In addition to these actions, Did

[96]   Cf. Kraft, *Barnabas and the Didache*, 167; Conzelmann, 'εὐχαριστέω κτλ.', 405; Wengst, *Didache (Apostellehre)*, 44.

[97]   Marcovich, *Iustini Martyris Apologiae*, 127; lines 1-10. See also Hänggi-Pahl, *Prex Eucharistica*, 70. For the instances in Ignatius of Antioch and Justin Martyr, see also Sandelin, *Wisdom as Nourisher*, 227 and Riggs, 'The Sacred Food', 270-71 and 276-77.

[98]   Clerici, *Einsammlung der Zerstreuten*, 13.

[99]   According to Tidwell ('Didache XIV:1'), the expression κατὰ κυριακὴν δὲ κυρίου in the opening phrase of Chap 14 is not a pleonasm but a clear Semitism. The occurrence of κυρίου without an article would reflect the Septuagintic tradition of using κυρίου to refer distinctively to the tetragrammaton, to Israel's God, rather than to Jesus. In this quality, the epithet is considered to be a case of the tetragrammaton employed in its superlative function. The force of the divine name in this expression would be to raise the κυριακή, the day of the Lord, to a preeminent degree. Since Yom Kippur is the day, preeminently, of the Jewish festival calender, the opening expression of 14:1 might well refer to a Jewish-Christian observance of Yom Kippur. However attractive this hypothesis may be, one objection is inevitable. In view of the evidence in 11:2, where the twofold usage of the noun κύριος without an article is likely to point to Jesus twice, it is questionable whether in the Didache this term is earmarked to refer to the tetragrammaton only. Further, see also Rordorf, *Der Sonntag*, 207-12.

14 speaks of "sacrifice" but there is no compelling reason for believing that "breaking bread," "giving thanks" and the "sacrifice" refer to separate rituals. It is also beside the point to contend that, since Did 14 is concerned with the Eucharist, Did 9-10 must deal with the *agape* celebration because the editor cannot have discussed the same subject twice. For, although the Eucharist depicted in Did 14 is none other than that of 9-10, it is not a mere repetition. The major issue of Chap. 14 is not the worship on the day of the Lord but confession and reconciliation to prepare for it.[100] Summarizing, we thus may argue with some assurance that one should reject any alleged difference between the uses of the term εὐχαριστεῖν or εὐχαριστία in Did 9-10 on the one hand and Did 14 on the other,[101] since the ritual in Did 14 is identical to the Eucharist described in Did 9-10.

THE CHARACTER OF THE DIDACHE EUCHARIST IN THE PERSPECTIVE OF ITS DIFFUSION

The structural and thematical similarity of Did 9 and 10 encourages the belief that the prayers in these chapters refer to a single meal, a ritual which is headed by one and the same rubric in 9:1: Περὶ δὲ τῆς εὐχαριστίας. On the grounds that important features (the silence about the death of Jesus and the sequence cup-bread) of this Eucharist differ too much from the evidence otherwise known to us from Christian antiquity, the ritual meal in the Didache is often dismissed from consideration as being anything but a Eucharist. We need not assume, however, that the Eucharist took the same shape everywhere. A liturgical text that is most common does not necessarily contain the most ancient form, and an unusual phenomenon, seemingly atypical of the period, may in fact be a rudimentary relic of a common ancient practice that somehow managed to escape a later unifying process. In this section, the widespread belief is put to the test whether the actual Eucharist described in Did 9-10 is the only exception to the general shape of the liturgy in the ancient church. Was this type of liturgy restricted to the community from which the Didache is derived or is there comparative material left suggesting that these eucharistic rites were diffused more widely? Our concern will be primarily with the rite opening the eucharistic supper in Did 9, where the blessing said over the cup precedes the blessing over the bread.

The structure of the rite opening the Eucharist in Did 9 is often considered anomalous[102] in Christian liturgy since the history of the eucharistic celebration always

---

[100] Niederwimmer, *Die Didache*, 12.234.

[101] For example, that the prayers in Chaps. 9-10 refer to a genuine meal, while Chap. 14 refers to the actual celebration of the Sunday Eucharist without a meal; see Drews, 'Untersuchungen zur Didache', 78-79 and, similarly, Knopf, *Die Lehre der zwölf Apostel*, 35.

[102] The observation that the sequence bread-cup appears in 9:5 and 10:3 would speak for an original sequence bread-cup (cf. J. Betz, 'The Eucharist in the Didache', 252) does not hold good. These verses refer to the sequence of elements in the course of the material satiation while the opening liturgy regards the ritual only: "Après les bénédictions sur la coupe et sur le pain, on mange d'abord et on boit ensuite

shows the inverted order, that is bread-cup. The normal bread-cup sequence is found in the accounts of the Last Supper as transmitted in Matt 26:26-29; Mark 14:22-25 and 1 Cor 11:23-25. On the other hand, the order cup-bread is not as peculiar as it may seem. The practice is reflected in the shorter Lukan institution account (22:15-19a), which omits any mention of the second cup. Luke's institution narrative has come down to us in two forms, a longer and a shorter text. Both these versions offer the report of Luke 22:15-18 but then diverge: the longer text adding vv. 19b-20 (τὸ ὑπὲρ ὑμῶν / "given for you" ... ἐκχυννόμενον / "poured out" at the end of v. 20) is read by all Greek manuscripts, with the exception of the Codex Bezae (D) and other witnesses of the Western text (a, d, ff², i, l) which represent the shorter version. The weight of the manuscript evidence thus favours the longer text. At the same time, it is important to note that there are serious objections to this assumption.[103] First, a basic rule of textual criticism applies here, that is that the shorter reading often is the older one. Second, it is more intelligible why the shorter text was extended into the canonical longer version than the reverse. An adaptation to other accepted institution accounts, especially to the one in 1 Cor 11:17-33 might have been felt necessary to establish the sequence bread-wine. Third, the long version contains several linguistic features which are non-Lukan and clearly reflect 1 Cor 11:24b-25. The verses probably are an interpolation in Luke 22:19b-20 which was based on the Pauline version of the Last Supper account.

The blessings in Did 9:2-3 introduce the celebration of the Eucharist. When someone recites a blessing, he or she declares that the food originally belonged to God, and that now it represents a gift. Specific blessings and the procedures for their recitation are listed in mBer 6. Nothing was to be eaten without God having first been blessed for it. It was unacceptable to 'enjoy anything in the world without a blessing.'[104] While, in fact, benedictions had to be recited for anything eaten, the bread and wine did not, of course, constitute the entire menu. These two elements are singled out, however, since they stood for the whole meal. The benediction over the bread exempted the other foods, except for wine, which required its own benediction. A number of Christian communities celebrated their communal meal in the same order as non-sectarian Jews did, with the blessing over the wine preceding the blessing over the bread.[105] This was the normal sequence

(cf. *Did*, 9,5; 10,3);" Rordorf-Tuilier, *La Doctrine des douze Apôtres*, 175, n. 7; cf. also Wengst, *Didache (Apostellehre)*, 45.

[103] See e.g. Lietzmann, *Messe und Herrenmahl*, 215-17; R.D. Richardson, 'A Further Inquiry', 224-37; Metzger, *A Textual Commentary*, 173-77; Amphoux, 'Luc 22/15-20'; Van Cangh, 'Le déroulement primitif', 194; Kilpatrick, 'Luke XXII, 19b-20'; cf. also Oesterley, *The Jewish Background*, 163; Burkitt, 'On Luke 22.17-20'; Finegan, *Die Ueberlieferung*,11; Schürmann, *Der Paschamahlbericht*, 123; Gamber, 'Die «Eucharistia»', 8-10. See also Jeremias, *Die Abendmahlsworte Jesu*, 133-153 (ET: 87-106), who decides, however, in favour of the longer text of Luke's account of the Last Supper.

[104] Cf. bBer 35 in Safrai, 'Religion in Everyday Life', 803. For a justification of the blessings before eating, cf. Bokser, '*Ma'al* and Blessings over Food'.

[105] There is no compelling reason to connect the wine-bread sequence in the Eucharist of the Didache with the *Kiddush*. The Kiddush is a rite performed at the eve of Shabbat or a feast-day before the meal and comprises a blessing over the cup (and, in a later period also over the bread) to dedicate the Sabbath

in the Eucharist of those early Christian communities in which the Didache and the shorter Lukan version were transmitted; and this order has continued to be the arrangement for the ordinary Jewish meal until today.

The pattern 'bread-cup', however, fits the Essene order.[106] An account of the communal meal of the Essenes is given in 1QS 6:4-5 and, with more detailed information, in 1QSa 2:17-22. In these passages, presumably reflecting actual practice in the Qumran community, the priestly blessings of the bread and the wine are said to take place at the beginning of the meal, in this order, the one immediately after the other.[107] There were Christian communities celebrating their communal meal in the same order as sectarian Jews did, with the bread preceding the wine. One may thus assume that both traditions containing the sequence 'bread-wine' as well as 'wine-bread' represent primitive Christian practice. In any case, the sequence 'bread-wine' became the official order for the Eucharist in the churches, and entered into most of the New Testament reports. In fact, it supplanted the former non-sectarian type in many Christian communities.[108]

Before looking at some additional indications supporting the cup-bread structure, it is useful to briefly review the appearance of the Last Supper in the New Testament. In the above discussion, it was established that the texts presenting the Last Supper are not identical in their description of the institution of the Eucharist.[109] We have basically two different reports about the Last Supper (Matt 26:26-29; Mark 14:22-25; 1 Cor 11:23-25 *and* Luke 22:15-19a), varying both in their cover-

---

or feast-day to God. The prayers, however, of the Eucharist in the Didache – neither the blessing over the wine, nor the blessing over the bread – do not mention the holiness of the day. See also Alon, 'Hahalakha ba-Torat 12 ha-Shelihim', 287, n. 59 (ET: 183, n. 59); Niederwimmer, *Die Didache*, 181-82, n. 4.

[106] See Flusser, 'The Last Supper'.

[107] The Essene order 'bread - wine' is now confirmed by the Temple Scroll from Qumran. See Yadin, *The Temple Scroll* 1, 140-42, note 73. Josephus also offers a description of the ordinary Essene meal in *Bellum* 2, 130-31, which in many respects agrees with the one presented in the Qumran texts (see Thackeray, *Josephus* 2 [LCL 203] 372). In this report, he doesn't say anything about a blessing over the wine or the wine as being a constituent of the meal. A few lines below this account, however, he mentions the Essenes' sobriety and "the limitation of their allotted portions of food (τροφήν) and drink (ποτόν)" (*Bellum* 2, 133). For a comparison between the rendering in Josephus and the two Qumran texts (IQS and IQSa), see K.G. Kuhn, 'Über den ursprünglichen Sinn'. See also Schiffman, *Sectarian Law*, 191-210.

[108] Van Cangh ('Le déroulement primitif', 215) has brought ancient witnesses for the Eucharist consisting only of bread (*sub una*); see also Luke 24:35 and Acts 2:42.46; 20:7.11. Although, in these instances of Acts, the occurrence of the expression "breaking of bread" does not necessarily preclude the use of wine, it is likely that wine did not always belong to the ritual meal. It was, after all, not as easily available as it is today; cf. also Vogel, 'Anaphores eucharistiques préconstantiniennes'; Rouwhorst, 'Bread and Cup', 35-36.

[109] The chronological attestations in the New Testament texts do not agree among themselves either. There are scholars who claim that the Last Supper was a Passover meal and they rely on the Synoptic gospels. On the other hand, there are others who reject this idea because they accept John's chronology as historical, which situates the Supper on the day "before the feast of the Passover" (13:1). An innovative effort at harmonization was made by A. Jaubert, who reaches the conclusion that Jesus ate the Passover meal on Tuesday and died on Friday; cf. her *La Date de la Cène*, 135; Id., 'Jésus et le calendrier de Qumrân', passim.

age of the sequence of actions of the Last Supper and in their rendering of the words used by Jesus. These ways of describing the celebration of the Last Supper are modelled after two quite different types of Jewish antecedents. The gospel accounts of this ceremony, then, are not accurate portrayals of an actual historical event but creations of the early Christian communities which in turn were influenced by liturgical practices in early Judaism. It is not advisable, therefore, to attempt a reconstruction of the Last Supper at the Passover.[110] On the contrary, it is far more likely that the daily ritual meal of a Christian community was originally not considered as having any connection with the Last Supper. Yet, since the liturgy described in the Synoptic gospels contains a number of details which are in correspondence with the Passover explanation,[111] the most that can be said is that the Last Supper took place in a Passover ambience.

Those favouring the originality of the tradition containing the structure 'cup - bread' might draw some extra support from the First Letter to the Corinthians. It is of particular interest to note that Paul, while referring to the Eucharist twice, uses both the order 'bread-cup' and 'cup-bread'. Let us discuss the authoritative bread-wine sequence first. This liturgical structure is found in 1 Cor 11:23-25. We have seen that Paul presents here the official church order which was in agreement with the Essene tradition:

> For I (Paul) received from the Lord what I also delivered to you, that the Lord Jesus on the night when he was betrayed took bread, and when he had given thanks, he broke it, and said, ...In the same way also the cup, after supper, saying ... (1Cor 11:23-25)

It is noteworthy, however, that in contrast to the rendering of the institution narrative in Mark and Matthew, the position of the cup and its blessing is the same as in the inserted verses of Luke 22:19b-20. The cup over which Jesus gives thanks was the cup used *after* dinner: "in the same way also the cup, after supper, ..." (ὡσαύτως καὶ τὸ ποτήριον μετὰ τὸ δειπνῆσαι ... / Luke: καὶ τὸ ποτήριον ὡσαύτως μετὰ τὸ δειπνῆσαι), which shows the close relation between the two texts. It is not impossible that according to Paul, a former Pharisee, the official bread-cup sequence was aberrant and this may be the reason why, when transmitting this apostolic tradition, he adds the use of the cup (accompanied by the relevant blessing) *after* the meal (μετὰ τὸ δειπνῆσαι). In that case, he must have been acquainted with the expression "cup of blessing" as a technical one in rabbinic literature (כוס של ברכה or כוס הברכה), which refers to one of the various cups

---

[110] Van Cangh, 'Le déroulement primitif', 210, n. 31; see also Ligier, 'The Origins of the Eucharistic Prayer', 161-63; *pace* Jeremias, *Die Abendmahlsworte Jesu.*

[111] It is not difficult to identify the cup of the Jewish Passover meal - or, according to the secondary text of Luke (22:15-20), the two cups - with one of the various cups of the Jewish ceremony. Moreover, Mark stresses the atmosphere of the Jewish feast by adding two items: in 14:20 (cf. Matt 26:23), the eating of vegetables before the meal is suggested (see Str-B 1, 989), and in 14:26, the participants are reported as hymn-singing (cf. Matt 26:30), which probably refers to the second section of the Hallel (Pss 115 [or 114]-118; see mPes 10:6). On the other hand, the early church did not celebrate the Eucharist according to the Passover ritual. One of the two liturgical variants of the procedure itself fits the rabbinic (wine-bread), and the other the Essene form of a solemn Jewish meal (bread-wine).

that were passed around after dinner.[112] If this tradition was operative in the mid-first century, Paul is likely to have referred in 1 Cor 11:25 to an autonomous rite of the cup, which – separate from the juxtaposed rites of cup and bread – took place at the end of a solemn Jewish meal, such as the Passover meal.

Even if the terminology τὸ ποτήριον τῆς εὐλογίας (the "cup of blessing") reflects a well established expression derived from Judaism,[113] concerning a cup that was handed around among the participants after the meal, yet it is difficult to decide whether the wording was reserved in Paul's days for this use only.[114] For in 1 Cor 10:16, he mentions the rite of the cup and the rite of the bread (in this reverse order!). Paul intends to demonstrate the importance of participating in the rite as a means to obtain communion with God/the gods. He refers to the lived experience of the Corinthians and probably resorts to a traditional terminology and pattern of the Lord's Supper. The rite of the cup and the rite of the bread are the elements which enable the Corinthians to commune with the blood and body of Christ: "The cup of blessing (τὸ ποτήριον τῆς εὐλογίας) which we bless, is it not a participation in the blood of Christ? The bread which we break, is it not a participation in the body of Christ?" In v. 17, he goes on to point to the unity implied in the bread of the Christian rite because there is only one body of Christ. When the "cup of blessing" was not yet bound to a particular ritual moment in first-century Judaism, its mention *before* the eucharistic bread may be particularly relevant to our subject. It would imply that Paul in 1 Cor 10 is reproducing the liturgy of the eucharistic supper as celebrated by the Christian community in Corinth and by himself. The first person plural of the various verbs in verses 16-17 (εὐλογοῦμεν, κλῶμεν, ἐσμεν, μετέχομεν) tells us what the church does in its assembly. In this letter, the two celebrations are different, the one (11:23-25) dealing with apostolic tradition about Jesus and confronting the Corinthians with a model to live after, while the other (10:16-17) considers the actual liturgy of the local community. Because the efficacy of the ceremony with regard to unity is formulated in rhetorical questions (οὐχί ... οὐχί), the rite of the cup and of the bread must be ritual facts, which the Corinthians were experiencing just as Paul describes them. Because the cup is mentioned first in 1 Cor 10:16-17 (and this sequence is repeated in 10:21!), one may conclude that Paul does not formally quote apostolic tradition but follows the more common Jewish order here.

The sparsity of the evidence makes it extremely difficult to draw definite conclusions about the form of the eucharistic celebrations of the early Christians. There

---

[112] Cf. the baraita in bBer51a and compare bBer 48a; see also Str-B 3, 419; 4, 628-31; for a discussion on the question which of the cups of the Passover Seder was the cup of institution, cf. Cohn-Sherbok, 'A Jewish Note on ΤΟ ΠΟΤΗΡΙΟΝ ΤΗΣ ΕΥΛΟΓΙΑΣ'; Sigal, 'Another Note to 1 Corinthians 10.16'; cf. also Id., 'Early Christian and Rabbinic Liturgical Affinities'.

[113] The expression כוס של ברכה is also found in Kal 1 (50b) (twice); KalR 1:7.8 (51b) and yBer 2,5b.

[114] For the following, see Mazza, *The Origins of the Eucharistic Prayer*, 66-97 (= Chap. III, which is a translation of an article published previously: 'L'eucaristia di 1 Corinzi 10:16-17'); Tomson, *Paul and the Jewish Law*, 141-42.

are clear indications, however, that initially there were two quite different types of eucharistic liturgy in the early church. First, the tradition reflected in Luke 22:15-19a, Did 9 and, possibly, 1 Cor 10:16 and, second, the canonical one, common to almost all versions of the institution report (cf. Matt 26:26-29; Mark 14:22-25 and 1 Cor 11:23-25). We have seen above that the rite of the blessing over the cup preceding the one over bread was derived from a common Jewish custom practised in other early Christian communities as well. In this kind of Christian liturgy, the institution narrative appears considerably reduced or nonexistent. Did 9 and Luke 22:15-19a give evidence of the persistence of this reverse order. Once, however, the canonical institution account had replaced the tradition reflected in Luke and the Didache, later generations did not want to preserve the latter. The tradition consequently ceases to appear in later canonical writings in that form. The argument of the omission of the actual account of institution thus has no weight whatsoever in the discussion about the character of the meal in Did 9-10, because it does not seem a necessary part of the ritual of the Eucharist in the first century. The idea that an institution report must be present if a ritual is to be assessed as truly eucharistic is merely a surmise based on a practice which became commonly accepted at a later stage only. The gospel message must not be the chief criterion in interpreting the eucharistic prayers of the Didache.

THE CHARACTER OF THE DIDACHE EUCHARIST IN THE PERSPECTIVE OF ITS HISTORY

Like Did 9:1.5 and part of 10:6-7, the passage in Did 10:1 makes up a liturgical rubric, an injunction to the Christian community addressed in the Didache. The phrase "When you have had your fill" (μετὰ δὲ τὸ ἐμπλησθῆναι) refers to a regular meal for the satisfaction of the believers. In the following pages, the focus will be primarily on some of the key issues in the eucharistic prayers of Did 9:2-10:5 which frame a genuine full-course dinner. These prayers, being older than the Didache, have their parallel in the Jewish rites that open and conclude a Jewish ritual meal. The attachment of the Didache community to the Judaism of their environment must still have been very strong, which is not surprising. For we may expect that the first converts continued to adhere to the pattern of daily prayer which was observed by Jews of the time. Let us consider the different successive elements of the Eucharist. First, in a source-critical approach, we will concentrate on the various sources of the extant form of the prayers. Next, in the subsequent sections, a tradition-historical treatment will be the line of approach, dealing with the development of the prayers in Did 9-10 over time.

The Jewish Sources of the Eucharistic Prayers in Did 9-10

The celebration begins with a prayer of thanksgiving over the cup followed by a thanksgiving over the bread (Did 9:2-3).[115] These separate prayers are both embodied now in the setting of the common meal and their structure reflects the sequence (cup-bread) of mainstream Judaism. They are close to the Jewish table blessing in content as well. In the Mishna, the Jewish blessing over the cup is rendered thus:

> (Blessed are you, O Lord, our God, King of the world,) who creates the fruit of the vine (mBer 6:1)

and over the bread:

> (Blessed are you, O Lord, our God, King of the world,) who brings forth bread from the earth (mBer 6:1).

Especially the thanksgiving over the cup in Did 9:2 recalls its Jewish origins. The mention of David twice in 9:2 and 10:6 - without a Christological connotation – is quite conceivable in a Jewish environment.[116] Moreover, the wording of 9:2 in itself is similar to its Jewish counterpart in two respects. First, the concept of the vine, directly bound up with the contents of the cup, is also found in the Jewish benediction over the cup. Second, the formula "for the holy vine" (ὑπὲρ τῆς ἁγίας ἀμπέλου) takes up the Jewish expression הגפן פרי ("fruit of the vine"),[117] which indicates the dependence on a traditional Jewish wine blessing.

The thanksgiving over the bread in Did 9:3 is somewhat longer because it is yoked to a petition for the unity of the church in 9:4. This supplication to assemble the church is taken up again in 10:5 and appears to play an important role in this liturgy. The idea reaches far back into biblical tradition and is linked with the expectation in the Hebrew bible that the dispersed of Israel will be gathered in the day of salvation. The four principal passages in the Bible speaking of the dispersion and the gathering of the people run as follows:

- ... then the Lord your God will restore your fortunes, and have compassion upon you, and he will gather you again from all the peoples where the Lord your God has scattered you. If your outcasts are in the uttermost parts of heaven, from there the Lord your God will gather you, and from there he will fetch you; and the Lord your God will bring you into the land which your fathers possessed, that you may possess it; ... (Deut 30:3-5a);

[115] Since the Greek verb εὐχαριστεῖν is used here, we speak of a 'thanksgiving' rather than 'blessing'. Its meaning is not equivalent to the Hebrew ברך (usually translated as εὐλογεῖν), as suggested by Audet, *La Didachè*, 377-98; see further, below in n. 151.

[116] See Wengst, *Didache (Apostellehre)*, 49; Niederwimmer, *Die Didache*, 184, n. 22 and Vööbus, *Liturgical Traditions*, 125-26. For the messianic connotation of the expression 'your servant', see 4 Ezra 13:32.37 and 7:28-29; see also Stone, *Fourth Ezra*, 208 and 393.

[117] The phrase γένημα τῆς ἀμπέλου in Matt 26:29; Mark 14:25 and Luke 22:18 comes even closer to the Hebrew expression הגפן פרי of the blessing of the cup.

- ... He will assemble the outcasts of Israel, and gather the dispersed of Judah from the four corners of the earth (Isa 11:12b-c);
- I will gather you from the peoples, and assemble you out of the countries where you have been scattered, and I will give you the land of Israel (Ezek 11:17b-d);
- Thus says the Lord God: Behold, I will take the people of Israel from the nations among which they have gone, and will gather them from all sides, and bring them to their own land (Ezek 37:21).[118]

The aspiration of being gathered also plays a special part in the stereotyped description of "Sin-Exile-Return" passages, often recurring in the Testaments of the Twelve Patriarchs. After the sins of the sons of the patriarchs, exile among the gentiles is mentioned and, finally, their return from captivity.[119] This desire that the people of Israel might be gathered and united was also kept alive in Jewish liturgical traditions. The tenth benediction of the Palestinian recension of the *tefilla* reads:

> lift up the banner for the gathering of our exiles; praised are you, O Lord, who gathers the dispersed of your people Israel[120]

and the Babylonian recension of the same supplication has:

> lift up the banner to gather all our exiles from the four ends of the earth into our land; praised are you, O Lord, who gathers the dispersed of your people Israel[121]

The prayers display the same hope of gathering the scattered from the "(four) ends of the earth." The Jewish petition is not reflected in the prayer of the Didache, however, to the extent that no longer is the gathering of Israel implored but the gathering of the church from the ends of the earth. More will be said shortly on the Christian use of this traditional Jewish theme (pp. 325-29).

As we can see in the rubric of Did 10:1 a regular meal follows upon these prayers, which is concluded by an additional prayer of thanksgiving. This is the second part of the eucharistic prayers of Did 9-10. According to an overwhelming consensus of scholarly opinion, this prayer is a reworking of the Birkat Ha-Mazon,

---

[118] See also Isa 27:13; 43:5-7; 56:8; Jer 23:8; 31:8.10; 39:37 (LXX); Ezek 28:25; 34:11-16; 39:27; Mic 4:12; Pss 106:47; 147:2; Neh 1:8-9; Zech 2:10 (LXX); 1 Chr 16:35; Sir 36:11; 2 Macc 1:27; 2:7.18; Tob 13:5; cf. Niederwimmer, *Die Didache*, 188 and n. 54. For the theme of the gathering of the dispersed in the LXX, in writings of the Second Temple period and in the New Testament, see Clerici, *Einsammlung der Zerstreuten*, 67-85.

[119] *T. Levi* 10; 14-15; 16; *T. Jud.* 18:1 + 23; *T. Iss.* 6; *T. Zeb.* 9:5-7.9; *T.Dan* 5:4a + 5.6-9; *T.Naph.* 4:1-3; *T. Asher* 7:2. 5-7; for these "Sin-Exile-Return" passages, cf. De Jonge, *The Testaments*, 83-86 and Hollander-De Jonge, *The Testaments*, 39-41 and 53-56.

[120] For a comparison in parallel columns of the prayers in Did 9-10 and their Jewish sources, see Riggs, 'From Gracious Table', 92-93; Middleton, 'The Eucharistic Prayers', 261-64.

[121] See Str-B 4/1, 212; Clerici, *Einsammlung der Zerstreuten*, 90. See also the Mussaf prayer for Rosh Hashana and the benediction before the Shema: "Bring us to peace from the four ends of the earth and lead us straight into our land."

the prayer that concludes the Jewish ritual meal.[122] This might also be inferred from the terminology in Did 10:1: "When you have had your fill" (μετὰ δὲ τὸ ἐμπλησθῆναι). Besides indicating that a material satiation from a meal is involved here, the verb ἐμπλησθῆναι also recalls the presciption in Deut 8:10 (LXX): "And you shall eat and be filled (καὶ φάγῃ καὶ ἐμπλησθήσῃ) and shall bless the Lord your God ...." The combination of φαγεῖν with ἐμπλησθῆναι ("to eat one's fill") appears to be a technical formula in the Bible aiming at the prosperous situation in the promised land (cf. also Deut 6:11; 8:12; Neh 9:25). In rabbinic sources, the Hebrew version of Deut 8:10 underlies the obligation to recite the Birkat Ha-Mazon[123] and this verse is considered so important that it is also at the basis of the second strophe of the Birkat Ha-Mazon.[124] The use of the term ἐμπλησθῆναι at the end of the meal may indicate that now the duty of reciting the prayer, enjoined in Deut 8:10, is performed.[125]

The first to examine closely the links between Did 10 to the Jewish Grace was Louis Finkelstein. He presented the two texts in parallel columns and in commenting on the strong similarities between the texts, he already noted in the Didache the inversion of the order of the first two pericopes and the "spiritualization" of the original text. He observes the "emphasis on the spiritual as opposed to the material blessing" in the replacement of physical by spiritual food and drink, of the land by the Name and of Jerusalem and the Temple by the church.[126] The connection, indeed, between the Birkat Ha-Mazon and Did 10 no longer requires demonstration. Admittedly, one must be careful about Finkelstein's reconstruction of the Hebrew text since the exact phraseology of the meal blessings may not yet have been fixed in the first century CE. There still might have been a degree of variation and verbal fluidity of the prayers and a plurality of their versions as well.[127] On the other hand, the materials extant from Qumran but of non-Qumranic

---

[122] See, for example, G. Klein, 'Die Gebete in der Didache', 140-41; Finkelstein, 'The Birkat Ha-Mazon', passim; Middleton, 'The Eucharistic Prayers', 263-64; Dibelius, 'Die Mahl-Gebete der Didache' (1956) 117.122-23; Audet, *La Didachè*, 410; Ligier, 'The Origins of the Eucharistic Prayer', 161-85; Riggs, 'From Gracious Table', 91-93; Rordorf-Tuilier, *La Doctrine des douze Apôtres*, 178-79, n. 3; Rouwhorst, 'Les oraisons de la table'; Wegman, 'Généalogie hypothétique'; Niederwimmer, *Die Didache*, 194-199; Mazza, *The Origins of the Eucharistic Prayer*, 16-30. *Contra:* Klinghardt (*Gemeinschaftsmahl und Mahlgemeinschaft*, 418-27) who especially refers to the different order of the prayers in Did 10 (423, n. 33). For this problem, see below.

[123] See yBer 7, 11a: ואכלה ושבעת וברכת זו ברכי הזימון – "and you shall eat and be full, and you shall bless (the Lord your God);" cf. also bBer 48b.

[124] See below, p. 315. Cf. also Mazza, 'Didache 9-10', 297; Id., *The Origins of the Eucharistic Prayer*, 23.

[125] Cf. Rordorf-Tuilier, *La Doctrine des douze Apôtres*, 178-79, n. 3; Mazza, *The Origins of the Eucharistic Prayer*, 16-17; Id., 'Didache 9-10', 298, n. 76.

[126] Cf. Finkelstein, 'The Birkat Ha-Mazon' (1928-29) 211-62; esp. 214.

[127] See J. Heinemann, *Prayer in the Talmud*, 37-64 and, concerning the Grace after meals, Safrai, 'Religion in Everyday Life', 802-03; Bradshaw, *The Search for the Origins*, 207; Reiff, 'The Early History'; Draper, 'Ritual Process and Ritual Symbol', 139.

origin affirm that the initial step in the shaping of fixed prayers was already taken in the Second Temple period.[128]

All this is not to say that Finkelstein's reconstruction of the original wording of the Birkat Ha-Mazon must be valued as a futile attempt. On the contrary. In our case, the sources indicate at least a basic, even solid framework in which wording and expression were certainly not totally free. The oldest Jewish prayer manuscripts dating back to the Middle Ages provide prayers which, in both structure and expression, parallel the prayer formulae of the Didache. The reconstructed version will therefore be utilized here, albeit just to a certain extent. Some confirmation of the antiquity of the form and wording restored by Finkelstein is provided by the Mishna and the Book of Jubilees. In contrast to its presentation of the text of the two food-blessings before the meal, the Mishna does not give the text of the Grace at the end of the meal. On the other hand, the general outline of the Birkat Ha-Mazon must by then have well been established, for it is referred to as comprising three berakhot by R. Gamliel II in mBer 6:8. Further evidence to a still earlier redactional layer of this tripartite structure in the Book of Jubilees will be considered in the next section.

The Reorganization of the Birkat Ha-Mazon in the Prayers of Did 9-10

In the above section, it was ascertained that blessings of the type found in mBer 6:1 underlie the first two thankgivings in Did 9:2-3, while a prayer like the tenth benediction of the *tefilla* probably is the source of the petition in 9:4. It also became clear that, according to a wide scholarly consensus, the prayer in Did 10 was grafted on the Birkat Ha-Mazon. Assessing the evidence, it is worth noting that the prayers in Did 9 are fused together from different sources which did not constitute an integral whole prior to their reception in the table prayer. On the other hand, while the individual elements of Did 9 had an independent existence before their incorporation in this prayer, the prayer after the meal in Did 10 comes from one coherent Jewish liturgical source. Assuming "that the closer we get to a primitive Jewish-Christian setting, the more likely it is that a prayer would have been composed from a single similar source" lacking a composite character, "Did 10 may well be the earlier prayer."[129] It thus appears that Did 10 was the starting point and that the literary form of the prayers before the meal as displayed in Did 9 were dependent on Did 10. The original shape of the two benedictions and the petition was re-arranged to bring it in line with the liturgical composition of the earlier prayer after the meal, which in its turn was based on the Jewish model of the Birkat Ha-Mazon. In view of the verbal agreement between the text of Did 9 and that of Did 10, however, it is likely that this process of harmonisation and adaptation did not begin until the prayers were translated into Greek.

---

[128] A text of the Grace after meals, however, was not found in Qumran. See above, n. 3.
[129] See Riggs, 'From Gracious Table', 93.

It is important to note that there was obviously an element of continuity in the general structure of themes of the Grace after meals but, on the other hand, of discontinuity in the precise contents of the prayer. In this section, the focus will primarily be on the variety and flexibility as well as on the consistency and constancy of Jewish prayer-content in the course of time. In comparing the Birkat Ha-Mazon with the eucharistic prayer in Did 10, one notes that both the pattern and wording of the Jewish Grace underwent significant developments. The successive strophes of Did 10 do not correspond with the structure of the underlying Jewish model. The Birkat Ha-Mazon displays a tripartite structure: a berakha or benediction (in the strict sense) for the gift of food, a hodaya (thanksgiving) for the gift of the land, the covenant, the Law, and a supplication for mercy on the people, the city of Jerusalem and the temple. Since, as will be established, an alteration took place of the threepartite Jewish Grace's pattern to a twofold pattern of thanksgiving and supplication in the Didache, the obvious questions arise: How are we to explain that the tripartite pattern of the Jewish Grace gave rise to a bipartite structure? Is the altered order of the prayers in comparison with the Birkat Ha-Mazon on which they are modelled due to a profound Christianization? Besides elasticity and transformation, however, also the consistent elements of the Birkat Ha-Mazon will be subject of discussion, since the substance of the prayer must have been in regular use long before the destruction of the Temple.

Let us first deal with the alterations in the Jewish Grace after meals and have a closer look at the strophes in Did 10:2 and 4. We must treat these two pericopes in combination because they match the second benediction of the Jewish Grace after meals (the 'benediction of the land'), comprising the thanksgiving for the gift of the land, the covenant and the Law. The thanksgiving in Did 10:2 begins with a sentence similar to the second verse of the preceding Chapter 9 ("We thank you, holy Father, for your holy name"). The continuation clearly resembles 9:3, although here thanksgiving is made for three ("knowledge" / γνῶσις), "faith" / πίστις and "immortality" / ἀθανασία) instead of the two goods of salvation ("life" and "knowledge") in 9:3. The strophe in 10:4a according to the Jerusalem manuscript reads "Above all (Πρὸ πάντων) we thank you, Lord, ...," and could be regarded in this version as a later addition. According the Coptic version, however, the text was: "For all things (Περὶ πάντων) we thank you, Lord, ..." The latter reading is probably correct since it has a clear parallel in the second Jewish benediction "For all these things we thank you ..." (... ועל כלם אנו מודים לך).[130] If the vv.

---

[130] See Finkelstein, 'The Birkat Ha-Mazon' (1928-29) 228-230 and 247-252. Finkelstein wrongly believes that the final statement beginning with the words ועל כלם is a secondary addition (229-230 / 351-352). Parallel phrases, however, underscore their authenticity. A clause close to this phrase in the Jewish Grace after meals (ועל הכל ה' אלהינו אנחנו מודים לך ומברכים אתך) is found in the benediction after the Sabbatical reading from the Prophets. And the similar wording (ועל כלם יתברך ויתרומם שמך) in the 17ᵗʰ benediction of the tefilla; cf. Finkelstein, 'The Development of the Amidah' (1972) 327-28. For a confirmation of the antiquity of Did 10:4, see also J.M. Robinson, 'Die Hodajot-Formel', 209, n. 42.
For a textual commentary on this phrase, see above, n. 87.

2 and 4 in Did 10 originally represent the second Jewish benediction, it is clear that the literary integrity of this strophe is disrupted by Did 10:3. As reconstructed by Finkelstein, the oldest version of the first benediction in the Hebrew prayer was: "Blessed are you, O Lord, our God, king of the universe, who feedest the whole world with goodness, with grace, and with mercy." The Didache prayer lacks the *barukh* formula now that this strophe is no longer the opening berakha. Nevertheless, also Did 10:3 first calls upon God, the almighty Lord (δεσπότης παντοκράτωρ) who created all things. The berakha is concerned with God as a creator and as the one who keeps the world in being by giving nourishment. With respect to the first benediction of the Hebrew Grace, the benediction in the Did 10:3 was extended, however, to include spiritual food and drink as well.

A look at the rendering of the first two strophes of the Birkat Ha-Mazon in Did 10:2.3.4 gives the effect of one thanksgiving articulated by doxologies at the middle and at the end.[131] But why did the inversion of the first two prayers or, better, the incorporation of the first Jewish benediction into the second Jewish one come about in the Didache? It is possible that the composer of the prayer in the Didache did not recognize that the verse in Did 10:3 was based on the first Jewish benediction of the Grace after meals and took 10:4 to be the sequel to 10:2. In order to better understand all this, attention should be paid to bBer 48b. An explanation for the insertion of the strophe in Did 10:3, based on the first Jewish benediction, is found in a *baraita* on this very page:

> R. Eliezer says: 'One who does not say the words "A goodly, pleasant and broad land" (in describing the Holy Land) in the second benediction ... has not fulfilled his duty. Nahum Ha-Zaken says: 'One must also mention (in the second benediction) thanks for the Covenant'. R. Yose says: 'One must also include the Tora.'[132]

The second benediction of the Jewish Grace ends with the words: "Blessed are You, O Lord, *for the land and for the food.*" This phrase depends on Deut 8:10: "And you shall *eat* and be full, and you shall bless the Lord your God for the *good land* he has given you." Because this biblical verse, as seen above, was basic to the very composition of the Birkat Ha-Mazon, the mention of the food and the land in the benediction is essential. At an early date, however, also items like the Covenant and the Tora (included in the report of bBer 48b) were incorporated in the actual Hebrew benediction. It stands to reason that after these insertions, a final summarizing conclusion was added: "For all [these things] we thank you...."

These considerations are meaningful for a deeper understanding of the emergence of Did 10:2.3.4 as a comprehensive unit. On the basis of the information in bBer 48b, one may assume that the second Jewish benediction after the meal was extended in the course of time to contain, in addition to the thanksgiving for the

---

[131] For the reorganization of the Grace in the Didache, cf. J.M. Robinson, 'Die Hodajot-Formel', 209-12; Talley, 'The Eucharistic Prayer', 145. A somewhat developed version of this paper is entitled 'From Berakah to Eucharistia', 123. See also Van Cangh, 'Le déroulement primitif', 203-06.

[132] See Finkelstein, 'The Birkat Ha-Mazon' (1928-29) 229.

land and the food, other gracious gifts of God as well.[133] A parallel tendency of recording additions is reflected in Did 10:2 and 4, where a list of God's benefits to the believers (God's 'holy name', 'knowledge', 'faith' and 'immortality') is produced. In this context of goods to be thankful for to God, it was probably considered fit to interpolate the catalogue of 10:3 including 'food and drink' and their spiritual counterparts. This procedure took place in spite of the fact that not the second topic of thanksgiving but the first Jewish benediction of creation was the background of Did 10:3. Then, after an expansion of the body of the thanksgiving, there would be no obstacle felt in finally returning to the theme of thanksgiving in Did 10:4: "For all things we thank you...." The first pericope of the prayer after the meal in this usage became absorbed by the second. One wonders, however, whether the displacement of the entire first Jewish benediction in favour of the second betrays the hand of a Hellenistic Jew or a Hellenistic Jewish Christian. In the next section we will attempt to show that it might have been the work of a Hellenistic Jew. For now, it may suffice to refer to passages in Philo which show that thanking God for all his benefits may imply both material and spiritual things.[134] Whoever the editor of the Didache prayer was, the person reversing the original order of the benedictions is not likely to have grasped the basic structure of the original Jewish Grace after meals.

The third strophe in the Didache prayer traces its origin in the third benediction of the Jewish Grace after meals, namely, the supplication for Jerusalem.[135] The city is not mentioned in the prayer of the Didache where, instead, the supplication is for the church and for its gathering into the kingdom. In Did 10:5, the prayer begins with the words: "Be mindful, Lord, of your church" (ἐκκλησία), while the third benediction begins with the words: "Have mercy, O Lord, our God, on your people of Israel and on your city of Jerusalem." The appeal in 10:5 is made specific in the three petitions "to preserve it," "to perfect it" and to "gather it from the four winds."

The above observations demonstrate that the Birkat Ha-Mazon was not always transmitted invariably. Yet, in spite of these differences, the Jewish Grace has some constant components throughout its historical development. From early times onward, there was consistency in the general structure and themes of the Grace after meals. Its all-encompassing outline and some fixed elements of the Grace appear in the three berakhot mentioned in mBer 6:8. Moreover, the general structure and themes of the Grace were already known to the composer of the Book of Jubilees in the second century BCE. The report in Jubilees is about Abraham who, after eating a "good thank offering" (22:5) pronounces his Grace after meals:

[133] See also Talley, 'The Eucharistic Prayer', 146-48 and id., 'From Berakah to Eucharistia', 125-27.
[134] Sandelin, *Wisdom as Nourisher*, 215.
[135] See e.g. Rordorf-Tuilier, *La Doctrine des douze Apôtres*, 181, note 7; Niederwimmer, *Die Didache*, 198-99; Finkelstein, 'The Birkat Ha-Mazon' (1928-29) 216. 230-33; Riggs, 'From Gracious Table', 93.94 and 97.

6. And he (Abraham) ate and drank and blessed God Most High who created heaven and earth and who made all the fat of the earth and gave it to the sons of man so that they might eat and drink and bless their Creator. 7. 'And now I thank you, my God, because you have let me see this day. Behold, I am one hundred and seventy-five years old .... 9. O, my God, may your mercy and your peace be upon your servant and upon the seed of his sons so that they might become an elect people for you and an inheritance from all the nations of the earth from henceforth and for all the days of the generations of the earth forever.'[136]

These verses 6-9 of Chap. 22 show a pattern very much like the later texts of the Birkat Ha-Mazon. On the lips of Abraham is put a three-part meal Grace, that is a benediction, a thanksgiving, and finally a supplication.[137]

Of course, the contents of the prayers in Jubilees were extensively reworked to avoid obvious anachronisms in the second and third strophes. The first unit in Jub 22:6 reflects the first Jewish benediction of God as creator and provider of food ("who feedest the whole world"). Only here does the prayer in Jubilees speak of God in the third person, because in the Hebrew bible and early Judaism the prayer form of the berakha – utilizing the passive participle *barukh* in reference to God – mostly praises God in the third person.[138] The unit in Jub 22:7-8 ("I thank you") corresponds to the second Jewish benediction, with the long life, protection, and sustenance granted to Abraham being equivalent to the benediction for the land. The final unit in Jub 22:9 is a parallel to the third Jewish benediction, the benediction of Jerusalem.[139] This is corroborated by the verbal agreement between the two prayers. The wording at the beginning of Jub 22:9 ("May your mercy be upon") reflects the opening of the third Jewish blessing:"... רחם על". Again, the petition for God's mercy and peace to Abraham and his people, the sons of Abraham, must be taken to be the equivalent of the benediction for Jerusalem. Neither in Did 10:5 nor in Jub 22:9 could the city be mentioned. It is skipped in the Didache, because the eucharistic prayer is characteristically Christian, and in Jubilees because the benediction is already said there by Abraham; but even so, Abraham begs God that his descendants may become God's "elect people and an inheritance from all the nations of the earth." The following diagram may illustrate the development – such as argued above – towards the eucharistic prayer in Did 10:2-5:

---

[136] ET: Wintermute, 'Jubilees', 97.

[137] Cf. Finkelstein, 'The Birkat Ha-Mazon' (1928-29) 219; Robinson, 'Die Hodajot-Formel', 205-06; Hruby, 'La «Birkat Ha-Mazon»', 206; Bradshaw, *The Search for the Origins*, 25; Talley, 'From Berakah to Eucharistia', 120-21; Mazza, *The Origins of the Eucharistic Prayer*, 156-159.

[138] Bradshaw, *Daily Prayer in the Early Church*, 11-16; Talley, 'The Eucharistic Prayer. Tradition and Development', 51. The structure of the prayer proper, starting with "who created ...," is well exposed in the lay-out of the edition by Charles, *The Apocrypha and Pseudepigrapha*, 45.

[139] The fourth benediction of the Birkat Ha-Mazon is neither reflected in Jub 22:6-9 nor in Did 10. It already existed in the Second Temple period, but became obligatory only after the Bar Kokhba War. See Alon, 'Ha-halakha ba-Torat 12 ha-Shelihim', 289-90 (ET: 187) and Finkelstein, 'The Birkat Ha-Mazon' (1928-29) 221-222.

Jub 22:6-9	*Jewish Grace*	*Did 10:2-5*

A. Jub 22:6
    food
	A. 1st benediction
	    food	

B. Jub 22:7-8
    God's blessings:
    "I thank you"
	B. 2nd benediction
	    God's blessings
	    1) "we thank you"
		B.
		    God's blessings
		    1) *Did 10:2*
		    "we thank you"

		A. *Did 10:3* food

	2) "for all (this) we
	    thank you"
		B. 2) *Did 10:4*
		    "For all (this) we thank
		    you"

C. Jub 22:9
    "May your mercy ... be
    upon your servant and
    upon the seed of his
    sons so that they might
    become   an   elect
    people"
	C. 3rd benediction
	    "May your mercy be
	    upon your people of
	    Israel, and on your city
	    of Jerusalem"
		C. *Did 10:5*
		    "Be mindful, Lord, of
		    your church"

The comparison of the three texts is instructive for the prehistory of the eucharistic prayer in Did 10. The Book of Jubilees clearly shows that the original order of the Grace after meals existed as early as the second century BCE. In the Didache form of the prayer, however, the initial arrangement was changed, thanksgiving now preceding the reference to God's gift of food. The praise for the food, at first coming at the beginning of the Jewish Grace, now came in second position and disrupted the original thanksgiving unit of 10:2.4. It was inserted in between the thanksgiving for God's blessings (Did 10:2) and the short summarizing statement in Did 10:4: "For all [this] we thank you." A related point is that the praise of God as the giver of food is now subsumed under the thanksgiving. For the history of the Christian term 'eucharist', it nevertheless remains important that this designation did not make its first appearance in the Didache. The pertinent verb already appeared in the Jewish Grace after meals at the time of the Book of Jubilees: "And now I thank you" (Jub 22:7).

A Postulated Hellenistic-Jewish Stratum between the Birkat Ha-Mazon and the Prayers in Did 9-10

Apart from the partial inversion of the first two strophes in the Didache, two deviations from the established text in the Birkat Ha-Mazon should be noted. First, there is the spiritualization. Is this a Christian characteristic, or Jewish, or is it both?

And second, there is the prevalence of a thanksgiving verb (εὐχαριστεῖν), rather than a verb of blessing (εὐλογεῖν). Why does the prayer in Did 9-10 show an unmistakable priority of the thanksgiving over against the benediction found in the Birkat Ha-Mazon? These questions may be summarized in a more comprehensive one which will be the substance of the last two sections of this chapter: is it possible to establish to what extent the Christian Eucharist deliberately steps beyond its Jewish model? Is the ritual in Did 9-10 a rather superficial Christianization of the Jewish prayer, or does it represent a substantial re-elaboration of Jewish thought expressed in the meal prayer?

As suggested above, the Christian benedictions in Did 9 and 10 probably depend on the Hebrew benedictions only indirectly. The connecting link may have consisted in hypothetical Greek benedictions which, though presumably current within Hellenistic Jewry, are lost nowadays. This means that the tendency towards spiritualization in the Didache - e.g., "the spiritual food and drink and eternal life" (10:3) – is likely to have originated in an intermediary, Jewish-Hellenistic stage of the prayer. In the following pages, we will pay attention to this possibility with respect to both the usage of thanksgiving verbs and the spiritualization.

Our interest will center first upon the thanksgiving (εὐχαριστεῖν) vocabulary. In early Judaism, several types of formal prayer were in use. The classical form of prayer was the *berakha* (ברכה or in Greek: εὐλογία), a liturgical benediction or blessing in reference to God. Its name is derived from the Hebrew verb in the Pi'el form *bērakh* (ברך), 'to bless', a verb normally translated as εὐλογεῖν in the absolute sense in the LXX, meaning to "say a benediction." The use of εὐλογεῖν without a direct object as a blessing in reference of God is not found in secular Greek (where it signifies "to praise") and thus may be considered a Semitism. The biblical *berakha* is less a prayer directly addressed to God than a confessional proclamation about God phrased in the third person throughout (Pss 89:52; 41:13; 106:48; 1 Chron 16:36 etc.). It includes a liturgical opening formula employing the passive participle ברוך (or in Greek: εὐλογητός), possibly further descriptive phrases and epitheta after the divine name, and a relative clause in the third person singular expressing the particular reasons for the blessing. An example showing these features is found in 1 Sam 25:32: "Blessed be the Lord, the God of Israel, who sent you ..." (and for additional instances, cf. Gen 24:27; Exod 18:10; 2 Sam 18:28; 1 Kgs 5:7). In due course, however, the use of the third person was dropped; a growing preference for the second person becomes visible: "Blessed are you, O Lord my God, and blessed is your holy and honoured name for ever. May ..." (Tob 3:11-12; see also Tob 8:5-8; 1 Esd. 4:60; 1 Macc 4:30-33), and the standardized form emerged: "Blessed are you, O Lord our God, King of the universe ...." It must be noted, however, that in most cases the relative clause was preserved in the third person as before.[140]

---

[140] See J. Heinemann, *Prayer in the Talmud*, 77-103; Falk, *Daily, Sabbath, and Festival Prayers*, 81-84 and, also for the following, Bradshaw, *Daily Prayer in the Early Church*, 11-16.

An alternative way of praising God is articulated in a formula using the hif'il form of the Hebrew verb ידה, that is הודה (*hodeh*). The verb is often used in the Thanksgiving Psalms from Qumran in the first person singular and is found frequently in the fixed prayer formula אודכה אדוני כי ("I praise you Lord, because"), which phrase has a precise parallel in Isa 12:1.[141] This prayer type, again a blessing, is addressed to God in the second person and in an active form. The primary significance of the verb הודה is 'to confess' or 'to acknowledge', and usually the term is rendered in the LXX by the compound forms ἐξομολογεῖσθαι (noun ἐξομολόγησις) and ἀνθομολογεῖσθαι (noun: ἀνθομολόγησις). Although the verb from its earliest appearance in the Bible is associated with thanksgiving and gratitude, it first of all expresses a general meaning of praise. We will say more on this shortly, but in the meantime it is in order to note that the prayer after the meal was generally introduced with the formula ברוך. Therefore it was called a *berakha*, which one even might consider to be a *terminus technicus* for the table prayer in liturgical usage.

The LXX hardly uses the verb εὐχαριστεῖν and expressions like χάριν ἔχειν or χάριν ἀποδιδόναι to translate ברך or הודה or similar Hebrew / Aramaic praise-words. When these Greek wordings are found in a few occurrences in biblical literature, it is generally in those books which betray the strongest Hellenistic influence. The examples include Jdt 8:25; Wis 18:2; 2 Macc 1:11; 10:7; 12:31; 3 Macc 7:16 (verb) and Esth 8:13; Wis 16:28; Sir 37:11; 2 Macc 2:27 (noun). In these instances, the verb has no Hebrew equivalent since these writings are extant in Greek only.[142] Further light on the development in the usage of the words εὐλογεῖν and εὐχαριστεῖν is shed by the way they appear in Josephus. In his description of the erection and dedication of the Temple of Solomon (1 Kgs 8:23-53), Josephus has added an important part to Solomon's prayer. Its introduction has been profoundly changed by inserting in *Ant.* 8,111-112 a theme dealing with the right way of praying. In the main, it comes down to the repudiation of the material sacrifices in favour of thanksgiving prayers. Two points may be of interest to us.

First, Josephus emphasizes that the introduction to the petition prayer proper is the thanksgiving, and in doing so he mentions a verb belonging to the χάρις group thrice: ἀποδοῦναι θεῷ χάριν – εὐχαριστεῖν – χάριν ... ἔχειν. Apparently he has taken Solomon's opening words of 1 Kgs 8:23-24 as being a prayer of

---

[141] 1QH 2:20.31; 3:19.37; 4:5; 7:6.26.34; 8:4 etc.; cf. Robinson, 'Die Hodajot-Formel', 194-98. There are also six instances, however, of the *barukh* formula in these *Hodayot* (10:14; 11:27.29.32; 16:8; frg. 4,15), which are cast in the second person (ברוך אתה) and, in case they have a 'motive clause' describing the action of God in the past, these are phrased in the second person too; cf. Schuller, 'Some Observations on Blessings', 134-38.

[142] Van Cangh, 'Le déroulement primitif', 201; Audet, *La Didachè*, 385-389. The substantive εὐχαριστία in Sir 37:11 has the Hebrew equivalent חסד תגמל (Ms. B); see Beentjes, *The Book of Ben Sira in Hebrew*, 64.

thanksgiving for God's benefactions.[143] Second, the technical meaning of verb εὐλογεῖν denoting "to bless (God)" was apparently not understood as such by a Roman reader. For this reason, Josephus adds τὴν σὴν ... μεγαλειότητα (thy [= God's] greatness) as a direct object of the verb εὐλογεῖν in *Ant.* 8,111: "But with that (gift of speech), O Lord, through which we have been made by Thee superior to other creatures, we cannot but praise (εὐλογεῖν) Thy greatness and give thanks (εὐχαριστεῖν) for Thy kindnesses to our house and the Hebrew people ... ."[144]

Even more interesting are the significations of the verbs in Philo. In his usage the praise words εὐχαριστεῖν and εὐλογεῖν remain for the most part interchangeable synonyms, but it is worthy of note that Philo uses εὐχαριστεῖν rather than εὐλογεῖν to refer to prayer at meals:[145]

- (It would be irreverent) ... and equally unlawful to enjoy and partake of any form of food for which thanks had not been offered (εὐχαριστήσαντας) in the proper and rightful manner[146]

and commenting on Exod 25:30:

- Wherefore He adds, 'before Me continually thou shalt place the loaves of bread', for 'continually' means that the gift of food is continual and uninterrupted, while 'before' (means) that it is pleasing and agreeable to God both to be gracious and to receive gratitude (εὐχαριστίαν)[147]

In those instances where one would expect the verb εὐλογεῖν, Philo adopts εὐχαριστεῖν and it is quite possible that in Philo's time this verb was the common word used for the blessing at table in Hellenistic Judaism[148]. This, at the same time, may imply that there were versions of Grace opening with the verb εὐχαριστεῖν.

The evidence in the New Testament may point in the same direction. The most important object of thanks are food and drink. Outside these pericopes, only Luke among the synoptics uses εὐχαριστεῖν without connection to a meal (17:16; 18:11). Because it is likely that the accounts of the multiplication of the loaves and

---

[143] "In den Worten Salomos in 1 Kön 8,23f. hat er den Dank des Königs für Gottes Wohltaten gelesen. Deshalb hat er im Anschluss an die griechische Sitte, die Philo auch für das hellenistische Judentum bezeugt, eine Eucharistie formuliert, mit der ein rechtes Gebet anzufangen hatte. Dabei hat er auch ausgesprochen, worin eine rechte Eucharistie besteht;" cf. Van Unnik, 'Eine merkwürdige liturgische Aussage', 369.

[144] ET: Thackeray, *Josephus* 5 (LCL 281) 632-33. See also Van Cangh, 'Le déroulement primitif', 202.

[145] See, also for additional examples, Laporte, *La Doctrine eucharistique chez Philon*, 82-84.

[146] *Spec. Leg.* II,175; for the ET, cf. Colson, *Philo* 7 (LCL 320) 414-417.

[147] Quaestiones et solutiones in Exodum II,72 (cf. II,69); see for the translation from the ancient Armenian version of the original Greek, Marcus, *Philo. Supplement* 2 (LCL 401) 121-22.

[148] Cf. Laporte, *La Doctrine eucharistique chez Philon*: "Nous pouvons conclure que, même si Philon utilisait *eulogein* lorsqu'il disait les «Grâces», ce dont nous ne sommes pas certains, du moins, il considérait ce geste comme une *eucharistia* et le dénommait ainsi. Et peut-être utilisait-il *eucharistein* dans la formule même de cette prière" (84). See also Drews, 'Untersuchungen zur Didache', 77; Wengst, *Didache (Apostellehre)*, 57, n. 192.

the fishes were affected by the Last Supper narrative (cf. Matt 15:36; Mark 8:6), we will focus on the accounts of the Last Supper. It is striking that, in the first two synoptic reports of the Last Supper, there are occurrences of εὐλογήσας in reference to the bread and of εὐχαριστήσας in reference to the cup (Matt 26:26 and Mark 14:22). At first glance, it would thus seem that the verb εὐχαριστεῖν in connection with meal in the gospels is interchangeable with the word for blessing (εὐλογεῖν). On the other hand, according to the usage of Philo, the verb εὐχαριστεῖν may denote giving thanks at meals. In this way it is also used in Luke 22:17.19, where a report of the Last Supper is found (cf. also Mark 8:6; Matt 15:36; John 6:11.23) and the same meaning for blessing at table may have been accidentally preserved in Rom 14:6; 1 Cor 10:30 and 1 Tim 4:3-5. Interestingly, Luke has probably replaced in 22:19a Mark's εὐλογεῖν with εὐχαριστεῖν in reference to the bread, which may reflect Luke's intention to distinguish between the 'eucharistic' meaning of the verb and the regular word for blessing.

These references to a blessing over food suggest that there were forms of Grace in Hellenistic Judaism which began with εὐχαριστεῖν.[149] Since the traditional translation of the Hebrew *bērakh* in the LXX is εὐλογεῖν, and since there are no examples of the word εὐχαριστεῖν actually being used to render the Hebrew *bērakh* in early Greek sources,[150] it would seem that the Hellenistic Jews preferred the second benediction of the Hebrew version of Jewish Grace to be the opening blessing. What is at issue is not a translation of the opening phrase of the first Jewish berakha, but the displacement of the entire paragraph in favour of the second, the thanksgiving. The second paragraph of the Grace which was already in the thanksgiving form, has been repositioned to become the opening of the prayer. At the same time, the original opening now comes after it, or rather, has been incorporated into it because this berakha also lists goods to be thankful to God for. The *barukh* formula has been deleted now that it is no longer the opening berakha. The Greek expression εὐχαριστοῦμέν σοι in the first strophe of the Christian prayer (Did 10:2.4) - which as a whole is based upon a Greek version of the Hebrew Vorlage - is ultimately a translation of the Hebrew נודה לך in the second benediction of the Birkat Ha-Mazon. The unmistakable priority given to the (second) thanksgiving over against the (first) benediction must have led to the deviation in structure from the established arrangement of the text. There is no question of using a form of the Greek *eucharistein* to translate the Hebrew *barukh*[151] because the pattern of the eucharistic prayer in the Didache may reflect

---

[149] For this view, see – besides Laporte, *La Doctrine eucharistique chez Philon*, 82-84 – also Jeremias, *Die Abendmahlsworte Jesu*, 167 and n. 4 (ET: 119 and n. 5); Ledogar, *Acknowledgment*, 127-28.

[150] Cf. Ledogar, *Acknowledgment*, 127.

[151] J.-P. Audet, however, takes the 'literary genre' of the *berakha* to be the forerunner or true parent of the Christian Eucharist and considers the three Greek verbs εὐλογεῖν, ἐξομολογεῖσθαι, and εὐχαριστεῖν interchangeably as equivalent to the Hebrew ברך; cf. *La Didachè*, 377-98 and (more developed) in his 'Literary Forms and Contents'. This article was published in an expanded version in his 'Esquisse historique du genre littéraire'. Likewise J. Betz, ('The Eucharist in the Didache' 258 and n. 53) follows Audet and considers εὐχαριστεῖν to be a translation of the Hebrew ברך. For criticism

a form of the Grace after meals as it was current in the Hellenistic synagogue. The result of all this confirms the view expressed in the above section (pp. 313-18), namely that the prayer in Did 10, although obviously derived from the Birkat Ha-Mazon, deviates from it in order to conform to a Hellenistic model containing the first and second pericopes in reversed order.

Turning now to the spiritualization, it is important to notice first of all that this phenomenon was not a Christian innovation either. Especially Karl-Gustav Sandelin has collected numerous parallels from Judaism within the Greco-Roman world which confirm the earlier thesis of Dibelius and others that Hellenistic Jewish prayers lie behind the formulations of the Didache.[152] Many sources, especially Wisdom literature, show this strand of Judaism, associated particularly with Alexandria and Philo. The present text of Did 10:3 could very well be a slightly Christianized form of a Hellenistic Jewish prayer, in which a distinction was made between earthly and spiritual food. While the first benediction of the Hebrew Grace was probably confined to God as creator and provider of food, it may well have been expanded within a Hellenistic milieu to include spiritual food and drink. The community which says the prayer is distinguished from all mankind: but "to us" God has given spiritual food and drink (πνευματικὴν τροφὴν καὶ ποτόν) and eternal life (ζωὴν αἰώνιον). It has been suggested that these gifts come from a spiritualizing Hellenistic model,[153] while also the distinction between two categories of men receiving different food each is found in Philo.[154] Consequently, there are reasons to think of a Hellenistic Jewish tradition underlying this deviation from the Birkat Ha-Mazon.

The second Hebrew benediction, the thanksgiving, is reflected in Did 10:2 and 4. The thanksgiving in Did 10:2 begins with a sentence ("We thank you, holy Father, for your holy name") similar to the second strophe of the preceding chapter 9 ("we thank you, our Father, for..."). The thanks in 10:2 is expressed for four goods of salvation: God's "Name" (ὄνομα), "knowledge" (γνῶσις), "faith" (πίστις) and "immortality" (ἀθανασία). Since the word "immortality" (ἀθανασία) is not found in those parts of the LXX which are translated from Hebrew but occurs in Wis 3:4; 4:1; 8:13.17; 15:3; 4 Macc 14:5; 16:13 and is often employed by Philo, it might be the result of an adaptation of the Hebrew prayer in a Hellenistic milieu. The word "faith" (πίστις), however, though paralleled in Hellenistic Judaism too, is often found in juxtaposition with γνῶσις in Paul's

---

of Audet's position and his clustering of the variety of first-century praise formulae into one single category, see Ledogar, *Acknowledgment*, 121-24; Talley, 'The Eucharistic Prayer', 139-41 and Id., 'From Berakah to Eucharistia', 118-20; Draper, *A Commentary on the Didache*, 182-88 and R.D. Richardson, 'A Further Inquiry', 385-91.

[152] For Sandelin, see his *Wisdom as Nourisher*, 186-228. Further, cf. Dibelius, 'Die Mahl-Gebete der Didache', passim. See also Alon, 'Ha-halakha ba-Torat 12 ha-Shelihim', 288, n. 67 (ET: 185, n. 67); Lietzmann, *Messe und Herrenmahl*, 233-34; Köster, *Synoptische Überlieferung*, 193; Wengst, *Didache (Apostellehre)*, 48-49. 53, n.177; Ledogar, *Acknowledgment*, 127-28; Kollmann, *Ursprung und Gestalten*, 80-89.

[153] Dibelius, 'Die Mahl-Gebete der Didache',123.

[154] *Mutat.*, 258-59; cf Sandelin, *Wisdom as Nourisher*, 213.

letters and might thus be a Christian accretion to a possibly Hellenistic Jewish strophe.[155]

The Eucharist prayer prefacing the meal (Did 9) may be dealt with likewise. The spiritual thanksgivings over the physical cup and bread replace the standard benedictions of the meal. Let us first examine Did 9:2 more closely. In the Hebrew Bible, the vine is used as a metaphor for Israel (Ps 80:9-12.15; Jer 2:21; Ezek 15:1-5; Hos 10:1), but it is conceivable that in this context the expression alludes to messianic salvation for the elected people. Hellenistic Judaism has spiritualized the wine to become the "holy vine of David." The subsequent designation, the messianic title "your servant," is attributed to Jesus and to David. However, since according to the Christian believers the messianic promise has already been fulfilled through Jesus, it is striking that the designation of Jesus in the Didache does not transcend that of David. The fact that identical designations were ascribed to Jesus and David, though one would have expected a clear inferiority of David, makes it hard to believe that the text in Did 9:2a was conceptualized in Christian circles. The Christian innovation in this strophe and the following ones (9:3; 10:2.3), might therefore not go further than the one phrase "through Jesus your servant." The hellenistic Jewish prayer of Did 9:2, then, acquired its meaning within a Christian community from the relative clause: "which you made known to us through Jesus your servant."[156]

The bread (Did 9:3) is similarly spiritualized as the life and knowledge made known to us through Jesus. The naming of these salvific goods may reflect the type of prayers used in the Greek synagogue of the first century.[157] In view of the liturgical variety, we have every reason to conjecture that the Hebrew prayers received new nuances when they were translated into Greek and transferred to a Greek setting.

The petitionary prayers in Did 9:4 for the union of the church for the most part run parallel with 10:5. The comparison between the gathering of the dispersed church and a piece of bread that is scattered and then gathered together (Did 9:4a) is striking.[158] One would, in fact, rather expect the image of seed that becomes one

---

[155] Sandelin, *Wisdom as Nourisher*, 210.

[156] "Sachlich verleiht die jeweils mittels des Relativsatzes ἧς ἐγνώρισας ἡμῖν διὰ ᾽Ιησοῦ τοῦ παιδός σου erfolgende Christologisierung der Gewissheit Ausdruck, dass sämtliche in den hellenistisch-jüdischen Gebetsvorlagen als Objekte des Dankes ausgewiesenen Gaben Gottes erst durch Jesus offenbar wurden. Dabei implizieren derartige Aussagen in der von starken Abgrenzungstendenzen gegenüber dem Judentum geprägten Did die Vorstellung, dass demzufolge ausschliesslich die Christliche Gemeinde wirklich an diesen Heilsgütern partizipiert. ...;" cf. Kollmann, *Ursprung und Gestalten*, 82. See also Dibelius, 'Mahl-Gebete', passim; Wengst, *Didache (Apostellehre)*, 48-52.

[157] "In beiden Eucharistien, der vor der Sättigung und der nach der Sättigung, ist der Gedankengang der gleiche. Zuerst wird für die Heilsgüter gedankt, die z.T. noch stark at.lich formuliert werden ("heiliger Weinstock Davids, Deines Knechts;" "Dein heiliger Name, den Du hast zelten lassen in unsern Herzen"), z.T. aber stark hellenistisch gefärbt sind: "Leben", "Erkenntnis", "Glaube", "Unsterblichkeit", "geistliche Speise und Trank fürs ewige Leben;" cf. Clerici, *Einsammlung der Zerstreuten*, 37. See also Sir 29:21 and Josephus, *Bellum* 2, 131.

[158] See Riesenfeld, 'Das Brot von den Bergen', 145-48; Clerici, *Einsammlung der Zerstreuten*, 92-94.

loaf, a symbolic language which would presuppose the dispersion as a sowing and the gathering together as a reaping. The phrase surely is a poetical innovation of the prayer and is similar to the terminology in 1 Cor 10:16-17, where the cup of wine and the bread symbolize the unity of the church: "Because there is one loaf, we, who are many, are one body, for we all partake of the one loaf" (see also Ign. *Eph.* 20:2). It has been pointed out above that the idea of the gathering and assembling most certainly testifies to a Jewish background. In the next section, we will see that the ideas articulated in the prayers were transferred to the Christian church in the first couple of centuries. For now it suffices to mention that these verses go back to a Hellenistic Jewish model, that is, to a petition for the Jewish people. The expression ἡ ἐκκλησία σου in 10:5 or σου ἡ ἐκκλησία in 9:4 (your church) may replace the original phrase ὁ λαός σου 'Ισραήλ (your people of Israel). Also sentences like "may your people of Israel be gathered from the ends of the earth into your kingdom" or "Be mindful, Lord, of your people of Israel ...," would be entirely conceivable within a (Hellenistic) Jewish environment.[159]

A Gentile-Christian Redaction of the Prayers in Did 9-10

The meal prayers of Did 9-10 derive from a pre-Didachic Greek-speaking community and, ultimately, from a current Hebrew form of Grace at meals. Considering the detailed attention given it, the Christian ritual in these chapters obviously stands out. In the same way in which the version of the Lord's Prayer in Did 8 is supposed to take the place of the Jewish *tefilla*, so the full text of the eucharistic prayers may have been inserted in the Didache as a replacement for the Jewish table prayer. In this respect, the Chapters Did 9-10 do not seem to be different from Did 8. It is well conceivable that some Christian communities continued to adhere to the pattern of the *tefilla* and to prayers at meals as observed by Jews at the time. At first sight, the community whose traditions are reflected in the extant Didache text seems to have been composed of Christian Jews whose religious life and outlook still remained close to their Jewish roots. Their prayer seems but superficially Christianized in Did 9-10 by specifically Christian phrases like διὰ 'Ιησοῦ τοῦ παιδός σου ("through Jesus your servant" in 9:2.3; 10:2.3) or διὰ 'Ιησοῦ Χριστοῦ ("through Jesus Christ" in 9:4). In fact, however, the strophes in Did 9:4 and 10:5 represent a movement away from Jews to gentiles. In these strophes, the central idea of the Jewish prayer in the tenth benediction of the *tefilla* and the final benediction of the Birkat Ha-Mazon are discredited to the advantage of the gentile Christian church.

The passages in Did 9:4 and 10:5 concern the hope for the future gathering of the Christian diaspora:

---

[159] See further Sandelin, *Wisdom as Nourisher*, 201-07; 215-19.

- Just as this fragment (of bread) lay scattered upon the mountains and became a single [fragment] when it had been gathered,
  so may your church be gathered from the ends of the earth into your kingdom (9:4).
- Be mindful, Lord, of your church, to preserve it from all evil and to perfect it in your love. And, once it is sanctified, gather it from the four winds, into the kingdom which you have prepared for it (10:5).

The gathering of the gentile church is a basic concept of earliest Christianity,[160] and because this theme figures prominently in the eucharistic prayers, it calls for a more elaborate comment at this point of our discussion. As has been shown above, the longing for a Christian gathering parallels the Jewish hope for the restoration of Israel and the gathering of the people.

The idea of the assembling of the church is already reflected in the (later stages of?) the gospels. In the so-called Synoptic Apocalypse in Mark, it says that when the Son of Man comes, "he will send out the angels and gather his elect from the four winds, from the ends of the earth to the ends of heaven" (Mark 13:27; cf. Matt 24:31). In John 11:52, the Jewish aspect is linked with the speculation about the gentile believers: Jesus did not come only for the Jewish nation but also for the scattered children of God, to bring them together and make them one (cf. also John 10:15-16). And according to the same gospel (John 12:32), Jesus is supposed to have said: "and I, when I am lifted up from the earth, will draw all men to myself" (see also 1 Thess 4:15-17 and 2 Thess 2:1).

It is probably justified to believe that the notion of the gathering of the scattered church and the idea of the final gathering of Israel were originally connected with one another. For the key concepts of the early church were closely intertwined with the Jewish views of the time and remained basically the same. Moreover, support for this position is found in the dialogue in Acts 1:6-8.[161] The apostles asked the resurrected Lord whether he was going to "*restore*" the sovereignty of Israel immediately and the question is no doubt imbued with a national-political colouring. In his answer, Jesus shifts the time of the kingdom to an indeterminate future and goes on to define their task as being his witnesses "in Jerusalem ... and to the *ends of the earth*."[162] This discussion might draw on God's uttering in Isa 49:6: "It

---

[160] For this notion, cf. also Flusser, *Jesus* (1998) 237-50; Id., 'Matthew's "Verus Israel"'; Clerici, *Einsammlung der Zerstreuten*, passim; Niederwimmer, *Die Didache*, 188-90.

[161] Although one may trace the warning of rejection in Acts (3:23; 7:51-53; 13:46; 18:6; 28:26-28), Luke still clings to a hope for Israel beyond the tensions described in these passages. For further discussion, see Helyer, 'Luke and the Restoration of Israel', 323-29; Tannehill, 'Israel in Luke-Acts', 84; Wainwright, 'Luke and the Restoration'. Indeed, Paul's quotation of a judgment oracle from Isa 6:9-10 in Acts 28:26-27 at first sight discloses Israel's failure to listen and God's announcement to finish speaking to his people. Then follows Paul's solemn announcement which might be compared to an "obituary" for the Jewish people: "Therefore let it be known to you that this salvation of God has been sent to the gentiles; and they will listen" (28:28). Also this statement, however, does not imply God's abandonment of Israel as a people; cf. Van de Sandt, 'Acts 28,28'.

[162] "... one may understand Jesus' reply as a redirection of priorities rather than a rejection of national aspirations. ... I conclude that the point of the question could hardly have been whether there would be a restoration but, rather, when it would occur;" cf. Helyer, 'Luke and the Restoration of Israel', 327.

is too small a thing for you (Israel) to be my servant to *restore* the tribes of Jacob and bring back the preserved of Israel. I will give you as a light for the gentiles, that my salvation may reach to the *ends of the earth.*" Allusions and references to this verse also appear in both Luke (2:32) and Acts (1:6-8;13:47; 26:23). In the declaration of Isa 49:6, the future restoration of the kingdom of Israel - or even the gathering of the dispersed tribes - is linked with an even greater promise, namely, that Israel will be "a light for the gentiles," to bring God's salvation "to the ends of the earth." It may have been the passage in Acts 1:6-8 that was the underlying cause of the obligation to propagate the Christian message until the end of the earth. The text, at any rate, is about the inclusion of the gentiles when the kingdom comes.[163]

It is thus only natural to assume that originally the gathering of the church was linked with the gathering of Israel. On the other hand, when gentile Christians gradually began to outnumber the Jewish Christians, the gentile element prevailed and the animosity against the historical (non-Christian) Israel – and a future reconstitution of a Jewish state – increased. A strong tension between the two concepts of gathering became patent: the gentile Christian gathering replaced the gathering of the 'historical' Israel. In the early second century CE, a kind of anti-Jewish gentile Zionism emerged which claimed that it is not the Jews but the gentile Christians who will inherit Jerusalem and the Holy Land. According to the (gentile) Christian view, God had disinherited and surpassed the people of Israel and transferred Israel's election to the gentile church. This new concept of supersession *vis-à-vis* Judaism becomes a form of exclusivism, and bans the Jews from Jerusalem. Justin Martyr insists that in the end gentile Christians will be gathered in the Holy Land and in Jerusalem, but the Jews who oppose Christianity "shall not inherit anything on the Holy Mountain, unless they repent. Whereas the gentiles, who believe in Christ ... shall receive the inheritance..." (*Dialogue* 26:1 and also 80:1; 113:3-4; 139:4-5).[164] A similar attestation that the future Jerusalem will be the dwelling place of gentile believers, gathered there together, is found

---

[163] See also Tiede, 'The Exaltation of Jesus', 285-86.
Paul may have followed this line, as can be inferred from his statement in Rom 15:18-24 that he has fully proclaimed the gospel of Christ "from Jerusalem and as far round as Illyricum" (v. 19). Since, in Paul's view, there was no further place for him to work in these regions, he plans to go to the West, to Spain: "Die Nennung Illyriens mag zwar so gemeint sein, nicht aber die Jerusalems. ἀπὸ 'Ιερουσαλήμ bezeichnet jedenfalls den Ausgangspunkt der Ausbreitung des Evangeliums, das Paulus »bis nach Illyrien hin« durch den ganzen Bereich des Ostens hindurch »vollstreckt« hat. Die gleiche geographische Vorstellung zeigt – unabhängig von Röm 15,19 – Lukas in Apg 1,8;" ... "Die konkrete geographische Vorstellung universaler Mission ist also in nachpaulinischer Zeit in verschiedenen Überlieferungsbereichen (vgl. auch Mt 28,19!) so selbstverständlich zum Gemeingut urchristlicher Mission geworden, dass man Anlass hat zu fragen, wieweit sie zur Zeit von Röm 15 auf Paulus allein beschränkt war." ... "Hinter Röm 15,19 steht eine heilsgeschichtliche Missionskonzeption... Wenn Paulus hier davon spricht, stellt er sich also gerade nicht mit *seiner* Mission exklusiv selbst heraus, sondern ordnet sie vielmehr in den übergreifenden Kontext einer universalen Evangeliums-Missions-Vorstellung ein, deren Geltung er als auch in Rom bekannt und anerkannt voraussetzen kann;" Wilckens, *Der Brief an die Römer* 3, 119-20.
[164] ET: Falls, *Saint Justin Martyr*, 186.

in the so-called Fifth Esdras. Here the Lord says to Ezra: "Inform my people that I will give them the kingdom of Jerusalem which I would have given to Israel. ... Ask and you will receive; pray for but a few days for yourselves [and] that they may be shortened; the kingdom is already prepared for you. ... " (2:10-13; see also 1:24-27 and 30-40).[165] A third source containing the same idea is the gospel of Matthew. Above, in Chap. 6, we have mentioned that the final redactor of this gospel fostered opinions similar to the ideas in the Fifth Esdras and to the eschatology contained in Justin Martyr's *Dialogue*. He believed that the kingdom – taken away from its previous sons and promised to a nation producing its fruits – would be realized in the new, earthly Jerusalem.[166]

The conclusions of the two eucharistic prayers in the Didache (9:4 and 10:5) belong to the same type of ideological complex emphasizing the hope of the gathering of the scattered church. The petitions ask for the gathering of the church into the kingdom which God has prepared for it (cf. especially Matt 21:43). Also the Fifth Esdras (2:10.13) mentions the kingdom which God has already made ready beforehand for gentile Christianity. On the other hand, Did 9:4 and 10:5 bring up neither the location of the kingdom, nor the spot where the church was to be gathered, and, likewise, the Jewish expectation of the gathering of Israel according to the flesh is omitted. A proper assessment of the situation represented by the Didache is impossible, because it is hard to find out to what extent the prayer for the gathering of the church reflects concrete historical beliefs. It does not show the symptoms of an exclusivist ecclesiology by the claim, for example, of possessing all the advantages of Israel and by propagating at the same time the absolute condemnation of the Jewish people. Nor do we meet here a continued concern for Jerusalem and the Holy land, which are remarkable features of the later gentile Christian tradition. Yet, in view of the refashioning – involving a gathering of the church as a substitute for the political restoration of Israel –, we have every reason to conjecture that the liturgical texts in Did 9 and 10 are a product of a largely non-Jewish Christian community. Both Did 9:4 and 10:5 represent a striking discontinuity in the people-of-God concept, since the gathering of the church into God's kingdom no longer has any connection to the gathering of Israel.[167]

---

[165] The Fifth Book of Esdras is the first two chapters of the apocryphal Fourth Book of Esdras. It probably was once an independent work, and is preserved in Latin only though it was originally written in Greek. It is of Christian provenance and was evidently written in the second century CE. The English translation used here is that of Myers, *I and II Esdras*, 140-158. Another translation has been produced by B.M. Metzger in Charlesworth, *The Old Testament Pseudepigrapha* 1, 525-528.

[166] See Chap. 1, pp. 33-34; Chap. 6, n. 35 (2nd part). Here it must suffice to present the two Matthean passages:

- Therefore I tell you, the kingdom of God will be taken from you [Israel] and given to a people which produces its fruit (Matt 21:43).
- Many, I tell you, will come from east and west to feast with Abraham, Isaac and Jacob in the kingdom of Heaven. But the sons of the kingdom will be driven out into the outer dark; there men will be wailing and gnashing their teeth (Matt 8:11-12).

[167] For the transfer of the election of Israel to the gentile church, see Skarsaune, *The Proof from Prophecy*, 326-74.

To sum up, the eucharistic prayer in the Didache can best be explained by postulating various layers of composition. We do not know what exactly was the form of the oldest prayer after meals, but we do know that it was already tripartite in its first stage (I). It is even likely that a version of the Birkat Ha-Mazon, although not yet in a completely standardized version, underlied this table prayer. Further-more, it is quite possible that also a first version of the berakhot before meals (certain fixed cup-and-bread sayings and the tenth berakha of the *tefilla*) came to be attached to meals at a certain point in this first stage. In early rabbinic Judaism, the recitation of a blessing before eating any food is described as a requirement. Interestingly, the sequence wine-bread fits the regular order of the Jewish blessings before the meal as reflected in Luke 22:17-19a.

Later, in a second stage (II), the Birkat Ha-Mazon was translated from Hebrew into Greek within Jewish Hellenistic circles, whether in Palestine or in the diaspora. In this period, a fundamental reorganization of the Birkat Ha-Mazon took place. The preference for the thanksgiving form over the blessing or berakha form goes far beyond the simple use of the verb εὐχαριστεῖν, as it involves the displacement of the entire first benediction in favour of the second. In this Jewish-Hellenistic milieu, the ancient table prayers continued to be prayed, albeit with new signifi-cance, since it was especially the spiritual purport of these prayers that was dis-covered and redefined. Also the benedictions before the meal are likely to have been rearranged in this time to make them conform to the liturgical composition of the Greek version of the Birkat Ha-Mazon.

In a third stage (III), these prayers were appropriated by a community of Christians who initially might have been Jews who believed in Jesus. The eucharistic prayer in the Didache does not contain many transformations over against the Greek version of the Birkat Ha-Mazon. Moreover, the ritual does not include the words of institution, nor touch upon the tradition of the Last Supper and the Lord's passion, nor even show any awareness of salvation through the sacrifice of Christ's death. In all these respects, the eucharistic prayer still remained close to the Jewish table prayer. Nonetheless, in substituting "your church" for an expression like "your people of Israel" in the petitions for an eschatological gathering, the community appears to have alienated itself from its Jewish back-ground and to have taken on the character of a primarily gentile Christian group. The fourth stage (IV) can be seen in the rubrical additions in 9:1.5; 10:1.6b-7. This is the stage when the compiler of the Didache obtained the prayers and redacted them to suit his purposes.

Chapter Nine

The Didache Community and its
Jewish Roots (Did 11-15)

The ritual observances prescribed in Did 7-10 are interrupted by a new introduction in 11:1-2. These verses form a transition to a kind of church order which ends in 15:4, just before the eschatological chapter 16. Chapters 11-15 give a glimpse of the local church or churches[1] for which the Didache was written. A variety of disciplinary measures is presented, designed particularly to correct abuses in the life of the Didache community. In Did 11:1-12:2, the emphasis is on testing Christians who would stop over at the Didache community. The passage provides guidelines by which to ascertain the legitimacy of these Christians, whether they claim to be apostles, prophets or just laymen. The next subject dealt with is the treatment of Christians who want to settle in the community. Here, too, the Didache carefully distinguishes between laymen and the different ministering roles with regard to the matter of provisions to be made (12:2-13:7). In chapter 14, the concern is no longer with the attitude of the local community towards outsiders, towards those who visit the community, but rather with circumstances within the settled community itself. The successive topics are loosely connected. The directives in chapter 14 concern the confession of sins and the reconciliation of comrades who are engaged in a dispute. Both rules are laid down as a requirement for the admission to the celebration of the Eucharist.[2] In 15:1-2, another theme is introduced. The community members are advised to select for themselves bishops and deacons who are qualified for their offices. They are explicitly warned not to despise them. The next statement in 15:3 reminds of the admonition in 14:3. Someone who, in spite of the congregation's correction, continues to wrong his brother has to be excluded from the community until he repents. At the end of the text, the community is called upon to conduct themselves in accordance with the requirements of the gospel.

In the following pages, attention will be drawn to three interrelated subjects. The literary composition of Did 11-15, still a hotly debated issue, will come up for discussion first (pp. 331-40). We will examine the various results of previous

---

[1] We believe that the Didache was originally written for a single community. Some elements (its title and Did 13:4) in the present form of the document seem to indicate that it was redacted in a later stage for use in other communities as well (see below, pp. 345-46 and 364).

[2] The primary theme is not the celebration itself, as in Chaps. 9-10; cf. Vööbus, *Liturgical Traditions in the Didache*, 75-78 and Niederwimmer, *Die Didache*, 234.

investigations in redaction criticism attempting to explain its *aporia* in terms of traditions and historical developments. It will become clear that chapters 11-13 essentially form a literary unit which was incorporated by the final composer of the Didache (the Didachist) into an extant Christian scheme of traditional materials underlying Did 8-10 and 14-15. A next section will focus on Did 11-13 where the apostles, prophets and teachers are dealt with (pp. 340-50). The directives in these chapters, which reflect the circumstances in the time and region of the Didachist, will help us to further present the milieu in which this unity (and probably the Didache in its entirety as well) was composed and transmitted. Finally, the focus will be directed toward the Jewish roots of the materials under discussion and, also in this respect, the chapters 11-13 will play an outstanding role (pp. 350-64). This examination will show that early Judaism has left a great impact on the present text of the Didache.

The Literary Composition of Didache 11-15

Modern scholarship has not yet reached a general consensus regarding the vexing problem of the disposition of the materials in Did 11-15. It has considerable consequences for the interpretation of Did 11-15 and the study of the community's history whether we consider this section as a collection of dissimilar traditional materials re-worked by an editor, or whether we look upon it as a literary unity composed by one author. The above survey may suggest that Did 11-15 in its present form does not represent a literary unit. The apparently incoherent character of the text and some discrepancies, which will be detailed below, make it difficult to accept that a single author is responsible for the arrangement of these chapters. The following discussion will show how scholars have tried to find a solution for the seemingly uncoordinated nature of this section. We will first examine the theories with regard to Did 11-13. Several researchers have taken this passage to be an expansion and elaboration of an originally separate tradition. They associate this tradition and the later additions in Did 11-13 with various stages in the historical development of the Didache community. A second line of research involves the entirety of Did 11-15 as it focusses upon the purported clash between Did 11-13 and 15. In this approach, problems are solved by compositional theories which assume a first edition of the Didache to which later materials were added in one or more redactional stages.

DIDACHE 11-13

Kurt Niederwimmer[3] has summarized some problems which render the section in Did 11-13 most confusing. He finds that Did 11:4-12 offers a set of rules about

---

[3] 'Zur Entwicklungsgeschichte', 147-53; Id., *Die Didache*, 209-246, esp. 210-11.

wandering apostles and prophets, a subject which is introduced in Did 11:3, but that the next chapter (Did 12) presents a third type of itinerant Christians (the laymen) without any preliminary mention. Niederwimmer has observed some further inconsistencies between Did 11 and 13. He ascertains that the regulation about the prophets, which presumably was discussed to the fullest possible extent in 11:7-12, reappears at the centre of attention in Did 13. Moreover, in the headline of 11:3, the apostles and prophets are mentioned and their roles are in fact evaluated in the succeeding lines. In Did 13, however, the apostles are lacking altogether and, at the same time, a new class of ministers, the teachers, turns up here in combination with the prophets. To account for these discrepancies, Niederwimmer suggests that chapters 11-13 derive from two different literary stages. The traditional materials used by the Didachist are found in Did 11:4-12. This source, containing a set of rules about the apostles and prophets, was revised at a later stage and resulted in the additions rendered in 11:1-3; 12:1-5 and 13:1-7. In his opinion, the original core in 11:4-12 reflects the life situation in a particular stage of the community's history, the *Sitz im Leben*. Under the pressure of historical developments, then, the Didachist expanded and actualized the ancient tradition for the community in his own day.[4]

Stephen J. Patterson[5] accepts Niederwimmer's redactional analysis in asserting that 11:4-12 represents a traditional source. However, he adds an additional layer of redaction from the hand of the Didachist, consisting of Did 11:1-3 as an introduction and 12:1-2a as a conclusion. In his opinion, these materials reflect the first stage of the Didachist's revision of his source while the section of 12:2b-13:7 represents a second redactional phase. To corroborate this view, reference is made to a Coptic papyrus sheet representing a text which corresponds to Did 10:3b-

---

[4] Niederwimmer's thesis remains problematic, however, in some respects. In his view, the itinerant apostles of 11:4-6 do not reappear in the remainder of Did 11-15 because they did not belong to the period of the Didachist ("Von Wander*aposteln* ist jetzt nicht mehr die Rede. Die Gruppe der Spiritualen setzt sich jetzt nicht mehr aus Aposteln und Propheten zusammen [so in 11,4-12], sondern aus Propheten und Lehrern [13,1-7; 15,1f];" cf. 'Zur Entwicklungsgeschichte', 161). But why would the editor bother to incorporate this material in his document at a point of time when the problem did not exist any more? "There would be no need to write instructions regulating a dead institution" (Draper, 'Torah and troublesome Apostles', 350-51). Furthermore, by assigning the topic of the wandering Christian laymen (12:1-5) to the changed circumstances in the period of the Didachist, it is ignored that itinerancy was not a common phenomenon before (cf. Niederwimmer, 'Zur Entwicklungsgeschichte', 160). For these objections, see also Wengst, *Didache (Apostellehre)* 23, n. 83. Against Wengst's claim that the Didachist probably would not apply irrelevant materials like those with regard to the apostles, Niederwimmer responds: "Gegenüber der Skepsis von Wengst bleibt aber das m.E. starke Argument, dass in 11,4-12 Wanderapostel und Wanderpropheten im Mittelpunkt stehen, in den späteren Passagen aber von den Aposteln nicht mehr die Rede ist, sondern statt dessen von Propheten und Lehrern ...;" (*Die Didache*, 211, n. 4). However, the reason for this change of actors might derive from the fact that Did 11:1-12:2 is concerned with itinerancy – an important characteristic of the apostles – whereas teachers probably lived within a local community and prophets were allowed to settle down in a particular congregation if they wished to do so (see below, pp. 342-43). Finally, also the reappearance of the prophets and the unexpected mention of the class of teachers in Chap. 13 can more easily be accounted for, as will be shown below (p. 335).

[5] '*Didache* 11-13: the Legacy'. See also Patterson-Jefford, 'A Note on *Didache* 12,2a'.

12:2a. Since this papyrus dates from the fourth or fifth century, it is the oldest preserved witness to this section of the Didache. Patterson attempts to prove that the end of the Coptic version in 12:2a was the actual conclusion of a papyrus roll which contained the Didache. This version, then, would represent an older recension of the document than the one preserved in the eleventh-century Hierosolymitanus 54. In his opinion, the Coptic Didache reflects the first stage of editorial development in which the traditional unit (11:4-12) was supplemented by 11:1-3 and 12:1-2a. At a later stage in the history of the community, conditions had changed. The arrival of traveling Christians aiming to settle in the community required an adjustment of the traditional rules. The adaptation to the new circumstances, the Didachist's second redaction, is represented by the addition of the remaining verses of Chaps. 12 and 13 in the recension of the eleventh-century Greek manuscript.[6]

The position of Jonathan A. Draper with respect to Did 11-13 seems to be somewhat related to that of Niederwimmer and Patterson. He takes 11:3-6 to represent the earliest stage of the text which originally may have been introduced in 11:3 with the title: περὶ δὲ τῶν ἀποστόλων, οὕτω ποιήσατε. This is the point of departure in his various examinations of the different strata of the materials from a redaction-critical view. He finds that in a later stage the community of the Didache still living within the bounds of the Tora experienced that apostles, former members of their congregation, taught a different doctrine, which threatened to subvert the observation of the law.[7] In the face of these new circumstances, the instructions on apostles in 11:3-6 were left intact in themselves but modified with regard to content by the addition of 11:1-2. This introduction would indicate that teachers should be received only if their teaching reaffirms the Jewish Tora and promotes the "Christian *halakah*."[8] In another article, Draper[9] suggested that also the unit in 11:3-6, which he still considers as representing the earliest layer of the text, was not left unchanged in the attempt by the community to maintain the observation of the Tora. He now believes that the repression of the earlier influential role of the apostles by the community is reflected not only in Did 11:1-2 but in Did 11:5-6 as well. Also the permission granted for one-night visits and the prohibition to collect money marginalized the apostles in a functional sense. In yet another publication, Draper suggested that besides the instructions in the unit of Did 11:3 (in its original form) to 11:6, presenting rules only about the reception

---

[6] Against this view, it must be observed that it is by no means certain that the sheet with the Coptic version was from the *end* of a roll which contained the Didache. See Jones-Mirecki, 'Considerations on the Coptic Papyrus', 74-83.

[7] Cf. Draper, 'Torah and troublesome Apostles', 348-60.

[8] Draper's contention that Did 11:1-2 was designed to correct those who advocate the abolition of the Tora cannot be substantiated from the text itself. His attempt to prove this point by reference to the (alleged) "close relationship of the language of Did 11,1-2 to the polemic in Mt. 5:17-20" (356) suffers from the weakness that the verbal agreements between the two passages is restricted to just two words, the verb καταλῦσαι and the noun δικαιοσύνη.

[9] 'Social Ambiguity', 294-95.

of apostles, the earliest layer also contained Did 12:1-5 since these verses "follow the same pattern and use the same language as 11:4-6."[10] He attempts to point out here that the instructions concerning the prophets are an insertion into this earlier text, indicating that the prophets have succeeded the apostles as the community leaders.

At first sight there does not appear to be an obvious rationale for the structure of Did 11-13. The above mentioned traditio-historical approaches represent an effort to explain the multifarious diversities in the text in terms of distinct embodied traditions. Nevertheless, our survey shows a great variety in the results of these theories,[11] and as yet no consensus has emerged. In this light, one wonders whether we can rely on the criteria adopted to establish earlier traditions available to the Didachist. The purported contradictions, *aporia,* and ruptures in Did 11-13 do not appear to be unambiguous marks to the extent that they allow a definite assessment of one or more traditions.

On the contrary. Upon closer consideration, Did 11-13 shows a coherent legal style and a logically consistent line of thought. The different topics are introduced with πᾶς ("all" / "every") and a subsequent participle, each time referring to the different categories of persons and objects considered. The rules applying to these categories are eventually differentiated by conditional propositions like εἰ δέ or εἰ μέν.[12] The following observations may demonstrate its mode of reasoning.[13] After a warning about traveling teachers in general[14] (11:1-2), the instruction in the remainder of Did 11 distinguishes between two classes of itinerants in accordance with their respective qualities and rights, namely, apostles and prophets.[15] Although these preachers could expect a hospitable reception within the community, they all had to be subjected to an examination. The community reserves the right to judge outsiders to prevent charlatans from taking advantage of its hospitality. The principles regulating the conduct of the community toward those who have

---

[10] Cf. Draper, 'Weber, Theissen, and "Wandering Charismatics"', 565.

[11] Two theories must be mentioned yet. It was Robert A. Kraft (*Barnabas and the Didache,* 1-3. 63-65) who coined the wording "evolved literature," characterizing the Didache as a product of a developing process within a living community. Kraft considers Did 11-13 as showing "indications of having been constructed from smaller, separate blocks of material" (62). After a tentative survey of the conglomerated ingredients in this section he concludes: "Any attempt to explain in detail how all these materials came together would be even more conjectural than the above analysis" (63).

Also of interest here is the historical critical analysis of Gottfried Schille, 'Das Recht der Propheten'. His approach is too complex to summarize in a few lines. For a critique, see Niederwimmer, 'Zur Entwicklungsgeschichte', 148-49, n. 8 and 165, n. 60 and Schöllgen, 'Die Didache als Kirchenordnung', 21, n. 120 (ET: 65, n. 120).

[12] Rordorf-Tuilier, *La Doctrine des douze Apôtres,* 50.

[13] See also the important article of Georg Schöllgen, 'Die Didache als Kirchenordnung', 11-17 (ET: 51-59) and cf. Schöllgen-(Geerlings), *Didache. Zwölf-Apostellehre,* 55-68.

[14] The text does not refer to teachers as designated officials, for whom the Didache reserves the title διδάσκαλος (cf. 13:2 and 15:1-2); see below, pp. 342-43.

[15] From 11:7-12 one cannot tell whether the prophets under discussion are itinerant or resident. However, the directive in Did 13:1, where prophets are in focus who wish to settle down in the community, indicates that they are considered as traveling figures.

no claim to any special status are laid down in Did 12. As stated in 12:1-2, even though these visiting laymen are entitled to a generous reception, they are not exempt from the testing and setting conditions. In 12:3-5, the subject has changed in the sense that details are presented about people who seek a permanent home, as distinct from the itinerants. Christians wishing to reside within the community will have to work for a living: "If he wants to settle in with you (εἰ δὲ θέλει πρὸς ὑμᾶς καθῆσθαι), ... , let him work and [thus] eat" (12:3). Consequently, those Christians wishing to settle down have no right to material support from the community. In this context, the passage in 13:1-7 is not some peculiar afterthought or a part not reflected upon in Did 11. The connection between Did 13 and 12:3-5 is clearly indicated in the phrase "wanting to settle in with you" (θέλων καθῆσθαι πρὸς ὑμᾶς) in 13:1 (cf. 12:3). Apparently, the instruction in Did 13 is meant to counteract the wording of 12:3-5 insofar as the classes of the prophets and teachers are regarded. Because the prophets and teachers are accorded prestige and respect (15:1-2), they, contrary to other wandering folk, are supported by the community as a reward for their labours.

The role of the apostles is lacking in Did 13, not because they belong to a far past and have disappeared from the scene, but simply because they are not supposed to settle down within the community. Therefore they are not mentioned in 15:1-2 either. On the other hand, the professional teachers (διδάσκαλοι) are discussed in 13:2 for the first time and grouped together with the prophets because these classes might reside in the local congregation.[16] It appears to be justified, then, to essentially appreciate the disposition of Did 11-13 as a literary integrity without the necessity of resorting to a multi-layered text. Of course, the composer might have been elaborating upon older traditions here, but as long as clear evidence from additional sources is lacking,[17] it is impossible to value the interruptions in the logical line of thought in Did 11-13 as a valid criterion for the assessment of editorial seams or interpolations in the text.

DIDACHE 11-15

What remains to be examined is the entirety of Did 11-15. According to J.-P. Audet and W. Rordorf– A. Tuilier, the Didache was the result of several stages of editing. Audet believes that one and the same author (an apostle) initially wrote Did 1:1-11:2 (= D1) and added 11:3-16:8 (= D2) some years later.[18] He suggests that

---

[16] See below, pp. 342-46.

[17] We will attempt, for example, to show below (pp. 360-64) that Did 13:3.5-7 existed at one time as a separate traditional unit on the basis of its content, style and contemporary Jewish materials.

[18] *La Didachè*, 104-120. His arguments:

1. Did 11:2 represents the ending point of a book
2. the number of στίχοι (lines) of the Didache according to the *Stichometry* of Nicephorus matches the total of D1

afterwards the so-called you-passages in the singular (1:3b-2:1; 6:2-3; 7:2-4 and 13:3.5-7) were interpolated by some contemporary redactor. Rordorf and Tuilier agree with Audet that the present form of the Didache cannot be assigned in its entirety to the same author but they assessed the data differently. Since they substantiated the relative youth of Did 14-15 on the basis of information in Did 11-15 it is of interest to look at their argument at this point.[19] Aside from the Two Ways treatise in Did 1-6, they essentially distinguished between Did 1-13 and a later addition in the Did 14-15 (16). They argued as follows. Whereas the teachers, apostles and prophets in Did 11-13 do not really occupy hierarchical offices, the text in Did 15 displays an entirely different situation. Contrary to the wandering apostles, prophets and teachers who come from outside the community, the bishops and deacons are chosen by the members of the community (15:1). The decline of authority and reputation of the itinerant charismatic leaders and the decrease of their number caused them to be replaced by bishops and deacons and thus a new set of local offices was created. Thus, the information given in Did 14-15 presupposes a development in the history of the community and needs to be attributed to a later period. In view of the changing circumstances, the text was expanded by additional elements in this section which stem from the contemporary milieu of the Didachist. According to Rordorf and Tuilier, Did 15:2 still reflects the problems involved in this process of change in that the recently-installed local officials appear not yet to be accepted by the community as equals of the charismatics.[20]

The interpretation of Did 11-15 as reflecting a process of gradual replacement of itinerant charismatics by local offices is widely attested[21] and was suggested for the first time by A. von Harnack.[22] Although Von Harnack did not distinguish between different layers in Did 11-13 and 14-15, reflecting corresponding stages in the administrative history of the community, he sketched a similar scenario of the earliest phase of the church's development on the basis of the materials in the Didache. In his view, there was originally a threefold universal charismatic ministry of apostles, prophets and teachers who wandered from community to

3. because the authority of the Lord is appealed to in the present tense in D2, whereas it is referred to in the past tense in D1, one may assume that D2 presupposes a written gospel.
He considers the phrases in 1:4a; 7:1b and 13:4 to be later glosses which of course are not related to the compositional history of the book but to the transmission of the text.
For objections against Audet's point of view, see P. Nautin, 'La composition de la "Didachê"',193-99; Rordorf-Tuilier, *La Doctrine des douze Apôtres*, 19 and Niederwimmer, *Die Didache*, 65.
[19]   For the following, see *La Doctrine des douze Apôtres*, 49; 63-64; 72-73 (and 92-93). See also Tuilier, 'La Doctrine des Apôtres', 234-35 and 251-52.
[20]   For a critical discussion of Rordorf-Tuilier, see Schöllgen, 'Die Didache als Kirchenordnung', 23-25 (ET: 67-70).
[21]   See, for example, Giet, *L'Énigme de la Didachè*, 241; Niederwimmer, 'Entwicklungsgeschichte', 164-67; Wengst, *Didache (Apostellehre)*, 42; Patterson, '*Didache* 11-13', 326-27; cf. also Kretschmar, 'Ein Beitrag zur Frage', 141-42.
[22]   For the following, see his *Lehre der zwölf Apostel*, 93-158; cf. 56-57; cf. id., *Die Mission* 1, 314-51.

community.[23] These charismatic offices existed side by side with the administrative church offices of bishop and deacon (and presbyters), whose authority was limited to the local communities. The Didache, so he believes, shows a development in which the resident bishops and deacons took the place of the visiting charismatics as the latter became scarce or lost importance. He maintains that no other document in early Christian literature is as significant for the history of the originating Catholic episcopate as is Did 15:1-2.[24] Thus, Von Harnack, as well as later interpreters, regard Did 15:1-2 as representing an important step in the process of community institutionalization.

On the basis of Did 15:1-2, however, it cannot be inferred that the offices of bishop and deacon represent a relatively new institution coupled with the increasing exclusion of teachers and prophets from their active role in the guidance of the community. In the first place, there is no evidence in the text itself supporting this assumption. Sometimes, the phrase in Did 15:1b that bishops and deacons "perform the functions (λειτουργοῦσι ... τὴν λειτουργίαν) of prophets and teachers" is taken as indicating a new set of offices.[25] It is unlikely, however, that the bishops and deacons were appointed in order to guarantee the continuation of eucharistic celebration.[26] Hence, the clause in Did 15:1c does not support the directive in 15:1a nor motivate the election of bishops and deacons. Moreover, not all Christian communities had a resident prophet (13:4), a fact which suggests that they were not indispensable to the worship of the local churches. The phrase referring to the performance of the functions of prophets and teachers is more properly seen as motivating the preceding list of qualities required for the leadership roles of bishops and deacons. In order to be eligible for the position of bishop and deacon candidates had to be "mild-tempered men who are not greedy, who are honest and

---

[23] Von Harnack later modified this thesis by suggesting that teachers were usually confined to particular local communities, while prophets could serve within their home community and in other Christian congregations as well: "Sie" (i.e. the prophets) "sind teils in einer einzelnen Gemeinde wirksam, teils gehen sie auch in andere Gemeinden (...) und haben ebenfalls ihre Standespflichten. Die Lehrer scheinen an einen Ort gebunden gewesen zu sein, so dass die Propheten zwischen ihnen und den Aposteln eine Mittelstellung einnehmen (Apostel und Propheten in der Apostellehre c. 11 und sonst; Propheten und Lehrer l.c. 15; AG 13,1f. und sonst). ..." cf. Von Harnack, *Entstehung und Entwickelung*, 18-19.

[24] "...; ja man darf geradezu behaupten, dass es in der gesammten urchristlichen Literatur keine zweite Stelle giebt, die für die Entstehungsgeschichte des katholischen Episkopats so wichtig ist wie die unsrige." (*Lehre der zwölf Apostel*, 141).

[25] So Rordorf-Tuilier, *La Doctrine des douze Apôtres*, 64. It also appears to be mistaken to assume that prophets normally presided over the community Eucharist, as they propose elsewhere with reference to Did 10:7 (where prophets have an idiosyncratic way of praying during the liturgy) and to the clause "your high priests" in 13:4 (52-53); cf. the discussion in Milavec, 'Distinguishing True and False Prophets', 122, 122-23, n. 7 and see also 131.

[26] Although the Greek wording (λειτουργοῦσι ... τὴν λειτουργίαν) might suggest that bishops and deacons perform their functions within the framework of cultic celebrations only, the criteria for their election, mentioned in 15:1b, imply a wider variety of tasks. Their duties seem at least to have included preaching and teaching as well as the control of community finances. Moreover, it is anything but certain whether the group of teachers had a liturgical function; cf. Schöllgen, 'Die Didache als Kirchenordnung', 18-19 and n. 109 (ET: 60-62 and n. 109).

have proved themselves, for (γάρ) they too perform the functions of prophets and teachers for you." They had to be worthy ministers because the prophets and teachers, with whom they shared many tasks, were generally regarded honourable and meritorious men. Consequently, the purport of 15:1 is not that bishops and deacons are to be elected for the first time, but that qualified men would be elected to whom the community was to accord a similar high esteem as it gave to the prophets and teachers.[27]

There are more reasons pleading against the possibility that Did 15:1-2 would suggest an innovation of offices. The mention of bishops (plural!) and deacons reflects a rather archaic situation which might be analoguous to the occurrence of the dual leadership in Phil 1:1. In this letter, which might have been written between 60 and 62 CE, Paul addresses "all the saints in Christ Jesus who are at Philippi, with the bishops and deacons."[28] The juxtaposition of bishops and deacons apparently reflects an early stage in the development of the community organizational structure. This view is confirmed by Ignatius of Antioch. He worked as a bishop in the geographical region where the Didache, as will be shown presently,

---

[27] See Schöllgen, 'Die Didache als Kirchenordnung', 19 (ET: 62). Schöllgen is right in opposing the contention that 15:1-2 reflects an innovation of the roles of bishops and deacons. He argues that the instruction to elect bishops and deacons in Did 15:1 "worthy of the Lord" and the subsequent list of qualities required for these leadership roles ("meek, not greedy, honest and tested") are designed to prevent an appointment of unsuitable occupants of these offices.

Schöllgen, however, considers this instruction to be a correction of an earlier practice. In the past, the office appears to have attracted some less motivated incumbents. He finds support for his argument in the subsequent statement of 15:2, where the congregation is explicitly warned not to despise the bishops and deacons but to regard them with respect "together with the prophets and teachers." The positions of bishops and deacons, so he argues, had fallen into disrepute as a result of the unworthy conduct by former officials. The enumeration of the qualities in 15:1 for the selection of proper bishops and deacons would probably not have needed such articulation if they were not somehow at risk. They are designed to correct the abuse of office in the past. According to Schöllgen, the text attempts to prevent the election of unfitting candidates who might continue to discredit these functions. See 'Die Didache als Kirchenordnung', 18-19 and 23-25 (ET: 60-62 and 67-70); cf. also Schöllgen-(Geerlings), *Didache. Zwölf-Apostellehre*, 70-73.

However attractive this view may be, it does not take into account the conventional setting of Did 15:1-2. The instructions in Did 15:1-2 are very similar to the ones in 1 Timothy in that they lay down corresponding demands and standards which the bishops and deacons have to comply with (see below). Rather than representing a response to an actual erosion of the local authorities at the time of the Didachist, these materials may more properly be seen as traditional.

[28] "...gesetzt, dass diese Parallele nicht eine zufällige ist, würden wir die Rückständigkeit der kirchenrechtlichen Entwicklung im Traditionsbereich der Did. erkennen (...);" Niederwimmer, *Die Didache*, 242. See also Wengst, *Didache (Apostellehre)*, 41, n. 141; Schille, 'Das Recht der Propheten', 85-86; De Halleux, 'Les ministères dans la *Didachè*', 20.

In addition to the occurrence in Phil 1:1, the juxtaposition of bishops and deacons also appears in *1 Clem.* 42:4-5 "They" (i.e. the apostles sent by Jesus Christ) "preached from district to district, and from city to city, and they appointed their first converts, testing them by the Spirit, to be bishops and deacons of the future believers. And this was no new method, for many years before had bishops and deacons been written of; ..." (cf. Lake, *The Apostolic Fathers* 1, 80-81). Thus Clement employs this terminology when speaking about religious leaders appointed by the apostles. Nevertheless, the dual designation of "bishops and deacons" was replaced in the second half of the first century by the label "elders"; cf. Dockx, 'Le Binôme: ἐπισκόποι καὶ διακόνοι', 321 and id., 'Date et Origine', 388-391.

was probably composed or compiled. Ignatius testifies that in his time, at the beginning of the second century, many churches had a single bishop who presided over the council of "elders" (presbyters) and was assisted by deacons.[29] The Didache still represents a collective leadership, a stage preceding the process of increasing subordination to the authority of the monarchical bishop as the exclusive leader of a Christian community.[30]

Moreover, the evidence found in 1 Timothy strongly suggests that the verses in Did 15:1-2 are constructed upon an extant tradition. The requirements listed in Did 15:1 for the offices of bishops and deacons belong to same literary type as those which are – to a greater extent – found in 1 Tim 3:1-13. More importantly, the requisite qualifications in this letter concern the very same functions of bishops and deacons. Furthermore, upon closer observation, the Didache not only exhibits material parallels to 1 Timothy but also a structural correspondence with this letter.[31] With the exclusion of Did 11:1-13:7 – the section which was established to constitute a literary unit – the materials of Did 8-15 represent the same sequence of topics as 1 Tim 2:1-3:13, that is, instructions regarding praying (Did 8:2-10:7 and 1 Tim 2:1-7), ethical conditions of a congregational worship (Did 14 and 1 Tim 2:8-15) and directives with regard to bishops and deacons (Did 15 and 1 Tim 3:1-13). In the subsequent chapters in Did 8-15 and 1 Tim 2:1-3:13 the same pattern is recognizable, that is to say that the subsequent development of themes in Did 8-15 (with the exception of chapters 11-13) might reflect an ancient scheme which was used both by the Didachist and the author of 1 Timothy. The mention of the prophets in 10:7 probably occasioned the interpolation of Did 11-13.[32] The apostles and prophets are discussed at such great length because they deal with a problem that was pressing at the time of the Didachist, that is, the arrival of itinerants who claimed to be apostles and prophets but in fact were wandering swindlers who exploited the credulity of the community. Thus, the model upon which Did 8-15

---

[29] Ignatius, *Magn.* 6:1; *Eph.* 2:1-2; 20:2; *Trall.* 3:1; *Philad.*, address, 4; *Smyrn.* 12:2; *Pol.* 6:1; cf. Schoedel, *Ignatius of Antioch*, 22-23. 45-47. 112-13;140-42.
Jefford ('Did Ignatius of Antioch know') has studied the potential relationship between the Didache and Ignatius. He reaches the conclusion that "it is entirely possible that there was some contact between Ignatius and certain, specific traditions which have been preserved in the text of the *Didache*" (349) and "... it appears much more plausible that Ignatius knew some early form of the *Didache* (a form which now is lost to us) and even more likely that he was familiar with materials and traditions which eventually were compiled by the Didachist" (351).
[30] Cf. Rordorf-Tuilier, *La Doctrine des douze Apôtres*, 78; Wengst, *Didache (Apostellehre)*, 41-42; esp. n.141; Schöllgen-(Geerlings), *Didache. Zwölf-Apostellehre*, 73.
[31] For the following, see Dibelius, *Geschichte der urchristlichen Literatur*, 151-52; Id. *Die Pastoralbriefe*, 5 and Vielhauer, *Geschichte der urchristlichen Literatur*, 727-28. See also Stempel, 'Der Lehrer', 209-17; esp. 214.
[32] Vööbus comes to the same conclusion with regard to the eucharistic contents of Did 9-10 and Did 14: "At the end of the second prayer he mentions the functions of the prophets" (cf. 10:7). "This touches off a new excursion. In the sections which follow, he deals with the prophets and eventually he comes back to the subject of the Eucharist. ... In the light of these observations, the Eucharist described in chapter XIV cannot be other than that described in chapters IX and X" (*Liturgical Traditions*, 78).

and 1 Tim 2:1-3:13 are moulded is ancient but the instructions themselves apparently are changed and amplified to meet the different situations.

The evidence presented thus far permits the conclusion that there is no need to assign the instructions about the election of bishops and deacons in 15:1-2 to an additional layer of editing. In fact, the Didachist basically framed the entirety of the chapters 8-15 according to a traditional design which is reflected in 1 Timothy as well. The temptation to read a preconceived theory of historical development into the Didache must be resisted. The text of Did 11-15 obviously does not reflect a stage in a *Katholisierungsprozess*, i.e., an institutional development of substituting a new set of local stable offices for the declining role of itinerant charismatic leaders. Rather than showing indications of a gradual cessation of the charismatic ministries and the innovation of the offices of bishops and deacons, the apostles and prophets do not belong to a past generation but appear to still be active in the church at the time of the editing of the Didache. It is fully justified, therefore, to assume that Did 11-15 is a compositional unity which has been created by one author[33] on the basis of a traditional pattern which he modified and expanded with additional materials in the face of the altered circumstances of his time. Since Did 11-13 represents a response to the excrescences of itinerancy in the time of the Didachist, this section ought to be read as an independent witness to the character and functioning of the apostles and prophets (and teachers) within early Christianity.

Teachers, Apostles, Prophets and the Milieu of the Didache Community

The author's central concern in Did 11-13 is with the relationship between itinerant authority figures (especially apostles and prophets) and the local community. At first glance, the injunctions in this section seem to reflect the suspicious attitude of a narrow-minded local church, lacking any tolerance and understanding toward outsiders. All Christians, whether they are spiritual leaders (11:1-12) or other Christan travelers (12:1) are to be examined with respect to their reliability. The major part of the criteria in ascertaining trustworthiness, however, are related to the apostles and prophets, which indicates that the community of the Didache must have been very familiar with these classes of individuals who singly or in small groups frequently visited the congregation. It can be inferred from other sources that the mobility of preachers was not unusual or exceptional in the first and second century CE. The wandering apostles and prophets of the Didache had counterparts in the contemporary religious teachers of the popular Hellenistic faith, among them

---

[33] In this respect, it is important to mention Audet (*La Didachè*, 113) who refers to the "parfaite unité de style de D1 and D2."

such illustrious figures as Apollonius of Tyana and Alexander of Abonuteichos.[34] The Cynic philosophers, in particular finding themselves on the fringes of society in rejecting home, family and property, represented a similar type of preacher.[35] Seemingly, these itinerant non-Christian proclaimers of a salvational doctrine played a significant part in the acceptability, preservation and diffusion of itinerant Christian charismatics in the Hellenistic world.

The injunctions of Did 11-13 are not directed, however, to the wandering preachers themselves but to the people who welcomed those idividuals into the settled community. By the time the Didachist wrote his manual, the number of itinerant religious propagandists apparently had increased to such an extent that it opened the door for abuses. The hospitality and generosity which Christians were expected to show towards visitors could easily be abused. Strong evidence of such a practice occurring in the Greco-Roman world is found in *De morte Peregrini* (Chaps. 11-13.16), written by Lucian of Samosata in the second half of the second Christian century. In this work, Lucian reports on Peregrinus of Parion about whom more will be said presently. The directives in Did 11:6 and 12 reflect these circumstances in rejecting any request for money by apostles and prophets (unless the latter give it to "others in need" 11:12). There is a good possibility that Hellenistic preachers exercised influence on Christian itinerants in asking for a remuneration for religous services. Admittedly, the Cynic philosopher Peregrinus made his appearance in the middle of the second century and is not likely to have been a contemporary of the Didachist. In 2 Cor 2:17, however, the same charge is leveled against false prophets. Here Paul accuses his opponents of being "peddlers of God's word (καπηλεύοντες τον λόγον τοῦ θεοῦ)." In the same terms, Apollonius of Tyana, who wandered as early as the first century CE, blames a competitive philosopher, Euphrates, for "doing anything for money." He, Apollonius, "tried to wean him of his love of filthy lucre and of huckstering his wisdom (καὶ τὴν σοφίαν καπη-λεύειν).[36] Thus, the directives in Did 11-13 surely do not air an unwarranted suspicion. On the contrary, the main problem facing the community was the question of which line of conduct should be followed towards wandering charismatics in order to protect the community against profiteers, frauds and swindlers.

---

[34] • Apollonius of Tyana was a Neopythagorean sage in the first century CE whose life was described by Philostratus in ΤΑ ΕΣ ΤΟΝ ΤΥΑΝΕΑ ΑΠΟΛΛΩΝΙΟΝ; cf. text and English translation in Conybeare, *Philostratus*; see also Petzke, *Die Traditionen über Apollonius von Tyana*.
• Lucian of Samosata offers a (hostile) account of Alexander of Abonuteichos in ΑΛΕΞΑΝΔΡΟΣ Η ΨΕΥΔΟΜΑΝΤΙΣ; cf. text and English translation in Harmon, *Lucian* 4, 174-253: *Alexander the False Prophet*. For the Greek text, cf. also Macleod, *Luciani Opera* 2, 331-359. See also Caster, *Etudes sur Alexandre* and Jones, *Culture and Society in Lucian*, 133-148.

[35] Cf. Theissen, 'Wanderradikalismus', 89.

[36] Cf. Conybeare, *Philostratus*, Chap. 13 (34-37). See also Crone, *Early Christian Prophecy*, 269-70 and 286.

TEACHERS, APOSTLES AND PROPHETS

The legislation of the Didache, while retaining the rules of hospitality,[37] aims at protecting the community from illegitimate preachers who made a profitable profession of their activity. The Didachist inserted chapters 11-13, which contained criteria for a serious evaluation of wandering preachers, into the ancient scheme handed down to him by tradition.

Teachers

The words "teaching" and "teachers" in Did 11:1-2; 13:2 and 15:2 has occasioned some scholarly disagreement in assessing the class or groups these terms refer to. It is undeniable that the occurrences of the noun διδαχή ("teaching") and its verbal cognate διδάσκω ("to teach") in Did 11:1-2 relate to people who instruct the community. A teaching individual (ὁ διδάσκων), so it says, should be received by the community, only if his instruction coheres with the doctrine of the Didache (chs. 1-10) itself. He is expected to teach in harmony with accepted tradition. It is also clear that the language used here suggests itinerancy. The instructor who "comes" (ὅς ἄν οὖν ἐλθών) is ordered to be "received" (δέξασθε αὐτόν). It is doubtful, however, whether the "teaching one" (ὁ διδάσκων) in Did 11:1-2 belongs to the same professional group as the teachers (διδάσκαλος / διδάσκαλοι), mentioned in Did 13:2 and 15:2.[38]

First of all, the wording διδάσκαλος or διδάσκαλοι is surprisingly absent in 11:1-2, which might indicate that only the noun διδάσκαλος is used in the Didache as a *terminus technicus* designating a distinct class of teachers. Moreover, Did 11:1-2 mentions guidelines to be followed towards itinerant instructors, but the criteria stated in the subsequent lines of 11:3-12 are restricted to itinerant apostles and prophets only. This section of 11:3-12 further refers to the teaching activity of prophets as well: "if any prophet teaching (διδάσκων) the truth does not do what he teaches (ἃ διδάσκει), he is a false prophet" (11:10). Obviously, teaching was one of the functions the prophets were expected to perform. Finally, at variance with the description of the instructing figure in 11:1-2, who is clearly itinerant, the professional teacher (διδάσκαλος) appears to be resident. He is mentioned for the first time in 13:2, in a context stating that genuine prophets and teachers deserve to be supported by the community without having to do any other work:

(1) Every true prophet who wants to settle in with you deserves his food. (2) In the same way, a true teacher (διδάσκαλος ἀληθινός), too, deserves his food, just as a worker does (13:1-2)

---

[37] Cf. Audet, *La Didachè*, 444-45; Schöllgen, 'Die Didache als Kirchenordnung', 12 (ET: 53).
[38] As is argued by Schöllgen, 'Die Didache als Kirchenordnung', 11 (ET: 51); Id., 'Wandernde oder sesshafte Lehrer'; Schöllgen-(Geerlings), *Didache. Zwölf-Apostellehre*, 58-59; Stempel, 'Der Lehrer', 210. 213.

The teacher's wish to settle down is lacking altogether, presumably because he already lives within a community. Neither here nor anywhere else in the text is an indication given that the teachers, this is the designated officials (διδάσκαλοι) of Did 13:2 and 15:2, were wandering teachers. Rather, they appear to have functioned within the framework of the local community.[39] The text is very explicit, however, about prophets wanting to reside within the community (θέλων καθῆσθαι) and subsequent verses (13:3-7) draw attention to the sustenance of prophets. This seems to suggest that the established right of the teacher to a permanent home is extended here to the prophets.[40] The warning in Did 11:1-2 concerns itinerants, probably the apostles and prophets who are dealt with in subsequent divisions.

Apostles

In Did 11:3-12, criteria are laid down for ascertaining the reliability of the apostles and prophets. The apostles (Did 11:4-6) are to be received "as the Lord" and their reception is limited to a maximum length of time. They are allowed to stop over for one day or two at the most and any apostle who exceeded this welcome for more than two days or asked for money was to be marked as a "false prophet."[41] It is clear that these apostles do not equal the college of the Twelve although this association obviously occurs in the heading of the Didache.[42] In Did 11:4-6 the number of apostles, just like in the letters of Paul, is not restricted to twelve and, furthermore, they do not represent the undisputed authority of the Twelve, reflected in the general heading of the document.[43]

---

[39] "XI,1.2 ist eine allgemeine Anordnung, die nicht nothwendig auf die professionsmässigen διδάσκαλοι (XIII,2. XV,1.2) bezogen werden muss;" so Von Harnack, *Lehre der zwölf Apostel*, 37. Cf. also Audet, *La Didachè*, 442; Wengst, *Didache (Apostellehre)*, 37.41; Zimmermann, *Die urchristlichen Lehrer*, 141-42.

[40] See Neymeyr, *Die Christlichen Lehrer*, 140-41 and 149-150.

[41] The term ψευδοπροφήτης is an equivalent of ψευδαπόστολος here. The word ψευδοπροφήτης is used repeatedly in the LXX, in early Greek Judaism, and in the New Testament; see Draper, 'Weber, Theissen', 564, n. 113. The term ψευδαπόστολος, however, which is seldom used in the earliest extant Christian texts, seems to be unknown to the composer of this section. It is found by Paul only once (2 Cor 11:13) where it might have been coined by Paul for this particular occasion. The term is lacking in the postapostolic literature; cf. Niederwimmer, 'Zur Entwicklungsgeschichte', 155, n. 26; Id., *Die Didache*, 216; Rordorf-Tuilier, *La Doctrine des douze Apôtres*, 52; Wengst, *Didache (Apostellehre)*, 38, n. 127.

[42] The longer title states: "The Teaching of the Lord through the Twelve Apostles to the Gentiles" while the shorter title says "Teaching of the Twelve Apostles." For our present purpose, it is irrelevant whether the longer or the shorter title is authentic. It is even more likely that neither title is original. See above, Chap. 3, pp. 84-85. Cf. also Rordorf-Tuilier, *La Doctrine des douze Apôtres*, 15-17; Vielhauer, *Geschichte der urchristlichen Literatur*, 722-725; Niederwimmer, *Die Didache*, 81-82.

[43] Wengst views the existence of the apostles in itself as an anachronism: "Im urchristlichen Vergleich erscheint es als ein erstaunliches, ja anachronistisches Phänomen, dass es in der Gegenwart der Didache Apostel gibt. Überall sonst in den späteren Schriften sind die Apostel eine Grösse der Vergangenheit" (*Didache [Apostellehre]*, 39); "Nicht nur nach den engen lukanischen Kriterien (Act 1,21f.), sondern

The directives with regard to the apostles are limited to their reception (11:4: ἐρχόμενος... δεχθήτω), stay (11:5: μενεῖ) and departure (11:6: ἐξερχόμενος). Although the itinerant apostle retained the basic right to receive hospitality, the regulation is even stricter towards them than it is towards laymen. The latter travelers were permitted to stay three days, if necessary, and even to settle down if they had a trade or were willing to work for their keep in other ways (12:2-5). The apostles were only allowed to pass through and the support of the congregation was restricted to bed and board and a single day's provision on the road. They were not to tax the community's resources. In addition, the limited ration of food for one day's march does not indicate that the wandering apostle had to bridge long distances and travel between big cities but rather seems to presuppose a network of stopping places, like hamlets, villages or small towns. These circumstances suggest that the community was located in a rural area.[44]

Prophets

A keyword which holds the passage about the prophets together is the repeated phrase of speaking "in the spirit" (ἐν πνεύματι; cf. 11:7.8.9.12). Because their messages were considered as being a command of God, the prophets were highly-valued figures. It has been pointed out that the Didache community shows a superstitious timidity towards prophets which seems to be totally unknown to Paul.[45] Whereas Paul recommends the utterances of the prophets to be judged critically by those present (1 Cor 12:10; 14:29; 1 Thess 5:19-21), the Didache forbids the evaluation of prophets speaking in the spirit. The exact nature of this pneumatic speech is not defined here, but it was probably a technique which could be mastered by true and false prophets. Because either type of prophets appealed to divine authority as standing behind their pronunciations the community might have had great difficulty in exposing false prophets as frauds. Prophecy, after all,

---

auch nach den weiteren paulinischen (vgl. 1Kor 9,1; 15,5-11; Gal 1,15f.) ist der Apostelkreis grundsätzlich auf eine bestimmte Personengruppe begrenzt" (id., n. 130); cf. also Rordorf-Tuilier, *La Doctrine des douze Apôtres*, 58-59.

In the present form of the Didache, the twelve apostles, under whose authority the directives of the document are issued, ironically serve to protect the unrestricted number of apostles and to safeguard the community from false apostles among them; cf. Sass, 'Die Apostel in der Didache', 239.

[44] Cf. Von Harnack, *Lehre der zwölf Apostel*, 168-70; Knopf, *Die Lehre der zwölf Apostel*, 3 and 34; Niederwimmer, 'Zur Entwicklungsgeschichte', 153; Theissen, 'Legitimation und Lebensunterhalt', 197 and id., 'Wanderradikalismus', 98-100 (with additional arguments in support of this setting); Wengst, *Didache (Apostellehre)*, 32-33. Schöllgen has opposed this thesis upon the basis of 13:3-7. He believes that the specific firstfruits, mentioned in this passage, do not necessarily deny an origin in an urban milieu because many citizens of ancient cities were farmers; cf. 'Die Didache – ein frühes Zeugnis'. It is doubtful, however, whether this single passage provides sufficient ground to settle this matter.

[45] Von Campenhausen, *Kirchliches Amt*, 78; see also Hahn, 'Prophetie und Lebenswandel', 528-34; cf. also Kraft, 'Vom Ende der urchristlichen Prophetie', 181.

was a gift of divine origin and, therefore, principally beyond man's examination. This view seems to underlie the statement in 11:7: "Do not test any prophet who speaks in spirit, and do not judge him, for every (other) sin will be forgiven, but this sin will not be forgiven." Evaluation of a prophecy would involve a judgment on the spirit at work in the prophet and might as such be a sin against the spirit.[46]

The general norm for distinguishing the true prophets from the false ones is neither the length of time for their stay (as it is for the apostles), nor what they teach but how they live. True prophets, so it says in 11:8, are recognizable by the "behaviour (τρόποι) of the Lord." An impression of this behaviour and, at the same time, of the criteria by which to judge prophetic conduct is given in the three illustrations of the subsequent verses 9-12.[47] A prophet may order a meal for others but must not eat it himself (v. 9), he should practise what he preaches (v. 10) and if he asks for money or other gifts, it must be for the benefit of the poor (v. 12). The usage of moral standards as a touchstone for examining prophecy was not uncommon in the early church. It is also found in other early Christian sources, like Matt 7:15-23; Hermas, *Mandate XI*,7.16 and the *Acts of Thomas*, 79.[48] It must be stressed, however, that the "behaviour (τρόποι) of the Lord" does not refer to the ascetic lifestyle of itinerant charismatics who turned away from village and family ties.[49] Because a trustworthy prophet according to Did 13:1-7 might settle down at a particular location if he wished to do so, itinerancy was not a constitutive characteristic for being a prophet. His stay was not limited to a maximum length of time and he could minister both within his home community and in other Christian congregations. If a legitimate prophet, someone who has built up a reputation, settles among the people, he may receive the support of the community consisting of firstfruits of the crops and of general profits. It is likely that by the time the Didachist inserted Chaps. 11-13, most prophets were not yet settled down. The section in 13:1-7 insists that the accepted attitude towards teachers, already

---

[46] Although the allusion to the unforgivable sin in 11:7 shows a close relationship with the saying in Mark 3:28-29, Matt 12:31-32, and Luke 12:10, it is neither related to the miracles of Jesus (like Mark) or to the son of man (like Matthew and Luke). It rather seems to represent an independent version of a tradition which is preserved in the synoptics as well; cf. Köster, *Synoptische Überlieferung*, 215-17; see also Boring, 'The Unforgivable Sin Logion'.

[47] In one case, however, the community is forbidden to evaluate a prophet's behaviour. A prophet who is certified and thus enjoys the community's confidence (πᾶς δὲ προφήτης δεδοκιμασμένος) may act "for the earthly mystery of the church" (ποιῶν εἰς μυστήριον κοσμικὸν ἐκκλησίας) as long as he does not teach others to the same (11:11). The meaning of the obscure phrase μυστήριον κοσμικὸν ἐκκλησίας is often taken to refer to a spiritual marriage of the prophet with his companion; cf., for example, Knopf, *Die Lehre*, 32-33; Von Campenhausen, *Kirchliches Amt*, 78, n.10; Adam, 'Erwägungen zur Herkunft der Didache', 43; Kretschmar, 'Ein Beitrag zur Frage', 137; Wengst, *Didache (Apostellehre)*, n. 100; Niederwimmer, *Die Didache*, 220-222.

[48] See Crone, *Early Christian Prophecy*, 223 and Aune, *Prophecy in Early Christianity*, 222-29. For Hermas, *Mandate XI*, see also Reiling, *Hermas and Christian Prophecy*, 70-71.

[49] As proposed by Theissen, 'Wanderradikalismus', 83. Against this presumption Draper correctly observes: "If wandering penury were the hallmark of the true prophet, how could a true prophet remain a true prophet if s/he settled in the community and received a stipend from the firstfruits of the community?" ('Social Ambiguity', 306).

resident and supported by the community, serve as a model for an arrangement with respect to the prophets who would opt for living in a local residence as well. Since the majority of prophets were itinerant while some might have settled down in individual churches, it is not surprising that at that point not every community had a prophet (13:4).

The privileges granted to teachers and prophets in Did 13:1-2 as well the prestige and respect granted to them according to 15:1-2 shows the authority these classes enjoyed within the established community of the Didache. On the other hand, even though the teachers and some prophets may have been permanent residents at the time of the Didachist, the text does not evidence that they were integrated in the organizational structure of the congregation. They are not said to be elected by the members of the community. Yet, they possibly were held in greater honour by the local Christians than their chosen leaders, the bishops and deacons. These circumstances, exhibiting an ambiguity of status which is not to be expected in a more developed organizational structure of larger Christian communities in urban regions, seem to further substantiate the impression that the community was located in a rural area.[50]

THE MILIEU OF THE DIDACHE COMMUNITY

Two features might help us to more specifically situate the environment in which Did 11-13 was composed, firstly, the three types of spiritual leaders in this section and, secondly, the itinerancy of the apostles and the majority of the prophets. Since A. von Harnack,[51] it has been widely accepted that the triad of leadership roles, the apostles, prophets and teachers, represents an ancient tradition. In Pauline literature, we come accross the same triad in 1 Cor 12:28-29: "And God has appointed in the church first apostles, second prophets, third teachers, ..." There is a good possibility that these three types of officials, reflecting the most important charismatics in the Pauline churches, were not original to Paul himself. He might have borrowed the triadic list from a primitive church order which ultimately stemmed from Antioch.[52] Support for Antioch as the probable place of origin of these offices is found in the information about "the church in Antioch" in Acts 13:1-3. Five persons, called prophets and teachers, are mentioned by name here and apparently they held a prominent position in the community. Out of their midst two men (Barnabas and Saul) were elected to be apostles according to the instruction of the Spirit. The information found in Acts 13:1-3 might be historical in substance since Luke takes great pains to pass on the names of the five prophets and teachers. From a comparison with the catalogues of names in Acts 1:13 / Luke

---

[50] Theissen, 'Wanderradikalismus', 99-100; see also Von Harnack, *Lehre der zwölf Apostel*, 168-70.
[51] See Von Harnack, *Lehre der zwölf Apostel*, 93-140; id., *Die Mission* 1, 314-31.
[52] Cf. Zimmermann, *Die urchristlichen Lehrer*, 110-13. The reference in Eph 4:11 may be dependent on 1 Cor 12:28; see also Crone, *Early Christian Prophecy*, 227.

6:14-16 with Mark 3:16-19, it is clear that he handled traditional materials with care, especially when names were concerned. An additional indication that Luke handed down extant materials is that Acts 13:1 is the only occurrence in Luke-Acts mentioning the term διδάσκαλοι.[53]

The two classes of wandering charismatics described in Did 11-13 are at variance with the picture presented in Paul, which mentions the itinerant lifestyle of apostles only. Because the prophets in the Pauline churches appear to have performed their ministry within the setting of the local community,[54] the letters of Paul do not suit our purpose of finding the appropriate geographical and historical framework for these itinerants. In this respect, the similarities between our section and the gospel of Matthew are particularly relevant.[55] Both the mission instruction for Christian messengers in Matt 10 and the rules for the reception of charismatics in Did 11-13 basically assume Christian itinerants whose lifestyle was dominated by their moving from place to place and remaining only briefly in any one community. In Matt 10:5-15.40-42 (cf. Luke 9:1-6; 10:1-12), Jesus addresses the Twelve and sets rules for their missionary assignment containing such values as the rejection of home, family and property. These passages seem to reflect the existence of a group of itinerant radicals within the Matthean community.[56] As far as the prophets in this congregation are concerned, it appears that at least some of them must have been illegitimate. The very number of references to false prophets in Matt 7:15-23; 24:11.24 suggests that they presented a special problem in the Matthean community.[57]

The circumstances reflected in Matt 10 may to a certain extent be compared with the social situation described in Did 11-13. This section, like Matt 10, presupposes a settled community that was frequently visited by teachers, i.e., apostles and prophets. Moreover, the guidelines instructing the community on the attitude which should be taken with regard to these itinerants provide us with similar ascetic values of homelessness, lack of family ties and the forsaking of material wealth. It is open to question, however, whether the Didachist used Matthew in its present form.[58] Modern scholarship disagrees on this point. Since it is difficult to substantiate a literary dependence on the gospel of Matthew as we have it, it seems more reasonable to assume that the Didachist drew on the same traditions as Matthew did. In order to face the crisis caused by dubious itinerant vagabonds, the Didachist

---

[53] See Zimmermann, *Die urchristlichen Lehrer*, 124-35; see also Rordorf-Tuilier, *La Doctrine des douze Apôtres*, 56-58.

[54] Greeven, 'Propheten, Lehrer, Vorsteher', 9; Von Campenhausen, *Kirchliches Amt*, 65-66.

[55] For the following, see also Theissen, 'Wanderradikalismus', 86-87; Aune, *Prophecy in Early Christianity*, 214-15; Crone, *Early Christian Prophecy*, 234-369 (264-65).

[56] Schweizer, *Matthäus und seine Gemeinde*, 140-48; see also Luz, *Das Evangelium nach Matthäus* 2, 151.

[57] Minear, 'False Prophecy' 80; Luz, *Das Evangelium nach Matthäus* 1, 403.

[58] For a discussion of this complicated issue, see Niederwimmer, *Die Didache*, 71-78; 214, n. 3; cf. also Rordorf-Tuilier, *La Doctrine des douze Apôtres*, 84. 87-89. The vast literature on this subject is too extensive to present here.

felt forced to confront his community with traditions transmitted in the form of an oral or written (apocryphal?) gospel.[59] He, therefore, introduced the required line of conduct towards traveling apostles and prophets as follows: "Act this way, according to the ordinance of the gospel" (κατὰ τὸ δόγμα τοῦ εὐαγγελίου οὕτω ποιήσατε) (11:3). Even though his community was familiar with the instructions, similar to some of the directions given in Matt 10, they appear to have only been partially or unevenly implemented. For our present purpose, it is of importance to ascertain that the Matthean community is generally located in the region of Syria (-Palestine)[60] in the last half of the first century CE.

Above the satire *De morte Peregrini* was mentioned.[61] Lucian of Samosata wrote this work in the second half of the second Christian century with the purpose of exposing Peregrinus of Parion, who burnt himself alive and was worshipped by his disciples. Indeed, Lucian's portrait of Peregrinus must be treated with considerable caution. Yet, although his information might be inaccurate and even tendentious, he no doubt presents us with a glimpse of the appearance of early Christianity in the eyes of an outsider at the time. According to Lucian's account, Peregrinus had been a Christian during one period of his lifetime. On one of his travels, he became a Christian, and was arrested for this and imprisoned by the governor of Syria. His fellow Christians left no stone unturned in trying to help him and provided financial support: "...much money came to him from them by reason of his emprisonment, and he procured not a little revenue from it" (Chap. 13).[62] Lucian offers various reasons for the generous attitude of the Christians (the belief in immortality, brotherhood of Christians, common property, etc.) and concludes: "So if any charlatan and trickster, able to profit by occasions, comes among them, he quickly acquires sudden wealth by imposing upon simple folk" (*ibid.*). Vagabonds moving from place to place would seem to receive a hospitable reception from local admirers who sustained and enriched them. After he was freed, Peregrinus returned to his native city (Parion) and after a while resumed his travels among the Christian communities. Lucian describes how he profited once

---

[59] The usage of the same gospel instance in both the Didache and Matthew might be reflected in the following example. In the passage of Did 13:1-2 it says: "Every true prophet who wants to settle in with you deserves his food (ἄξιός ἐστι τῆς τροφῆς αὐτοῦ). In the same way, a true teacher, too, deserves his food, just as a worker does (ἐστιν ἄξιος καὶ αὐτὸς ὥσπερ ὁ ἐργάτης τῆς τροφῆς αὐτοῦ)." The wording in these verses almost verbally agrees with the final clause in Matt 10:9-10 which belongs to Jesus' instructions for the mission of the twelve:"Take no gold, nor silver, nor copper in your belts, no bag for your journey, nor two tunics, nor sandals, nor a staff; for the labourer deserves his food (ἄξιος γὰρ ὁ ἐργάτης τῆς τροφῆς αὐτοῦ)." For the traditional character of the latter saying which is probably is linked to the halakha on field labour, see Tomson, *Paul and the Jewish Law*, 126-27.

[60] See above, Chap. 1, n. 139.

[61] Cf. above, p. 341. See H.D. Betz, 'Lukian von Samosata und das Christentum'; Id., *Lukian von Samosata und das Neue Testament*, 5-13; cf. also Bagnani, 'Peregrinus Proteus', 107-112 and Jones, *Culture and Society*, 117-132.

[62] See ΠΕΡΙ ΤΗΣ ΠΕΡΕΓΡΙΝΟΥ ΤΕΛΕΥΤΗΣ. For the English translation, see Harmon, *Lucian* 5, 3-51: *The Passing of Peregrinus*; for the Greek text, cf. also Macleod, *Luciani Opera* 3 (1980) 188-205.

more from Christian naivety and compassion: "He left home, then, for the second time, to roam about, possessing an ample source of funds in the Christians, through whose ministrations he lived in unalloyed prosperity" (Chap. 16). If the information provided by Lucian is reliable, Peregrinus wandered in Syria-Palestine while keeping up a pose of a Christian prophet. This might be a further indication of the diffusion of the phenomenon of traveling preachers in this region.

In other second and third century sources, early Christianity is pictured as a movement which was still dominated by wandering missionaries who moved from place to place. The two Ps-Clementine letters *Ad Virgines*, created in the early third century, describe the ethos of Syrian preachers, teachers, lectors, intercessors, exorcists and miracle workers who travelled through the region while visiting various Christian homes in the villages along the route of their journey.[63] In these letters, references are made to financial abuses for the sake of personal gain since there were wanderers who, as the text reads, "use attractive words to make a living with the name of Christ."[64] A significant difference with the type of itinerancy seen in Matthew and the Didache, however, is that ascetism has become a prominent characteristic of these charismatic wanderers to such an extent that teaching played but a subordinate role. Radical itinerancy was increasingly perceived as a road to personal perfection rather than a means of promoting the gospel.[65] Furthermore, the gospel of Thomas, which is closely connected with Syrian Christianity and was composed in 140 CE at the latest, focusses on the itinerant lifestyle. Some traditions here suggest that Thomasian Christians were also homeless vagabonds (*Gos.Thom.* 42, 86), without possessions (*Gos.Thom.* 95, 54, 36) and family ties (*Gos.Thom.* 55, 99, 101), who ate the food that was offered to them (*Gos.Thom.*

---

[63] See, for example, the following statement: "Wenn uns aber an einem Orte zufällig die Zeit (zum Übernachten) überrascht, sei es auf dem Lande oder in einem Dorfe oder in einer Stadt oder bei einer Wohnstätte oder wo wir uns gerade befinden, und es sind an jenem Orte Brüder vorhanden, so treten wir bei einem Bruder ein und rufen dorthin alle Brüder zusammen und reden mit ihnen Worte der Ermunterung und des Trostes" (II,1,3); cf. Duensing, 'Klemens von Rom', 180, 28-33. See also Kretschmar, 'Ein Beitrag zur Frage', 136-38.

[64] "... Da sie müssig sind und nichts tun, gehen sie unnötigen Dingen nach und machen mit Hilfe gewinnender Worte ein Geschäft mit dem Namen Christi." (I,10,4); cf. Duensing, 'Klemens von Rom', 175, 34-36; see also I, 11,4 (= 176, 10): "im Namen Christi ein Geschäft machen." The Syrian version, which has been lost at these places, might reflect the original Greek wording χριστέμπορος occurring in Did 12:5. Adam ('Erwägungen zur Herkunft der Didache') points out that the use of this expression is infrequent in early Christianity (38) and concludes as follows: "An ebensolche Gemeinden, wie sie aus den Briefen Ad Virgines zu erschliessen sind, muss die Didache gerichtet gewesen sein, um ihnen die erste Anleitung für die Aufrichtung einer zuchtvollen Ordnung zu geben" (39). A similar expression is also found in I,13,5 (= 179, 34-35): "Arbeiter, die Gottesfurcht und Gerechtigkeit für eine Erwerbsquelle halten."

[65] Cf. Von Harnack, 'Die pseudoclementinischen Briefe', 381: "Die Linie unserer Asketen reicht also bis zu den Ursprüngen des Christenthums zurück. Wohl ist hier eine Metamorphose vor sich gegangen – aus den freien Evangelisten und Lehrern, die *auch* enthaltsam waren, sind Enthaltsame geworden, die *auch* Lehrer sind –; aber die Continuität ist unverkennbar."

14). It demonstrates that in the latter first or early second century, the unconventional ethos advocated by wandering radicals was alive and well in Syria.[66]

The section being discussed here probably originated in a Greek-speaking part of Western Syria and might have been created within the class of accredited teachers. They, at least, are the only officials mentioned here who apparently did not present problems to the community. Moreover, they presumably were permanent residents who, like a number of prophets, enjoyed a great deal of respect (15:1-2) and particular privileges (13:1-2).

Didache 11-15 and its Jewish Roots

In the following section the vestiges of early Judaism, as reflected in Did 11-15, are traced. The exposition takes place in three phases. First, attention is given to specific elements in Did 14-15. The subsequent section deals with the classes of apostles, teachers and prophets again, but this time the discussion focusses primarily on their embedment in Jewish institutions and concepts. As the existence of (wandering) prophets appears to have been a common phenomenon in the Didache community, even though several ancient Jewish texts suggest that prophecy declined or ceased altogether in the Second Temple period, the question regarding the prophets and prophecy is addressed rather extensively in this section. In the final section, the passage in Did 13:3-7, which gives the impression of being derived from Jewish halakhic tradition, is examined. The materials up for discussion seem to reveal that the separation between the church as reflected in the Didache and the synagogue took place gradually and in a later period than, for example, Paul's missionary activities.

DIDACHE 14-15

In Did 14, the confession of sins and reconciliation is the central theme. Relevant to our present discussion is the temporal indication κατὰ κυριακὴν δὲ κυρίου ("on the Sunday of the Lord") with reference to the Eucharist in 14:1. This pleonastic phrase emphasizes the Sunday as the day of the Lord. The usage of this expression as an alternative to a phrase like καθ'ἡμέραν δὲ κυρίου or κατὰ κυριακήν might indicate a polemic against those who still preferred the Sabbath to the Lord's day for the weekly celebration of the Eucharist. Evidence from other sources (Gal 4:8-11; Col 2:16-17 and Ignatius, *Magn.* 9:1-2), indicating that some Christian circles continued to observe the Sabbath, strengthens this impression.

---

[66] Cf. Patterson, *The Gospel of Thomas*, 158-170.

The phrase, then, might suggest that these Christians should exchange the Sabbath for the Sunday as the day of the celebration of the Eucharist.[67] The text provides little information about the bishops and deacons (15:1-2). It states that they were elected from local community members and, in addition to the more general qualification of being "worthy of the Lord," it mentions the most important prerequisites for these offices. In the history of scholarly inquiry about the origins of the earliest Christian community organization, the episcopal office is frequently presented as borrowed from Greco-Roman institutions or as being typical of the gentile Christian churches. The episcopate might, however, not be as foreign and novel as is often suggested.[68] Although ἐπίσκοπος is used in non-biblical Greek for a civic, financial and religious "overseer", it is also found in the LXX and may thus have Jewish antecedents. One possibility is that the episcopacy was modelled on the *archisynagôgos* ("synagogue chief") of the Jewish synagogue, since the functions of both offices are similar.[69] In that case, however, the question remains how the title *episkopos* originated. With respect to the nomenclature (bishop = overseer), it is much more likely that the Jewish model of this office can be located in the community of the Qumran Essenes. The title is similar to that of the sectarian official מבקר which literally means "overseer".[70] Of course, it not

---

[67] For the argument, see Rordorf-Tuilier, *La Doctrine des douze Apôtres*, 64-65. Of course, the reference to Christian worship on a Sunday does not necessarily stand in opposition to Sabbath worship. Similarly, the choice of the primitive church for Wednesday and Friday may also have been affected by the use of the solar calendar among the Jewish sect of Qumran (see also above, Chap. 8, p. 293, n. 76). For a critique against the view that the Christians took over the Sunday from the sectarians, however, see Rordorf, *Der Sonntag*, 180-86. In the light of the additional features in the Didache differentiating Christians from Jews, as illustrated in Chaps. 8 and 1 (pp. 291-96.327-29 and 32-35), we consider these guidelines to be indications of an ongoing separation.
There are scholars who have argued that κυριακή would seem to refer to Easter Day; cf. Strobel, 'Die Passa-Erwartung', 184-85 and n. 104; Dugmore, 'Lord's Day and Easter', 275-78. This hypothesis, however, is doubtful; cf. Niederwimmer, *Die Didache*, 235, n. 8. According to a recent proposition of Tidwell ('Didache XIV:1'), the expression κατὰ κυριακὴν δὲ κυρίου in the opening phrase of Did 14 refers to a Jewish-Christian observance of Yom Kippur. For this suggestion, see above, Chap. 8, n. 99.
Another point requiring consideration is the quotation from Mal 1:11.14 in Did 14:3 in support of the purity of the sacrifice. Gordon established that the addition of καὶ χρόνῳ to the quotation from Mal 1:11 LXX (and MT) in the rendering of Did 14:3 seems, at first sight, to reflect Jewish exegesis as exhibited in Tg.Yon. He, however, considers it more likely that "both the Targum and *Didache* have adapted Mal 1,11 to suit their own particular doctrinal needs" ('Targumic parallels', 288).
[68] For a comprehensive account of the history of interpretation of early literary and archeological evidence for public offices in the earliest church, see Burtchaell, *From Synagogue to Church*, 1-179.
[69] Cf. e.g. Götz, *Petrus als Gründer*, 49-54.
[70] If the Damascus Rule (CD) represents a later stage in the development of the Qumran community than does the Community Rule (1QS), as is proposed by many authors (see Schürer, *The history of the Jewish People* 2, 396, n. 21), it is of interest to see that the Qumran institution of the מבקר, by analogy with the development of the episopal role in early Christianity, underwent some profound changes. Like the early Christian bishop, the Qumran "overseer" initially did not have a position of prominence. Only in a later stage, reflected in CD 13-14, did he exercise monarchical authority; cf. Reicke, 'The Constitution of the Primitive Church',149-55.
For the affinity between the Qumran מבקר and the early Christian ἐπίσκοπος, see also Greehy, 'The

implied here that early Christianity adopted this institution direct from Qumran but some connection between the two offices is not easily rejected.

The injunctions of this section come to a close in Did 15:3-4 and it is the mention of "the gospel" in these verses which arouses particular interest. Twice the expression ὡς ἔχετε ἐν τῷ εὐαγγελίῳ ("as you have it in the gospel;" 15:3) occurs, to which in 15:4 is added "of our Lord." Most scholars agree that this wording refers to some written gospel, but it is difficult to determine whether the text alludes to a canonical or apocryphal gospel. The content of the reference is the most explicit in 15:3a: "Correct one another not in anger but in peace, as you have it in the gospel." The text shows that the reader was to find this injunction in the gospel while the remainder of the verse, not quoted here, appears to be peculiar to the Didache itself. Now, it is often assumed that the directive draws upon Matt 18:15 (or 18:15-17).[71] While it is difficult to establish definitive connections between the two texts based simply upon the Matthean admonition of reprovement of a brother ("between you and him alone"), there is a good possibility that the instance in the Didache is influenced by Qumran materials. In the Community Rule or Manual of Discipline the focus is particularly on the circumstances in which mutual correction is to take place as it says: "They shall admonish one another in t[ruth], humility and affectionate love. He must not speak to him with anger or with a snarl, or with a [stiff] neck ...."(1QS 5:24-25).[72] The argument brought up here is the same as the one found in Did 15:3, i.e., the attendant conditions are not conflict, rage or agitation (ἐν ὀργῇ // בְּאַף) but harmony and friendliness (ἐν εἰρήνῃ // בְּא[נָ]מְה] וענוה ואהבת חסד).[73] An additional parallel is found in *T. Gad* 6:3: "Therefore, love one another from the heart, and if a man sins against you, speak to him in peace (ἐν εἰρήνῃ), ..."[74] Again, it is not our intention to claim that the Didachist is dependent on 1QS or on the Testament of Gad here, but rather that the "gospel" which is referred to in Did 14:3 might be a source which at some points, and at variance with our present gospel of Matthew, shows

Qumran Mebaqqer'; Fitzmyer, 'Jewish Christianity in Acts', 288-94; Tuilier, 'La Doctrine des Apôtres', 237-39; Rordorf-Tuilier, *La Doctrine des douze Apôtres*, 77 and n. 2.

Nauck also establishes a close correspondence between the directive for the "overseer" in CD 13:7-12 and a prayer in the liturgy on the occasion of the consecration of a bishop in Chap. 3 of the *Traditio Apostolica* (early third century CE) ascribed to Hippolytus, a document which shows strong Jewish influences. From the agreement between the two texts, Nauck draws the conclusion: "dass die Wendung im römischen Bischofsweihegebet auf alte Tradition zurückgeht, die, vom Judentum übernommen, in der frühen Kirche lebendig blieb;" cf. 'Probleme des frühchristlichen Amtsverständnisses', 207.

Josephus speaks of the Essene ἐπιμεληταί, which might well be his equivalent for the Hebrew מבקר: "The overseers (ἐπιμεληταί) of the common property are elected and each without distinction is appointed in the manner of all to the various offices;" *Bellum* 2, 123; cf. also 2, 134; see Schürer, *The history of the Jewish People* 2, 566 and n. 21.

[71] See Schenk-Ziegler, *Correctio fraterna im Neuen Testament*, 296-311; esp. 310. For additional references, cf. Niederwimmer, *Die Didache*, 245, n.10.

[72] ET: Wernberg-Møller, *The Manual of Discipline*, 29.

[73] Cf. Audet, *La Didachè*, 180 and Schenk-Ziegler, *Correctio fraterna*, 126-58; esp. 130-32.

[74] ET: Hollander-De Jonge, *The Testaments of the Twelve Patriarchs*, 331.

a marked affinity with Qumran concepts or with Jewish schools of thought close to these Sectarians.

DIDACHE 11-13: THE APOSTLES, TEACHERS AND PROPHETS

In the following, attention is given to the classes of leaders rooted in Jewish antecedents: the apostles, teachers and prophets. The first group to be considered here, the apostles, has a close parallel in the Jewish שליח (shaliah) institution. The shaliah was sent round to the communities of the Diaspora as an envoy of the central authorities in Jerusalem. Authorized by the Sanhedrin or the נשיא (nasi), i.e., the patriarch, these distinguished emissaries preserved the connection between the motherland and the congregations outside the land of Israel. Their commission was many-faceted. They preached in public, exercised surveillance, solved halakhic problems and conveyed circular letters. An additional important task was the collection of tributes for the patriarch, who used these funds to maintain his courts, the academies, and needy students. After the destruction of the temple, Jews in many parts of the world continued to make donations and they probably considered their contributions to be a replacement for the half shekel formerly sent to the temple. The שלוחים, the emissaries, would gather these monies from the scattered Jewish communities and transport them to Jerusalem. The sending of commissioned messengers continued during the rule of the patriarchate until 425 CE and this practice was renewed in the seventh century.[75] Although clear evidence about the date of origin is lacking, there is little reason to doubt that a basic form of this institution existed in the late Second Temple period and exercised a formative influence upon the Christian apostolate.[76]

---

[75] See Safrai, 'Eretz Israel weha-tefutsah ha-yehudit', 299-300; Id., 'Relations between the Diaspora', 205-209; Tomson, *Paul and the Jewish Law*, 147; David, 'Sheluhei Eretz Israel', 1358-61.

[76] It has been questioned whether the Jewish office of *shaliah* existed as early as the first century CE; cf. especially Schmithals, *Das Kirchliche Apostelamt*, 87-99; see also Klein, *Die zwölf Apostel*, 26-28; Schütz, *Paul and the Anatomy*, 27-28.

Evidence for the existence of a שליח institution is found in the Mishnah, in the Talmud, in the *Codex Theodosianus* XVI 8,14, and in patristic literature (main sources: Justin, Eusebius, Jerome and Epiphanius); see Krauss, 'Die jüdischen Apostel'; Von Harnack, *Die Mission* 1, 314-18; Str-B 3, 2-4; Rengstorf, 'ἀπόστολος'; Schille, *Die urchristliche Kollegialmission*, 17-18. Although the above-mentioned sources hardly suffice as witnesses to the existence of a *shaliah* office as early as the first century, the apparent commonness of this institution in these documents makes it highly improbable that this phenomenon would have been unknown in Judaism of the late Second Temple period. Moreover, Justin Martyr (*Dialogue* 17:1; cf. 108:2-3 and 117:3) affirms that, soon after the death and resurrection of Jesus, emissaries were dispatched all over the world by Jerusalem to counteract the Christian mission (cf. Hare, 'The Relationship', 447). Acts 9:1-2 too, testifies that Paul, prior to his vocation, went as a representative of the central authorities to Damascus, carrying letters of accreditation for the local synagogues. A significant difference, however, between the Jewish *sheluhim* and the Christian apostles must be noted. The Jewish emissaries had the primary function of acting as intermediaries between the Jewish communities and were not involved in what we should call missionary activity (cf. Rengstorf, 'ἀπόστολος', 418; see also Goodman, 'Jewish Proselytizing in the First Century', 53-78 and McKnight, *A Light among the Gentiles*, 49-77).

We turn to the appearance of the apostles in Did 11:4-6. It is not farfetched to assume that at least some features of the apostolic role described here are akin to the office of the Jewish *sheluhim*. Mobility is one such characteristic. In 11:4-6, the emphasis is placed on their coming and going from the community and this picture correlates with the remainder of Did 11-15. Unlike some prophets and the class of designated teachers who functioned within the framework of the religious community (13:1-2; cf. 15:2), the text never mentions or implies that the apostles are permanent residents. Little is specifically said in the Didache about the duties of the apostles. Did 11:4 seems to indicate that they have received their task by virtue of a divine commission. Because they are representatives of the Lord, they should be welcomed as the Lord Himself, a statement which recalls a principle frequently stated in rabbinic literature: שלוחו של אדם כמותו ("the one sent by a man is as the man himself").[77] Additional information about their function can be found outside the present passage. The introduction in 11:1-2 to the verses under consideration here (and to the subsequent admonishment in 11:7-12) indicates that teaching was one of the apostles' functions. Their role thus appears to be akin in several respects to specific features characterizing the Jewish *shaliah*.

More evidence favouring the Jewish roots of the apostles in the Didache is found in the two proscriptions themselves in Did 11:4-6. The first injunction stipulating that apostles are provided with a maximum of two days' food and lodging is likely to limit the community's generous hospitality. It is clear that a reduction of the duration of a visitor's reception to that extent would prevent the apostles from playing a teaching role of some consequence in the life of the community.[78] If they wished their labour to be influential, a longer stay in a community was needed, as is shown in the case of Paul, who remained in Corinth some eighteen months and in Ephesus two and a half years (Acts 18:1-18, resp.

A final indication for the existence of the Jewish שליח institution before the second century may be found in the use of the designation ἀπόστολος in biblical and secular Greek. The word is rarely found in the LXX and when it occurs in classical and *koine* Greek, it is predominantly used with reference to the experience of seafaring. In this light, it is surprising to discover the term ἀπόστολος as often as 80 times in the New Testament in the sense of (authorized) messenger. The word ἀπόστολος with this significance may have been known in secular Greek in NT times (Agnew, 'On the Origin of the term *Apostolos*', 53), but we lack the recorded use except for Josephus, *Ant*. 17, 300 (the text of the other possible instance, 1,146, is uncertain). The surprisingly large number of occurrences in the NT can be accounted for by only one explanation: "... the noun was already current in some Hellenistic-Jewish circles as an established rendering of שליח. On the Hebrew side, both verb and noun were current in the technical sense;..." (cf. Barrett, '*Shaliah* and Apostle', 99-100) The most natural Greek word qualified to translate the Jewish equivalent must have been ἀπόστολος. On the basis of the above data, one may safely assume that the Christian apostolate has firm roots in the Jewish שליח institution.

[77] The wording (δεχθήτω) ὡς κύριος is missing in the Coptic and Ethiopic versions. See, however, Niederwimmer, 'Textprobleme der Didache', 127. For parallels in rabbinic literature, see mBer 5:5; bNed 72b; bKidd 41b; bHag 10b; bNaz 12b; bBM 96a; bMen 93b. Cf. also Matt 10:40; John 13:16.20; Ignatius, *Eph*. 6:1. See also Rengstorf, 'ἀπόστολος', 415-16 and Tomson, '*If this be from Heaven...*', 132-34.

[78] Schöllgen-(Geerlings), *Didache. Zwölf-Apostellehre*, 60-61; Schöllgen, 'Die Didache als Kirchenordnung', 12 (ET: 53); Draper, 'Social Ambiguity', 294-95.

19:1-20:1). This also explains why the instruction of the apostles, at variance with the utterances of the prophets in 11:7-12, does not appear to have been an issue for the Didachist. We at least do not find any injunction demanding that their teaching should be examined. It is thus fair to assume the original teaching function of the apostles, still presupposed in the introduction, is severely subverted by the restriction of the length of their stay.

The second injunction prohibits them from asking for money (11:6). Of course, this regulation, like the first one, takes issue against swindlers who wished to exploit the community. Possibly, the instruction in 11:6 was also directed against people who sought remuneration for their services (cf. 11:12[79]). Yet, there might be an additional reason for this proscription. We know that Paul, as soon as he was recognized to be an apostle by the pillars of the Jerusalem church, was commissioned to collect money for the support of the Jerusalem church (Gal 2:10), a task which caused him a great deal of trouble (1 Cor 16:1-4; 2 Cor 8-9; Rom 15:25-28) and finally resulted in his death. In 2 Cor 8:23, Paul uses the phrase ἀπόστολοι ἐκκλησιῶν ("apostles of the churches") to denote the men who at his request were to escort him on his way to Jerusalem with the collection for the Christian community in that city which he had arranged in his gentile communities. In a similar sense, Epaphroditus, who on behalf of the congregation in Philippi was sent with a donation to Paul, is called ἀπόστολος (Phil 2:25). The collection was a duty imposed by Jerusalem, the spiritual benefactress of all the churches, on the gentile communities.

It is not inconceivable, then, that the apostles of Did 11:4-6, visiting the local community of the Didache, were charged with a similar commission. Admittedly, the text is silent about the specific tasks of the apostles as delegates from the mother church in Jerusalem. They were primarily authorized by the Lord. This need not indicate, however, that they were to break off relations with the officials and administrators in the earliest Christian community. The latter, after all, were appointed by Jesus in his stead. After 70 CE, however, the superior juridical status enjoyed by the Jerusalem church vanished. Once James the Just was executed, Jerusalem was destroyed, and the primatial church scattered, the preeminence of this Christian centre faded.[80] The decrease of respect for the centre may be reflected in Did 11:4-6. In that case, not only contemporary abuses but also the lower esteem for the Jerusalem church may have originated the disciplinary measures presented in the Didache forestalling any apostle from staying (and thus teaching) for an indeterminate period of time and collecting money in the community.[81]

---

[79] The injunction in Did 11:12, however, differs form the one in 11:6 in that the request of prophets in 11:12 is not confined to money only: δός μοι ἀργύρια ἢ ἕτερά τινα.

[80] See also Draper, 'Social Ambiguity', 294-95; id., 'Weber, Theissen', 570; cf. Von Harnack, *Die Mission* 1, 317 en id., *Entstehung und Entwickelung*, 20-22 and 30.

[81] The wording of Did 11:4-6 may even draw upon a rule that was applied in Jewish communities. It deals with the aid to a traveller who is poor and has no financial means to pay for lodging and board: They give to a poor man traveling from place to place no less than a loaf [of bread] worth a *dupondion* ...

Let us turn to the teachers (διδάσκαλοι) now. In the Didache, they appear twice (13:2 and 15:1-2) and are grouped together with the prophets on these occasions. The specific information about the class of teachers in the text is meagre, but it is clear that they are settled local officials who enjoyed the financial support of the community. The office of teachers was a traditional institution in early Judaism. The term is found 58 times in the New Testament (48 times in the gospels) and Jesus is often addressed as διδάσκαλε or ῥαββί. In John 1:38, these designations occur in juxtaposition. Jesus is called ῥαββί by the disciples of John the Baptist, which is rendered διδάσκαλε here for readers not acquainted with the Hebrew. The relationship between Jesus and his disciples thus seems to correspond to the relationship between the Jewish Sages and their disciples. Clear evidence for the linguistic affinity between διδάσκαλος and the rabbinic teacher in the late Second Temple period is found in three ossuary inscriptions dating from some time before 70 CE. These epigraphs, containing a declension of the Greek word διδάσκαλος (namely διδασκάλου), were discovered in 1930 on Mount Scopus in Jerusalem. They attest to the fact that some Jewish διδάσκαλοι were buried in the period before 70 CE.[82] Indications in Josephus and in the New Testament, both geographically and chronologically close to the evidence of the three ossuaries, enable us to determine more exactly the meaning of the word διδάσκαλος in the ossuary inscriptions. They appear to be religious teachers, probably Pharisaic Sages.[83] In addition to the evidence of Acts 13:1-2 and 1Cor 12:28, the appearance of this institution in Did 13:2 and 15:1-2 supports the assumption that the office of teacher was recognized to be a prestigeous institution in early Christianity, especially in Syria.[84] The term διδάσκαλος thus has a distinctively rabbinic character and is

[If such a poor person] stayed overnight,
they give him enough [to pay] for a night's lodging.
[If such a poor person] spent the Sabbath,
they give him food for three meals (mPea 8:7).
Cf. Milavec, 'Distinguishing True and False Prophets', 127, n. 14 and Moore, *Judaism* 2, 176-77. See also tPea 8:7 and yPea 8, 21a.

[82] See Zimmermann, *Die urchristlichen Lehrer*, 69-74. The designation διδάσκαλος (or διδασκάλου in these inscriptions) equates the Hebrew רב (*rav* = 'master' or, sometimes, 'teacher'). The Hebrew רבי (*rabbi*), the same noun with the pronominal first person suffix, must be ruled out as a possible equivalent here since the wording *rabbi* was used in these days as an address, meaning 'my master' and thus would correspond with the Greek διδάσκαλέ (μου). After the destruction of the temple, however, the Hebrew רבי (*rabbi*) became a fixed title, accorded to a Sage who was properly ordained; cf. Dalman, *Die Worte Jesu*, 272-80.

[83] Cf. Zimmermann, *Die urchristlichen Lehrer*, 85-86; See also Rengstorf, 'διδάσκω κτλ', 154-160.

[84] Zimmermann believes that the understanding of the διδάσκαλος in the second century was profoundly modified as compared to the ancient institution of Jewish Christian teachers. He ascribes this change of meaning to three factors, namely the exclusive Christocratic self-concept of the primitive Christian community, the bad experiences of the communities with these teachers, and the impact of the unabridged rule in Matt 23:8-10, where Jesus is the absolute διδάσκαλος (*Die urchristlichen Lehrer*, 209-14 and 218-19). In the presentation of the teachers in the Didache, however, we do not find traces of such a development.

linked with the Sage of early Judaism whose work lies within the sphere of the community.

The Jewish impact on the development of Christian *prophecy* needs some more consideration than the above topics of apostles and teachers. At first glance, it is impossible to find in early Judaism a functional model as a paradigm for the Christian prophets because our main Jewish sources express the view that, during the Second Temple period, prophecy has vanished altogether.[85] Postexilic Jews denied the possibility that God still communicated with his people by speaking directly to certain individuals. In rabbinic literature, the ability to prophesy is closely associated with the presence of the Spirit,[86] but both prophecy and the Spirit are recorded to be absent from Jewish religious experience. On the other hand, the Didache, which expresses a similar close affinity between prophecy and the Spirit (11:7.8.9.12), presents the prophets as practising prophecy on a regular basis. How is this phenomenon to be accounted for?

According to a number of texts in rabbinic literature, Josephus, Apocrypha, and Pseudepigrapha, the Spirit was taken from Israel after the fall of the first temple, or alternatively, after the death of the last canonical prophets (Haggai, Zechariah, and Malachi).[87] For the Sages of the Tannaitic period onward, genuine prophecy had ceased. Revelation was no longer mediated by the inspired prophet but by a בת קול (*bath qol*, i.e., a daughter of voice) which, however, was rather a poor compensation for a legitimate continuation of prophecy.[88] Veritable prophecy was dead and no one could claim the title 'prophet' until God was to fully realize the kingdom. Although some rabbis were held to be worthy of the title "prophet", the iniquity of the present age made it impossible for even the holiest of men, such as Hillel the Elder and Rabbi Akiva, to be called so.[89] Prophecy was limited to the period of the canonical prophets of the distant past and was expected to return in the endtime.[90] There is evidence that even Josephus shared the rabbinic view that

---

[85] There are authors who have challenged this consensus, like Aune, *Prophecy in Early Christianity*, 103-06; Overholt, 'The End of Prophecy'; Greenspahn, 'Why Prophecy Ceased'. For a critical discussion of their arguments, see Sommer, 'Did Prophecy Cease?'. Recently, however, J.R. Levison ('Did the Spirit withdraw from Israel?') has supported the objections against the assumption that prophecy was believed to have ceased during the Tannaitic period.

[86] Cf. Schäfer, *Die Vorstellung vom heiligen Geist*, 14-15 (with additional bibliographical references) and 21-26; Sjöberg, 'πνεῦμα', 381-82.

[87] Cf. SOlamR 30; bSot 48b; tSot 13:2-3; bSan 11a; bYom 9b. 21b etc. See also Schäfer, *Die Vorstellung vom heiligen Geist*, 89-110.

[88] Cf. tSot 13:3; bSot 48b; bSan 11a; bYom 9b; see Leivestad, 'Das Dogma von der prophetenlosen Zeit', 289-90. Some rabbis even warned against giving the *bath qol* a decisive role and an appeal to this surrogate-for-prophecy was sometimes challenged; cf. bBer 51b-52a; bBM 59a; bBB 59b; bEr 7a. 13b; bYev 14a and bPes 114a.

[89] Cf. tSot 13:3-4; bSan 11a; bSuk 28a; bBB 134a; cf. also ARN a 14; see Urbach, *The Sages* 1, 576-79.

[90] In this respect Ezek. 36:26-27 and Joel 3:1-2 were particularly important; cf. NumR 15,25 on Num. 11:17 (= Mirkin, *Midrash Rabbah* 2, 159); cf. also tSot 13:2 and Or. Sib. III, 582. See also Leivestad, 'Das Dogma von der prophetenlosen Zeit', 291.294-99; Schäfer, *Die Vorstellung vom heiligen Geist*, 112-15.

prophecy had ceased.[91] For him, as for most rabbis, prophecy consists principally in prediction and foreknowledge of the course of future events. He himself claims to have the gift of prophecy, which rested on a combination of exegetical skill and divine inspiration, and he ascribes a similar access to divine revelation to the Essenes who predicted the future by studying biblical texts.[92] Nevertheless, Josephus does not apply the term προφήτης ("prophet") to himself nor to those, who like himself, had prognostic gifts. He reserves the word for any but biblical prophets, while calling those who in his days abusively claimed to be messengers of God "false prophets."

It has been suggested that the rabbinic texts postulating the cessation of prophecy might reflect an apologetic attempt to subvert the prophetic claims of the early Christians.[93] There are reasons, however, to oppose that view. The comments of Josephus on the Essene seers accord with the more precise information we now have from the Dead Sea Scrolls about the application of Scriptural prophecies to contemporary events and figures. The scrolls also speak about the leading role of the "Teacher of Righteousness" who has received from God the understanding and illumination to interpret Scripture. Nevertheless, the community of Qumran does not call this kind of inspired interpretation נבואה ("prophecy") nor does it ever call its Teacher of Righteousness, as far as we know, a נביא ("prophet").[94] In addition, references in 1 Macc 4:46; 14:41 (cf. 9:27) prove that as early as the time of the Maccabees, the conviction had settled in that prophecy belonged to the normative age of the past and to the messianic age in the future.[95] Both texts propose that a final solution should be postponed while waiting for the eschatological prophet. In rabbinic sources, this vacuum was filled with the lively expectation of distinct prophetic figures at the endtime, in particular with the return of Elijah.[96]

The above evidence shows that prophecy in the late Second Temple period had considerably decreased and had become a strikingly infrequent phenomenon. On the other hand, evidence in Josephus does not permit us to entirely exclude prophetic activity at the time. He (briefly) describes popular figures in Judaea in the years between CE 40-70 who acted under the pretence of divine inspiration and

---

[91] Cf. Blenkinsopp, 'Prophecy and Priesthood', 240.256. However, the well-known utterance in *c. Ap.* 1, 41 with respect to the "failure of the exact succession of the prophets," which Blenkinsopp and others (see, e.g. Crone, *Early Christian Prophecy*, 143) often consider as proof of the cessation of prophecy, does not appear relevant in this matter; see Van Unnik, *Flavius Josephus*, 47-48.

[92] Cf. Blenkinsopp, 'Prophecy and Priesthood', 247; see also Aune, *Prophecy in Early Christianity*, 140-43.

[93] Urbach, 'Matai pasqah ha-Nevuah', 8-11.

[94] Cf. Crone, *Early Christian Prophecy*, 94-118; Leivestad, 'Das Dogma von der prophetenlosen Zeit', 297-98; Foerster, 'Der Heilige Geist im Spätjudentum', 123-25.132.

[95] See Leivestad, 'Das Dogma von der prophetenlosen Zeit', 294-96; Blenkinsopp, 'Prophecy and Priesthood', 250; see also Foerster, 'Der Heilige Geist im Spätjudentum', 121.

[96] The expectation of the return of Elijah was derived from Mal 3:23-24 (cf. Sir 48:10) and is found frequently in rabbinic sources: SifDeut 342 (= Finkelstein, *Siphre ad Deuteronomium*, 393-94); DeutR 6,7 (= Mirkin, *Midrash Rabbah* 11, 102); mEd 8:7; bPes 70b; bBer 33b etc. Cf. also Wiener, *The Prophet Elijah*.

falsely claimed to be prophets or were wrongly regarded as such.[97] These charismatics, who often promised signs and miracles, proclaimed a message of eschatological redemption. They gathered large crowds of followers around themselves and led them into the desert to await God's final deliverance from the Romans and a re-acquisition of the land. Josephus mentions in particular Theudas appearing during the procuratorship of Cuspius Fadus (*Ant.* 20, 97-99), the unnamed "charlatans" (*Bellum* 2, 258-59; *Ant.* 20, 167-68) and the "Egyptian" (*Bellum* 2, 261-63; *Ant.* 20, 169-72) attracting attention while Antonius Felix was procurator, the unidentified "charlatan" during the procuratorship of Porcius Festus (*Ant.* 20, 188) and the anonymous "false prophet" appearing while the temple was alight (*Bellum* 6, 284-86).[98] These prophets had in common the anticipation of some great act of eschatological redemption as an essential characteristic.[99] Although Josephus calls them "charlatans" (γοήτες) or "false prophets" (ψευδοπροφήτες), there is little doubt that these charismatic figures were believed to be prophets and were so designated.[100] They claimed prophetic authority to announce the messianic age of deliverance and showed a strong eschatological awareness. In this respect, they may be compared with John the Baptist and Jesus, who appear to be rooted in the same tradition.

This sequence of inspired prophets, on the face of it, seems to contradict the widely held rabbinic postulate that the voice of prophecy had ceased. Conversely, one may also argue that it makes perfectly good sense in the Jewish concept of prophecy, which was limited to the normative past prophecy and a hoped-for future. Many expected a prophetic figure to appear immediately before the end of the age (e.g., Elijah) and the endtime was widely regarded as imminent. The strong messianic overtones in the conflicts with the Romans in the three decades before the destruction and in the great revolt in 66-70 CE provided a breeding ground for a revival of prophecy. A charismatic figure appearing in this period who made a claim to prophecy was expected by his followers to conclude the prophetless interregnum. This type of prophecy, then, which became vital in an eschatological setting, in

---

[97] Cf. Hengel, *Die Zeloten*, 235-51; Horsley, '«Like One of the Prophets of Old»', 454-61; Horsley-Hanson, *Bandits, Prophets, and Messiahs*, 160-172. For a description of these movements, cf. Schürer, *The history of the Jewish People* 1, 455-70 and Stern, 'The Province of Judaea', 360-72.
It is noteworthy that Josephus, though never applying the title "prophet" to himself or to his contemporaries, does not deny the existence of prophetic activity in his time. In his opinion, God still made use of certain individuals as instruments to reveal future events and, besides claiming a prophetic status for himself, he refers to some Essenes (Judas and Menahem) as genuine seers and prognostics; cf. Blenkinsopp, 'Prophecy and Priesthood', 258; Horsley and Hanson, *Bandits, Prophets, and Messiahs*, 155-56; Horsley, '«Like One of the Prophets of Old»', 448.
[98] See Barnett, 'The Jewish Sign Prophets', 680-86; Gray, *Prophetic Figures*, 112-44. In the latter study, also a certain Yonatan is considered to be a Jewish sign prophet (*Bellum* 7, 437-50; *Vita*, 424-25), "a Sicarius refugee from Palestine who was active in Cyrene after the war" (112; see also 121-22).
[99] Hengel, *Die Zeloten*, 242-51.
[100] Barnett, 'The Jewish Sign Prophets', 689: "Each clearly was a *prophet*. A '*Sign*' was attempted by each man. A significant *locale* was involved on each occasion and a *crowd* of people was present." See also Horsley and Hanson, *Bandits, Prophets, and Messiahs*, 161-62.

a time that many considered to be the end of days, thus meets the notion of Second Temple Judaism limiting prophets and prophecy to the past and the future.[101]

Early Christianity, which in its initial stage was no doubt an eschatological movement, fits into this framework. In Acts 2, the prophecy of Joel is said to have burst out within the Christian community in Jerusalem. Symptomatic of the end of the present age is the Spirit of God being poured out on the entire people and providing all Israelites with the gift of prophecy. In a later stage of early Christianity, however, the understanding of prophecy was profoundly modified. When Christianity moved out of its Judaean heartland to the diaspora, including the Syrian region which we are particularly concerned with presently, prophecy became institutionalized.[102] Within the context of the Greco-Roman world, where oracles and divination generally were not connected with the end of age, prophecy became a de-eschatologized phenomenon. In contrast to early Judaism, which applies the term "prophet" to biblical and eschatological prophets, this designation was applied freely and without hesitation to contemporary figures who were regarded by themselves and others as inspired spokesmen (cf. Did 11:7-13:7; Acts 11:27-28; 13:1-2; 15:32). A new type of prophet and prophecy developed. The ability to prophesy was no longer linked with a strong eschatological awareness but was considered a natural manifestation of the presence of God in the church. However, the Jewish impact on the function of the Christian prophet in the Didache community is still clearly recognizable in the close cause-and-effect relationship between the Spirit and prophesying.

DIDACHE 13:3-7: THE COMMUNITY'S DUTY TO SUPPORT THE PROPHETS

We have yet to consider more closely a most remarkable passage in Did 13:3-7, dealing with the community's support of the prophets. In the preceding verses (12:2-5), the reception of those Christians who had no claim to any special status was limited to just a few days. This regulation needed correction with respect to prophets who wished to settle down in the community. They deserved sustenance by the community after the example of the class of teachers who already were established local officials. In the following pages we will attempt to show that the Didachist has adopted traditional materials in 13:3-7 to support the argument.

A closer examination indicates that this section has preserved and reworked a carefully arranged tradition which at one time existed as a separate unit.[103] The idiosyncrasy of this unit as compared to its context is easily noticed. As far as content is concerned, the section presents a specific regulation for the support of the prophets by detailing the "firstfruits" (ἀπαρχή). It also stands out from the

---

[101] Schäfer, *Die Vorstellung vom heiligen Geist*, 146 and Sommer, 'Did Prophecy Cease?', 36-37.

[102] Cf. Aune, *Prophecy in Early Christianity*, 194-95.

[103] For the following, see Schöllgen, 'Die Didache als Kirchenordnung', 15-17 (ET: 56-59); Giet, *L'Énigme de la Didachè*, 228-29.

preceding and subsequent verses (with the exception of verses 3b and 4) by the fact that the community is addressed here in the second person singular. Finally, the passage stylistically represents a unity as it has been construed according to a clear pattern. In verses 3a, 5, 6, and 7, the wording τὴν ἀπαρχήν (with a precise description of the items referred to) recurs in juxtaposition with the clause λαβὼν δός / δώσεις ("having taken [it], give..."). These clauses in their turn are then succeeded by the phrases τοῖς προφήταις ("to the prophets") and κατὰ τὴν ἐντολήν ("according to the commandment") alternately. The following pattern appears:

3a. Πᾶσαν οὖν ἀπαρχήν (succeeded by the produce one is expected to separate from) λαβὼν δώσεις τὴν ἀπαρχὴν τοῖς προφήταις· ...

5. Produce + τὴν ἀπαρχὴν λαβὼν δὸς κατὰ τὴν ἐντολήν.

6. Produce + τὴν ἀπαρχὴν λαβὼν δὸς τοῖς προφήταις·

7. Produce + λαβὼν τὴν ἀπαρχὴν ... δὸς κατὰ τὴν ἐντολήν.

Both the symmetrical structures of our passage and the recurrence of the same stereotyped wording, facilitating memorization, may indicate that this unit has been transmitted orally. It would be a reasonable hypothesis that a Jewish oral tradition was the section's original form since the specification of the firstfruits and the wording itself have the characteristic marks of a Jewish halakhic tradition. This basic tradition may have circulated in Jewish communities as a teaching about the firstfruits and tithes before it was reworked and incorporated in the Didache. This hypothesis, of course, must be tested.

Admittedly, tithes are not mentioned in Did 13:3-7. This objection, however, is apparent rather than real since it has been noticed that, in Jewish sources, the tithes are often implied in the designation "firstfruits".[104] In early Judaism, the priestly dues (תרומות) were separated from a person's produce and given to the priests. According to the Tora, a tenth from the remainder, the first tithe (מעשר ראשון), was assigned to the Levites who for their part gave a tenth of the first tithe to the priests. In spite of this biblical law, however, there is abundant evidence that they were in fact given to the priests in the last decades of the second Temple period.[105] After deducting the first tithe, the owner of the produce had yet another tenth of the produce to set apart. This second tithe (מעשר שני) was brought to Jerusalem and was consumed by him there in a state of ritual purity.[106] After the destruction of the temple, when the priests and Levites no longer had any sacerdotal functions to fulfill, the Sages encouraged people to keep on giving their tithes. It is possible that, as early as after the destruction, the tithes were granted to those priests and

---

[104] Cf. Alon, 'Ha-halakha ba-Torat 12 ha-Shelihim', 293; (ET: 191-92). Also in the LXX the term ἀπαρχή is not unambiguous as it renders both ראשית and תרומה; see Del Verme, *Giudaismo e Nuovo Testamento*, 217-228; esp. 220 and id., 'The Didache and Judaism', 116.

[105] Cf. Stern, 'Aspects of Jewish Society', 585; Oppenheimer, *The 'Am Ha-Aretz*, 38-40.

[106] Cf. Safrai, 'Religion in Everyday Life', 818; Oppenheimer, *The 'Am Ha-Aretz*, 23; Schürer, *The history of the Jewish People* 2, 263-64.

Levites who were rabbis, that is, to the Sages themselves.[107] They were thus allotted to those Sages who performed public functions and were the spiritual leaders of the Jewish community.

According to Jewish practice, tithes were levied on the products from the fields (grain, wine, oil) and cattle,[108] and the specifiations in Did 13:3a.5-6, mentioning the products of the winepress and the threshing floor, of cows and sheep (v. 3), of bread (v. 6), wine, oil (v. 6), appear to cover these items. In 13:7, however, a wider separation of tithes, like money, clothes, and chattel is recorded. Also in this respect, however, the Didache reflects established Jewish halakha. In a later period, the custom of tithing was extended to apply to other types of income as well, to goods and money in general, although this custom never was really widespread. Judging by Jewish sources indicating this practice,[109] it is likely that this tendency to tithe all profits had already emerged in the Second Temple period. In a time when trade, in addition to pasturage, became an important component of the nation's economy, this measure probably served as a means to treat the farmer and traders equally in the matter of tithes. The conclusion appears to be that the regulation in the Didache reflects contemporary Jewish halakha.[110]

If Did 13:3a.5-7 has preserved extant materials representing an initially oral tradition that was handed down in Jewish circles, one may assume that the terminology of this section would also show some affinity with the type of expression in rabbinic literature. In light of this, we refer to the repeated stereotyped phrase κατὰ τὴν ἐντολήν in Did 13:5 and 7. There is a good possibility that this Greek clause reflects the Hebrew or Aramaic wording כמצוה or כמצוותא because the word מצוה or מצוותא ("commandment / precept") was well established in similar contexts in the language of the Sages.[111] One might even argue that this expression ("according to the commandment") – whether it was in Hebrew, Aramaic, or Greek – was the original wording behind the alternate phrases of 13:3 and 6 as well and was replaced in a later stage by the wording τοῖς προφήταις. Because prophecy has never become a standard function in early Judaism, it is unlikely that prophets received a share of the firstfruits and tithes. The injunction to give the firstfruits "to the prophets" (τοῖς προφήταις) would be alien to the tradition rendered here.

An indication supporting a possible substitution of τοῖς προφήταις for κατὰ τὴν ἐντολήν is found in Did 13:3b. The passage 13:3b-4 interrupts the rigorous

---

[107] So Alon, *The Jews in their Land* 1, 257. According to Oppenheimer, however, "this view is not fully substantiated" (*The 'Am Ha-Aretz*, 46).

[108] For grain, wine and oil, see the biblical law in Lev 27:30; Num 18:27; Deut 12:17 and 14:13. Several passages in the Apocrypha and Philo also refer to a tithe of the cattle; cf. Alon, 'Ha-halakha ba-Torat 12 ha-Shelihim', 294 and Oppenheimer, *The 'Am Ha-Aretz*, 27, n. 6.

[109] Jub 32:2; CD 14:11-15; PesRK 10 (ed. B. Mandelbaum, 1962, 173); Luke 18:12; cf. Alon, 'Ha-halakha ba-Torat 12 ha-Shelihim', 294 (ET:193-94); Safrai, 'Religion in Everyday Life', 825; Oppenheimer, *The 'Am Ha-Aretz*, 46-47.

[110] See also Del Verme, *Giudaismo e Nuovo Testamento*, 217-228; esp. 219 and id., 'The Didache and Judaism', 115.

[111] Cf. Alon, 'Ha-halakha ba-Torat 12 ha-Shelihim', 293 (ET:192).

symmetrical structure of the basic tradition in 13:3a.5-7 and, in contrast to the immediate context, addresses the audience in the second person plural (ἀρχιερεῖς ὑμῶν in 3a and ἔχητε ... δότε ... in v. 4). Both the clause in v. 3b and the whole of v. 4 no doubt represent later additions to the basic tradition in 3a.5-7.[112] They are related to the injunction of v. 3a to give tithes to the prophets. This directive is underscored in v. 3b by equating the prophets with the high priests while v. 4 discusses the case when no prophet is available in the community. In order to further establish how the initially priestly gifts were transferred to the prophets, we have to delve more deeply into the phrase of 13:3b.

After the specification of the firstfruits and the succeeding standard phrase "you shall give the firstfruits to the prophets" in Did 13:3a, the directive continues in 13:3b as follows: "for they are your (ὑμῶν) high priests." The high priests are probably considered identical here to the priests to whom the firstfruits and tithes were generally given in the late Second Temple period. Their right to receive these gifts is now assigned to the prophets. We may ask, however, why precisely the high priests are mentioned in this instance, the more so since the association of the gift of prophecy with the office of high priest is not found elsewhere in early Christian literature.[113] To account for this phenomenon, we must turn to early Jewish sources again. It appears that a popular view connected prophetic powers with the office of the high priest during the late Second Temple period.[114] Although the existence of prophecy was generally held to have ended with the canonical prophets there is evidence of a widespread belief in the oracular prophecy of high priesthood at this time. The perception that true prophecy had ceased was apparently in no way at variance with the recognition that revelation or divination continued in some attenuated form. Our first witness to the belief in a prophetic endowment of the high priests is found in Josephus. He relates that John Hyrcanus (135-104 BCE), like the high priest Jaddus before him, was privileged to receive dream-oracles in the temple which enabled him to foresee the future (*Ant.* 11, 327; 13, 322). According to Josephus, the Hasmonean Hyrcanus united three of the highest privileges in his person: he was a civil ruler, high priest, and prophet (*Ant.* 13, 299-300). The connection of prophecy and high priesthood is probably not original to Josephus since the *T. Levi* (8:1-3.11-15) attests to a combination of these honoured positions as well. It is noteworthy, however, that Josephus, who generally confines prophecy to the biblical period, mentions this tradition without objection. Further evidence of prophecy being associated with the high priesthood

---

[112]   Cf. Schöllgen, 'Die Didache als Kirchenordnung',16, n. 88 (ET: 58, n. 88). With repect to v. 4, see also Rordorf-Tuilier, *La Doctrine des douze Apôtres*, 190-91, n. 5.

[113]   Von Harnack, *Lehre der zwölf Apostel*, 52: "Dass aber Propheten als Hohepriester bezeichnet werden, ist einzigartig." Niederwimmer notes that the Old Testament does not have prescriptions concerning the income of the high priests and continues: "Der in Did. vorliegende Irrtum wirft ein bezeichnendes Licht auf den Didachisten" (*Die Didache*, 232, n. 9).

[114]   For the following, see Blenkinsopp, 'Prophecy and Priesthood', 250-53; Bammel, ''ΑΡΧΙΕΡΕΥΣ ΠΡΟΦΗΤΕΥΩΝ'; Dodd, 'The Prophecy of Caiaphas',138-141.

is found in rabbinic sources[115] and in John 11:49-51. John attributes a saying to the high priest Caiaphas about the death of Jesus on which he comments in the next verse as follows: "He did not say this of his own accord, but being high priest (ἀρχιερεὺς ὢν)...he prophesied (ἐπροφήτευσεν)... ."

The above evidence supports the view that the materials in the segment of Did 13:3-7 draw upon two separate Jewish traditions. Although it is impossible to say with certainty how this section was given its present form, we propose the following reconstruction of its history. The carefully structured admonitions in Did 13:3a.5-7, which use a repetitive pattern as a mnemonic device, probably reflect an underlying oral unit of halakhic tradition specifying the firstfruits and tithes to be handed over to the priests. In a second stage, the instruction's original form merged with the traditional Jewish view which associated prophecy with the high priesthood. This fusion was meant to transfer the right to the firstfruits, previously assigned to the priest, to the class of prophets. The prophet has taken the position of the high priest and is therefore entitled to the priest's income. This secondary form of the basic instruction must have originated and been transmitted in a milieu where these Jewish traditions were alive and where prophets and prophecy existed as an established institution, that is, in Jewish Christian circles.[116] At this second stage, the diversity of these traditions was still clearly recognizable by the distinct position of v. 3b that interrupted the stylistic flow of speech and addressed the audience in the plural. This might have occasioned a further adjustment of the tradition right after v. 3b at a third stage. When this composite tradition was finally incorporated into the present form of the Didache, the redactor expanded these materials with an additional verse 4 so as to solve the problems of those communities which had till then been deprived of settled prophets. The Didachist also had to take into account the implications of his regulation for the congregations beyond the borders of his own community.

It would then appear that the section in Did 13:3-7 reflects several attempts (though awkward) to adapt an initially oral Jewish tradition. The underlying oral instruction in Did 13:3a.5-7 about the priestly gifts was reworked in later stages by Jewish Christians and the Didachist so as to embody in it certain ideas of their own.

---

[115] The high priests Yohanan heard from "the Holy of Holies" that the men who fought against Antioch "have been victorious." At the very hour of this revelation, they won the battle (tSot 13:5). In the same way the high priest Shimon the Righteous learned that "Casqelges" (probably Caligula) was killed and that his anti-Jewish decrees were annulled (tSot 13:6; cf. bSot 33a). For these and other references, see Schäfer, *Die Vorstellung vom heiligen Geist*, 135-36.

[116] The alternative view that the Didachist himself blended both traditions is less likely since he probably was a gentile Christian (cf. Did 8:1-2; 9:4; 10:5; 14:1; see also 6:2-3) and, therefore, not directly acquainted with these traditions; see also above, Chap. 1, pp. 32-35 and Chap. 8, pp. 292-96.327-29.

Abbreviations

Names of Biblical books, Apocrypha, Pseudepigrapha, Dead Sea Scrolls and Early Christian writings are abbreviated according to the usage of the Journal of Biblical Literature.

Josephus

Ant.	Flavius Josephus, Antiquitates Judaicae
Bellum	Flavius Josephus, De Bello Judaico
c. Ap.	Flavius Josephus, contra Apionem

Philo

Quis heres	Quis rerum divinarum heres
Decal.	De decalogo
Legat.	De legatione ad Gaium
Mutat.	De mutatione nominum
Omn. prob. lib.	Quod omnis probus liber sit
Praem.	De praemiis et poenis, de exsecrationibus
Spec. Leg.	De specialibus legibus
Conf. Ling.	De confusione linguarum
Vit. Cont.	De vita contemplativa
Virt.	De virtutibus

Rabbinic literature

Ar	Arakhin
ARN a/b	Avoth de-R. Natan (ed Schechter) vers. A/B
Av	Avot
AZ	Avoda Zara
b	Bavli (Babylonian Talmud)
BB	Bava Batra
Bekh	Bekhorot

Ber	Berakhot
Bik	Bikkurim
BK	Bava Kamma
BM	Bava Metsia
DER	Derekh Erets Rabba
DeutR	Deuteronomy Rabba (ed Mirkin)
DEZ	Derekh Erets Zuta
Ed	Eduyot
Er	Eruvin
ExR	Exodus Rabba
Frg.Tg	The Fragment-Targums of the Pentateuch (ed M.L. Klein)
GenR	Genesis Rabba (ed Theodor-Albeck)
Hag	Hagiga
Hul	Hullin
Jub	Jubilees
Kal	Kalla
KalR	Kalla Rabbati
Ker	Keritot
Ket	Ketubbot
Kidd	Kiddushin
LevR	Leviticus Rabba (ed Margulies)
m	Mishna
Meg	Megilla
Mekh	Mekhilta d'Rabbi Yishmael (ed Horovitz-Rabin)
MekhRSbY	Mekhilta d'Rabbi Sh. b. Yohai (ed Epstein-Melamed)
Men	Menahot
Mikw	Mikwaot
Naz	Nazir
Ned	Nedarim
NumR	Numbers Rabba (ed Mirkin)
Pes	Pesahim
PesR	Pesikta Rabbati (ed Friedmann)
PesRK	Pesikta de-R. Kahana (ed Mandelbaum)
Odes Sol.	Odes of Solomon
Pirqe R. El.	Pirqe Rabbi Eliezer
Ps. Sol.	Psalms of Solomon
San	Sanhedrin
SER	Seder Eliahu Rabba (ed Friedmann)
SOlamR	Seder Olam Rabba (ed Friedmann)
Shab	Shabbat
Shek	Shekalim
Shevu	Shevuot
SifDeut	Sifrei Deuteronomy (ed Finkelstein)
SifNum	Sifrei Numbers (ed Horovitz)
Sot	Sota

Suk	Sukka
t	Tosefta
Taan	Taanit
Tam	Tamid
Tg	Targum
TgOnq	Targum Onqelos
TgPs-Yon	Targum Pseudo-Yonatan (= TgYer)
Tg.Yon	Targum Yonatan
TgNeof	Targum Neofiti
y	Yerushalmi (Palestinian Talmud)
YalShim	Yalqut Shimoni
Yev	Yevamot
Yom	Yoma

Periodical, Reference Works and Related Abbreviations

AAA.A	Acta Academia Aboensis, ser. A
AASF.DHL	Annales Academiae Scientiarum Fennicae. Dissertationes Humanarum Litterarum
AB	Anchor Bible
ABRL	The Anchor Bible Reference Library
ACC	Alcuin Club Collections
AF	The Apostolic Fathers, R.M. Grant (ed)
AGJU	Arbeiten zur Geschichte des antiken Judentums und des Urchristentums
AK	Arbeiten zur Kirchengeschichte
ALGHJ	Arbeiten zur Literatur und Geschichte des Hellenistischen Judentums
AnBib	Analecta biblica
ANRW	Aufstieg und Niedergang der römischen Welt
ANTZ	Arbeiten zur neutestamentlichen Theologie und Zeitgeschichte
AOAT	Alter Orient und Altes Testament
ARL	Archiv für Liturgiewissenschaft
ASTI	Annual of the Swedish Theological Institute
ATANT	Abhandlungen zur Theologie des Alten und Neuen Testaments
ATR	Anglican Theological Review
AzF	Arbeiten zur Frühmittelalterforschung
AzK	Arbeiten zur Kirchengeschichte
BA	Biblical Archaeologist
BAug	Bibliothèque Augustinienne
BBB	Bonner biblische Beiträge
BETL	Bibliotheca ephemeridum theologicarum lovaniensium
BevT	Beiträge zur evangelischen Theologie
BFCT	Beiträge zur Förderung christlicher Theologie

BHT	Beiträge zur historischen Theologie
Bib	Biblica
Bibleb	Bibel und Leben
BibN	Biblische Notizen
BibU	Biblische Untersuchungen
BJRL	Bulletin of the John Rylands University Library of Manchester
BJS	Brown Judaic Studies
BKAT	Biblischer Kommentar: Altes Testament
BNTT	Beihefte zu Norsk Teologisk Tidsskrift
BPF	Biblische und Patristische Forschungen
BR	Biblical Research
BS	The Biblical Seminar
BSac	Bibliotheca Sacra
BSR	Brown Studies in Religion
BU	Biblische Untersuchungen
BZ	Biblische Zeitschrift
BZNW	Beihefte zur Zeitschrift für die Neutestamentliche Wissenschaft
CBET	Contributions to Biblical Exegesis and Theology
CBQ	Catholic Biblical Quarterly
CBQMS	Catholic Biblical Quarterly – Monograph Series
CChr.SL	Corpus Christianorum, Series Latina
CHLS	Cambridge Handbooks of Liturgical Study
CHR	Catholic Historical Review
CNT	Commentaire du Nouveau Testament
CPSSup	Cambridge Philological Society, Supplementary Volume
CQ	Church Quarterly
CQR	Church Quarterly Review
CRINT	Compendia rerum iudaicarum ad Novum Testamentum
CSCO	Corpus scriptorum christianorum orientalium
CSEL	Corpus Scriptorum Ecclesiasticorum Latinorum
CSHJ	Chicago Studies in the History of Judaism
CSS	Cistercian Studies Series
CT	Corpus Tannaiticum
CTSRR	College Theology Society Resources in Religion
DJD	Discoveries in the Judaean Desert
DRev	Downside Review
DSD	Dead Sea Discoveries
Ebib	Études Bibliques
ÉCent	Édition du Centenaire
EcOr	Ecclesia Orans
ÉHPR	Études d'histoire et de philosophie religieuses publiées par la Faculté de Théologie protestante de l'université de Strasbourg
EJ	Encyclopaedia Judaica
EKKNT	Evangelisch-katholischer Kommentar zum Neuen Testament
EL	Ephemerides Liturgicae

Ergb	Ergänzungsband
EstEc	Estudios Eclesiasticos
ÉtAug	Études Augustiennes
ETL	Ephemerides theologicae lovanienses
ETR	Etudes théologiques et religieuses
EvT	Evangelische Theologie
ExpTim	Expository Times
FB	Forschung zur Bibel
FC	Fathers of the Church
FdG	Forschungen zur deutschen Geschichte
FDV	Franz Delitzsch Vorlesungen
FFRS	Foundations and Facets – Reference Series
FJCD	Forschungen zum Jüdisch-Christlichen Dialog
FJS	Frankfurter Judaistische Studien
FO	Folia Orientalia
FRLANT	Forschungen zur Religion und Literatur des Alten und Neuen Testaments
FSt	Frühmittelalterliche Studien
GCS	Die griechischen christlichen Schriftsteller der ersten Jahrhunderte
GDQ	Geschichtliche Darstellungen und Quellen
GNS	Good News Studies
GTA	Göttinger theologische Arbeiten
H-E	Hermes-Einzelschriften
HNT	Handbuch zum Neuen Testament
HNTC	Harper's NT Commentaries
HNT.E	Handbuch zum Neuen Testament, Ergänzungsband
HSS	Harvard Semitic Studies
HTKNT	Herders theologischer Kommentar zum Neuen Testament
HTR	Harvard Theological Review
HUCA	Hebrew Union College Annual
HZaG	Historia: Zeitschrift für alte Geschichte
IEJ	Israel Exploration Journal
ICC	International Critical Commentary
JAC	Jahrbuch für Antike und Christentum
JAC.E	Jahrbuch für Antike und Christentum, Ergänzungsband
JAL	Jewish Apocryphal Literature
JBL	Journal of Biblical Literature
JBLMS	JBL Monograph Series
JE	The Jewish Encyclopedia
JECS	Journal of Early Christian Studies
JES	Journal of Ecumenical Studies
JETS	Journal of the Evangelical Theological Society
JJS	Journal of Jewish Studies
JQR	Jewish Quarterly Review

JR	Journal of Religion
JSHRZ	Jüdische Schriften aus der hellenistisch-römischer Zeit
JSJ	Journal for the Study of Judaism in the Persian, Hellenistic and Roman Period
JSNT	Journal for the Study of the New Testament
JSNTSup	Journal for the Study of the New Testament-Supplement Series
JSOT	Journal for the Study of the Old Testament
JSOTSup	Journal for the Study of the Old Testament, Supplement Series
JTS	Journal of Theological Studies
JTSA	Journal of Theology for Southern Africa
KAV	Kommentar zu den Apostolischen Vätern
KEK	Kritisch-exegetischer Kommentar über das neue Testament
KNT	Kommentar zum Neuen Testament
Kon	Konziliengeschichte
KTVÜ	Kleine Texte für Vorlesungen und Übungen
LBS	The Library of Biblical Studies
LC	Library of Early Christianity
LCL	Loeb Classical Library
LF	Liturgiegeschichtliche Forschungen
LLJC	The Littman Library of Jewish Civilization
LQF	Liturgiegeschichtliche Quellen und Forschungen
LUÅ	Lunds universitets årsskrift
MdlB	Le Monde de la Bible
MeyerK	Kritisch-exegetischer Kommentar über das Neue Testament, begr. von H.A.W. Meyer
MThSt	Marburger Theologische Studien
NCB	New Century Bible
nF	Neue Folge
NGSt	New Gospel Studies
NorTT	Norsk Teologisk Tidsskrift
NTAbh	Neutestamentliche Abhandlungen
NTD	Das Neue Testament Deutsch
NTS	New Testament Studies
NovT	Novum Testamentum
NovTSup	Supplements to Novum Testamentum
n.s.	new series
NVBS	New Voices in Biblical Studies
OBO	Orbis Biblicus et Orientalis
OCA	Orientalia Christiana analecta
OECT	Oxford Early Christian Texts
OrChr	Oriens christianus
PFES	Publications of the Finnish Exegetical Society
PFLUS	Publications de la Faculté des lettres de l'université de Strasbourg
PG	J.P. Migne, *Patrologia cursus completus, Series graeca*. Paris 1857ff

PIASH	Proceedings of the Israel Academy of Sciences and Humanities
PIBA	Proceedings of Irish Biblical Association
PL	J.P. Migne, *Patrologia cursus completus, Series latina*. Paris 1844ff
PoTh	Le Point Théologique
PTA	Papyrologische Texte und Abhandlungen
PTS	Patristische Texte und Studien
PVTG	Pseudepigrapha Veteris Testamenti Graece
QD	Questiones disputatae
QL	Questions Liturgiques
RAC	Reallexikon für Antike und Christentum
RArC	Rivista di archeologia cristiana
Rarch	Revue Archéologique
RAug	Recherches Augustiniennes
RB	Revue Biblique
RBén	Revue Bénédictine
RBS.Sup	Regulae Benedicti Studia. Supplementa
REJ	Revue des études juives
«Relieff»	«Relieff», Publications edited by the Department of Religious Studies of the University of Trondheim
ResQ	Restoration Quarterly
RevAM	Revue d'Ascétique et de Mystique
RevM	Revue Mabillon
RevQ	Revue de Qumran
RevScRel	Revue des sciences religieuses
RHR	Revue de l'histoire des religions
RQ	Römische Quartalschrift für christliche Altertumskunde und Kirchengeschichte
RSR	Recherches de science religieuse
RTAM	Recherches de Théologie ancienne et médiévale
RTP	Revue de Théologie et de Philosophie
SANT	Studien zum alten und neuen Testament
SAW	Studienhefte zur Altertumswissenschaft
SBA	Sammlung Bibliothekswissenschaftlicher Arbeiten
SBLDS	Society of Biblical Literature – Dissertation Series
SBLRBS	Society of Biblical Literature – Resources for Biblical Study
SBLSP	Society of Biblical Literature – Seminar Papers
SBS	Stuttgarter Bibelstudien
SfBS	Sources for Biblical Study
StBTh	Studia Biblica et Theologica
StBW	Studien der Bibliothek Warburg
SC	Sources Chrétiennes
SCBO	Scriptorum Classicorum Bibliotheca Oxoniensis
SCHNT	Studia ad Corpus Hellenisticum Novi Testamenti
SCJ	Studies in Christianity and Judaism

ScrCop	Scriptores coptici
SE	Studia Evangelica
SEÅ	Svensk Exegetisk Årsbok
SecC	Second Century
SF	Spicilegium Friburgense
SfBS	Sources for Biblical Study
SGKA	Studien zur Geschichte und Kultur des Altertums
SJS	Sanhedrin Jewish Studies
SJT	Scottish Journal of Theology
SKI	Studien zu Kirche und Israel
SL	Studia Liturgica
SNTSMS	Society for New Testament Studies Monograph Series
SNTIW	Studies of the New Testament and Its World
SPAW	Sitzungsberichte der königlichen preussischen Akademie der Wissenschaften
SQS	Sammlung ausgewählter kirchen- und dogmengeschichtlicher Quellenschriften
ST	Sammlung Töpelmann
StBTh	Studia Biblica et Theologica
STDJ	Studies on the Texts of the Desert of Judah
StDStD	Studi e Documenti di Storia e Diretto
SteT	Studi e Testi
StGKA	Studien zur Geschichte und Kultur des Altertums
StP	Studia Postbiblica
StPa	Studia Patristica
Str-B	Strack-Billerbeck, *Kommentar zum Neuen Testament*
StrThSt.S	Strassburger Theologische Studien, Supplementband
StudJud	Studia Judaica
SU	Schriften des Urchristentums
SUNT	Studien zur Umwelt des Neuen Testaments
SVTG	Septuaginta. Vetus Testamentum Graecum Auctoritate Societatis Litterarum Gottingensis editum
SVTP	Studia in Veteris Testamenti Pseudepigrapha
SWKGRS	Sammlung Wissenschaftlicher Kommentare zu griechischen und römischen Schriftstellern
SzG	Studien zur Geistesgeschichte
TANZ	Texte und Arbeiten zum neutestamentlichen Zeitalter
TBü	Theologische Bücherei
TC	Traditio Christiana
TEh	Theologische Existenz heute
ThH	Théologie Historique
ThJ	Theologische Jahrbücher
ThTL	Theological Translation Library
TLZ	Theologische Literaturzeitung
TQ	Theologische Quartalschrift

TRE	Theologische Realenzyklopädie
TRu	Theologische Rundschau
TSAJ	Texte und Studien zum Antiken Judentum
TS.JTS	Texts and Studies of the Jewish Theological Seminary of America
TSSO	Theologische Studien und Skizzen aus Ostpreussen
TST	Toronto Studies in Theology
TTZ	Trierer theologische Zeitschrift
TU	Texte und Untersuchungen
TWNT	Theologisches Wörterbuch zum Neuen Testament, G. Kittel and G. Friedrich (eds.)
TynBul	Tyndale Bulletin
TZ	Theologische Zeitschrift
UBS	United Bible Societies
UNT	Untersuchungen zum Neuen Testament
VC	Vigiliae christianae
VCSup	Supplements to Vigiliae Christianae
VetChr	Vetera Christianorum
VKSM	Veröffentlichungen aus dem Kirchenhistorischen Seminar München
VT	Vetus Testamentum
VTSup	Vetus Testamentum, Supplements
WBC	Word Biblical Commentary
WdF	Wege der Forschung
WMANT	Wissenschaftliche Monographien zum Alten und Neuen Testament
WS	Wiener Studien: Zeitschrift für klassische Philologie und Patristik
WUNT	Wissenschaftliche Untersuchungen zum Neuen Testament
ZKG	Zeitschrift für Kirchengeschichte
ZNW	Zeitschrift für die neutestamentliche Wissenschaft
ZPE	Zeitschrift für Papyrologie und Epigraphik
ZRGG	Zeitschrift für Religions- und Geistesgeschichte
ZTK	Zeitschrift für Theologie und Kirche
ZWT	Zeitschrift für wissenschaftliche Theologie

Bibliography

Abrahams, I., *Studies in Pharisaism and the Gospels* 1. Cambridge 1917 (= New York 1967)

Achtemeier, P.J., 'An Elusive Unity: Paul, Acts, and the Early Church'. *CBQ* 48 (1986) 1-26

Adam, A., 'Erwägungen zur Herkunft der Didache', in G. Ruhbach (ed.), *Sprache und Dogma. Untersuchungen zu Grundproblemen der Kirchengeschichte*. Gütersloh 1969, 24-70; published previously in *ZKG* 68 (1957) 1-47

Agnew, F., 'On the Origin of the term *Apostolos*'. *CBQ* 38 (1976) 49-53

Albertz, M., *Die Synoptischen Streitgespräche. Ein Beitrag zur Formengeschichte des Urchristentums.* Berlin 1921

Albright, W.F. and C.S. Mann, *Matthew*. (AB) New York 1971

Aldridge, R.E., 'The Lost Ending of the *Didache*'. *VC* 53 (1999) 1-15

—— 'Peter and the "Two Ways"'. *VC* 53 (1999) 233-64

Alexander, P.S., 'Jesus and the Golden Rule', in J.H. Charlesworth and L.L. Johns (eds.), *Hillel and Jesus. Comparative Studies of Two Major Religious Leaders*. Minneapolis 1997, 363-88

Allen, L.C., *Psalms 101-150*. (WBC 21) Waco (TX) 1983

Allen, W.C., *A Critical and Exegetical Commentary on the Gospel according to S. Matthew*. 3rd ed (ICC) Edinburgh 1972

Alon, G., *Studies in Jewish History in the Times of the Second Temple, the Mishna and the Talmud* 1-2. Tel Aviv 1958 (Hebr.)

—— *Jews, Judaism and the Classical World. Studies in Jewish History in the Times of the Second Temple and Talmud*. Jerusalem 1977

—— 'Ha-halakha ba-Torat 12 ha-Shelihim', in id., *Studies in Jewish History* 1, 274-94; published previously in *Tarbiz* 11 (1939-40) 127-145; ET: 'The Halacha in the Teaching of the Twelve Apostles', in Draper, *The Didache in Modern Research*, 165-94

—— 'Tumat Nokhrim', in *Studies in Jewish History* 1, 121-147; ET: 'The Levitical Uncleanness of Gentiles', in id., *Jews, Judaism and the Classical World*, 146-89

—— 'Le-jeshuva shel baraita achat', in id., *Studies in Jewish History* 2. 120-27

—— 'On Philo's Halakha', in id., *Jews, Judaism and the Classical World*, 89-137

—— *The Jews in their Land in the Talmudic Age (70-640 CE)* 1-2. Jerusalem 1980-84

Alpers, J., *Hercules in Bivio*. (Diss.) Göttingen 1912

Altaner, B., 'Zum Problem der Lateinischen Doctrina Apostolorum'. *VC* 6 (1952) 160-167

Altaner, B. and A. Stuiber, *Patrologie. Leben, Schriften und Lehre der Kirchenväter*. 8th ed Freiburg-Basel-Wien 1978

Amélineau, É., *Mémoires publiés par les membres de la Mission archéologique française au Caire, 1885-1886*, 4.1: *Monuments pour servir à l'histoire de l'Égypte chrétienne aux IVe et Ve siècles*. Paris 1888

Amir, Y., 'Die Zehn Gebote bei Philon von Alexandrien', in id., *Die Hellenistische Gestalt des Judentums bei Philon von Alexandrien*. (FJCD 5) Neukirchen-Vluyn 1983, 131-163

Amphoux, Chr. B., 'Luc 22/15-20'. *ETR* 56 (1981) 449-454

Andersen, F.I., '2 (Slavonic Apocalypse of) Enoch', in Charlesworth, *The Old Testament Pseudepigrapha* 1, 91-221

Anderson, H., '4 Maccabees', in Charlesworth, *The Old Testament Pseudepigrapha* 2. London 1985, 544-64

Angenendt, A., *Kaiserherrschaft und Königstaufe. Kaiser, Könige und Päpste als geistliche Patrone in der abendländischen Missionsgeschichte.* (AzF 15) Berlin-New York 1984

Arndt, W.F., *The Gospel according to St. Luke.* St Louis 1956

Arnold, A., *S. Athanasii archiep. Alex. Syntagma doctrinae ad clericos et laicos.* Paris 1685

Ascough, R.S., 'An Analysis of the Baptismal Ritual of the *Didache*'. *SL* 24 (1994) 201-13

Audet, J.-P., 'A Hebrew-Aramaic List of Books of the Old Testament in Greek Transcription'. *JTS* n.s. 1(1950) 135-154

— 'Affinités littéraires et doctrinales du <Manuel de Discipline>'. *RB* 59 (1952) 219-238; ET: 'Literary and Doctrinal Affinities of the "Manual of Discipline"', in Draper, *The Didache in Modern Research,* 129-47

— 'Literary Forms and Contents of a Normal Eucharistia in the First Century'. *SE* 1 (TU 73) (1959) 643-62

— 'Esquisse historique du genre littéraire de la "bénédiction" juive et de l'"eucharistie" chrétienne'. *RB* 65 (1958) 371-99

— *La Didachè. Instructions des Apôtres.* (Ebib) Paris 1958

Aune, D.E., *Prophecy in Early Christianity and the Ancient Mediterranean World.* Grand Rapids (MI) 1983

Baer, Y., 'The Historical Foundations of the Halakha'. *Zion* 27 (1962) 117-155 (Hebr.)

Bacher, W., *Die Agada der Tannaiten* 1-2. Strassburg 1884-90

— *Die Agada der palästinensischen Amoräer* 1 (1892); repr Hildesheim 1965

— *Die exegetische Terminologie der jüdischen Traditionsliteratur* 1-2 (1899-1905); repr Darmstadt 1965

Bacon, B.W., *Studies in Matthew.* London 1930

Badia, L.F., *The Qumran Baptism and John the Baptist's Baptism.* Lanham (Md) 1980

Baehrens, W.A. (ed.), *Origenes Werke,* VII,2: *Homilien zum Hexateuch in Rufins Übersetzung.* II: *Die Homilien zu Numeri, Josua und Judices.* (GCS 30) Leipzig 1921

Bagnani, G., 'Peregrinus Proteus and the Christians'. *HZaG* 4 (1955) 107-112

Baillet, M., *Qumrân Grotte 4* 3: *4Q482-4Q520.* (DJD 7) Oxford 1982

Baltzer, K., *Das Bundesformular.* (WMANT 4) 2nd ed Neukirchen-Vluyn 1964

Bamberger, B.J., *Proselytism in the Talmudic Period.* New York 1939

Bammel, E., ''ΑΡΧΙΕΡΕΥΣ ΠΡΟΦΗΤΕΥΩΝ'. *TLZ* 6 (1954) 351-56

— 'Pattern and Prototype of Didache 16', in Draper, *The Didache in Modern Research,* 364-72; published previously as 'Schema und Vorlage von *Didache* 16', in F.L. Cross (ed.), *Studia Patristica* 4. (TU 79) Berlin 1961, 253-62

Banks, R., 'Matthew's Understanding of the Law: Authenticity and Interpretation in Matthew 5:17-20'. *JBL* 93 (1974) 226-42

— *Jesus and the Law in the Synoptic Tradition.* (SNTSMS 28) Cambridge 1975

Bardenhewer, O., *Geschichte der altkirchlichen Literatur* 1-5. 2nd ed Freiburg 1913-1932; repr Darmstadt 1962

Barnard, L.W., 'The Problem of the Epistle of Barnabas'. *CQR* 159 (1958) 211-230

— *Studies in the Apostolic Fathers and their Background.* Oxford 1966

Barnett, P.W., 'The Jewish Sign Prophets – A.D. 40-70. Their Intentions and Origin'. *NTS* 27 (1981) 679-97

Barnikol, E., 'Die triadische Taufformel: Ihr Fehlen in der Didache und im Matthäusevangelium und ihr altkatholischer Ursprung'. *ThJ* 4-5 (1936-37) 144-52

Barré, H., *Les Homéliaires Carolingiens de l'école d'Auxerre. Authenticité – Inventaire – Tableaux comparatifs – Initia.* (SteT 225) Città del Vaticano 1962

Barrett, C.K., 'Shaliah and Apostle', in E. Bammel, C.K. Barrett and W.D. Davies (eds.), *Donum Gentilicium. New Testament Studies in Honour of David Daube.* Oxford 1978, 88-102

Barth, G., 'Das Gesetzesverständnis des Evangelisten Matthäus', in G. Bornkamm, G. Barth, H.J. Held (eds.), *Überlieferung und Auslegung im Matthäusevangelium*. (WMANT 1) 5th ed Neukirchen-Vluyn 1968, 54-154

— *Die Taufe in Frühchristliche Zeit*. Neukirchen-Vluyn 1981

Bartlet, J.V., 'Fragments of the Didascalia Apostolorum in Greek'. *JTS* 18 (1917) 301-09

Batiffol, P., 'Canones Nicaeni Pseudepigraphi'. *RArch* 3 ser. 6 (1885) 133-141

— *Didascalia CCCXVIII patrum pseudepigrapha e graecis codicibus rec. P. Batiffol, coptico contulit H. Hyvernat*. Paris 1887

— 'Le Syntagma Doctrinae dit de Saint Athanase', in id., *Studia Patristica. Études d'ancienne littérature chrétienne* fasc. 2. Paris 1890, 119-160

Bauer, W., *A Greek-English Lexicon of the New Testament and Other Early Christian Literature*. (ET by W.F. Arndt and F.W. Gingrich) 2nd ed Chicago-London 1979

Beare, F.W., *The Gospel according to Matthew. A Commentary*. Oxford 1981

Beasley-Murray, G.R., *Baptism in the New Testament*. Grand Rapids 1962; pb: Exeter 1972

Becker, J., *Das Heil Gottes. Heils- und Sündenbegriffe in den Qumrantexten und im Neuen Testament*. (SUNT 3) Göttingen 1964

— *Untersuchungen zur Entstehungsgeschichte der Testamente der zwölf Patriarchen*. (AGJU 8) Leiden 1970

— *Unterweisung in lehrhafter Form: Die Testamente der zwölf Patriarchen*. (JSHRZ III/1) Gütersloh 1974

Becker, O., *Das Bild des Weges und verwandte Vorstellungen im frühgriechischen Denken*. (H-E 4) Berlin 1937

Beeck, F.J. van, 'The Worship of Christians in Pliny's Letter'. *SL* 18 (1988) 121-131

Beentjes, P.C., *The Book of Ben Sira in Hebrew. A Text Edition of all extant Hebrew Manuscripts and a Synopsis of all Parallel Hebrew Ben Sira Texts*. (VTSup 68) Leiden-New York-Köln 1997

Behm, J. and E. Würthwein, 'μετανοέω, μετάνοια κτλ.', in *TWNT* 4, 972-1004

Bell, D. N., *Besa: The Life of Shenoute*. (CSS 73) Kalamazoo (MI) 1983

Benoit, P., 'Qumrân et Le Nouveau Testament'. *NTS* 7 (1960-61) 276-96

Benoit, A., *Le Baptême Chrétien au second siècle. La théologie des Pères*. (ÉHPR 43) Paris 1953

Bergemann, Th., *Q auf dem Prüfstand. Die Zuordnung des Mt/Lk-Stoffes zu Q am Beispiel der Bergpredigt*. (FRLANT 158) Göttingen 1993

Berger, K., *Die Gesetzesauslegung Jesu. Ihr historischer Hintergrund im Judentum und im Alten Testament* 1. (WMANT 40,1) Neukirchen 1972

— 'Hellenistische Gattungen im Neuen Testament', in *ANRW* II, 25,2. Berlin-New York 1984, 1031-1432. 1831-1885

— *Das Buch des Jubiläen*. (JSHRZ II/3) Gütersloh 1981

— *Die Weisheitsschrift aus der Kairoer Geniza. Erstedition, Kommentar und Übersetzung*. (TANZ 1) Tübingen 1989

— 'Apostelbrief und apostolische Rede / Zum Formular frühchristlicher Briefe'. *ZNW* 65 (1974) 190-231

Bergman, J., 'Zum Zwei-Wege-Motiv. Religionsgeschichtliche und exegetische Bemerkungen', in H. Riesenfeld (ed.), *SEÅ* 41-42, Uppsala (1976-77) 27-56

Berman, S., 'Law and Morality', in M. Elon (ed.), *The Principles of Jewish Law*. Jerusalem (1975) 153-57

Bernays, J., 'Philon's Hypothetika und die Verwünschungen des Buzyges in Athen', in id., *Gesammelte Abhandlungen* 1. H. Usener (ed.), Berlin 1885; repr Hildesheim-New York 1971, 262-282

Besch, B., *Der Dualismus in den Kernschriften von Qumran. Ein Beitrag zur Diskussion über Wesen und Herleitung des Qumranischen Dualismus*. (PSU) Rome 1996

Betz, H.D., *The Sermon on the Mount. A Commentary on the Sermon on the Mount, including the Sermon on the Plain (Matthew 5:3-7:27 and Luke 6:20-49)*. (Hermeneia) Minneapolis 1995

— *Essays on the Sermon on the Mount*. Philadelphia 1985

— 'The Sermon on the Mount (Matt. 5:3-7:27): Its Literary Genre and Function' (*JR* 59 [1979] 285-97); repr in id., *Essays*, 1-16

— 'The Hermeneutical Principles of the Sermon on the Mount (Matt. 5:17-20)', in id. *Essays*, 37-53; published previously in *JTSA* 42 (1983) 17-28; orig.: 'Die hermeneutischen Prinzipien in der Bergpredigt (Mt 5,17-20)', in E. Jüngel, J. Wallmann, W. Werbeck (eds.), *Verifikationen, Festschrift für Gerhard Ebeling zum 70. Geburtstag*. Tübingen 1982, 27-41

— 'Lukian von Samosata und das Christentum'. *NovT* 3 (1959) 226-37; repr in id. *Hellenismus und Urchristentum. Gesammelte Aufsätze* 1. Tübingen 1990, 10-21

— *Lukian von Samosata und das Neue Testament. Religionsgeschichtliche und paränetische Parallelen.* (TU 76) Berlin 1961

Betz, J., 'Die Eucharistie in der Didache'. *ARL* 11 (1969) 10-39; ET: 'The Eucharist in the Didache', in Draper, *The Didache in Modern Research*, 244-75

Betz, O., 'Die Proselytentaufe der Qumransekte und die Taufe im Neuen Testament'. *RevQ* 1 (1958-59) 213-34

— 'Was John the Baptist an Essene?', in H. Shanks (ed.), *Understanding the Dead Sea Scrolls: A Reader from the Biblical Archaeology Review.* New York 1992, 205-14

Bickell, J.W., *Geschichte des Kirchenrechts.* Giessen 1843

Bietenhard, H., 'ὄνομα, ὀνομάζω κτλ.', in *TWNT* 5, 242-83

— 'πνίγω κτλ.', in *TWNT* 6, 453-56

Bihlmeyer, K., *Die Apostolischen Väter. Neubearbeitung der Funkschen Ausgabe.* 3rd ed Tübingen 1970

Bischoff, B., 'Paläographische Fragen deutscher Denkmäler der Karolingerzeit'. *FSt* 5 (1971) 101-134

— *Die südostdeutschen Schreibschulen und Bibliotheken in der Karolingerzeit.* (SBA 49) Leipzig 1940

— *Die Abtei Lorsch im Spiegel ihrer Handschriften.* 2nd ed Lorsch 1989

Black, M., *The Book of Enoch or I Enoch.* (SVTP 7) Leiden 1985

Blaise A., *Dictionnaire latin-français des auteurs chrétiens*, Turnhout 1954

Blass, F., A. Debrunner and F. Rehkopf, *Grammatik des neutestamentlichen Griechisch.* Göttingen [15]1979

Blenkinsopp, J., 'Prophecy and Priesthood in Josephus'. *JJS* 25 (1974) 239-62

Blinzler, J., 'Qumran-Kalender und Passionschronologie'. *ZNW* 49 (1958) 238-51

Boccaccini, G., *Beyond the Essene Hypothesis: The Partying of the Ways between Qumran and Enochic Judaism.* Grand Rapids (MI) 1998

Bockmuehl, M., 'The Noachide Commandments and New Testament Ethics; with special Reference to Acts 15 and Pauline Halakhah'. *RB* 102 (1995) 72-101; repr in id., *Jewish Law in Gentile Churches. Halakhah and the Beginning of Christian Public Ethics.* Edinburgh 2000, 145-73

Böcher, O., 'Das sogenannte Aposteldekret', in H. Frankemölle and K. Kertelge (eds.), *Vom Urchristentum zu Jesus.* (FS. J. Gnilka) Freiburg-Basel-Wien 1989, 325-36

Böckenhoff, K., *Das apostolische Speisegesetz in den ersten fünf Jahrhunderten.* Paderborn 1903

Böhl, F., *Gebotserschwerung und Rechtsverzicht als ethisch-religiöse Normen in der rabbinischen Literatur.* (FJS 1) Freiburg i. B. 1971

Boehmer, H., 'Hat Benedikt von Nursia die Didache gekannt?'. *ZNW* 12 (1911) 287

Böttrich, C., *Das slavische Henochbuch* (JSHRZ V/7), Gütersloh 1995

Bogaert, P. (ed.), *Apocalypse de Baruch. Introduction, Traduction du Syriaque et Commentaire* 1-2. (SC 144-145) Paris 1969

Bokser, B.M., '*Ma'al* and Blessings over Food: Rabbinic Transformation of Cultic Terminology and Alternative Modes of Piety'. *JBL* 100 (1981) 557-74

Boman, Th., 'Das textkritische Problem des sogenannten Aposteldekrets'. *NovT* 7 (1964-65) 26-36

Bonnard, P., *L'Évangile selon Saint Matthieu.* (CNT 1) 2nd ed Neuchatel 1970

Borgen, P., 'The Golden Rule. With Emphasis on Its Usage in the Gospels', in id., *Paul Preaches Circumcision and Pleases Men. And Other Essays on Christian Origins.* («Relieff» 8) Trondheim 1983, 99-114; ET of 'Den såkalte gyldne regel (Matt. 7:12, Luk. 6:31), dens forekomst i Det nye testamentes omverden og dens innhold i evangelienes kontekst'. *NorTT* 67 (1966) 129-46

— 'Philo of Alexandria', in Stone, *Jewish Writings*, 233-82

Boring, M.E., 'The Unforgivable Sin Logion Mark III 28-29 / Matt. XII 31-32 / Luke XII 10: Formal Analysis and History of the Tradition'. *NovT* 18 (1976) 258-79

Bornkamm, G., 'Der Aufbau der Bergpredigt'. *NTS* 24 (1978) 419-32

Botte, B. (ed.), *La Tradition Apostolique d'après anciennes versions*. (SC 11bis) Paris 1984

Bouhot, J.-P., 'Alcuin et le <De catechizandis rudibus> de saint Augustin'. *RAug* 15 (1980) 176-240

— 'Explications du rituel baptismal à l'époque carolingienne'. *ÉtAug* 24 (1978) 278-301

— 'Un florilège sur le symbolisme du baptême de la seconde moitié du VIIIe siècle'. *RAug* 18 (1983) 151-82

Bourgeault, G., *Décalogue et morale chrétienne. Enquête patristique sur l'utilisation et l'interprétation chrétiennes du décalogue de c. 60 à c. 220*. Paris-Tournai-Montréal 1971

Bradshaw, P.F., *Daily Prayer in the Early Church. A Study of the Origin and Early Development of the Divine Office*. (ACC 63) 2nd ed London 1983

— *The Search for the Origins of Christian Worship. Sources and Methods for the Study of Early Liturgy*. London 1992

Branscomb, B.H., *Jesus and the Law of Moses*. New York 1930

Braumann, G., 'Zum Traditionsgeschichtlichen Problem der Seligpreisungen MT V 3-12'. *Nov.T* 4 (1960) 253-60

Braun, F.-M., 'Les Testaments des XII Patriarches et le problème de leur origine'. *RB* 67 (1960) 516-49

Braun, H., *Qumran und das Neue Testament* 1-2. Tübingen 1966

— *Spätjüdisch-häretischer und frühchristlicher Radikalismus. Jesus von Nazareth und die essenische Qumransekte* 1-2. (BHT 24) 2nd ed Tübingen 1969

Bridge, S.L., 'To Give or Not to Give? Deciphering the Saying of *Didache* 1.6'. *JECS* 5 (1997) 555-68

Brock, S., 'The Two Ways and the Palestinian Targum', in P.R. Davies and R.T. White (eds.), *A Tribute to G. Vermes. Essays on Jewish and Christian Literature and History*. (JSOTSup 100) Sheffield 1990, 139-152

Broer, I., 'Die Antithesen und der Evangelist Matthäus. Versuch eine alte These zu revidieren'. *BZ* nF 19 (1975) 50-63

— *Freiheit vom Gesetz und Radikalisierung des Gesetzes*. (SBS 98) Stuttgart 1980

— 'Anmerkungen zum Gesetzesverständnis des Matthäus' in K. Kertelge (ed.), *Das Gesetz im Neuen Testament*. (QD 108) Freiburg-Basel-Wien 1986, 128-145

— 'Das Ius Talionis im Neuen Testament'. *NTS* 40 (1994) 1-21.

Brownlee, W.H., 'John the Baptist in the New Light of Ancient Scrolls', in K. Stendahl (ed.), *The Scrolls and the New Testament*. London 1957, 33-53; published previously in *Interpretation* 9 (1955) 71-90

— 'A Comparison of the Covenanters of the Dead Sea Scrolls with Pre-Christian Jewish Sects'. *BA* 13 (1950) 50-72

Brox, N., *Der Hirt des Hermas*. (KAV 7) Göttingen 1991

Brun, L., 'Apostelkoncil und Aposteldekret', in L. Brun und A. Fridrichsen *Paulus und die Urgemeinde*. (BNTT 1) Giessen 1921, 1-52

Bruyne, D. De (ed.), 'Epistula Titi, Discipuli Pauli, De Dispositione Sanctimonii'. *RBén* 37 (1925) 47-72

— 'La première Règle de Saint Benoît'. *RBén* 42 (1930) 316-341

Buber, S. (ed.), *Midrasch suta. Hagadische Abhandlungen über Schir ha-Schirim, Ruth, Echah und Koheleth, nebst Jalkut zum Buche Echah*. Berlin 1894; repr Tel Aviv 1969

Budge, E.A.W. (ed.), *Miscellaneous Coptic Texts in the Dialect of Upper Egypt. With English Translations*. London 1915

Büchler, A., *Studies in Sin and Atonement*. London 1928

— *Types of Jewish-Palestinian Piety from 70 B.C.E. to 70 C.E. – The Ancient Pious Men*. London 1922; repr Westmead 1969

— 'Hearot al matsav ha-dati shel eved kanaani be-mea she-lifne hurban ha-bait we-she-le-acharav', in B. Schindler and A. Marmorstein (eds.), *Gaster Anniversary Volume. In Honour of M. Gaster's 80th Birthday*. (Occident and Orient) London 1936, 549-570

Büchsel, H.M.F., 'εἰδωλόθυτον', in *TWNT* 2, 375-76

Bultmann, R., *Theologie des Neuen Testaments*. 8th ed Tübingen 1968

— *Die Geschichte der synoptischen Tradition*. 8th ed (FRLANT 29) Göttingen1970 (1921); ET: *The History of the Synoptic Tradition*. New York rev. ed 1963

Burkitt, F.C., *Christian Beginnings*. London 1924

— 'On Luke 22.17-20'. *JTS* 28 (1927) 178-81

Burtchaell, J.T., *From Synagogue to Church. Public services and offices in the earliest Christian communities*. Cambridge 1992

Butler, E.C., 'The Rule of St Benedict'. *JTS* 11 (1910) 279-88 and 12 (1911) 261-68

Butler, B.C., 'The Literary Relations of Didache Ch. XVI'. *JTS* n.s. 11 (1960) 265-83

— 'The "Two Ways" in the Didache'. *JTS* n.s. 12 (1961) 27-38

Caird, G.B., *The Revelation of St. John the Divine*. (HNTC) New York and Evanston 1966

Campenhausen, H. von, *Kirchliches Amt und geistliche Vollmacht in den ersten drei Jahrhunderten*. (BHT 14) 2nd ed Tübingen 1963

— 'Taufen auf den Namen Jesu?', in id., *Urchristliches und Altkirchliches. Vorträge und Aufsätze*. Tübingen 1979, 197-216

Cangh, J.-P. van, 'Le déroulement primitif de la Cène (Mc 14,18-26 et par.)'. *RB* 102 (1995) 193-225

Carlston, C.E., 'The Things that Defile (Mark VII.14) and the Law in Matthew and Mark'. *NTS* 15 (1968-69) 75-96

Caster, M., *Etudes sur Alexandre ou le faux prophète de Lucien, Thèse supplémentaire*. Paris 1938

Catchpole, D.R., 'Paul, James and the Apostolic Decree'. *NTS* 23 (1977) 428-444

Charles, R.H., *The Apocrypha and Pseudepigrapha of the Old Testament in English* 2. Oxford 1913

— *The Revelation of St. John* 1. (ICC) Edinburgh 1920

Charlesworth, J.H., *The Old Testament Pseudepigrapha* 1-2. London 1983-85

— 'A Critical Comparison of the Dualism in 1QS III,13-IV,26 and the "Dualism" contained in the fourth Gospel'. *NTS* 15 (1968-69) 389-418

Chazon, E.G., 'Prayers from Qumran and Their Historical Implications'. *DSD* 1 (1994) 265-84

Chazon, E.G., T. Elgvin, E. Eshel *et alii*, *Qumran Cave 4 20: Poetical and Liturgical Texts* 2. (DJD 29) Oxford 1999

Clark, A.C., *The Acts of the Apostles: A Critical Edition with Introduction and Notes on Selected Passages*. Oxford 1933

Clerici, L., *Einsammlung der Zerstreuten. Liturgiegeschichtliche Untersuchung zur Vor- und Nachgeschichte der Fürbitte für die Kirche in Didache 9,4 und 10,5*. (LQF 44) Münster (Westf) 1965

Cody, A., 'The *Didache*: An English Translation', in Jefford, *The Didache in Context*, 3-14

Cohen, S.J.D., 'Was Judaism in Antiquity a Missionary Religion', in M. Mor (ed.), *Assimilation and Accomodation: Past Traditions, Current Issues and Future Perspectives*. Jerusalem 1992, 14-23

Cohn-Sherbok, D., 'A Jewish Note on ΤΟ ΠΟΤΗΡΙΟΝ ΤΗΣ ΕΥΛΟΓΙΑΣ'. *NTS* 27(1981) 704-09

Collins, A.Y., 'The Origin of Christian Baptism'. *SL* 19 (1989) 28-46

Collins, J.J., 'The Sibylline Oracles', in Stone, *Jewish Writings of the Second Temple Period*, 357-81

Colson, F.H., *Philo. With an English Translation* 1-10. *Supplement* (ET by R.A. Marcus) 1-2. (LCL) London-Cambridge MA 1929-53 and repr

Connolly, R.H., 'The Use of the Didache in the Didascalia'. *JTS* 24 (1923) 147-157

— 'The *Didache* in Relation to the Epistle of Barnabas'. *JTS* 33 (1932) 237-253

— 'Canon Streeter on the Didache'. *JTS* 38 (1937) 364-79

— 'The Didache and Montanism'. *DRev* 55 (1937) 339-47

Conybeare, F.C., 'The Eusebian form of the Text Matth. 28,19'. *ZNW* 2 (1901) 275-88

— *Philostratus. The Life of Apollonius of Tyana* 1-2. (LCL 16-17) Cambridge MA-London, 1912

Conzelmann, H., 'εὐχαριστέω κτλ.', in *TWNT* 9, 397-405

— 'χαίρω, χαρά, συγχαίρω κτλ.', in *TWNT* 9, 350-366 and 377-405

— *Der erste Brief an die Korinther*. (MeyerK 5) Göttingen 1969

Court, J.M., 'The Didache and St. Matthew's Gospel'. *SJT* 34 (1981) 109-20

Creed, J.M., 'The Didache'. *JTS* 39 (1938) 370-87

Crone, Th.M., *Early Christian Prophecy: A Study of its Origin and Function*. Baltimore Md 1973

Cross, F.M., *The Ancient Library of Qumran and Modern Biblical Studies*. 2nd ed Grand Rapids MI 1980

Cruel, R., *Geschichte der deutschen Predigt im Mittelalter*. Detmold 1879; repr Hildesheim 1966

Cuneo, B.H., *The Lord's Command to Baptize*. Washington 1923

Dahood, M., *Psalms III: 101-150*. (AB) Garden City NY 1970

Dalman, G., *Die Worte Jesu. Mit Berücksichtigung des nachkanonischen jüdischen Schrifttums und der aramäischen Sprache* 1. 2nd ed Leipzig 1930

— *Jesus – Jeshua, die drei Sprachen Jesu*. Leipzig 1922

Danby, H. (ed.), *The Mishnah*. Oxford 1933

Daniélou, J., 'Le traité De centesima, sexagesima, tricesima et le Judéo-Christianisme Latin avant Tertullien'. *VC* 25 (1971)171-181

Daube, D., *The New Testament and Rabbinic Judaism*. London 1956

David, A., 'Sheluhei Eretz Israel', in *EJ* 14, 1358-68

Davies, W.D., *The Setting of the Sermon on the Mount*. Cambridge 1964

Davies, W.D. and D.C. Allison, *A Critical and Exegetical Commentary on The Gospel according to Saint Matthew* 1. (ICC) Edinburgh 1988

Davis C., 'The *Didache* and early Monasticism in the East and West', in Jefford, *The Didache in Context*, 352-367

Dawes, G.W., 'The Danger of Idolatry: First Corinthians 8:7-13'. *CBQ* 58 (1996) 82-98

Dehandschutter, B., 'The Text of the *Didache*: Some Comments on the Edition of Klaus Wengst', in Jefford, *The Didache in Context*, 37-46

Dekkers, E. *et alii* (eds.), *Tertulliani Opera* 1: *Opera Catholica. Adversus Marcionem*. (CChr.SL 1) Turnhout 1954

Dekkers, E. and I. Fraipont (eds.), *Sancti Aurelii Augustini Enarrationes in Psalmos CI-CL* (CChr.SL 40), Turnhout 1956

Del Verme, M., *Giudaismo e Nuovo Testamento. Il Caso delle Decime*. Napoli 1989

— 'The Didache and Judaism: the ἀπαρχή of Didache 13:3-7', in E.A. Livingstone (ed.), *Studia Patristica* 26. Leuven 1993, 113-20

— 'Medio giudaismo e *Didaché*: il caso della comunione dei beni *(Did.* 4,8)'. *VetChr* 32 (1995) 293-320

Denaux, A., 'Der Spruch von den zwei Wegen im Rahmen des Epilogs der Bergpredigt (Mt 7,13-14Par. Lk 13,23-24). Tradition und Redaktion', in J. Delobel (ed.), *Logia. Les Paroles de Jésus – The Sayings of Jesus*. (BETL 59) Leuven 1982, 305-335

Descamps, A., 'Essai d'interprétation de Mt 5,17-48. Formgeschichte ou Redactionsgeschichte?'. *SE* 1 (1959) 156-73

— 'La Composition littéraire de Luc XVI 9-13'. *NovT* 1 (1956) 47-53

Dibelius, M., 'Die Mahl-Gebete der Didache'. *ZNW* 37 (1938) 32-41; repr in H. Kraft and G. Bornkamm (eds.), *Botschaft und Geschichte. Gesammelte Aufsätze von Martin Dibelius*. 2: *Zum Urchristentum und zur hellenistischen Religionsgeschichte*. Tübingen 1956, 117-27

— *Geschichte der urchristlichen Literatur*. (TBü NT 58) (1926); repr München 1975

— *Die Pastoralbriefe*. (HNT 13) 4th ed Tübingen 1966

— *Der Brief des Jakobus*. (KEK), H. Greeven (ed.); Göttingen [11]1964

— *Die Apostolischen Väter* 4: *Der Hirt des Hermas*. (HNT.E) Tübingen 1923

Dietrich, E.L., 'Die "Religion Noahs", ihre Herkunft und ihre Bedeutung'. *ZRGG* 1 (1948) 301-15

Dihle, A., *Die Goldene Regel. Eine Einführung in die Geschichte der antiken und frühchristlichen Vulgärethik*. (SAW 7) Göttingen 1962

Dimant, D., 'Qumran Sectarian Literature', in Stone, *Jewish Writings of the Second Temple Period*, 483-550

Dix, G., *The Shape of the Liturgy*. 2nd ed London 1945

Dockx, S., *Chronologies néotestamentaires et Vie de l'Église primitive. Recherches exégétiques*. Leuven 1984

— 'Le Binôme: ἐπισκόποι καὶ διακόνοι', in id., *Chronologies néotestamentaires*, 319-24

— 'Date et Origine de la Doctrine des Apôtres aux Gentils (Did. 7,1-10,7; 14,1-15,2)', in id., *Chronologies néotestamentaires*, 363-92

Dölger, F.J., *Der Exorzismus im altchristlichen Taufritual. Eine religionsgeschichtliche Studie*. (StGKA III, 1-2) Paderborn 1909

— *Die Sonne der Gerechtigkeit und der Schwarze. Eine religionsgeschichtliche Studie zum Taufgelöbnis*. (LF 2) Münster (Westf) 1918

Dodd, C.H., 'The Prophecy of Caiaphas (John XI 47-53)', in *Neotestamentica et Patristica*, 134-143

Dombrowski, B.W., 'היחד in 1QS and τὸ κοινόν. An Instance of Early Greek and Jewish Synthesis'. *HTR* 59 (1966) 293-307

Draper, J.A., *A Commentary on the Didache in the Light of the Dead Sea Scrolls and Related Documents*. (unpubl. Cambridge PhD diss.) 1983

— (ed.), *The Didache in Modern Research*. (AGJU 37) Leiden-New York-Köln 1996

— 'Torah and troublesome Apostles in the Didache Community', in id. *The Didache in Modern Research*, 340-363; published previously in *Nov.T* 33 (1991) 347-372

— 'The Didache in Modern Research: an Overview', in id. *The Didache in Modern Research*, 1-42

— 'Social Ambiguity and the production of Text: Prophets, Teachers, Bishops, and Deacons and the Development of the Jesus Tradition in the Community of the *Didache*', in Jefford, *The Didache in Context*, 284-312

— 'Christian Self-Definition against the "Hypocrites" in Didache VIII', in id. *The Didache in Modern Research*, 223-243

— 'The Jesus Tradition in the Didache', in D. Wenham (ed.), *Gospel Perspectives V: The Jesus Tradition Outside the Gospels*. (JSOT) Sheffield 1985, 269-89; slightly rev. in Draper, *The Didache in Modern Research*, 72-91

— 'The Development of "The Sign of the Son of Man" in the Jesus Tradition'. *NTS* 39 (1993) 1-21

— 'Barnabas and the Riddle of the Didache Revisited'. *JSNT* 58 (1995) 89-113

— 'Weber, Theissen, and "Wandering Charismatics" in the Didache'. *JECS* 6 (1998) 541-76

— 'Ritual Process and Ritual Symbol in Didache 7-10'. *VC* 54 (2000) 121-58

Drews, P., 'Untersuchungen zur Didache'. *ZNW* 5 (1904) 53-79

Drobner, H.R., *Lehrbuch der Patrologie*. Freiburg-Basel-Wien 1994

Duensing, H., 'Die dem Klemens von Rom zugeschriebenen Briefe über die Jungfräulichkeit'. *ZKG* 63 (1950-51) 166-188

Dugmore, C.W., 'Lord's Day and Easter', in *Neotestamentica et Patristica*, 272-81

Duhaime, J., 'Les voies des deux esprits (*1QS* iv 2-14). Une analyse structurelle'. *RevQ* 19 (2000) 349-67

Dumais, M., *Le Sermon sur la Montagne. État de la recherche. Interprétation. Bibliographie*. Québec 1995

Dumbrell, W.J., 'The Logic of the Role of the Law in Matthew V 1-20'. *NovT* 23 (1981) 1-23

Dupont, J., *Les Béatitudes* 1: *Le problème littéraire*. (Ebib) Paris 1969

— *Les Béatitudes* 3: *Les évangélistes* (Ebib) Paris 1973

Dupont-Sommer, A., *Les Écrits esséniens découverts près de la mer Morte*. 4th ed Paris 1980

Dupont-Sommer, A. et M. Philonenko (eds.), *Écrits intertestamentaires*. Paris 1992

Ebersohn, M., *Das Nächstenliebegebot in der synoptischen Tradition*. (MThSt 37) Marburg 1993

Ehrhard, A., *Die altchristliche Litteratur und ihre Erforschung von 1884-1900*. 1: *Die vornicänische Litteratur*. (StrThSt.S 1) Freiburg im B. 1900

Ehrman, B.D., 'The New Testament Canon of Didymus the Blind'. *VC* 37 (1983) 1-21

Eichholz, G., *Auslegung der Bergpredigt*. 2nd ed Neukirchen-Vluyn 1970

Eijk, T.H.C. van, *La résurrection des morts chez les pères apostoliques*. (ThH 25) Paris 1974

Elgvin, T., '4QThe Two Ways', in *Qumran Cave 4* 17: *Parabiblical texts* 3 (DJD XXII) Oxford 1996, 289-294

Ellis, E.E., 'The Old Testament Canon in the Early Church', in M.J. Mulder (ed.), *Mikra. Text. Translation. Reading and Interpretation of the Hebrew Bible in Ancient Judaism and Early Christianity*. (CRINT II,1) Assen/Maastricht-Philadelphia 1988, 653-690

Eppel, R., *Le piétisme Juif dans les Testaments des douze Patriarches*. (ÉHPR) Paris 1930

Epstein, J.N., *Mavo le-nosah ha-Mishna* 1-2. Jerusalem 1948; rev. ed. 1964

Epstein, J.N. and E.Z. Melamed (eds.), *Mekhilta d'Rabbi Šim'on b. Jochai*. Jerusalem 1955

Faivre, A., *Naissance d'une hiérarchie. Les premières étapes du cursus clérical*. (ThH 40) Paris 1977

—— 'La documentation canonico-liturgique de l'église ancienne'. *RevScRel* 54 (1980) 204-219.273-297

—— 'Le texte Grec de *La Constitution Ecclésiastique des Apôtres* 16-20 et ses sources'. *RevScRel* 55 (1981) 31-42

Falk, D.K., *Daily, Sabbath, and Festival Prayers in the Dead Sea Scrolls*. (STDJ 27) Leiden-Boston-Köln 1998

Falls, Th. B., *Saint Justin Martyr*. (FC 6) 3rd ed Washington D.C. 1977

Faust, U., 'Benediktiner, Benediktinerinnen', in G. Schwaiger (ed.), *Mönchtum, Orden, Klöster. Von den Anfängen bis zur Gegenwart. Ein Lexikon*. München 1993, 84-111

Fee, G.D., 'Εἰδωλόθυτα Once Again: An Interpretation of 1 Corinthians 8-10'. *Bib* 61 (1980) 172-97

Feldman, L.H., *Josephus. Jewish Antiquities XVIII-XX*. With an English Translation, in Thackeray, *Josephus* 9-10

Fendt, L., *Einführung in die Liturgiewissenschaft*. (ST II,5) Berlin 1958

Fiebig, P., *Jesu Bergpredigt. Rabbinische Texte zum Verständnis der Bergpredigt*. (FRLANT 20) Göttingen 1924

Fiensy, D.A., *Prayers Alleged to be Jewish. An Examination of the Constitutiones Apostolorum*. (BJS 65) Chico (Cal) 1985

Finegan, J., *Die Ueberlieferung der Leidens- und Auferstehungs-Geschichte Jesu*. Giessen 1934

Finkelstein, L., *Pharisaism in the Making. Selected Essays*, New York 1972

—— 'The Birkat Ha-Mazon', in id., *Pharisaism*, 333-384; published previously in *JQR* n.s. 19 (1928-29) 211-62

—— 'The Development of the Amidah'. *JQR* n.s. 16 (1925-26) 1-43.127-67; repr in id., *Pharisaism*, 245-329

—— (ed.), *Siphre ad Deuteronomium*. (CT III/2) Berlin 1939; repr New York 1969

Fischer, J.A., *Die apostolischen Väter*. (SU 1) 10th ed Darmstadt 1993 (1956)

—— 'Das sogenannte Apostelkonzil', in G. Schwaiger (ed.), *Konzil und Papst* (FS. H. Tüchle) München-Paderborn-Wien 1975, 1-17

Fisher, J.D.C., *Christian Initiation: Baptism in the Medieval West. A Study in the Disintegration of the Primitive Rite of Initiation*. (ACC 47) London 1965

Fitzmyer, J.A., *Essays on the Semitic Background of the New Testament*. (SfBS 5) London 1974

—— 'The Use of explicit Old Testament Quotations in Qumran Literature and in the New Testament', in id., *Essays on the Semitic Background*, 3-58; published previously in *NTS* 7 (1960-61) 297-333

—— 'Jewish Christianity in Acts in the Light of the Qumran Scrolls', in id., *Essays on the Semitic Background*, 271-303; orig. publ. in L.E. Keck and J.L. Martyn *Studies in Luke-Acts: Essays Presented in Honor of Paul Schubert*. London 1966, 233-57

—— *The Gospel According to Luke* 1-2. (AB) New York 1981-85

—— 'The Priority of Mark and the "Q" Source in Luke', in Miller, *Jesus and Man's Hope* 1, 131-170; repr in J.A. Fitzmyer *To Advance the Gospel: New Testament Studies*, New York 1981, 3-40

Flaskamp, F., *Die Missionsmethode des hl. Bonifatius*. (GDQ 8) Hildesheim 1929

Flusser, D., *Judaism and the Origins of Christianity* (collected articles) Jerusalem 1988

—— '"I am in the Midst of Them" (Mt. 18:20)', in id., *Judaism*, 515-25

—— 'The Dead Sea Sect and Pre-Pauline Christianity', in id., *Judaism*, 23-74; published previously in *Scripta Hierosolymitana IV: Aspects of the Dead Sea Scrolls* 1958, 215-66

—— 'An early Jewish-Christian Document in the Tiburtine Sibyl', in id., *Judaism*, 359-89; published previously in A. Benoit, M. Philonenko and C. Vogel (eds.), *Paganisme, Judaïsme, Christianisme: influences et affrontements dans le monde antique. Mélanges* (FS. M. Simon), Paris 1978, 153-83

—— 'Matthew's "Verus Israel"', in id., *Judaism*, 561-74

—— 'The Last Supper and the Essenes', in id., *Judaism*, 202-06; published previously in *Immanuel* 2 (1973) 23-27

— 'Two Anti-Jewish Montages in Matthew', in id., *Judaism*, 552-60; published previously in *Immanuel* 5 (1975) 37-45.
— 'A Rabbinic Parallel to the Sermon on the Mount', in id., *Judaism*, 494-508
— 'Blessed are the Poor in Spirit', in id., *Judaism*, 102-14; published previously in *IEJ* 10 (1960) 1-13
— 'Some Notes to the Beatitudes', in id., *Judaism*, 115-25; published previously in *Immanuel* 8 (1978) 37-47
— 'The Didache and the Noachic Commandments', in id., *Judaism*, 508
— 'A New Sensitivity in Judaism and the Christian Message', in id., *Judaism*, 469-89; published previously in *HTR* 61 (1968) 107-27
— 'Jesus' opinion about the Essenes', in id., *Judaism*, 150-68
— 'Die Tora in der Bergpredigt', in H. Kremers (ed.), *Juden und Christen lesen dieselbe Bibel.* Duisburg 1973, 102-113
— 'The Conclusion of Matthew in a New Jewish Christian Source'. *ASTI* 5 (1967) 110-120
— 'Testaments of the Twelve Patriarchs' in *EJ* 13, 184-86
— 'Tevilat Yohanan we-kat midbar Yehudah', in id., *Jewish Sources in Early Christianity. Studies and Essays*, 5th ed Tel Aviv (1994) 81-112; published previously in C. Rabin and Y. Yadin (eds.), *Essays on the Dead Sea Scrolls: In Memory of E.L. Sukenik.* Jerusalem 1961, 209-38
— *Jesus*. Jerusalem 1997; rev. ed. 1998
— 'The Parable of the Unjust Steward: Jesus' Criticism of the Essenes', in J.H. Charlesworth (ed.), *Jesus and the Dead Sea Scrolls.* (ABRL) New York-London-Toronto-Sydney-Auckland 1992, 176-197
— *Das Christentum – eine jüdische Religion*. München 1990
— 'Paul's Jewish-Christian Opponents in the Didache', in S. Shaked, D. Shulman and G.G. Stroumsa (eds.), *Gilgul. Essays on Transformation, Revolution and Permanence in the history of Religions.* (FS. Z. Werblowski) Leiden-New York-Copenhagen-Cologne 1987, 71-90; repr in Draper (ed.), *The Didache in Modern Research*, 195-211
— 'John Toland oder die ursprüngliche Absicht des Christentums', in H. Kremers and J.H. Schoeps (eds.), *Das jüdisch-christliche Religionsgespräch.* (SzG 9) Stuttgart-Bonn 1988, 198-209
— 'Noachitische Gebote: I. Judentum'. *TRE* 24 (1994) 582-85
— 'Shte Derakhim Hen', in id., *Jewish Sources in Early Christianity. Studies and Essays.* Jerusalem 1979, 235-52
— 'Ezohi Derekh Yashara Shiboor loo Ha-adam? (Avot 2,1)'. *Tarbiz* 60 (1991) 163-178
— *Das essenische Abenteuer. Die jüdische Gemeinde vom Toten Meer; Auffälligkeiten bei Jesus, Paulus, Didache und Martin Buber.* Winterthur 1994
— 'The Ten Commandments and the New Testament', in B.-Z. Segal and G. Levi (eds.), *The Ten Commandments in History and Tradition.* Jerusalem 1990, 219-46
— '"Miqtsat maase ha-Tora" u-Birkat ha-minim'. *Tarbiz* 61 (1992) 333-374
— 'Ostracon from Qumran throws a Light on the First Community'. *Jerusalem Perspective* 85 (1997) 12-15.
— '"Do not commit adultery", "Do not murder"', in S. Talmon (ed.), *Textus* 4. Jerusalem 1964, 220-224
— '«Den Alten ist gesagt» Zur Interpretation der sog. Antithesen der Bergpredigt'. *Judaica* 48 (1992) 35-39
Flusser, D. and S. Safrai, 'Das Aposteldekret und die Noachitischen Gebote', in E. Brocke und H.-J. Barkenings (eds.), *"Wer Tora vermehrt, mehrt Leben".* (FS. H. Kremers) Neukirchen-Vluyn 1986, 173-92
Foerster, W., 'Der Heilige Geist im Spätjudentum'. *NTS* 8 (1961-62) 117-34
Freedman, H. and M. Simon, *The Midrash Rabbah* 2: *Exodus-Leviticus.* London-Jerusalem-New York 1977
Frend, W.H.C., *Martyrdom and Persecution in the Early Church. A Study of a Conflict from the Maccabees to Donatus.* Oxford 1965
Friedlander, G., *The Jewish Sources of the Sermon on the Mount.* (LBS) New York 1969

Friedmann (Ish-Shalom), M. (ed.), *Pseudo-Seder Eliahu Zuta (Derech Ereç und Pirkê R. Eliezer)* Vienna 1904; repr (and, in addition, *Seder Eliahu Rabba and Seder Eliahu Zuta*) Jerusalem 1969
— (ed.), *Pesikta Rabbati. Midrasch für den Fest-Cyclus und die ausgezeichneten Sabbathe.* Vienna 1880; repr Tel Aviv 1963
Funk, F.X., 'Zur alten lateinischen Übersetzung der Doctrina apostolorum'. *TQ* 68 (1886) 650-655
— 'Die Apostolische Kirchenordnung'. in id., *Kirchengeschichtliche Abhandlungen und Untersuchungen* 1-2. Paderborn 1899, 236-251
— (ed.), *Didascalia et Constitutiones Apostolorum* 1. Paderborn 1905; repr Turin 1962
— *Doctrina duodecim Apostolorum. Canones Apostolorum ecclesiastici ac reliquae doctrinae de duabus viis expositiones veteres.* Tübingen 1887
Gamber, K., 'Die «Eucharistia» der Didache'. *EL* 101 (1987) 3-32
Gammie, J.G., 'Spatial and Ethical Dualism in Jewish Wisdom and Apocalyptic Literature'. *JBL* 93 (1974) 356-85
García Martínez, F., 'The Origins of the Essene Movement and of the Qumran Sect', in F. García Martínez and J.T. Barrera (eds.), *The People of the Dead Sea Scrolls: Their Writings, Beliefs and Practices.* Leiden 1995, 77-96
— 'Qumran Origins and Early History: A Groningen Hypothesis'. *FO* 25 (1988) 113-36
— *The Dead Sea Scrolls Translated. The Qumran Texts in English.* Leiden-New York-Köln 1994
Gauger, J.-D., *Sibyllinische Weissagungen. Griechisch-deutsch.* Darmstadt 1998
Gavin, F., *The Jewish Antecedents of the Christian Sacraments.* London 1928
Gebhardt, O. von, 'Ein übersehenes Fragment der Διδαχή in alter lateinischer Übersetzung', in A. von Harnack *Die Lehre der zwölf Apostel*, 275-86
Geffcken, J. (ed.), *Die Oracula Sibyllina.* (GCS 8) Leipzig 1902
— *Zwei griechische Apologeten.* (SWKGRS) Leipzig-Berlin 1907; repr Hildesheim-New York 1970
Gerhardsson, B., *Memory and Manuscript. Oral Tradition and Written Transmission in Rabbinic Judaism and Early Christianity.* 2nd ed Lund-Copenhagen 1964
Gerlo, A. *et alii* (eds.), *Tertulliani Opera* 2: *Opera Montanistica.* (CChr.SL 2/2) Turnhout 1954
Gero, S., 'The so-called Ointment Prayer in the Coptic Version of the Didache: A Re-evaluation'. *HTR* 70 (1977) 67-84
Geyser, A.S., 'The Youth of John the Baptist. A Deduction from the Break in the Parallel Account of the Lucan Infancy Story'. *NovT* 1 (1956) 70-75
Giet, St., *L'Énigme de la Didachè.* (PFLUS 149) Paris 1970
Gill, D., '*Trapezomata*: A Neglected Aspect of Greek Sacrifice'. *HTR* 67 (1974) 117-137
Ginzberg, L., *A Commentary on the Palestinian Talmud. A Study of the Development of the Halakah and Haggadah in Palestine and Babylonia* 1-4. (TS.JTS 10-12, 21) New York 1941-61 (Hebr.)
— 'Derek Erez Zuta', in *JE* 4, 528-530
Gladigow, B., 'Der Makarismus des Weisen'. *Hermes* 95 (1967) 404-33
Glover, R., 'The Didache's Quotations and the Synoptic Gospels'. *NTS* 5 (1958) 12-29
— 'Patristic Quotations and Gospel Sources'. *NTS* 31 (1985) 234-51
Gnilka, J., 'Der Missionsauftrag des Herrn nach Mt 28 und Apg 1'. *Bibleb* 9 (1968) 1-9
— 'Die essenischen Tauchbäder und die Johannestaufe'. *RevQ* 3 (1961-62) 185-207
— *Das Matthäusevangelium. I. Kommentar zu Kap. 1,1-13,58.* (HTKNT I/1) Freiburg-Basel-Wien 1986
Götz, K.G., *Petrus als Gründer und Oberhaupt der Kirche und Schauer von Gesichten nach den altchristlichen Berichten und Legenden.* (UNT 13) Leipzig 1927
Goldhahn-Müller, I., *Die Grenze der Gemeinde. Studien zum Problem der Zweiten Busse im Neuen Testament unter Berücksichtigung der Entwicklung im 2. Jh. bis Tertullian.* (GTA 39) Göttingen 1989
Gooch, P.D., *Dangerous Food. 1 Corinthians 8-10 in Its Context.* (SCJ 5) Waterloo 1993
Goodman, M., 'Jewish Proselytizing in the First Century', in J. Lieu *et alii*, *The Jews among Pagans and Christians in the Roman Empire*, 53-78
— *Mission and Conversion: Proselytizing in the Religious History of the Roman Empire.* Oxford 1994

Goodspeed, E.J. (ed.), *Die ältesten Apologeten. Texte mit kurzen Einleitungen.* Göttingen 1914; repr 1984
— 'The Didache, Barnabas and the Doctrina'. *ATR* 27 (1945) 228-247
Goppelt, L., *Christentum und Judentum im ersten und zweiten Jahrhundert.* (BFCT II, 55) Gütersloh 1954
— 'Das Problem der Bergpredigt', in id., *Christologie und Ethik.* Göttingen 1968, 28-43
Gordon, R.P., 'Targumic parallels to Acts XIII 18 and Didache XIV,3'. *NovT* 16 (1974) 285-289
Grant, R.M., *A Historical Introduction to the New Testament.* New York 1963
Gray, R., *Prophetic Figures in Late Second Temple Jewish Palestine. The Evidence from Josephus.* New York-Oxford 1993
Greehy, J., 'The Qumran Mebaqqer and the Christian Episkopos', in A. Mayes (ed.), *Church Ministry.* (PIBA 2) Dublin 1977, 29-36
Green, H.B., 'The Commandment to Baptize and Other Matthean Interpolations'. *SE* 4, Berlin 1968, 60-63
— *The Gospel according to Matthew.* (NCIB) Oxford 1975
Greenspahn, F., 'Why Prophecy Ceased'. *JBL* 108 (1989) 37-49
Greeven, H., 'Propheten, Lehrer, Vorsteher bei Paulus: zur Frage der "Amten" im Urchristentum'. *ZNW* 44 (1952-53) 1-43
Greiff, A., *Das älteste Pascharituale der Kirche, Did 1-10, und das Johannesevangelium.* (Johanneische Studien 1) Paderborn 1929
Grenfell, B.P. and A.S. Hunt, *The Oxyrhynchus Papyri* 10. London 1914
— *The Oxyrhynchus Papyri* 15. London 1922
Gronewald, M. (ed.), *Didymos der Blinde. Psalmenkommentar (Tura-Papyrus)* 3. (PTA 8) Bonn 1969
— *Didymos der Blinde. Kommentar zum Ecclesiastes (Tura-Papyrus)* 2. (PTA 22) Bonn 1977
Grundmann, W., *Das Evangelium nach Matthäus.* (THKNT 1) 3rd ed Berlin 1972
— *Das Evangelium nach Lukas.* (THKNT 3) 2nd ed Berlin 1969
Guelich, R.A., 'The Antitheses of Matthew 5,21-48: Traditional and/or Redactional'. *NTS* 22 (1976) 444-457
— *The Sermon on the Mount. A Foundation for Understanding.* 2nd ed Waco (TX) 1983
Guilbert, P., 'Le plan de la Règle de la Communauté' . *RevQ* 3 (1959) 323-344
Gundry, R.H., *Matthew. A Commentary on His Literary and Theological Art.* Grand Rapids (MI) 1982
Guttmann, M., *Das Judentum und seine Umwelt. Eine Darstellung der religiösen und rechtlichen Beziehungen zwischen Juden und Nichtjuden mit besonderer Berücksichtigung der talmudisch-rabbinischen Quellen* 1. Berlin 1927
Hadas, M., *The Third and Fourth Books of Maccabees.* (JAL) New York 1953
Haenchen, E., *Die Apostelgeschichte.* (MeyerK 3) 12th ed Göttingen 1959
Hänggi A. and I. Pahl, *Prex Eucharistica. Textus e Variis Liturgiis Antiquioribus Selecti.* (SF 12) Fribourg 1968
Hahn, F., 'Prophetie und Lebenswandel. Bemerkungen zu Paulus und zu zwei Texten der Apostolischen Väter', in H. Merklein (ed.), *Neues Testament und Ethik.* (FS. R. Schnackenburg) Freiburg-Basel-Wien 1989, 527-37
Hahn, H., 'Die angeblichen Predigten des Bonifaz'. *FdG* 24 (1884) 585-625
Hainz, J., *Koinonia. »Kirche« als Gemeinschaft bei Paulus.* (BU 16) Regensburg 1982
Hall, S.G. (ed.), *Melito of Sardis, on Pascha and Fragments.* (OECT) Oxford 1979
Halleux, A. de, 'Les ministères dans la *Didachè*'. *Irénikon* 53 (1980) 4-29; ET: 'Ministers in the Didache', in Draper, *The Didache in Modern Research*, 300-320
Hallinger, K., 'Das Kommentarfragment zu Regula Benedicti IV aus der ersten Hälfte des 8. Jahrhunderts'. *WS* 82 (1969) 211-234
Hamerton-Kelly, R., 'Attitudes to the Law in Matthew's Gospel. A Discussion of Matthew 5:18'. *BR* 17 (1972) 19-32
Hanslik, R., *Benedicti Regula.* (CSEL 75) Vienna 1960

Hare, D.R.A., 'The Relationship between Jewish and Gentile Persecution of Christians'. *JES* 4 (1967) 446-56

Harlow, D.C., *The Greek Apocalypse of Baruch (3 Baruch) in Hellenistic Judaism and Early Christianity*. (SVTP 12) Leiden 1996

Harmon, A.M., *Lucian* 4-5. (LCL 162 and 302) Cambridge (MA)-London 1925-36 and repr

Harms, W., *Homo viator in bivio. Studien zur Bildlichkeit des Weges*. (Medium Aevum 21) München 1970

Harnack, A. von, 'Die pseudoclementinischen Briefe de virginitate und die Entstehung des Mönchthums'. *SPAW* 21 (1891) 361-85

— *Die Lehre der zwölf Apostel nebst Untersuchungen zur ältesten Geschichte der Kirchenverfassung und des Kirchenrechts*. (TU 2,1) Leipzig 1884; repr Leipzig 1893

— *Die Mission und Ausbreitung des Christentums in der ersten drei Jahrhunderten* 1-2. 3rd ed Wiesbaden 1915; ET: *The Mission and Expansion of Christianity in the First Three Centuries* 1-2. (ThTL 19) New York 1908

— *Entstehung und Entwickelung der Kirchenverfassung und des Kirchenrechts in den zwei ersten Jahrhunderten*. Leipzig 1910; ET: *The Constitution and Law of the Church in the First Two Centuries*. London 1910

— *Beiträge zur Einleitung in das Neue Testament* 3-4. Leipzig 1908-1911

— 'Das Aposteldekret (Act. 15,29) und die Blass'sche Hypothese', in id., *Studien zur Geschichte des Neuen Testaments und der Alten Kirche, I: Zur neutestamentlichen Textkritik*. (AK 19) Berlin-Leipzig 1931, 1-32; published previously in *SPAW* 1, Berlin 1899, 150-76

— *Geschichte der altchristlichen Litteratur bis Eusebius, 1: Die Überlieferung und der Bestand*. Leipzig 1893

— *Die Apostellehre und die jüdischen Beiden Wege*. Leipzig 1886

Harrington, H.K., *The Impurity Systems of Qumran and the Rabbis: Biblical Foundations*. (SBLDS 143) Atlanta (Ga) 1993

Harrington, D.J., 'Pseudo-Philo', in Charlesworth, *The Old Testament Pseudepigrapha* 2, 297-377

Harrington, D.J. and J. Cazeaux (eds.), *Pseudo-Philon. Les antiquités bibliques* 1. (SC 229) Paris 1976

Harris, J.R., *The Teaching of the Apostles*. London-Baltimore 1887

— *Three Pages of the Bryennios Manuscript Reproduced by Photography for the Johns Hopkins University*. Baltimore 1885

Hartel, W., *S. Thasci Caecili Cypriani opera omnia 3: Opera spuria. Indices. Praefatio*. (CSEL 3,3) Vienna 1871

Hartman, L., 'Into the Name of Jesus'. *NTS* 20 (1974) 432-40

— *"Auf den Namen des Herrn Jesus". Die Taufe in den neutestamentlichen Schriften*. (SBS 148) Stuttgart 1992

Hasler, V., *Amen. Redaktionsgeschichtliche Untersuchung zur Einführungsformel der Herrenworte "Wahrlich ich sage euch"*. Zürich-Stuttgart 1969

Heer, J.M., *Ein Karolingischer Missions-Katechismus. Ratio de Cathecizandis Rudibus*. (BPF 1) Freiburg im B. 1911

Heinemann, I., *Philo's griechische und jüdische Bildung. Kulturvergleichende Untersuchungen zu Philons Darstellung der jüdischen Gesetze*. Breslau 1932; repr Hildesheim 1962

— 'Development of the Technical Terms for the Biblical Exegesis'. *Leshonenu* 15 (1947) 108-115 (Hebr.)

Heinemann, J., *Prayer in the Talmud. Forms ans Patterns*. (StudJud 9) Berlin-New York 1977

Heintz, J.-G., 'Royal Traits and Messianic Figures: A Thematic and Iconographical Approach', in J.H. Charlesworth (ed.), *The Messiah. Developments in Earliest Judaism and Christianity*. Minneapolis 1992

Helyer, L.R., 'Luke and the Restoration of Israel'. *JETS* 36 (1993) 317-329

Hengel, M., 'Zur matthäischen Bergpredigt und ihrem jüdischen Hintergrund'. *TRu* 52 (1987) 327-400

— *Judentum und Hellenismus*. (WUNT 10) Tübingen 1973

— *Die Zeloten. Untersuchungen zur jüdischen Freiheitsbewegung in der Zeit von Herodes I. bis 70 n. Chr.* (AGJU 1) Leiden-Köln 1976

Hennecke, E., 'Die Grundschrift der Didache und ihre Recensionen'. *ZNW* 2 (1901) 58-72

Hennecke, E. and W. Schneemelcher, *Neutestamentliche Apokryphen. In deutscher Übersetzung* 2: *Apostolisches, Apokalypsen und Verwandtes.* 5th ed Tübingen 1989

Higger, M. (ed.), *The treatises Derek Erez: Masseket Derek Erez; Pirke Ben Azzai; Tosefta Derek Erez* 1-2. New York 1935; repr Jerusalem 1970

— (ed.), *Seven Minor Treatises: Sefer Torah; Mezuzah; Tefillin; Zizit; 'Abadim; Kutim; Gerim.* New York 1930

— (ed.), *Minor Tractates (Massekhtot Ze'irot).* New York 1929; repr Jerusalem 1970

Hildesheimer, E. (ed.), *Sefer Halakhot Gedolot* 1. Jerusalem 1971

Hilgenfield, A., 'Das Apostel-Concil nach seinem ursprünglichen Wortlaut'. *ZWT* 42 (1899) 138-49

Hill, D., *Greek Words with Hebrew Meanings.* Cambridge 1967

— *The Gospel of Matthew.* (NCB) London 1972

Hitchcock, F.R.M., 'Did Clement of Alexandria know the *Didache*?'. *JTS* 24 (1923) 397-401

Hofius, O., *Der Christushymnus Philipper 2,6-11.* (WUNT 17) Tübingen 1976

Hollander, H.W. and M. de Jonge, *The Testaments of the Twelve Patriarchs. A Commentary.* (SVTP 8) Leiden 1985

Hoppe, R., 'Vollkommenheit bei Matthäus als theologische Aussage', in I. Oberlinner and P. Fiedler (eds.), *Salz der Erde – Licht der Welt. Exegetische Studien zum Matthäusevangelium.* (FS. A. Vögtle) Stuttgart 1991, 141-64

Horgan, M.P., *Pesharim: Qumran Interpretations of Biblical Books.* (CBQMS 8) Washington DC 1979

Horn, F.W., *Das Angeld des Geistes. Studien zur paulinischen Pneumatologie.* (FRLANT 154) Göttingen 1992

Horner, G.W., *The Statutes of the Apostles or Canones Ecclesiastici.* London 1904

— 'A New Papyrus Fragment of the *Didache* in Coptic'. *JTS* 25 (1924) 225-31

Horovitz, H. S. (ed.), *Siphre d'be Rab I: Siphre ad Numeros adjecto Siphre zutta.* (CT III/3,1) Leipzig 1917; corr. repr Jerusalem 1966

Horovitz, H.S. and I.A. Rabin, *Mechilta d'Rabbi Ismael.* 2nd ed Jerusalem 1970

Horsley, R.A., 'Gnosis in Corinth: I Corinthians 8. 1-6'. *NTS* 27 (1981) 32-51

— '«Like One of the Prophets of Old»: Two types of Popular Prophets at the Time of Jesus'. *CBQ* 47 (1985) 435-63;

Horsley, R.A. and J.S. Hanson, *Bandits, Prophets, and Messiahs. Popular Movements in the Time of Jesus.* (NVBS) San Francisco (orig. Minneapolis) 1985

Horst, P.W. van der, *The Sentences of Pseudo-Phocylides.* Leiden 1978

— 'Jews and Christians in Aphrodisias in the Light of their Relations in Other Cities of Asia Minor'. *NedTTs* 43 (1989) 106-121

— 'Gottesfürchtige', in *LTK* 4 (1995) 914-5

— 'Jewish Self-Definition by Way of Contrast in *Oracula Sibyllina* III 218-247' in id., *Hellenism – Judaism – Christianity. Essays on Their Interaction.* (CBET 8) 2nd enl. ed.: Leuven 1998, 93-110

Hruby, K., 'La «Birkat Ha-Mazon»', in *Mélanges Liturgiques.* (FS. B. Botte) Leuven (1972) 205-222

Hubbard, B.J., *The Matthean Redaction of a Primitive Apostolic Commissioning: An Exegesis of Matthew 28:16-20.* (SBLDS 19) Montana 1974

Hübner, H., *Das Gesetz in der synoptischen Tradition. Studien zur These einer progressiven Qumranisierung und Judaisierung innerhalb der synoptischen Tradition.* 2nd ed Göttingen 1986 (orig. Witten 1973)

Hummel, R., *Die Auseinandersetzung zwischen Kirche und Judentum im Matthäusevangelium.* (BEvT 33) 2nd ed München 1966

Hunkin, J.W., 'The Prohibitions of the Council at Jerusalem (Acts xv 28,29)'. *JTS* 27 (1926) 272-83

Hurd, J.C., *The Origin of 1 Corinthians.* London 1965

Hyman, D., D.N. Lerrer and I. Shiloni (eds.), *Yalqut Shim'oni al ha-Torah le Rabbenu Shim'on ha-Darshan* 1. Jerusalem 1973

Ireland, D.J., *Stewardship and the Kingdom of God. An Historical, Exegetical, and Contextual Study of the Parable of the Unjust Steward in Luke 16:1-13.* (NovTSup 70) Leiden-New York-Köln 1992

Irmscher, J., 'Das Buch des Elchasai', in Hennecke-Schneemelcher, *Neutestamentliche Apokryphen 2*, 619-23

Iselin, L.E., *Eine bisher unbekannte Version des ersten Teiles der "Apostellehre".* (TU 13/1b) Leipzig 1895

Jacquier, E., *Les Actes des Apôtres.* (Ebib) Paris 1926

Jaspert, B., 'Die Regula Benedicti-Forschung 1880-1980', in id., *Studien zum Mönchtum.* (RBS.Sup 7) Hildesheim 1982, 133-146

Jaubert, A., 'Jésus et le calendrier de Qumrân'. *NTS* 7 (1960) 1-30

— *La Date de la Cène. Calendrier biblique et liturgie Chrétienne.* (Ebib) Paris 1957

Jefford, C.N., *The Sayings of Jesus in the Teaching of the Twelve Apostles.* (VCSup 11) Leiden-New York-København-Köln 1989

— (ed.), *The **Didache** in Context. Essays on Its Text, History and Transmission.* (NovTSup 77) Leiden-New York-Köln 1995

— 'Did Ignatius of Antioch know the *Didache*?', in id., *The Didache in Context*, 330-51

Jellinek, A., *Bet ha-Midrasch* 6. 3rd ed Jerusalem 1967

Jeremias, J., *Die Kindertaufe in den Ersten Vier Jahrhunderten.* Göttingen 1958; ET: *Infant Baptism in the First Four Centuries.* London 1960

— *Neutestamentliche Theologie 1. Die Verkündigung Jesu.* Gütersloh 1971

— *Die Abendmahlsworte Jesu.* 3rd ed Göttingen 1960; ET (from the 2nd ed): *The Eucharistic Words of Jesus.* Oxford 1955

— 'πύλη, πυλών', in *TWNT* 6, 920-27

Joannou, P.-P., *Fonti. Discipline générale antique (IVe-IXe s.)* 2: *Les canons des Pères Grecs*, Rome 1963

Johnson, L.T., *The Literary Function of Possessions in Luke-Acts.* Missoula (MT) 1977

Johnson, S.E., 'A Subsidiary Motive for the Writing of the Didache', in M.H. Shepherd, Jr. and S.E. Johnson (eds.), *Munera Studiosa.* Cambridge (MA) 1946, 107-22

Jones, C.P., *Culture and Society in Lucian.* Cambridge (MA)-London 1986

Jones, C., G., Wainwright and E. Yarnold, *The Study of Liturgy.* London 1978

Jones, F.S. and P.A. Mirecki, 'Considerations on the Coptic Papyrus of the *Didache* (British Library Oriental Manuscript 9271)', in Jefford, *The Didache in Context*, 47-87

Jonge, M. de, *The Testaments of the Twelve Patriarchs: A Study of Their Text, Composition and Origin.* Assen 1953

— *The Testaments of the Twelve Patriarchs* (PVTG I/2), Leiden 1978

Kadushin, M., *Worship and Ethics. A Study in Rabbinic Judaism.* New York 1963

Kamlah, E., *Die Form der katalogischen Paränese im Neuen Testament.* (WUNT 7) Tübingen 1964

Karpp, H. (ed.), *Die Busse: Quellen zur Entstehung des altkirchlichen Busswesens.* (TC 1) Zürich 1969

Kasting, H., *Die Anfänge der urchristlichen Mission. Eine historische Untersuchung.* (BevT 55) München 1969

Kertelge, K., 'Der sogenannte Taufbefehl Jesu (Mt 28,19)', in *Zeichen des Glaubens. Studien zu Taufe und Firmung.* (FS. B. Fischer) Freiburg in Breisgau 1972, 29-40

Kilger, L., 'Die Taufvorbereitung in der frühmittelalterlichen Benediktinermission', in H.S. Brechter (ed.), *Benedictus. Der Vater des Abendlandes 547-1947.* München 1949, 505-521

Kilpatrick, G.D., *The Origins of the Gospel according to St. Matthew.* Oxford 1946

— 'Luke XXII, 19b-20', in J.K. Elliott (ed.), *The Principles and Practices of New Testament Textual Criticism. Collected Essays of G.D. Kilpatrick.* Leuven 1990, 319-326

Kingsbury, J.D., 'The Composition and Christology of Matt. 28,16-20'. *JBL* 93 (1974) 573-84

— *Matthew.* (Proclamation Commentaries) 2nd ed Philadelphia 1986

Kirsten, H., *Die Taufabsage. Eine Untersuchung zu Gestalt und Geschichte der Taufe nach den altkirchlichen Taufliturgien.* Berlin 1960

Klauser, Th., 'Taufet in Lebendigem Wasser! Zum religions- und kulturgeschichtlichen Verständnis von Didache 7,1/3', in E. Dassmann (ed.), *Gesammelte Arbeiten zur Liturgiegeschichte, Kirchengeschichte und Christlichen Archäologie*. (JAC.E 3) Münster (Westf) 1974, 177-83; published previously in Th. Klauser and A. Rücker (eds.), *Pisciculi. Studien zur Religion und Kultur des Altertums*. (FS. F.J. Dölger) Münster (Westf) 1939, 157-64

Klein, G., *Der älteste christliche Katechismus und die jüdische Propaganda-Literatur*. Berlin 1909

— 'Die Gebete in der Didache'. *ZNW* 9 (1908) 132-146

Klein, G., *Die zwölf Apostel. Ursprung und Gehalt einer Idee*. (FRLANT 77) Göttingen 1961

Klein, M.L. (ed.), *The Fragment-Targums of the Pentateuch; According to their Extant Sources* 1. (AnBib 76) Rome 1980

Klinghardt, M., *Gesetz und Volk Gottes. Das lukanische Verständnis des Gesetzes nach Herkunft, Funktion und seinem Ort in der Geschichte des Urchristentums*. (WMANT II, 32) Tübingen 1988

— *Gemeinschaftsmahl und Mahlgemeinschaft. Soziologie und Liturgie frühchristlicher Mahlfeiern*. (TANZ 13) Tübingen 1996

Kloppenborg, J.S., 'The Transformation of Moral Exhortation in *Didache* 1-5', in Jefford, *The Didache in Context*, 88-109

— 'Didache 16,6-8 and Special Matthaean Tradition'. *ZNW* 70 (1979) 54-67

Klostermann, E., *Das Matthäusevangelium*. (HNT) 4th ed Tübingen 1971

Knopf, R., *Die Lehre der zwölf Apostel. Die zwei Clemensbriefe*. (HNT.E 1) Tübingen 1920

Knox, W.L., *St. Paul and the Church of Jerusalem*. Cambridge 1925

Köhler, W.-D., *Die Rezeption des Matthäusevangeliums in der Zeit vor Irenäus*. (WUNT 24) Tübingen 1987

Körtner, U.H.J. und M. Leutzsch, *Papiasfragmente. Hirt des Hermas*. (SU 3) Darmstadt 1998

Köster, H., *Synoptische Überlieferung bei den apostolischen Vätern*. (TU 65) Berlin 1957

Kollmann, B., *Ursprung und Gestalten der frühchristlichen Mahlfeier*. (GTA 43) Göttingen 1990

Kooyman, A.C., *The Jewish Context of Matthew 5:31-32. A Contribution to the Debate on the Use of Rabbinic Texts for the Study of the New Testament*. (Diss. in Dutch; with a summary in English) Utrecht 1992

Kosmala, H., 'The Conclusion of Matthew'. *ASTI* 4 (1965) 132-47

— 'The three Nets of Belial. A Study in the Terminology of Qumran and the New Testament'. *ASTI* 4 (1965) 91-113

Kraabel, A.T., 'Immigrants, Exiles, Expatriates, and Missionaries', in L. Bormann, K. Del Tredici and A. Strandhartinger (eds.), *Religious Propaganda and Missionary Competition in the New Testament World*. (FS. Dieter Georgi) Leiden 1994, 71-88

Krämer, M., *Das Rätsel der Parabel vom ungerechten Verwalter, Lk 16:1-13*. Zürich 1972

Kraft, H., *Die Offenbarung des Johannes*. (HNT 16a) Tübingen 1974

— 'Vom Ende der urchristlichen Prophetie', in J. Panagopoulos (ed.), *Prophetic Vocation in the New Testament and Today*. (NovTSup 45) Leiden 1977, 162-185

Kraft, R.A., *Barnabas and the Didache*. (AF 3) Toronto-New York-London 1965

Kratz, R., 'πύλη', in *EWNT* 3, 474-476

Kraus, H.J., *Psalmen*. (BKAT XV/2) Neukirchen 1966

Krauss, S., 'Le traité talmudique «Déréch Éréç»'. *REJ* 36 (1897) 27-46.205-221

— 'Le traité talmudique «Déréch Éréç»'. *REJ* 37 (1898) 45-64

— 'Die jüdischen Apostel'. *JQR* 17 (1905) 370-83

Kretschmar, G., 'Die Geschichte des Taufgottesdienstes in der alten Kirche', in K.F. Müller und W. Blankenburg (eds.), *Leiturgia. Handbuch des evangelischen Gottesdienstes* 5. Kassel 1970, 1-348

— 'Ein Beitrag zur Frage nach dem Ursprung frühchristlicher Askese', in K. S. Frank (ed.), *Askese und Mönchtum in der Alten Kirche*. (WdF 409) Darmstadt 1975, 129-180; published previously in *ZTK* 61 (1964) 27-67

Küchler, M., *Frühjüdische Weisheitstraditionen. Zum Fortgang weisheitlichen Denkens im Bereich des frühjüdischen Jahweglaubens*. (OBO 26) Göttingen 1979

Kümmel, W.G., 'Jesus und der jüdische Traditionsgedanke'. *ZNW* 33 (1934) 105-30

— 'Die älteste Form des Aposteldekrets', in id., *Heilsgeschehen und Geschichte. Gesammelte Aufsätze 1933-1964* (E. Grässer, O. Merk und A. Fritz; eds.). (MThSt 3) Marburg 1965, 278-88; published previously in *Spiritus et Veritas* (FS. K. Kundzins) Eutin 1953, 83-98

Kuhn, H.W., 'Das Liebesgebot Jesu als Tora und als Evangelium. Zur Feindesliebe und zur christlichen und jüdischen Auslegung der Bergpredigt', in H. Frankemölle und K. Kertelge (eds.), *Vom Urchristentum zu Jesus*. (FS. J. Gnilka) Freiburg-Basel-Wien 1989, 194-230

Kuhn, K.G., 'Über den ursprünglichen Sinn des Abendmahles und sein Verhältnis zu den Gemeinschaftsmahlen der Sektenschrift'. *EvT* 10 (1950-51) 508-27; rev. and ET: 'The Lord's Supper and the Communal Meal at Qumran', in Stendahl, *The Scrolls*, 65-93

Kurfess, A. (ed.), *Sibyllinische Weissagungen*. Berlin 1951

Lake, K., *The Apostolic Fathers. With an English Translation* 1-2. (LCL 24-25) London-Cambridge MA 1912-13 and repr

— *The Earlier Epistles of St. Paul: Their Motive and Origin*. 2nd ed London 1914

— *The Acts of the Apostles* in F.J.F. Jackson and K. Lake (eds.), *The Beginnings of Christianity* 5; London 1933; repr Grand Rapids 1979

Lambert, D., 'Autour de la Règle du Maître'. *RevM* 32 (1942) 54-56

Lambrecht, J., *The Sermon on the Mount. Proclamation and Exhortation*. (GNS 14) Wilmington (Del) 1985

Lange, A., 'Wisdom and Predestination in the Dead Sea Scrolls'. *DSD* 2 (1995) 340-54

— *Weisheit und Prädestination. Weisheitliche Urordnung und Prädestination in den Textfunden von Qumran*. (STDJ 18) Leiden-New York-Köln 1995

Laporte, J., *La Doctrine eucharistique chez Philon d'Alexandrie*. (ThH 16) Paris 1972

Layton, B., 'The Sources, Date, and Transmission of *Didache* 1,3b-2,1'. *HTR* 61 (1968) 343-83

Leaney, A.R.C., *The Rule of Qumran and Its Meaning. Introduction, Translation and Commentary*. London 1966

Ledogar, R.J., *Acknowledgment. Praise-verbs in the Early Greek Anaphora*. Rome 1968

Lefort, L.-Th., *Les Pères apostoliques en copte* 1-2. (CSCO 135-36; ScrCop 17-18) Leuven 1952

Leipoldt, J., *Sinuthii Vita Bohairice*. (CSCO 41 – Scriptores Coptici 1) Leuven 1951

— *Die urchristliche Taufe im Lichte der Religionsgeschichte*. Leipzig 1928

Leivestad, R., 'Das Dogma von der prophetenlosen Zeit'. *NTS* 19 (1972-73) 288-99

Lemerle, P., *Le premier humanisme byzantin. Notes et remarques sur enseignement et culture à Byzance des origines au Xe siècle*. (Biliothèque Byzantine 6) Paris 1971

Lerner, M. B., 'The External Tractates', in Safrai *The Literature of the Sages* 1, 367-404

Levinskaya, I., *The Book of Acts in Its Diaspora Setting*, in B.W. Winter (ed.), *The Book of Acts in Its First Century Setting* 5. Grand Rapids (MI) – Carlisle (UK) 1996

Levison, J., 'A better Righteousness: The Character and Purpose of Matthew 5:21-48'. *StBTh* 12 (1982) 171-94

Levison, J.R., 'Did the Spirit withdraw from Israel? An Evaluation of the earliest Jewish Data'. *NTS* 43 (1997) 35-57

Licht, J., *The Rule Scroll. A Scroll from the Wilderness of Judaea: 1QS – 1QSa – 1QSb*. Jerusalem 1965 (Hebr.)

— 'An Analysis of the Treatise on the two Spirits in DSD'. *Scripta Hierosolymitana IV: Aspects of the Dead Sea Scrolls*, 88-100

Lichtenberger, H., 'Taufergemeinden und frühchristliche Tauferpolemik im letzten Drittel des I. Jahrhunderts'. *ZTK* 84 (1987) 36-57

Lichtenstein, A., 'Does Jewish Tradition Recognize An Ethic Independent of Halakha?', in M.M. Kellner *Contemporary Jewish Ethics*'. (SJS) 2nd ed New York 1979, 102-123

Lichtenstein, H., ' מגילת תענית (Die Fastenrolle)'. *HUCA* 8-9 (1931-32) 257-351

Lieberman, S., 'The Discipline in the So-Called Dead Sea Manual of Discipline'. *JBL* 71 (1952) 199-206

— *Greek in Jewish Palestine. Studies in the Life and Manners of Jewish Palestine in the II-IV Centuries C.E.*. New York 1942

— *Tosefta ki-Fshutah. A Comprehensive Commentary on the Tosefta* 1-8 (Zeraim-Nashim). New York 1955-73 (Hebr.)

Lietzmann, H., 'Der Sinn des Aposteldekrets und seine Textwandlung', in H.G. Wood (ed.), *Amicitiae Corolla, a Volume of Essays Presented to James Rendel Harris*. London 1933, 203-211; repr in id. *Kleine Schriften* 2: *Studien zum Neuen Testament*. (TU 68) Berlin 1958, 292-98

— 'Die liturgischen Angaben des Plinius', in *Geschichtliche Studien* (FS. A. Hauck) Leipzig 1916, 34-38; repr in id. *Kleine Schriften* 3: *Studien zur Liturgie- und Symbolgeschichte zur Wissenschaftsgeschichte*. (TU 74) Berlin 1962, 48-53

— (ed.), *Die Didache. Mit kritischem Apparat*. (KTVÜ 6) 6th ed Berlin 1962

— *Messe und Herrenmahl. Eine Studie zur Geschichte der Liturgie*. (AzK 8) Berlin 1926; ET: *Mass and Lord's Supper. A Study in the History of the Liturgy*, with Introduction and Further Inquiry by R.D. Richardson. Leiden 1979

Lieu, J., 'History and Theology in Christian views of Judaism', in J. Lieu, *et alii, The Jews among Pagans and Christians*, 79-96

Lieu, J., J. North and T. Rajak (eds.), *The Jews among Pagans and Christians in the Roman Empire*. London and New York 1992

Lightfoot, J.B., *The Apostolic Fathers* I/1-2: *S. Clement of Rome*. 2nd ed London 1890 (orig. 1869/1885)

Ligier, L., 'The Origins of the Eucharistic Prayer: From the Last Supper to the Eucharist'. *SL* 9 (1973) 161-85; published previously as 'Les origines de la prière eucharistique: de la cène du Seigneur à l'eucharistie'. *QL* 53 (1972) 181-202

Lilje, H., *Die Lehre der zwölf Apostel. Eine Kirchenordnung des ersten christlichen Jahrhunderts*. Hamburg 1956

Loader, W.R.G., *Jesus' Attitude towards the Law. A Study of the Gospels*. (WUNT 2/97) Tübingen 1997

Locke, J., *An Essay Concerning Human Understanding*. (The Clarendon Edition of the works of John Locke) Oxford 1975

Loewenstamm, S.E., 'Beloved is Man in that he was created in the Image', in *Comparative Studies in Biblical and Ancient Oriental Literatures*. (AOAT 204) Neukirchen 1980, 48-50; published previously in *Tarbiz* 27 (1957) 1-2 (Hebr.)

Lohmann, H., *Drohung und Verheissung. Exegetische Untersuchungen zur Eschatologie bei den Apostolischen Vätern*. (BZNW 55) Berlin-New York 1989

Lohmeyer, E., '"Mir ist gegeben alle Gewalt!" – Eine Exegese von Mt. 28:16-20', in W. Schmauch (ed.), *In Memoriam Ernst Lohmeyer*. Stuttgart 1951, 22-49

— *Das Evangelium des Matthäus*. (MeyerK) Göttingen 1967

Lohse, E., '"Ich aber sage euch"', in E. Lohse, Chr. Burchard und B. Schaller (eds.), *Der Ruf Jesu und die Antwort der Gemeinde*. (FS. J. Jeremias) Göttingen 1970, 189-203; repr in E. Lohse *Die Einheit des Neuen Testaments. Exegetische Studien zur Theologie des Neuen Testaments*. Göttingen 1973, 73-87

Longenecker, R.N., *The Christology of Early Jewish Christianity*. London 1970; repr Grand Rapids 1981

Longère, J., *La Prédication Médiévale*. (ÉtAug) Paris 1983

Loopik, M. van, *The Ways of the Sages and the Way of the World*. (TSAJ 26) Tübingen 1991

Lührmann, D., 'Liebet eure Feinde (Lk 6,27-36 / Mt 5,39-48)'. *ZTK* 69 (1972) 412-38

— *Die Redaktion der Logienquelle*. (WMANT 33) Neukirchen-Vluyn 1969

— 'Das Bruchstück aus dem Hebräerevangelium bei Didymos von Alexandrien'. *NovT* 29 (1987) 265-279

Luttikhuizen, G.P., *The Revelation of Elchasai. Investigations into the Evidence for a Mesopotamian Jewish Apocalypse of the Second Century and its Reception by Judeo-Christian Propagandists* (TSAJ 8) Tübingen 1985

Luz, U., *Das Evangelium nach Matthäus* 1-2 (Mt 1-7.8-17). (EKKNT I/1-2) Zürich-Neukirchen/Vluyn usw. 1985-90

Maclean, A.J., *The Ancient Church Orders*. (CHLS 1) Cambridge 1910

Macleod, M.D., *Luciani Opera* 1-4. (SCBO) Oxford 1972-87

Madec, G. and J. Pegon, *Oeuvres de Saint Augustin* 8: La Foi Chrétienne. (BAug) Paris 1982

Malina, B., 'Does *Porneia* mean Fornication?'. *NovT* 14 (1972) 10-17

Manning, E., 'Un texte de S. Augustin, source du chap. 4, v. 13-17 de la Règle bénédictine?'. *RTAM* 28 (1961) 331-333

— 'Une catéchèse baptismale devient Prologue de la Règle du Maître'. *RevM* 52 (1962) 61-73

Manson, T.W., 'The Lord's Prayer'. *BJRL* 38 (1970) 99-113

— *The Sayings of Jesus*. London 1950

Manzanera, M., '*Koinonia* en Hch 2:42. Notas sobre su Interpretación y Origen Historico-Doctrinal'. *EstEc* 52 (1977) 307-29

Marcovich, M. (ed.), *Iustini Martyris Apologiae pro Christianis*. (PTS 38) Berlin-New York 1994

— (ed.), *Hippolytus. Refutatio omnium Haeresium*. (PTS 25) Berlin-New York 1986

Margulies, M. (ed.), *Midrash Wayyikra Rabbah* 1-5. 3rd ed New York and Jerusalem 1993

Martène, E. and U. Durand, *Collectio amplissima ueterum scriptorum et monumentorum* 9. Paris 1733

Martin, R., *Carmen Christi: Philippians 2:5-11 in Recent Interpretation and in the Setting of Early Christian Worship*. rev. ed.: Grand Rapids 1983

Massaux, E., *Influence de l'Évangile de saint Matthieu sur la littérature chrétienne avant saint Irénée*. Leuven 1950; repr by F. Neirynck, suppl. Bibliogr. 1950-1985 by B. Dehandschutter. (BETL 75) Leuven 1986; ET: *The Influence of the Gospel of Saint Matthew on Christian Literature before Saint Irenaeus* 1-3. (NGSt 5/1-3) Leuven-Macon (GA) 1990-93

Mathys, H.-P., *Liebe deinen Nächsten wie dich selbst. Untersuchungen zum alttestamentlichen Gebot der Nächstenliebe (Lev. 19,18)*. (OBO 71) Freiburg (S)-Göttingen 1986

May, H.G., 'Cosmological Reference in the Qumran Doctrine of the Two Spirits and in Old Testament Imagery'. *JBL* 82 (1963) 1-14

Mazza, E., *The Origins of the Eucharistic Prayer*. ET Collegeville (Minn) 1995

— 'Didache 9-10: Elements of a Eucharistic Interpretation' in Draper, *The Didache in Modern Research*, 276-99

— 'L'eucaristia di 1 Corinzi 10:16-17 in rapporto a Didachè 9-10'. *EL* 100 (1986) 193-223

Mc Dermott, M., 'The Biblical Doctrine of KOINΩNIA'. *BZ* 19 (1975) 64-77. 219-233

McGinn, B., '*Teste David cum Sibylla*: The Significance of the Sibylline Tradition in the Middle Ages', in J. Kirshner and S.F. Wemple (eds.), *Women of the Medieval World*. (FS. J.H. Mundy) Oxford 1985 (pb: 1987) 7-35

McKitterick, R., *The Frankish Church and the Carolingian Reforms, 789-895*. London 1977

McKnight, S., *A Light among the Gentiles. Jewish Missionary Activity in the Second Temple Period*. Minneapolis (MN) 1991

McNamara, M., *The New Testament and the Palestinian Targum to the Pentateuch*. (AnBib 27A) 2nd ed Rome 1978

Meeks, W.A., *The Moral World of the First Christians*. (LC 6) Philadelphia (PA) 1986

Meier, J.P., *Law and History in Matthew's Gospel. A Redactional Study of Mt. 5:17-48*. (AnBib 71) Rome 1976

Merkelbach, R., 'Der Eid der Bithynischen Christen'. *ZPE* 21 (1976) 73-74

Merklein, H., *Die Gottesherrschaft als Handlungsprinzip. Untersuchung zur Ethik Jesu*. (FB 33) 2nd ed Würzburg 1981

Metso, S., *The Textual Development of the Qumran Community Rule* (STDJ 21) Leiden-New York-Köln 1997

Metzger, B.M., *A Textual Commentary on the Greek New Testament*. (UBS) 3rd ed Stuttgart 1975

Metzger, M., 'Nouvelles perspectives pour la prétendue *Tradition apostolique*'. *EcOr* 5 (1988) 241-59

Meyer, E., *Ursprung und Anfänge des Christentums* 1: *Die Evangelien*. Stuttgart 1982; repr 1921

Meyier, K.A. de, *Bibliotheca Universitatis Leidensis. Codices Manuscripti* 6: *Codices Vossiani Graeci et Miscellanei*. Leiden 1955

Micaelli C. and Ch. Munier, *Tertullien, La Pudicité (De pudicitia)* 1. (SC 394) Paris 1993

Michaelis, W., 'ὁδός κτλ.', in *TWNT* 5, 42-118

Middleton, R.D., 'The Eucharistic Prayers of the Didache'. *JTS* 36 (1935) 259-67

Milavec, A., 'The Pastoral Genius of the Didache: An Analytical Translation and Commentary', in J. Neusner, E.S. Frerichs and A.J. Levine (eds.), *Religious Writings and Religious Systems. Systemic Analysis of Holy Books in Christianity, Islam, Buddhism, Greco-Roman Religions, Ancient Israel, and Judaism* 2: *Christianity*. (BSR 2) Providence RI 1989, 89-125

— 'Distinguishing True and False Prophets: The Protective Wisdom of the Didache'. *JECS* 2 (1994) 117-136

Milik, J.T., *Ten Years of Discovery in the Wilderness of Judaea*. London 1959

Miller, D.G. (ed.), *Jesus and Man's Hope* 1. Pittsburgh 1970

Mimouni, S.C., *Le judéo-christianisme ancien; essais historiques*. (Patrimoines) Paris 1998

Minear, P.S., 'False Prophecy and Hypocrisy in the Gospel of Matthew', in J. Gnilka (ed.), *Neues Testament und Kirche*. (FS. R. Schnackenburg) Freiburg-Basel-Wien 1974, 76-93

Mirkin, M.A., *Midrash Rabbah* 1-11. Tel Aviv 1956-67

Mitchell, N., 'Baptism in the *Didache*', in Jefford, *The Didache in Context*, 226-255

Mohrlang, R., *Matthew and Paul; a comparison of ethical perspectives*. (SNTSMS 48) Cambridge 1984

Montefiore, C.G., *The Synoptic Gospels. Edited with an Introduction and a Commentary* 1-2. 2nd ed New York 1968 (orig. 1927)

— *Rabbinic Literature and Gospel Teachings*. New York 1970 (orig. 1930)

Montfaucon B. de, *Sancti patris nostri Athanasii archiep. Alexandrini Opera omnia quae extant vel quae ejus nomine circumferuntur* 1-3, Paris 1698

Moo, D.J., 'Jesus and the Authority of the Mosaic Law'. *JSNT* 20 (1984) 3-49

Moore, G.F., *Judaism in the first Centuries of the Christian Era. The Age of the Tannaim* 1-3. Cambridge (MA) 1927-30

Morin, G. (ed.), *Sancti Caesarii Arelatensis Sermones*. (CChr.SL 104) Turnholti 1953

Müller, K., *Tora für die Völker. Die noachidischen Gebote und Ansätze zu ihrer Rezeption im Christentum*. (SKI 15) Berlin 1994

Muilenburg, J., *The Literary Relations of the Epistle of Barnabas and the Teaching of the Twelve Apostles*. Marburg 1929

Murphy-O'Conner, J., 'The Essenes and Their History'. *RB* 81 (1974) 215-44

— 'The Damascus Document Re-visited'. *RB* 92 (1985) 223-46

Mussner, F., 'Das "Gleichnis" vom gestrengten Mahlherrn (Lk 13,22-30). Ein Beitrag zum Redaktionsverfahren und zur Theologie des Lukas'. *TTZ* 65 (1956) 129-143

Myers, J.M., *I and II Esdras. Introduction, Translation and Commentary*. (AB) New York 1974

Nauck, W., 'Probleme des frühchristlichen Amtsverständnisses (I Ptr 5,2f.)'. *ZNW* 48 (1957) 200-220

Nautin, P., 'La composition de la "Didachê" et son titre'. *RHR* 78 (1959) 191-214

Neirynck, F., 'Paul and the Sayings of Jesus', in A. Vanhoye (ed.), *L'Apôtre Paul*. (BETL 73) Leuven 1986, 265-321

Neotestamentica et Patristica. FS. O. Cullmann (NovTSup 6) Leiden 1962

Newsom, C., *Songs of Sabbath Sacrifice: A Critical Edition*. (HSS 27) Atlanta 1985

— 'Shirot 'Olat Hashabbat', in E. Eshel, H. Eschel, C. Newsom *et alii*, *Qumran Cave 4* 6: *Poetical and Liturgical Texts* 1. (DJD 11) Oxford 1998, 173-401

Neymeyr, U., *Die Christlichen Lehrer im zweiten Jahrhundert. Ihre Lehrtätigkeit, ihr Selbstverständnis und ihre Geschichte*. (VCSup 4) Leiden-New York-København-Köln 1989

Nickle, K.F., *The Collection: A Study in Paul's Strategy*. London 1966

Niebuhr, K.-W., *Gesetz und Paränese; Katechismusartige Weisungsreihen in der frühjüdischen Literatur*. (WUNT II/ 28) Tübingen 1987

Niederwimmer, K., 'Zur Entwicklungsgeschichte des Wanderradikalismus im Traditionsbereich der Didache'. *WS* nF 11 (1977) 145-167; ET: 'An Examination of the Development of Itinerant Radicalism in the Environment and Tradition of the Didache', in J.A. Draper (ed.), *The Didache in Modern Research*, 321-339

— *Die Didache*. (KAV 1) 2nd ed Göttingen 1993 (1989); ET: *The Didache*. (Hermeneia) Minneapolis 1998

— 'Der Didachist und seine Quellen', in Jefford, *The Didache in Context*, 15-36

— 'Textprobleme der Didache'. *WS* nF 16 (1982) 114-30
— 'Doctrina Apostolorum (Cod. Mellic. 597)', in H.-C. Schmidt-Lauber (ed.), *Theologia Scientia Eminens Practica*. (FS. F. Herbst) Vienna-Freiburg-Basel 1979, 266-272
Nissen, A., *Gott und der Nächste im Antiken Judentum. Untersuchungen zum Doppelgebot der Liebe.* (WUNT 15) Tübingen 1974
Nitzan, B., *Qumran Prayer and Religious Poetry*. (STDJ 12) Leiden-New York-Köln 1994
Nötscher, F., *Gotteswege und Menschenwege in der Bibel und in Qumran* (BBB 15), Bonn 1958
Novak, D., *The Image of the Non-Jew in Judaism. An Historical and Constructive Study of the Noahide Laws*. (TST 14) New York-Toronto 1983
Oepke, A., 'βάπτω, βαπτίζω κτλ.', in *TWNT* 1, 527-44
Oesterley, W.O.E., *The Jewish Background of the Christian Liturgy*. Gloucester (MA) 1925; repr 1965
Oppenheimer, A., *The 'Am Ha-Aretz. A Study in the Social History of the Jewish People in the Hellenistic-Roman Period*. (ALGHJ 8) Leiden 1977
Orbán, A.P., 'Die Frage der ersten Zeugnisse des Christenlateins'. *VC* 30 (1976) 214-238
Orlandis, J., and D. Ramos-Lisson, *Die Synoden auf der Iberischen Halbinsel bis zum Einbruch des Islam (711)*. (Kon A) Paderborn-München-Wien etc. 1981
Osten-Sacken, P. von der, *Gott und Belial. Traditionsgeschichtliche Untersuchungen zum Dualismus in den Texten aus Qumran*. (SUNT 6) Göttingen 1969
Overholt, Th., 'The End of Prophecy: No players without a Program'. *JSOT* 42 (1988) 103-15
Overman, J.A., *Matthew's Gospel and Formative Judaism. The Social World of the Matthean Community*. Minneapolis 1990
Paget, J.C., 'Jewish Proselytism at the Time of Christian Origins: Chimera or Reality?'. *JSNT* 62 (1996) 65-103
Palmer, G., *Ein Freispruch für Paulus. John Tolands Theorie des Judenchristentums. Mit einer Neuausgabe von Tolands 'Nazarenus' von C.-M. Palmer*. (ANTZ 7) Berlin 1996
Panikulam, G., *Koinōnia in the New Testament. A Dynamic Expression of Christian Life*. (AnBib 85) Rome 1979
Panofsky, E., *Hercules am Scheidewege und andere antike Bildstoffe in der neueren Kunst*. (StBW 18) Leipzig 1930
Pardee, D., 'A Restudy of the Commentary on Psalm 37 from Qumran Cave 4'. *RevQ* 8 (1972) 163-194
Pardee, N., 'The Curse That Saves (*Didache* 16,5)', in Jefford, *The Didache in Context*, 156-76
Patterson, S.J., *The Gospel of Thomas and Jesus*. (FFRS) Sonoma (CA) 1993
— '*Didache* 11-13: the Legacy of Radical Itinerancy in Early Christianity', in Jefford, *The Didache in Context*, 313-329
Patterson, S.J. and C.N. Jefford, 'A Note on *Didache* 12,2a (Coptic)'. *SecC* 9 (1989-90) 65-75
Pearson, J. *et alii* (eds.), *Critici Sacri, sive annotata doctissimorum virorum in Vetus ac Novum Testamentum* 1-9. London 1660
Peradse, G., 'Die "Lehre der zwölf Apostel" in der georgischen Überlieferung'. *ZNW* 31 (1932) 111-16
Percy, E., *Die Botschaft Jesu. Eine traditionskritische und exegetische Untersuchung*. (LUÅ n.s. 49) Lund 1953
Peterson, E., *Frühkirche. Judentum und Gnosis. Studien und Untersuchungen*. Rome-Freiburg-Vienna 1959
— 'Über einige Probleme der Didache-Überlieferung'. *RArC* 27 (1951) 37-68; repr in id., *Frühkirche. Judentum und Gnosis*, 146-82
— 'Die Behandlung der Tollwut bei den Elchasaiten nach Hippolyt'. *RSR* 34 (1947) 232-46; repr in id., *Frühkirche. Judentum und Gnosis*, 221-35
Petzke, G., *Die Traditionen über Apollonius von Tyana und das Neue Testament*. (SCHNT 1) Leiden 1970
Pez, B., *Thesaurus anecdotorum nouissimus: seu veterum monumentorum, praecipue Ecclesiasticorum, ex Germanicis potissimum Bibliothecis adornata collectio recentissima* 1-6. Augsburg 1721-29
Pines, S., 'The Jewish Christians of the Early Centuries of Christianity according to a New Source'. *PIASH* 2 (1968) 237-310

— 'The Oath of Asaph the Physician and Yohanan ben Zabda. Its Relation to the Hippocratic Oath and the Doctrina Duarum Viarum of the Didachè'. *PIASH* 5 (1971-76) 223-264

Piper, J., *'Love your enemies'. Jesus' love command in the synoptic gospels and in the early Christian paraenesis*. (SNTSMS 38) Cambridge-London-New York etc. 1979

Plummer, A., *A Critical and Exegetical Commentary on the Gospel according to S. Luke*. (ICC) Edinburgh 1896

Pope, M.H., *Song of Songs*. (AB) Garden City NY 1977

Popkes, W., 'Die Gerechtigkeitstradition im Matthäus-Evangelium'. *ZNW* 80 (1989) 1-23

Posner, R., 'Ablution', in *EJ* 2, 81-86

Poschmann, B., 'Busse: Christlich' in *RAC* 2 (1954) 805-12

Preuschen, E. (ed.), *Analecta. Kürzere Texte zur Geschichte der Alten Kirche und des Kanons* 2: *Zur Kanonsgeschichte*. (SQS 1,8,2) 2nd ed Tübingen 1910

Prigent, P., 'Une thèse nouvelle sur la Didachè'. *RTP* 3rd series, 10 (1960) 298-304

— *L'Apocalypse de Saint Jean*. (CNT 14) Paris 1981

Prigent. P. et R.A. Kraft, *Épître de Barnabé*. (SC 172) Paris 1971

Prostmeier, F.R. (ed.), *Der Barnabasbrief*. (KAV 8) Göttingen 1999

Przybylski, B., *Righteousness in Matthew and his world of thought*. (SNTSMS 41) Cambridge etc. 1980

Quasten, J., *Patrology* 1-3. Utrecht-Antwerp 1950-1963

Qimron E. and J.H. Charlesworth, 'Rule of the Community (1QS; cf. 4QS MSS A-J, 5Q11)', in J.H. Charlesworth (ed.), *The Dead Sea Scrolls: Hebrew, Aramaic, and Greek Texts with English Translations* 1: *Rule of the Community and Related Documents*. Tübingen-Louisville 1994, 1-107

Rabin, Ch., *The Zadokite Documents*. Oxford 1954

— *Qumran Studies*. (StudJud 2) Oxford 1957

Radice, B., *Pliny. Letters and Panegyricus* 2. (LCL 59) Cambridge 1969

Räisanen, H., *Paul and the Law*. (WUNT 29) Tübingen 1983

Raphael, Y. (ed.), *Sefer Hamanhig. Rulings and Customs. R. Abraham ben Nathan of Lunel* 2. Jerusalem 1978

Rehm, B. (ed.), *Die Pseudoklementinen* 1: *Homilien*. (GCS 42) Berlin-Leipzig 1953

— (ed.), *Die Pseudoklementinen* 2: *Rekognitionen in Rufins Übersetzung*. (GCS 51) Berlin 1965

Reichert, E., *Die Canones der Synode von Elvira. Einleitung und Kommentar*. (Dissertation) Hamburg 1990

Reicke, B., 'The Constitution of the Primitive Church in the Light of Jewish Documents', in K. Stendahl (ed.), *The Scrolls and the New Testament*. New York 1957, 143-56; published previously as: 'Die Verfassung der Urgemeinde im Lichte jüdischer Dokumente'. *TZ* 10 (1954) 95-113

Reiff, S.C., 'The Early History of Jewish Worship', in P.F. Bradshaw and L.A. Hoffman (eds.), *The Making of Jewish and Christian Worship*. Notre Dame 1991, 109-36.

Reiling, J., *Hermas and Christian Prophecy. A Study of the Eleventh Mandate*. Leiden 1973

Reitzenstein, R., 'Eine frühchristliche Schrift von den dreierlei Früchten des christlichen Lebens'. *ZNW* 15 (1914) 60-90

Rengstorf, K.H., 'ἀπόστολος', in *TWNT* 1, 406-446

— 'διδάσκω κτλ', in *TWNT* 2, 138-168

Resch, G., *Das Aposteldecret nach seiner ausserkanonischen Textgestalt*. (TU nF XIII,3) Leipzig 1905

Revillout, E., *Le concile de Nicée d'après les textes coptes et les diverses collections canoniques* 1-2. Paris 1881 and 1918

Reynolds, J. and R. Tannenbaum, *Jews and Godfearers at Aphrodisias*. (CPSSup 12) Cambridge 1987

Richardson, C.C., *Early Christian Fathers*. New York 1970

Richardson, R.D., 'A Further Inquiry into Eucharistic Origins with Special Reference to New Testament Problems', in H. Lietzmann, *Mass and Lord's Supper*, 217-748

Riedmatten, H. de, 'La Didachè: solution du problème ou étape décisive?'. *Angelicum* 36 (1959) 415-429

Riesenfeld, H., 'Das Brot von den Bergen. Zu Did. 9,4'. *Eranos* 54 (1956) 142-50

Riesner, R., 'A Pre-Christian Jewish Mission?', in J. Ådna and H. Kvalbein (eds.), *The Mission of the Early Church to Jews and Gentiles*. (WUNT 127) Tübingen 2000, 211-50

Riggenbach, E., *Der trinitarische Taufbefehl Matth. 28,19 nach seiner ursprünglichen Textgestalt und seiner Authentie untersucht.* (BFCT 7) Gütersloh 1903

Riggs, J.W., 'From Gracious Table to Sacramental Elements: The Tradition-History of Didache 9 and 10'. *SecC* 4 (1984) 83-101

— 'The Sacred Food of *Didache* 9-10 and Second-Century Ecclesiologies', in Jefford, *The Didache in Context*, 256-83

Robinson, J.A., *Barnabas, Hermas and the Didache. Being the Donnellan Lectures delivered before the University of Dublin in 1920.* London 1920

Robinson, J.A.T., 'The Baptism of John and the Qumran Community: Testing a Hypothesis', in id., *Twelve New Testament Studies*, London 1962, 11-27; published previously in *HTR* 50 (1957) 175-91

— *Redating the New Testament.* London 1976

Robinson, J.M., 'Die Hodajot-Formel in Gebet und Hymnus des Frühchristentums', in *Apophoreta*. (BZNW 30; FS. E. Haenchen) Berlin 1964, 194-235

Rochais, H. et E. Manning (eds.), *Règle de Saint Benoît.* (ÉCent) Rochefort 1980

Ropes, J.H., *The Text of Acts* in *The Beginnings of Christianity* 1: *The Acts of the Apostles* 3. pb: Grand Rapids (Mich) 1979

— *Die Sprüche Jesu, die in den kanonischen Evangelien nicht überliefert sind.* (TU 14/2) Leipzig 1896

Rordorf, W., *Liturgie, Foi et Vie des premiers Chrétiens. Études Patristiques.* (ThH 75) Paris 1986

— 'Le Baptême selon la *Didachè*', in id. *Liturgie, Foi et Vie*, 175-85; published previously in *Mélanges liturgiques.* (FS. B. Botte) Leuven 1972, 499-509; ET: 'Baptism according to the Didache', in Draper, *The Didache in Modern Research*, 212-222

— 'Un chapitre d'éthique Judéo-Chrétienne: les deux voies', in id., *Liturgie, Foi et Vie*, 155-174; published previously in *RSR* 60 (1972) 109-128; ET: 'An Aspect of the Judeo-Christian Ethic: The Two Ways' in Draper, *The Didache in Modern Research*, 148-164

— 'L'Eucharistie des premiers chrétiens: la Didachè', in id., *Liturgie, Foi et Vie*, 187-208; published previously as 'La Didachè', in *L'Eucharistie des premiers chrétiens.* (PoTh 17) Paris 1976, 7-28; ET: 'The Didache', in W. Rordorf *et alii* (eds.), *The Eucharist of the Early Christians.* New York 1978, 1-23

— 'Le problème de la transmission textuelle de Didachè 1,3b.-2,1', in F. Paschke (ed.), *Überlieferungsgeschichtliche Untersuchungen.* (TU 125) Berlin 1981, 499-513; repr in id., *Liturgie, Foi et Vie*, 139-153

— 'Does the Didache contain Jesus Tradition independently of the Synoptic Gospels?', in H. Wansbrough (ed.), *Jesus and the Oral Gospel Tradition.* (JSNTSup 64) Sheffield 1991, 394-423

— 'Die Mahlgebete in *Didache* Kap. 9-10. Ein neuer Status Quaestionis'. *VC* 51 (1997) 229-46

— *Der Sonntag. Geschichte des Ruhe- und Gottesdiensttages im ältesten Christentum.* (ATANT 43) Zürich 1962; ET: *Sunday. The History of the Day of Rest and Worship in the Earliest Centuries of the Christian Church.* London-Philadelphia 1968

Rordorf, W. et A. Tuilier, *La Doctrine des douze Apôtres (Didachè).* (SC 248 bis) 2nd ed Paris 1998

Rouwhorst, G., 'Bénédiction, action de grâces, supplication. Les oraisons de la table dans le Judaïsme et les célébrations eucharistiques des Chrétiens syriaques'. *QL* 61 (1980) 211-40

— 'Bread and Cup in Early Christian Eucharist Celebrations', in Ch. Caspers, G. Lukken and G. Rouwhorst (eds.), *Bread of Heaven. Customs and Practices Surrounding Holy Communion.* (Liturgia condenda 3) Kampen 1995, 11-40

Rousseau, A. (ed.), *Irénée de Lyon, Contre les Hérésies* 2. (SC 100) Paris 1965

Rowley, H.H., 'Jewish Proselyte Baptism and the Baptism of John'. *HUCA* 15 (1940) 313-34

Rüger, H.P., *Die Weisheitsschrift aus der Kairoer Geniza. Text, Übersetzung und philologischer Kommentar.* (WUNT 53) Tübingen 1991

Ruiz Bueno, D. (ed.), *Padres Apostólicos. Edición bilingüe completa.* (Biblioteca de autores cristianos 65) Madrid 1950

Ruzer, S., 'The Technique of composite Citation in the Sermon on the Mount (Matt 5:21-22, 33-37)'. *RB* 103 (1996) 65-75

Safrai, S., 'The Synagogue', in Safrai and Stern, *The Jewish People in the First Century* 2, 908-44

— 'Religion in Everyday Life', in Safrai and Stern, *The Jewish People in the First Century* 2, 793-833
— 'Eretz Israel weha-tefutsah ha-yehudit', in id., *In Times of Temple and Mishnah. Studies in Jewish History* 1. Jerusalem 1994, 294-310; published previously in S. Safrai, Y. Tsafrir and M. Stern (eds.), *Eretz Israel me-hurban beit sheni we-ad ha-kibush ha-muslimi* 1. Jerusalem 1982, 456-72
— (ed.), *The Literature of the Sages* 1. (CRINT II, 3) Assen / Maastricht / Philadelphia 1987
— 'Teaching of Pietists in Mishnaic Literature'. *JJS* 16 (1965) 15-33
— 'Hasidim we-Anshei Maase'. *Zion* 50 (1984-85)133-154
— 'Jesus and the Hasidim'. *Jerusalem Perspective* 42-44 (1994) 3-22
— 'Home and Family', in Safrai and Stern, *The Jewish People in the First Century* 2, 728-92
— 'Jesus and the Hasidic Movement' (Hebr.), in I.M. Gafni, A. Oppenheimer and D.R. Schwartz (eds.), *The Jews in the Hellenistic-Roman World. Studies in Memory of Menahem Stern*. Jerusalem 1996, 413-36
— 'Relations between the Diaspora and the Land of Israel', in Safrai-Stern, *The Jewish People in the First Century* 1, 184-215
Safrai, S. and M. Stern (eds.), *The Jewish People in the First Century. Historical Geography, Political History, Social, Cultural and Religious Life and Institutions* 1-2. (CRINT I,1-2) edited in co-operation with D. Flusser and W.C. van Unnik. Assen/Philadelphia 1974-76
Sahlin, H., 'Die drei Kardinalsünden und das neue Testament'. *ST* 24 (1970) 93-112
Saldarini, A.J., 'The Gospel of Matthew and Jewish-Christian Conflict in the Galilee', in L.I. Levine (ed.), *The Galilee in Late Antiquity* Cambridge MA-London 1992, 23-38
— *Matthew's Christian-Jewish Community*. (CSHJ) Chicago-London 1994
Sand, A., *Das Gesetz und die Propheten: Untersuchungen zur Theologie des Evangeliums nach Matthäus*. (BibU 11) Regensburg 1974
Sandelin, K.-G., *Wisdom as Nourisher. A Study of an Old Testament Theme, its Development within Early Judaism and its Impact on Early Christianity*. (AAA.A: Humaniora 64,3) Åbo 1986
Sanders, E.P., *Jewish Law from Jesus to the Mishnah. Five Studies*. London-Philadelphia 1990
— *Judaism. Practice and Belief, 63 BCE – 66 CE*. London-Philadelphia 1992
Sandt, H. van de, 'Research into Rom. 8,4a: The Legal Claim of the Law'. *Bijdragen* 37 (1976) 252-69
— 'An Explanation of Rom. 8,4a'. *Bijdragen* 37 (1976) 361-78
— 'Didache 3,1-6: A Transformation of an Existing Jewish Hortatory Pattern'. *JSJ* 23 (1992) 21-41
— 'Acts 28,28: No Salvation for the People of Israel? An Answer in the Perspective of the LXX'. *ETL* 70 (1994) 341-58
Santos Otero, A. de, 'Der Pseudo-Titus-Brief', in Hennecke-Schneemelcher, *Neutestamentliche Apokryphen* 2, 50-70
Sass, G., 'Die Apostel in der Didache', in W. Schmauch (ed.), *In Memoriam Ernst Lohmeyer*. Stuttgart 1951, 233-239
Savi, P., 'La dottrina degli apostoli'. *StDStD* 14 (1893) 3-48
Schäfer, P., *Die Vorstellung vom heiligen Geist in der rabbinischen Literatur*. (SANT 28) München 1972
Schaff, Ph., *The Oldest Church Manual, Called the Teaching of the Twelve Apostles*. 2nd ed New York 1886
Schechter, S., 'The Rabbinic Conception of Holiness'. *JQR* 10 (1898) 1-12
— 'Some Rabbinic Parallels to the New Testament'. *JQR* 12 (1900) 415-33
— *Aspects of Rabbinic Theology: Major Concepts of the Talmud*. New York 1961 (orig. 1909)
— (ed.), *Aboth de Rabbi Nathan*. Vienna 1887; repr New York 1945; corr. repr New York 1967
Schenk-Ziegler, A., *Correctio fraterna im Neuen Testament. Die "brüderliche Zurechtweisung" in biblischen, frühjüdischen und hellenistischen Schriften*. (FB 84) Würzburg 1997
Schermann, Th., 'Eine neue Handschrift zur Apostolischen Kirchenordnung'. *OrChr* 2 (1902) 398-408
— *Eine Elfapostelmoral oder die X-Rezension der "beiden Wege"*. (VKSM II,2) München 1903
— *Die allgemeine Kirchenordnung, frühchristliche Liturgien und kirchliche Überlieferung* 1: *Die allgemeine Kirchenordnung des zweiten Jahrhunderts*. (StGKA Ergb 3,1) Paderborn 1914
Schiffman, L.H., *Who was a Jew?*. Hoboken (NJ) 1985

— *Sectarian Law in the Dead Sea Scrolls. Courts, Testimony and the Penal Code.* Chico (Cal) 1983

Schille, G., 'Das Recht der Propheten und Apostel – gemeinderechtliche Beobachtungen zu Didache Kapitel 11-13', in P. Wätzel and G. Schille (eds.), *Theologische Versuche.* Berlin 1966, 84-103

— *Die urchristliche Kollegialmission.* Zürich 1967

Schlatter, A., *Der Evangelist Matthäus. Seine Sprache, sein Ziel, seine Selbständigkeit.* 6th ed Stuttgart 1963

Schlecht, J., *Doctrina XII Apostolorum, una cum antiqua versione latina prioris partis de Duabus viis.* Freiburg im Breisgau 1900

— *Doctrina XII Apostolorum. Die Apostellehre in der Liturgie der katholischen Kirche.* Freiburg im Breisgau 1901

Schlesinger, Simon S., 'Derekh Erez'. *EJ* 5, 1551

Schmahl, G., 'Die Antithesen der Bergpredigt. Inhalt und Eigenart ihrer Forderungen'. *TTZ* 83 (1974) 284-97

Schmidt, C., 'Das koptische Didache-Fragment des British Museum'. *ZNW* 24 (1925) 81-99

Schmithals, W., *Das Kirchliche Apostelamt. Eine historische Untersuchung.* (FRLANT nF 63) Göttingen 1961

Schneider, J., *Die Taufe im Neuen Testament.* Stuttgart 1952

Schneider, G., *Die Apostelgeschichte* 2. (HTKNT V/2) Freiburg-Basel-Wien 1982

Schoedel, W.R., *Ignatius of Antioch. A Commentary on the Letters of Ignatius of Antioch.* (Hermeneia) Philadelphia 1985

Schöllgen, G., 'Die Didache als Kirchenordnung. Zur Frage des Abfassungszweckes und seinen Konsequenzen für die Interpretation', in *JAC* 29 (1986) 5-26; ET: 'The Didache as a Church Order: An Examination of the Purpose for the Composition of the Didache and its Consequences for its Interpretation', in Draper, *The Didache in Modern Research*, 43-71

— 'Wandernde oder sesshafte Lehrer in der Didache?'. *BibN* 52 (1990) 19-26

— 'Die Didache – ein frühes Zeugnis für Landgemeinden?'. *ZNW* 76 (1985) 140-43

— 'Die literarische Gattung der syrischen Didaskalie', in H.J.W. Drijvers *et al* (eds.), *IV Symposium Syriacum 1984. Literary Genres in Syriac Literature* (OCA 229) Rome (1987)149-59

— 'Pseudapostolizität und Schriftgebrauch in den ersten Kirchenordnungen', in G. Schöllgen and C. Scholten (eds.), *Stimuli. Exegese und ihre Hermeneutik in Antike und Christentum.* (FS. E. Dassmann) (JAC.E 23) Münster (Westf) 1996, 96-121

Schöllgen, G. und W. Geerlings (eds.), *Didache. Zwölf-Apostellehre / Traditio Apostolica. Apostolische Überlieferung.* (Fontes Christiani 1) Freiburg-Basel-Wien etc. 1991

Schümmer, J., *Die altchristliche Fastenpraxis. Mit besonderer Berücksichtigung der Schriften Tertullians.* (LQF 27) Münster (Westf.) 1933

Schürer, E., *The History of the Jewish People in the Age of Jesus Christ (175 B.C.-A.D. 135)* 1-3/2. rev by G. Vermes, F. Millar and M. Goodman, Edinburgh 1973-1987

Schürmann, H., *Der Paschamahlbericht Lk 22, (7-14.) 15-18* 1: *Einer Quellenkritischen Untersuchung des Lukanischen Abendmahlsberichtes Lk 22,7-38* (NTAbh XIX,5) Münster (Westf.) 1953

— '"Wer daher eines dieser geringsten Gebote auflöst ..." Wo fand Matthäus das Logion Mt 5,19?'. *BZ* 4 (1960) 238-50

Schütz, J.H., *Paul and the Anatomy of Apostolic Authority.* Cambridge 1975

Schuller, E.M., *Non-Canonical Psalms from Qumran: Pseudepigraphic Collection.* (HSS 28) Altlanta 1986

— 'Some Observations on Blessings of God in Texts from Qumran', in H.W. Attridge, J.J. Collins and T.H. Tobin (eds.), *Of Scribes and Scrolls. Studies on the Hebrew Bible, Intertestamental Judaism, and Christian Origins* (FS. J. Strugnell). (CTSRR 5) Lanham-New York-London 1990, 133-43

— 'Prayer, Hymnic and Liturgical Texts from Qumran', in *The Community of the Renewed Covenant: The Notre Dame Symposium on the Dead Sea Scrolls.* Notre Dame 1994, 153-71

— 'Hodayot' in Chazon-Elgvin-Eshel *e.a*, *Qumran Cave 4* 20, 69-254

Schulz, S., *Die Stunde der Botschaft. Einführung in die Theologie der vier Evangelisten.* Hamburg 1967

Schwartz, E. (ed.), *Eusebius II: Die Kirchengeschichte*: II/1-2:. *Die Bücher I-V. VI-X*. (GCS 9,1-2) Leipzig 1903-08

Schwartz, D.R., *Studies in the Jewish Background of Christianity*. Tübingen 1992

Schweizer, E., *Matthäus und seine Gemeinde*. Stuttgart 1974

— 'Matth. 5,17-20. Anmerkungen zum Gesetzesverständnis des Matthäus', in id., *Neotestamentica. Deutsche und Englische Aufsätze 1951-1963*. Zürich-Stuttgart 1963, 399-406; published previously in *TLZ* 77 (1952) 479-84

— *Das Evangelium nach Matthäus*. (NTD 2) Göttingen 1976; ET: *The Good News according to Matthew*. London 1976

Scobie, C.H.J., *John the Baptist*. Philadelphia 1964

Seccombe, D.P., *Possessions and the Poor in Luke-Acts*. (SUNT B 6) Linz 1983

Seeberg, A., *Der Katechismus der Urchristenheit*. Leipzig 1903; repr München 1966

— *Das Evangelium Christi*. Leipzig 1905

— *Die Beiden Wege und das Aposteldekret*. Leipzig 1906

— *Die Didache des Judentums und der Urchristenheit*. Leipzig 1908.

Seeliger, H.R., 'Erwägungen zu Hintergrund und Zweck des apokalyptischen Schlusskapitels der *Didache*', in E.A. Livingstone (ed.), *Studia Patristica* 21. Leuven 1989, 185-92

Segal, A.F., *Paul the Convert. The Apostolate and Apostasy of Saul the Pharisee*. New Haven-London 1990

— 'Matthew's Jewish Voice', in D.L. Balch (ed.), *Social History of the Matthean Community. Cross-Disciplinary Approaches*. Minneapolis 1991, 3-37

Seitz, O.J.F., 'Love Your Enemies'. *NTS* 16 (1969-70) 39-54

Selwyn, E .G., *The First Epistle of St. Peter. The Greek Text with Introduction, Notes and Essays*. 2nd ed Grand Rapids 1983 (orig. 1946)

Sharvit, S., 'Traditions of Interpretations and their Relations to Traditions of Textual Readings in the Mishnah', in *Studies in Talmudic Literature, Bible and the History of Israel*. (FS. E.Z. Melamed) Ramat Gan 1983, 115-134 (Hebr.)

Siegert, F., 'Gottesfürchtige und Sympathisanten'. *JSJ* 4-6 (1973-75) 109-164

Sievers, J., '"Where Two or Three ...": The Rabbinic Concept of *Shekhinah* and Matthew 18,20', in A. Finkel and L. Frizzell (eds.), *Standing before God. Studies on Prayer in Scriptures and in Tradition with Essays*. (FS. J. Oesterreicher) New York 1981, 171-182

Sigal, Ph., 'Another Note to 1 Corinthians 10.16'. *NTS* 29 (1983) 134-39

— 'Early Christian and Rabbinic Liturgical Affinities: Exploring Liturgical Acculturation'. *NTS* 30 (1984) 63-90

— *The Halaka of Jesus of Nazareth according to the Gospel of Matthew*. Lanham 1986

Sim, D.C., *The Gospel of Matthew and Christian Judaism. The History and Social Setting of the Matthean Community*. (SNTIW) Edinburgh 1998

Simon, M., 'The Apostolic Decree and its Setting in the Ancient Church'. *BJRL* 52 (1969-70) 437-460

— 'Gottesfürchtiger', in *RAC* 11 (1981) 1060-70

Simonetti, M. (ed.), *Rufin. Opera*. (CChr.SL 20) Turnhout 1961

Sjöberg, E., 'πνεῦμα', esp. 'Geist in Judentum', in *TWNT* 6, 366-387

— *Gott und die Sünder im Palästinischen Judentum*. (BWANT 79) Stuttgart-Berlin 1938

Skarsaune, O., *The Proof from Prophecy. A Study in Justin Martyr's Proof-Text Tradition: Text-Type, Provenance, Theological Profile*. (NovTSup 56) Leiden 1987

Skehan, P.W., '*Didache* 1,6 and Sirach 12,1'. *Bib* 44 (1963) 533-36

Skehan, P.W. and A.A. di Lella, *The Wisdom of Ben Sira*. (AB) New York 1987

Smit, J., '1 Cor 8,1-6: A Rhetorical *Partitio*'. A Contribution to the Coherence of 1 Cor 8,1-11,1, in R. Bieringer (ed.), *The Corinthian Correspondence*. (BETL 125) Leuven 1996, 577-91

Smith, D., *The Life and Letters of St. Paul*. New York 1919

— 'Jewish Proselyte Baptism and the Baptism of John'. *ResQ* 25 (1982) 13-32

Smith, M., 'Mt. 5:43 "Hate Thine Enemy"'. *HTR* 45 (1952) 71-73

— *Tannaitic Parallels to the Gospels*. (JBLMS 6) Philadelphia 1951

Snodgrass, K., 'Matthew and the Law'. *SBLSP*. Missoula (MT) 1988, 536-554

Snyder, G.F., *The Apostolic Fathers* 6: *The Shepherd of Hermas*. London 1968

Sommer, B.D., 'Did Prophecy Cease? Evaluating a Reevaluation'. *JBL* 115 (1996) 31-47

Sommer, J.G., *Das Aposteldekret. Entstehung, Inhalt und Geschichte seiner Wirksamkeit in der Christlichen Kirche*. (TSSO 1) Königsberg 1887

Sperber, D., *Masechet Derech Eretz Zutta and Perek Ha-Shalom*. 3rd ed Jerusalem 1994

Stanton, G., 'The Origin and Purpose of Matthew's Gospel. Matthean Scholarship from 1945 to 1980', in *ANRW* II, 25,3, Berlin-New York 1985, 1889-1951

— *A Gospel for a New People. Studies in Matthew*. Edinburgh 1992; repr 1993

— 'Other early Christian writings: "Didache", Ignatius, "Barnabas", Justin Martyr', in J. Barclay and J. Sweet (eds.), *Early Christian thought in its Jewish context* (FS. M.D. Hooker) Cambridge 1996, 174-90

Stegemann, H., *The Library of Qumran. On the Essenes, Qumran, John the Baptist, and Jesus*. Grand Rapids (Mich)-Cambridge (UK) 1998; published originally as *Die Essener, Qumran, Johannes der Täufer und Jesus*. (Spektrum 4128) Freiburg-Basel-Wien 1993

— 'Zu Textbestand und Grundgedanken von *1QS* III,13-IV,26'. *RevQ* 13 (1988) 95-131

Steidle, B., *Die Benediktusregel*. 4th ed Beuron 1980

Steimer, B., *Vertex Traditionis. Die Gattung der altchristlichen Kirchenordnungen*. (BZNW 63) Berlin-New York 1992

Stempel, H.-A., 'Der Lehrer in der "Lehre der zwölf Apostel"'. *VC* 34 (1980) 209-17

Stenzel, M., 'Der Bibelkanon des Rufin von Aquileja'. *Bib* 23 (1942) 43-61

Stern, M., 'The Province of Judaea', in Safrai-Stern, *The Jewish People in the First Century* 1, 308-76

— 'Aspects of Jewish Society. The Priesthood and other Classes', in Safrai and Stern, *The Jewish People in the First Century* 2, 561-630

— 'The Jews in Greek and Latin Literature', in Safrai-Stern, *The Jewish People in the First Century* 2, 1101-1159

— (ed.), *Greek and Latin Authors on Jews and Judaism* 1-3. Jerusalem 1976-84

Stommel, E., 'Σημεῖον ἐκπετάσεως (Didache 16,6)'. *RQ* 48 (1953) 21-42

Stone M.E. (ed.), *Jewish Writings of the Second Temple Period: Apocrypha, Pseudepigrapha, Qumran Sectarian Writings, Philo, Josephus*. (CRINT II,2) Assen-Philadelphia 1984

— 'The Dead Sea Scrolls and the Pseudepigrapha'. *DSD* 3 (1996) 270-95

— *Fourth Ezra*. (Hermeneia) Minneapolis 1990

Strack, H.L. und P. Billerbeck, *Kommentar zum neuen Testament aus Talmud und Midrasch* 1-4/2. München 1922-28

Strack, H.L. und G. Stemberger, *Einleitung in Talmud und Midrasch*. (Beck'sche Elementar bücher) 7th ed München 1982; ET: *Introduction to the Talmud and Midrash*. Edinburgh 1991

Strecker, G., 'Die Antithesen der Bergpredigt (Mt 5,21-48 par)'. *ZNW* 69 (1978) 36-72

— *Die Bergpredigt. Ein exegetischer Kommentar*. Göttingen 1984

— *Der Weg der Gerechtigkeit. Untersuchung zur Theologie des Matthäus*. (FRLANT 82) 2nd ed Göttingen 1966

— 'Kerugmata Petrou' in Hennecke-Schneemelcher, *Neutestamentliche Apokryphen* 2, 479-88

Streeter, B.H., *The Four Gospels. A Study of Origins*. 5th ed London 1936 (1924)

— 'The Much-Belaboured Didache'. *JTS* 37 (1936) 369-374

Strobel, A., 'Die Passa-Erwartung als urchristliches Problem in Lc. 17,20f'. *ZNW* 49 (1958) 157-96

Stroker, W.D., *Extracanonical Sayings of Jesus*. (SBLRBS 18) Atlanta (GA) 1989

Strothotte, G., *Das Apostelkonzil im Lichte der Jüdischen Rechtsgeschichte*. Erlangen 1955 (unpubl. diss.)

Stroumsa, G.G., 'Form(s) of God: Some Notes on Metatron and Christ'. *HTR* 76 (1983) 269

Stuiber, A., '"Das ganze Joch des Herrn" (Didache 6,2-3)', in F.L. Cross (ed.), *Studia Patristica* 4. (TU 79) Berlin 1961, 323-29

Suggs, M.J., 'The Antitheses as Redactional Products', in G. Strecker (ed.), *Jesus Christus in Historie und Theologie*. (FS. H. Conzelmann) Tübingen 1975, 433-444; repr in R. Fuller (ed.), *Essays on the Love Commandment*. Philadelphia 1978, 93-107

— *Wisdom, Christology and Law in Matthew's Gospel*. Cambridge (MA) 1970

— 'The Christian Two Ways Tradition: Its Antiquity, Form, and Function', in D.E. Aune (ed.), *Studies in New Testament and Early Christian Literature*. (NovTSup 33; FS. A.P. Wikgren) Leiden 1972, 60-74

Sullivan, R.E., 'Carolingian Missionary Theories'. *CHR* 62 (1956) 273-295

Syreeni, K., *The Making of the Sermon on the Mount. A procedural analysis of Matthew's redactoral activity*. Part I: *Methodology & Compositional Analysis*. (AASF.DHL 44) Helsinki 1987

— 'Matthew, Luke, and the Law. A study in hermeneutical exegesis', in T. Veijola (ed.), *The Law in the Bible and in its Environment*. (PFES 51) Göttingen 1990, 126-55

Talley, Th.J., 'The Eucharistic Prayer of the Ancient Church According to Recent Research: Results and Reflections', in *SL* 11 (1976) 138-58

— 'From Berakah to Eucharistia: A Reopening Question'. *Worship* 50 (1976) 115-37

— 'The Eucharistic Prayer. Tradition and Development', in K. Stevenson (ed.), *Liturgy Reshaped*. London 1982, 48-64

Tannehill, R.C., 'Israel in Luke-Acts: A Tragic Story'. *JBL* 104 (1985) 69-85

Taylor, C., *The Teaching of the Twelve Apostles, with illustrations from the Talmud*. Cambridge 1886

Taylor, J.E., 'John the Baptist and the Essenes'. *JJS* 47 (1996) 256-85

— *The Immerser: John the Baptist within Second Temple Judaism*. Grand Rapids (Mich)-Cambridge (UK) 1997

Taylor, V., *The Formation of the Gospel Tradition. Eight Lectures*. London 1953 (repr of 2nd ed, 1935)

Thackeray, H.St.J. et al., *Josephus. With an English Translation* (LCL) 1-10. Cambridge MA – London 1926-65

Theissen, G., 'Wanderradikalismus. Literatursoziologische Aspekte der Überlieferung von Worten Jesu im Urchristentum', in id., *Studien zur Soziologie des Urchristentums*. (WUNT 19) Tübingen 1979, 79-105; published previously in *ZTK* 70 (1973) 245-71; ET: 'Itinerant Radicalism: The Tradition of Jesus' Sayings from the Perspective of the Sociology of Literature'. *Radical Religion* 2 (1976) 84-93

— 'Legitimation und Lebensunterhalt: ein Beitrag zur Soziologie urchristlicher Missionare'. *NTS* 21 (1975) 192-221

Theodor, J. and Ch. Albeck (eds.), *Midrash Bereshit Rabba. Critical Edition with Notes and Commentary* 1-3. Berlin 1912-36; repr Jerusalem 1965

Thiering, B.E., 'Qumran Initiation and New Testament Baptism'. *NTS* 27 (1980-81) 615-31

— 'Inner and Outer Cleansing at Qumran as a Background for New Testament Baptism'. *NTS* 26 (1979-80) 266-77

Tidner, E. (ed.), *Didascalia Apostolorum, Canonum Ecclesiasticorum, Traditionis Apostolicae versiones latinae*. (TU 75) Berlin 1963

Tidwell, N.L.A., 'Didache XIV:1 (KATA KYPIAKHN ΔE KYPIOY) Revisited'. *VC* 53 (1999) 197-207

Tiede, D.L., 'The Exaltation of Jesus and the Restoration of Israel in Acts 1'. *HTR* 79 (1986) 278-86

Toland, J., *Nazarenus: or Jewish, Gentile, and Mahometan Christianity*. London 1718

Tomson, P.J., *Paul and the Jewish Law: Halakha in the Letters of the Apostle to the Gentiles*. (CRINT III,1) Assen/Maastricht-Minneapolis 1990

— *'If this be from Heaven,,,'. Jesus and the New Testament Authors in their Relationship to Judaism*. (BS 76) Sheffield 2001

Torrance, T.F., 'Proselyte Baptism'. *NTS* 1 (1954) 150-54

Torrey, C.C. and O. Eissfeldt, 'Ein griechisch transkribiertes und interpretiertes hebräisch-aramäisches Verzeichnis der Bücher des Alten Testaments aus dem 1. Jahrhundert n. Chr.'. *TLZ* 77 (1952) 249-54

Travers Herford, R., *Christianity in Talmud and Midrash*. New York 1903; repr 1975

Trilling, W., *Das wahre Israel: Studien zur Theologie des Matthäus-Evangeliums*. (SANT 10) 3rd ed München 1964

Tripp, D.H., 'Pliny and the Liturgy — yet again'. *Studia Patristica* 15. 1984, 581-85

— 'The Letter of Pliny', in Jones, Wainwright and Yarnold, *The Study of Liturgy*, 51-52

Tuckett, C.M., 'Synoptic Tradition in the Didache', in J.-M. Sevrin (ed.), *The New Testament in Early Christianity*. Leuven 1989, 197-230; repr in Draper, *The Didache in Modern Research*, 92-128

Tuilier, A., 'La Doctrine des Apôtres et la hiérarchie dans l'Église primitive'. *StPa* 18 (1989) 229-262

Unnik, W.C. van, 'Josephus' Account of the Story of Israel's Sin with Alien Women in the Country of Midian (Num 25:1ff.)', in M.S.H.G. Heerma van Voss, Ph.H.J. Houwink ten Cate, N.A. van Uchelen (eds.), *Travels in the World of the Old Testament*. (FS. M.A. Beek) Assen 1974, 241-61

— 'Eine merkwürdige liturgische Aussage bei Josephus. Jos Ant 8,111-113', in O. Betz, K. Haacker und M. Hengel (eds.), *Josephus – Studien. Untersuchungen zu Josephus, dem antiken Judentum und dem Neuen Testament*. (FS. O. Michel) Göttingen 1974, 362-69

— *Flavius Josephus als historischer Schriftsteller*. (FDV 1972) Heidelberg 1978

— 'De la Règle Μήτε προσθεῖναι μήτε ἀφελεῖν dans l'histoire du Canon'. *VC* 3 (1949) 1-36

Urbach, E.E., 'Matai pasqah ha-Nevuah'. *Tarbiz* 17 (1945-46) 1-11

— *The Sages – Their Concepts and Beliefs* 1-2. Jerusalem 1975

— (ed.), *Pitron Torah: A Collection of Midrashim and Interpretations*. Jerusalem 1978

Vaillant, A., *Le livre des secrets d'Hénoch: Texte slave et traduction française*. Paris 1952; repr 1976

VanderKam, J.C., *The Dead Sea Scrolls Today*. Grand Rapids (MI) 1994

Verheul, A., 'La prière eucharistique dans la Didachè'. *QL* 80 (1999) 337-47

Vermes, G., *Scripture and Tradition in Judaism. Haggadic Studies*. (StP 4) Leiden 1961

— *The Dead Sea Scrolls: Qumran in Perspective*. London 1982

— *The Dead Sea Scrolls in English*. (Penguin Books) 3rd ed London 1987

Vielhauer, Ph., *Geschichte der urchristlichen Literatur. Einleitung in das Neue Testament, die Apokryphen und die Apostolischen Väter*. Berlin-New York 1975

— 'Das Schlusskapitel der Didache', in Hennecke-Schneemelcher, *Neutestamentliche Apokryphen* 2, 535-37

Vööbus, A., *Liturgical Traditions in the Didache*. Stockholm 1968

— 'Die Entdeckung der alteste Urkunde für die syrische Übersetzung der Apostolische Kirchenordnung'. *OrChr* 63 (1979) 37-40

— (ed.), *The Didascalia Apostolorum in Syriac* (CSCO 401-02. 407-08; Scriptores Syri 175-76. 179-80) Leuven 1979

Vogel, C., 'Anaphores eucharistiques préconstantiniennes. Formes non traditionnelles'. *Augustinianum* 20 (1980) 401-10

Vogüé, A. de, *La Règle du Maître* 1. (SC 105) Paris 1964

— '"Ne haïr personne". Jalons pour l'histoire d'une maxime'. *RevAM* 44 (1968) 3-9

— *La Règle de Saint Benoît* 4. (SC 184) Paris 1971

— *La Règle de Saint Benoît* 7. (SC 186A) Paris 1977

Vokes, F.E., *The Riddle of the Didache. Fact or Fiction, Heresy or Catholicism?*. (S.P.C.K.) London-New York 1938

— 'The Ten Commandments in the New Testament and in First Century Judaism'. *SE* V,2 (1968) 146-154

— 'The Didache – Still Debated'. *CQ* 3 (1970) 57-62

Vouga, F., *Jésus et la Loi selon la Tradition synoptique*. (MdlB) Genève 1988

Wacholder, B.Z., *The Dawn of Qumran: The Sectarian Torah and the Teacher of Righteousness*. Cincinnati 1983

Wainwright, W., 'Luke and the Restoration of the Kingdom to Israel'. *ExpTim* 89 (1977-78) 76-79

Walls, A.F., 'A Note on the Apostolic Claim in the Church Order Literature', in E.A. Livingstone (ed.), *Studia Patristica* 2. 1957, 83-92

Wander, B., *Gottesfürchtige und Sympathisanten. Studien zum heidnischen Umfeld von Diasporasynagogen*. (WUNT 104) Tübingen 1998

Warfield, B.B., 'Text, Sources and Contents of "The Two Ways" or first section of the Didache'. *BSac* 43 (1886) 100-61

Watson, F., *Paul, Judaism and the Gentiles. A Sociological Approach.* (SNTSMS 56) Cambridge 1986

Webb, R.L., *John the Baptizer and Prophet. A Socio-Historical Study.* (JSNTSup 62) Sheffield 1991

Wegman, H., 'Généalogie hypothétique de la prière eucharistique'. *QL* 61 (1980) 263-78

Wehnert, J., *Die Reinheit des »christlichen Gottesvolkes« aus Juden und Heiden. Studien zum historischen und theologischen Hintergrund des sogenannten Aposteldekrets.* (FRLANT 173) Göttingen 1997

Weinfeld, M., 'The Charge of Hypocrisy in Matthew 23 and in Jewish Sources'. *Immanuel* 24/25 (1990) 52-58

— 'Traces of Kedushat Yotzer and Pesukey De-Zimra in the Qumran Literature and in Ben-Sira'. *Tarbiz* 45 (1976) 15-26 (Hebr.)

— 'The Prayers for Knowledge, Repentance and Forgiveness in the "Eighteen Benedictions" – Qumran Parallels, Biblical Antecedents, and Basic Characteristics'. *Tarbiz* 48 (1979) 186-200 (Hebr.)

— 'The Morning Prayers (Birkoth Hashachar) in Qumran and in the Conventional Jewish Liturgy'. *RevQ* 13 (1988) 481-94

— 'Grace After Meals at the Mourner's House in a Text from Qumran'. *Tarbiz* 61 (1991) 15-23

— 'Grace After Meals in Qumran'. *JBL* 111 (1992) 427-40

Weiss, J. H. (ed.), *Sifra d'Be Rab. Hu' Sefer Torat Kohanim.* Vienna 1862; repr New York 1947

Wengst, K., *Didache (Apostellehre). Barnabasbrief. Zweiter Klemensbrief. Schrift an Diognet.* (SU 2) Darmstadt 1984

— *Tradition und Theologie des Barnabasbriefes.* (AK 42) Berlin-New York 1971

Wernberg-Møller, P., *The Manual of Discipline.* (STDJ 1) Leiden 1957

— 'A Reconsideration of the Two Spirits in the Rule of the Community (1QSerek III,13-IV,26)'. *RevQ* 3 (1961-62) 413-441

Wettstein, J., *Novum Testamentum Graecum* 1-2. Amsterdam 1752; repr Graz 1962

Wibbing, S., *Die Tugend- und Lasterkataloge im Neuen Testament und ihre Traditionsgeschichte unter besonderer Berücksichtigung der Qumran-Texte.* (BZNW 25) Berlin 1959

Wiener, A., *The Prophet Elijah in the Development of Judaism. A Depth-Psychological Study.* (LLJC) London-Boston (MA) 1978

Wiesmann, H., *Sinuthii Vita Bohairice.* (CSCO 129 – Scriptores Coptici 16) Leuven 1951

Wilckens, U., *Der Brief an die Römer* 3. Teilband: *Röm 12-16.* (EKKNT VI,3) Neukirchen-Vluyn 1982

Wilcox, M., *The Semitisms of Acts.* Oxford 1965

Will, E. and C. Orrieux, *Prosélytisme juif? Histoire d'une erreur.* Paris 1992

Wilmart, D.A., 'Le Discours de Saint Basile sur l'ascèse en Latin'. *RBén* 27 (1910) 226-233

Wilson, S.G., *Luke and the Law,* Cambridge-London-New York etc. 1983

Wilson, W.T., *The Mysteries of Righteousness. The Literary Composition and Genre of the Sentences of Pseudo-Phocylides.* (TSAJ 40) Tübingen 1994

Windisch, H., *Der zweite Korintherbrief.* Göttingen 1924

Winter, P. , 'Ben Sira and the teaching of the "Two Ways"'. *VT* 5 (1955) 315-18.

Wintermute, O.S., 'Jubilees', in Charlesworth, *The Old Testament Pseudepigrapha* 2, 35-142

Wistinetzki, J. (ed.), *Sefer Hasidim.* Berlin 1891

Witherington, B., 'Not so idle Thoughts about *Eidolothuton*'. *TynBul* 44 (1993) 237-54

Wohleb, L., *Die lateinische Übersetzung der Didache; kritisch und sprachlich untersucht.* (StGKA VII,1) Paderborn 1913; repr 1967

Wrege, H.-T., *Die Überlieferungsgeschichte der Bergpredigt.* (WUNT 9) Tübingen 1968

Yadin, Y., *The Temple Scroll* 1. Jerusalem 1983

Young, D. (ed.), *Theognis, Ps-Pythagoras, Ps-Phocylides.* Leipzig 1961

Zahn, Th., *Die Apostelgeschichte des Lucas.* (KNT V/2) Leipzig-Erlangen 1921

Ziegler, J., *Sapientia Iesu Filii Sirach.* (SVTG XII,2) Göttingen 1965

Zimmermann, A.F., *Die urchristlichen Lehrer. Studien zum Tradentenkreis der διδάσκαλοι im frühen Urchristentum.* (WUNT II,12) 2nd ed Tübingen 1988

Ziwsa, C. (ed.), *Optatus von Mileve*. (CSEL 26) Prag-Wien-Leipzig 1893
— (ed.), 'Gesta apud Zenophilum', in id., *Optatus von Mileve*, 185-197
Zuckermandel, M.S. (ed.), *Tosephta*. Pasewalk 1881; repr Jerusalem 1970
Zycha, I. (ed.), *Sancti Aureli Augustini*. (CSEL 41) Prague-Vienna-Leipzig 1900

Indices

- The source index includes the references to actual documents. References to oral traditions, hypothetical documents, and literary categories appear in the subject index.
- Verse subdivisions by means of letters (1a, etc.) are suppressed in the index.
- Page indications in bold print indicate that the passage or subject concerned is central and detailed references to it are restricted there.
- In the index of modern authors, translators and editors of ancient texts are not included.

1. Index of Sources

Greek Jewish Writers

Other Early Christian Writings

Rabbinic Literature

Medieval Jewish Literature

Pagan Greek and Latin Authors

Ancient Manuscripts and Papyri

2. Index of Subjects

3. Index of Ancient and Mediaeval Personal Names

4. Index of Modern Authors